THE WORLD OF

L A W

The Law *as* Literature

A treasury of great writing about and in the law—
from Plato to the present

Edited by Ephraim London

SIMON AND SCHUSTER : NEW YORK

"DADDY" AND "PEACHES." From *Trials and Other Tribulations* by Damon Runyon. Copyright 1926, 1927, 1929, 1931, 1933 by International News Service; copyright 1947 by King Features, Inc. Published by J. B. Lippincott Company. Reprinted with the permission of the publishers.

THE SCOPES TRIAL by H. L. Mencken. From *A Treasury of the World's Great Speeches*, edited by Louis L. Snyder and Richard R. Morris. Copyright 1949 by Simon and Schuster, Inc. Reprinted by permission of The Mencken Estate, *The Baltimore Sun*, *The New York Times* and Simon and Schuster, Inc.

THE CASE OF SACCO AND VANZETTI: A CRITICAL ANALYSIS by Felix Frankfurter. Copyright 1927 by Felix Frankfurter. Reprinted by permission of Little, Brown & Company.

THE TRIAL OF QUEEN CAROLINE. From *For the Defense* by Lloyd Paul Stryker. Copyright 1947 by Lloyd Paul Stryker. Used by permission of Doubleday & Company, Inc.

"J'ACCUSE! . . ." by Emile Zola. From *Zola and His Time* by Matthew Josephson. Reprinted by permission of Harold Ober Associates, Inc.

THE BERTRAND RUSSELL CASE: A SCANDALOUS DENIAL OF JUSTICE by Morris R. Cohen. Copyright 1946 by Henry Holt, Inc. Reprinted by permission of Harry N. Rosenfield, Administrator, Estate of Morris R. Cohen.

THE TRIAL OF DR. ADAMS: THE FIRST DAY. From *The Trial of Dr. Adams* by Sybille Bedford. Copyright © 1958 by Sybille Bedford. Reprinted by permission of Simon and Schuster, Inc., and William Collins & Son, Ltd. (London).

THE TRIAL OF LIZZIE BORDEN. Reprinted by permission of Charles Scribner's Sons from *Verdict in Dispute* by Edgar Lustgarten. Copyright 1950 by Charles Scribner's Sons.

ON THE NUREMBERG TRIAL. From *A Train of Powder* by Rebecca West. Copyright 1946, 1955 by Rebecca West. First published in *The New Yorker*. Reprinted by permission of The Viking Press, Inc.

JOAN OF ARC: TESTIMONY GIVEN AT HER TRIAL FOR HERESY AND WITCHCRAFT. From *The Trial of Joan of Arc* published by The Folio Society, Ltd. Reprinted by permission of the publishers.

SUMMATION IN THE SWEET CASE.

Contents

vii

TESTIMONY AND ARGUMENT AS LITERATURE

JUDGMENTS, OBSERVATIONS AND REFLECTIONS ON THE LAW

Contents : ix

ACCOUNTS OF NOTABLE AND NOTORIOUS CASES

Damon Runyon

:

"DADDY" AND "PEACHES"

Carmel, New York, January 23, 1927

That gallus old codger, "Daddy" Browning, and his flapper wife, the celebrated "Peaches," go to bat with their matrimonial pains and aches here tomorrow morning.

The veterans of the press benches of Somerville are massed behind their typewriters and telegraph keys nearly a hundred strong in this pastoral little town, and a pleasant time is anticipated by one and all when Daddy and Peaches start telling the low-down on each other.

Some say it will be very low-down.

The populace expects to hear more or less "dirt." It would be a terrible blow to the nation if this should turn out to be a dull narration of conjugal incompatibility without any paprika in it. You can hear those kickless stories anywhere.

If you have followed the public prints to any extent the past year, you know that Daddy Browning is Edward W. Browning, a New York real estate man of reputed wealth, and of at least fifty-one years of age, giving him plenty the best of it, who likes his girl friends young.

He is what you might call a "chick chaser." That, I believe, is the term for old guys who choose 'em very youthful. Old girls who like young men are called "veal hunters." Thus the English language is enriched every day.

When it comes to the dolls, old Daddy Browning seems to be of

3

the genus sap. Moreover, he appears to have a strong yen for publicity, and who shall say he has not had plenty of it since he married Frances Heenan Browning, the "Peaches" aforesaid, at the glowing, mature age of fifteen?

Now he is endeavoring to shake Peaches off the Browning family tree, and the matter comes up at this time in the form of a plea by Daddy for separation. Peaches has filed a countersuit against Daddy that will come up later. Daddy, dear old Daddy, was more like a step-father to her, she says.

Sometimes Daddy is called "Bunny," so I understand. He is also called other things less endearing by coarse persons who do not comprehend the influence of sweet love on a gent's heart and blood pressure.

Daddy Browning is a dressy old boy. They tell me he has more neckties than Sulka's, with pants to match. Much of his publicity after his marriage to the fifteen-year-old Peaches came from the way he threw his bankroll around in her behalf, though Peaches now says he always had a rope tied to it. She says he wears fishhooks in his pockets so that when he gets his hand in 'em he can't get it out.

Prior to the advent of Peaches, the old boy broke into print through an advertisement for a girl companion for Dorothy "Sunshine" Browning, a child now ten years old, whom he adopted when she was about six. Many young women were almost trampled to death in the ensuing crush of applicants for the job, and Daddy finally nominated Miss Mary Spas and adopted her, also.

A condition of the advertisement was that the girl must be under sixteen. Captious observers of Mary said they would hate to be hanging since she was sixteen, and finally it came out that she had omitted the winters in calculating her summers. Daddy gave her the air, but Mary now has suits pending against Daddy for something like half a million, and mentions an attempted assault at the Kew Gardens Inn among other things.

You can readily see that Daddy is having his troubles with those kids, but not half as much trouble as he might have had if he had gone pestering around fifteen-year-old children out in—well, let me say out in Trinidad, Colorado. You see, I know Trinidad, Colorado.

But the effete East seems more blasé about these things, and thus we have the great moral spectacle in this modern civilization of a legal hearing involving a gray-haired old wowser and a child-wife attracting more attention than the League of Nations. Such life in the snow-clad hills of Putnam County, New York.

I say snow-clad because it has been snowing all day, and the chances are Daddy and Peaches will have to travel to the old, picturesque colonial court house tomorrow morning on skis. Carmel has a population of about five hundred, and it squats on the shore of Lake Glendida, which is part of the reservoir system of New York City.

The lake is frozen tighter than Daddy Browning's pocketbook as described by Peaches, and skating would be fine if anybody had any skates, or the desire to skate. The natives and the visiting firemen spent the day hived up in the tepees of Carmel, speculating on the outcome of the trial and its effect on business in Carmel.

There have been a few mild squawks among the visiting firemen because the price of bed and board has been jacked up to some extent in Carmel, but one can scarcely blame the citizenry. They do not get a crack at outsiders as often as other communities. They may never get another Browning trial.

There is some chatter that the hearing may be moved to White Plains, or possibly to Poughkeepsie. I hope and trust that in the latter case it will not produce at dear old Vassar the drastic steps taken by the head of a local seminary for young ladies. I am informed that they have been instructed to keep away from public places during the hearing.

I am wondering if this order is by any chance a reflection upon any of the visiting Apollos and Adonises of the New York press, or merely a wise precaution against Daddy Browning.

The hearing is before Supreme Court Justice Albert H. S. Seeger. There will be no jury. One of Daddy's attorneys is John E. Mack, of Poughkeepsie, who was appointed guardian ad litem for baby Stillman in the Stillman divorce squabble, another of our historical moral episodes of this century. His attorney of record is Francis C. Dale, an able barrister of Cold Springs and New York City.

It was at Cold Springs that Daddy married Peaches last April. He had met her at a dance after the episode with Mary Spas, during which Daddy became known as "the Cinderella man." This was because he loaded Mary up with clothes and what not, and drove her around in a Rolls-Royce. It is said now that this Rolls-Royce was hired, but a hired Rolls-Royce is none the less a Rolls-Royce.

Henry Epstein is Peaches' attorney. Peaches was married to Daddy with the consent of her mother, Mrs. Catherine Heenan, and it is said that Mother Heenan's ears feel like they are all afire just from what Daddy is thinking about her. Mother Heenan is expected to figure in this hearing tomorrow no little.

There was a mysterious incident in the romance of Daddy and Peaches that may be cleared up during the hearing. Someone threw a lot of acid in Peaches' face, and she still wears the scars. Some say this and some say that about the acid-throwing. Now it can be told, as Sir Philip Gibbs said of the war.

Mary Spas tossed off a hooker of iodine after her jam with Daddy Browning at the Kew Gardens Inn, so it is related, but nothing came of it. However, it was considered another quite thrilling chapter in the life, and so forth, of Daddy. He was a divorcé. Some say his income is around $300,000 per year. If it was about $1,200 you would never have heard a whisper of him.

Organizations devoted to the welfare of children have made various motions toward getting Dorothy Sunshine Browning away from Daddy at different times, alleging that he is an unfit guardian, but she is still with him, and, moreover, is very fond of him. I do not know Daddy's exact pose in life, but some say he regards himself as a philanthropist. It may be so.

Anyway, Carmel is all agog—in fact, I might say it is all agoggogga— over the events of tomorrow. The court house is in apple pie order, the telegraph wires are tuned in to the Queen's taste, and your correspondent's typewriter is well oiled.

January 24, 1927

I regret to report that the opening scene of the great moral opus, entitled "The Saps of 1927," and featuring the inimitable Daddy and Peaches Browning, fell a little flat today.

It was not the fault of the principals. It was their material. There was no "dirt" whatever. Nothing came out that you couldn't mention freely in any modern drawing room or speakeasy.

The upshot of the whole business today was this:

A couple of witnesses, telling pallid, colorless tales, were examined in Daddy's suit for separation against Peaches, that buxom matron of sixteen, who sat encased in a mink coat and in a rather blubbery state of mind and emotion during the hearing.

Daddy charged that Peaches abandoned him, and wouldn't come back. The testimony of the witnesses was designed to prove this to Supreme Court Justice Seeger.

Then Henry Epstein, Peaches' attorney, made a brace of motions, one that the suit be dismissed as to the abandonment on the ground that no proof had been presented, the other to dismiss the suit as to Peaches' refusal to return on the same ground—no proof.

Judge Seeger denied the second motion and withheld decision on the first, but sustained a motion by Epstein to hold the hearing at White Plains beginning tomorrow morning.

And that was that.

The good citizens of Putnam County, who packed the little low-ceilinged court room, noisily stamping the snow from their galoshes, and removing their mufflers and ear-tippets as they entered, seemed somewhat disappointed.

Some were almost indignant, especially when it was decided to take the show over to White Plains tomorrow afternoon. The taxpayers of Putnam County didn't get as much as one bedtime story for their money. It may be made an issue in the next election. True they got $1.50 per pair of mutton chops, but I doubt if that makes up for their loss of what they expected.

They came with their wives, grandmothers, maiden aunts, and one little baby in arms. Some of the ladies brought their tatting, anticipating startlement that might cause them to drop a few stitches. The baby howled at intervals, then stopped so suddenly that everybody looked around, thinking perhaps a heartless mother had stuffed a galosh in its maw.

But it seems that the mother had merely whispered to the baby that Daddy Browning was entering the room. It was a girl baby.

Daddy Browning—the old boy himself—rolled up to the vintage court house in a blue Rolls-Royce, and faced the cameras like a man. In fact, like several men. He had more law attending him than a rich bootlegger, as he stalked into court.

Daddy wore a blue sack coat, with thin white penciling, and the coat was a tight fit. He had the bottom button fastened so that his chest protruded in front like a platter, and his pistol pocket stuck out so far behind that several of his lawyers following in his rear couldn't get through the doorway until he was well in the clear.

A rattle of applause broke out among the spectators as Daddy Browning came down an aisle, walking first on one foot, and then on the other. Judge Seeger hammered his desk, and said he would clear the court room if there were any more such demonstrations. The judge is an iron-gray man in a pepper-and-salt suit, and an air of determination.

When the applause started, Daddy looked around as if he had some idea of taking a bow. Some say he probably brought his own claque with him, but I am inclined to scout this theory, as I saw my sorrel secretary, The Bull, in the background leading the applause.

The Bull is one of the lads from the neighborhood of Sixty-ninth Street and West End Avenue and he jockeyed your correspondent over the snowy roads from New York to this spot in a roadster. Feeling certain that The Bull knows nothing of the merits of the case, I asked him why he had applauded Daddy, and he said:

"Well, I thought he was Leon Errol coming in to do some funny falls for us."

You see how much a man may be mistaken.

Daddy is of medium height, and his figure is probably not what it used to be. Only the last button on the coat gives him a waistline. He has a florid complexion and gray hair, that has been worn off the top of his head like the nap on a wool coat.

He has dark eyes that are constantly shifting their gaze. Daddy's eyes remind me of the orbs of Mr. Harry K. Thaw, that other celebrated connoisseur of feminine youth. I say this with all due respect to both Daddy and Mr. Harry K. Thaw.

Peaches was already in the court room when Daddy arrived. In the shuffle of the entrance, and being propelled forward by the solid movement of his attorneys behind him, Daddy was shunted so close to her chair that he could have reached out and touched her. He gave her one swift peek, and sharply turned away.

Peaches immediately opened a handbag about the size of a laundry sack, fumbled therein and extracted a handkerchief, which she applied to her eyes. Her mother, Mrs. Catherine Heenan, who sat beside her, leaned forward and whispered in her ear, but Peaches continued somewhat lachrymose throughout the hearing.

One of my sage ancestors once told me that whenever I contemplated matrimony I should go around and take a look at the girl's old lady, meaning her mother, and see what twenty years had done for the parent. I should say that a decade hence Peaches will be the present Mrs. Heenan to the life. She is the image of her Maw.

Peaches is large and blonde. Her hair is a straw color. She is one of those expansive, patient looking blondes, who are sometimes very impatient. She has blue eyes which contain an expression of resignation. She has stout legs. I hesitate to expatiate on so delicate a matter, but they are what the boys call "piano legs." Her feet are small. She had them encased in neat brown ties.

Under her mink coat, which probably cost a couple of thousand dollars, she wore a blue dress, blue being a color that matches her complexion well. Her hat was blue, and fitted close over her hair. There were wisps of brown feathers on either side of the hat. She wore a big diamond pin on her breast and a diamond pendant around her neck.

Take her by and large, she was gotten up very expensively, and if you care for the large type in blondes she is reasonably pulchritudinous. I mean to say she is what you would call good looking—if you like 'em in her style. They say she was fifteen when she married Daddy. She could pass for twenty, and nobody would bat an eye.

Her mother was dressed in black, with a black fur coat around her, black hat, and black shoes and stockings of a color that I believe the girls call "nude." Mrs. Heenan, too, suggested that she had spent some money on her appearance. She sat close to her chick and child, and she took a couple of offhand glares at Daddy that would have done him no good if glances were lethal weapons.

Peaches' mouth droops in an adenoidal manner. She smiled wanly at a couple of acquaintances in the press seats, crossed her stout legs, and tried to compose herself as the proceedings opened. She had a spray of orchids pinned to her mink coat, but she was scarcely the picture of a forlorn little child-wife that I had expected. It is very difficult for any one to look forlorn in a mink coat.

There was an informal, jovial aspect to the brief hearing. The bench and bar made humorous sallies, especially Mr. John E. Mack, who did the talking for Daddy's side, and who has a Texas hair cut and looks like a Missouri statesman of the period of Bill Bryan. He is of Poughkeepsie, I believe.

It developed at once that both Daddy and Peaches have suddenly been overtaken by a yearning for privacy in the discussion of their matrimonial caterwauling. They want it behind closed doors. Up to this time neither Daddy nor Peaches has been a shrinking violet in the matter of publicity, especially Daddy, who has eagerly held his jowly countenance up to every camera in New York City, while Peaches has told her story almost from the housetops.

But Henry Epstein, a small, neat-looking man, with a close-clipped black mustache, and a low, confiding voice, asked Judge Seeger for a hearing in chambers as soon as the session opened this morning. He requested that the press and public be excluded, intimating that the testimony might be such as to be inimical to public morals, something Daddy, at least, hasn't apparently given much thought to in the past.

Epstein is said to be related to Max Steuer, the great trial lawyer of Manhattan Island. His request was not altogether unexpected. Mack supported it, saying that while Daddy himself wished a public hearing he disagreed with his client on that point and thought that public decency should be considered.

Judge Seeger said he would rule on the point later, but he suggested that the parties to the matter hadn't manifested any desire for secrecy in the past. He added that he had received a letter from a women's organization in Carmel asking that the hearing be private. Carmel, at least, will not be further troubled by the publicity of the case.

It is doubtful that Judge Seeger will grant the request for a private hearing, perhaps on the ground that publicity may serve as a deterrent to other cases of a similar nature. A private hearing would compel the newspaper men and women who were banked in the jury box and the spectators' seats in the court room today to get their information as to the progress of the case outside the court room, perhaps from Daddy or Peaches themselves.

The first witness called by Mr. Mack for Daddy's side was Edward P. Kearney, a chauffeur in the employ of one John J. Goishow, of New York. He drove the Rolls-Royce that was Peaches' envied chariot in the early days of her married bliss or what-have-you. It was supposed to be Daddy's own car, but it later developed that he merely rented it.

Anyway, Kearney, a solid, chauffeurish looking gent, told of taking Peaches and her Maw and her trunks from Daddy's apartment in the Kew Gardens Inn to Mrs. Heenan's home in One Hundred and Seventy-fifth Street and of hearing Peaches say: "Money isn't everything after all."

An astonishing discovery, as the reader must admit. This was the occasion when Peaches is supposed to have quit Daddy's home—when she gave him what is technically known as "the air."

Epstein cross-examined him, but briefly—so briefly that you might think he had little interest in the testimony of the mahout of the Rolls-Royce. He denied that he worked for Browning. He said Goishow, a name that led to quaint repartee between Mr. Mack and the bench, was his employer.

John P. Gorman, a bald man, who said he is Daddy's secretary, testified to listening in at Daddy's request to a telephone conversation between Daddy and Peaches' mother after Peaches had quit Daddy.

Gorman said he often listened to conversations between Daddy and other persons, at Daddy's request via an extension phone.

He said Daddy asked Mrs. Heenan to let him talk with Peaches, and that Mrs. Heenan said: "Peaches is through with you, Mr. Browning."

Kearney's testimony was designed to show the court that Peaches had abandoned Daddy, and Gorman's testimony to prove that she wouldn't come back to Daddy. As Gorman concluded, Mack said his side rested.

Epstein was as brief with Gorman as with the other witnesses. He asked Gorman how much money he got from Daddy, and Gorman said his salary is $3,000 per year. Epstein demanded:

"Didn't you thank Mrs. Browning for getting you a raise?"

The witness said no. And that's all there was to the hearing, save that Epstein presented his application for a transfer of the case to White Plains, and it was granted. It seems that the attorneys on both sides had agreed to such a transfer beforehand.

There was some applause as the first witness left the stand, and again Judge Seeger admonished the spectators. I looked around hastily, and did not see The Bull slapping his hands together. He was, in fact, asleep. One might infer from the applause that Daddy's side is the favorite side in this community, but they might have applauded just as hard had Peaches had an inning. Applause often goes with the fellow in front at the moment.

As Daddy and Peaches left the court room to take their respective cars, Daddy his Rolls-Royce, and Peaches a less pretentious buggy, they were surrounded by the crowd. Both stood for more photos, but not together. It is not of record that they were asked for a group-posing, and it is no cinch it couldn't have been had.

The typewriters were hastily folded up tonight and the procession moves on to White Plains. But I must warn Daddy and Peaches that the great American public will not tolerate many more pale performances such as they gave this morning. If they haven't got any scandal to offer, they might as well send for Mr. Cain, the theatrical warehouse man, and put their show in storage. He has a lot better shows as it is.

White Plains, New York, January 25, 1927

Your correspondent's manly cheeks are still suffused with blushes as he sits down to write of a few peeks into the bridal chamber of dear old Daddy Browning and his Peaches.

He is almost sorry now that Judge Seeger did not grant the application of Peaches' attorney for a private hearing. Your correspondent would have been spared the embarrassment of listening to Peaches' narrative of the strange didoes of Daddy.

But the thing being public, your correspondent, in common with the rest of the world, risked one eye at the keyhole, as you might say, and heard the buxom and at times blubbery Peaches tell about Daddy on the nuptial night—and on many other nights, too.

How that old boy did carry on, hear Peaches tell it! Hey, hey! Not a word to the major, as the girls say.

The gods on Mount Olympus, or wherever it is the gods assemble, must have held their sides with laughter today—and probably their noses, too—as they looked down and watched the earthworms wriggling in the muck heap of a modern-day matrimonial squabble.

They must have guffawed, these gods, as they saw a court room jammed with men and women and young girls, with their ears distended, and a street packed with people almost rioting in their desire to get a peep at the principals in a duel of defamation.

The gods must scent familiar odors rising from this particular spot on the globe and perhaps wonder if somebody didn't bury a load of limburger cheese hereabouts and go away and forget it, for it was in the court house in White Plains that the Rhinelander case of unfragrant memory almost asphyxiated the populace.

It was in another court room, however, than the one in which Peaches sat prattling away this afternoon when a recess was taken until tomorrow morning, and Daddy Browning went bouncing down the court house steps to the cheers of the assembled citizens.

In this instance I think the cheers were inspired, largely by a crafty newspaper photographer who desired to get some good action pictures of the multitude, and who bawled, "Three cheers for Daddy."

I think few citizens resist an impulse to cheer when properly approached. Thus the White Plains welkin rang with a couple of strong yip-yips. The third was not so strong. Somebody said, "Tiger," and I distinctly heard the unmistakable noise that you make when the tongue flutters between the teeth.

But Daddy bowed in all directions. He was a little bit flustered on emerging from the court house after hearing Peaches tell those tales out of school about his alleged abnormalities and one thing and another.

I would not think of disclosing some of the allegations in a family newspaper. Your Uncle Samuel would bar it from his mails. They are the things that are only put in plays nowadays—the kind of plays that Mayor Jimmy Walker often speaks of censoring.

They were pretty raw. Peaches herself did not want to blurt them out before the crowded court room, and she looked appealingly at Judge Seeger when Mr. Henry Epstein, her attorney, pressed her for answers to certain questions. She asked, "Must I tell all these people?"

Judge Seeger said softly, "Yes."

Peaches cried into her handkerchief, and told.

At one point she broke down and sobbed so lustily that Mr. Epstein asked for a brief recess. Peaches' mother was stitting back among the witnesses today, and hurried to her daughter's comfort when Peaches was taken into an ante-room.

I thought that perhaps the testimony might cause some of the female spectators to step outside for a breath of air, but not one stirred.

I think that possibly, next to your correspondent, Mr. Henry Epstein was perhaps the most embarrassed person in Westchester County as he questioned his client. He had asked to have the hearing in private, but when Judge Seeger denied the motion at the opening of the hearing, Mr. Epstein set his teeth and plunged on in, like a man hopping into a cold tub.

When he got to the point where he wanted Peaches to tell the Court those things that I cannot tell you, he again asked that the room be cleared, but the Court said no.

Mr. Epstein turned quite pale, wiped his close-clipped little black mustache with a neat handkerchief, took a big swig of water, fumbled with a pencil, and questioned Peaches in a low, soft voice. Embarrassment leaked out all over him.

Peaches left her expensive looking fur coat in her chair when she took the stand. Some say this is a sable coat that cost $20,000. I believe Daddy himself claims he paid $5,500 for it. I classed it as a mink, but these girls are wearing so many different animal skins nowadays that one is apt to get confused.

It probably cost even less than Daddy himself says, if Peaches' tales of his economy in other respects are true.

She wore the same blue dress and the same blue hat that she wore at Carmel yesterday when the hearing was transferred to White Plains.

A close-up of Peaches takes away none of the buxomness of a distant view, but it removes some of the expensiveness of her get-up of a first impression. She had a little round watch suspended from a chain around her neck, an article of jewelry that cost not over $30, and she wore her monogram in near-diamonds on her breast.

A huge but not expensive slave-bracelet was around one arm. The best piece of jewelry that she displayed today was her wedding ring, a diamond circlet that she said cost Daddy $200.

However, under cross-examination she admitted that he had given her one ring that cost $3,500 and a bracelet that stood him $2,500. She said she got $50 per week for pin money, and Daddy paid all her living expenses. Moreover, her mother got an allowance from him.

She weighed 140 pounds when she was married in April and had shot up to 160 pounds when she quit him six months later. She is certainly a bit to the hefty side, although she is only sixteen. Her chin and neck are sadly disfigured by the mysterious acid burns that she got one morning while asleep shortly before her marriage to Daddy.

These acid burns came in for some investigation by John Mack, who is a peremptory sort of man in handling a witness, but given to joviality. She said she had no idea at the time she received the burns who could have thrown the acid on her, but today on cross-examination she said she thought Daddy might have had something to do with them.

At least she expressed the opinion that she wouldn't have been burned if she had never met Daddy. She was a bit hazy as to just how she arrived at this conclusion.

She struck me at times as a little bit more sophisticated than her years would suggest when Mr. Mack was cross-examining her. She used very precise language, but now and then she would grow a bit tempery, and would say "sure," and "positively." She called a bell-boy, a "bell hop," which I believe is accepted English in some circles, but not always in the best. She invariably said "gittin'." Her voice and manner are quite mature.

Daddy listened to her with interest. He frowned when she spoke of some of his antics, and laughed at her recital of others. There was a matter of a goose, described by Peaches as an African honking goose, which was brought home by Daddy in jocular mood one evening, and which caused Peaches much pain and mental anguish, she said.

It seems that the goose was a live goose, and it caused disorder in the apartment that tickled Daddy no end. Then he put it in a cage on the back of his car and journeyed to Long Beach with the goose honking all the way. Mack suggested jovially, "You didn't think you had married a goose?"

Peaches answered with an attempt at severity, "No."

She admitted a photograph taken of her and the goose at Long Beach, however, but said that was Daddy's doings.

January 26, 1927

Our legal pulling and hauling here in the interests of the moral uplift of the nation came to a halt today until Monday.

The pause is not, as you might suspect, to give the sanitary authorities of this pleasant Westchester County town a chance to fumigate the premises. It is to give Daddy Browning's attorneys time to marshal testimony to refute the many, many things that Peaches said about that great big gander man.

Also what some of Peaches witnesses said about him today, which was plenty. There was one witness, for instance, who came along at the afternoon session, a Miss Marion Tussey, of New York, one of Peaches' friends, who testified that as late as last Saturday Daddy came snooping around her house asking her if she hadn't taken Peaches on nude parties, and hadn't she chaperoned Peaches to a doctor for an illegal operation?

All this before Peaches' marriage to Daddy, you understand. Miss Tussey said she told Daddy she hadn't done anything of the sort, wherefore, so she testified, Daddy remarked that it would be worth her while if she could think up something to that effect, and would get her a lot of publicity. It probably would.

Miss Tussey is a young woman who is a bit on the fleshy side. I mean to say she is plumpish. She was one of a quartette of ladies who came in together today, and who all appeared on the stand, the party including Peaches herself, Peaches' mother, a Mrs. Catherine Mayer, and Miss Tussey.

Put 'em all together, they spelt hefty.

But by Monday morning Daddy expects to have enough evidence assembled in White Plains to prove that everything Peaches and her witnesses said is all dead wrong, and that he is the nicest, whitest, kindliest, and possibly the happiest fifty-two-year-oldster that ever joined hands in wedlock with a fifteen-year-old flapper.

Barring certain alleged abnormalities, Peaches has so far merely made Browning out a little bit dizzy for a gent of his years. The most serious charge she made against him was an innuendo in reference to ten-year-old Dorothy Sunshine Browning, his adopted daughter.

I gathered from a statement made this morning by John E. Mack that he expects to produce some snappy testimony on behalf of his client. The folks can hardly wait to hear it. The folks have been somewhat disappointed so far. The testimony has been putrid in spots, but it might have been worse.

Peaches confessed to a little fib at the morning session through her attorney, the abashed Henry Epstein. He got up and told Judge Seeger, in a soft, low voice, that last evening after leaving the court house, Peaches had sent for him and told him that the red-backed diary she produced in court yesterday as a diary she had kept before her marriage was not the original manuscript.

Mr. Epstein seemed pained as he mentioned this circumstance. He said he asked her if she had the original diary, and she admitted she had. Then he told Peaches to produce it in court today. Mr. Epstein said gently:

"I consider that my duty as an officer of this court and as attorney for my client requires that the truth and all of the truth should be known."

Mr. Mack took hold of that with avidity. Peaches was on the stand, still under cross-examination at the time, and he asked for the original diary. She pointed to her handbag, on her attorney's table, and another red-backed book, somewhat similar to the one she displayed yesterday, was produced.

Peaches said she had kept the diary until the day she was married. It seems that she made record of the little episodes of her girlhood such as casual "neckings" with the flaming youth of her acquaintance. I believe they call it "necking" now, but when your correspondent was a "necker" of no mean standing back in the dim and misty past, they called it "lally-gagging." Times have changed. The girls didn't keep diaries then, thank heaven.

Well, Peaches had set down the names of the "neckers" or "neckees," as the case might be, so she said, but she had great respect for the boys she went out with, they were all very nice to her, and she wished to keep them out of the court record. The diary she had produced yesterday was one she had written at the suggestion of a young man, Joseph Morris, she said. Joseph is in the court record, anyway. Mr. Mack inquired:

"Were the boys mentioned in the original diary, boys that you had made love to, and that had made love to you?"

Peaches answered, "They were."

The world do move, my friends. Talk of "love" at fifteen and less. The world do move.

In her copy she had omitted all names.

Some of the pages had been torn out of the original diary, and Mr. Mack inquired about them. Peaches said there had been nothing on those pages. She admitted, as Mr. Mack read from her testimony of yesterday, that she had fibbed about the diary. Her cheeks were scarlet against the blue of her hat as she confessed the little lie.

Mr. Mack wanted to put both diaries in evidence, and Mr. Epstein objected on the ground that they pertained to events before Peaches' marriage and therefore could have nothing to do with the present hearing. Mr. Mack said:

"Your Honor will find in the diaries, unless I am mistaken, and I am satisfied that I am not, the writings of this young lady to show that she was a woman of the world, even though young. They are extremely important as bearing upon her story that she was an innocent girl at the time of her marriage, and knew nothing of the usual marriage relations."

Peaches answered sharply, "I was a good girl when I married."

Mr. Mack went on:

"They are part of the res gestae, and with the letters which I intend to offer will give Your Honor a picture of this marriage of December and May and bring into Your Honor's mind, in my opinion, the conviction that the story which this lady told on the stand is, under all circumstances and all the evidence, unbelievable."

But Judge Seeger sided with Mr. Epstein and would not admit the diaries, though he said Mr. Mack might file briefs to support another similar motion.

Peaches was finally excused after she had identified a mass of letters shown her by Mr. Mack as her handwriting, and a number of copies of a newspaper containing the tale of her marital woes with the elderly Daddy.

Daddy dug these letters and papers out of a huge, black valise, of the "telescope" variety. Both Peaches and Daddy seem to be disregarding this royal opportunity for sartorial display, as she has worn the same dress and hat since the trial started, and though Daddy is said to be the owner in fee simple of a thousand neckties, he has worn the same one, of a scrambled-egg pattern, from the beginning, and the same suit.

Peaches said she got $15 per week in the auditing department of Bedell's before her marriage and attended Textile High. Large round tears welled up in her eyes a couple of times, but she did not break down, though her mother, Mrs. Catherine Heenan, sat right at her side ready to render first aid in case of a collapse.

Even a case-hardened old sinner, such as your correspondent, must feel a little sympathy for Peaches, regardless of the merits of her case against Daddy. He is no rose-geranium any way you take him. The child-wife seems to be a victim of circumstances in many respects. She is disfigured for life, how and why, has not been made clear, but perhaps, as she says, it wouldn't have happened if she had never met Daddy, though she admits he didn't burn her.

She is marked for life spiritually, as well as physically—a tough break for a sixteen-year-old girl, however you look at it. The pity is, so far as she is concerned, that Daddy had more than two dollars. Otherwise you would never have heard his name—or her name, for that matter.

Old friend mother-in-law was with us much of the morning session in the person of Mrs. Heenan. You have seen her, my brothers, full many a time and oft. Yes.

Of about the shape and heft of Willie Meehan, the old time roly-poly of the manly art of scrambling ears. Willie was shaped like an apple. She wore a black hat and a dark blue dress, drawn a bit tightly and skittishly about her hips. She smiled at her daughter as she sat down in the witness chair.

She followed to the stand one Mrs. Catherine Mayer, a woman of middle age, with a middle-age bob, who wore eye-glasses and a black satin dress and who told of quarrels between Peaches and Daddy while in the first bloom of their honeymoon at Cold Springs. Mrs. Mayer lives with Mrs. Heenan and corroborated much of Peaches' tales with reference to the battling at Cold Springs.

Daddy gave Mother Heenan a good strong son-in-law glare as she said, "He always called me mother."

She said Peaches was born in Columbus, Ohio, and that she herself was divorced in 1918 from her husband. She asked Mr. Mack coyly, "Do I have to tell my age?"

"Certainly not."

She replied, bridling, "I am forty-three."

Mr. Epstein produced Peaches' birth certificate which she identified and which Mr. Mack examined carefully and then objected to. The objection was not sustained.

Mrs. Heenan, too, told of Cold Springs. She said she had gone there and leased a house at Daddy's instructions with money furnished by him, because Daddy's attorney, Captain Dale, told her they wanted everything legal in case of any action by the Children's Society, which was threatening steps against her as unfit guardian of Peaches.

She said she noticed her daughter was unhappy at once, and heard Peaches and Daddy quarreling with great vim.

Mrs. Heenan said she was with Peaches and Daddy at the battles of Cold Springs, the Fairfield and the Gramatan hotels, but always at Daddy's invitation, whereupon Daddy's countenance took on a wry expression as if he had bitten into a lemon.

She said Daddy gave her daughter the name of Peaches. Others always called her Frances. Under cross-examination by Mr. Mack, she told about Daddy coming home one night with his face very red, and said he produced a bottle from his pocket and said, "Mother, I'm drunk."

It was on this occasion, she said, that he threatened to shoot Peaches and her, but became very contrite when she threatened to call the police.

Mr. Mack demanded:

"How big was that bottle? You're a nurse and familiar with ounces, how many ounces would that bottle contain?"

Mrs. Heenan replied, "About two ounces."

Mr. Mack looked startled. A two-ounce bottle is not much of a bottle, when you are talking about liquor.

He continued to press the lady for more information.

Mr. Mack, still on the subject of Daddy's condition, demanded, "Did he stagger like this?"

Then the counsel gave a very life-like stagger around his table, and Mrs. Heenan brightened. She said, "Just like that."

She said she had advised her daughter to return to Daddy and had always tried to keep peace between them, but that her daughter failed in health until after she left Daddy. Then she picked right up again.

At the afternoon session, Arthur Leduc, a reporter on the *Evening Journal,* testified briefly to having received pictures from Daddy, and to having interviewed Daddy and Peaches time and again. He said Daddy sent for him after the separation, and wanted to know how many times he had kissed Peaches and would he testify to the calculation. Leduc denied ever having kissed the blushing bride.

The attorneys on both sides filed a stipulation to defer the matter of investigating Daddy's financial status, which is involved in the squabble, until after the main issue had been settled.

Miss Tussey was the last witness of the day. She said a man named Proctor called at her apartment last Saturday evening and she refused to see him; then her landlord, one Croner, called her downstairs and introduced her to Proctor. She pointed out Proctor, sitting next to Daddy in the court room. He is of Daddy's legal squad.

Proctor gave her $5 and a subpoena, she said. Then Daddy came in, and wanted to know about those alleged nude parties, and that alleged illegal operation, as related at the beginning of this long-winded tale. Also, she said, Daddy wanted to know if Mrs. Heenan had ever belonged to a "call house," a "call house," my friends, being an institution of great iniquity, indigenous only to this great moral country.

Then Daddy and Peaches were left free to fight their way through the crowd that jammed the court room, the corridors and the street outside, though the ozone hereabouts was so nippy today that only a case of this nature could have kept the populace waiting out in the cold.

You could scarcely stir in the court room this afternoon, the crowd was so dense. At one stage the entire grand jury, on leave of absence for the moment from its arduous duty of making the rain of justice fall on the unjust, filed into the room, and stood listening with palpitating eardrums to the recitals.

Daddy got a mild cheer as he proceeded to his waiting Rolls-Royce, from which his chauffeur and footman had to clear a pile of rubbish made up of notes tossed into the car by ladies with strangely shaped heads. Peaches also got a few scattering whoops as she appeared before the public gaze.

This is a great country, my friends!

January 31, 1927

Some heavy emoting by that buxom matron of sixteen summers and 160 pounds, Mrs. Peaches Browning, was perhaps the high blood pressure point in our little sextravaganza in the Westchester County Court House today.

One James P. Mixon, black-haired, blocky-built, young man, in a blue serge suit, well shined in spots from much sitting down, came along testifying for old Daddy Browning that he had once been one of Peaches' little playmates in her flippery-flappery days before she married that great big rubber egg man.

This James P. Mixon did not get a chance to tell just how they played, but it was suggested in questions by John E. Mack, the bland, Bryanesque-looking, up-State attorney for Daddy, that brought Peaches to her feet, denouncing James P. Mixon as a liar in spades.

James P. Mixon gave his address as No. 65 Patchen Avenue, Brooklyn, no occupation stated. He said he was born in Louisiana, and nine Southern gentlemen in the court room suddenly keeled over as they thought of the possibility that his answers to Mack's interrogations might have been, "Yes, indeed."

Henry Epstein, the bashful attorney for Peaches, who seems to be growing more forward as he becomes inured to the slush, filed an objection to each question asked James P. Mixon as fast as it was asked by Mack, and Justice Seeger in each instance sustained the objection.

But meantime the questions as presented gave one and all something of a background for speculation over their morning's morning.

Peaches and her mother, who sat side by side at their counsel's table, looked somewhat startled as James P. Mixon eased his way through the journalists jammed in the jury box, and slumped down in the witness stand.

He had a black, beetling brow and rather a snarly expression. He did not state his age, but I would guess it as in the mid-twenties.

After Mack's first few questions it dawned on the assembled multitude what James P. Mixon's errand might be, and I think no one envied him his situation, though he was examined with great care by those present who might be interested in those odd specimens of human fauna that you come upon from time to time in the nooks and crevices of life.

Of course it is only fair to give James P. Mixon the benefit of the doubt and suggest that he might have answered no to Mack's questions, but so far the witnesses in the jolly little matrimonial muck-heaving between Peaches and Daddy have run to expected form.

James P. Mixon said he had met Peaches on the Strand Roof before her marriage to Daddy, and then he sat silent in the witness chair, looking somewhat uncomfortable, as Mack queried and Epstein objected.

Mack asked:

"Did you give her money to buy underwear?"

"Did you accompany her to a room in a hotel?"

"Did she take a bath and come out in the underwear and ask you how you liked her?"

"Did you and Peaches stay over night in the hotel room?"

All these, and others the witness was not permitted to answer.

Justice Seeger said, "That's far enough."

"Do you think I'm going too far?" Mack asked as if surprised.

Apparently the Court did. You see we must have some delicacy somewhere in this matter, and not reach a point where we might offend good taste. I believe my readers will appreciate this restraint.

"Do you see this girl sitting there?"

Epstein asked it when he took the witness for cross-examination. Epstein's face was white with anger, and his index finger trembled violently as he aimed it at Peaches, whose blue eyes had been fixed on Mack's amiable countenance with an expression of alarm as he presented his interrogations.

Occasionally she looked at the witness with scorn. Her mother looked at him with several scorns. I suppose it is just as well for all hands that glances do not produce sudden strangulation, or James P. Mixon might have been lugged out of the court room feet foremost.

Mrs. Heenan remains the most remarkable parent I have ever clapped these old orbs on. The remarkable thing to me is that she can sit in the court room and hear all this junk about her child without having attacks of vertigo.

Anyway, James P. Mixon said yes, he did see Peaches, though his glance at her was what you might call casual. Epstein shouted, "Is she the one you are talking about?"

"Yes."

Peaches cried, her blue eyes bubbling tears: "He lies! I never saw him before in my life."

"That's the one, is it?"

Mack roared it, his voice clattering right behind Epstein's question and also taking a good point at Peaches.

"There's no question about that, is there?"

"No."

Peaches hopped to her feet and hammered her fist on the table, shouting, "I never saw him before in my life! He's perjuring himself!"

"You keep quiet!"

Epstein admonished her thus, a trifle ungallantly, so Peaches dissolved into tears and her mother wept with her.

Old Daddy seemed to enjoy this scene. He came in this morning wearing a black overcoat piped with silk, a blue suit and a very speedy tie. He always has a battery of three fat cigars jutting out of the upper outside pocket of his coat.

He had a pair of eye-glasses perched precariously on his aquiline beak, and was industriously poring over papers of one kind and another all day, but he listened with both ears wagging as Mack queried James P. Mixon.

Also Daddy smiled when Peaches went into her big scene.

Mixon said a man who said his name was Alexander came to him after Peaches' marriage and wanted to pay him to keep still about his relations with her. Mack asked Epstein, "Is Alexander one of your investigators?"

"I never employed an investigator at any time in this action."

It seems the witness married after an alleged hotel incident with Peaches, and Mack brought out from him that Mrs. Mixon gave him the well-known ozone when she heard of his terrible past in connection with Peaches.

Mrs. Mixon appeared on the stand, a slight, dark, little woman in a pink hat and black dress, and said she had seen photos of Peaches in her husband's possession and had torn up letters signed "Frances."

You must understand that no actual testimony bearing on all this innuendo contained in Mack's questions is in the records. Justice Seeger held that anything pertaining to Peaches' life before her marriage is not germane to this hearing.

Mack's idea was to prove by incidents in Peaches' past that she could not have been as mortified and chagrined as she alleges in her demand for separation from Daddy by the matters she sets up in said demand, such as being required to appear before him *au naturel,* so to speak.

Justice Seeger did permit Mixon to testify about an alleged telephone conversation with Peaches after her marriage, in which they wished plenty of happiness to each other, Mixon having meantime become wrapped up in those holy bonds of matrimony.

We had no little comedy today, and there was a genial atmosphere to the proceedings, with the Court and counsel bandying quips.

"Are you trying to establish that the lady didn't wear clothing in the dining-room?"

So inquired Justice Seeger, as Mack queried employees of the Kew Gardens Inn as to Peaches' manner of apparel in those jolly days of her honeymoon.

Then again, when Frank W. Golden, headwaiter at the inn, seemed to hesitate in answering questions by Epstein as to Daddy's liberality in tips, Justice Seeger said:

"You can tell what he gave you. We will not take it away from you."

I mention this to show you that we are far from acrimony as we go forward in this matter. The only ill-feeling today was developed in the crowd that stormed the court house because some of the New York newspapers have deplored the publicity given the hearing, and said that there really ought to be a censorship of everything.

I really felt sorry for the officers of the law on guard over the court room doors and feel that something should be done to insure their protection in the future.

They were viciously assaulted by infuriated women trying to shove past them to listen to the testimony and determine for themselves if it is as terrible as they hear. Hell hath no fury like a woman trying to break into a court room.

The more dangerous were mainly women past thirty and they stepped on the cops' corns and snatched buttons off the cops' jackets, and threatened to tweak the cops' noses if the cops got too gay with them.

One of the court room doors was broken down. The court room was jammed until the seams spread. Many of the women were standing on chairs to get a peek over the heads of those fortunate enough to grab seats, and Justice Seeger admonished them of danger.

"I warn you that if anybody stands on chairs it is at her own risk. You may get hurt if the chairs give way."

The street outside the court house and the corridors inside, were jammed before the morning session began. Everybody wished to get a look at Peaches and Daddy as they made their entrance. It was the biggest day in point of excitement and attendance since the hearing began.

Charlotte Mills, that drab, troubled looking little reminder of the Hall-Mills trial at Somerville, was an early arrival, and sat in the jury box. She wore a rose-colored turban, and a black coat. Charlotte is said to have been called as a witness.

There were a lot of distinguished looking citizens in the crowd, including Lady So-and-so. I have really forgotten the moniker.

Grandmotherly looking old women, stout, housewifely looking dames and skittish looking young dolls stood all morning and all afternoon on their two feet listening in.

Occasionally gusts of laughter would roll over the room, and once there was a scattering of applause as one of Daddy's witnesses was testifying.

I am told that many a dress was torn in the struggle for the doors.

I do not see how the girls were able to stand so long. Had their husbands required it of them under any other circumstances, it would be considered cruel and inhuman treatment and grounds for alimony.

The men were just as bad. They were outnumbered by the women only because the women are more adept in a struggle for a given point through long experience at bargain counters, and also because courtesy demands that the women and children be first.

Mack tried to get Peaches' original diary of incidents prior to her marriage admitted at the morning session, also some letters by which he said he expected to prove that she was a woman of the world and had once attended a game of "strip poker" before Daddy took her for better or for worse.

All this the Court ruled out.

"Strip poker," I might explain, is a little pastime with cards wherein the loser sheds garments until—well, you really cannot talk at any length about it.

Also, Mack said in his argument on the admission of the diary and letters, he expected to prove that Peaches knew more about men before her marriage than Ford knows about flivvers. At this point Peaches cried and her mother soothed her.

Miss Marion Tussey was recalled for further cross-examination by Epstein on her testimony some days ago. She is that auburn-haired, chubby young lady friend of Peaches who said Daddy had asked her to testify for him that she knew of Peaches' relations with men before her marriage, also that Mrs. Heenan had once been connected with a house that was not a nice house.

This proposition, Miss Tussey said, had been made in the presence of her landlord, one Bondy Croner, of No. 72 West Seventy-fifth Street, and Bondy disclosed himself presently as a German who might have stepped out of an old-time tintype.

He wore a high collar and a black bow tie, a long coat, and a reddish gray moustache.

Moreover, he had an accent, and was disposed to be quite discursive as he related that Miss Tussey had told him some indelicate things about Peaches and how Miss Tussey was by no means propositioned by Daddy as she claimed.

He admitted that he got $5 on two occasions from Proctor, one of Daddy's legal representatives, when he was served with a subpoena.

"Did you give either of the $5 fees to Miss Tussey?"

"No, she already had $5."

His wife, Louise Croner, a kindly looking old German woman, wearing gold-rimmed spectacles and a black dress with a lace jabot, was even more voluble than her husband as she sat with hands folded in her lap and discoursed of her knowledge of the visit of Daddy to her house to see Miss Tussey. Epstein asked, "What did he say?"

"He said good evening."

The witness uttered it simply, and the spectators laughed uproariously. After that, Mrs. Croner said, Daddy did not open his mouth.

Margaret Lou, a rather nice, neat-looking German girl, testified to hearing part of the conversation between Croner and Miss Tussey, and also disclosed Croner as a big-hearted fellow. She said he paid her $20 a month and her room and board for her labors as a maid in his household.

Leslie Fullenwider, a slight, well-groomed young fellow wearing a pince-nez with great aplomb and employing a Southern accent, testified to buying two great contributions to literature—"The Diary of Peaches," by Peaches, and "Why I Married Peaches," by the old boy himself, for a newspaper syndicate operated by Fullenwider and Lorman Wardell.

Fullenwider gave vent to many words but not much explicit information. His favorite reply was, "I'll have to leave that to someone else."

When he was asked who wrote the diary, he said, "I don't know that 'wrote' is exactly correct. John S. Garden assembled it."

Mack asked jovially, "You distinguish between wrote and rot?"

He said Daddy had visited him and wanted to know if he and Peaches had engaged in osculation, which Fullenwider said they had not.

Lorman Wardell also testified as to the activities of the syndicate in the "assembling" of Peaches' literary life work.

He took her to his home in Demarest, N. J., and to other points, after the separation, to escape the newspaper reporters, and paid her $1,000 for the diary. They got $1,000 for it from one newspaper and about thirty-five other papers used it, he said.

John S. Garden, another slight man, young, and with an intellectual expression behind his horn rims, said he compiled the diary for the syndicate. Epstein demanded:

"You are the hot writer, the red-hot man for the syndicate, are you?"

Mr. Garden denied this, blushing vigorously.

Belle Edwards, in a big raccoon coat, said she is a waitress at the Kew Gardens Inn and waited on Peaches and Daddy and that Daddy seemed to be an ever-loving husband.

He always had flowers on the table, "which was unusual because no one else had them," said Belle Edwards, handing the other husbands of Kew Gardens a gentle jab.

Looking at Belle and looking at Peaches the casual observer was moved to reflect on the irony of life that one should be waiting on the other. Belle was a right nifty looking young woman.

There was other testimony along this line. Golden, the headwaiter; Edward F. McDonald, manager of Kew Gardens Inn, and Leo Ehrenreich, a resident of Kew Gardens, who had entertained the Brownings, testified that Daddy seemed devoted to his Peaches.

You got a fair cross-section of life in Kew Gardens from the testimony.

Frank Dolan, a young and handsome newspaper reporter, and obviously of many sterling personal characteristics, testified succinctly, and I might say very well, about seeing Peaches under photographic fire, and other incidents.

Then came the afternoon session, and James P. Mixon, and his wife, followed by Roman Androwsky, a baldish, foreign looking young man, with an accent and mixed metaphor, who described himself as a "sallisman." This was finally interpreted as a salesman for the National Insurance Company.

"What do you sell, insurance?"

"Correct."

Androwsky was what you might call the big laugh of the day as he told of hearing a conversation between Peaches and another woman on Riverside Drive, in which Peaches was asked by the woman as to whether she cared for Daddy. Her alleged remark was:

"Don't be foolish. I never could love any man, but so far I've got what I wanted and I'll have more before I'm through."

February 1, 1927

Well, folks, it was pretty sticky up here in White Plains today in the way of testimony, as old Daddy Browning sat on the witness stand and prattled his tale of woe against the weighty young Peaches, and they finally put the cover back on their matrimonial garbage can for a couple of weeks.

Both sides rested after Daddy had denied all, as the tabloid headline writers say, and after Peaches had also denied all once more, just for good measure, and Supreme Court Justice Seeger, who has been hearing the case, gave the attorneys two weeks in which to submit briefs in place of oral argument.

Poor Henry Epstein, the bashful barrister who is representing Peaches, was quite overcome during his cross-examination of Daddy, probably by the fumes of Daddy's testimony. Mr. Epstein sat down very suddenly during the afternoon session while Daddy was fumbling with answers to questions. Mr. Epstein's face was quite white and his hands shook.

He asked plaintively for a little air.

Judge Seeger promptly ordered a few windows opened, while bailiffs hurried water to Mr. Epstein's succor. Peaches and her Ma, Mrs.

Frances Heenan, who were seated at Mr. Epstein's table, leaned forward solicitously.

Someone dashed out into the crowded main stem of White Plains, fighting his way through the packed corridors of the court house, and returned with some spirits of ammonia. Mr. Epstein inconsiderately drank the ammonia instead of sprinkling it about the premises.

A five-minute recess was given Mr. Epstein by Judge Seeger and everybody managed to revive more or less and continue listening to Daddy. The court room was packed to what you might call suffocation and the ladies present seemed to stand it better than the men. In fact, they proved themselves gluttons for punishment, as the boys say. Some removed their modish helmets that they might not miss a word that fell from Daddy's pendant lips.

At the conclusion of the hearing Judge Seeger remarked that if he ever had another case like this he would hear it in private. He gently chided the newspaper reporters for adding comment to their reports, but I hope and trust that the Court will not deem it comment if I add one little word to his statement that other cases of this kind will be heard in private. The word is "Amen."

But it was a big day for old Daddy Browning as he sat up there on the witness stand, with his wife eyeing him, now disdainfully, and now rather wistfully, but always eyeing him. Daddy's ma-in-law also eyed him, using two eyes for the purpose. Daddy kept his own eyes, which are rather glittering eyes, on other points of the compass. He scarcely ever glanced at the wife and her parent.

He wore a blue suit and a high turn-down linen collar that seemed about to strangle him. He kept jerking his head forward to free his neck from the embrace of the collar like an old snapping-turtle popping its beezer out of its shell.

Daddy had a reddish purplish complexion, peculiar to golfers, or Scotch inhalers, though he took occasion to deny vehemently that he ever drank to any extent in the fifty-two years of his life. He said fifty-two. He looked older, what with the wattles on his jowls, and his thin white hair.

He wore a very fancy necktie, with a diamond set in gold stuck in it. An inside pocket of his coat bulged with papers. Three fat cigars peeped out of the upper outside pocket of his coat, as usual. They must be "prop" cigars, or Daddy replaces them every day.

He kept his hands folded in his lap, twiddling the fingers from time to time as he pondered some question. Occasionally he wrinkled up his forehead, and peered at the ceiling as he thought over some interrogation. When he talked, he talked so rapidly that the words fairly tumbled over one another. Once or twice, under cross-examination, he got quite excited and yelled his answers.

One occasion was when Mr. Epstein, in a most abashed manner, handed him a photograph and asked him if it was one that he had taken home to Peaches, and said to be a photograph of Marion Dockerill. Daddy recoiled as the bailiff poked the picture at him, and bawled:

"No, that's a filthy picture. I'd be ashamed to show it if I were you."

Your ever-blushing correspondent got a fleeting glimpse of the photo as it was passed from hand to hand, and he violates no confidence in stating that it was, and doubtless still is, a photographic reproduction of a lady who seems to be posing with no drapes of any consequence about her person, not even as much as the proverbial fig leaf. Epstein asked:

"But you weren't ashamed to show it to your wife?"

"Yes, I was—maybe you showed it to her. That's a filthy picture. I understand you stole it out of some place to frame me with."

This statement was ordered stricken out by the Court. Daddy fingered the picture very gingerly, but he refused to identify it as a likeness of Marion Dockerill.

As I gathered, Miss Dockerill is an exponent of some mysterious art of science known as numerology. Daddy said she gave both him and Peaches "readings," but Peaches didn't care for hers. Then Mr. Epstein handed him what purported to be a picture of Miss Dockerill taken from a newspaper and asked Daddy to compare this with the one he shrank from and say if they were from the same person.

Daddy handled the pictures as if he feared they might bit him, and finally remarked, somewhat cryptically, "Well, in one she seems to have a hat on."

There was some disappointment among the spectators that the original photo was not handed around more freely. It was no worse than some of the testimony, at that, though it might cause more of a sensation if hung in a hotel lobby.

Daddy hemmed and hawed no little with Peaches' attorney and had Mr. Epstein quite impatient at times. Also Judge Seeger got a bit impatient with Mr. Epstein and mildly rebuked the attorney for some of his questions to Daddy. On direct examination at the hands of his own attorney, John E. Mack, Daddy answered with surprising swiftness.

It was when Mr. Epstein asked Daddy about Peaches' charges concerning his relations with Dorothy Sunshine Browning, his ten-year-old adopted daughter, that Daddy let out another yell.

"I think more of that child than I do of my life."

He bellowed that he had never even heard of some of the other things that Peaches alleges against him. Daddy has quite a resounding voice when he puts all his lung power behind it, though it was dropping to a low whisper at times during the cross-examination. He has what you might call a "Bowery" accent—saying "boid" for "bird" and "poifect" for "perfect."

His tale was mainly the sad, sad tale of what the Broadway boys term a "sap say," meaning a "sap" trying to catch up with a little youth after he has passed that old fifty-yard line. By the way, the Roaring Forties contributed a few listeners-in today. They never heard anything like this downtown.

They called him to the stand at 11:25 this morning, and Daddy, for some reason, did not move with alacrity. He got up from his chair slowly, whispered a moment to Attorney Mack, then ambled to the witness chair. He somehow seemed very, very old as he hoisted his frame to the chair. Peaches and Mrs. Heenan watched him very closely, and Peaches' face broke into a wide smile when Daddy denied that she had walked up to him when he was talking with some other girls at a dance at the McAlpin, was introduced to him and asked him to dance with her.

Daddy rather gave the impression that Peaches, then fifteen years old, pursued him hotly in those dear, dead days of some months ago, calling him up, and one thing and another. So they were married, as the movies say, and as you must know by this time.

That mysterious burning of Peaches by acid came into Daddy's discourse, but he could throw no light on it. He said the Heenans had little to eat, and their rent and radio instalments were unpaid, and that he took care of all those little matters, besides giving Peaches $300 for clothes to enter the Spence, Central or Scudder school, all quite fashionable institutions.

Instead, he said, she had gone to Earl Carroll's theater and got a job, not as a bathtub exhibit,* but as an extra girl. This disappointed him no

* An allusion to Joyce Hawley, who sprawled in a bathtub of champagne at a party staged by Earl Carroll—an incident that produced another big-headline story in

end, Daddy said. He told her it was no life for a girl. After the acid incident he paid Mrs. Heenan $50 per week to take care of Peaches, and paid a Mrs. Mayer as a night nurse. Mack asked:

"Did you call at the Heenan home until the Pizzaro incident?"

Mr. Epstein objected to that question forthwith. There has been nothing said about Mr. Pizzaro. Who was Mr. Pizzaro, anyway?

Well, it came out that Mr. Pizzaro had been hanging around the Heenans, muttering about getting evidence to put Peaches in an institution.

So Daddy figured there was only one way out. Peaches would make him a good wife. So they were married, as I have said before. Then Daddy proceeded to a categorical denial of each and every incident of the nuptial night and thereafter, alleged by Peaches, as reflecting on his character as a gentleman and scholar, and causing her mental pain and anguish.

He took her everywhere, parties, dances, theaters. He spent his dough on her for clothes and jewelry, Russian sable and ermine coats. He called her up two or three times a day. He never hurled phone books at her, never slugged her, never set off an alarm clock in her ear, never crawled around on his hands and knees in her bed chamber and said "woof, woof" (as she had testified).

He said, "I may have crawled around on my hands and knees when I was a baby, but never since."

Mack asked, "You are not in your second childhood, then?"

"I hope not."

Oh, yes, about the gander—the African honking gander, that has been going kah-donking through the hearing. It seems that they were at a lawn party one day, at the home of some folks named Reeves, and they had the gander, and Peaches thought it would be just dandy to own the gander.

So, eager to grant her slightest wish, Daddy borrowed the gander and Peaches tied a ribbon around its neck, and down to Long Beach they went to parade the honker along the boardwalk, and have it photographed. That was that, Daddy said. He never threatened to kill Peaches and her mother, and never got drunk. The sandpapering of his shoe-trees, mentioned by Peaches as one of the causes of her mental

the Twenties and put Carroll (because of his forgetfulness of the details) in a Federal cooler.

anguish, was nothing more than a little cobbling on one of Peaches' own shoes. It was tight, so he sandpapered it for her.

Incidentally, Daddy mentioned that he often wore Peaches' tennis shoes and house slippers, and that she wore his, because they fit both ways, which statement caused some of the curious in the court to try to get a peek at Peaches' feet. Mr. Epstein learned from Daddy that he wears a No. 6 shoe. He said Peaches wanted an apartment on Park Avenue with "all corner rooms," which would have been a lot of corner in any man's town, and that furthermore, she wanted six or seven rooms, because her mother wanted two dogs while Peaches wanted three.

Mack asked, "Did you have any idea that your wife or mother-in-law was going to leave you?"

"Not my wife."

"And your mother-in-law?"

"I er-ah-er—I was hoping so."

Mrs. Heenan laughed loudly.

This was about the only dig Daddy took at Mrs. Heenan, and he seemed ashamed of it, for he quickly added, "I didn't mean that—I didn't mind her staying with us."

But he said under cross-examination that he was scarcely ever alone at any time with Peaches, and that the marriage relation was never truly that of man and wife. I believe that is the polite expression among us polite people.

A lot of those mysterious little letters that Daddy has been trying to get into the record were finally produced by Mr. Mack. They were notes written to Daddy by Peaches in his office when she would be waiting for him, and they were simple little epistles. In fact they were so simple you might call 'em childish.

She wrote one poem to him in which she sang:

> I love you.
> I love you—
> You are the idle of my dreams.

That is the way she spelled it. We can give Peaches about 89 in spelling.

When Mr. Epstein brought Peaches back to the witness stand as one of his last witnesses, she said she had written these things at Daddy's request.

Peaches denied ever having seen the fellow, James P. Mixon, whom she denounced as a liar yesterday when he claimed to be one of her former boy friends.

Also she denied the testimony of one Swint that she used baseball players' language.

Peaches wore exactly the same outfit of blue dress and hat, and sable coat that she started out with at Carmel, and her face showed signs of strain.

About the only allegation of Peaches that Daddy admitted was buying a dozen green handkerchiefs for a St. Patrick's Day ball. Peaches said he "had hundreds" in his pocket, but Daddy defied anybody to get that many 'kerchiefs in one pocket.

Mr. Epstein examined him at great length as to his living expenses, and brought out that Daddy pays about $800 a month for the famous hired Rolls-Royce and its crew of two, but the two work in his office when not escorting him.

He said he had spent between $10,000 and $12,000 on clothes and one thing and another for Peaches, but didn't expect her to go through life as Mrs. Browning at that clip. Mr. Epstein spent some time over the matter of Daddy's ownership of a pistol, and read at length from interviews and stories printed in newspapers purporting to quote Daddy. Daddy admitted some, and denied others. Epstein asked:

"When was the first time you kissed your wife?"

Daddy puffed both cheeks full of wind, stared at the ceiling and the crowd roared.

"Wife, or before she was my wife?"

Then he admitted that the first time he had committed osculation with Peaches was on a trip to Yonkers.

Oh, yes, about that Japanese princess that Peaches said Daddy told her he would buy her when she said she wanted children. Daddy said he couldn't seem to remember a thing about any Japanese princess, and as for Peaches wishing children—well.

And then the cross-examination went past the precincts of pure literature. In reply to a question if he had ever requested his wife to sit at the dinner table at Cold Springs, in his presence, quite nude, as Peaches asserted, Daddy said, "Absolutely not. It was very cold. It would have been foolish to ask her."

As a final witness, Mr. Epstein recalled Dr. George A. Blakeslee, a neurological expert, who said he had much experience with psycho-neurosis with the Eighty-second Division during the war.

The purport of a long question was, would all the things set forth by Peaches against Daddy, including the goose, rubber eggs, sandpapering and all the rest, cause the nervous disorder to which Peaches is said to be prone. The doctor said he thought it would.

At the morning session, Mr. and Mrs. Frank J. Farney, of Evanston, Ill., testified for Daddy. They were guests at the Kew Gardens Inn when Daddy and Peaches were living there, and the couples made a jolly foursome on many occasions. It came out that Farney, who makes nurs-ery furniture, and is of the go-getter type of mid-westerner, was the vic-tim of Daddy's rubber egg joke.

Farney said he thought it was a riot of a joke, at that. Moreover, he took the egg home with him. Both he and Mrs. Farney, a classy look-ing matron, said Daddy seemed devoted to Peaches and gave her so many things "it made me feel like a piker," as Farney put it. He said there had been chatter about children to and fro on occasion, and he offered to provide Daddy and Peaches with the nursery, but Peaches said not for her, or words to that effect.

Miss Emma R. Steiner, a picturesque woman with a rakish black hat over her white hair, testified to knowing Daddy for twenty-eight years. She said she is an orchestral conductor and that her last direction was of the Metropolitan Orchestra, at which statement the customers sat up and took notice.

She had a kind word for all, including Mrs. Heenan. She said Daddy was always devoted to his mother and she thought his relations with Peaches were ideal. She made a tremendous impression. She was frank, outspoken, and no trace of rancor marked any of her statements. The folks smiled on her as she left the stand.

Miss Margaret MacDonald, who said she is a journalist and publicist, and Mrs. Norma Drupyke, president of the Victory Club, of 106 West Fifty-ninth Street, New York, where Daddy gave his famous birthday party for Peaches, testified that Daddy always seemed a kind and loving hubby to Peaches.

Then came Daddy.

As both sides rested, Epstein moved the dismissal of the first cause of action by Daddy, which is cruelty, but Judge Seeger said, while he thought the motion should be granted, he would reserve decision until he heard the arguments, which the attorneys agreed should be in written form.

Mr. Mack thanked the Court for his patience, to which Judge Seeger replied he had enjoyed it as much as one could be expected to enjoy such a case, rather leaving the impression that this isn't much enjoyment after all.

He said he had held the hearing in public only for fear he might have been misunderstood had he held it in private, what with great wealth on one side. But he made it clear that if the lawyers have more cases like this that they desire heard in public, they had better forget his address.

Some days after the trial's end, the Court awarded Mrs. Browning, "Peaches," the decree of separation she sought.

In the meantime—on the morning after the curtain fell on the big show at White Plains—a New York newspaper gave it a sour review. Runyon was moved to write in the New York American:

I have just read an editorial in one of the leading public prints deploring the publicity that is being given our little presentation at White Plains, the Daddy-Peaches Browning atrocity.

It is a good editorial, at that, well written, and timely, and it appears on a page hard by one carrying advertisements of some highly moral and uplifting plays now running on Broadway, and dealing with such interesting topics as miscegenation, male and female perversion, divorce, seduction, Negro honky-tonks, night life deadfalls, larceny, assault and battery, bootlegging, burglary, forgery, murder, and perhaps some lesser peccadilloes of this great human race.

Also there are advertisements on this page of other shows that go in largely and liberally for female nudity, preferably young, which is hung on curtains like skinned sheep on meat hooks, or disposed in picturesque posture about the theatrical premises in the name, I believe, of Art.

Our modest offense at White Plains is out-nuded ten to one by any one of these undraped casts.

The editorial inveighed against the tabloids for making much of the Daddy-Peaches outrage, though I can remember when the newspaper in which the editorial appeared was one of the loudest organs in the land when it came to playing on our social disorders. I would like to place its accounts of the Thaw trial alongside the tabloid report on

Daddy and Peaches, and show you how strong it went in those days.

But I suppose a newspaper is only human, after all.

You take a fellow who has massed a ton or two of money after a humble beginning carrying a pack, or peddling peanuts, or gathering junk, and he eventually yearns for social position for himself and his family.

And if he attains it, he is usually one of the first to deplore the manifestations of the masses, and to fail to understand them.

I suppose a newspaper that has picked up a lot of circulation and prosperity in its younger days by the huffle-scuffle, whoop-tee-do methods of presenting the news that they used to call yellow journalism, finally comes upon the same yearning.

I would not be surprised to see the tabloids one day wearing journalistic high hats and deploring some new and popular form of newspaper enterprise, just as they are now high-hatted and deplored by some of their venerable reformed brethren.

But, if you ask me, I think the publicity that is being given Daddy and Peaches is a good thing.

I do not mean to say that the case itself is a good thing. On the contrary, I am as hearty a deplorer as the writer of the editorial I have been talking about when it comes to deploring the case. But as long as such cases are permitted in the courts of law they ought to get plenty of publicity, if only because it mirrors to the rest of humanity the sappiness of some of its representatives, and perhaps of the law, too, and thus may possibly act as a deterrent to other saps.

The whole trouble is with the New York law that requires, or permits, the kind of testimony that has been produced in the Daddy-Peaches case. As I understand it, Peaches wouldn't live with Daddy on a bet, and she is about as welcome now to that dizzy old beezark as a case of smallpox.

But under the law they have to go into court and give a lot of odious reasons why they no longer desire any part of each other's company.

In other States, the mere statement of desertion, or incompatibility, or any one of a dozen other causes is sufficient ground for a split-out between unhappy couples.

In New York you must have trimmings, and the result is generally unfit for publication. I do not say the New York law is wrong. I merely speak of net results.

I hear lawyers criticizing the newspapers for publicizing incidents like the Daddy-Peaches affair; but what of the legal fraternity that files proceedings of this nature as hooks for the publicity?

I believe if I had been Peaches' attorney I would have rested on the African honking gander, and had I been representing Daddy I would have closed with my cross-examination of Maw-in-law, showing that she was on deck at all times right from the bell.

Supreme Court Justice Seeger, who is presiding at the hearing, had it in mind to hold the thing in private when it first opened at Carmel. His chief thought was to protect Peaches as a minor. But his decision to hold it in public was, I think, quite sound, because, as he said, the parties to the case had never before shrunk from publicity. On the contrary, they had sought it with astonishing avidity.

I was greatly relieved by Judge Seeger's decision. My years and my spats would make it most unseemly and undignified for me to be eavesdropping at keyholes and waylaying witnesses hot off the stand in quest of news of the proceedings. Anyway, I might have gotten my second-hand information garbled up by the time I presented it to the public, and I can garble it first-hand good enough to suit any one.

You may be sure the newspapers would get the news, even if the case were held behind closed doors. And as a newspaper reader you would expect it of your favorite publication, and cavil at its lack of enterprise did it fail.

They would have gotten it, if all other sources were shut off, from Daddy and Peaches themselves, with fresh photographic postures of them after each session.

As one of my readers remarked to me the other day:

"I am astonished at the newspapers printing that awful stuff—but, say, tell me just what it was they had to leave out, will you?"

Peaches capitalized on her notoriety in vaudeville. It was estimated that she earned $125,000 before the vaudeville public lost interest in seeing her "in person."

Browning died in 1934. A codicil to his will said Mrs. Browning had caused him "great mental distress" and "unnecessary expenditure of money," and declared he did not want her to get a widow's share of his estate. His will devised ninety per cent of his money to charitable institutions, and provided for payment of $14,000 a year to the other Browning protégé, Dorothy Sunshine, whom he had gone through the legal formality of adopting as a daughter.

Peaches sued for a widow's third of the estate, and evidence was presented that the Wall Street debacle of 1929 had deflated Mr. Browning's estate and ego considerably. Peaches settled her claim for $170,000, of which, of course, lawyers took their usual share.

Peaches soon acquired another husband. The marriage lasted about a year. Another marriage, and still another, followed, to swell her scrapbooks.

Twenty years after the epic trial in White Plains, Peaches was still living her life in headlines.

Early in 1947, her fourth husband, who was described in newspapers as a "member of a wealthy, meat-packing family of Columbus, O.," asked a San Francisco court to declare his marriage with Peaches null and void on the ground that her divorce from her third husband had not been concluded when the fourth marriage occurred.

About the same time, her father, William B. Heenan, aged 69, applied to her publicly for financial assistance. He said he hadn't heard from her in three years.

Her mother announced: "My daughter is the wisest of all the girls who made the headlines in the Twenties. Most of them are broke but Frances has all her money in real estate."

William Makepeace Thackeray

:

THE CASE OF PEYTEL

IN A LETTER TO EDWARD BRIEFLESS,
ESQUIRE, OF PUMP COURT, TEMPLE

Paris, November 1839

MY DEAR BRIEFLESS,—Two months since, when the act of accusation first appeared, containing the sum of the charges against Sebastian Peytel, all Paris was in a fervor on the subject. The man's trial speedily followed, and kept for three days the public interest wound up to a painful point. He was found guilty of double murder at the beginning of September; and since that time, what with Maroto's disaffection and Turkish news, we have had leisure to forget Monsieur Peytel, and to occupy ourselves with τί νέον. Perhaps Monsieur de Balzac helped to smother what little sparks of interest might still have remained for the murderous notary. Balzac put forward a letter in his favor, so very long, so very dull, so very pompous, promising so much, and performing so little, that the Parisian public gave up Peytel and his case altogether; nor was it until today that some small feeling was raised concerning him, when the newspapers brought the account how Peytel's head had been cut off at Bourg.

He had gone through the usual miserable ceremonies and delays which attend what is called, in this country, the march of justice. He had made his appeal to the Court of Cassation, which had taken time to consider the verdict of the Provincial Court, and had confirmed it. He had made his appeal for mercy; his poor sister coming up all the way from Bourg (a sad journey, poor thing!) to have an interview with the King, who had refused to see her. Last Monday morning, at nine o'clock, an hour before Peytel's breakfast, the Greffier of Assize Court, in company with the Curé of Bourg, waited on him, and informed him that he had only three hours to live. At twelve o'clock Peytel's head was off his body: an executioner from Lyons had come over the night before, to assist the professional throat-cutter of Bourg.

I am not going to entertain you with any sentimental lamentations for this scoundrel's fate, or to declare my belief in his innocence, as Monsieur de Balzac has done. As far as moral conviction can go, the man's guilt is pretty clearly brought home to him. But any man who has read the "Causes Célèbres," knows that men have been convicted and executed upon evidence ten times more powerful than that which was brought against Peytel. His own account of his horrible case may be true; there is nothing adduced in the evidence which is strong enough to overthrow it. It is a serious privilege, God knows, that society takes upon itself at any time to deprive one of God's creatures of existence. But when the slightest doubt remains, what a tremendous risk does it incur! In England, thank Heaven, the law is more wise and more merciful. An English jury would never have taken a man's blood upon such testimony; an English judge and Crown advocate would never have acted as these Frenchmen have done—the latter inflaming the public mind by exaggerated appeals to their passions; the former seeking, in every way, to draw confessions from the prisoner, to perplex and confound him, to do away, by fierce cross-questioning and bitter remarks from the bench, with any effect that his testimony might have on the jury. I don't mean to say that judges and lawyers have been more violent and inquisitorial against the unhappy Peytel than against any one else. It is the fashion of the country: a man is guilty until he proves himself to be innocent; and to batter down his defense, if he have any, there are the lawyers, with all their horrible ingenuity, and their captivating passionate eloquence. It is hard thus to set the skillful and tried champions of the law against men unused to this kind of combat—nay, give a man all the legal aid that he can purchase or procure, still, by this plan, you take him at a cruel, unmanly disadvantage; he has to fight against the law, clogged with the dreadful weight of his presupposed guilt. Thank God that, in England, things are not managed so.

However, I am not about to entertain you with ignorant disquisitions about the law. Peytel's case may, nevertheless, interest you; for the tale is a very stirring and mysterious one, and you may see how easy a thing it is for a man's life to be talked away in France, if ever he should happen to fall under the suspicion of a crime. The French "Acte d'accusation" begins in the following manner:—

"Of all the events which, in these latter times, have afflicted the department of the Ain, there is none which has caused a more profound and lively sensation than the tragical death of the lady, Félicité Alcazar, wife of Sebastian Benedict Peytel, notary, at Belley. At the end of October, 1838, Madame Peytel quitted that town, with her husband, and their servant Louis Rey, in order to pass a few days at Macon. At midnight the inhabitants of Belley were suddenly awakened by the arrival of Monsieur Peytel, by his cries, and by the signs which he exhibited of the most lively agitation. He implored the succors of all the physicians in the town; knocked violently at their doors; rung at the bells of their houses with a sort of frenzy, and announced that his wife, stretched out and dying, in his carriage, had just been shot, on the Lyons road, by his domestic, whose life Peytel himself had taken.

"At this recital a number of persons assembled, and what a spectacle was presented to their eyes!

"A young woman lay at the bottom of a carriage, deprived of life. Her whole body was wet, and seemed as if it had just been plunged into the water. She appeared to be severely wounded in the face; and her garments, which were raised up, in spite of the cold and rainy weather, left the upper part of her knees almost entirely exposed. At the sight of this half-naked and inanimate body, all the spectators were affected. People said that the first duty to pay to a dying woman was, to preserve her from the cold, to cover her. A physician examined the body, he declared that all remedies were useless—that Madame Peytel was dead and cold.

"The entreaties of Peytel were redoubled; he demanded fresh succors, and, giving no heed to the fatal assurance which had just been given him, required that all the physicians in the place should be sent for. A scene so strange and so melancholy; the incoherent account given by Peytel of the murder of his wife; his extraordinary movements; and the avowal which he continued to make, that he had dispatched the murderer, Rey, with strokes of his hammer, excited the attention of Lieutenant Wolf, commandant of gendarmes. That officer gave orders for the immediate arrest of Peytel; but the latter threw himself into the arms of a friend, who interceded for him, and begged the police not immediately to seize upon his person.

"The corpse of Madame Peytel was transported to her apartment; the bleeding body of the domestic was likewise brought from the road, where it lay; and Peytel, asked to explain the circumstances, did so."

Now, as there is little reason to tell the reader, when an English counsel has to prosecute a prisoner on the part of the Crown for a capital offense, he produces the articles of his accusation in the most moderate terms, and especially warns the jury to give the accused person the benefit of every possible doubt that the evidence may give or may leave. See how these things are managed in France, and how differently the French counsel for the Crown sets about his work.

He first prepares his act of accusation, the opening of which we have just read. It is published six days before the trial, so that an unimpassioned, unprejudiced jury has ample time to study it, and to form its opinions accordingly, and to go into court with a happy, just prepossession against the prisoner.

Read the first part of the Peytel act of accusation. It is as turgid and declamatory as a bad romance, and as inflated as a newspaper document by an unlimited penny-a-liner:—"The department of the Ain is in a dreadful state of excitement; the inhabitants of Belley come trooping from their beds, and what a sight do they behold!—a young woman at the bottom of a carriage, *toute ruisselante,* just out of a river; her garments, in spite of the cold and rain, raised, so as to leave the upper part of her knees entirely exposed, at which all the beholders were affected, and cried that the *first duty* was to cover her from the cold." This settles the case at once: the first duty of a man is to cover the legs of the sufferer; the second to call for help. The eloquent "Substitut du Procureur du Roi" has prejudged the case, in the course of a few sentences. He is putting his readers, among whom his future jury is to be found, into a proper state of mind. He works on them with pathetic description, just as a romance-writer would: the rain pours in torrents; it is a dreary evening in November; the young creature's situation is neatly described; the distrust which entered into the breast of the keen old officer of gendarmes strongly painted; the suspicions which might, or might not, have been entertained by the inhabitants, eloquently argued. How did the advocate know that the people had such? Did all the bystanders say aloud, "I suspect that this is a case of murder by Monsieur Peytel, and that his story about the domestic is all deception"? or did they go off to the mayor and register their suspicion? or was the advocate there to hear them? Not he; but he paints you the whole scene, as though it had existed, and gives full accounts of suspicions, as if they had been facts, positive, patent, staring, that everybody could see and swear to.

Having thus primed his audience, and prepared them for the testimony of the accused party—"Now," says he, with a fine show of justice, "let us hear Monsieur Peytel"; and that worthy's narrative is given as follows:—

"He said that he had left Macon on the 31st October, at eleven o'clock in the morning, in order to return to Belley, with his wife and servant. The latter drove, or led, an open car; he himself was driving his wife in a four-wheeled carriage drawn by one horse. They reached Bourg at five o'clock in the evening; left it at seven, to sleep at Pont d'Ain, where they did not arrive before midnight. During the journey, Peytel thought he remarked that Rey had slackened his horse's pace. When they alighted at the inn, Peytel bade him deposit in his chamber 7,500 francs, which he carried with him; but the domestic refused to do so, saying the inn gates were secure, and there was no danger. Peytel was, therefore, obliged to carry his money upstairs himself. The next day, the 1st November, they set out on their journey again at nine o'clock in the morning. Louis did not come, according to custom, to take his master's orders. They arrived at Tenay about three, stopped there a couple of hours to dine, and it was eight o'clock when they reached the bourg of Rossillon, where they waited half an hour to bait the horses.

"As they left Rossillon the weather became bad, and the rain began to fall. Peytel told his domestic to get a covering for the articles in the open chariot; but Rey refused to do so, adding, in an ironical tone, that the weather was fine. For some days past Peytel had remarked that his servant was gloomy, and scarcely spoke at all.

"After they had gone about five hundred paces beyond the bridge of Andert, that crosses the river Furans, and ascended to the least steep part of the hill of Darde, Peytel cried out to his servant, who was seated in the car, to come down from it, and finish the ascent on foot.

"At this moment a violent wind was blowing from the south, and the rain was falling heavily. Peytel was seated back in the right corner of the carriage, and his wife, who was close to him, was asleep, with her head on his left shoulder. All of a sudden he heard the report of a fire-arm (he had seen the light of it at some paces' distance), and Madame Peytel cried out, 'My poor husband, take your pistols.' The horse was frightened, and began to trot. Peytel immediately drew the pistol, and fired, from the interior of the carriage, upon an individual whom he saw running by the side of the road.

"Not knowing as yet that his wife had been hit, he jumped out at one side of the carriage, while Madame Peytel descended from the other; and he fired a second pistol at his domestic, Louis Rey, whom he had just recognized. Redoubling his pace, he came up with Rey, and struck him, from behind, a blow with the hammer. Rey turned at this, and raised up his arm to strike his master with the pistol which he had just discharged at him; but Peytel, more quick than he, gave the domestic a blow with the hammer which felled him to the ground (he fell his face forwards), and then Peytel, bestriding the body, dispatched him, although the brigand asked for mercy.

"He now began to think of his wife, and ran back, calling out her name repeatedly, and seeking for her in vain on both sides of the road. Arrived at the bridge of Andert, he recognized his wife stretched in a field, covered with water, which bordered the Furans. This horrible discovery had so much the more astonished him, because he had no idea until now that his wife had been wounded. He endeavored to draw her from the water; and it was only after considerable exertions that he was enabled to do so, and to place her, with her face towards the ground, on the side of the road. Supposing that here she would be sheltered from any further danger, and believing as yet that she was only wounded, he determined to ask for help at a lone house situated on the road towards Rossillon; and at this instant he perceived, without at all being able to explain how, that his horse had followed him back to the spot, having turned back of its own accord from the road to Belley.

"The house at which he knocked was inhabited by two men of the name of Thannet, father and son, who opened the door to him, and whom he entreated to come to his aid, saying that his wife had just been assassinated by his servant. The elder Thannet approached to and examined the body, and told Peytel that it was quite dead. He and his son took up the corpse and placed it in the bottom of the carriage, which they all mounted themselves, and pursued their route to Belley. In order to do so they had to pass by Rey's body on the road, which Peytel wished to crush under the wheels of his carriage. It was to rob him of 7,500 francs, said Peytel, that the attack had been made."

Our friend, the Procureur's Substitut, has dropped here the eloquent and pathetic style altogether, and only gives the unlucky prisoner's narrative in the baldest and most unimaginative style. How is a jury to listen to such a fellow? they ought to condemn him, if but for making such an uninteresting statement. Why not have helped poor Peytel with some of those rhetorical graces which have been so plentifully bestowed in the opening part of the act of accusation? He might have said,—

"Monsieur Peytel is an eminent notary at Belley. He is a man distinguished for his literary and scientific acquirements; he has lived long in the best society of the capital; he had been but a few months married to that young and unfortunate lady, whose loss has plunged her bereaved husband into despair—almost into madness. Some early differences had marked, it is true, the commencement of their union; but these—which, as can be proved by evidence, were almost all the unhappy lady's fault—had happily ceased, to give place to sentiments far more delightful and tender. Gentlemen, Madame Peytel bore in her bosom a sweet pledge of future concord between herself and her husband: in three brief months she was to become a mother.

"In the exercise of his honorable profession (in which, to succeed, a man must not only have high talents, but undoubted probity—and, gentlemen, Monsieur Peytel *did* succeed, *did* inspire respect and confidence, as you, his neighbors, well know)—in the exercise, I say, of his high calling, Monsieur Peytel, towards the end of October last, had occasion to make a journey in the neighborhood, and visit some of his many clients.

"He traveled in his own carriage, his young wife beside him. Does this look like want of affection, gentlemen? or is it not a mark of love —of love and paternal care on his part towards the being with whom his lot in life was linked—the mother of his coming child—the young girl who had everything to gain from the union with a man of his attainments of intellect, his kind temper, his great experience, and his high position? In this manner they traveled, side by side, lovingly together. Monsieur Peytel was not a lawyer merely, but a man of letters and varied learning; of the noble and sublime science of geology he was, especially, an ardent devotee."

(Suppose, here, a short panegyric upon geology. Allude to the creation of this mighty world, and then, naturally, to the Creator. Fancy the conversations which Peytel, a religious man,* might have with his young wife upon the subject.)

"Monsieur Peytel had lately taken into his service a man named Louis Rey. Rey was a foundling, and had passed many years in a regiment— a school, gentlemen, where much besides bravery, alas! is taught; nay, where the spirit which familiarizes one with notions of battle and

---

* He always went to mass; it is in the evidence.

death, I fear, may familiarize one with ideas, too, of murder. Rey, a dashing, reckless fellow from the army, had lately entered Peytel's service; was treated by him with the most singular kindness; accompanied him (having charge of another vehicle) upon the journey before alluded to; and *knew that his master carried with him a considerable sum of money*—for a man like Rey an enormous sum—7,500 francs. At midnight on the 1st of November, as Madame Peytel and her husband were returning home, an attack was made upon their carriage. Remember, gentlemen, the hour at which the attack was made; remember the sum of money that was in the carriage; and remember that the Savoy frontier *is within a league of the spot* where the desperate deed was done."

Now, my dear Briefless, ought not Monsieur Procureur, in common justice to Peytel, after he had so eloquently proclaimed, not the facts, but the suspicions which weighed against that worthy, to have given a similar florid account of the prisoner's case? Instead of this, you will remark that it is the advocate's endeavor to make Peytel's statements as uninteresting in style as possible; and then he demolishes them in the following way:—

"Scarcely was Peytel's statement known, when the common-sense of the public rose against it. Peytel had commenced his story upon the bridge of Andert, over the cold body of his wife. On the 2nd November he had developed it in detail, in the presence of the physicians, in the presence of the assembled neighbors—of the persons who, on the day previous only, were his friends. Finally, he had completed it in his interrogatories, his conversations, his writings, and letters to the magistrates; and everywhere these words, repeated so often, were only received with a painful incredulity. The fact was that, besides the singular character which Peytel's appearance, attitude, and talk had worn ever since the event, there was in his narrative an inexplicable enigma; its contradictions and impossibilities were such that calm persons were revolted at it, and that even friendship itself refused to believe it."

Thus Mr. Attorney speaks, not for himself alone, but for the whole French public—whose opinions, of course, he knows. Peytel's statement is discredited *everywhere*—the statement which he had made over the cold body of his wife—the monster! It is not enough simply to prove that the man committed the murder, but to make the jury violently angry against him, and cause them to shudder in the jury-box as he exposes the horrid details of the crime.

"Justice," goes on Mr. Substitut (who answers for the feelings of everybody), *"disturbed by the pre-occupations of public opinion,* commenced, without delay, the most active researches. The bodies of the victims were submitted to the investigations of men of art; the wounds and projectiles were examined; the place where the event took place explored with care. The morality of the author of this frightful scene became the object of rigorous examination; the *exigeances* of the prisoner, the forms affected by him, his calculating silence, and his answers, coldly insulting, were feeble obstacles, and justice at length arrived, by its prudence, and by the discoveries it made, to the most cruel point of certainty."

You see that a man's demeanor is here made a crime against him, and that Mr. Substitut wishes to consider him guilty because he has actually the audacity to hold his tongue. Now follows a touching description of the domestic, Louis Rey:—

"Louis Rey, a child of the Hospital at Lyons, was confided, at a very early age, to some honest country people, with whom he stayed until he entered the army. At their house, and during this long period of time, his conduct, his intelligence, and the sweetness of his manners were such that the family of his guardians became to him as an adopted family, and that his departure caused them the most sincere affliction. When Louis quitted the army, he returned to his benefactors, and was received as a son. They found him just as they had ever known him" (I acknowledge that this pathos beats my humble defense of Peytel entirely), "except that he had learned to read and write; and the certificates of his commanders proved him to be a good and gallant soldier.

"The necessity of creating some resources for himself obliged him to quit his friends, and to enter the service of Monsieur de Montrichard, a lieutenant of gendarmerie, from whom he received fresh testimonials of regard. Louis, it is true, might have a fondness for wine and a passion for women; but he had been a soldier, and these faults were, according to the witnesses, amply compensated for by his activity, his intelligence, and the agreeable manner in which he performed his service. In the month of July 1839, Rey quitted, voluntarily, the service of M. de Montrichard; and Peytel, about this period, meeting him at Lyons, did not hesitate to attach him to his service. Whatever may be the prisoner's present language, it is certain that, up to the day of Louis's death, he served Peytel with diligence and fidelity.

"More than once his master and mistress spoke well of him. *Everybody* who has worked, or been at the house of Madame Peytel, has spoken in praise of his character; and, indeed, it may be said that these testimonials were general.

"On the very night of the 1st of November, and immediately after the catastrophe, we remark how Peytel begins to make insinuations against his servant, and how artfully, in order to render them more sure, he disseminates them through the different parts of his narrative. But, in the course of the proceeding, these charges have met with a most complete denial. Thus we find the disobedient servant who, at Pont d'Ain, refused to carry the money-chest to his master's room, under the pretext that the gates of the inn were closed securely, occupied with tending the horses after their long journey; meanwhile Peytel was standing by, and neither master nor servant exchanged a word, and the witnesses who beheld them both have borne testimony to the zeal and care of the domestic.

"In like manner, we find that the servant, who was so remiss in the morning as to neglect to go to his master for orders, was ready for departure before seven o'clock, and had eagerly informed himself whether Monsieur and Madame Peytel were awake, learning from the maid of the inn that they had ordered nothing for their breakfast. This man, who refused to carry with him a covering for the car, was, on the contrary, ready to take off his own cloak and with it shelter articles of small value; this man, who had been for many days so silent and gloomy, gave, on the contrary, many proofs of his gaiety—almost of his indiscretion—speaking at all the inns in terms of praise of his master and mistress. The waiter at the inn at Dauphin says he was a tall young fellow, mild and good-natured: 'we talked for some time about horses, and such things; he seemed to be perfectly natural, and not preoccupied at all.' At Pont d'Ain, he talked of his being a foundling; of the place where he had been brought up, and where he had served; and finally, at Rossillon, an hour before his death, he conversed familiarly with the master of the port, and spoke on indifferent subjects.

"All Peytel's insinuations against his servant had no other end than to show, in every point of Rey's conduct, the behavior of a man who was premeditating attack. Of what, in fact, does he accuse him? Of wishing to rob him of 7,500 francs, and of having had recourse to assassination in order to effect the robbery. But, for a premeditated crime, consider what singular improvidence the person showed who had determined on committing it, what folly and what weakness there is in the execution of it.

"How many insurmountable obstacles are there in the way of committing and profiting by crime! On leaving Belley, Louis Rey, according to Peytel's statement, knowing that his master would return with money, provided himself with a holster pistol, which Madame Peytel had once before perceived among his effects. In Peytel's cabinet there were some balls: four of these were found in Rey's trunk, on the 6th of November. And in order to commit the crime, this domestic had brought away with him a pistol and no ammunition; for Peytel has informed us that Rey, an hour before his departure from Macon, purchased six balls at a gunsmith's. To gain his point, the assassin must immolate his victims: for this he has only one pistol, knowing perfectly well that Peytel, in all his travels, had two on his person; knowing that, at a late hour of the night, his shot might fail of effect, and that in this case he would be left to the mercy of his opponent.

"The execution of the crime is, according to Peytel's account, still more singular. Louis does not get off the carriage until Peytel tells him to descend. He does not think of taking his master's life until he is sure that the latter has his eyes open. It is dark, and the pair are covered in one cloak; and Rey only fires at them at six paces' distance. He fires at hazard, without disquieting himself as to the choice of his victim; and the soldier, who was bold enough to undertake this double murder, has not force nor courage to consummate it. He flies, carrying in his hand a useless whip, with a heavy mantle on his shoulders, in spite of the detonation of two pistols at his ears, and the rapid steps of an angry master in pursuit, which ought to have set him upon some better means of escape. And we find this man, full of youth and vigor, lying with his face to the ground, in the midst of a public road, falling without a struggle, or resistance, under the blows of a hammer!

"And suppose the murderer had succeeded in his criminal projects, what fruit could he have drawn from them? Leaving, on the road, the two bleeding bodies; obliged to lead two carriages at a time for fear of discovery; not able to return himself, after all the pains he had taken to speak, at every place at which they had stopped, of the money which his master was carrying with him; too prudent to appear alone at Belley; arrested at the frontier by the excise officers, who would present an impassable barrier to him till morning—what could he do, or hope to do? The examination of the car has shown that Rey, at the moment of the crime, had neither linen, nor clothes, nor effects of any kind. There was found in his pockets, when the body was examined, no passport nor certificate. One of his pockets contained a ball of large caliber, which he had shown, in play, to a girl at the inn at Macon, a little horn-handled knife, a snuff-box, a little packet of gunpowder, and a purse containing only a halfpenny and some string. Here is all the baggage with which, after the execution of his homicidal plan, Louis Rey intended to take refuge in a foreign country.* Besides these absurd contradictions, there is another remarkable fact which must not be passed over; it is this—the pistol found by Rey is of antique form, and the original owner of it has been found. He is a curiosity merchant at Lyons; and though he cannot affirm that Peytel was the person who bought this pistol of him, he perfectly recognizes Peytel as having been a frequent customer at his shop!

"No, we may fearlessly affirm that Louis Rey was not guilty of the crime which Peytel lays to his charge. If, to those who knew him, his mild and open disposition, his military career, modest and without a stain, the touching regrets of his employers, are sufficient proofs of his innocence—the calm and candid observer, who considers how the crime was conceived, was executed, and what consequences would have resulted from it, will likewise acquit him, and free him of the odious imputation which Peytel endeavors to cast upon his memory.

"But justice has removed the veil with which an impious hand endeavored to cover itself. Already, on the night of the 1st of November, suspicion was awakened by the extraordinary agitation of Peytel; by those excessive attentions towards his wife, which came so late; by that excessive and noisy grief, and by those calculated bursts of sorrow, which are such as nature does not exhibit. The criminal, whom the public conscience had fixed upon; the man whose frightful combinations have been laid bare, and whose falsehoods, step by step, have been exposed, during the proceedings previous to the trial; the murderer, at whose hands a heart-stricken family, and society at large, demands an account of the blood of a wife—that murderer is Peytel!"

When, my dear Briefless, you are a judge (as I make no doubt you will be, when you have left off the club all night, cigar-smoking of mornings, and reading novels in bed), will you ever find it in your heart to order a fellow-sinner's head off upon such evidence as this? Because a romantic Substitut du Procureur du Roi chooses to compose and recite a little drama, and draw tears from juries, let us hope that severe Rha-

* This sentence is taken from another part of the "Acte d'accusation."

damanthine judges are not to be melted by such trumpery. One wants but the description of the characters to render the piece complete, as thus:—

PERSONAGES		COSTUMES
SEBASTIAN PEYTEL...............Meurtrier...................		Habillement complet de notaire perfide: figure pâle, barbe noire, cheveux noirs.
LOUIS REY...........................	Soldat rétiré, bon, brave, franc, jovial, aimant le vin, les femmes, la gaieté, ses maîtres surtout; vrai Français enfin	Costume ordinaire; il porte sur ses épaules une couverture de cheval.
WOLF	Lieutenant de gendarmerie.	
FÉLICITÉ D'ALCAZAR................	Femme et victime de Peytel.	

Médecins, Villageois, Filles d'Auberge, Garçons d'Ecurie, etc., etc.

La scène se passe sur le pont d'Andert, entre Macon et Belley. Il est minuit. La pluie tombe; les tonnerres grondent. Le ciel est couvert de nuages, et sillonné d'éclairs.

All these personages are brought into play in the Procureur's drama: the villagers come in with their chorus; the old lieutenant of gendarmes with his suspicions; Rey's frankness and gaiety, the romantic circumstances of his birth, his gallantry and fidelity, are all introduced, in order to form a contrast with Peytel, and to call down the jury's indignation against the latter. But are these proofs, or anything like proofs? And the suspicions that are to serve instead of proofs, what are they?

"My servant, Louis Rey, was very somber and reserved," says Peytel; "he refused to call me in the morning, to carry my money-chest to my room, to cover the open car when it rained." The Prosecutor disproves this by stating that Rey talked with the inn maids and servants, asked if his master was up, and stood in the inn-yard grooming the horses, with his master by his side, neither speaking to the other. Might he not have talked to the maids, and yet been somber when speaking to his master? Might he not have neglected to call his master, and yet have asked whether he was awake? Might he not have said that the inn gates were safe, out of hearing of the hostler witness? Mr. Substitut's answers to Peytel's statements are no answer at all. Every word Peytel said might be true, and yet Louis Rey might not have committed the murder; or every word might have been false, and yet Louis Rey might have committed the murder.

"Then," says Mr. Substitut, "how many obstacles are there to the commission of the crime? And these are—

"1. Rey provided himself with *one* holster pistol, to kill two people, knowing well that one of them had always a brace of pistols about him.

"2. He does not think of firing until his master's eyes are open—fires at six paces, not caring at whom he fires, and then runs away.

"3. He could not have intended to kill his master, because he had no passport in his pocket, and no clothes; and because he must have been detained at the frontier until morning; and because he would have had to drive two carriages, in order to avoid suspicion.

"4. And, a most singular circumstance, the very pistol which was found by his side had been bought at the shop of a man at Lyons, who perfectly recognized Peytel as one of his customers, though he could not say he had sold that particular weapon to Peytel."

Does it follow, from this, that Louis Rey is not the murderer, much more that Peytel is? Look at argument No. 1. Rey had no need to kill two people; he wanted the money, and not the blood. Suppose he had killed Peytel, would he not have mastered Madame Peytel easily?—a weak woman, in an excessively delicate situation, incapable of much energy at the best of times.

2. "He does not fire till he knows his master's eyes are open." Why, on a stormy night, does a man driving a carriage go to sleep? Was Rey to wait until his master snored? "He fires at six paces, not caring whom he hits";—and might not this happen too? The night is not so dark but that he can see his master, in *his usual place,* driving. He fires and hits —whom? Madame Peytel, who had left her place, *and was wrapped up with Peytel in his cloak.* She screams out, "Husband, take your pistols." Rey knows that his master has a brace, thinks that he has hit the wrong person, and, as Peytel fires on him, runs away. Peytel follows, hammer in hand. As he comes up with the fugitive, he deals him a blow on the back of the head, and Rey falls—his face to the ground. Is there anything unnatural in this story?—anything so monstrously unnatural, that is, that it might not be true?

3. These objections are absurd. Why need a man have change of linen? If he had taken none for the journey, why should he want any for the escape? Why need he drive two carriages? He might have driven both into the river, and Mrs. Peytel in one. Why is he to go to the *douane,* and thrust himself into the very jaws of danger? Are there not a thousands ways for a man to pass a frontier? Do smugglers, when they

have to pass from one country to another, choose exactly those spots where a police is placed?

And, finally, the gunsmith of Lyons, who knows Peytel quite well, cannot say that he sold the pistol to him—that is, he did *not* sell the pistol to him; for you have only one man's word, in this case (Peytel's), to the contrary, and the testimony, as far as it goes, is in his favor. I say, my lud, and gentlemen of the jury, that these objections of my learned friend, who is engaged for the Crown, are absurd, frivolous, monstrous; that to *suspect* away the life of a man upon such suppositions as these is wicked, illegal, and inhuman; and, what is more, that Louis Rey, if he wanted to commit the crime—if he wanted to possess himself of a large sum of money, chose the best time and spot for so doing, and, no doubt, would have succeeded, if fate had not, in a wonderful manner, caused Madame Peytel *to take her husband's place,* and receive the ball intended for him in her own head.

But whether these suspicions are absurd or not, hit or miss, it is the advocate's duty, as it appears, to urge them. He wants to make as unfavorable an impression as possible with regard to Peytel's character; he therefore must, for contrast's sake, give all sorts of praise to his victim, and awaken every sympathy in the poor fellow's favor. Having done this, as far as lies in his power—having exaggerated every circumstance that can be unfavorable to Peytel, and given his own tale in the baldest manner possible—having declared that Peytel is the murderer of his wife and servant, the Crown now proceeds to back this assertion by showing what interested motives he had, and by relating, after its own fashion, the circumstances of his marriage.

They may be told briefly here. Peytel was of a good family, of Macon, and entitled, at his mother's death, to a considerable property. He had been educated as a notary, and had lately purchased a business, in that line, at Belley, for which he had paid a large sum of money; part of the sum, 15,000 francs, for which he had given bills, was still due.

Near Belley, Peytel first met Félicité Alcazar, who was residing with her brother-in-law, Monsieur de Montrichard; and, knowing that the young lady's fortune was considerable, he made an offer of marriage to the brother-in-law, who thought the match advantageous, and communicated on the subject with Félicité's mother, Madame Alcazar, at Paris. After a time Peytel went to Paris to press his suit, and was accepted. There seems to have been no affection of love on his side, and some little repugnance on the part of the lady, who yielded, however, to the wishes of her parents, and was married. The parties began to quarrel on the very day of the marriage, and continued their disputes almost to the close of the unhappy connection. Félicité was half blind, passionate, sarcastic, clumsy in her person and manners, and ill-educated; Peytel, a man of considerable intellect and pretensions, who had lived for some time at Paris, where he had mingled with good literary society. The lady was, in fact, as disagreeable a person as could well be, and the evidence describes some scenes which took place between her and her husband, showing how deeply she must have mortified and enraged him.

A charge very clearly made out against Peytel is that of dishonesty: he procured from the notary of whom he bought his place an acquittance in full, whereas there were 15,000 francs owing, as we have seen. He also, in the contract of marriage, which was to have resembled, in all respects, that between Monsieur Broussais and another Demoiselle Alcazar, caused an alteration to be made in his favor, which gave him command over his wife's funded property, without furnishing the guarantees by which the other son-in-law was bound. And, almost immediately after his marriage, Peytel sold out of the funds a sum of 50,000 francs that belonged to his wife, and used it for his own purposes.

About two months after his marriage, *Peytel pressed his wife to make her will.* He had made his, he said, leaving everything to her, in case of his death. After some parley, the poor thing consented.* This is a cruel suspicion against him, and Mr. Substitut has no need to enlarge upon it. As for the previous fact, the dishonest statement about the 15,000 francs, there is nothing murderous in that—nothing which a man very eager to make a good marriage might not do. The same may be said of the suppression, in Peytel's marriage contract, of the clause to be found in

---

* "Peytel," says the act of accusation, "did not fail to see the danger which would menace him, if this will (which had escaped the magistrates in their search of Peytel's papers) was discovered. He, therefore, instructed his agent to take possession of it, which he did, and the fact was not mentioned for several months afterwards. Peytel and his agent were called upon to explain the circumstance, but refused, and their silence for a long time interrupted the 'instruction' [getting up of the evidence]. All that could be obtained from them was an avowal that such a will existed, constituting Peytel his wife's sole legatee; and a promise, on their parts, to produce it before the court gave its sentence." But why keep the will a secret? The anxiety about it was surely absurd and unnecessary. The whole of Madame Peytel's family knew that such a will was made. She had consulted her sister concerning it, who said, "If there is no other way of satisfying him, make the will"; and the mother, when she heard of it, cried out, "Does he intend to poison her?"

Broussais', placing restrictions upon the use of the wife's money. Mademoiselle Alcazar's friends read the contract before they signed it, and might have refused it, had they so pleased.

After some disputes, which took place between Peytel and his wife (there were continual quarrels, and continual letters passing between them from room to room), the latter was induced to write him a couple of exaggerated letters, swearing "by the ashes of her father that she would be an obedient wife to him, and entreating him to counsel and direct her. These letters were seen by members of the lady's family, who, in the quarrels between the couple, always took the husband's part. They were found in Peytel's cabinet, after he had been arrested for the murder, and after he had had full access to all his papers, of which he destroyed or left as many as he pleased." The accusation makes it a matter of suspicion against Peytel, that he should have left these letters of his wife's in a conspicuous situation.

"All these circumstances," says the accusation, "throw a frightful light upon Peytel's plans. The letters and will of Madame Peytel are in the hands of her husband. Three months pass away, and this poor woman is brought to her home, in the middle of the night, with two balls in her head, stretched at the bottom of her carriage, by the side of a peasant.

"What other than Sebastian Peytel could have committed this murder? —whom could it profit?—who but himself had an odious chain to break, and an inheritance to receive? Why speak of the servant's projected robbery? The pistol found by the side of Louis's body, the balls bought by him at Macon, and those discovered at Belley among his effects, were only the result of a perfidious combination. The pistol, indeed, which was found on the hill of Darde, on the night of the 1st of November, could only have belonged to Peytel, and must have been thrown by him near the body of his domestic, with the paper which had before enveloped it. Who had seen this pistol in the hands of Louis? Among all the gendarmes, work-women, domestics employed by Peytel and his brother-in-law, is there one single witness who had seen this weapon in Louis's possession? It is true that Madame Peytel did, on one occasion, speak to M. de Montrichard of a pistol, which had nothing to do, however, with that found near Louis Rey."

Is this justice, or good reason? Just reverse the argument, and apply it to Rey. "Who but Rey could have committed this murder?—who but Rey had a large sum of money to seize upon?—a pistol is found by his side, balls and powder in his pocket, other balls in his trunks at home.

The pistol found near his body could not, indeed, have belonged to Peytel: did any man ever see it in his possession? The very gunsmith who sold it, and who knew Peytel, would he not have known that he had sold him this pistol? At his own house, Peytel has a collection of weapons of all kinds; everybody has seen them—a man who makes such collections is anxious to display them. Did any one ever see this weapon? Not one. And Madame Peytel did, in her lifetime, remark a pistol in the valet's possession. She was short-sighted, and could not particularize what kind of pistol it was, but she spoke of it to her husband and her brother-in-law." This is not satisfactory, if you please; but, at least, it is as satisfactory as the other set of suppositions. It is the very chain of argument which would have been brought against Louis Rey, by this very same compiler of the act of accusation, had Rey survived instead of Peytel, and had he, as most undoubtedly would have been the case, been tried for the murder.

This argument was shortly put by Peytel's counsel:—*"If Peytel had been killed by Rey in the struggle, would you not have found Rey guilty of the murder of his master and mistress?"* It is such a dreadful dilemma, that I wonder how judges and lawyers could have dared to persecute Peytel in the manner which they did.

After the act of accusation, which lays down all the suppositions against Peytel as facts, which will not admit the truth of one of the prisoner's allegations in his own defense, comes the trial. The judge is quite as impartial as the preparer of the indictment, as will be seen by the following specimens of his interrogatories:—

JUDGE: The act of accusation finds in your statement contradictions, improbabilities, impossibilities. Thus your domestic, who had determined to assassinate you, in order to rob you, and who *must have calculated upon the consequence of a failure,* had neither passport nor money upon him. This is very unlikely, because he could not have gone far with only a single halfpenny, which was all he had.

PRISONER: My servant was known, and often passed the frontier without a passport.

JUDGE: *Your domestic had to assassinate two persons,* and had no weapon but a single pistol. He had no dagger, and the only thing found on him was a knife.

PRISONER: In the car there were several turner's implements, which he might have used.

JUDGE: But he had not those arms upon him, because you pursued him immediately. He had, according to you, only this old pistol.

PRISONER: I have nothing to say.

JUDGE: Your domestic, instead of flying into woods which skirt the road, ran straight forward on the road itself; *this, again, is very unlikely.*

PRISONER: This is a conjecture I could answer by another conjecture; I can only reason on the facts.

JUDGE: How far did you pursue him?

PRISONER: I don't know exactly.

JUDGE: You said "two hundred paces."

No answer from the prisoner.

JUDGE: Your domestic was young, active, robust, and tall. He was ahead of you. You were in a carriage, from which you had to descend; you had to take your pistols from a cushion, and *then* your hammer: how are we to believe that you could have caught him if he ran? It is *impossible.*

PRISONER: I can't explain it; I think that Rey had some defect in one leg. I, for my part, run tolerably fast.

JUDGE: At what distance from him did you fire your first shot?

PRISONER: I can't tell.

JUDGE: Perhaps he was not running when you fired.

PRISONER: I saw him running.

JUDGE: In what position was your wife?

PRISONER: She was leaning on my left arm, and the man was on the right side of the carriage.

JUDGE: The shot must have been fired *à bout portant,* because it burned the eyebrows and lashes entirely. The assassin must have passed his pistol across your breast.

PRISONER: The shot was not fired so close. I am convinced of it; professional gentlemen will prove it.

JUDGE: *That is what you pretend, because you understand perfectly the consequences of admitting the fact.* Your wife was hit with two balls —one striking downwards, to the right, by the nose; the other going horizontally through the cheek, to the left.

PRISONER: The contrary will be shown by the witnesses called for the purpose.

JUDGE: *It is a very unlucky combination for you* that these balls, which went, you say, from the same pistol, should have taken two different directions.

PRISONER: I can't dispute about the various combinations of firearms; professional persons will be heard.

JUDGE: According to your statement, your wife said to you, "My poor husband, take your pistols."

PRISONER: She did.

JUDGE: In a manner quite distinct?

PRISONER: Yes.

JUDGE: So distinct that you did not fancy she was hit?

PRISONER: Yes; that is the fact.

JUDGE: *Here, again, is an impossibility,* and nothing is more precise than the declaration of the medical men. They affirm that your wife could not have spoken; their report is unanimous.

PRISONER: I can only oppose to it quite contrary opinions from professional men likewise; you must hear them.

JUDGE: What did your wife do next?

JUDGE: You deny the statements of the witnesses (*they related to Peytel's demeanor and behavior, which the judge wishes to show were very unusual—and what if they were?*). Here, however, are some mute witnesses, whose testimony you will not perhaps refuse. Near Louis Rey's body was found a horse-cloth, a pistol, and a whip. . . . Your domestic must have had this cloth upon him when he went to assassinate you—it was wet and heavy. An assassin disencumbers himself of anything that is likely to impede him, especially when he is going to struggle with a man as young as himself.

PRISONER: My servant had, I believe, this covering on his body; it might be useful to him to keep the priming of his pistol dry.

The president caused the cloth to be opened, and showed that there was no hook, or tie, by which it could be held together; and that Rey must have held it with one hand, and, in the other, his whip, and the pistol with which he intended to commit the crime—which was impossible.

PRISONER: These are only conjectures.

And what conjectures, my God! upon which to take away the life of a man. Jeffreys, or Fouquier Tinville, could scarcely have dared to make such. Such prejudice, such bitter persecution, such priming of the jury, such monstrous assumptions and unreason—fancy them coming from an impartial judge! The man is worse than the public accuser.

"Rey," says the Judge, "could not have committed the murder, *because he had no money in his pocket to fly in case of failure.*" And what is the precise sum that his lordship thinks necessary for a gentleman to have before he makes such an attempt? Are the men who murder for money usually in possession of a certain independence before they begin? How much money was Rey, a servant, who loved wine and women, had been stopping at a score of inns on the road, and had probably an annual income of 400 francs—how much money was Rey likely to have?

"Your servant had to assassinate two persons." This I have mentioned before. Why had he to assassinate two persons,* when one was enough? If he had killed Peytel, could he not have seized and gagged his wife immediately?

"Your domestic ran straight forward, instead of taking to the woods by the side of the road; this is very unlikely." How does his worship know? Can any judge, however enlightened, tell the exact road that a man will take who has just missed a *coup* of murder, and is pursued by a man who is firing pistols at him? And has a judge a right to instruct a jury in this way, as to what they shall or shall not believe?

"You have to run after an active man, who has the start of you; to jump out of a carriage, to take your pistols, and *then* your hammer. *This is impossible.*" By heavens! does it not make a man's blood boil to read such blundering, blood-seeking sophistry? This man, when it suits him, shows that Rey would be slow in his motions, and, when it suits him, declares that Rey ought to be quick; declares *ex cathedrâ* what pace Rey should go, and what direction he should take—shows, in a breath, that he must have run faster than Peytel; and then, that he could not run fast, because the cloak clogged him; settles how he is to be dressed when he commits a murder, and what money he is to have in his pocket; gives these impossible suppositions to the jury, and tells them that the previous statements are impossible; and, finally, informs them of the precise manner in which Rey must have stood, holding his horse-cloth in one hand, his whip and pistol in the other, when he made the supposed attempt at murder. Now, what is the size of a horse-cloth? Is it as big as a pocket-handkerchief? Is there no possibility that it might hang over one shoulder—that the whip should be held under that very arm?

---

* M. Balzac's theory of the case is, that Rey had intrigued with Madame Peytel, having known her previous to her marriage, when she was staying in the house of her brother-in-law, Monsieur de Montrichard, where Rey had been a servant.

Did you never see a carter so carry it, his hands in his pockets all the while? Is it monstrous, abhorrent to nature, that a man should fire a pistol from under a cloak on a rainy day? that he should, after firing the shot, be frightened, and run—run straight before him, with the cloak on his shoulders, and the weapon in his hand? Peytel's story is possible, and very possible—it is almost probable. Allow that Rey had the cloth on, and you allow that he must have been clogged in his motions; that Peytel may have come up with him, felled him with a blow of the hammer—the doctors say that he would have so fallen by one blow—he would have fallen on his face, as he was found; the paper might have been thrust into his breast, and tumbled out as he fell. Circumstances far more impossible have occurred ere this, and men have been hanged for them who were as innocent of the crime laid to their charge as the judge on the bench who convicted them.

In like manner, Peytel may not have committed the crime charged to him; and Mr. Judge, with his arguments as to possibilities and impossibilities, Mr. Public Prosecutor, with his romantic narrative and inflammatory harangues to the jury, may have used all these powers to bring to death an innocent man. From the animus with which the case has been conducted from beginning to end, it was easy to see the result. Here it is, in the words of the provincial paper:—

Bourg, 28 October, 1839

"The condemned Peytel has just undergone his punishment, which took place four days before the anniversary of his crime. The terrible drama of the bridge of Andert, which cost the lives of two persons, has just terminated on the scaffold. Mid-day had just sounded on the clock of the Palais; the same clock tolled midnight when, on the 30th of August, his sentence was pronounced.

"Since the rejection of his appeal in Cassation, on which his principal hopes were founded, Peytel spoke little of his petition to the King. The notion of transportation was that which he seemed to cherish most. However, he made several inquiries from the jailer of the prison, when he saw him at meal-time, with regard to the place of execution, the usual hour, and other details on the subject. From that period, the words *'Champ de Foire'* (the fair-field, where the execution was to be held) were frequently used by him in conversation.

"Yesterday, the idea that the time had arrived seemed to be more strongly than ever impressed upon him, especially after the departure of the curé, who latterly has been with him every day. The documents connected with the trial had arrived in the morning. He was ignorant of this circumstance, but sought to discover from his guardians what they tried to hide from him, and to find out whether his petition was rejected, and when he was to die.

"Yesterday, also, he had written to demand the presence of his counsel, M. Margerand, in order that he might have some conversation with him, and regulate his affairs, before he—— He did not write down the word, but he left in its place a few points of the pen.

"In the evening, whilst he was at supper, he begged earnestly to be allowed a little wax candle, to finish what he was writing; otherwise, he said, *time might fail*. This was a new, indirect manner of repeating his ordinary question. As light, up to that evening, had been refused him, it was thought best to deny him in this, as in former instances; otherwise his suspicions might have been confirmed. The keeper refused his demand.

"This morning, Monday, at nine o'clock, the Greffier of the Assize Court, in fulfillment of the painful duty which the law imposes upon him, came to the prison, in company with the curé of Bourg, and announced to the convict that his petition was rejected, and that he had only three hours to live. He received this fatal news with a great deal of calmness, and showed himself to be no more affected than he had been on the trial. 'I am ready; but I wish they had given me four-and-twenty hours' notice,' were all the words he used.

"The Greffier now retired, leaving Peytel alone with the curé, who did not thenceforth quit him. Peytel breakfasted at ten o'clock.

"At eleven, a piquet of mounted gendarmerie and infantry took their station upon the place before the prison, where a great concourse of people had already assembled. An open car was at the door. Before he went out, Peytel asked the jailer for a looking-glass, and having examined his face for a moment, said, 'At least, the inhabitants of Bourg will see that I have not grown thin.'

"As twelve o'clock sounded, the prison gates opened, an aide appeared, followed by Peytel, leaning on the arm of the curé. Peytel's face was pale. He had a long black beard, a blue cap on his head, and his greatcoat flung over his shoulders, and buttoned at the neck.

"He looked about at the place and the crowd. He asked if the carriage would go at a trot; and on being told that that would be difficult, he said he would prefer walking, and asked what the road was. He immediately set out, walking at a firm and rapid pace. He was not bound at all.

"An immense crowd of people encumbered the two streets through which he had to pass to the place of execution. He cast his eyes alternately upon them and upon the guillotine, which was before him.

"Arrived at the foot of the scaffold, Peytel embraced the curé, and bade him adieu. He then embraced him again—perhaps for his mother and sister.

He then mounted the steps rapidly, and gave himself into the hands of the executioner, who removed his coat and cap. He asked how he was to place himself, and, on a sign being made, he flung himself briskly on the plank, and stretched his neck. In another moment he was no more.

"The crowd, which had been quite silent, retired, profoundly moved by the sight it had witnessed. As at all executions, there was a very great number of women present.

"Under the scaffold there had been, ever since the morning, a coffin. The family had asked for his remains, and had them immediately buried, privately; and thus the unfortunate man's head escaped the modelers in wax, several of whom had arrived to take an impression of it."

Down goes the axe; the poor wretch's head rolls gasping into the basket; the spectators go home, pondering; and Mr. Executioner and his aides have, in half an hour, removed all traces of the august sacrifice, and of the altar on which it had been performed. Say, Mr. Briefless, do you think that any single person, meditating murder, would be deterred therefrom by holding this—nay, a thousand more executions? Is it not for moral improvement, as I take it, nor for opportunity to make appropriate remarks upon the punishment of crime, that people make a holiday of a killing-day, and leave their homes and occupations to flock and witness the cutting off of a head. Do we crowd to see Mr. Macready in the new tragedy, or Mademoiselle Ellssler in her last new ballet and flesh-colored stockinet pantaloons, out of a pure love of abstract poetry and beauty; or from a strong notion that we shall be excited, in different ways, by the actor and the dancer? And so, as we go to have a meal of fictitious terror at the tragedy, of something more questionable in the ballet, we go for a glut of blood to the execution. The lust is in every man's nature, more or less. Did you ever witness a wrestling or boxing match? The first clatter of the kick on the shins, or the first drawing of blood, makes the stranger shudder a little; but soon the blood is his chief enjoyment, and he thirsts for it with a fierce delight. It is a fine grim pleasure that we have in seeing a man killed; and I make no doubt that the organs of destructiveness must begin to throb and swell as we witness the delightful, savage spectacle.

Three or four years back, when Fieschi and Lacenaire were executed, I made attempts to see the execution of both, but was disappointed in both cases. In the first instance, the day for Fieschi's death was purposely kept secret; and he was, if I remember rightly, executed at some

remote quarter of the town. But it would have done a philanthropist good
to witness the scene which we saw on the morning when his execution
did *not* take place.

It was carnival time, and the rumor had pretty generally been carried
abroad that he was to die on that morning. A friend, who accompanied
me, came many miles, through the mud and dark, in order to be in at
the death. We set out before light, floundering through the muddy
Champs Elysées, where, besides, were many other persons floundering,
and all bent upon the same errand. We passed by the Concert of Musard,
then held in the Rue St. Honoré; and round this, in the wet, a number
of coaches were collected. The ball was just up, and a crowd of people,
in hideous masquerade, drunk, tired, dirty, dressed in horrible old frip-
pery, and daubed with filthy rouge, were trooping out of the place—
tipsy women and men, shrieking, jabbering, gesticulating, as French will
do; parties swaggering, staggering forwards, arm in arm, reeling to and
fro across the street, and yelling songs in chorus. Hundreds of these were
bound for the show, and we thought ourselves lucky in finding a vehicle
to the execution place, at the Barrière d'Enfer. As we crossed the river
and entered the Enfer Street, crowds of students, black workmen, and
more drunken devils from more carnival balls, were filling it; and on the
grand place there were thousands of these assembled, looking out for
Fieschi and his cortège. We waited and waited; but, alas! no fun for us
that morning—no throat-cutting, no august spectacle of satisfied justice
—and the eager spectators were obliged to return disappointed of their
expected breakfast of blood. It would have been a fine scene that execution, could it but have taken place in the midst of the mad mountebanks
and tipsy strumpets who had flocked so far to witness it, wishing to wind
up the delights of their carnival by a *bonne-bouche* of a murder.

The other attempt was equally unfortunate. We arrived too late on the
ground to be present at the execution of Lacenaire and his co-mate in
murder, Avril. But as we came to the ground (a gloomy round space,
within the barrier—three roads lead to it; and, outside, you see the
wine-shops and restaurateurs' of the barrier looking gay and inviting)—
as we came to the ground, we only found, in the midst of it, a little pool
of ice, just partially tinged with red. Two or three idle street-boys were
dancing and stamping about this pool; and when I asked one of them
whether the execution had taken place, he began dancing more madly
than ever, and shrieked out with a loud fantastical, theatrical voice,
"Venez tous Messieurs et Dames, voyez ici le sang du monstre Lecenaire,

et de son compagnon le traître Avril," or words to that effect; and straightway all the other gamins screamed out the words in chorus, and took hands and danced round the little puddle.

O august Justice, your meal was followed by a pretty appropriate grace! Was any man, who saw the show, deterred, or frightened, or moralized in any way? He had gratified his appetite for blood, and this was all. There is something singularly pleasing, both in the amusement of execution-seeing, and in the results. You are not only delightfully excited at the time, but most pleasingly relaxed afterwards; the mind, which has been wound up painfully until now, becomes quite complacent and easy. There is something agreeable in the misfortunes of others, as the philosopher has told us. Remark what a good breakfast you eat after an execution; how pleasant it is to cut jokes after it, and upon it. This merry, pleasant mood is brought on by the blood tonic.

But, for God's sake, if we are to enjoy this, let us do so in moderation; and let us, at least, be sure of a man's guilt before we murder him. To kill him, even with the full assurance that he is guilty, is hazardous enough. Who gave you the right to do so?—you who cry out against suicides, as impious and contrary to Christian law. What use is there in killing him? You deter no one else from committing the crime by so doing. You give us, to be sure, half an hour's pleasant entertainment; but it is a great question whether we derive much moral profit from the sight. If you want to keep a murderer from further inroads upon society, are there not plenty of hulks and prisons, God wot—treadmills, galleys, and houses of correction? Above all, as in the case of Sebastian Peytel and his family, there have been two deaths already: was a third death absolutely necessary? And taking the fallibility of judges and lawyers into his heart, and remembering the thousand instances of unmerited punishment that have been suffered, upon similar and stronger evidence, before, can any man declare, positively and upon his oath, that Peytel was guilty, and that this was not *the third murder in the family?*

H. L. Mencken

:

THE SCOPES TRIAL

Be it enacted—that it shall be unlawful for any teacher in any of the universities, normals, and all other public schools in the state, which are supported in whole or in part by the public school funds of the state, to teach the theory that denies the story of the divine creation of man as taught in the Bible, and to teach instead that man has descended from a lower order of animals.

This statute was passed by the legislature of the state of Tennesse on March 21, 1925. It was a climax in a struggle that had split American Protestants into two warring camps. On the one side were the fundamentalists—those who believed in the letter of the Bible and who refused to accept any teaching that conflicted with it. On the other side were the modernists (or liberals), who, like the medieval scholastics, tried to reconcile faith with reason. The Tennessee legislature, dominated by fundamentalists, decided to deliver a powerful blow to the body of the modernists.

A few strong-minded liberals in the small town of Dayton, Tennessee, decided to put the law to a test. They persuaded John Thomas Scopes, a teacher of biology at the local high school, to allow himself to be caught red-handed in the act of teaching evolution to his pupils. Thus began a drama that was soon ballyhooed by an irreverent press into a great national circus occupying the attention of the entire world through the summer days of 1925. William Jennings Bryan, the Great Commoner—famous orator, leader of the free-silver forces, thrice-defeated candidate for President of the United States, former Secretary of State, and zealous, indefatigable champion of the Bible—volunteered his services to the prosecution. Clarence

Darrow, agnostic and liberal—a pleader of unpopular causes, the criminal lawyer who only recently had saved Richard Loeb and Nathan Leopold, wealthy young Chicago thrill slayers, from execution—accepted the appeal of the Civil Liberties Union to become chief counsel for Scopes. It was a natural—the battle of the century between Bryan, the unreconstructed fundamentalist, and Darrow, the hard-bitten friend of the underdog.

The hot spotlight of national publicity glared down on the sleepy little town of Dayton as the battle of the giants got under way. Gaunt Gothic Americans flocked to the scene from the surrounding mountains, eager to learn about this high-falutin' talk of monkeys and even more determined to defend their way of life against the outlanders. It was a kind of Tennessee Roman holiday, with all the world eavesdropping. Hot-dog and lemonade stands were set up in the streets. Book hawkers offered tracts on evolution at cut rates. Revivalists had a field day, posting such signs as this:

DO YOU WANT TO BE A SWEET ANGEL?

FORTY DAYS OF PRAYER.

ITEMIZE YOUR SINS.

COME CLEAN!

Bryan strode into Dayton as the shining knight in armor of the fundamentalists. Among the mass of gratuitous advice was this hint from Billy Sunday, the revivalist: "If man evolved from a monkey, why are there so many monkeys left? Why didn't they all evolve into humans?" Aimee Semple McPherson, the highly publicized evangelist of the gaudy Four-Square Gospel shrine in California, telegraphed "the lionhearted champion of the Bible":

CONSTANT PRAYER DURING WEEK ALL NIGHT PRAYER SATURDAY NIGHT STOP SUNDAY AFTERNOON BIBLE PARADE MASS MEETING AND TRIAL WITH HANGING AND BURIAL OF MONKEY TEACHERS TENNESSEE CAN COUNT ON US

An even more encouraging wire came from Smackover, Arkansas:

MY DEAR BROTHER BRYAN FIGHT THEM EVOLUTIONS UNTIL HELL FREEZES OVER AND GIVE THEM A ROUND OF THE ICE GOD BLESS YOU IN YOUR TIME OF TRIALS AND GIVE YOU WISDOM AND GRACE TO DO WHAT DEAR JESUS WILL SMILE UPON

YOUR UNACQUAINTED BROTHER

HAPPY GORDON MEAD

Into the supercharged atmosphere of Dayton came a mercurial newspaperman from Baltimore, who found a happy hunting ground for his peculiar talents. From the end of World War I to the brisk days of the New Deal, Henry Louis Mencken turned the blasts of his highly personal rhetoric on what he felt to be the stuffy spiritual, moral, and cultural institutions of the republic. Thoroughly enjoying the bizarre aspects of the American scene, he lashed out in all directions in a style composed of unequal parts of Boccaccio, Erasmus, Rabelais, and Mencken. He was fascinated by the stupidity of the common man and by the prevalence of mental vacuity in what he was fond of calling the "Bible Belt" or "Cow States." "The time-serving demagogues in public office," comments *Newsweek,* "the bigots in the pulpits, the editorial puritans, the pedagogical practitioners of timidity, gentility, and sanctimony in our institutions of learning, the bluenoses who imposed Prohibition upon the country, the prudes and Philistines and peasants who set themselves in vulgar opposition to culture—these felt the Mencken whiplash." A whole generation of college students swore by or at the Wagnerian rhythm of Mencken's prose.

This was the reporter sent by the Baltimore *Evening Sun,* along with the *Sunpapers'* Essary, Kent, Hyde, and Duffy, to cover the Scopes trial in Tennessee. Nothing could have made Mencken happier. He took the opportunity to investigate the Holy Roller cult in the mountains behind Dayton, where the yearning mountaineers' souls needed nightly reconversion.

DEEP IN "THE COCA-COLA BELT"

The Sun, Baltimore, July 13, 1925

Dayton, Tennessee, July 13—There is a Unitarian clergyman here from New York, trying desperately to horn into the trial and execution of the infidel Scopes. He will fail. If Darrow ventured to put him on the stand the whole audience, led by the jury, would leap out of the courthouse windows and take to the hills. Darrow himself, indeed, is as much as they can bear. The whisper that he is an atheist has been stilled by the bucolic make-up and by the public report that he has the gift of prophecy and can reconcile Genesis and evolution. Even so, there is ample space about him when he navigates the streets. The other day a newspaperwoman was warned by her landlady to keep out of the courtroom when he was on his legs. All the local sorcerers predict that a bolt from heaven will fetch him in the end. The night he arrived there was a violent storm, the town water turned brown, and horned cattle in the lowlands were afloat for hours. A woman back in the mountains gave birth to a child with hair four inches long, curiously bobbed in scallops.

The Book of Revelation has all the authority, in these theological uplands, of military orders in time of war. The people turn to it for light upon all their problems, spiritual and secular. If a text were found in it denouncing the antievolution law, then the antievolution law would become infamous overnight. But so far the exegetes who roar and snuffle in the town have found no such text. Instead they have found only blazing ratifications and reinforcements of Genesis. Darwin is the devil with seven tails and nine horns. Scopes, though he is disguised by flannel pantaloons and a Beta Theta Pi haircut, is the harlot of Babylon. Darrow is Beelzebub in person, and Malone is the Crown Prince Friedrich Wilhelm.

I have hitherto hinted an Episcopalian down here in the Coca-Cola belt is regarded as an atheist. It sounds like one of the lies that journalists tell, but it is really an understatement of the facts. Even a Methodist, by Rhea County standards, is one a bit debauched by pride of intellect. It is the four Methodists on the jury who are expected to hold out for giving Scopes Christian burial after he is hanged. They all made it plain, when they were examined, that they were freethinking and independent men, and not to be run amuck by the superstitions of the lowly. One actually confessed that he seldom read the Bible, though he hastened to add that he was familiar with its principles. The fellow had on a boiled shirt and a polka-dot necktie. He sits somewhat apart. When Darrow withers to a cinder under the celestial blowpipe, this dubious Wesleyan, too, will lose a few hairs.

Even the Baptists no longer brew a medicine that is strong enough for the mountaineers. The sacrament of baptism by total immersion is over too quickly for them, and what follows offers nothing that they can get their teeth into. What they have is a continuous experience of the divine power, an endless series of evidence that the true believer is a marked man, ever under the eye of God. It is not enough to go to a revival once a year or twice a year; there must be a revival every night. And it is not enough to accept the truth as a mere statement of indisputable and awful fact; it must be embraced ecstatically and orgiastically, to the accompaniment of loud shouts, dreadful heavings and gurglings, and dancing with arms and legs.

This craving is satisfied brilliantly by the gaudy practices of the Holy Rollers, and so the mountaineers are gradually gravitating toward the Holy Roller communion, or, as they prefer to call it, the Church of God. Gradually, perhaps, is not the word. They are actually going in by whole villages and townships. At the last count of noses there were 20,000 Holy Rollers in these hills. The next census, I have no doubt, will show many more. The cities of the lowlands, of course, still resist, and so do most of the county towns, including even Dayton, but once one steps off the state roads the howl of holiness is heard in the woods, and the yokels carry on an almost continuous orgy.

A foreigner in store clothes going out from Dayton must approach the sacred grove somewhat discreetly. It is not that the Holy Rollers, discovering him, would harm him; it is simply that they would shut down their boiling of the devil and flee into the forests. Wc left Dayton an hour after nightfall and parked our car in a wood a mile or so beyond the little hill village of Morgantown. Far off in a glade a flickering light was visible and out of the silence came a faint rumble of exhortation. We could scarcely distinguish the figure of the preacher; it was like looking down the tube of a dark field microscope. We got out of the car and sneaked along the edge of a mountain cornfield.

Presently we were near enough to see what was going on. From the great limb of a mighty oak hung a couple of crude torches of the sort that car inspectors thrust under Pullman cars when a train pulls in at night. In their light was a preacher, and for a while we could see no one else. He was an immensely tall and thin mountaineer in blue jeans, his collarless shirt open at the neck and his hair a tousled mop. As he preached he paced up and down under the smoking flambeaux and at each turn he thrust his arms into the air and yelled, "Glory to God!" We crept nearer in the shadow of the cornfield and began to hear more of his discourse. He was preaching on the day of judgment. The high kings of the earth, he roared, would all fall down and die; only the sanctified would stand up to receive the Lord God of Hosts. One of these kings he mentioned by name—the king of what he called Greece-y. The King of Greece-y, he said, was doomed to hell.

We went forward a few more yards and began to see the audience. It was seated on benches ranged round the preacher in a circle. Behind him sat a row of elders, men and women. In front were the younger folk. We kept on cautiously, and individuals rose out of the ghostly gloom. A young mother sat suckling her baby, rocking as the preacher paced up and down. Two scared little girls hugged each other, their pigtails down their backs. An immensely huge mountain woman, in a gingham dress cut in one piece, rolled on her heels at every "Glory to God." On one side, but half visible, was what appeared to be a bed. We found out afterward that two babies were asleep upon it.

The preacher stopped at last and there arose out of the darkness a woman with her hair pulled back into a little tight knot. She began so quietly that we couldn't hear what she said, but soon her voice rose resonantly and we could follow her. She was denouncing the reading of books. Some wandering book agent, it appeared, had come to her cabin and tried to sell her a specimen of his wares. She refused to touch it. Why, indeed, read a book? If what was in it was true, then everything in it was already in the Bible. If it was false, then reading it would imperil the soul. Her syllogism complete, she sat down.

There followed a hymn, led by a somewhat fat brother wearing silver-rimmed country spectacles. It droned on for a half a dozen stanzas, and then the first speaker resumed the floor. He argued that the gift of tongues was real and that education was a snare. Once his children could read the Bible, he said, they had enough. Beyond lay only infidelity and damnation. Sin stalked the cities. Dayton itself was a Sodom. Even Morgantown had begun to forget God. He sat down, and the female aurochs in gingham got up.

She began quietly, but was soon leaping and roaring, and it was hard to follow her. Under cover of the turmoil we sneaked a bit closer. A couple of other discourses followed, and there were two or three hymns. Suddenly a change of mood began to make itself felt. The last hymn ran longer than the others and dropped gradually into a monotonous, unintelligible chant. The leader beat time with his book. The faithful broke out with exultations. When the singing ended there was a brief palaver that we could not hear and two of the men moved a bench into the circle of light directly under the flambeaux. Then a half-grown girl emerged from the darkness and threw herself upon it. We noticed with astonishment that she had bobbed hair. "This sister," said the leader, "has asked for prayers." We moved a bit closer. We could now see faces plainly and hear every word.

What followed quickly reached such heights of barbaric grotesquerie that it was hard to believe it real. At a signal all the faithful crowded up to the bench and began to pray—not in unison, but each for himself. At another they all fell on their knees, their arms over the penitent. The leader knelt, facing us, his head alternately thrown back dramatically or buried in his hands. Words spouted from his lips like bullets from a machine gun—appeals to God to pull the penitent back out of hell, defiances of the powers and principalities of the air, a vast impassioned jargon of apocalyptic text. Suddenly he rose to his feet, threw back his head, and began to speak in tongues—blub-blub-blub, gurgle-

gurgle-gurgle. His voice rose to a higher register. The climax was a shrill, inarticulate squawk, like that of a man throttled. He fell headlong across the pyramid of supplicants.

A comic scene? Somehow, no. The poor half-wits were too horribly in earnest. It was like peeping through a knothole at the writhings of a people in pain. From the squirming and jabbering mass a young woman gradually detached herself—a woman not uncomely, with a pathetic homemade cap on her head. Her head jerked back, the veins of her neck swelled, and her fists went to her throat as if she were fighting for breath. She bent backward until she was like a half of a hoop. Then she suddenly snapped forward. We caught a flash of the whites of her eyes. Presently her whole body began to be convulsed—great convulsions that began at the shoulders and ended at the hips. She would leap to her feet, thrust her arms in air, and then hurl herself upon the heap. Her praying flattened out into a mere delirious caterwauling, like that of a tomcat on a petting party.

I describe the thing as a strict behaviorist. The lady's subjective sensations I leave to infidel pathologists. Whatever they were they were obviously contagious, for soon another damsel joined her, and then another and then a fourth. The last one had an extraordinarily bad attack. She began with mild enough jerks of the head, but in a moment she was bounding all over the place, exactly like a chicken with its head cut off. Every time her head came up a stream of yells and barking would issue out of it. Once she collided with a dark, undersized brother, hitherto silent and stolid. Contact with her set him off as if he had been kicked by a mule. He leaped into the air, threw back his head, and began to gargle as if with a mouthful of BB shot. Then he loosened one tremendous stentorian sentence in the tongues and collapsed.

By this time the performers were quite oblivious to the profane universe. We left our hiding and came up to the little circle of light. We slipped into the vacant seats on one of the rickety benches. The heap of mourners was directly before us. They bounced into us as they cavorted. The smell that they radiated, sweating there in that obscene heap, half suffocated us. Not all of them, of course, did the thing in the grand manner. Some merely moaned and rolled their eyes. The female ox in gingham flung her great hulk on the ground and jabbered an unintelligible prayer. One of the men, in the intervals between fits, put on his spectacles and read his Bible.

Beside me on the bench sat the young mother and her baby. She suckled it through the whole orgy, obviously fascinated by what was going on, but never venturing to take any hand in it. On the bed just outside the light two other babies slept peacefully. In the shadows, suddenly appearing and as suddenly going away, were vague figures, whether of believers or of scoffers I do not know. They seemed to come and go in couples. Now and then a couple at the ringside would step back and then vanish into the black night. After a while some came back. There was whispering outside the circle of vision. A couple of Fords lurched up in the wood road, cutting holes in the darkness with their lights. Once someone out of sight loosed a bray of laughter.

All this went on, for an hour or so. The original penitent, by this time, was buried three deep beneath the heap. One caught a glimpse, now and then, of her yellow bobbed hair, but then she would vanish again. How she breathed down there I don't know; it was hard enough ten feet away, with a strong five-cent cigar to help. When the praying brothers would rise up for a bout with the tongues their faces were streaming with perspiration. The fat harridan in gingham sweated like a longshoreman. Her hair got loose and fell down over her face. She fanned herself with her skirt. A powerful mortal she was, equal in her day to obstetrics and a week's washing on the same morning, but this was worse than a week's washing. Finally, she fell in a heap, breathing in great, convulsive gasps.

We tired of it after a while and groped our way back to our automobile. When we got to Dayton, after eleven o'clock—an immensely late hour for these parts—the whole town was still gathered on the courthouse lawn, hanging upon the disputes of theologians. The Bible champion of the world had a crowd. The Seventh Day Adventist missionaries had a crowd. A volunteer from faraway Portland, Oregon, made up exactly like Andy Gump, had another and larger crowd. Dayton was enjoying itself. All the usual rules were suspended and the curfew bell was locked up. The prophet Bryan, exhausted by his day's work for Revelations, was snoring in his bed up the road, but enough volunteers were still on watch to keep the battlements manned.

Such is human existence among the fundamentalists, where children are brought up on Genesis and sin is unknown. If I have made the tale too long, then blame the spirit of garrulity that is in the local air. Even newspaper reporters, down here, get some echo of the call. Divine inspiration is as common as the hookworm. I have done my best to show you what the great heritage of mankind comes to in regions where the Bible is the beginning and end of wisdom, and the mountebank Bryan, parading the streets in his seersucker coat, is pointed out to sucklings as the greatest man since Abraham.

Three days later William O. McGeehan, the sports writer, who covered the Scopes trial for the *New York Herald Tribune,* reported that in the midst of a booming peroration by Dudley Field Malone, "Mr. H. L. Mencken fell off his chair with a crash that startled the courtroom."

"It is a jedgment," said one of the sisters. "The walls are falling in, and Mr. Mencken is the first to go, and he won't go to glory, either."

The great scene of the trial came on the seventh day, when Bryan and Darrow locked horns in a savage encounter under extraordinary circumstances. Immediately preceding the cross-examination, Darrow insisted that a sign ten feet long with huge letters READ YOUR BIBLE! be removed from in front of the jury. A prosecution attorney objected, saying "It is time for us to tear up all the Bibles, throw them into the fire, and let the country go to hell." A court officer rapped for order: "People, this is no circus. There are no monkeys up here. This is a lawsuit. Let us have order." Bryan made an unctuous little speech: "If having that up there during the trial makes our brother to offend, I would take it down during the trial."

The crowd was so great in the afternoon that Judge Raulston had removed the court to the lawn. There under the maple trees hundreds of spectators formed fundamentalist and modernist cheering sections. The weather was oppressively hot and humid. All the participants stripped to their shirt sleeves —Bryan in a pongee shirt, Darrow with lavender suspenders, and Judge Raulston with judicial galluses.

Bryan started out calmly and confidently, but he was soon stung to anger by the relentless, barbed questioning of Darrow. Finally, in a burst of fury he and Darrow both came to their feet and shook fists at one another. Although publicly humiliated, Bryan refused to acknowledge defeat.

Here is *The New York Times'* report of the main event—the intellectual battle of the century between William Jennings Bryan, the plumed knight of the fundamentalists, and Clarence Darrow, the agnostic with lavender galluses.

MONKEY BUSINESS IN TENNESSEE

The New York Times, July 21, 1925

At last it has happened. After days of ineffective argument and legal quibbling, with speeches that merely skirted the edges of the matter which everyone wanted discussed in this Scopes antievolution trial, William Jennings Bryan, fundamentalist, and Clarence Darrow, agnostic and pleader of unpopular causes, locked horns today under the most remarkable circumstances ever known to American court procedure.

It was on the courthouse lawn, where Judge Raulston had moved so that more persons could hear, with the Tennessee crowds whooping for their angry champion, who shook his fist in the quizzical, satiric face of Mr. Darrow, that Mr. Bryan was put on the stand by the defense to prove that the Bible need not be taken literally.

With an airplane whizzing overhead, Mr. Darrow asked Mr. Bryan about Jonah and the whale, Joshua and the sun, where Cain got his wife, the Flood, and the Tower of Babel, until the youthful Attorney General Stewart, desperately trying to bring the performance within legal bounds, asked, "What is the meaning of all this harangue?"

"To show up fundamentalism," shouted Mr. Darrow, lifting his voice in one of the few moments of anger he showed, "to prevent bigots and ignoramuses from controlling the educational system of the United States."

Mr. Bryan sprang to his feet, his face purple, and shook his fist in the lowering, gnarled face of Mr. Darrow, while he cried:

"To protect the word of God from the greatest atheist and agnostic in the United States."

A roar of applause broke from the crowd under the trees and Mr. Darrow, looking down at them, called out sarcastically:

"Why don't you folks cheer?"

At the end of a day so crowded with unexpected happenings all Dayton tonight is holding its head, overcome by the drama of the unprecedented trial.

Mr. Darrow was cited in contempt as soon as court opened this morning for his defiance of the judge on Friday, and ordered to show cause why he should not be punished.

In the afternoon he apologized to Judge Raulston, who in a talk that was almost a prayer, his voice shaken with emotion, brought Mr. Darrow to the "mourner's bench," forgave him, and told him to go back home and learn in his heart the words of the man who said, "Come unto Me and receive eternal life."

All morning the crowds packed into the courtroom to hear what everybody assumed would be the final argument of the case, until in the afternoon the building was jammed. Judge Raulston did not wish to shut anybody out, and in order that all might hear he moved to a platform built against the wall of the courthouse, under the maple trees, where a week ago Mr. Bryan delivered a sermon. On the benches in front nearly everyone could get a seat, and hundreds stood, forming themselves into opposing modernist and fundamentalist cheering sections, although liberals present were in a small minority.

It was a striking scene. Judge Raulston sat at a little table in the center, with the state attorneys at his left and the defense at his right, while about them were a few newspapermen and fortunate persons who managed to squeeze by the guard. In front was a sea of upturned faces, waiting for what they presumed would be an ordinary argument, faces which became eager when Mr. Darrow announced that he would call Mr. Bryan as a witness for the defense.

And then for nearly two hours, while those below broke into laughter or applause or cried out encouragement to Mr. Bryan, Mr. Darrow goaded his opponent. In a blue shirt and suspenders he leaned against the edge of his table, Bible in hand, and asked Mr. Bryan if he really believed that the serpent had always crawled on its belly because it tempted Eve, and if he believed that Eve was made from Adam's rib.

Mr. Bryan started off as sweetly as a cooing dove. He wanted to confound this agnostic Darrow, he told the court; he wanted to testify to his faith in the revealed word of God and show that scientists did not know what they were talking about.

He overruled the objection of Attorney General "Tom" Stewart, who saw his lawsuit vanishing in the battle smoke of debate, but as Mr. Darrow prodded him with all the power of his logical mind, the admissions wrung from Mr. Bryan roused him to anger, and in a burst of fury he denounced Mr. Darrow as having only the purpose of casting slurs on the Bible.

"I have merely the purpose of showing up your fool ideas that no intelligent Christian believes in," shouted Mr. Darrow, stung to anger, and the judge, in the midst of confusion as both antagonists rose to their feet and shook their fists at each other, adjourned the court.

Mr. Darrow drew from Bryan that he knew little of comparative religion, very little of geology, nothing of physiology, and hardly anything that would interest a man seeking light on the vast questions of evolution and religion on which he has written for years. He took refuge again and again in his faith in the written word of the Bible. If what science he had learned did not agree with that he did not believe it and did not want to know.

"I have all the information I need to live by and die by," he declared vehemently.

But his insistence upon the literal acceptance of the Bible was weakened somewhat, for he admitted when questioned about Joshua making the sun stand still that it was one of those things that "anybody can put his own construction upon," and explained that although there was no doubt that the earth moved around the sun the Bible was "inspired by the Almighty, and He may have used language that could be understood at that time."

The problem of what was meant by "days" in the Genesis account of creation was also one on which Mr. Bryan said things pleasing to Mr. Darrow, for he admitted that "days" probably meant "periods," and that creation might have lasted for millions of years.

All those under the trees were completely absorbed in the conflict between the two men, each representing a point of view as to religion so diametrically opposed. It was as if all the voices of these two great divisions of religious thought, rationalism and faith, were debating in the persons of Mr. Darrow and Mr. Bryan. It was a burning vital issue to those people of Rhea County who were present, and to the little group of liberals who clustered in front.

Jonah and the whale should be taken literally, said Mr. Bryan, for he believed "in a God who can make a whale and can make a man, and make both do what He pleases."

"You don't know whether it was the ordinary mine-run of fish, or made for that purpose?" asked Mr. Darrow with quiet sarcasm.

"You may guess," replied Mr. Bryan, calmly, fanning himself with a palm-leaf fan, "an evolutionist guess."

"You are not prepared to say whether that fish was made especially to swallow a man or not?"

"The Bible doesn't say, so I'm not prepared to say," replied Mr. Bryan, and that was his attitude on nearly every question raised. It was a miracle, and one miracle was just as easy to believe as another, said Mr. Bryan.

"A miracle is a thing performed beyond what man performs," he said. "When you get beyond what man can do, you get within the realm of miracles, and it is just as easy to believe in the miracle of Jonah as any other miracle in the Bible."

The attorneys for the state were chuckling over the way Mr. Bryan was acquitting himself by this time, but they did not look so pleased as the afternoon wore on.

Joshua and the sun was another miracle that Mr. Darrow wanted to know about. How did it happen that the sun stood still, when the earth moves around the sun?

It was the language of the day, Mr. Bryan said, and if anything stopped it must have been the earth.

"Now, Mr. Bryan, have you ever pondered what would have happened to the earth if it had stood still?"

"No," replied Mr. Bryan. "The God I believe in could have taken care of that, Mr. Darrow."

"Don't you know it would have been converted into a molten mass of matter?"

"You testify to that when you get on the stand," retorted Mr. Bryan. "I will give you a chance," he said, for he had announced that he would call all the defense counsel if they called him, much to the delight of everyone present.

Then they got onto the flood, and attempted to fix the date of it by the Bible, and against the opposition of Mr. Stewart, Mr. Bryan told the court to let Mr. Darrow have all the latitude he wanted.

"I am going to have some latitude when he gets through," he said grimly.

"You can have latitude and longitude," said Mr. Darrow.

"These gentlemen have not had much chance," said Mr. Bryan, rising to his feet from the witness chair. "They did not come here to try this case. They came here to try revealed religion. I am here to defend it, and they can ask me any questions they please."

The applause from the yard brought a snort of disgust from Mr. Darrow, and in reproach for what Mr. Bryan called his insults, he raised his fist and shouted at him:

"You insult every man of science and learning in the world because he does not believe in your fool religion."

Judge Raulston calmed them both, and Mr. Stewart again stepped forward to protest.

"I have a public duty to perform under my oath," said the earnest young attorney general, who, with his case, had been crowded into the background. "I ask the court to stop it."

"How long ago was the flood, Mr. Bryan?" asked Mr. Darrow, and the debate was on again. They figured it up with the help of Bishop Usher's chronology, as being 2348 B.C. Mr. Bryan thought the fish might have lived, but everything else was destroyed.

"Don't you know there are any number of civilizations that are traced back to more than five thousand years?" asked Darrow.

"I know we have people who trace things back according to the number of ciphers they have," replied Bryan; "but I am not satisfied they are accurate. I am satisfied by no evidence that I have found, that would justify me in accepting the opinions of these men against what I believe to be the inspired word of God."

There was a civilization before the flood, said Mr. Bryan, but when he was asked if he knew a scientific man in the world who believed that all the animals and all the races now inhabiting the world had come here since the flood, he took refuge in saying that he was more interested in what Christians were doing now than in what happened in the past.

"You have never had any interest in the age of the various races and people and civilizations and animals that exist upon the earth today, is that right?" asked Mr. Darrow.

"I have never felt a great deal of interest in the effort that has been made to dispute the Bible by the speculation of men, or the investigations of men," replied Mr. Bryan.

The mild manner in which the "evangelical leader of the prosecution," as Mr. Malone has called him, seated himself in his chair, was vanishing rapidly. His face flushed under Mr. Darrow's searching words, and he writhed in an effort to keep himself from making heated replies. His eyes glared at his lounging opponent, who stood opposite him, glowering under his bulging brow, speculatively tapping his arm with his spectacles. No greater contrast in men could be imagined. The traps of logic fell from Mr. Darrow's lips as innocently as the words of a child, and so long as Mr. Bryan could parry them he smiled back, but when one stumped him he took refuge in his faith and either refused to answer directly or said in effect:

"The Bible states it; it must be so."

"Have you ever investigated to find out how long man has been on the earth?" asked Darrow.

"I have never found it necessary," said Mr. Bryan.

Mr. Bryan's complete lack of interest in many of the things closely connected with such religious questions as he has been supporting for many years was strikingly shown again and again by Mr. Darrow. He had never made a study of the ancient civilizations of China, or Egypt, he did not know that they couldn't go back beyond the time of creation as given in the Bible.

Mr. Bryan was of the opinion that he had heard of records of archeologists which describe the flood, but he did not know that there were many old religions with traditions of the flood. The origins of religion had not interested him much, either.

"The Christian religion has satisfied me," he said, "and I have never felt it necessary to look up some competitive religions."

The word competitive interested Mr. Darrow, and Bryan finally qualified it by saying he meant "religious unbelievers" in the Christian religion. The religions of Confucius and Buddha he did not regard as competitive, because he thought them inferior, and he insisted on telling Mr. Darrow what he thought of both. He did not know, however, how old the religions of Confucius, Buddha, or Zoroaster were.

"I think it much more important to know the differences between them than to know their age."

Mr. Darrow asked him if he knew how many men were on earth at various times, and when told he was the first man Mr. Bryan had ever met who was interested in it, he asked:

"Mr. Bryan, am I the first man you ever heard of who has been interested in the age of human societies and primitive man?"

He asked Mr. Bryan if he did not know there were thousands of books in the libraries on the subjects he had been asking about, and Mr. Bryan said he did not, but would take his word for it. He said he hadn't read much on primitive man, and when Mr. Darrow asked him if he had ever in his life tried to find out about the civilizations of the earth, how long they had existed, he replied:

"No, sir, I have been so well satisfied with the Christian religion that I have spent no time trying to find arguments against it."

"You don't care how old the earth is, how old man is, and how long the animals have been here?"

"I am not so much interested in that," said Mr. Bryan.

And then he drew from Mr. Bryan the admission that he had never studied anything on the subject he had written about.

"You have never made an investigation to find out?" he was asked.

"No, sir, I have never," Mr. Bryan answered.

Mr. Bryan said that Buddhism was a religion of agnosticism, because he had seen in Rangoon that the Buddhists were to send a delegation to the agnostics' congress to be held in Rome.

After more colloquy about the Tower of Babel and some more objections from Mr. Stewart, General Ben McKenzie said the defense would no more file Colonel Bryan's testimony as part of the record for the Appellate Court than they would file a rattlesnake.

Mr. Darrow, Dudley Field Malone, and Arthur Garfield Hays burst out as one man:

"We will file it, we will file it."

"File it from Dan to Beersheba," Mr. Bryan said in his deep rumble.

On the morning of July 21, Judge Raulston mercifully put an end to the unequal struggle. It was clear that Bryan, now old and flabby, could not possibly win a clear-cut victory over the wily Darrow. Unable to get any scientific evidence before the jury, Scopes' lawyers saw that their only hope lay in taking the fight up to the Tennessee Supreme Court. Scopes was quickly found guilty and fined one hundred dollars, which the Baltimore *Sunpapers* paid.

Bryan was closer to death than he had realized. During the trial, H. L. Mencken had reported that "there was a vague, unpleasant manginess about Bryan's appearance . . . the hair was gone behind his ears, in the obscene manner of the late Samuel Gompers." It was a shrewd observation. The Great Commoner died a week after the trial.

A brilliant post-mortem story on Bryan was sent in to the *St. Louis Post-Dispatch* by Paul Y. Anderson, which had this lead:

"In a rambling old white house on the outskirts of Dayton, where the maples rustle placidly and the fragrance of the harvest lingers on the air, rests today the majestic clay which was William Jennings Bryan.

"Little groups of men lie in the grass under the maples and converse in subdued tones. At intervals people tiptoe into the house, stay a minute and emerge. A cricket sings among the petunias in the side yard. A rocking chair creaks momentarily on the long front porch."

In Dayton, Ohio, a fiery cross was burned "in memory of William Jennings Bryan, the greatest Klansman of our time." It was an undeserved slur.

—NOTES BY LOUIS SNYDER AND
RICHARD MORRIS

Felix Frankfurter

:

THE CASE OF SACCO AND VANZETTI
A Critical Analysis (1927)

CHAPTER I

For more than six years the Sacco-Vanzetti case has been before the courts of Massachusetts. Such extraordinary delay, in a state where ordinarily murder trials are promptly dispatched, in itself challenges attention. A long succession of disclosures has aroused interest far beyond the boundaries of Massachusetts and even of the United States, until the case has become one of those rare *causes célèbres* which are of international concern. My aim is to give in brief compass an accurate résumé of the facts of the case from its earliest stages to its present posture. The following account is based upon the record of the successive court proceedings through which the case has gone, with such references to extrinsic facts as are necessary for understanding what transpired in court. Obviously, to tell the story within limited space requires drastic compression. The necessary selection of material has been guided by canons of relevance and fairness familiar to every lawyer called upon to make a disinterested summary of the record of a protracted trial. The entire record, spread over many thousand pages, is accessible to anyone who desires to examine for himself the ground herein traveled.

At about three o'clock in the afternoon of April 15, 1920, Parmenter, a paymaster, and Berardelli, his guard, were fired upon and killed by two men armed with pistols, as they were carrying two boxes containing the pay roll of the shoe factory of Slater and Morrill, amounting to $15,776.51, from the company's office building to the factory through the main street of South Braintree, Massachusetts. As the murder was being committed a car containing several other men drew up to the spot. The murderers threw the two boxes into the car, jumped in themselves, and were driven away at high speed across some near-by railroad tracks. Two days later this car was found abandoned in woods at a distance from the scene of the crime. Leading away from this spot were the tracks of a smaller car. At the time of the Braintree holdup the police were investigating a similar crime in the neighboring town of Bridgewater. In both cases a gang was involved. In both they made off in a car. In both eyewitnesses believed the criminals to be Italians. In the Bridgewater holdup the car had left the scene in the direction of Cochesett. Chief Stewart of Bridgewater was therefore, at the time of the Braintree murders, on the trail of an Italian owning or driving a car in Cochesett. He found his man in one Boda, whose car was then in a garage awaiting repairs. Stewart instructed the garage proprietor, Johnson, to telephone to the police when anyone came to fetch it. Pursuing his theory, Stewart found that Boda had been living in Cochesett with a radical named Coacci. Now on April 16, 1920, which was the day after the Braintree murders, Stewart, at the instance of the Department of Justice, then engaged in the rounding-up of Reds, had been to the house of Coacci to see why he had failed to appear at a hearing regarding his deportation. He found Coacci packing a trunk and apparently very anxious to get back to Italy as soon as possible. At the time (April 16), Coacci's trunk and his haste to depart for Italy were not connected in Chief Stewart's mind with the Braintree affair. But when later the tracks of a smaller car were found near the murder car, he surmised that this car was Boda's. And when he discovered that Boda had once been living with Coacci, he connected Coacci's packing, his eagerness to depart, his actual departure, with the Braintree murders, and assumed that the trunk contained the booty. In the light of later discoveries Stewart jumped to the conclusion that Coacci, Boda's pal, had "skipped with the swag." As a matter of fact, the contents of the trunk, when it was intercepted by the Italian police on arrival, revealed nothing. In the meantime, however, Stewart continued to work on his theory, which centered around Boda: that whosoever called for Boda's car at Johnson's garage would be suspect of the Braintree crime.

On the night of May 5, Boda and three other Italians did in fact call.

To explain how they came to do so let us recall here the proceedings for the wholesale deportation of Reds under Attorney-General Palmer in the spring of 1920. In particular the case of one Salsedo must be borne in mind—a radical who was held incommunicado in a room in the New York offices of the Department of Justice on the fourteenth floor of a Park Row building. Boda and his companions were friends of Salsedo. On May 4 they learned that Salsedo had been found dead on the sidewalk outside the Park Row building, and, already frightened by the Red raids, bestirred themselves to "hide the literature and notify the friends against the federal police." For this purpose an automobile was needed and they turned to Boda. Such were the circumstances under which the four Italians appeared on the evening of May 5 at the Johnson garage. Two of them were Sacco and Vanzetti. Mrs. Johnson telephoned the police. The car was not available and the Italians left, Sacco and Vanzetti to board a street car for Brockton, Boda and the fourth member, Orciani, on a motor cycle. Sacco and Vanzetti were arrested on the street car, Orciani was arrested the next day, and Boda was never heard of again.

Stewart at once sought to apply his theory of the commission of the two "jobs" by one gang. The theory, however, broke down. Orciani had been at work on the days of both crimes, so he was let go. Sacco, in continuous employment at a shoe factory in Stoughton, had taken a day off (about which more later) on April 15. Hence, while he could not be charged with the Bridgewater crime, he was charged with the Braintree murders; Vanzetti, as a fish peddler at Plymouth and his own employer, could not give the same kind of alibi for either day, and so he was held for both crimes.* Stewart's theory that the crime was

---

* In an account of the joint trial of Sacco and Vanzetti the details of Vanzetti's separate trial cannot find a place, but Vanzetti's prosecution for the Bridgewater job grew out of his arrest for, and was merely a phase of, the Braintree affair. The evidence of identification of Vanzetti in the Bridgewater case bordered on the frivolous, reaching its climax in the testimony of a little newsboy who, from behind the telegraph pole to which he had run for refuge during the shooting, had caught a glimpse of the criminal and "knew by the way he ran he was a foreigner." Vanzetti was a foreigner, so of course it was Vanzetti! There were also found on Vanzetti's person, four months after the Bridgewater attempt, several shells, one of which was claimed to be of a type similar to shells found at the scene of the Bridgewater crime. The innocent possession of these shells was accounted for at the Dedham trial. More than twenty people swore to having seen Vanzetti in Plymouth on December 24, among them those who remembered buy-

committed by these Italian radicals was not shared by the head of the state police, who always maintained that it was the work of professionals.

Charged with the crime of murder on May 5, Sacco and Vanzetti were indicted on September 14, 1920, and put on trial May 31, 1921, at Dedham, Norfolk County. The setting of the trial, in the courthouse opposite the old home of Fisher Ames, furnished a striking contrast to the background and antecedents of the prisoners. Dedham is a quiet residential suburb, inhabited by well-to-do Bostonians with a surviving element of New England small farmers. Part of the jury was specially selected by the sheriff's deputies from persons whom they deemed "representative citizens," "substantial" and "intelligent." The presiding judge was Webster Thayer of Worcester. The chief counsel for these Italians, Fred H. Moore, was a Westerner, himself a radical and a professional defender of radicals. In opinion, as well as in fact, he was an "outsider." Unfamiliar with the traditions of the Massachusetts bench, not even a member of the Massachusetts bar, the characteristics of Judge Thayer unknown to him, Moore found neither professional nor personal sympathies between himself and the Judge. So far as the relations between court and counsel seriously, even if unconsciously, affect the temper of a trial, Moore was a factor of irritation and not of appeasement. Sacco and Vanzetti spoke very broken English, and their testimony shows how often they misunderstood the questions put to them. A court interpreter was used, but his conduct raised such doubts* that the defendants brought their own interpreter to check his questions and answers. The trial lasted nearly seven weeks, and on July 14, 1921, Sacco and Vanzetti were found guilty of murder in the first degree.

---

ing eels from him for the Christmas Eve feasts. Of course all these witnesses were Italians. The circumstances of the trial are sufficiently revealed by the fact that Vanzetti, protesting innocence, was not allowed by his counsel to take the witness stand for fear his radical opinions would be brought out and tell against him disastrously. From a verdict of conviction counsel took no appeal. The judge and district attorney were Judge Webster Thayer and Mr. Katzmann, as also in the Braintree trial. The Bridgewater conviction was played up with the most lurid publicity when Vanzetti faced his trial for the Braintree crime.

* Some time after the trial this interpreter was convicted of larceny.

CHAPTER II

So far as the crime is concerned we are dealing with a conventional case of pay-roll robbery resulting in murder. At the trial the killing of Parmenter and Berardelli was undisputed. The only issue was the identity of the murderers. Were Sacco and Vanzetti two of the assailants of Parmenter and Berardelli, or were they not? This was the beginning and the end of the inquiry at the trial; this is the beginning and the end of any judgment now on the guilt or innocence of these men. Every other issue, no matter how worded, is relevant only as it helps to answer that central question.

On that issue there was at the trial a mass of conflicting evidence. Fifty-nine witnesses testified for the Commonwealth and ninety-nine for the defendants. The evidence offered by the Commonwealth was not the same against both defendants. The theory of the Commonwealth was that Sacco did the actual shooting and that Vanzetti sat in the car as one of the collaborators in a conspiracy to murder. Witnesses for the Commonwealth testified to having seen both defendants in South Braintree on the morning of April 15; they claimed to recognize Sacco as the man who shot the guard Berardelli and to have seen him subsequently escape in the car. Expert testimony (the character of which, in the light of subsequent events, constitutes one of the most important features of the case) was offered seeking to connect one of four bullets removed from Berardelli's body with the Colt pistol found on Sacco at the time of his arrest. As to Vanzetti, the Commonwealth adduced evidence placing him in the murder car. Moreover, the Commonwealth introduced the conduct of the defendants, as evinced by pistols found on their persons and lies admittedly told by them when arrested, as further proof of identification in that such conduct revealed "consciousness of guilt."

The defense met the Commonwealth's eyewitnesses by other eyewitnesses, slightly more numerous than those called by the Commonwealth and at least as well circumstanced to observe the assailants, who testified that the defendants were not the men they saw. Their testimony was confirmed by witnesses who proved the presence of Sacco and Vanzetti elsewhere at the time of the murder. Other witnesses supported Sacco's testimony that on April 15—the day that he was away from work—he was in Boston seeing about a passport to Italy, whither he was planning shortly to return to visit his recently bereaved father. The truth of his statement was supported by an official of the Italian consulate in Boston who deposed that Sacco visited his consulate at 2:15 P.M. If this were true, it was conceded that Sacco could not have been a party to this murder. The claim of Vanzetti that on April 15 he was pursuing his customary trade as fish peddler was sustained by a number of witnesses who had been his customers that day.

From this summary it must be evident that the *trustworthiness* of the testimony which placed Sacco and Vanzetti in Braintree on April 15 is the foundation of the case.

I. *As to Sacco:*

The character of the testimony of the five witnesses who definitely identified Sacco as in the car or on the spot at the time of the murder demands critical attention. These witnesses were Mary E. Splaine, Frances Devlin, Lola Andrews, Louis Pelzer, Carlos E. Goodridge.

1. Splaine and Devlin were working together on the second floor of the Slater and Morrill factory, with windows giving on the railroad crossing. Both heard the shot, ran to the window, and saw an automobile crossing the tracks. Splaine's identification of Sacco, as one of the occupants of this escaping car, was one of the chief reliances of the prosecution. Splaine, viewing the scene from a distance of from 60 to 80 feet, saw a man previously unknown to her, in a car traveling at the rate of from 15 to 18 miles per hour; she saw him only for a distance of about 30 feet, that is to say, for from one and a half to three seconds; and yet she testified:

The man that appeared between the back of the front seat and the back seat was a man slightly taller than the witness. He weighed possibly from 140 to 145 pounds. He was muscular, an active looking man. His left hand was a good sized hand, a hand that denoted strength.

Q: So that the hand you said you saw where?

A: The left hand, that was placed on the back of the front seat, on the back of the front seat. He had a gray, what I thought was a shirt,—had a grayish, like navy color, and the face was what we would call clear-cut, clean-cut face. Through here [indicating] was a little narrow, just a little narrow. The forehead was high. The hair was brushed back and it was between, I should think, two inches and two and one-half inches in length and had dark eyebrows, but the complexion was a white, peculiar white that looked greenish.

Q: Is that the same man you saw at Brockton?
A: It is.
Q: Are you sure?
A: Positive.

The startling acuity of Splaine's vision was in fact the product of a year's reflection. Immediately after Sacco's arrest the police, in violation of approved police methods for the identification of suspects, brought Sacco alone into Splaine's presence. Then followed in about three weeks the preliminary hearing at which Sacco and Vanzetti were bound over for the grand jury. At this hearing Splaine was unable to identify Sacco:

Q: You don't feel certain enough in your position to say he is the man?
A: I don't think my opportunity afforded me the right to say he is the man.

When confronted with this contradiction between her uncertainty forty days after her observation and her certainty more than a year after her observation, she first took refuge in a claim of inaccuracy in the transcript of the stenographer's minutes. This charge she later withdrew and finally maintained:

From the observation I had of him in the Quincy court and the comparison of the man I saw in the machine, on reflection I was sure he was the same man.

Then followed this cross-examination:

Q: Your answer in the lower court was you didn't have opportunity to observe him. What did you mean when you said you didn't have opportunity sufficient, kindly tell us, you didn't have sufficient opportunity to observe him?
A: Well, he was passing on the street.
Q: He was passing on the street and you didn't have sufficient opportunity to observe him to enable you to identify him?
A: That is what I meant.
Q: That is the only opportunity you had?
A: Yes, sir.
Q: You have had no other opportunity but that one fleeting glance?
A: The remembrance of that.

Let Dr. Morton Prince, professor of abnormal and dynamic psychology at Harvard University, comment on this testimony:

I do not hesitate to say that the star witness for the government testified, honestly enough, no doubt, to what was psychologically impossible. Miss

Splaine testified, though she had only seen Sacco at the time of the shooting from a distance of about 60 feet for from 1½ to three seconds in a motor car going at an increasing rate of speed at about 15 to 18 miles an hour; that she saw and at the end of a year she remembered and described 16 different details of his person, even to the size of his hand, the length of his hair as being between two and 2½ inches long, and the shape of his eyebrows! Such perception and memory under such conditions can be easily proved to be psychologically impossible. Every psychologist knows that—so does Houdini. And what shall we think of the animus and honesty of the state that introduces such testimony to convict, knowing that the jury is too ignorant to disbelieve?

How came Miss Splaine to become acquainted with these personal characteristics of Sacco?

The answer is simple. Sacco had been shown to her on several occasions. She had had an opportunity to study him carefully. More than this, he sat before her in the court. At the preliminary hearing in the police court she was not asked to pick Sacco from among a group of other men. Sacco was shown alone to her. Every one knows that under such circumstances the image of a person later develops, or may develop, in an observer's mind and becomes a false memory. Such a memory is produced by suggestion. Every lawyer knows the unconscious falsification of memory due to later acquired knowledge, though ignorant of the psychology of the phenomenon. And yet Miss Splaine's testimony was offered by the state to the jury.

Why was not Miss Splaine asked to pick out Sacco from among a group of men? If this had been done, this unconscious falsification of memory would have been avoided.

As a matter of fact "the good-sized hand" by which Splaine identified Sacco and on which, in a later affidavit, she rests her identification almost entirely, did not exist. Sacco has hands smaller than the average. Also, since the trial it has been shown that Splaine had identified another person as the man whom she later identified as Sacco, after it appeared that the person previously identified by her was in jail on April 15, 1920.

2. Devlin, a little over a month after the murders, thus testified:

He (Sacco) looks very much like the man that stood up in the back seat shooting.

"Q. Do you say positively he is the man?" and you answered: "A. I don't say positively."

At the trial, over a year later, she had no doubt, and when asked: "Have you at any time had any doubt of your identification of this man?" replied: "No." The obvious discrepancy of an identification reaching certainty by lapse of time, without any additional opportunity for verification, she explained thus:

> At the time there I had in my own mind that he was the man, but on account of the immensity of the crime and everything, I hated to say right out and out.

The inherent improbability—not to say, as does Dr. Prince, "impossibility"—of making any such accurate identification on the basis of a fleeting glimpse of an unknown man in the confusion of a sudden alarm is affirmed by the testimony of two other eyewitnesses. Ferguson and Pierce, from a window above Splaine and Devlin, on the next floor of the factory, had substantially the same view as the two women. They found it impossible to make any identification.

Thus Ferguson:

> He thinks that he did testify at the inquest in response to the question "How did that man look?" as follows: "I can't tell it [*sic*] all. I only had a quick glimpse of him. He looked like an Italian with a growth of beard. It seems just as he shot he just got up from the front seat, and it seems to me he was pulling his cap over his hair."
>
> He did testify at the inquest in response to the question "If you saw a picture, could you recognize him?" as follows: "I feel pretty sure I could not."
>
> Q: And you can't recognize him now?
> A: No, sir.

Then Pierce:

> Q: Would you be able to tell the men, the chauffeur, and the man in the front seat?
> A: I don't think so. I have had pictures shown me by the state police and if it was a matter of looking at a million pictures I couldn't say. I just saw a dark man with a gun, that is all.

3. Pelzer, a young shoe-cutter, swore that when he heard the shooting he pulled up his window, took a glance at the scene, and saw the man who murdered Berardelli:

> Q: How long did you stay in the window?
> A: Oh, about,—I would say about a minute. . . .
> Q: Then what did you do?
> A: I seen everything happen about that time, about in a minute.

This was the foundation for the following identification:

Q: Do you see in the court room the man you saw shooting Berardelli that day?

A: Well, I wouldn't say it was him but he is a dead image of him.

   Witness points out Mr. Sacco.

Q: Have you seen him since that time until you saw him in the court room?

A: No, sir.

   Witness was shown picture of him by Mr. Williams today.

Q: You say you wouldn't say it is him, but he is the dead image of him? What do you mean by that?

A: Well, he has got the same appearance.

On cross-examination Pelzer admitted that immediately after Sacco's arrest, on May 6 or 7, he was unable to make any identification:

I did not see enough to be able to identify anybody.

Pelzer's inability in May 1920 to make the identification which he did make in June 1921 was confirmed by three fellow workmen, at work in the same room on the day of the murder. Two of them testified that instead of pulling up the window he took shelter under a bench, and the third added:

Q: Did you hear him later talk about the shooting?

A: I think I did, but I am not sure.

Q: That day?

A: Yes, sir. . . .

Q: What did you hear Pelser say?

A: Well, I heard him say that he did not see anybody. . . . That is all.

Q: Is that all you recollect that you heard him say?

A: Yes, sir.

Pelzer's tergiversations and falsifications extracted from the District Attorney, Mr. Katzmann, the following eulogy:

He was frank enough here, gentlemen, to own that he had twice falsified before to both sides, treating them equally and alike, and he gave you his reason. I think he added that he had never been in court before. If not, somebody has and I confused him. It is of little consequence. He is big enough and manly enough now to tell you of his prior falsehoods and his reasons for them. If you accept them, gentlemen, give such weight to his testimony as you say should be given.

4. Lola Andrews, a woman of doubtful reputation, testified that at about 11 A.M. on the day of the murders, while in company with a

Mrs. Campbell, she saw an automobile standing outside the Slater and Morrill factory. She saw a "very light" man inside the car (concededly neither Sacco nor Vanzetti) and another man "bending over the hood of the car," whom she characterized as a "dark-complexioned man." She went into the factory in search of a job and at the time "had no talk with either of the men." When she came out "fifteen minutes later" the dark man "was down under the car like he was fixing something" and she asked him the way to another factory. He told her. That was the whole conversation between them. After Sacco's arrest she was taken to the Dedham jail and identified Sacco as the dark-complexioned man. She again identified him at the trial.

How came she to connect the dark man under the car with the murder which took place four hours later?

Q: Would you say that the man had a fuller or more slender face [than the man in a photograph shown to the witness]?
A: I don't know. He had a funny face. . . .
Q: Meaning by that a face that was not a kindly face, a kind of brutal face?
A: He did not have a real good looking face.
Q: [By the Commonwealth] What came to your mind, if anything, when you learned of the shooting? . . .
A: Why, the only way I can answer that is this: When I heard of the shooting I somehow associated the man I saw at the car.

Four reputable witnesses completely discredited the Andrews testimony.

A. Mrs. Campbell, an elderly woman who was with Andrews throughout the episode, testified that, while they saw an automobile in front of the factory, the man they accosted for information was not the man under the automobile but a man "in khaki clothes" standing near:

When they came out neither she nor Mrs. Andrews spoke to a man at the automobile in front of the Slater & Morrill factory.
Q: Did you hear Mrs. Andrews have any talk with any man who was working around an automobile that morning?
A: No, sir.
Q: Did Mrs. Andrews speak to a man?
A: No, sir.
Q: (continued) Who was working about an automobile that morning?
A: No, sir.

B. Harry Kurlansky testified as follows:

He is in business at Quincy, at 1466 Hancock Street. He has been in business there since 1909 or 1910. He knows Mrs. Lola Andrews and has known her for the last seven or eight years. Sometime in February of this year he had a talk with her. "I was right on my door step and Lola Andrews went by . . . It was just between six or seven; I should judge it was about half past six."

Q: Now, tell us what was said.

A: As I sat on my door step and as I know her I always spoke to her when she went by. I said to her, "Hello, Lola," and she stopped and she answered me. While she answered me I said, "You look kind of tired." She says, "Yes." She says, "They are bothering the life out of me." I says, "What?" She says, "I just come from jail." I says, "What have you done in jail?" She says, "The Government took me down and want me to recognize those men," she says, "and I don't know a thing about them. I have never seen them and I can't recognize them." She says, "Unfortunately I have been down there to get a job and I have seen many men that I don't know and I have never paid any attention to anyone."

This patently ingenuous witness was subjected to the following questioning by Judge Thayer:

THE COURT: Mr. Witness, I would like to ask you one question. Did you attempt to find out who this person was who represented the Government who was trying to get her to take and state that which was false?

THE WITNESS: Did I what?

MR. JEREMIAH MC ANARNEY: What is that question?

THE COURT: Did you try to find out who it was who represented the Government?

THE WITNESS: No.

THE COURT: Why not?

THE WITNESS: Well, it didn't come into my mind. I wasn't sure, you know. It didn't—

THE COURT: Did you think the public interest was served by anybody representing the Government to try to get a woman—

THE WITNESS: I don't think of anything—

THE COURT: —To identify somebody? . . .

THE WITNESS: I don't think of anything like that, just simply what she tell you.

THE COURT: Don't you think it would be a good idea to find out, if you could?

THE WITNESS: I think it would be.

THE COURT: I am trying to find out why you didn't do it.

This cross-examination must appear strange to anyone familiar with the usual conduct of Massachusetts trial judges. For Judge Thayer to insist that it was the duty of a small shopkeeper, poorly educated and struggling with imperfect English, to ferret out intimations of police improprieties conveyed in the course of a casual conversation was to draw a "red herring" across the trail. It undoubtedly served to discredit Kurlansky in the eyes of the jury and thereby to obliterate the effect of important testimony adverse to the Commonwealth. Only the extraordinary features of this case, as they will unfold in the course of the subsequent discussion, can account for the incident.

C. In February 1921, Andrews complained to the police of an assault on herself in her apartment in Quincy. George W. Fay, a Quincy policeman who was called in to investigate the matter, gave the following account of his conversation with Andrews:

> I asked her if the man who assaulted her, if she thought that he was one of the men she saw at Braintree on the day of the shooting, and she said she could not tell because she did not see the faces of the Braintree men. I asked her how he compared in appearance with the men at Braintree that she saw. She said that she could not tell.
>
> I asked her if his clothes were like the clothes that any of the men wore at Braintree, she said she could not tell.

D. Alfred Labrecque, a Quincy newspaper man and secretary of the Quincy Chamber of Commerce, testified to a conversation with Andrews substantially to the same effect as Fay's.

The District Attorney not only offered the Andrews testimony for the consideration of the jury, but gave it the weightiest possible personal sponsorship:

> Gentlemen, there is some responsibility upon the Commonwealth. There is some responsibility upon a prosecutor who produces witnesses whose evidence tends to prove murder. He may think well. He should think long, and he should always have his intelligence and his conscience with him before he puts the stamp of approval of the Commonwealth of Massachusetts upon him as a creditable witness before he takes the stand seeking to prove the guilt of men and if proven will result in their death.
>
> And then there is Lola Andrews. I have been in this office, gentlemen, for now more than eleven years. I cannot recall in that too long service for the Commonwealth that ever before I have laid eye or given ear to so convincing a witness as Lola Andrews.

5. Carlos E. Goodridge (who after the trial was discovered to be a fugitive from justice in another state and to have given evidence under a false name) swore that, at the time of the shooting, he was in a poolroom in South Braintree, heard shots, stepped to the door, saw an automobile coming toward him, and when he got to the sidewalk a man in the automobile "poked a gun over towards him," whereupon he "went back into the poolroom." About seven months later, he identified Sacco as that man for the first time and identified him again at the trial.

Four witnesses squarely contradicted Goodridge's belated identification.

A. Goodridge reported the affray to his employer, Andrew Manganaro, an hour afterward without revealing any identification. Manganaro further testified:

> Later at the time that Sacco and Vanzetti were arrested there was another talk between the witness and Goodridge. The witness read of the arrest in the newspapers and the same day went to the South Braintree store and told Mr. Goodridge that he should go and see if he could recognize these people that were arrested, whether they were the ones or not.
>
> Q: What did he say?
>
> A: He said he could not do it because when he saw the gun he was so scared he run right in from where he was. He could not possibly remember the faces. I told him as a matter of justice, "if you think you do remember the faces do go over there and I will pay you just the same."

Finally, Manganaro testified without contradiction that Goodridge's reputation for veracity was bad.

. . . .

Even when completely disinterested, identification testimony runs all the grave hazards due to the frailties and fallibilities of human observation and memory. But Goodridge's testimony was, in addition to everything else, tainted with self-interest. At the time he was a witness for the Commonwealth, he was facing jail under an indictment for larceny to which he had pleaded guilty. The case "had been filed,"—that is, no sentence had been imposed,—and Goodridge had been placed on probation. The Judge did not allow the defense to show that Goodridge's testimony on behalf of the Commonwealth was influenced by leniency previously shown to him by the District Attorney in connection with the confessed charge of larceny, and by fear of losing his immunity. In the light of settled principles of the law of evidence this ruling, though later

sustained by the Supreme Judicial Court of Massachusetts, is inde-
fensible.

II. *As to Vanzetti:*

The Commonwealth offered two witnesses who claimed to identify
Vanzetti as an occupant of the murder car. Of these one, Dolbeare,
claimed to have seen him hours before the murder, leaving only a single individual, LeVangie, who claimed to have seen him on the spot.
Before dealing with Dolbeare and LeVangie, a few words will dispose
of two other witnesses who claimed to have seen Vanzetti during the
day of the murder elsewhere than at Plymouth, but not at South Braintree. One witness, Faulkner, testified to recollecting a fellow passenger
on a train going from Cochesett to Boston who got out at East Braintree at 9:54, and identified Vanzetti as that passenger. The basis of
Faulkner's recollection was so frail and was so fully destroyed by three
other witnesses (McNaught, Pratt, and Brooks), all railroad men, that
we deem it superfluous to make a further recital of his testimony. Finally Reed, a crossing tender, purported to recognize Vanzetti as the
man sitting on the front seat of a car which he claimed to identify as
the murder car. This was at some distance more than an hour after the
murder. Reed's testimony placing Vanzetti on the front seat of the car
ran counter to the theory of the Commonwealth that Vanzetti was at
the rear. Moreover, Reed testified that "the quality of the English
[of Vanzetti] was unmistakable and clear" while at the trial Vanzetti's
English was found to be so imperfect that an interpreter had to be employed.

1. Harry E. Dolbeare testified that somewhere between 10 and 12
A.M. he saw a car going past him in South Braintree with five people in
it, one of whom he identified as Vanzetti:

Q: There was nothing that attracted your attention in this case except one
man leaning forward as though he was talking to another man?
A: Yes, there was.

He then stated that there was something that attracted his attention to
this man before the car got opposite him,—it was the appearance of the whole
five that attracted his attention. They appeared strange to him, as strangers to
the town, as a carload of foreigners. He hardly knows how to express himself. He knows how he felt at the time. "I felt it was a tough looking bunch.
That is the very feeling that came to my mind at the time. . . . I guess that
is all. That is all I recall now."

Q: And it is nothing unusual to see an automobile with three or five or seven foreigners in it, is it?

A: No.

Q: And those automobiles go through to Holbrook, to Randolph, and all through that district from the Fore River with those workmen, don't they?

A: Yes, sir.

He cannot give any description of the men who were on the front seat of the automobile. He did not take any particular notice of them. "This one man attracted my attention."

There is nothing other than what he has already given by which he characterizes these men as a tough looking bunch. He does not know whether the other two men who sat on the back seat had mustaches or beards of any kind. He does not know what kind of a hat or cap the man in the middle, who leaned forward to speak, wore. He does not know whether this man had a cap with a visor projecting out or whether he had on a slouch hat.

2. LeVangie, the gate tender of the New Haven railroad, was on duty at the South Braintree grade crossing on the day of the murder. According to his testimony, the murder car drove up to the crossing just as he was lowering the gate, and a man inside forced him at the point of a revolver to let the car through before the advancing train. Le-Vangie identified Vanzetti as the man who was driving the car. Le-Vangie's testimony was discredited by the testimony of McCarthy, a locomotive fireman of the New Haven, who testified that three quarters of an hour after the murder he had the following conversation with Le-Vangie:

LeVangie said "There was a shooting affair going on." I says, "Some one shot?" I says, "Who?" "Some one, a fellow got murdered." I said, "Who did it?" He said he did not know. He said there was some fellows went by in an automobile and he heard the shots, and he started to put down the gates, and as he started to put them down one of them pointed a gun at him and he left the gates alone and ducked in the shanty. I asked him if he knew them. He said, no, he did not. I asked him if he would know them again if he saw them. He said "No." He said all he could see was the gun and he ducked.

Moreover, LeVangie was discredited by all the other identification witnesses on both sides, who insisted that the driver of the car was a young, small, light-haired man, whereas Vanzetti was middle-aged, dark, with a black mustache. But, though the District Attorney had to repudiate LeVangie, he characteristically held on to LeVangie's identification. The following quotation from the District Attorney's summing

up reveals the worthlessness of LeVangie's testimony; it throws no less
light on the guiding attitude of the prosecution:

> They find fault, gentlemen, with Levangie. They say that Levangie is
> wrong in saying that Vanzetti was driving that car. I agree with them, gentle-
> men. I would not be trying to do justice to these defendants if I pretended
> that personally so far as you are concerned about my personal belief on that,
> that Vanzetti drove that car over the crossing. I do not believe any such
> thing. You must be overwhelmed with the testimony that when the car started
> it was driven by a light haired man who showed every indication of being
> sickly.
> We cannot mold the testimony of witnesses, gentlemen. We have got to
> take them as they testify on their oath, and we put Levangie on because
> necessarily he must have been there. He saw something. He described a light
> haired man to some of the witnesses. They produced Carter, the first witness
> they put on, to say that he said the light haired man,—the driver was a light
> haired man. That is true. I believe my brothers will agree with me on that
> proposition, but he saw the face of Vanzetti in that car, and is his testimony
> to be rejected if it disagrees with everybody else if you are satisfied he
> honestly meant to tell the truth?
> And can't you reconcile it with the possibility, no, the likelihood or more
> than that, the probability that at that time Vanzetti was directly behind the
> driver in the quick glance this man Levangie had of the car going over when
> they were going up over the crossing. . . .
> Right or wrong, we have to take it as it is. And I agree if it depends on the
> accuracy of the statement that Vanzetti was driving, then it isn't right, because
> I would have to reject personally the testimony of witnesses for the defense
> as well as for the Commonwealth who testified to the contrary. I ask you to
> find as a matter of commonsense he was, in the light of other witnesses, in
> the car, and if on the left side that he may well have been immediately behind
> the driver.

In other words, obliged to repudiate the testimony of LeVangie that
Vanzetti was on the front seat, the Commonwealth urged the jury to
find that although LeVangie said that Vanzetti was on the front seat, he
meant he was on the back seat. At the time that he offered this testimony of LeVangie, the District Attorney had held interviews with, and
had in his possession written statements of, the only two persons who
had an extended opportunity to observe the driver of the car. The detailed description given by them absolutely excluded Vanzetti. (Kelly
and Kennedy Affidavits.) The reliability of these observers and of their
statements has not been challenged. Yet they were not called by the

District Attorney; instead he called LeVangie. Unfortunately, the existence of Kelly and Kennedy was until very recently unknown to the defense and of course, therefore, their testimony was unavailable for Sacco and Vanzetti at the trial.

The alibi for Vanzetti was overwhelming. Thirty-one eyewitnesses testified positively that no one of the men that they saw in the murder car was Vanzetti. Thirteen witnesses either testified directly that Vanzetti was in Plymouth selling fish on the day of the murder, or furnished corroboration of such testimony.

What is the worth of identification testimony even when uncontradicted? The identification of strangers is proverbially untrustworthy. The hazards of such testimony are established by a formidable number of instances in the records of English and American trials. These instances are recent—not due to the brutalities of ancient criminal procedure. In England the case of Adolf Beck, who was twice convicted as a swindler on the confident identification of numerous witnesses but subsequently proven innocent, disclosed so serious a miscarriage of justice as to lead to the establishment of a Court of Criminal Appeals, with broad revisory powers over the action of juries and trial judges. The circumstances of the Beck case led to the appointment of a Royal Commission, headed by the Master of the Rolls, which thus expressed itself on identification testimony:

> Evidence as to identity based on personal impressions, however *bona fide,* is perhaps of all classes of evidence the least to be relied upon, and therefore, unless supported by other facts, an unsafe basis for the verdict of a jury.

In the Sacco-Vanzetti case the elements of uncertainty were intensified. All the identifying witnesses were speaking from casual observation of men they had never seen before, men of foreign race, under circumstances of unusual confusion. Thus one witness, Cole, "thought at the first glance that Vanzetti was a Portuguese fellow named Tony that he knew." Afterward he was sure the man was Vanzetti. The old song, "All Coons Look Alike to Me," represents a deep experience of human fallibility. Moreover, the methods pursued by the police in eliciting identification in this case fatally impair its worth. In England, such methods would have discredited the testimony and nullified a verdict based upon it. The recognized procedure is to line up the suspect with others, and so far as possible with individuals of the same race and class, so as not to provoke identification through accentuation. In defiance of these necessary safeguards, Sacco and Vanzetti after their arrest were shown singly to persons brought there for the purposes of identification, not as part of a "parade." Moreover, Sacco and Vanzetti were not even allowed to be their natural selves; they were compelled to simulate the behavior of the Braintree bandits. Under such conditions identification of foreigners is a farce.

To anticipate our story, after the conviction Judge Thayer himself abandoned the identification of Sacco and Vanzetti as the ground on which the jury's verdict rested. In denying a motion for a new trial, based on the discovery of a new eyewitness with better opportunities for observation than any of the other witnesses on either side, who in his affidavit swore that Sacco was not the man in the car, Judge Thayer ruled that this evidence

would simply mean one more piece of evidence of the same kind and directed to the same end, and in my judgment, would have no effect whatever upon the verdicts. For these verdicts did not rest, in my judgment, upon the testimony of the eye witnesses, for the defendants, as it was, called more witnesses than the Commonwealth who testified that neither of the defendants were in the bandit car.

The evidence that convicted these defendants was circumstantial and was evidence that is known in law as "consciousness of guilt."

To this "consciousness of guilt" we shall now address ourselves.

CHAPTER III

By "consciousness of guilt" Judge Thayer meant that the conduct of Sacco and Vanzetti after April 15 was the conduct of murderers. This inference of guilt was drawn from their behavior on the night of May 5, before and after arrest, and also from their possession of firearms. It is vital to keep in mind the exact data on which, according to Judge Thayer, these two men are to be sentenced to death. There was no claim whatever at the trial, and none has ever been suggested since, that Sacco and Vanzetti had any prior experience in holdups or any previous association with bandits; no claim that the sixteen thousand dollars taken from the victims ever found its way into their pockets; no claim that their financial condition, or that of Sacco's family (he had a wife and child, and another child was soon to be born), was in any way changed after April 15; no claim that after the murder either Sacco or Vanzetti changed his manner of living or employment. Not at all! Neither of these men had ever been accused of crime before their arrest. Nor, during the three weeks between the murder and their arrest, did they behave like men who were concealing the crime of murder. They did not go into hiding; they did not abscond with the spoils; they did not live under assumed names. On the contrary they maintained their old lodgings; they pursued openly their callings, within a few miles of the town where they were supposed to have committed murders in broad daylight; and when arrested Sacco was found to have in his pocket an announcement of a forthcoming meeting at which Vanzetti was to speak.* Was this the behavior of men eluding identification?

What, then, was the evidence against them?

1. Sacco and Vanzetti, as we have seen, were two of four Italians who called for Boda's car at Johnson's garage on the evening of May 5. It will be remembered that in pursuance of a prearranged plan Mrs. Johnson, under pretext of having to fetch some milk, went to a neighbor's house to telephone the police. Mrs. Johnson testified that the two defendants followed her to the house on the opposite side of the street and when, after telephoning, she reappeared they followed her back. Thereafter the men, having been advised by Mr. Johnson not to run the car without the current year's number plate, left without it:

Q: Now, Boda came there to get his car, didn't he?

A: Yes.

Q: There were no 1920 number plates on it?

A: No.

Q: You advised him not to take the car and run it without the 1920 number plates, didn't you?

A: Yes.

Q: And he accepted your view?

A: He seemed to.

* The manifesto ran as follows:—

"You have fought all the wars. You have worked for all the capitalists. You have wandered over all the countries. Have you harvested the fruits of your labors, the price of your victories? Does the past comfort you? Does the present smile on you? Does the future promise you anything? Have you found a piece of land where you can live like a human being and die like a human being? On these questions, on this argument, and on this theme, the struggle for existence, Bartolomeo Vanzetti will speak. Hour —— day —— hall ——. Admission free. Freedom of discussion to all. Take the ladies with you."

Q: He seemed to. And after some conversation went away?
A: Yes.

This was the whole of the testimony on the strength of which Judge Thayer put the following question to the jury:

> Did the defendants, in company with Orciani and Boda, leave the Johnson house because the automobile had no 1920 number plate on it, or because they were conscious of or became suspicious of what Mrs. Johnson did in the Bartlett house? If they left because they had no 1920 number plates on the automobile, then you may say there was no consciousness of guilt in consequence of their sudden departure, but if they left because they were consciously guilty* of what was being done by Mrs. Johnson in the Bartlett house, then you may say that is evidence tending to prove consciousness of guilt on their part.

2. Following their departure from the Johnson house, Sacco and Vanzetti were arrested by a policeman who boarded their street car as it was coming into Brockton. Three policemen testified as to their behavior after being taken into custody:

> [As to Vanzetti] He went down through the car and when he got opposite to the seat he stopped and he asked them where they were from. "They said 'Bridgewater.' I said, 'What was you doing in Bridgewater?' They said 'We went down to see a friend of mine.' I said, 'Who is your friend?' He said, 'A man by the—they call him "Poppy."' 'Well,' I said, 'I want you, you are under arrest.' Vanzetti was sitting on the inside of the seat."
>
> Q: When you say "on the inside," you mean toward the aisle or toward the window?
>
> A: Toward the window. The inside of the car; and he went, put his hand in his hip pocket and I says, "Keep your hands out on your lap, or you will be sorry."
>
> THE DEFENDANT VANZETTI: You are a liar!
>
> [As to Sacco] I told them when we started that the first false move I would put a bullet in them. On the way up to the Station Sacco reached his hand to put it under his overcoat and I told him to keep his hands outside of his clothes and on his lap.
>
> Q: Will you illustrate to the jury how he placed his hand?
>
> A: He was sitting down with his hands that way (indicating), and he moved his hand up to put it in under his overcoat.
>
> Q: At what point?

---

* These are Judge Thayer's words. His meaning must, presumably, have been "guiltily conscious."

A: Just about the stomach there, across his waistband, and I says to him, "Have you got a gun there?" He says "No." He says, "I ain't got no gun." "Well," I says, "Keep your hands outside of your clothes." We went along a little further and he done the same thing. I gets up on my knees on the front seat and I reaches over and I puts my hand under his coat but I did not see any gun. "Now," I says, "Mister, if you put your hand in there again, you are going to get into trouble." He says, "I don't want no trouble."

3. In statements made to the District Attorney and to the Chief of Police, at the police station after their arrest, both Sacco and Vanzetti lied. By misstatements they tried to conceal their movements on the day of their arrest, the friends they had been to see, the places they had visited. For instance, Vanzetti denied that he knew Boda.

What of this evidence of "consciousness of guilt"? The testimony of the police that Sacco and Vanzetti were about to draw pistols was emphatically denied by them. These denials, it was urged, were confirmed by the inherent probabilities of the situation. Did Sacco and Vanzetti upon arrest reveal the qualities of the perpetrators of the Braintree murders? Those crimes were committed by desperadoes—men whose profession it was to take life if necessary and who freely used guns to hold bystanders at bay in order to make their "getaway." Is there the slightest likeness between the behavior of the Braintree bandits and the behavior of Sacco and Vanzetti, when the two were arrested by one policeman? Would the ready and ruthless gunmen at Braintree so quietly have surrendered themselves into custody on a capital charge of which they knew themselves to be guilty? If Sacco and Vanzetti were the holdup men of Braintree, why did they not draw upon their expert skill and attempt to make their escape by scattering shots? But, if not "gunmen," why should Sacco and Vanzetti have carried guns? The possession of firearms in this country has not at all the significance that it would have, say, in England. The extensive carrying of guns by people who are not "gunmen" is a matter of common knowledge. The widespread advertisement of firearms indicates that we may not unfairly be described as a gun-carrying people. The practice is unfortunately rife for a variety of reasons. Sacco and Vanzetti had credible reasons, wholly unrelated to professional banditry. Sacco acquired the habit of carrying a pistol while a night watchman because, as his employer testified, "night watchmen protecting prop-

erty do have guns." Vanzetti carried a revolver, "because it was a very
bad time, and I like to have a revolver for self defense":

Q: How much money did you use to carry around with you?
A: When I went to Boston for fish, I can carry eighty, one hundred dollars,
one hundred and twenty dollars.
There were many crimes, many hold-ups, many robberies at that time.

The other evidence from which "consciousness of guilt" was drawn
the two Italians admitted. Sacco and Vanzetti acknowledged that they
behaved in the way described by Mrs. Johnson, and freely conceded
that when questioned at the police station they told lies. What was their
explanation of this conduct? To exculpate themselves of the crime of
murder they had to disclose elaborately their guilt of radicalism. In order to meet the significance which the prosecution attached to the incidents at the Johnson house and those following, it became necessary
for the defendants to advertise to the jury their offensive views, and
thereby to excite the deepest prejudices of a Norfolk County jury,
picked for its respectability and sitting in judgment upon two men of
alien blood and abhorrent philosophy.

Innocent men, it is said, do not lie when picked up by the police. But
Sacco and Vanzetti knew they were not innocent of the charge on
which they *supposed* themselves arrested, and about which the police
interrogated them. For when apprehended they were not confronted
with the charge of murder; they were not accused of banditry; they
were not given the remotest intimation that the murders of Parmenter
and Berardelli were laid at their door. They were told they were arrested as "suspicious characters" and the meaning which that carried
to their minds was rendered concrete by the questions that were put to
them:

(As to Vanzetti) Did you tell Mr. Katzmann the truth about Pappi and
why you—
A: About Pappi, yes, but I don't say that I was there to take the automobile
and I don't speak about the literature . . . I don't tell him about the meeting on next Sunday. Yes, I told them, I explained to them the meeting, I
think.
Q: Tell us all you recall that Stewart, the chief, asked of you?
A: He asked me why we were in Bridgewater, how long I know Sacco, if I
am a Radical, if I am an anarchist or Communist, and he asked me if I
believe in the government of the United States.

Q: Did either Chief Stewart at the Brockton police station or Mr. Katzmann tell you that you were suspected of robberies and murder?

A: No.

Q: Was there any question asked of you or any statement made to you to indicate to you that you were charged with that crime on April 15th?

A: No.

Q: What did you understand, in view of the questions asked of you, what did you understand you were being detained for at the Brockton police station?

A: I understand they arrested me for a political matter. . . .

Q: . . . Why did you feel you were being detained for political opinions?

A: Because I was asked if I was a Socialist. I say, "Well,—"

Q: You mean by reason of the questions asked of you?

A: Because I was asked if I am a Socialist, if I am I. W. W., if I am a Communist, if I am a Radical, if I am a Blackhand.

(As to Sacco) What did you think was the time when the crime that you were arrested for had been committed?

A: I never think anything else than Radical.

Q: What?

A: To the Radical arrest, you know, the way they do in New York, the way they arrest so many people there.

Q: What made you think that?

A: Because I was not registered, and I was working for the movement for the working class, for the laboring class.

Q: What occurred with Mr. Stewart [Chief of Police] that made you think you were being held for Radical activities?

A: Well, because the first thing they asked me if I was an anarchist, a communist or socialist.

Plainly their arrest meant to Sacco and Vanzetti arrest for radicalism. That being so, why should they evade police inquiries; what fear governed them in making lies to escape that charge?

The early winter of 1919-20 saw the beginning of an elaborately planned campaign by the Department of Justice under Attorney-General Mitchell Palmer for the wholesale arrest and deportation of "Reds" —aliens under suspicion of sympathy with the Communist régime. The details of these raids, their brutality and their lawlessness, are set forth authoritatively in decisions of United States courts condemning the misconduct of the Department of Justice. These findings the Attorney-General never ventured to have reviewed by the higher courts.*

* See Report upon the Illegal Practices of the United States Department of Justice by Roscoe Pound et al. (May 1920) which former Justice Charles E. Hughes thus summarized: "Very recently information has been laid by responsible citizens at

Boston was one of the worst centers of this lawlessness and hysteria. Its proximity to industrial communities having a large proportion of foreign labor and a history of past ugly industrial conflicts lent to the lawless activities of the government officials the widespread support of influential public opinion.* One of the leading citizens of Boston, Mr. John F. Moors, himself a banker, has called attention to the fact that "the hysteria against 'the reds' was so great, at the time when these men were convicted, that even the most substantial bankers in this city [Boston] were carried away to the extent of paying for full-page advertisements about the red peril." Sacco and Vanzetti were notorious Reds. They were associates of leading radicals. They had for some time been on the list of suspects of the Department of Justice, and were especially obnoxious because they were draft-dodgers.

The press made them daily anxious for their safety. The newspapers, it will be recalled, were filled with lurid accounts of what the Reds had done and were planning, and equally lurid accounts of the methods of the Government in dealing with the Reds. Not only were Sacco and Vanzetti living in this enveloping atmosphere of apprehension; the terrorizing methods of the Government had very specific meaning for them. Two of their friends had already been deported. Deportation, they knew, meant not merely expulsion and uprooting from home. What it did mean they had just learned. Among Vanzetti's radical group in Boston the arrest of the New York radical Salsedo, and his detention incommunicado by the Department of Justice, had been for some weeks a source of great concern. Vanzetti was sent to New York by this group to confer with the Italian Defense Committee having charge of the case of Salsedo and all other Italian political prisoners. On his return, May 2, he reported to his Boston friends the advice which had been given to the Italian Defense Committee by their New York lawyer: to dispose of their radical literature and thus eliminate

---

the bar of public opinion of violations of personal rights which savor of the worst practices of tyranny." (Address at Centennial Celebration of Harvard Law School, June 21, 1920.)

* In 1923 Mr. Moorfield Storey thus characterized the situation: ". . . on a small scale a 'reign of terror' [was produced] in which some thousands of innocent people were very cruelly treated and exposed to much suffering and loss. . . . The safeguards of the Constitution were ignored, and any true American must blush at what was done and the indifference with which he and all but a handful of his countrymen tolerated it." (Introduction to Post, *Deportations Delirium*, xii-xiii.)

the most damaging evidence in the deportation proceedings they feared.

THE WITNESS [SACCO]: Vanzetti come into the hall. He told us we are to get ready and advise our friends, any friend who knows a friend as a Socialist and active in the movement of labor, why, they are advised to get the books and literature to put at some place and hide not to find by the police or the state. And another thing he says nobody know why they arrest Salsedo and Elia.

THE COURT: Nobody knows—

THE WITNESS: Why, for what charge they did arrest Salsedo and Elia and Cammiti, and some of the other fellows before. So they say after all over in New York, a spy to find out the Radicals and they find out the same, the money, all the friends that been sending from Massachusetts and all over New England, been sending the money for the defending of Salsedo and Elia,—who is the man receiving it, who is the man responsible for those things, so we decided and Vanzetti decided it was same time, the quicker we come and get literature and anything out of the Radical's house, the Socialists, and to hide it. That is all he said. That is why I remembered. He probably said some more, but I could not remember all the conversation we had, because he been talking an hour, pretty near an hour and a half, and I could not remember all he says.

The urgency of acting on this advice was intensified by the tragic news of Salsedo's death after Vanzetti's return from New York. It was to carry out this advice that Vanzetti and his friends were trying to get Boda's car from Johnson's garage on May 5. The day before had come the news of Salsedo's death.

Q: Any one time you mentioned that you were afraid, what did you mean by that?

A: I mean that I was afraid, for I know that my friends there in New York have jumped down from the jail in the street and killed himself. The papers say that he jump down, but we don't know.

Q: You now allude to who? Who is that man?

A: Salsedo.

Q: When did you learn of Salsedo's death?

A: On the day, in the day, fourth, 4th of May.

Though Salsedo's death was unexplained, to Sacco and Vanzetti it conveyed only one explanation. It was a symbol of their fears and perhaps an omen of their own fate.

*

Let us now resume the story of the trial. The witnesses for the Commonwealth had dealt with identification of men and of bullets, and the suspicious conduct of Sacco and Vanzetti at the time of arrest. On the witness stand Sacco and Vanzetti accounted for their movements on April 15. They also accounted for their ambiguous behavior on May 5. Up to the time that Sacco and Vanzetti testified to their radical activities, their pacifism and their flight to Mexico to escape the draft, the trial was a trial for murder and banditry; with the cross-examination of Sacco and Vanzetti patriotism and radicalism became the dominant emotional issues. Of course, these were not the technical issues which were left to the jury. But, as Mr. Justice Holmes has admonished us, "in spite of forms [juries] are extremely likely to be impregnated by the environing atmosphere." Outside the courtroom the Red hysteria was rampant; it was allowed to dominate within. The prosecutor systematically played on the feelings of the jury by exploiting the unpatriotic and despised beliefs of Sacco and Vanzetti, and the judge allowed him thus to divert and pervert the jury's mind. Only a detailed knowledge of the conduct of the prosecutor, sanctioned by the Court, can give an adequate realization of the extent to which prejudice, instead of being rigorously excluded, was systematically fostered.

The opening question on cross-examination of Vanzetti by the District Attorney discloses a motif that he persistently played upon:

Q (By Mr. Katzmann): So you left Plymouth, Mr. Vanzetti, in May, 1917, to dodge the draft, did you?

A: Yes, sir. . . .

Q: When this country was at war, you ran away, so you would not have to fight as a soldier?

A: Yes.

Q: You were going to advise in a public meeting men who had gone to war? Are you that man?

A: Yes, sir, I am that man, not the man you want me, but I am that man.

This method was elaborated when Sacco took the stand:

Q (By Mr. Katzmann): Did you say yesterday you love a free country?

A: Yes, sir.

Q: Did you love this country in the month of May, 1917?

A: I did not say,—I don't want to say I did not love this country.

Q: Did you love this country in that month of 1917?

A: If you can, Mr. Katzmann, if you can give me that,—I could explain—

Q: Do you understand that question?

A: Yes.

Q: Then will you please answer it?

A: I can't answer in one word.

Q: You can't say whether you loved the United States of America one week before the day you enlisted for the first draft?

A: I can't say in one word, Mr. Katzmann.

Q: Did you love this country in the last week of May, 1917?

A: That is pretty hard for me to say in one word, Mr. Katzmann.

Q: There are two words you can use, Mr. Sacco, yes or no. Which one is it?

A: Yes.

Q: And in order to show your love for this United States of America when she was about to call upon you to become a soldier you ran away to Mexico.

Q: Did you go to Mexico to avoid being a soldier for this country that you loved?

A: Yes.

Q: And would it be your idea of showing your love for your wife that when she needed you, you ran away from her?

A: I did not run away from her.

MR. MOORE: I object.

THE WITNESS: I was going to come after if I need her.

THE COURT: He may answer. Simply on the question of credibility, that is all.

Q: Would it be your idea of love for your wife that you were to run away from her when she needed you?

MR. JEREMIAH MC ANARNEY: Pardon me. I ask for an exception on that.

THE COURT: Excluded. One may not run away. He had not admitted he ran away.

Q: Then I will ask you, didn't you run away from Milford so as to avoid being a soldier for the United States?

A: I did not run away.

Q: You mean you walked away?

A: Yes.

Q: You don't understand me when I say "run away," do you?

A: That is vulgar.

Q: That is vulgar?

A: You can say a little intelligent, Mr. Katzmann.

Q: Don't you think going away from your country is a vulgar thing to do when she needs you?

A: I don't believe in war.

Q: You don't believe in war?

A: No, sir.

Q: Do you think it is a cowardly thing to do what you did?

A: No, sir.

Q: Do you think it is a brave thing to do what you did?

A: Yes, sir.

Q: Do you think it would be a brave thing to go away from your own wife?

A: No.

Q: When she needed you?

A: No.

Q: Why didn't you stay there, down there in that free country, and work with a pick and shovel?

A: I don't think I did sacrifice to learn a job to go to pick and shovel in Mexico.

Q: Is it because,—is your love for the United States of America commensurate with the amount of money you can get in this country per week?

A: Better conditions, yes.

Q: Better country to make money, isn't it?

A: Yes. . . .

Q: Is your love for this country measured by the amount of money you can earn here? . . .

A: I never loved money.

Q: Is standing by a country when she needs a soldier evidence of love of country?

MR. JEREMIAH MC ANARNEY: That I object to, if your Honor please. And I might state now I want my objection to go to this whole line of interrogation.

THE COURT: I think you opened it up.

MR. JEREMIAH MC ANARNEY: No, if your Honor please, I have not.

THE COURT: It seems to me you have. Are you going to claim much of all the collection of the literature and the books was really in the interest of the United States as well as these people and therefore it has opened up the credibility of the defendant when he claims that all that work was done really for the interest of the United States in getting his literature out of the way?

MR. JEREMIAH MC ANARNEY: That claim is not presented in anything tantamount to the language just used by the Court, and in view of the record as it stands at this time I object to this line of inquiry.

THE COURT: Is that not your claim, that the defendant, as a reason that he has given for going to the Johnson house, that they wanted the automobile to prevent people from being deported and to get this literature all out of the way? Does he not claim that that was done in the interest of the United States, to prevent violation of the law by the distribution of this literature? I understood that was the—

MR. JEREMIAH MC ANARNEY: Are you asking that as a question to me?

THE COURT: Yes.

MR. JEREMIAH MC ANARNEY: Absolutely we have taken no such position as that, and the evidence at this time does not warrant the assumption of that question.

THE COURT: Are you going to claim that what the defendant did was in the interest of the United States?

MR. JEREMIAH MC ANARNEY: Your Honor please, I now object to your Honor's statement as prejudicial to the rights of the defendants and ask that this statement be withdrawn from the jury.

THE COURT: There is no prejudicial remark made that I know of, and none were intended. I simply asked you, sir, whether you propose to offer evidence as to what you said to me.

MR. JEREMIAH MC ANARNEY: If your Honor please, the remarks made with reference to the country and whether the acts that he was doing were for the benefit of the country. I can see no other inference to be drawn from those except prejudicial to the defendants. . . .

THE COURT: All I ask is this one question, and it will simplify matters very much. Is it your claim that in the collection of the literature and the books and papers that that was done in the interest of the United States?

MR. JEREMIAH MC ANARNEY: No, I make no such broad claim as that. . . .

MR. KATZMANN: Well, he [Sacco] stated in his direct examination yesterday that he loved a free country, and I offer it to attack that statement made in his examination by his own counsel.

THE COURT: That is what I supposed, and that is what I supposed that remark meant when it was introduced in this cross-examination, but counsel now say they don't make that claim.

MR. KATZMANN: They say they don't make the claim that gathering up the literature on May 5th at West Bridgewater was for the purpose of helping the country, but that is a different matter, not released [sic] to May 5th.

Q: Do you remember speaking of educational advantages before the recess?

A: Yes, sir.

Q: Do you remember speaking of Harvard University?

A: Yes, sir.

Q: Do you remember saying that you could not get an education there unless you had money? I do not mean you used those exact words. I do not contend you did, but, in substance, didn't you say that?

A: They have to use money in the rule of the Government.

Q: No. You don't understand. Did you hear it, perhaps?

A: I can't understand.

Q: I will raise my voice a little bit. Did you say in substance you could not send your boy to Harvard?

A: Yes.

Q: Unless you had money. Did you say that?

A: Of course.

Q: Do you think that is true?

A: I think it is.

Q: Don't you know Harvard University educates more boys of poor people free than any other university in the United States of America? [The Court having overruled his counsel's objection, Sacco answered.]

A: I can't answer that question, no.

Q: So without the light of knowledge on that subject, you are condemning even Harvard University, are you, as being a place for rich men? . . .

Q: Did you intend to condemn Harvard College? [Objection overruled.]

A: No, sir.

Q: Were you ready to say none but the rich could go there without knowing about offering scholarships? [Objection overruled.]

A: Yes.

Q: Does your boy go to the public schools?

A: Yes.

Q: Are there any schools in the town you came from in Italy that compare with the school your boy goes to? [Objection.]

Q: Does your boy go to the public school?

A: Yes.

Q: Without payment of money?

A: Yes.

Q: Have you free nursing where you come from in Stoughton?

A: What do you mean?

Q: A district nurse?

A: For the boys?

Q: For anybody in your family who is ill?

A: I could not say. Yes, I never have them in my house.

Q: Do you know how many children the city of Boston is educating in the public schools?—[Objection.] free?

Q: Do you know?

A: I can't answer yes or no.

Q: Do you know it is close to one hundred thousand children? [Objection.]

A: I know millions of people don't go there.

MR. JEREMIAH MC ANARNEY: Wait. When there is objection, don't answer. I object to that question.

THE COURT: He says he doesn't know.

MR. JEREMIAH MC ANARNEY: I object to that answer. I object to the question and the answer.

THE COURT: The question may stand, and the answer also.

MR. JEREMIAH MC ANARNEY: Will your Honor save an exception?

Q: The question is this: As far as you understood Fruzetti's views, were yours the same? [Objection overruled.]

Q: Answer please.

A (Through the interpreter): I cannot say yes or no.

Q: Is it because you can't or because you don't want to?

A (Through the interpreter): Because it is a very delicate question.

Q: It is very delicate, isn't it, because he was deported for his views?

Q: Do you know why Fruzetti was deported?

A (Through the interpreter): Yes.

Q: Was it because he was of anarchistic opinions?

THE INTERPRETER: He says he understands it now.

Q: Was it because Fruzetti entertained anarchistic opinions?

A: One reason, he was an anarchist. Another reason, Fruzetti been writing all the time on the newspapers, and I am not sure why the reason he been deported. . . .

Q: Was Fruzetti, before deportation, a subscriber to the same papers that you had in your house on May 5th?

A: Probably he is. [Objection.] . . .

Q: Who was the other man that you said was deported from Bridgewater?

A: I did not say; I am sure there is another man been deported, but I do not know the name.

Q: See if I can refresh your recollection. Was it Ferruccio Coacci?

A: He is one. There is another one.

Q: Who was the other man?

A: I do not remember the name.

Q: Did you believe that they had in their homes books similar to the ones you had in your house?

A: Yes.

Q: And the books which you intended to collect were books relating to anarchy, weren't they?

A: Not all of them.

Q: How many of them?

A: Well, all together. We are Socialists, democratic, any other socialistic information, Socialists, Syndicalists, Anarchists, any paper.

Q: Bolshevist?

A: I do not know what Bolshevism means.

Q: Soviet?

A: I do not know what Soviet means.

Q: Communism?

A: Yes. I got some on astronomy, too.

Q: You weren't going to destroy them?

A: I was going to keep them.

Q: You were going to keep them and when the time was over, you were going to bring them out again, weren't you?

A: Yes.

Q: And you were going to distribute circulars?

A: Education literature.

Q: And you were going to distribute circulars, weren't you?

A: It cost money to sacrifice.

Q: You were going to distribute those papers, weren't you?

MR. JEREMIAH MC ANARNEY: The question, were you?

Q: Were you?

A: What do you mean, destroy?

Q: No, not destroy them. After the time had gone by, were you going to bring them out, going to distribute the knowledge contained in them?

A: Certainly, because they are educational for books, educational.

Q: An education in anarchy, wasn't it?

A: Why, certainly. Anarchistic is not criminals.

Q: I didn't ask you if they are criminals or not. Nor are you to pass upon that, sir. Was it equally true as to the book and papers and periodicals that you expected to pick up at your friends' houses, that they were not to be destroyed?

A: Just to keep them, hide them.

Q: And then bring them forth afterwards when the time was over?

A: I suppose so.

Q: And you are a man who tells this jury that the United States of America is a disappointment to you?

MR. JEREMIAH MC ANARNEY: Wait a minute. I object.

MR. KATZMANN: On the question of intelligence, if your Honor please.

THE COURT: Not quite, and you assume, too.

MR. KATZMANN: I assumed on the question of intelligence?

THE COURT: You assumed "you are the man."

MR. KATZMANN: "Are you the man?" That this man passed judgment on the United States of America?

MR. JEREMIAH MC ANARNEY: I object.

THE COURT: He may answer, yes or no.

MR. JEREMIAH MC ANARNEY: Will your Honor save an exception to the question and the answer?

THE COURT: Certainly.

Q: Are you, Mr. Sacco?

A: I don't,—I can't understand this word.

Q: "Passed judgment?"

A: Yes, sir.

Q: Well, told us about how disappointed you were, and what you did not find and what you expected to find. Are you that man?

A: Yes.

In the Anglo-American system of criminal procedure the rôle of a public prosecutor is very different from that of an advocate in a private cause. In the words of a leading New York case:

> Language which might be permitted to counsel in summing up a civil action cannot with propriety be used by a public prosecutor, who is a *quasi*-judicial officer, representing the People of the state, and presumed to act impartially in the interest only of justice. If he lays aside the impartiality that should characterize his official action to become a heated partisan, and by vituperation of the prisoner and appeals to prejudice seeks to procure a conviction at all hazards, he ceases to properly represent the public interest, which demands no victim, and asks no conviction through the aid of passion, sympathy or resentment.

In 1921 the temper of the times made it the special duty of a prosecutor and a court, engaged in trying two Italian radicals before a jury of native New Englanders, to keep the instruments of justice free from the infection of passion or prejudice:—

> On these dates [1918] it was not necessary to inflame the passions of jurors by talking about the enemies of our country, rather was it a time to caution jurors against allowing their prejudices and patriotism from swaying their judgment. But the Assistant United States Attorney so far transcended his duty as a prosecuting officer that we are clearly of the opinion that the conviction of the defendant ought not to stand. The language used speaks for itself. It must have produced a situation in the minds of the jurors that destroyed a calm consideration of the rights of the defendant. The United States cannot afford to convict her citizens in this manner.*

In the case of Sacco and Vanzetti no such restraints were respected. By systematic exploitation of the defendants' alien blood, their imperfect knowledge of English, their unpopular social views, and their opposition to the war, the District Attorney invoked against them a riot of political passion and patriotic sentiment; and the trial judge connived at—one had almost written, coöperated in—the process. Upon this conduct of Judge Thayer Mr. William G. Thompson, in his argument on appeal, made this eminently just comment:

---

* *August v. United States*, 257 Fed. 388, 393 (1919).

The persistent attempt of the Court in the presence of the jury to suggest that the defendants were claiming that the suppression of the Socialist literature was "in the interest of the United States," to which exception was taken, was even more objectionable and prejudicial. It seems incredible that the Court could have believed from any testimony that had been given by Vanzetti or Sacco that their purpose in collecting and suppressing the Socialist literature had anything to do with the interest of the United States. *If anything had been made plain, it was that they were actuated by personal fear of sharing the fate of Salsedo, not merely deportation, but death by violence while awaiting deportation.* Yet the Court eight times, in the face of as many explicit disclaimers from Mr. McAnarney, suggested that that was the defendants' claim. Had that claim been made it would, of course, have been the grossest hypocrisy, and might well have sealed the fate of both defendants with the jury. The repeated suggestion of the Court in the presence of the jury that that *was* the claim amounted to a violation by the Court of the defendants' elementary constitution right to a fair and impartial trial. It was not cured by the Court's disclaimer made immediately after the exception was taken to the effect that he did not intend "to prejudice the rights of either of these defendants." Whatever the Court intended, he had fatally prejudiced their right to a fair trial, and no general disclaimer could undo the harm.

That the real purpose of this line of the prosecutor's cross-examination was to inflame the jury's passions is revealed by the professed ground on which, with the Court's sanction, it was conducted. The Commonwealth claimed that Sacco and Vanzetti's alleged anxiety on the evening of their arrest, and the lies they told, could only be explained by the fact that they were the murderers of Parmenter and Berardelli. The defense replied that their conduct was clearly accounted for by the fact that the men were Reds, in terror of the Department of Justice. To test the credibility of this answer the District Attorney proposed to examine Sacco and Vanzetti to find out whether they were really radicals or only pretending to be. It was on this theory that the Court allowed the cross-examination. The Commonwealth undertook to show that the defendants were impostors, that they were spurious Reds. In fact, it made not the least attempt to do so. It never disputed their radicalism; it could not be disputed, certainly not by Mr. Katzmann. For we now know he had been in close connection with the Department of Justice before the trial, and well knew that Sacco and Vanzetti were bona fide Reds, sought as such by the Government. Instead of undermining the claim of the defendants by which their conduct was explained, the District Attorney adopted their confession of radicalism, exaggerated and exploited it. He thereby wholly destroyed the basis of his original claim, for what reason was there any longer to suppose that the "consciousness of guilt" was consciousness of murder, rather than of radicalism?

CHAPTER IV

The deliberate effort to excite the emotions of jurors still in the grip of war fever is not unparalleled in the legal history of the times. During the years 1918-19 in the United States, forty-four convictions were reversed by appellate courts for misconduct of the trial judge or the public prosecutor; thirty-three of them for inflammatory appeals made by the district attorney on matters not properly before the jury. Appellate courts interfere reluctantly in such cases and only where there has been a flagrant abuse, so that we may safely assume that the above figures indicate an even more widespread evil. In a New York case the district attorney urged on the jury that the name of the accused (Esposito) meant "bastard," and that he was an alien and within the draft age. The New York Court of Appeals set aside the conviction, and happily appellate courts in general have taken a firm stand against such practices. What *is* unparalleled is that such an abuse should have succeeded in a Massachusetts court.

As things were, what wonder the jury convicted? The last words left with them by Mr. Katzmann were an appeal to their solidarity against the alien:

Gentlemen of the jury, do your duty. Do it like men. Stand together, you men of Norfolk!

The first words of Judge Thayer's charge revived their memories of the war and sharpened their indignation against the two draft-dodgers whose fate lay in their hands:

The Commonwealth of Massachusetts called upon you to render a most important service. Although you knew that such service would be arduous, painful and tiresome, yet you, like the true soldier, responded to that call in the spirit of supreme American loyalty. There is no better word in the English language than "loyalty."

It had been to the accompaniment of this same war motif that the jurors were first initiated into the case; by the license allowed to the prosecution it had been dinned into their ears; and now by the final and authoritative voice of the Court it was a soldier's loyalty which was made the measure of their duty.

The function of a judge's charge is to enable the jury to find its way through the maze of conflicting testimony, to sift the relevant from the irrelevant, to weigh wisely, and to judge dispassionately. A trial judge is not expected to rehearse all the testimony; in Massachusetts he is not allowed to express his own opinion on it. But in drawing together the threads of evidence and marshaling the claims on both sides he must exercise a scrupulous regard for relevance and proportion. Misplaced emphasis here and omission there may work more damage than any outspoken comment. By his summing-up a judge reveals his estimate of relative importance. Judge Thayer's charge directs the emotions only too clearly. What guidance does he give to the mind? The charge occupies twenty-four pages. Of these, fourteen are consumed in abstract legal generalities and moral exhortations, paying lip service to the ideals of justice. Having allowed the minds of the jurors to be impregnated with war feeling, Judge Thayer now invited them to breathe "a purer atmosphere of unyielding impartiality and absolute fairness." Unfortunately the passion and prejudice systematically instilled during the course of a trial cannot be exorcised by the general, placid language of a charge after the mischief is done. (Every experienced lawyer knows that it is idle to ask jurors to dismiss from their memory what has been deposited in their feelings.)

In this case, surely the vital issue was identification. That the whole mass of conflicting identification testimony is dismissed in two pages out of twenty-four is a fair measure of the distorted perspective in which the Judge placed the case. He dealt with identification in abstract terms and without mentioning the name of any witness on either side. The alibi testimony he likewise dismissed in two paragraphs, again without any reference to specific witnesses. In striking contrast to this sterile treatment of the issue whether or not Sacco and Vanzetti were in South Braintree on April 15 was his concrete and elaborate treatment of the inferences which might be drawn from the character of their conduct on the night of their arrest. Five pages of the charge are given over to "consciousness of guilt," set forth in great detail and with specific mention of the testimony given by the various police officials and by Mr. and Mrs. Johnson. The disproportionate consideration which Judge Thayer gave to this issue, in the light of his comments during the trial, must have left the impression on the jury that the case turned on "consciousness of guilt." As we have seen, Judge Thayer himself did in fact so interpret the jury's verdict afterward.

As to motive, the Court expatiated for more than a page on its legal conception and the undisputed claim of the Commonwealth that the motive of the murder of Parmenter and Berardelli was robbery, but made no comment whatever on the complete failure of the Commonwealth to trace any of the stolen money to either defendant or to connect them with the act of robbery. Undoubtedly, great weight must have been attached by the jury, as it was by the Court, to the identification of the fatal bullet taken from Berardelli's body as having passed through Sacco's pistol. This is a point soon to be dealt with in detail. Here the summary statement must suffice that the Court instructed the jury that Captain Proctor and another expert had testified in effect that "it was his [Sacco's] pistol that fired the bullet that caused the death of Berardelli" when in fact, as we shall see, that was not Captain Proctor's testimony. Of course, if the jury believed Proctor's testimony as interpreted by Judge Thayer Sacco was doomed. In view of the temper of the times, the nature of the accusation, the opinions of the accused, the tactics of the prosecution, and the conduct of the Judge, no wonder the "men of Norfolk" convicted Sacco and Vanzetti!

Hitherto the prejudicial methods pursued by the prosecution, which explain the convictions, rested on inferences, however compelling. But recently facts have been disclosed, and not denied by the prosecution, to show that the case against Sacco and Vanzetti for murder was part of a collusive effort between the District Attorney and agents of the Department of Justice to rid the country of these Italians because of their Red activities. In proof of this we have the affidavits of two former officers of the Government, one of whom served as post-office inspector for twenty-five years, and both of whom are now in honorable civil employment. The names of Sacco and Vanzetti were on the files of the Department of Justice "as radicals to be watched"; the Department was eager for their deportation, but had not evidence enough to secure it, and inasmuch as the United States District Court for Massachusetts had checked abuses in deportation proceedings the Department had become chary of resorting to deportation without adequate legal basis. The arrest of Sacco and Vanzetti, on the mistaken theory of Stewart, furnished the agents of the Department of Justice their opportunity. Although the opinion of the agents working on the case was that "the South Braintree crime was the work of professionals" and that Sacco and Vanzetti "although anarchists and agitators, were not highway robbers, and had nothing to do with the South Braintree crime" yet they collaborated with the District Attorney in the prosecution of Sacco and Vanzetti for murder. For "it was the opinion of the Department agents here that a conviction of Sacco and Vanzetti for murder would be one way of disposing of these two men." Here, to be sure, is a startling allegation. But it is made by a man of long years of important service in the Government's employ; it is supported by the now admitted installation of a government spy in a cell adjoining Sacco's with a view to "obtaining whatever incriminating evidence he could . . . after winning his confidence" by the insinuation of an "under cover man" into the councils of the Sacco-Vanzetti Defense Committee, by the proposed placement of another spy as a lodger in Mrs. Sacco's house, and by the supplying of information about the radical activities of Sacco and Vanzetti to the District Attorney by the agents of the Department of Justice. These joint labors between Boston agents of the Department of Justice and the District Attorney led to a great deal of correspondence between the agent in charge and the District Attorney and to reports between the agents of the Department and Washington:

> There is, or was, a great deal of correspondence on file in the Boston office between Mr. West [the then agent in charge] and Mr. Katzmann, the District Attorney, and there are also copies of reports sent to Washington about the case. Letters and reports were made in triplicate; two copies were sent to Washington and one retained in Boston. The letters and documents on file in the Boston office would throw a great deal of light upon the preparation of the Sacco-Vanzetti case for trial, and upon the real opinion of the Boston office of the Department of Justice as to the guilt of Sacco and Vanzetti of the particular crime with which they were charged.

These records have not been made available, nor has their absence been accounted for. An appeal to Attorney-General Sargent proved fruitless, although supported by Senator Butler of Massachusetts, requesting that West "be authorized to talk with [counsel for Sacco and Vanzetti] and to show me whatever documents and correspondence are on file in his office dealing with the investigations made by the Boston agents before, during, and after the trial of Sacco and Vanzetti." The facts upon which this appeal was made stand uncontradicted. West made no denial whatever, and Katzmann only emphasized his failure to deny the facts charged by the two former agents of the Department of Justice by an affidavit confined to a denial of some of the statements of a former government spy. The charge that the principal agent of the Department of Justice in Boston and the District Attorney collaborated to secure the conviction of Sacco and Vanzetti is denied neither by the agent nor by the District Attorney. Instead, Stewart takes it upon himself to say that the officials of the Department "had nothing whatsoever to do with the preparation of this case for trial." Instead of making a full disclosure of the facts, the representative of the Commonwealth* indulged in vituperation against the former officers of the Department of Justice as men who were guilty of "a breach of loyalty" because they violated the watchword of the Department of Justice "Do not betray the secrets of your departments." To which Mr. Thompson rightly replied: "What are the secrets which they admit? . . . A government which has come to value its own secrets more than it does the lives of its citizens has become a tyranny. . . . Secrets, secrets! And he says you should abstain from touching this verdict of your jury because it is so sacred. Would they not have liked to know something about the secrets? The case is admitted by that inadvertent concession. There are, then, secrets to be admitted." Yet Judge Thayer found in these circumstances only opportunity to make innuendo against a former official of the Government, well known for his long and honorable service. He indulged in much patriotic protestation, but is wholly silent about the specific acts of wrongdoing and lawlessness connected with the Red raids of 1920. The historian who relied on his opinion would assume that the charge of lawlessness and misconduct in the deportation of outlawed radicals was the traitorous invention of a diseased mind.

CHAPTER V

The verdict of guilty was brought in on July 14, 1921. The exceptions which had been taken to rulings at the trial were made the basis of an application for a new trial, which Judge Thayer refused. Subsequently

* It has seemed best to depart from the chronological summary of the successive stages of the case by quoting at this point from the arguments and the decision upon the last motion for a new trial.

a great mass of new evidence was unearthed by the defense, and made the subject of other motions for a new trial, all heard before Judge Thayer and all denied by him. The hearing on the later motions took place on October 1, 1923, and was the occasion of the entry into the case of Mr. William G. Thompson, a powerful advocate bred in the traditions of the Massachusetts courts. The espousal of the Sacco-Vanzetti cause by a man of Mr. Thompson's professional prestige at once gave it a new complexion and has been its mainstay ever since. For he has brought to the case not only his great ability as a lawyer, but the strength of his conviction that these two men are innocent and that their trial was not characterized by those high standards which are the pride of Massachusetts justice.

Some of the motions presented are technical in the extreme, and here no more can be attempted than to indicate their contents in the barest outline, reserving only one of them, the so-called Proctor motion, for more detailed treatment.

.　　.　　.　　.　　.　　.　　.　　.　　.　　.　　.　　.

3. *Hamilton motion.* Hamilton, an expert of fifteen years' experience in the microscopic examination of exhibits in criminal cases, who had been called in 165 homicide cases from Maine to Arizona, gave in the form of an affidavit the result of his examination under a compound microscope of the bullet taken from Berardelli's body and the revolver found on Vanzetti, supported by photographs taken under powerful magnification. In his opinion minute comparison of the scratches on the bullet and the grooves inside the barrel of Sacco's pistol conclusively disproved the claim of the Commonwealth that it was from Sacco's pistol that the fatal bullet was fired.

4. *Gould motion.* Gould, who was in the business of selling razor paste to employees of factories, gave an affidavit to the following effect. He arrived in South Braintree on April 15, 1920, at about 3 P.M. and inquired where the shoe employees were paid off. Someone told him, "There goes the paymaster now; follow him," and he started to follow Parmenter and Berardelli down the street, when suddenly the shooting began. An automobile passed him within five feet; he saw a man with a revolver in his hand climb from the back to the front seat on the right-hand side of the driver and that man pointed a revolver at him and fired, the bullet passing through his overcoat. Gould had thus a better view of the man alleged to be Sacco than any witness on either side. He gave his name and address to the police, but was never called

upon to testify. When, after the trial, Gould saw Sacco and Vanzetti, he was flat and unqualified in his statement that neither was the man he saw in the car. Judge Thayer's decision denying the Gould motion contains an extraordinary instance of his inaccuracy in matters of fact, which deserves quotation, not as unique, but as typical. By way of discrediting the affidavit he remarks that Gould did not see Sacco from April 15, 1920, until November 10, 1921, and yet was able to carry a correct picture of him in his mind all this time—eighteen months. The whole burden of Gould's affidavit was that the man he saw on April 15, 1920, was *not* Sacco, and therefore, far from carrying a mental picture of Sacco in his mind for eighteen months, he had never seen Sacco before he saw him in the jail.

5. *Proctor motion.* We have now reached a stage of the case the details of which shake one's confidence in the whole course of the proceedings and reveal a situation which in and of itself undermines the respect usually to be accorded to a jury's verdict. By prearrangement the prosecution brought before the jury a piece of evidence apparently most damaging to the defendants, when in fact the *full* truth concerning this evidence was very favorable to them. Vital to the identification of Sacco and Vanzetti as the murderers was the identification of one of the fatal bullets as a bullet coming from Sacco's pistol. The evidence excluded the possibility that five other bullets found in the dead bodies were fired either by Sacco or by Vanzetti. When Judge Thayer placed the case in the jury's hands for judgment he charged them that the Commonwealth had introduced the testimony of two experts, Proctor and Van Amburgh, to the effect that the fatal bullet went through Sacco's pistol. Such was not the belief of Proctor; he refused to accede to this view in the course of the preparation of the case, and the District Attorney knew that such was not intended to be his testimony. These startling statements call for detailed proof.

Proctor at the time of his testimony was head of the state police and had been in the Department of Public Safety for twenty-three years. On the witness stand he was qualified at length as an expert who had for twenty years been making examination of and experiments with bullets and revolvers and had testified in over a hundred capital cases. His testimony was thus offered by the State as entitled to the greatest weight. If the jury could be convinced that the bullet found in Berardelli's body came out of Sacco's pistol, the State's case was invincible. On this crucial issue Captain Proctor testified as follows at the trial:—

Q: Have you an opinion as to whether bullet No. 3 [Exhibit 18] was fired from the Colt automatic, which is in evidence [Sacco's pistol]?

A: I have.

Q: And what is your opinion?

A: My opinion is that it is consistent with being fired from that pistol.

The Government placed chief reliance on the expert testimony. In his closing argument the District Attorney told the jury: "You might disregard all the identification testimony, and base your verdict on the testimony of these experts." It weighed heavily in the Court's charge. In simple English Judge Thayer interpreted the evidence to mean that

it was his [Sacco's] pistol that fired the bullet that caused the death of Berardelli. To this effect the Commonwealth introduced the testimony of two witnesses, Messrs. Proctor and Van Amburgh.

Naturally the Court's interpretation became the jury's. By their silence, both the District Attorney and the counsel for the defense apparently acquiesced in the Court's interpretation. After the conviction Proctor in an affidavit swore to the following account of his true views and the manner in which they were phrased for purposes of the trial. After giving his experience and stating the fact that he had had the custody of the bullets, cartridges, shells, and pistols in the case, he swore that one of the bullets

was, as I then testified and still believe, fired from *a* Colt automatic pistol of 32 calibre. During the preparation for the trial, my attention was repeatedly called by the District Attorney and his assistants to the question: whether I could find any evidence which would justify the opinion that the particular bullet taken from the body of Berardelli, which came from *a* Colt automatic pistol, came from the particular Colt automatic pistol taken from Sacco. I used every means available to me for forming an opinion on this subject. I conducted, with Captain Van Amburgh, certain tests at Lowell, about which I testified, consisting in firing certain cartridges through Sacco's pistol. At no time was I able to find any evidence whatever which tended to convince me that the particular model bullet found in Berardelli's body, which came from *a* Colt automatic pistol, which I think was numbered 3 and had some other exhibit number, came from Sacco's pistol, and I so informed the District Attorney and his assistant before the trial. This bullet was what is commonly called a full metalpatch bullet and although I repeatedly talked over with Captain Van Amburgh the scratch or scratches which he claimed tended to identify this bullet as one that must have gone through Sacco's pistol, his statements concerning the identifying marks seemed to me entirely unconvincing.

At the trial, the District Attorney did not ask me whether I had found any evidence that the so-called mortal bullet which I have referred to as number 3 passed through Sacco's pistol, nor was I asked that question on cross-examination. The District Attorney desired to ask me that question, but I had *repeatedly* told him that if he did I should be obliged to answer in the negative; consequently, he put to me this question:

Q: Have you an opinion as to whether bullet number 3 was fired from the Colt automatic which is in evidence? To which I answered, "I have." He then proceeded.

Q: And what is your opinion?

A: My opinion is that it is consistent with being fired by that pistol.

He proceeded to state that he is still of the same opinion,

but I do not intend by that answer to imply that I had found any evidence that the so-called mortal bullet had passed through this particular Colt automatic pistol and the District Attorney well knew that I did not so intend and framed his question accordingly. Had I been asked the direct question: whether I had found any affirmative evidence whatever that this so-called mortal bullet had passed through this particular Sacco's pistol, I should have answered then, as I do now without hesitation, in the negative.

This affidavit of Proctor's was made the basis of Mr. Thompson's motion for a new trial before Judge Thayer. Here was a charge going to the vitals of the case, made by a high official of the police agencies of the state. How did the District Attorney meet it? Mr. Katzmann and his assistant, Mr. Williams, filed affidavits in reply. Did they contradict Proctor? They could not deny his testimony or the weight that the prosecution and the Court had attached to it. These were matters of record. Did they deny the prearrangement which he charged? Did they deny that he told them he was unable to identify the mortal bullet as Sacco's bullet? Let their affidavits speak.

Katzmann stated that,

prior to his testifying, Captain Proctor told me that he was prepared to testify that the mortal bullet was consistent with having been fired from the Sacco pistol; that I did not *repeatedly* ask him whether he had found any evidence that the mortal bullet had passed through the Sacco pistol, nor did he *repeatedly* tell me that if I did ask him that question he would be obliged to reply in the negative.

Williams's affidavit, after setting forth that Captain Proctor told him before the trial that comparisons of the mortal bullet with bullets "pushed by him through various types of pistols" showed that "the mortal bullet had been fired in *a* Colt automatic pistol," proceeded:—

He [Proctor] said that all he could do was to determine the width of the landmarks upon the bullet. His attention was not repeatedly called to the question, whether he could find any evidence which would justify the opinion that this bullet came from the Sacco pistol. I conducted the direct examination of Captain Proctor at the trial and asked him the question quoted in his affidavit, "Have you an opinion as to whether bullet number 3 was fired from the Colt automatic which is in evidence?"

This question was suggested by Captain Proctor himself as best calculated to give him an opportunity to tell what opinion he had respecting the mortal bullet and its connection with the Sacco pistol. His answer in court was the same answer he had given me personally before.

Proctor's disclosures remain uncontradicted: he was unable to identify the murder bullet as Sacco's bullet; he told Katzmann and Williams that he was unable to do it; he told them that if he were asked the question on the witness stand he would have to testify that he could not make the identification; a form of words was therefore found by which, without committing perjury, he could convey the impression that he had testified to the identification. The only contradiction by Katzmann and Williams of Proctor's account affects the number of times that he told them that he was unable to make the identification, he having sworn that he told them "repeatedly" and they denying that he told them "repeatedly." Can there be any dissent among impartial minds from the way in which Mr. Thompson characterized this transaction in his argument before Judge Thayer:

In your closing charge, your honor, you disclosed the importance which you attached to the testimony of these experts. The former District Attorney and the present District Attorney do not deny that the jury got an erroneous understanding, and that your honor got an erroneous understanding of the testimony of one of these witnesses. They heard your honor's charge. Did they rise in their seats to correct you? No, they sat by and said never a word. They profited by Captain Proctor's testimony. How can that be reconciled with a desire to be fair to men on trial for their lives? The more I reflect upon this matter, the worse it grows.

Yet Judge Thayer found no warrant in the Proctor incident for directing a new trial. And why?

1. The Judge quotes the Proctor questions and answers and argues that the questions were clear and must have been perfectly understood by Captain Proctor. Of course, the questions were clear and clearly understood by Proctor. The whole meaning of Captain Proctor's affidavit was that the questions and answers were prearranged and that by this prearrangement Court and jury were misled with terrible harm to the defendants.

2. Judge Thayer then inquires whether there was anything "unfair or improper" in the questions put by the District Attorney and whether they did not "invite Captain Proctor to state his true opinion at that time." Here again the entire point of Proctor's affidavit was perverted. The questions and answers are significant, not in themselves, but because of the prearrangement to ask and to answer them. The issue is the propriety of this prearrangement between the District Attorney and Captain Proctor and the effect of this prearrangement upon the jury's mind.

3. The Judge next asks why Captain Proctor did not, in answer to the question put to him, say that he had found no "affirmative evidence whatever that this so-called mortal bullet had passed through this particular Sacco's pistol." This is another amazing twist of the meaning of the Proctor affidavit. Captain Proctor swore that by prearrangement with the District Attorney the direct question whether he had found such evidence was avoided and a question formulated which would enable him to mislead the jury as it misled the Court. If the "direct question" had been put to him he would, as he says, have been obliged to answer in the negative and thereby, of course, would have disastrously affected the Commonwealth's case.

4. The Judge is extraordinarily versatile in misinterpreting the true purport of the Proctor affidavit. Thus, he seriously asks why, if Captain Proctor at the trial was "desirous of expressing his true opinion," he used the phrase "consistent with," language selected by himself. The crux of the Proctor motion was that Captain Proctor at the trial was not "desirous of expressing his true opinion," that the District Attorney was very desirous that he should not do so, and that between them they agreed on a form of words to avoid it.

5. Judge Thayer thus indicates the real question in issue:

I am asked to believe that when Captain Proctor testified in court to the effect that when he said it was consistent with being fired through the Sacco pistol, he intended to mean that it might have been fired through any .32 calibre Colt automatic, and that was all.

The affidavits of Proctor, Katzmann, and Williams leave no doubt of what was intended. It was arranged that the jury should understand that Proctor meant that in his opinion the bullet had passed through Sacco's pistol. Proctor knew and the District Attorney knew, but they did not intend the jury to know, that he had found no evidence in support of that opinion.

6. The Court then proceeds to charge Mr. Thompson with this argument on the strength of the Proctor incident:

That the District Attorney, knowing that Captain Proctor honestly believed that the mortal bullet was not fired through the Sacco pistol, by prearrangement with Captain Proctor prevailed on him to compromise the truth, in that Captain Proctor should testify that it was his opinion that it was consistent with its having been fired through the Sacco pistol. In other words, that Captain Proctor, by prearrangement (which means intentional) compromised the truth with the District Attorney by his (Captain Proctor's) testifying knowingly to something that was false.

Here again the Court tortures the Proctor material out of shape. No one suggested that Captain Proctor "honestly believed that the mortal bullet was not fired through the Sacco pistol." What he says he believed, and what nobody denies he believed, was that there was no evidence whatever to show it was fired through that pistol and not some other Colt automatic pistol of the same caliber. Nor did Mr. Thompson contend that Proctor testified "knowingly to something that was false." A more subtle mischief was involved in the prearrangement between the District Attorney and Proctor. Proctor used language which was true in one sense but false in the meaning it conveyed to those not privy to the arrangement. It was hoped that it would be understood in the false sense and it *was* understood in the false sense by the Judge himself in charging the jury. Formal accuracy was consciously resorted to as a means of misleading the Court and jury.

7. The Judge next tries to belittle the significance of the Proctor incident by seeking to reduce Proctor's qualifications and authority as an expert, two years after he was offered by the Commonwealth with elaborate reliance as a most important expert. We cannot go into the details of numerous misstatements of incontrovertible fact by which the Judge thus seeks to escape the harm that Proctor wrought on the jury's

mind. We must dwell, however, on one amazing statement of the Court. "With his limited knowledge," says Judge Thayer,

Captain Proctor did not testify that the mortal bullet did pass through Sacco's pistol, but that from his examination of the facts it was simply consistent with it.

Why did not Judge Thayer say this to the jury when he charged them with determining the guilt or innocence of Sacco, instead of discovering that it is what Captain Proctor testified, more than three years after the verdict of the jury found him guilty? Why did the Judge charge the jury that Captain Proctor *did* testify that the mortal bullet passed through Sacco's pistol? And why, having in October 1924, for the purpose of denying the Proctor motion, minimized the Proctor testimony by saying that Proctor testified that the passing of the mortal bullet through Sacco's pistol was "simply consistent with" the facts, does he two years later, in order to show how strong the case was at the original trial, state that the "experts testified in their judgment it [the mortal bullet] was *perfectly* consistent with" having been fired through the Sacco pistol? In his charge Judge Thayer misled the jury by maximizing the Proctor testimony as the prearrangement intended that it should be maximized. When the prearrangement was discovered and made the basis of a motion for a new trial, Judge Thayer depreciated Proctor's qualifications as an expert and minimized Proctor's actual testimony. Finally, when confronted with new evidence pointing not only away from Sacco and Vanzetti but positively in another direction, in order to give the appearance of impressiveness to the facts before the jury, Judge Thayer again relies upon the weightiness of Proctor's expert testimony and maximizes his evidence at the trial, but not to the extent that he did in charging the jury, because Proctor's affidavit now prevents him from so doing.

8. The battledore-and-shuttlecock method is further illustrated by the Court's treatment of his own understanding of Captain Proctor's testimony at the trial as indicated by his charge:

It is not the duty of the Court, in charging a jury, to deal with the weight and probative effect of testimony of witnesses.

True! But the Court assumed it to be his duty to state the testimony and that is what Judge Thayer undertook to do in this case. Presumably the Court stated to the jury the effect of Captain Proctor's testimony as he understood it at the time and as it was intended by Captain Proctor and the District Attorney that it should be understood. Certainly the jury could have been in no possible doubt as to how Captain Proctor's testimony lay in Judge Thayer's mind.

9. Finally, Judge Thayer characterized the affidavits of Katzmann and Williams as "clear and convincing"; but not a word as to what is made clear by them and of what they convinced the reader. He concludes by saying that he "never observed anything" on the part of Katzmann and Williams "but what was consistent with the highest standard of professional conduct."

This is the attitude of mind which has guided the conduct of this case from the beginning; this is the judge who has, for all practical purposes, sat in judgment upon his own conduct. Having heard Proctor testify at the trial that the fatal bullet was "consistent with having gone through" Sacco's pistol, he charged the jury that Proctor had in effect testified it did go through. Having read the uncontradicted affidavit of Proctor that he could not have testified, and did not mean to testify, that the mortal bullet was Sacco's, he denies the motion for retrial, partly because the questions that were put to Proctor and the answers that were given were unequivocal. Having decided that the Proctor incident was unimportant, two years later in reviewing the whole case he nevertheless changes his own interpretation of the testimony of Proctor from the damaging form in which he gave it to the jury. Even now, however, instead of quoting the language of Proctor, that the fatal bullet "was consistent with being fired through the Sacco pistol," Judge Thayer gives the testimony as *"perfectly* consistent."

.   .   .   .

In an opinion of sixty pages handed down on May 12, 1926, the Supreme Judicial Court of Massachusetts found "no error" in any of the rulings of Judge Thayer, and so the verdicts were allowed to stand. It is important to realize what issues were argued before the Court and decided by it, and what issues were not presented to the Court or passed upon because outside the scope of its authority. A distinction familiar to every lawyer must be emphasized because Judge Thayer has since misconstrued what the Court did. The guilt or innocence of the defendants was not retried in the Supreme Judicial Court. That Court could not even inquire whether the facts as set forth in the printed record justified the verdict. Such would have been the scope of judicial review had the case come up before the New York Court of Appeals or the English Court of Criminal Appeal. In those jurisdictions a judgment upon the facts as well as upon the law is open, and their courts decide whether convictions should stand in view of the whole record. A much more limited scope in reviewing convictions prevails in Massachusetts. What is reviewed, in effect, is the conduct of the trial judge; only so-called questions of law are open. For instance, it was a question of law, and therefore subject to review by the Supreme Judicial Court, whether evidence should be admitted to prove that at the time Goodridge was testifying on behalf of the Commonwealth the District Attorney let him go unpunished in a case of larceny to which he had pleaded guilty; whether any inference of self-interest discrediting Goodridge's testimony of identification should be drawn would be a question of fact for the jury, and so outside the Supreme Court's power to review.

The merits of the legal questions raised by the Goodridge and other exceptions cannot be discussed here. Suffice it to say, with all deference, that some of the Supreme Judicial Court rulings are puzzling in the extreme. One question of law, however, can be explained within small compass, and that is the question which is the crux of the case: Did Judge Thayer observe the standards of Anglo-American justice? In legal parlance, was there "abuse of judicial discretion" by Judge Thayer? This is the theme which permeates the whole opinion of the Court. Recurring again and again we find such phrases as "this ruling also was within the discretionary power of the Court," "no abuse of discretion is shown." What, then, is "judicial discretion"? Is it a technical conception? Is it a legal abracadabra, or does it imply standards of conduct within the comprehension of the laity in whose interests they are enforced? The present Chief Justice of Massachusetts has given an authoritative definition:

> Discretion in this connection means a sound judicial discretion, enlightened by intelligence and learning, controlled by sound principles of law, of firm courage combined with the calmness of a cool mind, free from partiality, not swayed by sympathy nor warped by prejudice nor moved by any kind of influence save alone the overwhelming passion to do that which is just. It may be assumed that conduct manifesting abuse of judicial discretion will be reviewed and some relief afforded.*

* *Davis* v. *Boston Elevated Ry.,* 235 Mass. 482, 496-7.

This is the test by which Judge Thayer's conduct must be measured. The Supreme Judicial Court found no abuse of judicial discretion on the record presented at the first hearing before it. In other words, the Court was satisfied that throughout the conduct of the trial and the proceedings that followed it Judge Thayer was governed by "the calmness of a cool mind, free from partiality, not swayed by sympathy nor warped by prejudice nor moved by any kind of influence save alone the overwhelming passion to do that which is just."

The reader has now had placed before him fairly, it is hoped, however briefly, the means of forming a judgment. Let him judge for himself!

CHAPTER VI

Hitherto the defense has maintained that the circumstances of the case all pointed away from Sacco and Vanzetti. But the deaths of Parmenter and Berardelli remained unexplained. Now the defense has adduced new proof, not only that Sacco and Vanzetti did *not* commit the murders, but also, positively, that a well-known gang of professional criminals *did* commit them. Hitherto a new trial has been pressed because of the character of the original trial. Now a new trial has been demanded because an impressive body of evidence tends to establish the guilt of others.

Celestino F. Madeiros, a young Portuguese with a bad criminal record, was in 1925 confined in the same prison with Sacco. On November 18, while his appeal from a conviction of murder committed in an attempt at bank robbery was pending in the Supreme Court, he sent to Sacco through a jail messenger the following note:

> I hear by confess to being in the South Braintree shoe company crime and Sacco and Vanzetti was not in said crime.
>
> CELESTINO F. MADEIROS

The confession of a criminal assuming guilt for a crime laid at another's door is always suspect, and rightly so. But, as we cannot too strongly insist, the new evidence is not *contained in* the Madeiros confession. His note to Sacco was only the starting point which enabled the defense to draw the network of independent evidence around the Morelli gang of Providence.

As soon as Sacco's counsel was apprized of this note he began a searching investigation of Madeiros's claim. It then appeared that Madeiros had tried several times previously to tell Sacco that he knew the real perpetrators of the Braintree job, but Sacco, fearing he was a spy who tried to ensnare him, as Sacco well might, had disregarded what he said. An interview with Madeiros revealed such circumstantiality of detail that his examination, both by the defense and the Commonwealth, was plainly called for. Several affidavits given by Madeiros and a deposition of one hundred pages, in which he was cross-examined by the District Attorney, tell the following story.

In 1920 Madeiros, then eighteen years old, was living in Providence. He already had a criminal record and was associated with a gang of Italians engaged in robbing freight cars. One evening, when they were talking together in a saloon in Providence, some members of the gang invited him to join them in a pay-roll robbery at South Braintree. A holdup was a new form of criminal enterprise for him, but they told him "they had done lots of jobs of this kind" and persuaded him to come along. As an eighteen-year-old novice he was to be given only a subordinate part. He was to sit in the back of a car with a revolver and "help hold back the crowd in case they made a rush." Accordingly a few days later, on April 15, 1920, the plan was carried into execution. In the party, besides Madeiros, were three Italians and a "kind of a slim fellow with light hair," who drove the car. In order to prevent identification they adopted the familiar device of using two cars. They started out in a Hudson, driving to some woods near Randolph. They then exchanged the Hudson for a Buick brought them by another member of the gang. In the Buick they proceeded to South Braintree, arriving there about noon. When the time came the actual shooting was done by the oldest of the Italians, a man about forty, and one other. The rest of the party remained near by in the automobile. As the crime was being committed they drove up, took aboard the murderers and the money, and made off. They drove back to the Randolph woods, exchanged the Buick again for the Hudson, and returned to Providence. The arrangement was that Madeiros should meet the others in a saloon at Providence the following night to divide the spoils. Whether this arrangement was kept and whether he got any of the Braintree loot Madeiros persistently refused to say.

This refusal was in pursuance of Madeiros's avowed policy. From the outset he announced his determination not to reveal the identity of his associates in the Braintree job, while holding nothing back which seemed to implicate himself alone. To shield them he obstinately declined to answer questions and, if necessary, frankly resorted to lies. Thus, examination could not extort from him the surnames of the gang, and he further sought to cover up their identity by giving some of them false Christian names. He showed considerable astuteness in evading what he wanted to conceal. But in undertaking to tell the story of the crime without revealing the criminals he set himself an impossible task. In spite of his efforts, a lawyer as resourceful as Mr. Thompson was able to elicit facts which, when followed up, established the identity of the gang and also strongly corroborated the story of Madeiros.

Madeiros said that the gang "had been engaged in robbing freight cars in Providence." Was there such a gang whose composition and activities verified Madeiros's story and at the same time explained the facts of the Braintree crime? There was the Morelli gang, well known to the police of Providence and New Bedford as professional criminals, several of whom at the time of the Braintree murders were actually under indictment in the United States District Court of Rhode Island for stealing from freight cars. Five out of nine indictments charging shoe thefts were for stealing consignments from *Slater and Morrill at South Braintree* and from Rice and Hutchins, the factory next door. In view of their method of operations, the gang must have had a confederate at Braintree to spot shipments for them. The Slater and Morrill factory was about one hundred yards from the South Braintree railroad station and an accomplice spotting shipments would be passed by the paymaster on his weekly trip. It will be recalled that the pay roll was that of the Slater and Morrill factory and that the murders and the robbery occurred in front of the Slater and Morrill and Rice and Hutchins factories. The Morellis under indictment were out of jail awaiting trial. They needed money for their defense; their only source of income was crime. They were at large until May 25, when they were convicted and sent to Atlanta.

Madeiros did not name the gang, but described the men who were with him at Braintree. How did his descriptions fit the Morelli gang? The leader of the gang was Joe, aged thirty-nine. His brothers were Mike, Patsy, Butsy, and Fred. Other members were Bibba Barone, Gyp the Blood, Mancini, and Steve the Pole. Bibba Barone and Fred Morelli were in jail on April 15, 1920. According to Madeiros there were five, including himself, in the murder car, three of whom were

Italians, and the driver "Polish or Finland or something northern Europe." The shooting was done by the oldest of the Italians, a man of about forty and another called Bill. A fourth Italian brought up the Buick car for exchange at Randolph. As far as his descriptions carry, Madeiros's party fits the members of the Morelli gang. But the testimony of independent witnesses corroborates Madeiros and makes the identification decisive. One of the gravest difficulties of the prosecution's case against Sacco and Vanzetti was the collapse of the Government's attempt to identify the driver of the murder car as Vanzetti. It will be recalled that the District Attorney told the jury that "they must be overwhelmed with the testimony that when the car started it was driven by a light-haired man, who gave every appearance of being sickly." Steve the Pole satisfies Madeiros's description of the driver as well as the testimony at the trial. To set the matter beyond a doubt two women who were working in the Slater and Morrill factory identified Steve the Pole as the man they saw standing for half an hour by a car outside their window on that day. Two witnesses who testified at the trial identified Joe Morelli as one of the men who did the shooting and another identified Mancini. The Morellis were American-born, which explains the testimony at the trial that one of the bandits spoke clear and unmistakable English, a thing impossible to Sacco and Vanzetti.

Plainly the personnel of the Morelli gang fits the Braintree crime. What of other details? The mortal bullet came out of a 32 Colt; Joe Morelli had a 32 Colt at this time; Mancini's pistol was of a type and caliber to account for the other five bullets found in the victims. The "murder car" at the trial was a Buick. Madeiros said a Buick was used; and Mike Morelli, according to the New Bedford police, at this time was driving a Buick, which disappeared immediately after April 15, 1920. In fact, the police of New Bedford, where the Morelli gang had been operating, suspected them of the Braintree crime, but dropped the matter after the arrest of Sacco and Vanzetti. Shortly after the Braintree job, Madeiros was sent away for five months for larceny of an amount less than $100. But immediately after his release, he had about $2800 in bank, which enabled him to go on a pleasure trip to the West and Mexico. The $2800 is adequately accounted for only as his share of the Braintree booty: the loot was $15,776.51, and according to his story there were six men in the job. Joe Morelli, we know, was sent to Atlanta for his share in the robbery of the Slater and Morrill shoes.

While confined he made an arrangement with a fellow prisoner whereby the latter was to furnish him with an alibi if he ever needed it, placing Morelli in New York on April 15, 1920.

Even so compressed a précis of the evidence of many witnesses will have made it clear that the defense has built up a powerful case, without the resources at the command of the State in criminal investigations. The witnesses other than Madeiros of themselves afford strong probability of the guilt of the Morellis. What of the intrinsic credibility of Madeiros's confession, which if believed, settles the matter? A man who seeks to relieve another of guilt while himself about to undergo the penalty of death does not carry conviction. The circumstances of Madeiros's confession, however, free it from the usual suspicion and furnish assurances of its trustworthiness. Far from having nothing to lose by making the confession, Madeiros stood to jeopardize his life. For while, to be sure, at the time of his confession he was under sentence for another murder, an appeal from this conviction was pending, which was in fact successful in getting him a new trial. Could anything be more prejudicial to an effort to reverse his conviction for one crime than to admit guilt for another? So clearly prejudicial in fact was his confession that by arrangement with the District Attorney it was kept secret until after the outcome of his appeal and the new trial which followed it. Moreover, the note of confession sent by Madeiros to Sacco on November 18 was not, as we have seen, his first communication to Sacco. Nor was it his first explicit confession. The murder for which he had been convicted, together with a man named Weeks,—the Wrentham bank crime,—was a holdup like the Braintree job. Weeks, under life sentence in another jail, when questioned, revealed that in planning the Wrentham job Madeiros drew on his experience at Braintree. During their partnership Madeiros, he said, frequently referred to the Braintree job, saying it was arranged by the Morelli gang (whom Weeks knew), and at one time identifying a speak-easy in which they found themselves as the one the gang visited before the Braintree holdup. In planning the Wrentham job Madeiros further told Weeks that he "had had enough of the Buick in the South Braintree job." Before the Wrentham crime he had talked to the couple who kept the roadhouse where for a time he was a "bouncer" of his part in the Braintree crime, and said "that he would like to save Sacco and Vanzetti because he knew they were perfectly innocent."

These earlier disclosures by Madeiros refute the theory that he was led to make his latest confession by the hope of money. It is suggested that in November 1925 he had seen the financial statement of the Sacco-Vanzetti Defense Committee. But the State conceded that there was no evidence that "aid of any description had been promised to Madeiros" on behalf of the defendants. Secondly, he could not have had knowledge of this statement before he talked to Weeks and the others, and when he attempted the prior communications to Sacco, because it was not then in existence. It is incredible that a man fighting for his life on a charge for one murder would, in the hope of getting money, falsely accuse himself of another murder. He knew the danger of a confession, for his conviction in the Wrentham case largely rested upon confessions made by him. Why should he be believed and suffer death when he confesses one crime and not be believed when he confesses another of the same character? Is not his own statement in accordance with the motives even of a murderer?

I seen Sacco's wife come up here [jail] with the kids and I felt sorry for the kids.

In the light of all the information now available, which is the more probable truth: that Sacco and Vanzetti or the Morelli gang were the perpetrators of the Braintree murders? The Morelli theory accounts for all members of the Braintree murder gang; the Sacco-Vanzetti theory for only two, for it is conceded that if Madeiros was there, Sacco and Vanzetti were not. The Morelli theory accounts for all the bullets found in the dead men; the Sacco-Vanzetti theory for only one out of six. The Morelli explanation settles the motive, for the Morelli gang were criminals desperately in need of money for legal expenses pending their trial for felonies, whereas the Sacco-Vanzetti theory is unsupported by any motive. Moreover Madeiros's possession of $2800 accounts for his share of the booty, whereas not a penny has ever been traced to anybody or accounted for on the Sacco-Vanzetti theory. The Morelli story is not subject to the absurd premise that professional holdup men who stole automobiles at will and who had recently made a haul of nearly $16,000 would devote an evening, as did Sacco and Vanzetti the night of their arrest, to riding around on suburban street cars to borrow a friend's six-year-old Overland. The character of the Morelli gang fits the opinion of police investigators and the inherent facts of the situation, which tended to prove that the crime was the work of professionals, whereas the past character and record of Sacco and Vanzetti have always made it incredible that they should spontaneously become perpetrators of a bold murder, executed with the utmost expertness. A good worker regularly employed at his trade but away on a particular day which is clearly accounted for, and a dreamy fish peddler, openly engaged in political propaganda, neither do nor can suddenly commit an isolated job of highly professional banditry.

Can the situation be put more conservatively than this? Every reasonable probability points away from Sacco and Vanzetti; every reasonable probability points toward the Morelli gang.

Surely, no jury of disinterested and informed lawyers would hesitate for a moment to hold that, if the evidence concerning the Braintree crime and the Morelli gang came before a magistrate, he would be bound to commit for the action of a grand jury; that a grand jury would clearly be justified in presenting a true bill against them; and that on trial a judge would submit such facts for a jury's verdict. The jury that tried and convicted Sacco and Vanzetti had no such facts before it; a jury trying them would in every likelihood find in the new facts controlling considerations for ascertaining the guilt or innocence of Sacco and Vanzetti.

How did these facts appear to Judge Thayer?

CHAPTER VII

At the outset, the scope of Judge Thayer's duty toward the motion for a new trial based upon this new evidence must be kept in mind. It was not for him to determine the guilt of the Morellis or the innocence of Sacco and Vanzetti; it was not for him to weigh the new evidence as though he were a jury, determining what is true and what is false. Judge Thayer's duty was the very narrow one of ascertaining whether here was new material fit for a new jury's judgment. May honest minds, capable of dealing with evidence, reach a different conclusion, because of the new evidence, from that of the first jury? Do the new facts raise debatable issues? Could another jury, conscious of its oath and conscientiously obedient to it, reach a verdict contrary to the one that was reached on a record wholly different from the present, in view of evidence recently discovered and not adducible by the defense at the time of the original trial? To all these questions Judge Thayer says, "No." This amazing conclusion he reached after studying the motion "for several weeks without interruption," and set forth in an opinion of 25,000 words! One can wish for nothing more than that every reader who has proceeded thus far should study the full text of this latest Thayer opinion. Space precludes its detailed treatment here. To quote it, to analyze it, adequately to comment upon would require a volume in itself. Having now put the materials for detailed judgment at the disposal of readers, space permits only a few summary observations.

By what is left out and by what is put in, the uninformed reader of Judge Thayer's opinion would be wholly misled as to the real facts of the case. Speaking from a considerable experience as a prosecuting officer, whose special task for a time it was to sustain on appeal convictions for the Government, and whose scientific duties since have led to the examination of a great number of records and the opinions based thereon, I assert with deep regret, but without the slightest fear of disproof, that certainly in modern times Judge Thayer's opinion stands unmatched, happily, for discrepancies between what the record discloses and what the opinion conveys. His 25,000-word document cannot accurately be described otherwise than as a farrago of misquotations, misrepresentations, suppressions, and mutilations. The disinterested inquirer could not possibly derive from it a true knowledge of the new evidence that was submitted to him as the basis for a new trial. The opinion is literally honeycombed with demonstrable errors, and infused by a spirit alien to judicial utterance. A study of the opinion in the light of the record led the conservative *Boston Herald,* which long held the view that the sentence against these men should be carried out, to a frank reversal of its position:—

As months have merged into years and the great debate over this case has continued, our doubts have solidified slowly into convictions, and reluctantly we have found ourselves compelled to reverse our original judgment. We hope the Supreme Judicial Court will grant a new trial on the basis of the new evidence not yet examined in open court. . . . We have read the full decision in which Judge Webster Thayer, who presided at the original trial, renders his decision against the application for a new trial, and we submit that it carries the tone of the advocate rather than the arbitrator.

Commenting on the restraint of the *Herald's* characterization of Judge Thayer's opinion, Dr. Morton Prince writes that any expert psychologist reading the Thayer opinion "could not fail to find evidences that portray strong personal feeling, poorly concealed, that should have no place in a judicial document." One or two illustrations must suffice. Mr. William G. Thompson is one of the leaders of the Boston bar. He has brought to the defense of these men the vigor of mind and the force of character which have given him his commanding position in the profession. Judge Thayer, however, thus characterized Mr. Thompson's activities in behalf of these two Italians:

> Since the trial before the Jury of these cases, a new type of disease would seem to have developed. It might be called "lego-psychic neurosis" or hysteria which means: "a belief in the existence of something which in fact and truth has no such existence."

And this from a judge who gives meretricious authority to his self-justification by speaking of the verdict which convicted these men as "approved by the Supreme Judicial Court of this Commonwealth"! The Supreme Court never approved the verdict; nor did it pretend to do so. The Supreme Court passed on technical claims of error, and "finding no error the verdicts are to stand." Judge Thayer knows this, but laymen may not. Yet Judge Thayer refers to the verdict as "approved by the Supreme Judicial Court."

No wonder that Judge Thayer's opinion has confirmed old doubts of the guilt of these two Italians and aroused new anxieties concerning the resources of our law to avoid grave miscarriage of justice. The courageous stand taken by the *Boston Herald* has enlisted the support of some of the most distinguished citizens of Massachusetts. President Comstock of Radcliffe College; Dr. Samuel M. Crothers; Mrs. Margaret Deland, the novelist; Professor W. E. Hocking, the philosopher; Mr. John F. Moors; Professor Samuel E. Morison, the historian; President Neilson of Smith College; Mr. Reginald H. Smith, author of *Justice and the Poor;* Dean Sperry of the Harvard Theological School; Professor Frank W. Taussig, the economist, are among those who have asked for a dispassionate hearing on all the facts. The *Independent* has thus epitomized this demand:

> Because of the increasing doubt that surrounds the question of the guilt of these men, springing from the intrinsic character of Judge Thayer's decision, and instanced by the judgment of the *Herald* editorial writer and other observers whose impartiality is unquestioned, we strongly hope that a new trial will be granted. It is important to note that the appeal is being made on the basis of new evidence never passed on before by the Supreme Court.

No narrow, merely technical, question is thus presented. The Supreme Judicial Court of Massachusetts will be called upon to search the whole record in order to determine whether Judge Thayer duly observed the traditional standards of fairness and reason which govern the conduct of an Anglo-American judge, particularly in a capital case. This Court has given us the requirements by which Judge Thayer's decision is to be measured and the tests which it will use in determining whether a new trial shall be granted. Nor must a new trial be withheld, where in justice it is called for, because thereby encouragement will be given to improper demands for a new trial. For, as the Chief Justice of Massachusetts has announced, courts cannot close "their eyes to injustice on account of facility of abuse."

With these legal canons as a guide, the outcome ought not to be in doubt.

I have sought to give in perspective, and so far as possible through the mouths of judge and witnesses, the facts of a particular case which has attracted world-wide attention, and not to call into question the Anglo-American system of criminal justice in general, or that of Massachusetts in particular. American criminal procedure has its defects. That we know on the authority of all who have made a special study of its working. But its essentials have behind them the vindication of centuries. Only ignorant and uncritical minds will find in an occasional striking illustration of its fallibilities an attack upon its foundations or lack of loyalty to its purposes. All systems of law, however wise, are administered through men, and therefore may occasionally disclose the frailties of men. Perfection may not be demanded of law, but the capacity to correct errors of inevitable frailty is the mark of a civilized legal mechanism. Grave injustices, as a matter of fact, do arise even under the most civilized systems of law and despite adherence to the forms of procedure intended to safeguard against them.

By way of illustration let us recall three striking instances in which the machinery of the criminal law worked injustice which was later corrected. The effectiveness of English criminal justice is properly held up to us for our imitation. Yet it was that system which, in a case turning on identification, sent Adolf Beck to prison for five years, although it was subsequently established that Beck was as innocent of the crime as the judge who sentenced him. It was this grave miscarriage of justice which led, in 1907, to the establishment of the English Court of Criminal Appeal, with its very wide power of revision of criminal cases. In 1922 a Chinese student named Wan was convicted of murder in the courts of the city of Washington. The Court of Appeals of the District of Columbia (ordinarily the final court of appeal in such cases) affirmed the conviction. Luckily the Supreme Court of the United States, doubtless influenced by the intervention of Mr. John W. Davis, exercised its prerogative of grace and allowed an appeal. The Court then unanimously found both the trial court and the Court of Appeals in error, reversed the conviction, and ordered a new trial because of a singularly abhorrent resort by the police to "third degree" methods in extorting confessions from the Chinaman. Wan was twice put on trial, twice thereafter the juries refused to convict, and the Government thereupon quashed the indictments; and Wan—after seven years in jail under harrowing circumstances—was given his liberty. It should be noted that the review exercised by the Supreme Court in this case is seldom assumed by that Court. But for this unusual intervention Wan would have been executed, despite all the formal observances of the criminal procedure of the District of Columbia; and high-minded men and women, without opportunity or time to exercise independent judgment on the case, would have assumed that the trial court and the Court of Appeals of the District of Columbia had served as ample safeguards against an unwarranted hanging carried out under the forms of law. Finally, last year the Governor of New Jersey pardoned an Italian named Morello convicted of murdering his wife because later investigation showed that a fatally wrong meaning was given to his testimony through misunderstandings of the interpreter. The efforts that were made to secure revision of judicial judgment in the Beck case, in the Wan case, and in the Morello case in no wise imply an attempt to undermine the necessary safeguards of society against crime in England, or in the District of Columbia, or in New Jersey. Rather do they reveal confidence in our institutions and their capacity to rectify errors. They also serve to warn against too marked an assumption that, because ordinarily the criminal machinery affords ample safeguards against perversions of justice, a situation may not arise where extraordinary circumstances have deflected the operation of the normal procedure.

[EDITOR'S NOTE: A few months after Mr. Frankfurter's analysis of their case was written, Sacco and Vanzetti were put to death. On the eve of their execution Vanzetti wrote the following letter to Sacco's son]:

August 21, 1927. From the Death House
of Massachusetts State Prison

My Dear Dante:

I still hope, and we will fight until the last moment, to revindicate our right to live and to be free, but all the forces of the State and of the money and reaction are deadly against us because we are libertarians or anarchists.

I write little of this because you are now and yet too young to understand these things and other things of which I would like to reason with you.

But, if you do well, you will grow and understand your father's and my case and your father's and my principles, for which we will soon be put to death.

I tell you now that all that I know of your father, he is not a criminal, but one of the bravest men I ever knew. Some day you will understand what I am about to tell you. That your father has sacrificed everything dear and sacred to the human heart and soul for his fate in liberty and justice for all. That day you will be proud of your father, and if you come brave enough, you will take his place in the struggle between tyranny and liberty and you will vindicate his (our) names and our blood.

If we have to die now, you shall know, when you will be able to understand this tragedy in its fullest, how good and brave your father has been with you, your father and I, during these eight years of struggle, sorrow, passion, anguish and agony.

Even from now you shall be good, brave with your mother, with Ines and with Susie [friend of Mrs. Sacco]—brave, good Susie—and do all you can to console and help them.

I would like you to also remember me as a comrade and friend to your father, your mother and Ines, Susie and you, and I assure you that neither have I been a criminal, that I have committed no robbery and no murder, but only fought modestly to abolish crimes from among mankind and for the liberty of all.

Remember Dante, each one who will say otherwise of your father and I, is a liar, insulting innocent dead men who have been brave in their life. Remember and know also, Dante, that if your father and I would have been cowards and hypocrits and rinnegetors of our faith, we would not have been put to death. They would not even have convicted a lebbrous dog; not even executed a deadly poisoned scorpion on such evidence as that they framed against us. They would have given a new trial to a matricide and abitual felon on the evidence we presented for a new trial.

Remember, Dante, remember always these things; we are not criminals; they convicted us on a frame-up; they denied us a new trial; and if we will be executed after seven years, four months and seventeen days of unspeakable tortures and wrong, it is for what I have already told you; because we were for the poor and against the exploitation and oppression of the man by the man.

The documents of our case, which you and other ones will collect and preserve, will prove to you that your father, your mother, Ines, my family and I have sacrificed by and to a State Reason of the American Plutocratic reaction.

The day will come when you will understand the atrocious cause of the above written words, in all its fullness. Then you will honor us.

Now Dante, be brave and good always. I embrace you.

P.S. I left the copy of *An American Bible* to your mother now, for she will like to read it, and she will give it to you when you will be bigger and able to understand it. Keep it for remembrance. It will also testify to you how good and generous Mrs. Gertrude Winslow has been with us all. Good-bye Dante.

Bartolomeo

Stephen Crane

:

AN ELOQUENCE OF GRIEF

The windows were high and saintly, of the shape that is found in churches. From time to time a policeman at the door spoke sharply to some incoming person. "Take your hat off!" He displayed in his voice the horror of a priest when the sanctity of a chapel is defied or forgotten. The courtroom was crowded with people who sloped back comfortably in their chairs, regarding with undeviating glances the procession, and its attendant and guardian policemen, that moved slowly inside the spear-topped railing. All persons connected with a case went close to the magistrate's desk before a word was spoken in the matter, and then their voices were toned to the ordinary talking strength. The crowd in the courtroom could not hear a sentence; they could merely see shifting figures, men that gestured quietly, women that sometimes raised an eager eloquent arm. They could not always see the judge, although they were able to estimate his location by the tall stands surmounted by white globes that were at either hand of him. And so those who had come for curiosity's sweet sake wore an air of being in wait for a cry of anguish, some loud painful protestation that would bring the proper thrill to their jaded, world-weary nerves—wires that refused to vibrate for ordinary affairs.

Inside the railing the court officers shuffled the various groups with speed and skill; and behind the desk the magistrate patiently toiled his way through mazes of wonderful testimony.

In a corner of this space devoted to those who had business before

145

the judge, an officer in plain clothes stood with a girl that wept constantly. None seemed to notice the girl, and there was no reason why she should be noticed, if the curious in the body of the courtroom were not interested in the devastation which tears bring upon some complexions. Her tears seemed to burn like acid, and they left fierce pink marks on her face. Occasionally the girl looked across the room, where two well-dressed young women and a man stood waiting with the serenity of people who are not concerned as to the interior fittings of a jail.

The business of the court progressed, and presently the girl, the officer, and the well-dressed contingent stood before the judge. Thereupon two lawyers engaged in some preliminary fire-wheels, which were endured generally in silence. The girl, it appeared, was accused of stealing fifty dollars' worth of silk clothing from the room of one of the well-dressed women. She had been a servant in the house.

In a clear way, and with none of the ferocity that an accuser often exhibits in a police-court, calmly and moderately, the two young women gave their testimony. Behind them stood their escort, always mute. His part, evidently, was to furnish the dignity, and he furnished it heavily, almost massively.

When they had finished, the girl told her part. She had full, almost Afric lips, and they had turned quite white. The lawyer for the others asked some questions, which he did—be it said, in passing—with the air of a man throwing flowerpots at a stone house.

It was a short case and soon finished. At the end of it the judge said that, considering the evidence, he would have to commit the girl for trial. Instantly the quick-eyed court officer began to clear the way for the next case. The well-dressed women and their escort turned one way and the girl turned another, toward a door with an austere arch leading into a stone-paved passage. Then it was that a great cry rang through the courtroom, the cry of this girl who believed that she was lost.

The loungers, many of them, underwent a spasmodic movement as if they had been knifed. The court officers rallied quickly. The girl fell back opportunely for the arms of one of them, and her wild heels clicked twice on the floor. "I am innocent! Oh, I am innocent!"

People pity those who need none, and the guilty sob alone; but, innocent or guilty, this girl's scream described such a profound depth of woe, it was so graphic of grief, that it slit with a dagger's sweep the curtain of commonplace, and disclosed the gloom-shrouded specter that sat in the young girl's heart so plainly, in so universal a tone of the mind, that a man heard expressed some far-off midnight terror of his own thought.

The cries died away down the stone-paved passage. A patrolman leaned one arm composedly on the railing, and down below him stood an aged, almost toothless wanderer, tottering and grinning.

"Plase, yer honor," said the old man as the time arrived for him to speak, "if ye'll lave me go this time, I've niver been dhrunk befoor, sir."

A court officer lifted his hand to hide a smile.

Henry James

:

CONTEMPORARY NOTES ON
WHISTLER v. RUSKIN

The London public is never left for many days without a *cause célèbre* of some kind. The latest novelty in this line has been the suit for damages brought against Mr. Ruskin by Mr. James Whistler, the American painter, and decided last week. Mr. Whistler is very well known in the London world, and his conspicuity, combined with the renown, of the defendant and the nature of the case, made the affair the talk of the moment. All the newspapers have had leading articles upon it, and people have differed for a few hours more positively than it had come to be supposed that they could differ about anything save the character of the statesmanship of Lord Beaconsfield. The injury suffered by Mr. Whistler resides in a paragraph published more than a year ago in that strange monthly manifesto called *Fors Clavigera,* which Mr. Ruskin had for a long time addressed to a partly edified, partly irritated, and greatly amused public. Mr. Ruskin spoke at some length of the pictures at the Grosvenor Gallery, and, falling foul of Mr. Whistler, he alluded to him in these terms:

"For Mr. Whistler's own sake, no less than for the protection of the purchaser, Sir Coutts Lindsay ought not to have admitted works into the gallery in which the ill-educated conceit of the artist so nearly approached the aspect of wilful imposture. I have seen and heard much of cockney impudence before now, but never expected to hear a coxcomb ask 200 guineas for flinging a pot of paint in the public's face."

Mr. Whistler alleged that these words were libellous, and that, coming from a critic of Mr. Ruskin's eminence, they had done him, professionally, serious injury; and he asked for £1,000 damage. The case had a two days' hearing, and it was a singular and most regrettable exhibition. If it had taken place in some Western American town, it would have been called provincial and barbarous; it would have been cited as an incident of a low civilization. Beneath the stately towers of Westminster it hardly wore a higher aspect.

A British jury of ordinary tax-payers was appealed to decide whether Mr. Whistler's pictures belonged to a high order of art, and what degree of "finish" was required to render a picture satisfactory. The painter's singular canvases were handed about in court, and the counsel for the defense, holding one of them up, called upon the jury to pronounce whether it was an "accurate representation" of Battersea Bridge. Witnesses were summoned on either side to testify to the value of Mr. Whistler's productions, and Mr. Ruskin had the honor of having his estimate of them substantiated by Mr. Frith. The weightiest testimony, the most intelligently, and apparently the most reluctantly delivered, was that of Mr. Burne-Jones, who appeared to appreciate the ridiculous character of the process to which he had been summoned (by the defense) to contribute, and who spoke of Mr. Whistler's performance as only in a partial sense of the word pictures—as being beautiful in color, and indicating an extraordinary power of representing the atmosphere, but as being also hardly more than beginnings, and fatally deficient in finish. For the rest the crudity and levity of the whole affair were decidedly painful, and few things, I think, have lately done more to vulgarize the public sense of the character of artistic production.

The jury gave Mr. Whistler nominal damages. The opinion of the newspapers seems to be that he has got at least all he deserved—that anything more would have been a blow at the liberty of criticism. I confess to thinking it hard to decide what Mr. Whistler ought properly to have done, while—putting aside the degree of one's appreciation of his works—I quite understand his resentment. Mr. Ruskin's language quite transgresses the decencies of criticism, and he has been laying about him for some years past with such promiscuous violence that it gratifies one's sense of justice to see him brought up as a disorderly character. On the other hand, he is a chartered libertine—he has possessed himself by prescription of the function of a general scold. His literary bad manners are recognized, and many of his contemporaries have suffered from them without complaining. It would very possibly, therefore, have been much wiser on Mr. Whistler's part to feign indifference. Unfortunately, Mr. Whistler's productions are so very eccentric and imperfect (I speak here of his paintings only; his etchings are quite another affair, and altogether admirable) that his critic's denunciation could by no means fall to the ground of itself. I wonder that before a British jury they had any chance whatever; they must have been a terrible puzzle.

The verdict, of course, satisfies neither party; Mr. Ruskin is formally condemned, but the plaintiff is not compensated. Mr. Ruskin too, doubtless, is not gratified at finding that the fullest weight of his disapproval is thought to be represented by the sum of one farthing.

James McNeill Whistler

:

ON THE TRIAL OF WHISTLER v. RUSKIN

PROLOGUE

Professor John Ruskin in *Fors Clavigera,* July 2, 1877.

"For Mr. Whistler's own sake, no less than for the protection of the purchaser, Sir Coutts Lindsay ought not to have admitted works into the gallery in which the ill-educated conceit of the artist so nearly approached the aspect of wilful imposture. I have seen, and heard, much of cockney impudence before now; but never expected to hear a coxcomb ask two hundred guineas for flinging a pot of paint in the public's face."

JOHN RUSKIN

THE ACTION

Lawsuit for Libel against Mr. Ruskin, Nov. 15, 1878.

In the Court of Exchequer Division on Monday, before Baron Huddleston and a special jury, the case of Whistler *v.* Ruskin came on for hearing. In this action the plaintiff claimed £1000 damages.

Mr. Serjeant Parry and Mr. Petheram appeared for the plaintiff; and the Attorney-General and Mr. Bowen represented the defendant.

MR. SERJEANT PARRY, in opening the case on behalf of the plaintiff, said that Mr. Whistler had followed the profession of an artist for many years, both in this and other countries. Mr. Ruskin, as would be prob-

151

ably known to the gentlemen of the jury, held perhaps the highest position in Europe and America as an art critic, and some of his works were, he might say, destined to immortality. He was, in fact, a gentleman of the highest reputation. In the July number of *Fors Clavigera* there appeared passages in which Mr. Ruskin criticized what he called "the modern school," and then followed the paragraph of which Mr. Whistler now complained, and which was: "For Mr. Whistler's own sake, no less than for the protection of the purchaser, Sir Coutts Lindsay ought not to have admitted works into the gallery in which the ill-educated conceit of the artist so nearly approached the aspect of wilful imposture. I have seen, and heard, much of cockney impudence before now; but never expected to hear a coxcomb ask two hundred guineas for flinging a pot of paint in the public's face." That passage, no doubt, had been read by thousands, and so it had gone forth to the world that Mr. Whistler was an ill-educated man, an impostor, a cockney pretender, and an impudent coxcomb.

MR. WHISTLER, cross-examined by the ATTORNEY-GENERAL, said: "I have sent pictures to the Academy which have not been received. I believe that is the experience of all artists. . . . The nocturne in black and gold is a night piece, and represents the fireworks at Cremorne."

"Not a view of Cremorne?"

"If it were called a view of Cremorne, it would certainly bring about nothing but disappointment on the part of the beholders. (*Laughter.*) It is an artistic arrangement. It was marked two hundred guineas."

"Is not that what we, who are not artists, would call a stiffish price?"

"I think it very likely that that may be so."

"But artists always give good value for their money, don't they?"

"I am glad to hear that so well established. (*A laugh.*) I do not know Mr. Ruskin, or that he holds the view that a picture should only be exhibited when it is finished, when nothing can be done to improve it, but that is a correct view; the arrangement in black and gold was a finished picture, I did not intend to do anything more to it."

"Now, Mr. Whistler. Can you tell me how long it took you to knock off that nocturne?"

. . . "I beg your pardon?" (*Laughter.*)

"Oh! I am afraid that I am using a term that applies rather perhaps to my own work. I should have said, 'How long did you take to paint that picture?' "

"Oh, no! permit me, I am too greatly flattered to think that you apply, to work of mine, any term that you are in the habit of using with reference to your own. Let us say then how long did I take to—'knock off,' I think that is it—to knock off that nocturne; well, as well as I remember, about a day."

"Only a day?"

"Well, I won't be quite positive; I may have still put a few more touches to it the next day if the painting were not dry. I had better say then, that I was two days at work on it."

"Oh, two days! The labor of two days, then, is that for which you ask two hundred guineas!"

"No;—I ask it for the knowledge of a lifetime." (*Applause.*)

"You have been told that your pictures exhibit some eccentricities?"

"Yes; often." (*Laughter.*)

"You send them to the galleries to incite the admiration of the public?"

"That would be such vast absurdity on my part, that I don't think I could." (*Laughter.*)

"You know that many critics entirely disagree with your views as to these pictures?"

"It would be beyond me to agree with the critics."

"You don't approve of criticism then?"

"I should not disapprove in any way of technical criticism by a man whose whole life is passed in the practice of the science which he criticizes; but for the opinion of a man whose life is not so passed I would have as little regard as you would, if he expressed an opinion on law."

"You expect to be criticized?"

"Yes; certainly. And I do not expect to be affected by it, until it becomes a case of this kind. It is not only when criticism is inimical that I object to it, but also when it is incompetent. I hold that none but an artist can be a competent critic."

"You put your pictures upon the garden wall, Mr. Whistler, or hang them on the clothes-line, don't you—to mellow?"

"I do not understand."

"Do you not put your paintings out into the garden?"

"Oh! I understand now. I thought, at first, that you were perhaps again using a term that you are accustomed to yourself. Yes; I certainly do put the canvases into the garden that they may dry in the open air while I am painting, but I should be sorry to see them 'mellowed.' "

"Why do you call Mr. Irving 'an arrangement in black'?"

MR. BARON HUDDLESTON: "It is the picture, and not Mr. Irving, that is the arrangement."

A discussion ensued as to the inspection of the pictures, and incidentally Baron Huddleston remarked that a critic must be competent to form an opinion, and bold enough to express that opinion in strong terms if necessary.

The ATTORNEY-GENERAL complained that no answer was given to a written application by the defendant's solicitors for leave to inspect the pictures which the plaintiff had been called upon to produce at the trial. The WITNESS replied that Mr. Arthur Severn had been to his studio to inspect the paintings, on behalf of the defendant, for the purpose of passing his final judgment upon them and settling that question forever.

Cross-examination continued: "What was the subject of the nocturne in blue and silver belonging to Mr. Grahame?"

"A moonlight effect on the river near old Battersea Bridge."

"What has become of the nocturne in black and gold?"

"I believe it is before you."

The picture called the nocturne in blue and silver was now produced in Court.

"That is Mr. Grahame's picture. It represents Battersea Bridge by moonlight."

BARON HUDDLESTON: "Which part of the picture is the bridge?"

(*Laughter.*) His Lordship earnestly rebuked those who laughed. And witness explained to his Lordship the composition of the picture.

"Do you say that this is a correct representation of Battersea Bridge?"

"I did not intend it to be a 'correct' portrait of the bridge. It is only a moonlight scene, and the pier in the center of the picture may not be like the piers at Battersea Bridge as you know them in broad daylight. As to what the picture represents, that depends upon who looks at it. To some persons it may represent all that is intended; to others it may represent nothing."

"The prevailing color is blue?"

"Perhaps."

"Are those figures on the top of the bridge intended for people?"

"They are just what you like."

"Is that a barge beneath?"

"Yes. I am very much encouraged at your perceiving that. My whole scheme was only to bring about a certain harmony of color."

"What is that gold-colored mark on the right of the picture like a cascade?"

"The 'cascade of gold' is a firework."

A second nocturne in blue and silver was then produced.

WITNESS: "That represents another moonlight scene on the Thames looking up Battersea Reach. I completed the mass of the picture in one day."

The Court then adjourned. During the interval the jury visited the Probate Court to view the pictures which had been collected in the Westminster Palace Hotel.

After the Court had re-assembled the "Nocturne in Black and Gold" was again produced, and MR. WHISTLER was further cross-examined by the ATTORNEY-GENERAL: "The picture represents a distant view of Cremorne with a falling rocket and other fireworks. It occupied two days, and is a finished picture. The black monogram on the frame was placed in its position with reference to the proper decorative balance of the whole."

"You have made the study of Art your study of a lifetime. Now, do you think that anybody looking at that picture might fairly come to the conclusion that it had no peculiar beauty?"

"I have strong evidence that Mr. Ruskin did come to that conclusion."

"Do you think it fair that Mr. Ruskin should come to that conclusion?"

"What might be fair to Mr. Ruskin I cannot answer."

"Then you mean, Mr. Whistler, that the initiated in technical matters might have no difficulty in understanding your work. But do you think now that you could make *me* see the beauty of that picture?"

The witness then paused, and examining attentively the Attorney-General's face and looking at the picture alternately, said, after apparently giving the subject much thought, while the Court waited in silence for his answer:

"No! Do you know I fear it would be as hopeless as for the musician to pour his notes into the ear of a deaf man.

"I offer the picture, which I have conscientiously painted, as being worth two hundred guineas. I have known unbiased people express the opinion that it represents fireworks in a night-scene. I would not complain of any person who might simply take a different view."

The Court then adjourned.

The ATTORNEY-GENERAL, in resuming his address on behalf of the defendant on Tuesday, said he hoped to convince the jury, before his case closed, that Mr. Ruskin's criticism upon the plaintiff's pictures was perfectly fair and *bonâ fide;** and that, however severe it might be, there was nothing that could reasonably be complained of. . . . Let them examine the nocturne in blue and silver, said to represent Battersea Bridge. What was that structure in the middle? Was it a telescope or a fire-escape? Was it like Battersea Bridge? What were the figures at the top of the bridge? And if they were horses and carts, how in the name of fortune were they to get off? Now, about these pictures, if the plaintiff's argument was to avail, they must not venture publicly to express an opinion, or they would have brought against them an action for damages.

After all, Critics had their uses.† He should like to know what would become of Poetry, of Politics, of Painting, if Critics were to be extinguished? Every Painter struggled to obtain fame.

No artist could obtain fame, except through criticism.‡

. . . As to these pictures, they could only come to the conclusion that

---

* "Enter now the great room with the Veronese at the end of it, for which the painter (*quite rightly*) was summoned before the Inquisition of State."—Prof. John Ruskin: *Guide to Principal Pictures, Academy of Fine Arts, Venice.*

† "I have now given up ten years of my life to the single purpose of enabling myself to judge rightly of art . . . earnestly desiring to ascertain, and *to be able to teach,* the truth respecting art; also knowing that this truth was *by time and labor* definitely ascertainable."—Prof. Ruskin: *Modern Painters,* Vol. III.

"Thirdly, that TRUTHS OF COLOR ARE THE LEAST IMPORTANT OF ALL TRUTHS."— Mr. Ruskin, Prof. of Art: *Modern Painters,* Vol. I, Chap. V.

"And that color is indeed a most unimportant characteristic of objects, would be further evident on the slightest consideration. The color of plants is constantly changing with the season . . . but the nature and essence of the thing are independent of these changes. An oak is an oak, whether green with spring, or red with winter; a dahlia is a dahlia, whether it be yellow or crimson; and if some monster hunting florist should ever frighten the flower blue, still it will be a dahlia; but not so if the same arbitrary changes could be effected in its form. Let the roughness of the bark and the angles of the boughs be smoothed or diminished, and the oak ceases to be an oak; but let it retain its universal structure and outward form, and though its leaves grow white, or pink, or blue, or tri-color, it would be a white oak, or a pink oak, or a republican oak, but an oak still."— John Ruskin, Esq., M.A., Teacher and Slade Prof. of Fine Arts: *Modern Painters.*

‡ "Canaletto, had he been a great painter, might have cast his reflections wherever he chose . . . but he is a little and a bad painter."—Mr. Ruskin, Art Critic.

"I repeat there is nothing but the work of Prout which is true, living, or right in its general impression, and nothing, therefore, so inexhaustively *agreeable"* (sic).—J. Ruskin, Art Professor: *Modern Painters.*

they were strange fantastical conceits not worthy to be called works of Art.

. . . Coming to the libel, the Attorney-General said it had been contended that Mr. Ruskin was not justified in interfering with a man's livelihood. But why not? Then it was said, "Oh! you have ridiculed Mr. Whistler's pictures." If Mr. Whistler disliked ridicule, he should not have subjected himself to it by exhibiting publicly such productions. If a man thought a picture was a daub* he had a right to say so, without subjecting himself to a risk of an action.

He would not be able to call Mr. Ruskin, as he was far too ill to attend; but, if he had been able to appear, he would have given his opinion of Mr. Whistler's work in the witness-box.

He had the highest appreciation for *completed pictures;*† and he required from an artist that he should possess something more than a few flashes of genius!‡

Mr. Ruskin entertaining those views, it was not wonderful that his attention should be attracted to Mr. Whistler's pictures. He subjected the pictures, if they chose,§ to ridicule and contempt. Then Mr. Ruskin spoke of "the ill-educated‖ conceit of the artist, so nearly approaching the action of imposture." If his pictures were mere extravagances, how could it redound to the credit of Mr. Whistler to send them to the Grosvenor Gallery to be exhibited? Some artistic gentleman from Manchester, Leeds, or Sheffield might perhaps be induced to buy one of the pictures because it was a Whistler, and what Mr. Ruskin meant was that he might better have remained in Manchester, Sheffield, or Leeds, with his money in his pocket. It was said that the term "ill-educated conceit"

---

* "Now it is evident that in Rembrandt's system, while the contrasts are not more right than with Veronese, the colors are all wrong from beginning to end."—John Ruskin, Art Authority.

† "I was pleased by a little unpretending modern German picture at Dusseldorf, by Bosch, representing a boy carving a model of his sheep dog in wood."—J. Ruskin: *Modern Painters.*

‡ "I have just said that every class of rock, earth, and cloud must be known by the painter with geologic and meteorologic accuracy."—Slade Prof. Ruskin: *Modern Painters.*

§ "Vulgarity, dullness, or impiety will indeed always express themselves through art, in brown and gray, as in Rembrandt."—Prof. John Ruskin: *Modern Painters.*

‖ "It is physically impossible, for instance, rightly to draw certain forms of the upper clouds with a brush; nothing will do it but the palette knife with loaded white after the blue ground is prepared."—John Ruskin, Prof. of Painting.

ought never to have been applied to Mr. Whistler, who had devoted the whole of his life to educating himself in Art;* but Mr. Ruskin's views† as to his success did not accord with those of Mr. Whistler. The libel complained of said also, "I never expected to hear a coxcomb ask two hundred guineas for flinging a pot of paint in the public's face." What was a coxcomb? He had looked the word up, and found that it came from the old idea of the licensed jester who wore a cap and bells with a cock's comb in it, who went about making jests for the amusement of his master and family. If that were the true definition, then Mr. Whistler should not complain, because his pictures had afforded a most amusing jest! *He did not know when so much amusement had been afforded to the‡ British Public as by Mr. Whistler's pictures.* He had now finished. Mr. Ruskin had lived a long life without being attacked, and no one had attempted to control his pen through the medium of a jury. Mr. Ruskin said, through him, as his counsel, that he did not retract one syllable of his criticism, believing it was right. Of course, if they found a verdict against Mr. Ruskin, he would have to cease writing,§ but it would be an evil day for Art, in this country, when Mr. Ruskin would be prevented from indulging in legitimate and proper criticism, by pointing out what was beautiful and what was not.||

* "And thus we are guided, almost forced, by the laws of nature, to do right in art. Had granite been white and marble speckled (and why should this not have been, but by the definite Divine appointment for the good of man?), the huge figures of the Egyptian would have been as oppressive to the sight as cliffs of snow, and the Venus de Medicis would have looked like some exquisitely graceful species of frog."—Slade Professor John Ruskin.

† "The principal object in the foreground of Turner's 'Building of Carthage' is a group of children sailing toy boats. The exquisite choice of this incident . . . is quite as appreciable when it is told, as when it is seen—it has nothing to do with the technicalities of painting; . . . such a thought as this is something far above all art."—John Ruskin, Art Professor: *Modern Painters.*

‡ "It is especially to be remembered that drawings of this simple character [Prout's and W. Hunt's] were made for these same middle classes, exclusively; and even for the second order of middle classes, more accurately expressed by the term 'bourgeoisie.' They gave an unquestionable tone of liberal-mindedness to a sub-urban villa, and were the cheerfullest possible decorations for a moderate-sized breakfast parlor, opening on a nicely mown lawn."—John Ruskin, Art Professor: *Notes on S. Prout and W. Hunt.*

§ "It seems to me, and seemed always probable, that I might have done much more good in some other way."—Prof. John Ruskin, Art Teacher: *Modern Painters,* Vol. V.

|| "Give thorough examination to the wonderful painting, *as such,* in the great Veronese . . . and then, for contrast with its reckless power, and for final image to be remembered of sweet Italian art in its earnestness . . . the Beata Catherine Vigri's St. Ursula. . . . I will only say in closing, as I said of the Vicar's picture

Evidence was then called on behalf of the defendant. Witnesses for the defendant, Messrs. Edward Burne-Jones, Frith, and Tom Taylor.

MR. EDWARD BURNE-JONES called.

MR. BOWEN, by way of presenting him properly to the consideration of the Court, proceeded to read extracts of eulogistic appreciation of this artist from the defendant's own writings.*

The examination of witness then commenced; and in answer to MR. BOWEN, MR. JONES said: "I am a painter, and have devoted about twenty years to the study. I have painted various works, including the 'Days of Creation' and 'Venus's Mirror,' both of which were exhibited at the Grosvenor Gallery in 1877. I have also exhibited 'Deferentia,' 'Fides,' 'St. George,' and 'Sybil.' I have one work, 'Merlin and Vivian,' now being exhibited in Paris. In my opinion complete finish ought to be the object of all artists. A picture ought not to fall short of what has been for ages considered complete finish.

MR. BOWEN: "Do you see any art quality in that nocturne, Mr. Jones?"

MR. JONES: "Yes . . . I must speak the truth, you know" . . . (*Emotion.*)

MR. BOWEN: ! . . . "Yes. Well, Mr. Jones, what quality do you see in it?"

MR. JONES: "Color. It has fine color, and atmosphere."

MR. BOWEN: "Ah. Well, do you consider detail and composition essential to a work of Art?"

MR. JONES: "Most certainly I do."

MR. BOWEN: "Then what detail and composition do you find in this nocturne?"

MR. JONES: "Absolutely none." †

MR. BOWEN: "Do you think two hundred guineas a large price for that picture?"

---

in beginning, that it would be well if any of us could do such things nowadays;— and more especially if our vicars and young ladies could."—John Ruskin, Prof. of Fine Art: *Guide to Principal Pictures, Academy of Fine Arts Venice.*

* "Of the estimate which shall be formed of Mr. Jones's own work . . .

"His work, first, is simply the only art-work at present produced in England which will be received by the future as 'classic' in its kind—the best that has been or could be."—Prof. Ruskin: *Fors Clavigera,* July 2, 1877.

† REFLECTION: There is a cunning condition of mind that *requires to know.* On the Stock Exchange this insures safe investment. In the painting trade this would induce certain picture-makers to cross the river at noon, in a boat, before negotiating a Nocturne, in order to make sure of detail on the bank, that honestly the purchaser might exact, and out of which he might have been tricked by the Night!

MR. JONES: "Yes. When you think of the amount of earnest work done for a smaller sum."

Examination continued: "Does it show the finish of a complete work of art?"

"Not in any sense whatever. The picture representing a night scene on Battersea Bridge is good in color, but bewildering in form; and it has no composition and detail. A day or a day and a half seems a reasonable time within which to paint it. It shows no finish—it is simply a sketch. The nocturne in black and gold has not the merit of the other two pictures, and it would be impossible to call it a serious work of art. Mr. Whistler's picture is only one of the thousand failures to paint night. The picture is not worth two hundred guineas."

MR. BOWEN here proposed to ask the witness to look at a picture of Titian,* in order to show what finish was.†

MR. SERJEANT PARRY objected.

MR. BARON HUDDLESTON: "You will have to prove that it is a Titian."

MR. BOWEN: "I shall be able to do that."

MR. BARON HUDDLESTON: "That can only be by repute. I do not want to raise a laugh, but there is a well-known case of 'an undoubted' Titian being purchased with a view to enabling students and others to find out how to produce his wonderful colors. With that object the picture was rubbed down, and they found a red surface, beneath which they thought was the secret, but on continuing the rubbing they discovered a full-length portrait of George III. in uniform!"

The witness was then asked to look at the picture, and he said: "It is a portrait of Doge Andrea Gritti, and I believe it is a real Titian. It shows finish. It is a very perfect sample of the highest finish of ancient art.‡ The

* "I believe the world may see another Titian, and another Raffaelle, before it sees another Rubens."—Mr. Ruskin.

† . . . "The Butcher's Dog, in the corner of Mr. Mulready's 'Butt,' displays, perhaps, the most wonderful, because the most dignified, finish . . . and assuredly the most perfect unity of drawing and color which the entire range of ancient and modern art can exhibit. Albert Durer is, indeed, the only rival who might be suggested."—John Ruskin, Slade Professor of Art: *Modern Painters.*

‡ . . . "I feel entitled to point out that the picture by Titian, produced in the case of Whistler *v.* Ruskin, is an early specimen of that master, and does not represent adequately the style and qualities which have obtained for him his great reputation—one obvious point of difference between this and his more mature work being the far greater amount of finish—I do not say completeness—exhibited in it . . . and as the picture was brought forward with a view to inform the jury as to the nature of the work of the greatest painter, and more especially as to the high finish introduced in it, it is evident that it was calculated to produce an

flesh is perfect, the modeling of the face is round and good. That is an 'arrangement in flesh and blood!' "

The witness having pointed out the excellences of that portrait, said: "I think Mr. Whistler had great powers at first, which he has not since justified. He has evaded the difficulties of his art, because the difficulty of an artist increases every day of his professional life."

Cross-examined: "What is the value of this picture of Titian?"—"That is a mere accident of the saleroom."

"Is it worth one thousand guineas?"—"It would be worth many thousands to me."

MR. FRITH was then examined: "I am an R.A.; and have devoted my life to painting.* I am a member of the Academies of various countries. I am the author of the 'Railway Station,' 'Derby Day,' and 'Rake's Progress.' I have seen Mr. Whistler's pictures, and in my opinion they are not serious works of art. The nocturne in black and gold is not a serious work to me. I cannot see anything of the true representation of water and atmosphere in the painting of 'Battersea Bridge.' There is a pretty color which pleases the eye, but there is nothing more. To my thinking, the description of moonlight is not true. The picture is not worth two hundred guineas. Composition and detail are most important matters in a picture. In our profession men of equal merit differ as to the character of a picture. One may blame, while another praises, a work. I have not exhibited at the Grosvenor Gallery. I have read Mr. Ruskin's works."

Mr. Frith here got down.†

MR. TOM TAYLOR—Poor Law Commissioner, Editor of *Punch,* and so forth—and so forth: "I am an art critic of long standing. I have been engaged in this capacity by the *Times,* and other journals, for the last

---

erroneous impression on their minds, if indeed any one present at the inquiry can hold that those gentlemen were in any way fitted to understand the issues raised therein.—I am, Sir, your obedient servant,

"A. Moore.

"Nov. 28."

Extract of a letter to the Editor of the *Echo.*

* "It was just a toss up whether I became an Artist or an Auctioneer."—W. P. Frith, R.A.

REFLECTION:

He must have tossed up.

REFLECTION:

† A decidedly honest man—I have not heard of him since.

twenty years. I edited the 'Life of Reynolds,' and 'Haydon.' I have *always* studied art. I have seen these pictures of Mr. Whistler's when they were exhibited at the Dudley and the Grosvenor Galleries. The 'Nocturne' in black and gold I do not think a serious work of art." The witness here took from the pockets of his overcoat copies of the *Times,* and, with the permission of the Court, read again with unction his own criticism, to every word of which he said he still adhered. "All Mr. Whistler's work is unfinished. It is sketchy. He, no doubt, possesses artistic qualities, and he has got appreciation of qualities of tone, but he is not complete, and all his works are in the nature of sketching. I have expressed, and still adhere to the opinion, that these pictures only come 'one step nearer pictures than a delicately tinted wallpaper.' " *

This ended the case for the defendant.

Verdict for plaintiff.   Damages one farthing.

ART & ART CRITICS†

The *fin mot* and spirit of this matter seems to have been utterly missed, or perhaps willingly winked at, by the journals in their comments. Their correspondents have persistently, and not unnaturally as writers, seen nothing beyond the immediate case in law—viz., the difference between Mr. Ruskin and myself, culminating in the libel with a verdict for the plaintiff.

Now the war, of which the opening skirmish was fought the other day in Westminster, is really one between the brush and the pen; and involves literally, as the Attorney-General himself hinted, the absolute "raison d'être" of the critic. The cry, on their part, of "Il faut vivre," I most certainly meet, in this case, with the appropriate answer, "Je n'en vois pas la nécessité."

Far from me, at that stage of things, to go further into this discussion than I did, when, cross-examined by Sir John Holker, I contented myself with the general answer, "that one might admit criticism when

---

* REFLECTION: To perceive in Ruskin's army Tom Taylor, his champion—whose opinion he prizes—Mr. Frith, his ideal—was gratifying. But to sit and look at Mr. Burne-Jones, in common cause with Tom Taylor—whom he esteems, and Mr. Frith—whom he respects—conscientiously appraising the work of a *confrère*—was a privilege!!

† Whistler's article on the case of Whistler v. Ruskin.

emanating from a man who had passed his whole life in the science which he attacks." The position of Mr. Ruskin as an art authority we left quite unassailed during the trial. To have said that Mr. Ruskin's prose among intelligent men, as other than a *littérateur,* is false and ridiculous, would have been an invitation to the stake; and to be burnt alive, or stoned before the verdict, was not what I came into court for.

Over and over again did the Attorney-General cry out aloud, in the agony of his cause, "What is to become of painting if the critics withhold their lash?"

As well might he ask what is to become of mathematics under similar circumstances, were they possible. I maintain that two and two the mathematician would continue to make four, in spite of the whine of the amateur for three, or the cry of the critic for five. We are told that Mr. Ruskin has devoted his long life to art, and as a result—is "Slade Professor" at Oxford. In the same sentence, we have thus his position and its worth. It suffices not, Messieurs! a life passed among pictures makes not a painter—else the policeman in the National Gallery might assert himself. As well allege that he who lives in a library must needs die a poet. Let not Mr. Ruskin flatter himself that more education makes the difference between himself and the policeman when both stand gazing in the Gallery.

There they might remain till the end of time; the one decently silent, the other saying, in good English, many high-sounding empty things, like the cracking of thorns under a pot—undismayed by the presence of the Masters with whose names he is sacrilegiously familiar; whose intentions he interprets, whose vices he discovers with the facility of the incapable, and whose virtues he descants upon with a verbosity and flow of language that would, could he hear it, give Titian the same shock of surprise that was Balaam's, when the first great critic proffered his opinion.

This one instance apart, where collapse was immediate, the creature Critic is of comparatively modern growth—and certainly, in perfect condition, of recent date. To his completeness go qualities evolved from the latest lightnesses of to-day—indeed, the *fine fleur* of his type is brought forth in Paris, and beside him the Englishman is but rough-hewn and blundering after all; though not unkindly should one say it, as reproaching him with inferiority resulting from chances neglected.

The truth is, as compared with his brother of the Boulevards, the Briton was badly begun by nature.

To take himself seriously is the fate of the humbug at home, and destruction to the jaunty career of the art critic, whose essence of success lies in his strong sense of his ephemeral existence, and his consequent horror of *ennuyer*ing his world—in short, to perceive the joke of life is rarely given to our people, whilst it forms the mainspring of the Parisian's *savoir plaire.* The finesse of the Frenchman, acquired in long loafing and clever *café* cackle—the glib go and easy assurance of the *petit crevé,* combined with the *chic* of great habit—the brilliant *blague* of the ateliers—the aptitude of their *argot*—the fling of the *Figaro,* and the knack of short paragraphs, which allows him to print of a picture "C'est bien écrit!" and of a subject, "C'est bien dit!"— these are elements of an *ensemble* impossible in this island.

Still, we are "various" in our specimens, and a sense of progress is noticeable when we look about among them.

Indications of their period are perceptible, and curiously enough a similarity is suggested, by their work, between themselves and the vehicles we might fancy carrying them about to their livelihood.

Tough old Tom, the busy City 'Bus, with its heavy jolting and many halts; its steady, sturdy, stodgy continuance on the same old much-worn way, every turning known, and freshness unhoped for; its patient dreary dullness of daily duty to its cheap company—struggling on to its end, nevertheless, and pulling up at the Bank! with a flourish from the driver, and à joke from the cad at the door.

Then the contributors to the daily papers: so many hansoms bowling along that the moment may not be lost, and the *à propos* gone for ever. The one or two broughams solemnly rolling for reviews, while the lighter bicycle zigzags irresponsibly in among them for the happy Halfpennies.

What a commerce it all is, to be sure!

No sham in it either!—no "bigod nonsense!" they are all "doing good"—yes, they all do good to Art. Poor Art! what a sad state the slut is in, and these gentlemen shall help her. The artist alone, by the way, is to no purpose, and remains unconsulted; his work is explained and rectified without him, by the one who was never in it—but upon whom God, always good, though sometimes careless, has thrown away the knowledge refused to the author—poor devil!

The Attorney-General said, "There are some people who would do away with critics altogether."

I agree with him, and am of the irrationals he points at—but let me be clearly understood—the *art* critic alone would I extinguish. That writers should destroy writings to the benefit of writing is reasonable. Who but they shall insist upon beauties of literature, and discard the demerits of their brother *littérateurs?* In their turn they will be destroyed by other writers, and the merry game goes on till truth prevail. Shall the painter then—I foresee the question—decide upon painting? Shall *he* be the critic and sole authority? Aggressive as is this supposition, I fear that, in the length of time, his assertion alone has established what even the gentlemen of the quill accept as the canons of art, and recognize as the masterpieces of work.

Let work, then, be received in silence, as it was in the days to which the penmen still point as an era when art was at its apogee. And here we come upon the oft-repeated apology of the critic for existing at all, and find how complete is his stultification. He brands himself as the necessary blister for the health of the painter, and writes that he may do good to his art. In the same ink he bemoans the decadence about him, and declares that the best work was done when he was not there to help it. No! let there be no critics! they are not a "necessary evil," but an evil quite unnecessary, though an evil certainly.

Harm they do, and not good.

Furnished as they are with the means of furthering their foolishness, they spread prejudice abroad; and through the papers, at their service, thousands are warned against the work they have yet to look upon.

And here one is tempted to go further, and show the crass idiocy and impertinence of those whose dicta are printed as law.

How he of the *Times* has found Velasquez "slovenly in execution, poor in color—being little but a combination of neutral grays and ugly in its forms"—how he grovelled in happiness over a Turner—that was no Turner at all, as Mr. Ruskin wrote to show—Ruskin! whom he has since defended. Ah! Messieurs, what our neighbors call "la malice des choses" was unthought of, and the sarcasm of fate was against you. How Gerard Dow's broom was an example for the young; and Canaletto and Paul Veronese are to be swept aside—doubtless with it. How Rembrandt is coarse, and Carlo Dolci noble—with more of this kind. But what does it matter?

"What does anything matter!" The farce will go on, and its solemnity adds to the fun.

Mediocrity flattered at acknowledging mediocrity, and mistaking mystification for mastery, enters the fog of dilettantism, and, graduating connoisseur, ends its days in a bewilderment of bric-à-brac and Brummagem!

"Taste" has long been confounded with capacity, and accepted as sufficient qualification for the utterance of judgment in music, poetry, and painting. Art is joyously received as a matter of opinion; and that it should be based upon laws as rigid and defined as those of the known sciences, is a supposition no longer to be tolerated by modern cultivation. For whereas no polished member of society is at all affected at admitting himself neither engineer, mathematician, nor astronomer, and therefore remains willingly discreet and taciturn upon these subjects, still would he be highly offended were he supposed to have no voice in what is clearly to him a matter of "Taste"; and so he becomes of necessity the backer of the critic—the cause and result of his own ignorance and vanity! The fascination of this pose is too much for him, and he hails with delight its justification. Modesty and good sense are revolted at nothing, and the millennium of "Taste" sets in.

The whole scheme is simple; the galleries are to be thrown open on Sundays, and the public, dragged from their beer to the British Museum, are to delight in the Elgin Marbles, and appreciate what the early Italians have done to elevate their thirsty souls! An inroad into the laboratory would be looked upon as an intrusion; but before the triumphs of Art, the expounder is at his ease, and points out the doctrine that Raphael's results are within the reach of any beholder, provided he enroll himself with Ruskin or hearken to Colvin in the provinces. The people are to be educated upon the broad basis of "Taste," forsooth, and it matters but little what "gentleman and scholar" undertake the task.

Eloquence alone shall guide them—and the readiest writer or wordiest talker is perforce their professor.

The Observatory at Greenwich under the direction of an Apothecary! The College of Physicians with Tennyson as President! and we know that madness is about. But a school of art with an accomplished *littérateur* at its head disturbs no one! and is actually what the world receives as rational, while Ruskin writes for pupils, and Colvin holds forth at Cambridge.

Still, quite alone stands Ruskin, whose writing is art, and whose art is unworthy his writing. To him and his example do we owe the outrage of proffered assistance from the unscientific—the meddling of the immodest—the intrusion of the garrulous. Art, that for ages has hewn its own history in marble, and written its own comments on canvas, shall it suddenly stand still, and stammer, and wait for wisdom from the passer-by?—for guidance from the hand that holds neither brush nor chisel? Out upon the shallow conceit! What greater sarcasm can Mr. Ruskin pass upon himself than that he preaches to young men what he cannot perform! Why, unsatisfied with his own conscious power, should he choose to become the type of incompetence by talking for forty years of what he has never done!

Let him resign his present professorship, to fill the chair of Ethics at the university. As master of English literature, he has a right to his laurels, while, as the popularizer of pictures he remains the Peter Parley of painting.

John Peter Zenger

:

THE TRIAL OF JOHN PETER ZENGER

When, in 1644, in his *Areopagitica,* John Milton asserted: "Give me the liberty to know, to utter, and to argue freely according to conscience, above all liberties," he was championing the cause of all early newspapermen. Editors spent almost as much time in jail as they did in the printing office. Defoe, a habitué of debtors' jail, was sentenced to a year in Newgate for a satire on religious intolerance. John Wilkes, another stouthearted reporter, was committed to the Tower and expelled from the House of Commons for daring to assert in his newspaper, *The North Briton,* in 1763, that the King, in a speech to Parliament, had not told the truth. American colonial newsmen fared no better. Before coming to this country, Benjamin Harris was pilloried, fined, and imprisoned for criticizing the King. His colonial venture, *Publick Occurrences,* the first newspaper in the English colonies, was suppressed four days after its initial appearance in 1690 for daring to report that the English armed forces had allied themselves with "miserable" savages. When James Franklin, the editor of *The New England Courant,* was jailed for attacking the colonial government, he had his half brother, Ben, then sixteen years old, and destined to be the most famous of colonial editors, carry on the enterprise in his own name. By this flimsy subterfuge he evaded the censors for a time.

None of these early newsmen served the cause of freedom more effectively than did the German immigrant, John Peter Zenger, whose *New-York Weekly Journal,* from its first issue in 1733, infused an independent and even truculent spirit into American colonial journalism. Backed by the ousted chief justice of New York, Lewis Morris, and by two prominent attorneys, James Alexander and William Smith, Zenger proceeded to attack the highhanded administration of Governor William Cosby. With grim, Swiftian humor he

168

published mock advertisements of strayed animals recognizable as political foes. Although the major articles were undoubtedly contributed by his sponsors, Zenger was legally responsible for them. In the fall of 1734 the authorities ordered certain issues of the *Journal* containing doggerel rhymes burned. Arrested and remanded to prison when unable to furnish the excessive bail demanded, Zenger, during his ten months' confinement, arranged to have his paper appear every Monday, the business being managed by his wife, who received her instructions from her husband "through the Hole of the Door of the Prison."

In April term, 1735, Zenger was brought to trial for criminal libel. An information accused him of having declared that the liberties and property of the people of New York were in jeopardy, "men's deeds destroyed, judges arbitrarily displaced, new courts erected without consent of the legislature," trial by jury "taken away when a governor pleases," and men of property "denied the vote." Zenger pleaded not guilty. When his counsel, Smith and Alexander, attacked the judges for their bias, they were promptly disbarred. Then Andrew Hamilton of Philadelphia appeared for the prisoner. Zenger's report of the trial follows:

THE TRIAL OF JOHN PETER ZENGER

A Brief Narrative of the Case and Tryal of John Peter Zenger
(New York, 1736)

MR. HAMILTON: May it please Your Honor; I am concerned in this cause on the part of Mr. Zenger, the defendant. The information against my client was sent me, a few days before I left home, with some instructions to let me know how far I might rely upon the truth of those parts of the papers set forth in the information and which are said to be libelous. And though I am perfectly of the opinion with the gentleman who has just now spoke, on the same side with me, as to the common course of proceedings, I mean in putting Mr. Attorney upon proving that my client printed and published those papers mentioned in the information; yet I cannot think it proper for me (without doing violence to my own principles) to deny the publication of a complaint, which I think is the right of every freeborn subject to make, when the matters so published can be supported with truth; and therefore I'll save Mr. Attorney the trouble of examining his witnesses to that point; and I do (for my client) confess that he both printed and published the two newspapers set forth in the information, and I hope in so doing he has committed no crime.

MR. ATTORNEY: Then if Your Honor pleases, since Mr. Hamilton has confessed the fact, I think our witnesses may be discharged; we have no further occasion for them.

MR. HAMILTON: If you brought them here, only to prove the printing and publishing of these newspapers, we have acknowledged that, and shall abide by it.

MR. CHIEF JUSTICE: Well, Mr. Attorney, will you proceed?

MR. ATTORNEY: Indeed, sir, as Mr. Hamilton has confessed the printing and publishing these libels, I think the jury must find a verdict for the King; for supposing they were true, the law says that they are not the less libelous for that; nay, indeed, the law says their being true is an aggravation of the crime.

MR. HAMILTON: Not so neither, Mr. Attorney, there are two words to that bargain. I hope it is not our bare printing and publishing a paper that will make it a libel. You will have something more to do before you make my client a libeler; for the words themselves must be libelous, that is, *false, scandalous, and seditious* or else we are not guilty.

MR. ATTORNEY: The case before the court is whether Mr. Zenger is guilty of libeling His Excellency the Governor of New York, and indeed the whole administration of the government. Mr. Hamilton has confessed the printing and publishing, and I think nothing is plainer than that the words in the information are *scandalous, and tend to sedition, and to disquiet the minds of the people of this province.* And if such papers are not libels, I think it may be said there can be no such thing as a libel.

MR. HAMILTON: May it please Your Honor; I cannot agree with Mr. Attorney: for though I freely acknowledge that there are such things as libels, yet I must insist at the same time that what my client is charged with is not a libel; and I observed just now that Mr. Attorney, in defining a libel, made use of the words *scandalous, seditious, and tend to disquiet the people;* but (whether with design or not I will not say) he omitted the word *false.*

MR. ATTORNEY: I think I did not omit the word *false.* But it has been said already that it may be a libel notwithstanding it may be true.

MR. HAMILTON: In this I must still differ with Mr. Attorney; for I depend upon it, we are to be tried upon this information now before the court and jury, and to which we have pleaded *Not Guilty,* and by it we are charged with printing and publishing *a certain false, malicious, seditious, and scandalous libel.* This word *false* must have some meaning, or else how came it there?

MR. CHIEF JUSTICE: You cannot be admitted, Mr. Hamilton, to give the truth of a libel in evidence. A libel is not to be justified; for it is nevertheless a libel that it is *true.*

MR. HAMILTON: I am sorry the court has so soon resolved upon that piece of law; I expected first to have been heard to that point. I have not in all my reading met with an authority that says we cannot be admitted to give the truth in evidence upon an information for a libel.

MR. CHIEF JUSTICE: The law is clear that you cannot justify a libel.
(*Hamilton then cites cases to support his contention that the truth of a libel is admissible in evidence.*)
Here the court had the case under consideration a considerable time, and every one was silent.

MR. CHIEF JUSTICE: Mr. Hamilton, the court is of opinion you ought not to be permitted to prove the facts in the papers: these are the words of the book, *"It is far from being a justification of a libel that the contents thereof are true, or that the person upon whom it is made had a bad reputation, since the greater appearance there is of truth in any malicious invective so much the more provoking it is."*

MR. HAMILTON: These are Star Chamber cases, and I was in hopes that practice had been dead with the court.

MR. CHIEF JUSTICE: Mr. Hamilton, the court have delivered their opinion, and we expect you will use us with good manners; you are not to be permitted to argue against the opinion of the court.

MR. HAMILTON: With submission, I have seen the practice in very great courts, and never heard it deemed unmannerly to——

MR. CHIEF JUSTICE: After the court have declared their opinion, it is not good manners to insist upon a point in which you are overruled.

MR. HAMILTON: I will say no more at this time; the court, I see, is against us in this point; and that I hope I may be allowed to say.

MR. CHIEF JUSTICE: Use the court with good manners, and you shall be allowed all the liberty you can reasonably desire.

MR. HAMILTON: I thank Your Honor. Then, gentlemen of the jury, it is to you we must now appeal, for witnesses to the truth of the facts we have offered, and are denied the liberty to prove; and let it not seem strange that I apply myself to you in this manner. I am warranted so to do both by law and reason. The last supposes you to be summoned *out of the neighborhood where the fact is alleged to be committed;* and the reason of your being taken out of the neighborhood is *because you are supposed to have the best knowledge of the fact that is to be tried.* And were you to find a verdict against my client, you must take upon you to say the papers referred to in the information, and which we acknowledge we printed and published, are *false, scandalous, and seditious;* but of this I can have no apprehension. You are citizens of New York; you are really what the law supposes you to be, *honest and lawful men;* and, according to my brief, the facts which we offer to prove were not committed in a corner; *they are notoriously known to be true;* and therefore in your justice lies our safety. And as we are denied the liberty of giving evidence, to prove the truth of what we have published, I will beg leave to lay it down as a standing rule in such cases *that the suppressing of evidence ought always to be taken for the strongest evidence;* and I hope it will have that weight with you.

It is true in times past it was a crime to speak truth, and in that terrible Court of Star Chamber many worthy and brave men suffered for so doing; and yet even in that court, and in those bad times, a great and good man durst say, what I hope will not be taken amiss of me to say in this place, *to wit, the practice of informations for libels is a sword in the hands of a wicked king, and an arrant coward to cut down and destroy the innocent; the one cannot, because of his high station, and the other dares not, because of his want of courage, revenge himself in another manner.*

MR. ATTORNEY: Pray, Mr. Hamilton, have a care what you say, don't go too far neither, I don't like those liberties.

MR. HAMILTON: Sure, Mr. Attorney, you won't make any applications; all men agree that we are governed by the best of kings, and I cannot see the meaning of Mr. Attorney's caution, my well-known principles, and the sense I have of the blessings we enjoy under his present Majesty, makes it impossible for me to err, and, I hope, even to be suspected, in that point of duty to my king. May it please Your Honor, I was saying that notwithstanding all the duty and reverence claimed by Mr. Attorney to men in authority, they are not exempt from observing the rules of common justice, either in their private or public capacities; the laws of our mother country know no exemption.

I hope to be pardoned, sir, for my zeal upon this occasion: it is an old and wise caution *that when our neighbor's house is on fire, we ought to take care of our own.* For though, blessed be God, I live in a government where liberty is well understood and freely enjoyed, yet experience has shown us all (I'm sure it has to me) that a bad precedent in one government is soon set up for an authority in another; and therefore I cannot but think it mine and every honest man's duty that (while we pay all due obedience to men in authority) we ought at the same time to be upon our guard against power, wherever we apprehend that it may affect ourselves or our fellow subjects.

I am truly very unequal to such an undertaking on many accounts. And you see I labor under the weight of many years, and am borne down with great infirmities of body; yet old and weak as I am, I should think it my duty, if required, to go to the utmost part of the land where my service could be of any use in assisting to quench the flame of prosecutions upon informations, set on foot by the government, to deprive a people of the right of remonstrating (and complaining too) of the arbitrary attempts of men in power. Men who injure and oppress the people under their administration provoke them to cry out and complain; and then make that very complaint the foundation for new oppressions and prosecutions. I wish I could say there were no instances of this kind.

But to conclude: the question before the court and you, gentlemen of the jury, is not of small nor private concern, it is not the cause of a poor printer, nor of New York alone, which you are now trying. No! It may in its consequence affect every freeman that lives under a British government on the Main of America. It is the best cause. It is the cause of liberty; and I make no doubt but your upright conduct this day will not only entitle you to the love and esteem of your fellow citizens; but every man who prefers freedom to a life of slavery will bless and honor you as men who have baffled the attempt of tyranny, and, by an impartial and uncorrupt verdict, have laid a noble foundation for securing to ourselves, our posterity, and our neighbors that to which nature and the laws of our country have given us a right —the liberty both of exposing and opposing arbitrary power (in these parts of the world, at least) by speaking and writing truth.

MR. CHIEF JUSTICE: Gentlemen of the jury. The great pains Mr. Hamilton has taken to show how little regard juries are to pay to the opinion of the judges, and his insisting so much upon the conduct of some judges in trials of this kind, is done, no doubt, with a design that you should take but very little notice of what I may say upon this occasion. I shall therefore only observe to you that, as the facts or words in the information are confessed: the only thing that can come in question before you is whether the words, as set forth in the information, make a libel. And that is a matter of law, no doubt, and which you may leave to the court. But I shall trouble you no further with anything more of my own, but read to you the words of a learned and upright judge in a case of the like nature.

"To say that corrupt officers are appointed to administer affairs is certainly a reflection on the government. If people should not be called to account for possessing the people with an ill opinion of the government, no government can subsist. For it is necessary for all governments that the people should have a good opinion of it. And nothing can be worse to any government than to endeavor to procure animosities; as to the management of it, this has been always looked upon as a crime, and no government can be safe without it be punished."

MR. HAMILTON: I humbly beg Your Honor's pardon; I am very much misapprehended if you suppose what I said was so designed.

Sir, you know I made an apology for the freedom I found myself under a necessity of using upon this occasion. I said there was nothing personal designed; it arose from the nature of our defense.

The jury withdrew, and in a small time returned, and being asked by the clerk whether they were agreed of their verdict, and whether John Peter Zenger was guilty of printing and publishing the libels in the information mentioned, they answered by Thomas Hunt, their foreman: *Not Guilty.* Upon which there were three huzzas in the hall, which was crowded with people, and the next day I was discharged from my imprisonment.

Since in those days the common law strictly construed criminal libel ("the greater the truth, the greater the libel"), Hamilton's plea for the right of the jury to inquire into the truth or falsity of the libel took the issue from hostile court to friendly jury. Zenger's acquittal may therefore be considered the first great victory for the freedom of the press, and it foreshadowed many later jury verdicts of "not guilty of publishing." His account of the trial aroused tremendous interest both in the colonies and in Great Britain and went through numerous editions. Ben Franklin's *Poor Richard* endorsed the verdict. However, it took another half century before the British government enacted into law the precedent established in the case—the right of the jury in seditious libel to judge the truth of the matter published.

—NOTES BY LOUIS SNYDER AND
RICHARD MORRIS

Lloyd Paul Stryker

:

THE TRIAL OF QUEEN CAROLINE

from *For the Defense*

On June 6, the very day Caroline arrived at Dover, her husband sent a message to the House of Lords. . . . "The King thinks it necessary," he wrote, "in consequence of the arrival of the Queen, to communicate to the House of Lords certain papers respecting the conduct of Her Majesty since her departure from this kingdom, which he recommends to the immediate and serious attention of this House." He had the fullest confidence, he said, that the Lords would now adopt "that course of proceeding which the justice of the case and the honor and dignity of His Majesty ever may require."

It was two hundred and eighty-seven years since any English king had taken such a step. In 1533 Henry VIII, having failed to secure a divorce from Catherine of Aragon by the Papal Court, compelled an English court to grant it, and three years later forced a jury of her peers to convict Anne Boleyn of adultery and send her to her death. Now another English king was seeking for his wife the combined fates of Catherine of Aragon and Anne Boleyn; for the adultery of a queen was grounds not only for divorce but for a conviction of high treason, the penalty for which was death.

Small wonder that the plain people of England were aroused at the prospect of this threatened tragedy. Small wonder, too, that Henry Brougham, knowing, as only able lawyers know, how uncertain is the prospect of a litigation, knowing also of the mass of evidence collected at Milan, fearing that with so much smoke some fire might be discovered, and aware as well that his case would come before a servile House of Peers, had advised his client not to face the risks. Nor was it strange that a woman of her courage had misunderstood, resented what she felt to be the counsel of timidity, and, womanlike, mistrusted him.

Not long after she arrived in London a drunken messenger (one of Wood's election agents) found Denman in the lobby of the House of Commons and summoned him to the Queen's presence. Going instantly to the alderman's house in South Audley Street, he conferred there with his famous client, thinking at that time he might be her only lawyer, but completely loyal to his confrere. After paying him some general compliments, the Queen proceeded with great animation: "If they wished me to stay abroad, why not leave me there in peace? No woman could submit to the insults they have offered." The conduct of the Ministers, she said, had forced her to come back to England. "And so here I am."

She expressed her exasperation against Brougham. Like many of her sex, it was clear that she would not prove too tractable a client.

Denman obtained her permission to bring Brougham back to dinner and hurried off to Berkeley Square to insure his coming. Here, Denman wrote later, "in the most alarming manner he laid open to me all his apprehension on the subject of the Queen's case. He had received from various quarters the most sinister reports, and with too much credulity. I shall never forget the tone and manner with which he said to me, at the close of a long series of awkward statements, 'So now we are in for it, Mr. Denman.'" Both proceeded to South Audley Street for their conference with the Queen. When they had finished, she suffered Brougham to leave first, and, detaining Denman, said to him: "He is afraid."

"She was certainly right," Denman later wrote, "but his fears were on her account, not on his own."

At the close of Denman's narrative of these events his memoirs proceed: "Let me here state, once for all, that from this moment I am sure that Brougham thought of nothing but serving and saving his client. . . . He felt that the battle must be fought, and resolved to fight it manfully and to the uttermost."

Immediately following the King's message on June 6, a committee of fifteen peers was appointed to examine the contents of the Green Bag.* Erskine became a member of that committee. Liverpool attempted

* Containing evidence against the Queen.

to secure a similar committee in the Commons, and a violent debate ensued. "Is it true," a member named Bennet asked, "that Lord Hutchinson was instructed by the government to persuade the Queen to sell her title for £50,000 sterling?" Wilson, another member, denounced the treatment she had been accorded in foreign courts with the connivance of the English Government. Lord Hamilton excoriated her exclusion from the Liturgy, and asked if it were fitting for the King at one and the same time to constitute himself an accuser and a judge.

Canning, although now President of the Council for India and therefore a member of the Cabinet, came manfully to the Queen's aid. "There was no society in Europe," he said, "of which she would not be the life, grace, and ornament. . . . I for one will never, so help me God, place myself in the situation of her accuser."

During the debates in the House of Commons, Brougham presented a communication from the Queen protesting against the "appointment of a secret tribunal for the examination of documents privately prepared by her adversaries."

It was a moving appeal, but Brougham's own speech overshadowed all else in the debate, and doomed the appointment of an examining committee in the Commons. As he began, the resentment that he felt for Wood's intervention at once displayed itself, and when he referred to the alderman as "Absolute Wisdom," the House shook with laughter. The name stuck. But he had not advanced far in his denunciations of the charges before laughter turned to fear, and fear gave way to terror among the country gentlemen who listened. Half a dozen of them, one after another, rose to implore Lord Castlereagh to drop the whole affair. "Not," wrote Denman, "from any sense of attachment to the despicable King, but because they thought their property might be compromised by the proceeding. They spoke and acted just in the same spirit as when an agricultural tax is to be repealed, or the price of corn raised by Act of Parliament."

Caroline's distrust of Brougham had not yet cooled, nor was it lessened by the proddings of the alderman, of Lady Anne Hamilton, and Dr. Parr. Denman here adds a comment that should be of interest to the wives of all great advocates. Knowing how thoroughly he deserved his client's trust, Brougham's failure thus far to win it had led to a certain coolness on his part, in return reflected by his wife, who failed to call on the returned voyager—a failure that all Whig ladies of quality were also following. "If," wrote Denman, "he had sent Mrs. Brougham

unmistakably at Leach, the great promoter of the Milan Commission, he quoted from *Othello:*

> *"I will be hang'd, if some eternal villain,*
> *Some busy and insinuating rogue,*
> *Some cogging, cozening slave, to get some office,*
> *Have not devised this slander. . . ."*

There was still time for the King's side to yield, but that his supporters had no such idea appeared on July 4, when the secret committee of the Lords reported that the charges made against the Queen required a "special inquiry," and that this inquiry would "best take the form of parliamentary procedure."

On the following day Lord Liverpool introduced the famous "Bill of Pains and Penalties." Its title was: "A Bill to Deprive Her Majesty Caroline Amelia Elizabeth of the Titile, Prerogatives, Rights, Privileges, and Pretentions of Queen Consort of this Realm, and to Dissolve the Marriage between His Majesty and the Said Queen."

Preceding the enacting clause there were four long recitals. "Whereas," the first one ran, "in the year one thousand eight hundred and fourteen, Her Majesty Caroline Amelia Elizabeth, the Princess of Wales and now Queen Consort of this Realm, being at Milan in Italy engaged in her service, in a menial situation, one Bartolomo Bergami, otherwise Bartolomo Pergami, a foreigner of low station, who had before served in a similar capacity":

"And whereas, after the said . . . Bergami had so entered the service of the said . . . Princess of Wales, a most unbecoming and degrading intimacy commenced between Her Royal Highness and the said . . . Bergami":

The third recital set forth that "Her Royal Highness not only advanced the said . . . Bergami to a high situation in her . . . household, and received into her service many of his near relatives . . . but bestowed upon him other great and extraordinary marks of favor and distinction, obtained for him orders of knighthood and titles of honor, and conferred upon him a pretended order of knighthood, which Her Royal Highness had taken upon herself to institute without any just and lawful authority."

The draftsman of this bill was well versed in the art of climax, and thus made the three preceding paragraphs a prelude to the crescendo of the fourth. "And whereas," the fourth recital read, "her said Royal

Highness . . . conducted herself toward the said . . . Bergami . . . both in public and private in the various places and countries which Her Royal Highness visited, with indiscreet and offensive familiarity and freedom, and carried on a licentious, disgraceful, and adulterous intercourse with the said . . . Bergami which continued for a long period of time during her . . . residence abroad. . . ."

Therefore, the bill concluded, "be it enacted . . . that her said Majesty Caroline . . . hereby be deprived of the title of Queen and of all the prerogatives . . . pertaining to her as Queen Consort of this realm . . . and . . . that the marriage between His Majesty and the said Caroline . . . be . . . forever wholly dissolved, annulled, and made void. . . ."

Thus did a servile Ministry succumb to the wishes of their master. Thus did those pliant tools, who but a little earlier had warned the King against the reliability of his proofs, give aid to the most unconscionable libertine in England and the most disloyal husband in the world, against a wife in whose guilt they had expressed themselves as not convinced. They had chosen for him the coward's way. They had selected a procedure whereby the husband would not stand boldly forth as the accuser. There would be no indictment for high treason, no action for divorce, wherein the guilt or innocence of the husband could be brought in question. There would be only an accused, but no accuser.

That which is known to history as the "Trial of Queen Caroline," which we shall presently attend, was in reality no trial at all. But it was decided that her legal advisers, even though members of the House of Commons, would be permitted to be heard and to conduct her defense at the bar of the Lords. "What was usually called the Queen's trial," wrote Denman, "was in form an examination before the House of Lords of the truth of the recitals set forth in the preamble of the Bill of Pains and Penalties." The whole proceeding, wrote Lord Holland, was "anomalous."

Whatever kind of trial it was to be, Caroline was more than ready for the fray. "Adultery," she snorted, when she heard that the bill had been at last introduced. "I am not altogether blameless, for *I have* committed adultery with Mrs. Fitzherbert's husband."

The trial was scheduled to begin on August 17, and as the time approached, popular excitement increased, nor was it diminished by the expected arrival of the witnesses from Italy, nor by the preparations that the government was making to receive them. A large space next

Westminster Bridge was barricaded so as to prevent all access save from the river. Many houses were refurnished and stored with food for the "Italian herd." High walls were run up at the extremity of the gardens so that the London populace might not see the discharged maids and valets who presently would seek to swear away the honor of a Queen.

Upon the completion of these preparations, as gunboats patrolled the river and a military force stood guard at the dock, the first boatload of Italian witnesses was landed at the stairs on July 12. By August 17 the whole company of paid perjurers had arrived, and as they rioted upon the sumptuous fare provided for their pleasure and amused themselves with their national dances, "the London mob," wrote Lord Albemarle, "would howl like a cat round the cage of a canary."

Like other Londoners, both inside and outside the House of Lords, Erskine watched all that was taking place about him. Did he watch, one can but wonder, with a pang of deep regret that in the coming trial his role must be the dull one of a judge instead of that of advocate for an outraged and persecuted woman? Of this, at all events, we may be sure, that it was without jealousy or envy that he beheld the younger lawyers who were now preparing for the role he had filled so gloriously in former years. Or could it be that he would now seize this last opportunity for ingratiating himself with a king whose friendship as a prince he once enjoyed?

It was more than forty years before that the young voice of the unknown Erskine had moved Lord Mansfield in the Baillie case. The voice of an old man, an aged hero of so many legal battlefields, had not lost its power to still his listeners with rapt attention.

"It is a criminal charge," he said, "or it is nothing. Her Majesty is not charged with any specific act of adultery, but with 'an adulterous intercourse'—and this not at any specified time or times, but during her whole absence from England, for six years together—which exposes her to criminating evidence, not only as to acts but general deportment on every one day or hour of the day throughout all that time. . . . This unparalleled generality of accusation creates an unparalleled difficulty of defense and renders a list of witnesses indispensably necessary to the ends of justice."

The words came trippingly as he spoke, and his face shone with the old fire of combat. He was pleading once again for justice. He had pleaded fourteen years before for an unknown shoemaker accused of high treason; with the same fervor he was now speaking for a queen.

"Another analogy," he said, "between this Bill of Pains and Penalties and a trial for high treason arises from the punishment to be inflicted on conviction. What, my Lords, is death, which in a moment ends us, to the lingering and degrading suffering, which the accused may, under our judgment, be sentenced to endure?

"Born a princess," he continued, "of the same illustrious house as the King her consort, and now raised to wear the imperial crown of the greatest nation that ever flourished on the earth—she may suddenly be cast down to shame and sorrow—and not only excluded from the society of her exalted kindred, but forever deprived of the esteem and affection of the whole female world. For my own part, my Lords, this appears to me the heaviest and most intolerable punishment which any human tribunal can inflict."

It was unnecessary for him to remind his fellow peers, although he did so, that he held no bias for the Queen. His early intimacy and friendship for the King when he was still the Prince of Wales would, had he been guided by his leanings, have led him to the King's side. But he said: "The habits of my professional life are, I hope, a useful shield against any bias whatsoever. I was bred in my youth to two professions, the characteristic of which is honor. But after the experience of very many years I can say with truth that they cannot stand higher for honor than the profession of the law."

No lawyer ever loved his own profession more. "Amidst unexampled temptations," he continued, "which through human frailty have produced their victims, the great bulk of the members of it are sound; and the cause is obvious—there is something so beautiful and exalted in the faithful administration of justice, and departure from it is so odious and disgusting, that a perpetual monitor is raised up in the mind against the accesses of corruption."

Pleading now with those who presently would be called upon to judge a queen, he exhorted them to remember that to deny her the plain rights accorded ordinary citizens in lower courts would cast a shadow upon England's fame, and warned them to remember that the powers they held were held in trust. "It may be superstition, perhaps, but I cannot alter the nature and character of my understanding, which, as long as I can look back, has dictated to me as a comforting truth that the *Divine Providence* singles out particular nations and perhaps even individual men, to carry on the slow and mysterious system of the world.

"This island," he went on, "although placed on the very margin of civilization, has been its example and protector, spreading the blessings of a pure religion and of equal laws to the remotest ends of the earth. My impression, my Lords, has always been that such an unparalleled dominion is but a more exalted trust, and that if we fall off from the character which bestowed it, and which fitted us for its fulfillment, we shall deservedly be treated like sentinels who desert, or who sleep upon their posts."

Presently he and all his fellow peers must sit in judgment on this case. "My Lords," he closed, "I have not made these observations from any desire to disappoint or obstruct the course we are engaged in. When the court assembles, I will do my duty as if all the angels of heaven were taking notes of whatever passes through my mind on this subject."

He had finished. An old man sank back into his seat.

With profound respect and in deep silence the House of Lords had heard him through. But it was no impartial jury he was addressing. He was speaking to "a blank wall." Displaying their intent to carry out a preconcerted plan, his motion to furnish the list of witnesses to the Queen was rejected by a vote of 78 to 28.

Ten days later, on July 24, Erskine, undaunted, once again arose, this time to present a communication from the Queen deploring the Lords' failure to grant her a list of witnesses, and praying for "a specification of the place or places in which the criminal acts charged upon her are alleged to have been committed. . . ." This application, like the first, was foredoomed to failure. If she could not gain a sympathetic ear within the House of Lords, however, her unsuccessful pleas did not fall on deaf ears in humbler houses and upon the streets and squares of London. As the hour of her ordeal approached, the fervor of the people mounted, and everywhere, throughout the capital, the air was rent with shouts of "Long live the Queen!"

Nor was the excitement lessened when Queen Caroline addressed a letter to the King, a letter that somehow, and without delay, was printed in the newspapers of the capital. It was written in the best Brougham style and sparkled with the eloquence of a master advocate. "After the unparalleled and unprovoked persecution," it began, "which during a series of years has been carried on against me under the name and authority of Your Majesty . . . it is not without a great sacrifice of private feelings that I now, even in the way of remonstrance, bring myself to address this letter to Your Majesty."

But, she went on: "I cannot refrain from laying my grievous wrongs once more before Your Majesty in the hope that the justice which Your Majesty may, by evil-minded counselors, be still disposed to refuse the claims of a dutiful, faithful, and injured wife, you may be induced to yield to considerations connected with the honor and dignity of your Crown. . . ."

A sense of what was due her character and her sex, she said, forbade her "to refer minutely to the real causes of our domestic separation, or to the numerous unmerited insults offered to me . . . ; but leaving to Your Majesty to reconcile with the marriage vow the act of driving, by such means, a wife from beneath your roof, with an infant in her arms, Your Majesty will permit me to remind you that that act was entirely your own. . . . From the very threshold of Your Majesty's mansion the mother of your child was pursued by spies and traitors, employed, encouraged, and rewarded to lay snares for the feet, and to plot against the reputation and life of her whom Your Majesty had so recently and solemnly vowed to honor, to love, and to cherish."

So long as George III lived, "his unoffending daughter-in-law had nothing to fear." On his death, "To calumniate your innocent wife was now the shortest road to royal favor, and to betray her was to lay the sure foundation of boundless riches and titles of honor."

Each paragraph more eloquent than the last, she continued: "Bereft of parent, brother, and father-in-law, shunned from motives of selfishness by those who were my natural associates, living in obscurity . . . I had one consolation left—the love of my dear and only child. To permit me to enjoy this was too great an indulgence. To see my daughter; to fold her in my arms, to mingle my tears with hers, to receive her cheering caresses, and to hear from her lips assurances of never-ceasing love; thus to be comforted, consoled, upheld, and blessed, was too much to be allowed me."

Bereft of the society of her child, she continued: "I resolved on a temporary absence in the hope that time might restore me to her in happier days. Those days, alas! were never to come. . . . Your Majesty had torn my child from me; you had deprived me of the power of being at home to succor her; you had taken from me the possibility of hearing of her last prayers for her mother. You saw me bereft, forlorn and brokenhearted; and this was the moment you chose for redoubling your persecutions."

There was nothing that could move King George IV, but the people of England read with indignation and profound sympathy this eloquent recital of the Queen's wrongs. "Let the world pass its judgment," she wrote, "on the constituting of a commission, in a foreign country, consisting of inquisitors, spies, and informers, to discover, collect, and arrange matters of accusation against your wife, without any complaint having been communicated to her. Let the world judge of the employment of ambassadors in such business, and of the enlisting of foreign courts in the enterprise; but on the measures which have been adopted to give final effect to those preliminary proceedings it is for me . . . to apprise you of my determination."

And what was that determination? With moving brevity she thus expressed it: "I have always demanded a fair trial. This is what I now demand, and this is refused me. Instead of a fair trial, I am to be subjected to a sentence by the Parliament, passed in the shape of a law. . . . The injustice of refusing me a clear and distinct charge, of refusing me the names of the witnesses, of refusing me the names of the places where the alleged acts have been committed—these are sufficiently flagrant and revolting; but it is against the *Constitution of the Court itself* that I particularly object, and that I most solemnly protest."

How could she expect justice from the House of Lords? "I could expect no justice at its hands. Your Majesty's Ministers have advised this prosecution; they are responsible for the advice they give; they are liable to punishment if they fail to make good their charges; and not only are they a part of my *judges,* but it is they who have *brought in the bill.* It is too notorious that they have always a majority in the House; so that without any other, here is ample proof that the House will decide in favor of the bill and against me."

There were still other reasons why the King's Ministers could marshal a majority in this case. "Your Majesty is the *plaintiff,*" she went on; "to you it belongs to appoint and elevate peers. Many of the present peers have been raised to that dignity by yourself, and almost the whole can be, at your will and pleasure, further elevated. The far greater part of the peers hold by themselves and their families, offices, pensions, and other emoluments, solely at the will and pleasure of Your Majesty, and these of course Your Majesty can take away whenever you please. There are more than four fifths of the peers in this situation, and there are many of them who might be thus deprived of the far better part of their incomes. . . . To regard such a body as a *Court of Justice* would be to calumniate that sacred name. . . ."

On this ground, she wrote, "I protest against this species of trial. I demand a court where the jurors are taken impartially from amongst the people; and where the proceedings are open and fair. Such a trial I court, and to no other will I willingly submit. If Your Majesty persevere in the present proceeding, I shall even in the Houses of Parliament face my accusers. But I shall regard any decision they may make against me as not in the smallest degree reflecting on my honor; and I will not, except compelled by actual force, submit to any sentence which shall not be pronounced by a *Court of Justice.*"

At last this feminine philippic, though conceived by the masculine brain of Henry Brougham, drew on to its climactic close: "You have cast upon me every shame to which the female character is open. . . . You sent me sorrowing through the world, and even in my sorrow pursued me with unrelenting persecution. Having left me nothing but my innocence, you would now, by a mockery of justice, deprive me even of the reputation of possessing that. The poisoned bow and the poignard are means more manly than perjured witnesses and partial tribunals; and they are less cruel, inasmuch as life is less valuable than honor."

And then this final thrust: "If my life would have satisfied Your Majesty, you should have had it on the sole condition of giving me a place in the same tomb with my child. But since you would send me dishonored to the grave, I will resist the attempt with all the means that it shall please God to give me."

This just jeremiad against the cad who sat upon the throne of England, this passionate plea for simple English justice, was, of course, of no avail with him to whom it was addressed. To plain Englishmen, already seething with good English hatred of oppression, the letter of the Queen was like oil poured on a roaring furnace.

Five days later the Princess Lieven sat writing to her lover: "In a few days there will be a serious crisis in this country. The Queen's trial begins next week. The Opposition believes there will be a revoultion. . . . There are fears of serious trouble."

The trial so long awaited began at last on the seventeenth of August, and all London that morning had eyes and ears for nothing else. It was not only London that was watching. In Moscow and Vienna, in

Rome, in Paris, and The Hague, even in the far-distant America of James Monroe, men waited feverishly for the news. The whole world was watching.

There had been rioting and disorder in the capital for many weeks, but now a large force of soldiers had been brought to town. In private homes adjoining both Houses of Parliament more troops were in reserve. Wooden beams a foot square had been made into strong barricades across the street between St. Margaret's Church and the Court of King's Bench, and there were heavy wooden barriers to block off all the streets that led to the Houses of Parliament. Between these barricades men of the Royal Guard, assisted by innumerable constables sworn in for this purpose, formed themselves into a living fence. Large bodies of infantry and cavalry patrolled the city.

Even this display of force was not enough to curb the populace. The experience of the Princess Lieven on that morning was typical of all who sought an access to the trial. "The crowd was terrific," she wrote. "I was stopped and they wanted me to shout 'Long live the Queen!' and my servants to take off their hats."

Since six in the morning every foot of ground from St. James's Square to the Houses of Parliament was occupied by the expectant throngs, and as the day advanced the restlessness of the people grew.

On their way to the trial, all those known to be hostile to the Queen were booed or mishandled. One of these was the Duke of Wellington. Waterloo was quite forgotten as the crowd watched a known enemy of Caroline proceeding to the House of Lords. "A moment after I passed," wrote Creevey, "I heard an uproar with hissing and shouting. On turning round I saw it was directed against Wellington on horseback."

Patience at last rewarded the excited Londoners for their vigil; a roar of voices all along the route announced the Queen's coming. When at last the six horses of her coach came into sight, ridden by servants in the royal liveries of scarlet and gold with purple velvet caps like those worn by the coachmen of King George III, and as the Queen bowed from the windows of her great state carriage, the exultation of the watching throngs was unrestrained. From ten thousand throats came cries of "God bless Your Majesty!" "We'll give our blood for you," "The Queen or death!" and "May you overcome your enemies!" Behind her coach came carriages containing her supporters. Among these were Mr. Keppel Craven and Sir John Gell who had once been in her service but had left it. They came that morning to disprove the current rumors as to the causes of their departure, and to demonstrate their confidence in her innocence.

Troops were posted along the whole route, and as the procession—for it was such—passed Carlton House, the crowds watched sharply to see whether the soldiers stationed there would present arms. They did so smartly, and seemingly with enthusiasm; and renewed cheering burst forth from the populace.

Meanwhile, the trial had gotten under way in the chamber of the House of Lords. It was a small but lovely room. At one end was the throne with velvet canopies, while on either side were two long balconies, each supported by eight graceful columns. Rounded windows with square panes let in the light of day, while for its evening sessions four great chandeliers of beautiful design hung from the ceilings with their galaxy of wax candles. It was a smaller but more impressive room than the converted chamber of St. Stephen's Chapel so long occupied by the House of Commons.

Underneath the balconies on long benches against the wall two hundred and fifty of the peers of England sat. Sixty had been excused because of age, infirmities, or the profession of the Catholic faith. Directly opposite the throne, and at the extreme end of the room, the tables and seats for counsel were arranged, while immediately in front of these was a gilt-and-crimson chair that had been set apart for the Queen's use. This chair stood vacant as the preliminary motions were attended to. Suddenly from outside came the blare of trumpets, the roll of drums, and human voices swelling ever louder. The Queen was approaching. At last she entered. The Lords rose to their feet as she swept to the chair prepared for her.

She wore a dress of black figured gauze with a high ruff. A black wig with profuse curls was surmounted by a gypsy hat with a huge bow in front. Her face was hidden by a thick white veil of handsome texture. Whatever the women present thought, her costume was not calculated to attract the men, if Creevey's strictures may be credited. And he occupied a point of vantage. With characteristic enterprise, "I got into the Lords," he wrote, "and to a place within two yards of the chair placed for the Queen."

The Duke of Wellington had by this time found his seat, and by every mark of disapprobation open to him was showing his strong disrespect for the accused. "Your friend Wellington," the Princess Lieven wrote to Metternich two days later, "did something in very bad taste.

He was the only person who kept his hat on, during the first hearing, in the Queen's presence."

As the Queen entered, her counsel Denman was on his feet addressing the Lords assembled. "This is undoubtedly a divorce bill," he was saying, "because its result will be that of dissolving the marriage heretofore contracted between the King and Queen, and to confer upon the King freedom to enter upon a fresh marriage. In that case why is the ordinary procedure not followed? Why, then, not make inquiry if the complainant himself comes before the court with clean hands, and if he has a legal right of complaint? . . . If this bill should become law, may it not one of these days perhaps be provocative of the greatest calamity which can befall a nation—I would say of a civil war resulting from a dispute as to the succession of the Crown?"

The Queen was thrilled and everyone was listening with amazement as her counsel launched into this bold peroration: "I beg to say, my Lords, that whatever may be enacted, whatever may be done by the exertions of any individual, by the perversion of truth or by the perjury of witnesses, whatever may be the consequences which may follow, and whatever she may suffer—I will for one never withdraw from her those sentiments of dutiful homage and respect which I owe to her rank, to her situation, to her superior mind, to her great and royal heart. Nor, my Lords, will I ever pay to anyone who may usurp Her Majesty's station that respect and duty which belong alone to her whom the laws of God and man have made the consort of his present Majesty, and the Queen of the kingdoms."

"My God, what a beautiful speech!" his client said to him a few hours later. He had good reason to believe also that he had made a strong impression on her judges.

With what cynical contempt Denman's argument was regarded by the Crown lawyers appeared at once when Solicitor General Sir John Singleton Copley, Jr., rose to reply. This Boston-born son of the American painter, who had started his political career in England as an extreme Whig, if not a Jacobin, had lately discovered the more luxuriant fields of the Tory party, and only the year before had been made Solicitor General by the government of Lord Liverpool. He did not intend to stop there. His eyes were focused on the far horizons of ambition. And here in the persecution of the Queen he saw the opportunity for advancing his career. How correct an estimate he made would appear in 1824 when he became Attorney General, in 1826 Master of the

Rolls, and in 1827 when as Lord Lyndhurst, he would be made Chancellor of England.

A sneer played on his lips as he said: "The Queen's counsel appears to imagine that adultery is an action equally culpable in persons of either sex; but this is ludicrously absurd, since in the man adultery is never punished."

All preliminary motions having been decided—of course adversely to the Queen—on Saturday, the nineteenth of August, Lord Chancellor Eldon turning to Sir Robert Gifford said: "Mr. Attorney General, you will proceed to open your case."

With the traditional unction of the prosecutor he told the Lords, as though with sadness, how heavy was his responsibility of marshaling the evidence that would be offered to support the charges set forth in the preamble of the bill.

With all the minute and traditionally boring detail of a travelogue, he proceeded then to follow the Queen upon her long and endless journeys from the very moment when she arrived in Italy. It was during the first three months of her stay in Milan, he said, that "a person was received into her service whose name occurs in the preamble of this bill, and whose name will frequently occur in the course of these proceedings—a person of the name of Bergami, who was received into her service as a courier, or footman, or *valet de place*."

To the English only is reserved the power of crowding into a single word their class-conscious scorn for the lowborn. With that scorn the word "person" was enunciated by Sir Robert. This "person" and the conduct of Caroline toward him, all the facts of their relationship it would now be, he said, his "melancholy duty to relate." How this servant, who once waited at her table, was finally given a place at it. How the distance between their sleeping chambers was constantly diminished, and the accessibility of the one to the other was constantly increased. The exact condition of the bed linen. How another servant once observed that Bergami's bed "bore evident marks of having been slept in by two persons." How another thought he heard them kissing—these and a hundred other nauseating details occupied the remainder of the day.

On Monday, August 21, the Attorney General continued his arraignment of the Queen. No alleged fact, no minute circumstance was omitted: how one servant had seen Bergami holding Caroline on his knees; how at Carlsruhe another espied Her Majesty sitting on

Bergami's bed with his arms around her neck; how "upon two or three occasions it was observed that either at night or at an unreasonably early hour in the morning, when the rest of the family were retired to rest, Bergami was seen coming from his sleeping apartment and going into that of Her Majesty and there remaining." These things and much else did the Attorney General promise to prove.

Thus had the King's chief law officer rummaged among the polluted contents of the Green Bag, spreading them out with meticulous and all but loving care before the prurient gaze of the peers of England. His speech was well put together, and long before he finished he had so surcharged the chamber of the House of Lords with thoughts of adultery that even the most trifling circumstance began to assume the air of irrefragable and unanswerable truth. He was poisoning the minds of his judges, poisoning them so much, he hoped, that no evidence ever would dislodge ideas so sedulously and insidiously planted.

There was one obstacle that must be overcome: the proof of all his facts would be the testimony of Italian witnesses.

Knowing full well the deep distrust of Anglo-Saxons for the Latin character then prevailing, and that this prejudice was shared by all Englishmen, peers and commoners alike, the Attorney General before he took his seat resolved to break down, if he could, this obstacle. This case, he said, would be proved by those only "whose avocations and humble employments gave them opportunities of seeing the conduct of the parties from time to time and of examining the beds and bedrooms." English servants could not prove this, because they had all abandoned her when at Milan "she seemed anxious to forget that she was or should be an Englishwoman."

Did not a suspicion of foreign witnesses, he asked, amount to saying: "Go abroad, commit what crime you please, you never can be convicted in an English court of justice. And why? Because the fact can only be proved by foreign witnesses; and they, we tell you before we hear them, are branded with infamy."

"Now her danger begins," wrote Creevey, "and I am quite unable to conjecture the degree of damage she will sustain from the publication of this opening. I say degree, because of course it is quite impossible that a very great effect should not be produced upon the better orders of people by the production of this cursed, disgusting narrative, however overstated it may eventually prove to be. . . ."

Just as the Attorney General's opening speech concluded the sound of distant drums announced the Queen's approach. She arrived as the first witness for the Crown was called. It was Theodore Majocchi, who had entered her service as a liveried lackey in the latter part of 1815.

As he advanced to take the oath, the Queen looked at him and exclaimed: "Theodore! No, no!" and then abruptly left the House. Was it surprise or fear that prompted her dramatic outbreak? That night she was copiously bled.

Majocchi spoke Italian only, and so interpreters were required. For the Crown, Di Spinato was sworn for this purpose, and Binetto Cohen for the Queen.

Majocchi was not only the first but the most important witness for the prosecution, and as he stepped forward all eyes were fastened on him. Heavy curls encircled his large head, and luxuriant sideburns seemed to give his face a kind of dignity. He had been a courier of General Pinto, and had then met Bergami who, as *valet de chambre,* had been his fellow servant with three livres a day for his wages. When he entered the Queen's service Bergami was her equerry.

This questioning then ensued:

Q: Can you describe the relative situation of the sleeping rooms of Bergami and the Princess?

A: I remember them.

Q: Describe them.

A: From the room of the Princess to that of Bergami there was a small corridor and a cabinet and immediately on the left there was the bedroom of Bartolomo Bergami.

There was an occasion when Bergami had been kicked by a horse. In consequence of that accident Majocchi had been directed to sleep in that cabinet near the fireplace.

Q: Did you during the nighttime see any person pass through your room?

A: I do remember seeing someone passing.

Q: Did you say there was a fire in the room?

A: Always a fire.

Q: Who was the person who passed through your room?

A: Her Royal Highness.

Q: Describe the manner in which she passed through your room, in what way she walked.

A: Very softly; and when near to my bed stopped to look and then passed on.

Q: After the Princess had entered the bedroom of Bergami, did you hear any conversation or anything else pass between them?
A: Only some whispers.

In endless detail Majocchi was then interrogated as to the sleeping arrangements of the Princess in the various places where she stopped. While in Milan, Bergami and the Queen occupied apartments separated only by a wall.

Q: Was there a staircase or landing place near to these two rooms?
A: There was.

Q: Was there any door that went out of Bergami's apartment on to that landing place?
A: There was a door that led on to this landing place.

Q: Was there also a door that went out of the Princess's apartment to this same staircase?
A: There was.

Q: How far were those doors from each other?
A: About seven or eight feet.

There was a similar proximity of sleeping apartments at the Grande Brittania in Venice, so also at the villa of Villani at Lake Como, and in a house they occupied in Messina and at Syracuse. At Messina, the witness said, he had seen Bergami, on departing on some errand, take the Princess by the hand and kiss her lips.

Q: Do you remember Bergami at any time before going to Syracuse go into the room of the Princess without being entirely dressed?
A: I remember it.

Q: What part of his dress had he on?
A: He had that morning gown on, which Her Royal Highness had given to him, with his stockings and his under small clothes or drawers.

At the Scala Nova he had seen the Princess sitting on the bed of Bergami. On the journey between Acuna and Jerusalem they had slept under the same tent. On their return from Jerusalem they had embarked at Jaffa.

Q: Do you remember on her embarking at Jaffa, on her voyage home, any tent being raised on deck?
A: I do.

Q: What beds were placed under that tent?
A: A sofa.

Q: Was there a bed besides the sofa?
A: A traveling bed.

Q: Of the Princess?

A: A traveling bed of the Princess.

Q: Did the Princess sleep under the tent generally on the voyage from Jaffa home?

A: She slept always under that tent during the whole voyage from Jaffa to the time she landed.

Q: Did anybody sleep under the same tent?

A: Bartolomo Bergami.

Q: That was on the deck?

A: Yes, on the deck.

Q: Did this take place every night?

A: Every night.

Q: Were they shut in, were the sides of the tent drawn in, so as to shut them entirely in?

A: When they went to sleep the whole was enclosed, shut up.

Majocchi had slept in the dining room, he said, directly below the deck where the tent for Bergami and the Queen was pitched.

Q: Did you on any occasion at night, while the Princess and Bergami were in the tent, hear any motion over you?

A: I heard a noise.

Q: What did that noise resemble?

A: The creaking of a bench.

With this and much else Monday's session at last came to an end.

On Tuesday, August 22, the direct examination of Majocchi was continued, and despite her copious bleeding of the night before, the Queen was there to watch him. "I never saw a human being so interesting," Denman later wrote. "Her face was pale, her eyelids a little sunken, her eyes fixed on the ground, with no expression of alarm or consciousness, but with an appearance of decent distress at being made the object of such revolting calumnies, and a noble disdain of her infamous accusers."

Majocchi's direct examination thus far had been devastating in its effect. Yet the increasing peril of the Queen's plight seemed only to increase public sympathy—a sympathy that had grown particularly strong among the troops. After the conclusion of his first day in the witness box "the Guards in their undress trousers and foraging caps," Brougham later wrote, "came to where they supposed the Queen was, or her family and friends, and they said: 'Never mind, it may be going badly; but, better or worse, we are all with you.'"

This and other encouragements, supported by her own strong courage, enabled her to come that day to the House of Lords. Majocchi, under the further proddings of Sir John Copley, added to his previous description of the Queen's sleeping arrangements. Did he remember what they were at Carlsruhe? Ah, yes. And in Nuremburg, Vienna, and Trieste? Yes indeed. In these places as in so many others, according to this ready witness, the rooms of Bergami and the Queen communicated with each other.

Compared with that of the previous day, however, his testimony was relatively unimportant, and much of it was broken up by argument. On one occasion the Solicitor General was proceeding to inquire as to a conversation supposed to have taken place between Bergami and the witness. Here Erskine interposed with the first but by no means the last of his interruptions. "It can have no connection with the case," he said, "if it proceeded from the mouth of Bergami without the presence of the Queen."

Finally, after about half an hour, the direct examination was concluded. The strategy of the Solicitor General has been plain. "Majocchi had been examined in chief," Brougham later wrote, "and Copley had purposely protracted his examination until it was too late for us to take off the effect of his evidence by cross-examination, of which we complained, because it made its impression, unaffected by our attacks the whole of that evening in the House of Lords, and the next day also in the town."

Brougham was not unready for the task of cross-examination, which was suddenly thrust upon him. Shortly before the beginning of the trial the Queen's legal staff had been augmented by the addition of four able lawyers: Lushington, Williams, Wilde, and Tindall. Wilde had been bred as an attorney, a fact enough to damn him in the eyes of any barrister. He had, moreover, been brought into the case by Alderman Wood's influence and without consulting either Brougham or Denman. Despite a handicap so great, "we were no sooner acquainted with him," said Denman, "than our prejudices vanished. He thought of nothing but success, and contributed most largely toward it. Extremely able and acute, generally very judicious, always active and persevering in the highest degree, his habits as an attorney qualified him for many things to which counsel are incompetent."

It was generous praise for a barrister to give. Almost equally so was Brougham's comment: "We always felt that Wilde had been put upon us as more fully trusted by the secret advisers of the Queen then we were.

We very soon found how utterly groundless these suspicions were. . . ."

When, therefore, Tindall and Wilde, along with Denman, called at Brougham's chambers in Lincoln's Inn Fields in the late evening after Majocchi's first day in the box, he received them gladly, although he had already gone to bed. They had with them their own "shorthand writers' " notes, and they had come to offer their suggestions as to the cross-examination. "We went through the different parts of the evidence that most pressed upon us," wrote Brougham, "and they went away. But something further having occurred to them, they came back immediately, and found me fast asleep." The consultation continued, and Brougham tells us that he "undoubtedly profited by their remarks." When at last he heard them through, like the able cross-examiner that he was, he reached the clear conclusion that his work could not follow a set pattern, and that his cross-examination must be guided chiefly by the first answers he received and by the demeanor of the witness as he gave them.

The time had now come. As he stood up to face Majocchi, the witness and the lawyer eyed each other as two fencers will, or prize fighters in the ring. A hush fell on the chamber. All the Lords including Erskine—Erskine especially—leaned forward to observe the contest. There stood the man whose direct testimony, if believed, would damn the Queen forever. The wily Italian had performed well for his masters, and a sneer played on his face, daring Brougham to unhorse him. He had been well schooled. His dark eyes shone like stiletto points. Before him stood the forty-two-year-old Henry Brougham, handsome, strong, and eager for the fray. He had nothing of Majocchi's cunning, but his sinewy Scottish mind was tough and ready.

He was convinced that Majocchi was a conscienceless and well-trained perjurer. Of all witnesses the cross-examiner confronts, the schooled liar is the most difficult. Especially is this true where there is unavailable a single letter or a scrap of paper to rely upon. The only material that Brougham had was the direct examination; that, and the demeanor of the witness. Yet, if his client were to be saved, somehow this imported rascal must be broken down.

In cross-examination, as in the field of pugilism, a knockdown blow, if scored at the very outset, may be decisive of the contest. If, in the first minute, the witness can be forced into a discreditable admission, his confidence may be destroyed. And so Brougham began:

Q: You have told us that you left General Pinto's service; was it not on account of killing a horse, or something of that sort?

A: No.

Q: You never killed a horse at all?

A: Never, never; oh, never.

Q: You never told anyone you had?

A: Never, never.

Three questions, and all failures! Then three more about Majocchi's reasons for quitting that employ; and again failure. The Italian's confidence was gaining. The attack must be shifted to another quarter. Turning suddenly from the subject of his previous questions, Brougham asked: "At the second table of the Queen's house at Naples, the table of the gentlemen, did not Sir William Gell's servant sit also?" It was an innocuous and seemingly innocent question, and the witness answered: "I do not remember." His actual words were: *"Non mi ricordo."*

There was a lilt and music in those words. *"Non mi ricordo"* rang through the crowded chamber. They rang, too, in Henry Brougham's brain, and brought an inspiration with them. The wily Majocchi had testified for many hours upon direct examination; he had remembered everything: names, dates, places, and the exact arrangement of the various sleeping quarters—*everything that could be made adverse to the Queen.* His memory had been perfect. It was perfect as to all the facts on which he had been carefully prepared. But, if he really remembered them, he must remember others of the same kind as well. If not, why not? Why, save for the reason that he did not in truth remember what he had been swearing to, but was repeating a prepared and well-drilled narrative.

Here was an opening. Brougham must approach it carefully. His next question was: "Do you remember another English servant of Mr. Craven, another of the gentlemen of Her Royal Highness's suite dining at that table?" And the answer came: "I do not remember that." So far so good; but Brougham wanted a repetition of the first answer in the same words: *"Non mi ricordo."* He plied Majocchi as to his memory of the names of other servants; he remembered them. And then: "In the Princess's house at Naples, where did William Austin sleep?" And the answer: *"Non mi ricordo."*

Q: Will you swear that he did not sleep in the next room to Her Royal Highness?

A: That I cannot remember.

Then many questions as to the passages between Bergami's and the Princess's rooms in Naples. On his direct examination Majocchi swore that there was but one corridor between the rooms and that it passed through the cabinet in which he slept. The Lords remembered well his graphic narrative of how the Queen came through that cabinet at midnight; "very softly." She had been willing then, if this were true, to risk detection only because there was no other way in which to hold this deep nocturnal rendezvous. Brougham now asked if there were not some other passage, knowing that if there had been the unlikelihood of the Queen not using it would stamp the witness as a perjurer. For several questions the witness answered persistently: "I have seen no other passage," and then finally: "There might have been, but I have seen no other."

Brougham was gradually gaining.

Q: Will you swear that if a person wished to go from the Princess's room, he or she could not go any other way than through the cabinet in which you slept?

A: There was another passage to go into the room of Bergami.

Q: Without going through the cabinet where you slept?

A: Yes.

And then:

Q: Where did Hieronimus sleep in this house?

A: *Non mi ricordo.*

Q: Where did Sir William Gell's servant sleep?

A: *Non mi ricordo.*

Q: And you do not remember where Mr. Craven's servant slept neither, I take for granted?

A: *Non mi ricordo.*

Brougham knew that he was now succeeding in his purpose. As he later wrote: "I indicated my sense of the advantage I had got which alarmed Denman, and he whispered words of caution. But I felt secure, and then poured question after question into him, and got him to repeat his *non mi ricordo* as often as I chose."

To drive home the words with which the Lords' chamber had so long been echoing, he asked his interpreter to translate *"Non mi ricordo."* The translation was: "I do not remember." He pursued the same strategy still further, asking about the Queen's sleeping arrangements at the Grande Brittania in Venice.

Q: Where did Hieronimus sleep?
A: *Non mi ricordo.*
Q: Was Victorine, Bergami's child, there?
A: *Non mi ricordo.*

In rapid succession more questions and more *"Non mi ricordos."* He now had the witness in his power, and he was slashing him as with a whip. The perjurer was cowering before him. As he cowered, the interpreter intervened, saying: "I do find it difficult to make myself understood; the witness is frightened out of his wits; he does not understand the most common words; I can't make him understand the question."

Brougham moved in, plying and slashing him with his questions, and making him repeat his *"Non mi ricordo,"* till the very galleries rang with the telling words.

The Lords had not forgotten Majocchi's story about the sea trip from Jaffa, where a tent was pitched upon the deck and the Queen and Bergami, according to the witness, had slept under it. And how Majocchi, sleeping on the deck below it, heard the creaking of a bench. Brougham had not forgotten either, and his cross-examination drove into this subject, asking first about the tent on the land journey.

Q: What sort of sofas were they that were put under the tent on those occasions; was not one an iron bedstead and the other a sofa?
A: There was first a Turkish sofa, or rather a sofa placed by the Turks, and then I placed an iron bedstead.
Q: Are you understood rightly that no bedclothes were put upon the sofa?
A: I do not remember that.
Q: Will you swear you ever saw, either on the land journey in Palestine, or on board the ship, during the voyage, one stitch of linen bedclothes, sheets, blankets, or coverlids upon that bed?
A: This I do not recollect.
Q: You have told us how and by whom the bed was made at night; who removed the beds in the morning on the voyage?
A: *Non mi ricordo.*

Another *"Non mi ricordo!"* Brougham pressed him further:

Q: Will you swear that it was not yourself?
A: I do not recollect. In the evening I was ordered to make the bed, and I carried the cushions; then in the morning I was called and took away the cushions; for it was not a matrimonial bed, but they were merely small cushions which I placed when people would rest.

Q: Did you ever happen to see Billy Austin, William Austin, rest under the tent in the same way, on the voyage, or on land?

A: I do not recollect.

Q: Did you ever see Hieronimus rest in the same way in the tent?

A: I do not recollect.

Q: Will you swear that they both of them have not so rested in the tent?

A: I do not recollect.

Q: In the room below the cabin on board the polacre where did Hieronimus sleep in general?

A: I do not recollect.

Q: Where did Mr. Hownam sleep?

A: I do not recollect.

Q: Where did William Austin sleep?

A: I do not remember—*"Non mi ricordo!"*

Majocchi was then forced to swear that during that sea journey he was sick most of the time. "Did you not," Brougham then asked, "when you were ill during the voyage sleep below under the deck?"

The witness answered: "Under the deck."

"In the hold?" shot Brougham with a flash of inspiration, and the witness answered: "Yes, at the bottom of the ship."

That answer spelled destruction for the witness. The impossibility of his hearing from the bottom of the ship the creaking of a bed on deck was self-evident. Self-evident, too, was it that a perjurer had been thrown hard in his tracks.

Having made so palpable a point, Brougham might well have stopped there, but he did not. For the remainder of the day and part of the next he pursued the Italian, never for a moment permitting his spent victim to recover, and driving him from one absurdity to another, forcing him again and again to answer *"Non mi ricordo."*

The retreat of the Italian was now a rout. The battle had become a contest between a red-hot poker and a tallow candle. Majocchi left the witness box discredited and despised. And through every street of London the phrase *"Non mi ricordo"* was repeated with loud shouts of derisive laughter. "Everyone," wrote the Princess Lieven a day or two later, "is using the catchword *'Non mi ricordo.'* "

Mistaking another room for his consultation chamber, Brougham entered it one day to find the Duke of Clarence and Sir Walter Scott in conference. He started to withdraw, but the Duke good-humoredly invited him to come in. Looking at him with a smile, the future King of

England said: "Of one thing I am quite sure: whatever your client may be in other respects, she is not what you have represented her, 'a defense-less woman.' " The conversation then drifted to the *Waverley Novels,* the authorship of which was then unknown, and the Duke began plying Scott with questions on this subject. "Sir," replied Sir Walter, "I must give Your Royal Highness the favorite answer of the day, *'Non mi ricordo.'* "

From the twenty-first of August until the ninth of September the Crown's twenty-six witnesses followed one another to the witness box in rapid succession. Of these all but two were foreigners. Samuel Pechell and Thomas Briggs, both British naval officers and captains respectively of the *Clorinda* and the *Leviathan,* were the only English witnesses, and their evidence was not damaging. With the exception of a German serv-ant at the hotel at Carlsruhe and a French-Swiss waiting woman, all others were Italians.

Lack of space, if not safety of the reader, precludes excursion fur-ther amid soiled sheets and the even more contaminated testimony of paid witnesses. That they were paid, drilled, marshaled, imported, and provided for by the Crown, was sufficiently established by their own admissions.

We have neither time nor inclination to listen to the testimony of Paturzo, Gargiulo, Birillo, Cuchi, or Raggazoni. We may not pause even to watch Louisa Demont, or to hear the devastating cross-examination of her made by associate counsel Williams, whose work of demolition here was as complete as that of Brougham of Majocchi.

Throughout the testimony of these and others of the Crown witnesses, innumerable arguments were made and rulings sought on points of evi-dence, and as a witness stepped up to the box there frequently ensued debate as to the kind of oath by which he should be sworn. In many of these discussions Erskine was engaged, showing increasingly, as the trial proceeded, his sympathy for the accused; and contending always for a rule that would not exclude but would let in the truth. Sometimes his arguments were filled with reminiscence, often they were enriched by precedents established in his own cases many years before. From his place on the Peers' bench he rose when the occasion offered to take part in the fray.

He had not forgotten the healing properties of a smile, or that to raise a laugh will generally alleviate the pressure of the prosecution's case and help despel the somber clouds, with which, as with the coils of a strong net, the prosecutor seeks always to enmesh his victims.

When, therefore, on one occasion the question as to the exact form of oath was argued, Erskine caused his fellow peers to smile as he arose and said: "My Lords, when I was counsel in a cause tried in the Court of King's Bench, an important witness called against me without describing himself to be of any particular sect, so as to be entitled to indulgence stated, that from certain ideas in his own mind he could not swear according to the usual form of the oath; that he would hold up his hand and would swear but that he would not kiss the book. I have no difficulty in saying that I wished very much to get rid of that witness; and I asked what was his reason for refusing to be sworn in the usual form? He gave a reason which seemed to me a very absurd one: 'Because it is written in the "Revelation" that the angel standing on the sea held up his hand.' I said, 'This does not apply to your case; for in the first place you are no angel. Secondly, you cannot tell how the angel would have sworn if he had stood on dry ground as you do.' "

On another occasion, when a debate ensued as to the admission of certain evidence, Erskine said that he had often seen such evidence admitted, and that while his "remembrance might not perhaps be of much avail" unless he were "completely superannuated," he could "not believe that questions were inadmissible which were calculated to elicit the truth." At another point he said that he "could not concur in any practice which had the effect of shutting out evidence capable of throwing light upon the testimony of the witness."

At still another time Erskine referred to the precedents established in the Hardy trial in 1794 where Lord Chancellor Eldon, then Sir John Scott, had conducted the prosecution as the Crown's Attorney General. In reply Eldon said that he had forgotten nearly all the circumstances of the case, except that he had made "a very tedious speech which very nearly killed himself and quite sickened his hearers," and suggested, too, that Erskine had forgotten the main points there. But with his old alertness and no little of his old fire, Erskine retorted tartly that he "remembered all the main features of the case as well as if they had occurred yesterday."

Forever removed from the role of advocate, Erskine, increasingly aroused at the injustice sought to be visited on the accused, determined that as a judge—if only one of two hundred and fifty—he would do all within his power to see justice done, both by his arguments on points of evidence and by his own cross-examination.

"I can bear witness," wrote Brougham years later in his memoirs, "to the warmest of feeling as well as the skill and judgment which Lord Erskine showed at the end of his life in the great case of the Queen."

Comparing him with the other peers, Brougham wrote: "It is needless to say how eminently Erskine shone above all the rest. His conduct throughout had all the excellence of the judicial character, combined with the most perfect skill in eliciting the truth by his examination. His leanings were all on our side, from his thorough conviction of the gross injustice and cruelty with which the Queen had been always treated."

Not only did Brougham and the House of Peers take notice of what Erskine did, but all England noticed. Everywhere in London where the Queen's sympathizers met, and they were everywhere, Erskine's name was applauded. A generation had grown up since the great treason trials, but the young, as well as those old enough to have celebrated the acquittal of Horne Tooke and Hardy, joined in their acclaim for the defender of the rights and liberties of Englishmen.

As the march of the Crown witnesses proceeded and their Italian answers filled the House of Lords with a strange tongue, the anger of plain Englishmen increased. Great as was the disaffection of the people, a greater source of apprehension to the government was the attitude now openly displayed by the armed forces. So loud did their espousals of the Queen become that one day a battalion of the Guards began a mutiny, and in Charing Cross that evening a crowd of many thousands milled before the barracks in the King's Mews, shouting: "Queen forever," and encouraging the soldiers there to do the same.

There was an instantaneous compliance, and as the carriages of the well-to-do passed by, their footmen and their coachmen were forced to take off their hats to the barracks in honor of the troops. This continued until the Life Guards came and drove the crowds away.

The mutinous battalion was marched off to Portsmouth, but as they marched they shouted: "Queen forever!" This battalion, however, was not alone among the regiments in registering their disaffection. The King's own regiment, the 10th Hussars, stationed at Hampton Court, displayed it too. And one evening as Grey-Bennett was passing through the taproom of Toy Tavern he saw a soldier lift his pot of porter and shout out to his comrades: "Come, lads, the Queen!" And all drank to her health.

As August drew to a close, the Princess Lieven wrote her lover: "I have come back from London not at all edified by what I learned there. Things are going badly . . . the crowd swells and every day increases the Queen's popularity and the unwillingness of the people to believe in the Italian witnesses. . . . Every day the Duke of Wellington is handled more and more roughly by the mob. Yesterday he was nearly pulled off his horse. Evidently they are getting bolder."

Meanwhile, from all over England addresses bidding her to stand firm rained in upon the Queen. One of these was from the married women, containing fifteen thousand signatures. Another from the artisans of London was signed with forty thousand names. Many were brought to Brandenburgh House by large deputations. One consisted of the members of the Common Council headed by the Lord Mayor.

From a distant part of England at this time Brougham's old mother wrote him in alarm of a regiment of cavalry stopping on its march at Penith where they drank to the Queen's health, swearing that they "would fight up to their knees in blood" for her. The fear was now general of an outbreak either in the capital or elsewhere. "Daily," Brougham himself later wrote, "there were loud demonstrations as different peers passed, great cheering of some, and much hissing and yelling at others."

Such was the state of public opinion when, on September 7, the last of the Crown witnesses had been examined and Solicitor General Copley rose to sum up for the prosecution.

It was an able speech, and it was hoped by the King's friends that it might serve to rehabilitate the Italian witnesses in the public mind. To that end the means most likely to achieve it would be to deny the Queen's defenders the right to open their defense unless they agreed to follow it immediately with their witnesses. Thus, as Copley finished, counsel for the Queen were asked "whether they proposed now to proceed, or to ask for delay previous to entering upon their case." To this Brougham answered that he was "not prepared at the present moment to commence opening the case of Her Majesty," but that he might be prepared by twelve o'clock tomorrow.

The House adjourned then, and the next day Brougham advised the peers that he was ready to proceed with his opening, after which he could not say whether he would ask for a delay in order to secure the testimony of those "not now in this country," or whether he might present no evidence at all. He was told that while he might have any reasonable adjournment, if he chose to open the next day he must follow it immediately with his evidence.

"Of all the scandalous perversions of justice of which she had so much reason to complain," Denman later wrote, "the most revolting was the prohibition to enter upon our defense the moment the case against us was closed, unless we undertook to proceed with our witnesses immediately. . . . Every counsel has a right to enter upon the defense of his client the moment the accusation is brought to an end, and to make up his mind from observing the effect he produces on his judges, whether he will call any witnesses or not."

On September 9, after consulting with his associates, Brougham told the House that he would be ready to proceed three weeks from the coming Tuesday. It was only of his amusement at the discomfiture of the peers that Creevey thought when at Brooks's that evening he sat writing to Miss Ord: "The House of Lords is adjourned to Tuesday three weeks. . . . You can form no conception of the rage of the Lords at Brougham fixing this time; it interferes with everything—pheasant shooting, Newmarket, etc., etc."

And as Denman later wrote, "the case against the Queen was permitted to circulate through the world and sink deep into every mind during the three weeks of adjournment."

Not long before the Crown's case had closed, the increasing outcries of the people for a persecuted queen had at last made an impression on Lord Liverpool. There must be some appeasement of the popular discontents. Moreover, it was well known that the bishops might not cast their vote in favor of the bill because of the divorce clause. "The Archbishop of York told me," wrote the Princess Lieven on September 6, "that neither he nor any of the ecclesiastical members of the House would vote for the bill; that they could not do so without dishonoring their calling; and that on this point their party was absolutely firm. This will be a very strong argument for the Queen in the eyes of the public. The clergy say the act of degradation may be passed, but not the divorce clause; and that no ecclesiastical court could grant a divorce in the present circumstances of the King and Queen respectively."

How accurate was the information of the Russian Ambassadress appeared the following day when, at the close of the Solicitor General's summing up, Lord Liverpool, in response to a question of Lord Lonsdale, told the Lords that "if it was the wish of the religious part of the House and of the community that this clause should be withdrawn, His Majesty had no personal wish in having it made part of the bill."

"Well, my archbishop and my premonitions were both right. The bill has been cut in two," wrote Metternich's mistress the next day.

Almost at the same hour Creevey sat writing to his stepdaughter from the House of Lords; "You know the Queen went down the river yesterday. I saw her pass the House of Commons on the deck of her state barge; the river and the shores of it were then beginning to fill. Erskine, who was afterwards at Blackfriars Bridge, said he was sure there were 200,000 people collated to see her. . . . There was not a single vessel in the river that did not hoist their colors and man their yards for her, and it was with the greatest difficulty that the watermen on the Thames, who are all her partisans, are kept from destroying the hulk which lies off the House of Commons to protect the witnesses in Cotton Garden."

A few days after the adjournment he again wrote: "I heard a noise of hurraing and shouting in the street so I ran out to see. It was, I may say, the Navy of England marching to Brandenburgh House with an address to the Queen. I have seen nothing like this before; nothing approaching it. There were thousands of seamen, all well dressed, all sober; the best-looking, the finest men you could imagine.

"Every man," he continued, "had a new white silk or satin cockade in his hat. They had a hundred colors, at least, or pieces of silk with sentiments upon them, such as *'Protection to the Innocent,'* etc. M'Donald asked one of them how many there were, to which he answered very civilly: 'I don't know exactly, sir, but we are many thousands, and should have been many more, but we would not let any men above forty come, because we have so far to walk.' Remember what I say—this procession decides the fate of the Queen. When the seamen take a part, the soldiers can't fail to be shaken."

October 3, 1820. A crowded House of Lords was filled to overflowing, and there was dead silence as Henry Brougham stood up to open the Queen's case.

Some lawyers, Brougham began, in defending their accused clients must contend against the weight of public opinion, but he himself was laboring under no such disadvantage. "Public opinion," he said, "has already decided on this case, and I have nothing to fear but the consequences of perjury."

"My Lords," he said, "the Princess Caroline of Brunswick arrived in this country in the year 1795—the niece of our sovereign, the intended consort of his heir apparent, and herself not a very remote heir to the throne of these realms. But I now go back to that period only for the purpose of passing over all the interval which elapsed between her arrival then and her departure in 1814."

The King's friends breathed freer. All of his adulteries, his marriage with Mrs. Fitzherbert—all that would have defeated him as a plaintiff in an action for divorce, would apparently be passed over.

But hark! "I rejoice that for the present, at least," Brougham continued, "the most faithful discharge of my duty permits me to draw this veil; but I cannot do so without pausing for an instant to guard myself against a misrepresentation to which I know this cause may not unnaturally be exposed, and to assure Your Lordships most solemnly that if I did not think that the cause of the Queen, as attempted to be established by the evidence against her, not only does not require recrimination at present—not only imposes no duty of even uttering one whisper, whether by way of attack or by way of insinuation, against her illustrious husband—but that it rather prescribes to me for the present, silence upon this great and painful head of the case. . . ."

"For the present!" The full import of this phrase three times repeated was not lost upon his listeners. For the present, silence. But what about the future? Brougham knew of the King's marriage to Mrs. Fitzherbert. He was in possession of a copy of the former's will made in her favor, signed with his own hand, in which he called her his dear wife. He did not have the marriage certificate itself—eighty-five years would pass before it saw the light of day.* But he did have Mrs. Fitzherbert's uncle, Mr. Errington, who was present at the marriage. This was in Brougham's mind, and fears of this were in the minds of the King's Ministers when he said that he would not attack the King "for the present."

The present state of the evidence, he said, did not require it. But, he went on, "I solemnly assure Your Lordships that but for this conviction my lips on that branch would not be closed; for . . . in postponing for the present the statement of that case of which I am possessed, I . . .

* "In 1905 the documents were examined. The marriage certificate was among them." The *Greville Diary*, Vol. I, p. 102.

am abstaining from the use of materials which are mine. And let it not
be thought, my Lords, that if either now I did conceive, or if hereafter I
should be so far disappointed in my expectation that the case against me
will fail, as to feel it necessary to exercise that right,—let no man vainly
suppose, that not only I but any of the youngest members of the profession would hesitate one moment in the fearless discharge of his paramount duty."

He now launched forth into an assertion of the lawyer's duty that men
still quote, some with misgivings as to its boldness, some with strong
dissent; but all with admiration for the exalted plane on which he placed
the duty of an English advocate.

"I once before," he said, "took leave to remind Your Lordships—
which was unnecessary, but there are many whom it may be needful to
remind—that an advocate by the sacred duty which he owes his client
knows, in the discharge of that office, but one person in the world, *that
client and none other.* To save that client by all expedient means, to protect that client at all hazards and costs to all others, and among others
to himself, is the highest and most unquestioned of his duties. And he
must not regard the alarm, the suffering, the torment, the destruction
which he may bring upon any other. Nay, separating the duties of a
patriot from those of an advocate, and casting them if need be to the
wind, he must go on reckless of the consequences, if his part it should
unhappily be to involve his country in confusion for his client's protection."

In startled amazement the House of Lords heard these bold assertions;
yet no one seemed to realize their full import. Little did they guess the
real ground of defense that Brougham was holding in reserve. "The
ground then," Brougham later wrote, "was neither more nor less than
impeaching the King's own title, by proving that he had forfeited the
Crown. He had married a Roman Catholic (Mrs. Fitzherbert) while heir
apparent, and this is declared by the Act of Settlement to be a forfeiture
of the Crown 'as if he were naturally dead.' "

Such were the concealed weapons that Brougham held. Such was the
threat that he held out to the King of England.

In a speech that lasted the whole day Brougham ripped and tore the
prosecution's case. The Italian witnesses and their purchased testimony

were held up to vitriolic ridicule and were castigated with contempt. In every form of utterance he expressed strong English hatred for the Latin perjury of imported character assassins.

On October 4 he went on with his denunciation and finally closed: "Such, my Lords, is the case now before you, and such is the evidence by which it is attempted to be upheld. It is evidence inadequate to prove any proposition; impotent to deprive the lowest subject of any civil right; ridiculous to establish the least offense; scandalous to support a charge of the highest nature; monstrous to ruin the honor of a Queen of England. What shall I say of it then as evidence to support a judicial act of legislature; *an ex post facto law?*"

"My Lords," said Brougham, "I call upon you to pause. You stand on the brink of a precipice. If your judgment shall go out against your Queen it will be the only act that ever went out without effecting its purpose. It will return to you upon your own heads. Save the country. Save yourselves. Rescue the country; save the people, of whom you are the ornaments; but severed from whom you can no more live than the blossom that is severed from the root and tree on which it grows."

Spent though he was, the Queen's defender launched into this final exhortation: "Save the country, therefore, that you may continue to adorn it. Save the Crown which is threatened with irreparable injury. Save the aristocracy which is surrounded with danger. Save the altar which is no longer safe when its kindred throne is shaken. You see that when the church and the throne would allow of no church solemnity in behalf of the Queen, the heartfelt prayers of the people rose to Heaven for her protection. I pray Heaven for her, and I pour forth my fervent supplications at the throne of mercy, that mercies may descend on the people of this country, richer than their rulers have deserved, and that your hearts may be turned to justice."

At half-past one that afternoon Creevey was again writing to his stepdaughter: "Brougham has just finished his opening . . . I never heard anything like the perfection he has showed in all ways. . . . In short, if he can prove what he has stated in his speech, I for one believe she is innocent, and the whole case a conspiracy."

The next day he again wrote her: "Brougham's speech not only astonished but has shaken the aristocracy, though Lord Grenville did tell me at parting this morning not to be too confident of that, for that the House of Lords was by far the stupidest and most obstinate collection of men that could be selected from all England."

From October 3 until the tenth of November the Queen's advocates called witness after witness who had accompanied her on her journeys or had seen her at some point in her wanderings. The general tenor of their testimony was that they had observed no impropriety in her conduct or any undue familiarity with Bergami.

The Queen, said Lady Charlotte Lindsay, had always conducted herself toward Bergami as "a mistress would conduct herself toward a servant." Her reason for resigning from the Queen's service was not disapproval of her behavior, but because of personal and family reasons. On the evening of October 5, when she concluded her direct testimony, Creevey wrote: "The witness of all witnesses has just closed her examination in chief—Lady Charlotte Lindsay. In your life you never heard such testimony as hers in favor of the Queen—the talent, the perspicuity, the honesty of it. . . ."

On cross-examination, however, Lady Charlotte proved less satisfactory to the defense. Far less. Asked if she had seen Her Royal Highness walking arm in arm with Bergami, she answered that she had no "recollection of it," but would not swear that it did not happen. Asked then if she herself had not said that she left the Queen's service because she considered that "no woman with any regard for her character could remain in the service of Her Royal Highness," she replied that she did "not recollect ever having stated any such thing in such words," and that she thought it "extremely improbable" that she should have done so. Pressed further on this subject by the Solicitor General, she repeated the same answer and then burst into tears.

She nevertheless made a strong impression, and that evening Creevey wrote: "Wonders will never cease. Upon my soul! This Queen must be innocent after all." He was, however, perhaps a shade too optimistic when he added: "Lady Charlotte went on her cross-examination, and could never be touched; though she was treated most infamously; so much so as to make her burst out a-crying."

Whatever effect she may have made, Brougham and his associates felt sure that in Lientenant Flynn they had a witness no cross-examination could impair. On October 9 they called him with high confidence, and he came through his direct examination with flying colors. He was a strong and handsome man with the straightforward look characteristic of naval officers. He had been in the Royal Navy for the past sixteen years.

He had first met the Queen in 1815, he swore and had been in command of the polacre on which Her Royal Highness had made her "voyage to Constantinople and other places." He described the suite accompanying her and the location of their sleeping apartments.

The tent in which the Princess slept during the voyage covered a passageway from below decks, and he had had occasion, when the maneuvering of the ship required it, to pass through that tent at night. Bergami did not sleep there. At no time had he ever seen them kissing.

He was then asked this sweeping question: "During the whole time that you had the management of this vessel, and that Her Royal Highness was on board, did you see the slightest impropriety or indecency in her behavior toward Bergami or toward any other person?"

Flynn answered with a firm "No."

The Solicitor General rose to cross-examine. In search of any opportunity, he was determind to destroy this witness if he could; he was not long in finding his first opening. Asked how many days it took to sail from Tunis to Jaffa, Flynn answered that he did not know exactly, and begged leave "to look at a memoir" he had made. When was this memorandum made, he was asked next, and he answered that what he held was a copy only.

Copley now plied him with question after question about this paper: when was the original made; where was it made; when was the copy made and where? With rapid fire the baffled Flynn was interrogated. Without permitting him to examine the memorandum in his hand, Copley asked him how long it had taken him to sail from Jaffa to Syracuse. At this point, as so often in the trial, Erskine intervened with an objection. "If the witness were not allowed to refresh his recollection by his memorandum, it was unfair," he said, "to tax the memory in the way attempted."

Pushed and badgered as to who slept where upon the ship, as the day's session was about closing, Flynn was asked:

Q: Have you any doubt that during that voyage and the whole of it Bergami slept upon that bed under the tent?

A: I cannot say where he slept. I never went to look after Mr. Bergami; when he was wanted, or where he slept, it is impossible for me to say; I can only repeat that I never saw him in bed.

The witness had begun to slip, and all saw that the Solicitor General had him in his power. But the sanguine Creevey wrote that afternoon: "Captain Flynn of the polacre is just called. He is mad, and in trying to do too much has, for the present, done harm; but it will be all set right tomorrow."

A brave man at sea, no doubt, poor Lieutenant Flynn was shivering with fear as he stood again in the witness box on the morning of October 10 and faced the relentless eyes of Sir John Copley. In the memorandum voluntarily produced by the witness the Solicitor General had struck pay dirt. Who had made the original?

"The account was written by the clerk," feebly replied the naval officer, who was now floundering in a heavy sea.

Was the clerk an Italian or an Englishman?

"I do not know what he was," the witness whispered. Then he said that the clerk referred to was an Italian, and Copley pressed him:

Q: Did you not just now say that you did not know what countryman he was?

A: I believed him to be an Italian or a Sicilian; I do not know what he was; he was on board the ship.

The Solicitor General crowded in upon his victim. Was the log written in Italian or English? Italian, Flynn answered, and then he added that it was written both in English and Italian. The sweat was streaming from his forehead; he had turned deathly white. Suddenly he fell to the floor in a dead faint.

At two o'clock that afternoon Creevey sat writing from the House of Lords: "This cursed Flynn is still going on. He has perjured himself three or four times over, and his evidence and himself have both gone to the devil. He is evidently a crack-brained sailor. . . . He has fainted away once and been obliged to be carried out."

Two days later the Princess Lieven wrote to Metternich: "How boring London will be when there is no more Queen to be tried. . . . For the last two days her stock has been very low. An unfortunate English lieutenant, bent on saving her, by ill luck made an indiscreet remark which had no reference to her; and from this followed a string of contradictions which so played on the poor man's nerves that he fainted in the House. The impression against her was unmistakable. Perhaps the fate of the trial rests with the lieutenant."

Something must be done. If one naval officer had failed, perhaps another would succeed, so the defense rushed Lientenant Joseph Hownam to the witness box. He had been Caroline's private secretary since 1815 and her devoted partisan. Once at Milan he had challenged Ompteda to a duel, but through the intervention of the Princess it had not come off. Now, on his direct examination, like Lieutenant Flynn, he gave firm testimony for the defense. On all their travels he had never seen the least impropriety between Bergami and the Queen.

On the morning of October 11 he was turned over to the Attorney General, and Brougham and his staff were praying that he would not fail them as the previous licutenant so lamentably had; but men who never feared an aroused ocean, have more than once quailed under the tidal wave of cross-examination. Hownam would prove that he was no exception to this rule. Attorney General Sir Robert Gifford had not gone far before a frightened witness was in trouble.

Q: Where did Bergami sleep on the return from Jaffa?

A: I do not know where he slept.

Q: Have you never seen him under the tent upon the bed?

A: In the nighttime?

Q: By day or night.

A: I have seen him under the tent in the day as everybody else was there.

Sir Robert now pressed harder:

Q: You have stated that Bergami at first slept in the cabin which you have mentioned—that he afterwards slept in the dining room; do you know where he slept on his way home from Jaffa?

A: I never saw him sleeping anywhere after that, therefore I cannot declare where he slept.

The Attorney General now moved in for the kill.

Q: You have said that you did not know where Bergami slept; upon your oath do you not believe he slept under the tent?

A: I have heard he did sleep under the tent.

Q: I do not wish to know what you have heard.

A: And I believe he did sleep under the tent.

With this answer the young lientenant had done the Queen far greater injury than all of the Italian witnesses. Sir Robert was determined to nail these answers down. It would have been good judgment to let them stand; further pursuit of the same subject might give the witness time to think and perhaps to wriggle out of his predicament. It was a bold chance for the cross-examiner to take, but something told him that he would not fail, and he was justified by the result. A silent House of Lords and the strained counsel for the Queen listened as the questioning went on.

Q: Do you believe that on the return from Jaffa, Bergami slept constantly under the tent?

A: I have heard that he slept under the tent, and I believe he did sleep under the tent.

Q: Without referring to what you have heard, do you not believe that he slept under the tent?

A: I have already said so.

Why so able a lawyer as Henry Brougham did not object to Hownam's "belief" upon this subject, or what he had "heard" about it, when he had not sworn to the fact of his own knowledge, we do not understand. The psychology of the lawyer in the middle of the battle is often difficult to fathom. Brougham perhaps thought it preferable to rest under the testimony as it was than to object and find the witness stating as a fact what he had theretofore given only as hearsay and opinion.

Be that is it may, Lieutenant Hownam, far more than Flynn, had massacred the Queen's case, and the promoters of the bill were jubilant. A buzz rang through the House that they would disregard all the evidence from Italy and rely solely on the testimony of this English naval officer.

"By jove, my dear," wrote Creevey to Miss Ord, just as Hownam left the stand, "we are coming to critical times, such as no man can tell the consequences of. It is quite understood that the Lords, at the suite of the Ministers, are resolved to pass this bill upon the sole point of the Queen being admitted to have slept under the tent on board the polacre, while Bergami slept there likewise. . . ."

Flynn and Hownam had so damaged the Queen's case that many thought the injury beyond repair. The defense was in retreat. How could the tide of battle be turned? It was a time for boldness, a time to recognize that in a court as on the battlefield the best of all defenses is the offense. What of the Milan Commission? Why not attack it now by proving its corruptions, by laying bare its purchase of testimony?

Many days before, during the prosecution's case, Giuseppi Restelli had been called by the Solicitor General. His evidence of what he claimed one day to have witnessed in a carriage called a *padovanello*, amounted almost to actual proof of sexual intercouse between Bergami and the Queen.

Restelli had been the head superintendent of the Queen's stables. He had been discharged. He had later been sought out by the Milan Commission and had become its active agent in procuring witnesses. His activities in this field had been extensive, and he had been well paid for them. On his cross-examination he had denied that he had ever offered any money to a prospective witness.

Now, on October 13, his evidence was recalled when Brougham called Giuseppi Giarolini to the witness box. At the Villa d'Este Giarolini had made great repairs at the Queen's request. He had done the work, but he had not been paid. A hundred forty-five thousand, five hundred livres had been owing to him. Restelli got wind of this and thereafter sought him out. The questioning of the witness then continued:

Q: Did Restelli offer you any money?

A: He told me if my account was not liquidated to send it to him, and he would contrive to see me paid.

Q: What did Restelli say you were to do for that?

A: He told me to give my account to him, for there were Englishmen at Milan, and he would see me paid.

Q: Did Restelli say to you at that time, what you were to do in order to get that bill paid?

A: He told me that if I had anything to say against Her Royal Highness (for I had been a long time in her service), to tell it to him and he would endeavor to make me paid.

Giarolini was asked whether he had had further conversation with Restelli about what he "was doing as a witness." At this point the Solicitor General objected. An argument ensued in which, before long, Erskine took part. Contending that the question was admissible, it was essential, he said, that "all the light should be let in upon this dark transaction." Either the question must be allowed, or Restelli should be recalled. He expressed the opinion that "it would be the better course to call back Restelli." . . .

A few days earlier Brougham had discovered that Restelli had been sent back to Italy. When, after a few more questions to the witness, it developed that his bill had been settled and that other witnesses had been paid, it was a startled House that watched the Queen's chief counsel as he stood up and, facing the Solicitor General, said: "I wish to know of my learned friend whether we can have access to Restelli? Is he here? Is he in this country?"

All eyes turned toward Sir John Copley, but there was no answer. From the space occupied by Crown counsel there came no reply; only a reverberating silence.

"My Lords," said Brougham, "I wish Restelli to be called."

As the air grew tense, the Solicitor General replied: "If my learned friend wishes to call Restelli, he certainly can call him."

The disingenuousness of this answer was soon established as Brougham now persisted: "I wish to know if Restelli is in the country, and, if in the country, where is he?"

With a cold official sneer the Attorney General replied: "Whether Restelli is in this country or not my learned friend must take the ordinary means to procure his attendance." Here the Lord Chancellor broke in: "Mr. Attorney, is Restelli here?"

Backed thus into a corner, the Attorney General answered: "No. He is sent to Milan."

A veritable tempest broke loose. As the medley of confusion grew, and one peer after another clamored to be heard, Brougham shouted: "I wish to know, my Lords, whether under these circumstances . . . I am to be obliged to go on with this bill?" The Attorney General feebly answered that "Restelli had been sent to Milan with dispatches, under the idea that he would not be wanted again."

Lord Holland rose in his place, saying that "the fact which has just come out at Your Lordship's bar that subornation had been practiced to a considerable extent, is absolutely monstrous. . . . What is the case, my Lords? Here is Restelli . . . upon whom suspicion now rests that he has been engaged in suborning witnesses for the prosecution, not merely escaping, but sent away by the government. . . . Considering all the circumstances as forming a prima facie case of the existence of a conspiracy to pervert justice, you would do well to get rid of the disgust and fatigue of this infamous proceeding."

Among the many peers rising to denounce the government for its perversion of justice was Lord Erskine. "I am ready to vote," he said, "to put an end to the whole proceeding."

During the veritable turmoil of excitement Lord Alvaney sought to learn "who was the individual that had sent Restelli to Milan," and if that person was "one of the Milan Commissioners." To which the Earl of Liverpool replied that it was Mr. Powell.

"As Mr. Powell's name has been mentioned," observed Earl Grey, "he ought to be called to the bar to account for his conduct."

The Chancellor here suggested that since it was then half-past four, "it might be better" to call him the next morning.

But an angered House of Lords would hear of no delay, and Powell —John Allan Powell—was immediately produced and examined, not by counsel, but by the Lords themselves.

Along with Colonel Browne, Powell had been one of the chief agents of the Milan Commission—he had been its very life and soul.

Under oath he gave a fumbling explanation for having sent Restelli back to Italy. Some of the Italian witnesses who had arrived at Dover had been ill-treated by the crowds, he said, and he had therefore sent Restelli back to reassure their families.

"My Lords," said Brougham, "I wish to ask the witness one question: Who is your employer in this case?" There were cries of "Order," "order," but Brougham held his ground. With consummate skill he had chosen the precise moment to focus attention once again upon the fact that in this case the real plaintiff had not avowed himself. It was, of course, to the King of England that Brougham referred when he said: "Whatever may be the name of this unknown—this interesting unknown . . . if I am told who he is, I may be able to trace his lineaments, and at length to bring out the mighty secret who and what he is from his own mouth. If he have one."

The question was not allowed, and Powell was at last excused. By his move in calling for Restelli, Brougham had turned the prosecution's flank. The accused was now accuser. The rout of the English naval lieutenants was forgotten. In London the sole topic of discussion was the Crown's purchase of its Italian witnesses and its spiriting away of one of them. The Milan Commission had been placed on trial.

Fifteen more witnesses were called, and on October 24, when the evidence on both sides was closed, Denman stood up to make his final plea for the accused Queen. It was the great opportunity of his life and he had been long preparing for it.

During a great part of the trial he later wrote: "Lord and Lady Holland had most kindly insisted on my passing the Sundays and part of the Saturdays and Monday at Holland House, where I luxuriated in an admirable library and the best company in the world; at the same time recruiting my health in good air and delicious gardens. I generally occupied Mr. Fox's chamber, and was as happy as a man could be."

He began his speech with a close analysis of the evidence, declaring at the end of this that "Her Royal Highness had been the victim of perjury and conspiracy by these Italian witnesses who had come over here to dethrone a queen. . . ."

He was exhausted when the session of October 24 at last drew to a close, but on the following morning he again rang the changes on Majocchi's *"Non mi ricordo,"* and despite Hownam's testimony, showed how utterly unreliable was the story of what happened in the tent on the polacre.

He turned then to the balcony where the Duke of Clarence sat. This aging scion of the House of Hanover was next in the line of succession, and in a little less than ten years would reign as King William IV of England. Denman knew that, ever since the trial began, this father of many bastards had been muttering denunciation of the Queen both inside and outside the House of Lords.

Glancing up at him, Denman continued: "I know that rumors are abroad of the most vague but at the same time of the most injurious character. I have heard them, even at the very moment we are defending Her Majesty against charges which, compared with the rumors, are clear, comprehensible, and tangible. We have heard, and hear daily with alarm, that there are persons and those not of the lowest condition, and not confined to individuals connected with the public press—not even excluded from your august assembly, who are industriously circulating the most odious and atrocious calumnies against Her Majesty."

All eyes were turned toward a future king of England. The Duke of Clarence shifted uneasily in his place as Denman, staring directly up at him, now went on: "Can this fact be? And yet can we live in the world in these times and not know it to be a fact? We know that if a juryman upon such an occasion should be found to possess any knowledge on the subject of inquiry, we should have the right to call him to the bar as a witness. 'Come forward,' we might say, 'and let us confront you with our evidence.' . . ."

He continued: "To any man who would ever be suspected of so base a practice as whispering calumnies to judges, distilling venom into the ears of jurors, the Queen might well exclaim, 'Come forth, thou slanderer, and let me see thy face! If thou wouldst equal the respectability even of an Italian witness, come forth and depose in open court! As thou art, thou art worse than an Italian assassin! Because while I am boldly and manfully meeting my accusers, thou art planting a dagger unseen in my bosom, and converting the poisoned stiletto into the semblance of the sword of justice!' "

Spellbound, the Lords listened as this commoner turned loose the vials of his wrath upon his future sovereign. These lawyers for a persecuted Queen were without fear, and there is no weapon, either on the battlefield or in the courtroom, comparable with fearlessness.

For many hours Denman talked, combining analysis of the evidence equally with eloquence—analysis so clear as in itself to be eloquence. Never for an instant did he spare King George IV. For this case, he said, he could find no parallel in English history and must, therefore, turn back to the story of imperial Rome. "Scarcely had Octavia become the wife of Nero, when, almost on the day of marriage, she became also the object of his disgust and aversion. She was repudiated and dismissed on a false and frivolous pretext. A mistress was received into her place, and before long she was even banished from the dwelling of her husband."

His excursions thus far into Roman annals seemed similar enough to the case on trial, but he would make the story of Octavia and Nero still more like that of Caroline and George Augustus, and so he continued: "A conspiracy was set on foot to impute to her a licentious amour with a slave, and it was stated by the great historian of corrupted Rome that on that occasion some of her servants were induced, not by bribes but by tortures, to depose to facts injurious to her reputation; but the greater number persisted in maintaining her innocence. It seemed that though the people were convinced of her purity, the persecutor persevered in asserting her guilt, and finally banished her from Rome. Her return was like a flood. The generous people received her with those feelings which ought to have existed in the heart of her husband."

He returned then to the case of Queen Caroline and again and again asserted that "the whole of the generous population had enlisted themselves with ardor on the side of the innocent and the injured," and if it were true, he said, that there were "also some apostles of mischief lurking in a corner, meditating a blow at the Constitution . . . generous sympathy . . . would be aggravated by a verdict of guilty; while those mischievous and disaffected men would deprecate nothing half so much as to see Your Lordships in the face of the power of the Crown, venturing to pronounce a verdict of acquittal for a defendant so prosecuted."

He went on: "I trust Your Lordships will not allow the idea of having fear imputed to you to divert you from the straight course of your duty; it would be the worst of injustice to the accused and the worst of cowardice in yourselves. I say, therefore, that if your own minds have been satisfied that all that has been proved has been scattered 'like dewdrops from the lion's mane' you will never hold yourselves justified in pronouncing a verdict contrary to the evidence, because your conduct may be imputed to the dread of a mob; or, to use the jargon of the day, which I detest, the apprehension of a Radical attack."

"You have but one course to pursue and that course is straightforward; it is to acquit Her Majesty at once of these odious charges. . . . This is an inquiry, my Lords, unprecedented in the history of the world . . . but the great day when the secret of all hearts shall be disclosed!

> " 'He who the sword of Heaven will bear,
> Should be as holy as severe.' "

He had traversed literature and history, and so far the assistance of his good friend Dr. Parr had stood him in good stead. Thus far he had avoided all the pitfalls that literary or historical allusions spread before the feet of the unwary.

Oh, that he might have finished with his reference to the sword of Heaven! But he did not. "If Your Lordships have been furnished with powers which I might almost say scarcely Omniscience itself possesses, to arrive at the secrets of this female, you will think it your duty to imitate the justice . . . of that Benignant Being, who, not in a case like this, when innocence is manifest, but when guilt was detected, and vice revealed, said—'if no accuser can come forth to condemn thee, neither do I condemn thee; go and sin no more.' "

His last words rang like a pistol shot, and as the impact of his *faux pas* began to dawn upon the House, the looks of serious attention which hitherto had followed him gave way to smiles, and smiles almost to laughter. "Go and sin no more!" If Caroline had not already sinned, how could she "sin no more"? What was intended as the climax of his appeal had become a plain admission of his client's guilt; although, of course, not so intended.

It was an unfortunate quotation; the use of it a bad mistake. It was one, Denman later wrote, that "has given me some of the bitterest moments of my life." It came into his mind after ten hours' speaking, which might, he said, "account in some degree for an indiscretion which nothing can fully justify."

Though Denman's bad mistake had caused a temporary smile, it was lost sight of in the vast splendor of his moving speech.

The thunders of his eloquence still rang throughout the commonplace address of his colleague Lushington. They rang still as the Attorney General began to make his final plea at the next session. The Crown's chief law officer had not gone far before he was interrupted. All eyes turned toward the bar where Brougham stood with a parcel of letters in his hand. These, he said, are "proved to be in the handwriting of Baron Ompteda . . . and were for the purpose of suborning witnesses to give evidence against Her Royal Highness."

Looking straight at Brougham, for a moment all that the Attorney General could do was to express "surprise that further evidence should be offered after the case was closed." The Earl of Liverpool, with a justice that no fair chronicler can gainsay, mildly observed that "whatever might be the importance of the papers they ought not to be introduced in the middle of the Attorney General's speech."

Satisfied, perhaps, that he had sufficiently broken up his opponent's address, Brougham dropped the matter and the Attorney General went on. He was followed next day by the Solicitor General, who concluded the Crown's closing plea three days later. As he finished, Brougham once again applied for leave to introduce Ompteda's letters.

As he was arguing for their admission the Attorney General interrupted, protesting against this application, and branding it as "the most extraordinary" he had ever heard. He pointed out that Brougham "had not said one word of the dates of the letters or to whom they were addressed."

"Oh, I have not the least objection," replied Brougham, "to read them to my learned friend," and the House of Lords at this was shaken with loud laughter.

By a vote of 145 to 16 the letters were excluded; but this final colloquy had dulled the whole force of what the Solicitor General had said.

Lord Chancellor Eldon rose from the woolsack to address the House. Forgetting, or, at least, hoping that others had forgotten, how fourteen years before, during the Delicate Investigation he had championed the cause of Caroline, had been the recipient of her many confidences and her frequent hospitality, he threw his whole weight into the scales against her. "I cannot," he finally concluded, "withdraw myself from what appears to me to be my imperative duty; namely, to express my firm belief that an adulterous intercourse has taken place."

All eyes were upon the wily old Chancellor, but there was none who gave him greater scrutiny than Lord Erskine. Watching as he had watched him sixteen years before in the great treason trials, the smell of battle was upon him and he rose like an old war horse to the fray. The years seemed to have rolled from Erskine as he stood facing once again his former adversary.

He began with an excoriation of the Ministers who had advised the King to strike the Queen's name from the Liturgy. Then, turning squarely first toward Lord Eldon, then toward the attorney and solicitor generals, his eyes flashing, he continued: "And yet in the face of this flagrant injustice we are talked to about holding the scales of justice even and not condemning anyone unheard." He was greeted by loud cheers.

Encouraged, he went on, and again referring to the omission of the Queen's name from the ritual, he said: "When this monstrous act was committed, I thought that the Ministers had at least an irresistible case against Her Majesty; but what was my astonishment, when the Ministers in the House of Commons, while the Green Bag lay on the table unopened, declared that the proceedings against her would be 'derogatory from the dignity of the Crown and injurious to the interests of the empire.' " Once again his speech was punctuated by loud cheering.

"I am now," he went on, "drawing near to the close of a long life, and I must end it as I began it. If you strike out of it, my Lords, some efforts to secure the sacred principles of impartial trial to the people of this country, and by example to spread it throughout the world, what would be left to me? What else seated me here? What else should there be to distinguish me from the most useless and insignificant among mankind? Nothing. Just nothing!"

Amazed to hear him display the energy and the fire of his indomitable youth, the peers strained forward on their benches as Erskine continued: "Proceedings of this kind, my Lords, have never been countenanced but in the worst of times; and have afterwards not only been reversed but stigmatized."

Those nearest him could see that he was breathing harder, yet he launched into an analysis of the evidence, devoting himself to what had taken place beneath the tent on board the polacre, as all else, he said, had "been abandoned by his noble and learned friend."

He pointed out that when the Queen first came on board all the beds had been arranged below the decks. "Now I would ask Your Lordships," he said, "if an adulterous intercourse was sought by Her Royal Highness, would she not have had the beds kept below where intercourse of that description would be less open to observation? Instead of this, what took place? Her Royal Highness went on deck where her actions were not only exposed to the observations of her attendants, but also to those of the ship's crew."

His words came harder now, and he was growing pale, but he managed to say that all evidence taken together fell short of establishing the preamble of the bill. Then, suddenly, he paused. His pause at first was not much noticed. Perhaps it was rhetorical—or perhaps, as he seemed to be doing, he was looking over the minutes of the trial that lay before him. But he did not go on. As he continued silent some of his fellow peers moved toward him in alarm. Now the anxiety of the whole House was aroused as Erskine lurched slowly forward, and, with a loud crash, fell senseless upon the table.

There were cries of "Open the windows." "Some water." The Lord Chancellor and Lord Liverpool, with the assistance of Earls Grey and Carnarvon and Lord Holland, raised him. But his speech was gone, his color was gone. Not knowing whether he had breathed his last, they bore him to an adjoining chamber.

There were not wanting at this time those who believed that Erskine never would regain consciousness, but after a quarter of an hour he was sufficiently restored to be taken home.

Revived by a night's rest, the next morning Erskine was in his seat again, and, after listening a while to the debate, he rose. "It is no longer my intention," he said, "to minutely examine the evidence which I was proceeding to do when attacked by sudden indisposition. . . . I now offer myself to Your Lordships rather as a kind of authority from long professional habits than as a debater. . . . The defendant certainly has laid before you the most positive evidence of the foulest practices to corrupt the sources of justice. A dark cloud hangs over the very beginning of the prosecution; and when we find the accusation to have been hatched in secret, and to have been supported by all the power and influence of foreign governments, when we see that some of the witnesses have been thrust forward by force, and others by the same force have been kept back—and that the foulest subornation has been detected—what security could we have had for the truth of any part of the evidence, even if it had not been impeached by the palpable perjuries which have been exposed."

Spent though he was, he was once again warming to his subject. "If Her Majesty be really guilty," he went on, "and the prosecution is therefore a just one, no false testimony could exist. False testimony is never found when a prosecution could be supported by truth, and one detected falsehood takes away from the credulity of testimony brought forward by the same party, although it stands without direct contradiction. . . . If I were in the Queen's situation and I were convicted of adultery by Your Lordships on such evidence as this, I would cast your decision in your faces, and appeal to the other House of Parliament—to the representatives of the people. The House of Commons cannot pass the bill against their own convictions and against the national nolle prosequi which resounds from every quarter of the island."

This was his final plea: "Of the legal proof of adultery I cannot be ignorant, having conducted every important case of that kind for thirty years not only in Westminster Hall, but likewise on the circuits; and I am sure, my Lords, it is impossible to infer that the opinion I have formed on this unfortunate subject has risen from prejudice or from partial inclination. To the King, who cannot be an indifferent spectator of this proceeding, I have many, many obligations from the warm interest formerly taken by His Majesty in my advancement and credit, and for my belief that I am still held by him in the same personal regard—although political changes have removed me to a greater distance from his person. If His Majesty should ever be exposed to any injurious treatment, I shall be ready to protect him at the peril of my life. I would contribute to his happiness by every sacrifice but that of my duty. My principles I have never deserted, and never will desert."

Slowly he sank into his seat while every corner of the House of Lords resounded with a loud and prolonged cheering.

The peers then proceeded to a second reading of the bill. When the count was taken there was a majority of 28 in favor of its passage. A third reading, however, was yet to come. Would the enemies of Caroline again triumph? Would she then, following the advice of Erskine, cast their decision in their faces and appeal to the representatives of the people? Or would the Lords at last become persuaded of the folly of their course?

The answer to these questions came upon the morning of November 10. There was more debate, in which Erskine again joined, saying, "if it were the last word I had to utter in this world I should pronounce the evidence to be wholly insufficient to support the charge, and I am certain that it would not be held sufficient in any court in which justice is duly administered."

The vote on the third reading was now recorded: 108 votes for the bill and 99 against. It had been carried by the slim margin of nine votes.

What now, my Lords? With a majority so thin, will you dare submit your bill to the House of Commons?

Brougham summoned Denman to prepare a petition to be signed by the Queen, praying that counsel should be again heard against the passage of the bill. It was hastily drawn up, and as their client signed "Caroline," she looked up and said, "Regina, in spite of them!"

Brougham left the room but Denman stayed behind. "At this moment," he later wrote, "I was seized with a sudden impulse that I could not resist, and believing that the seal was finally affixed to the sentence of degradation of the House of Lords, I went up to the Queen and requested a favor I had never enjoyed or solicited before, that of being permitted to kiss her hand. She held it out to me with great emotion and a profusion of tears."

Outside in the main chamber Lord Liverpool had risen wearily to his feet. "I cannot be ignorant," he slowly said, "of the state of the public feeling with regard to this measure, and it appears to be the opinion of this House that the bill should be read a third time only by a majority of nine votes. Had the third reading been carried by a considerable number of peers as the second, I and my colleagues would have felt it our duty to persevere, and to send the bill down to the other branch of the Legislature. In the present state of the country, however, and with Your Lordships so nearly balanced, we have come to the resolution not to proceed further with it. I move, therefore, that the further consideration of the bill be adjourned to this day six months."

Nemine contradicente, and almost by acclamation, the motion of Lord Liverpool was carried.

*

More than sixscore years have passed since the end of that six months' adjournment, but in that time the bill has never been revived. Neither that nor any similar attempt to flout justice has been essayed within the House of Lords. It was a triumph for Queen Caroline, but it was a greater triumph for the integrity of British justice.

As the vote was announced Lord Erskine once more took the floor, for the last time in that trial, and could he have but known it, in any other. "I see the fate of this odious measure consummated," he said, "and I heartily rejoice in the event. My Lords, I am an old man, and my life, whether it has been for good or for evil, has been passed under the sacred rule of the law. In this moment I feel my strength renovated by that rule being restored. The accursed charge wherewithal we had been menaced has passed over our heads. There is an end of that horrid and portentous excrescence of a new law—retrospective, oppressive, and iniquitous. Our Constitution is once more safe."

The trial was over. An injured but exonerated woman moved slowly from the scene of her long ordeal. In Denman's narrative she stands before us in the majesty of her exoneration, and at the end of his account there is this stark and nearly flawless sentence: "The Queen after a short delay, ascended her state carriage, and weeping and in silence proceeded to Brandenburgh House."

Emile Zola

:

"J'ACCUSE! . . ."

An Open Letter on the Dreyfus Case

January 13, 1898

Mr. President,

Permit me, I beg you, in return for the gracious favors you once accorded me, to be concerned with regard to your just glory and to tell you that your record, so fair and fortunate thus far, is now threatened with the most shameful, the most ineffaceable blot.

You escaped safe and sane from the basest calumnies; you conquered all hearts. You seem radiant in the glory of a patriotic celebration . . . and are preparing to preside over the solemn triumph of our Universal Exposition, which is to crown our great century of work, truth and liberty. But what a clod of mud is flung upon your name—I was about to say your reign—through this abominable Dreyfus affair. A court-martial has but recently, by order, dared to acquit one, Esterhazy—a supreme slap at all truth, all justice! And it is done; France has this brand upon her visage; history will relate that it was during your administration that such a social crime could be committed.

Since they have dared, I too shall dare. I shall tell the truth because I pledged myself to tell it if justice, regularly empowered did not do so, fully, unmitigatedly. My duty is to speak; I have no wish to be an accomplice. My nights would be haunted by the specter of the innocent

229

being, expiating under the most frightful torture, a crime he never committed.

And it is to you, Mr. President, that I shall speak out this truth, with all the force of my revolt as an honest man. To your honor, I am convinced that you are ignorant of the crime. And to whom, then, shall I denounce the malignant rabble of true culprits, if not to you, the highest magistrate in the country?

The truth first on the trial and condemnation of Dreyfus. One pernicious individual arranged, planned, concocted everything—Lieutenant-Colonel du Paty de Clam, then only Major. He is the whole Dreyfus Affair; we shall only understand it after an honest inquiry shall have definitely established all his acts and responsibilities. He appears as the foggy, complicated ruling-spirit, haunted by romantic intrigues, devouring serial novels, titillating himself with stolen papers, anonymous letters, strange trysts, mysterious women who come by night to sell crushing testimony, secrets of state. He it was who conceived the idea of studying the man in a room entirely lined with mirrors. . . . I declare simply that Major du Paty de Clam, designated as prosecuting officer, is the one who is first and most of all guilty of the fearful miscarriage of justice.

The *"bordereau"* had been for some time previously in the hands of the late Colonel Sandherr, head of the Secret Service. "Leaks" had been discovered, papers had disappeared, as they still do, today; when a perfectly arbitrary guess suggested that the author of the document could only be an artillery-officer, attached to the General Staff; manifestly a double error, which reveals in what a superficial manner the *bordereau* had been studied, for a reasonable examination shows that it could only have emanated from a line officer.

A search was made then; handwritings were examined, at home; it was all a family affair; a traitor was to be found right under their noses, and to be expelled. . . . And Major du Paty de Clam enters as the first suspicion falls on Dreyfus. Henceforth it is he who conceives, creates Dreyfus; the affair becomes his affair; he extends himself to confound the traitor, to precipitate him into complete confessions. There is also the Minister of War, General Mercier, at work, whose intellect seems but mediocre; there is also the chief-of-staff, General Boisdeffre, who seems to yield to his clerical passions; and there is the under-chief of the General Staff, General Gonse, whose conscience adjusts itself readily to many things. But at bottom, there is at first no one so busily involved as Major du Paty de Clam, who leads them all, who hypnotizes them, for he is also interested in spiritism, occultism, he talks with spirits. The experiments to which he had the unfortunate Dreyfus submitted, the traps he laid, seem incredible; the mad investigations, the monstrous hoax, a whole harrowing dementia.

Ah, that first affair is a nightmare for whoever knows it in its true details! . . . And thus the charges were drawn up, as in some tale of the 15th Century, in an atmosphere of mystery, brutal tricks, expedients, all based on a single, inane accusation, that of having written the idiotic *"bordereau,"* for the famous secrets delivered were found to be almost valueless. And, I insist, the core of the problem is here: it is from here on that the real crime issues, the shocking denial of justice which renders all France sick. I could wish to have everyone visualize how the judicial error was made possible, how it was born in the machinations of Major du Paty de Clam, how Generals Mercier, Boisdeffre, and Gonse permitted themselves to be taken in, entangling themselves little by little in the error which not long after they deem it necessary to impose upon us as the Holy Truth itself, a truth which is beyond all question and all discussion! At the outset their part had involved nothing more than negligence and silliness. At the most it had been a yielding to the religious prejudices of their circles, and to the bigotry of their party-spirit. They suffered the error to be made.

But here is Dreyfus before the court-martial. The most rigorous secrecy is preserved. A traitor might have opened the frontier to the enemy and led the German emperor clear to the Nôtre Dame cathedral and no more extreme measures of silence and mystery would have been taken. The nation is horror-stricken, the most terrible details are whispered of monstrous treasons that make all history cry out; obviously, the whole nation bows to the court. No punishment is severe enough for the criminal; the country will applaud the public degradation, she will want the guilty man to stay eternally on his rock of infamy, devoured by remorse. Is there any truth in those whispered unmentionable things, capable of setting all Europe aflame, that they must needs be buried in the deep secrecy of star-chamber proceedings? No. Behind those doors there were only romantic and insane notions, and the imaginings of a Major du Paty de Clam. All these efforts were merely to hide the most ridiculous and bizarre of serial romances. To be assured of that one has only to study carefully the bill of indictment read before the court-martial.

Ah! the inanity of that accusation! That a man could have been condemned on such a charge is a prodigy of iniquity. I challenge honest people to read it and not be overcome with indignation, and not cry out their revulsion at the superhuman expiation of the man on Devil's Island.

Dreyfus, it is shown, knows several languages: crime; he works hard: crime; no compromising papers are found in his home; crime; he goes occasionally to the country of his origin: crime; he endeavors to learn everything: crime; he is not easily worried: crime; he is worried: crime. And the simplicity of all these concoctions, pompous assertions in a vacuum! We were told of fourteen charges in the accusation; in the end we find only one, that of the *"bordereau";* and we learn even, that the experts were not unanimous on this, that one of them, M. Gobert, was roughly handled for not having come to the desired conclusion. . . . It is a family trial, one is completely among friends, and it must be remembered, finally, that the General Staff made the trial, judged it, and has just merely reaffirmed its judgment.

And so there remained nothing but the *"bordereau"* which was attributed (not unanimously) to Dreyfus. It is said that in the council chamber, the judges were naturally in favor of acquittal. And therefore, to justify the condemnation we may understand the desperate obstinacy with which they maintained the existence of a secret paper (emanating from a foreign office), something overwhelming, impossible ever to reveal, which legitimizes everything done, before which, in short, we must bow as we do to the almighty and unknowable God!

And this, I deny! I deny that paper! I deny it with all my power! One exists, yes. A ridiculous paper, something in which there is mention of a little woman, and wherein a certain D . . . (?) is spoken of as too extortionate; some cuckold doubtless wailing that he is not paid well enough for the use of his wife. But a paper involving the defense of the nation, that could not be produced without war being declared tomorrow —no, no! it is a lie. And it is the more odious and sardonic that they may lie with impunity and beyond the reach of argument. They muster all France, they hide behind her legitimate emotion, they shut up mouths by disturbing hearts, by perverting the mind. I know of no greater civic crime.

Here then, Mr. President, are the facts that explain how a judicial error could have been committed; and the moral proofs, the prosperous situation of Dreyfus, the absence of motives, his continual cry of innocence, combine to show him a victim of the extraordinary imaginings of Major du Paty de Clam, and of the clerical milieu in which he found himself, of the whole persecution, in short, of "the dirty Jews" that dishonors our time.

And now we arrive at the Esterhazy affair.

I shall not make an exposition of the doubts, then the certainty of M. Scheurer-Kestner. But while he was making researches for his part, grave incidents were taking place within the General Staff itself. Colonel Sandherr had died, and Lieutenant-Colonel Picquart had succeeded him as chief of the Secret Service. It was in this function that the latter found one day a little dispatch addressed to Major Esterhazy by the agents of a foreign power. His duty was to open an investigation. It is clear that he never acted against the wishes of his superiors. He reported his findings to General Gonse, then General Billot, then Minister of War. These researches lasted from May to September, 1896, and what must be cried out loud to all is that General Gonse was convinced of the guilt of Esterhazy, that General Billot and General Boisdeffre never doubted that the *"bordereau"* was the work of Esterhazy; the inquest of Picquart's had made that conclusion inevitable. But the emotion was extraordinary, for the condemnation of Esterhazy involved fatedly the revision of the Dreyfus verdict and it was this of all things that the General Staff wished to avoid at all cost.

There must have been, then, a psychological moment steeped in anguish for them. Observe that General Billot, new Minister of War, was as yet in no way compromised in the previous affair. His hands were clean; he could have established the truth. He dared not; in terror no doubt of public opinion, certainly also in fear of abandoning the whole General Staff, Boisdeffre, Gonse and the others, not to mention numerous subordinates involved. And so there was nothing but a moment of struggle between his conscience and what he felt to be the army's interests. When that moment had passed, it was already too late. He had involved himself, he was compromised. And since then his responsibility has only grown; he has taken upon his own account the crimes of others; he is more guilty than they for he was in a position to render justice, and he has done nothing. Do you understand that! Here it is a year since Generals Billot, Boisdeffre and Gonse know that Dreyfus is innocent and they keep the fearful thing to themselves! And those men sleep, and they have wives and children they love!

Colonel Picquart had done his duty as an honest man. In the name of justice he argued, he pleaded, he indicated how impolitic were their delays, in the face of the terrible storm that was gathering and would break with dreadful force when the truth were known. . . . No! The crime had been committed, the General Staff could no longer acknowledge its crime. And Colonel Picquart was sent upon a "mission"; he was ordered to go farther and farther away in Africa, . . . and they would honor his courage some day by entrusting him with a service that would surely have been his death, and yet he was not in disgrace; General Gonse maintained friendly correspondence with him. But there are secrets which one does ill to discover.

At Paris, Truth was on the march, indefatigable, unconquerable. It is known in what manner the awaited storm broke. M. Mathieu Dreyfus denounced Major Esterhazy as the true author of the *"bordereau"* at the same moment that M. Scheurer-Kestner was about to place in the hands of the Keeper of the Seals, a demand for the revision of the Dreyfus Trial. And it is at this point, for the first time that Major Esterhazy appears. Witnesses show him maddened at first, prone to suicide or flight. Then suddenly, he gambles on a daring front, he amazes all Paris by the violence of his gestures and attitudes. Help had come to him; he had received an anonymous letter warning him of the foul projects of his enemies—a mysterious veiled woman had even taken the trouble to visit him at night and return a paper stolen from the General Staff, which was to save him. And I cannot avoid perceiving in all these shifts the hand of Colonel du Paty de Clam, revealing as they do the qualities of his fertile imagination. His masterpiece, the established guilt of Dreyfus, was in danger, and he naturally desired to defend his achievement. Revision of the trial—but that would have meant the utter ruin of an extravagant tragic serial romance, whose horrible dénouement takes place in Devil's Island! . . . From now on, a duel is fought between Col. Picquart and Colonel du Paty de Clam, the one with frank, open face, the other masked. We shall find them both soon before the bar of civil justice. But at bottom, remember, it is always the General Staff defending itself, refusing to avow a crime whose consequences pile up from hour to hour.

Who, people asked in amazement, could be the defenders of Major Esterhazy? There is first, Colonel du Paty de Clam; there is next, General Boisdeffre, General Gonse, General Billot himself, all compelled now to have the Major acquitted, since they cannot permit the innocence of Dreyfus to be recognized without having the whole war department demolished by the public wrath. And the beautiful result of this preposterous situation is that the man who is supremely honest, who alone of all men, has done his duty, is to be the victim, is to be subjected to derision and punishment.

O justice, what horrible despair strikes the heart! They say even that he was the forger, that he fabricated the dispatch in order to betray Esterhazy! But, good Lord, why? To what end? Is he also paid by the Jews? . . . Ah, we witness the infamous spectacle of men weighed down with debts and crimes being proclaimed to all the world as innocent and virtuous, while the very soul of honor, a man without a stain, is dragged in the mire! When a country, when a civilization has come to this, it must fall apart in decay.

This then, Mr. President, is the Esterhazy affair: a guilty man who had to be exculpated for "reasons of state." For two months past we have been forced to look at this fine spectacle, hour by hour. . . . And we have seen General Pellieux, then Major Ravary conduct a dishonorable investigation from which scoundrels emerge purified and honest men besmirched. And then, at length, they convoked the court-martial. . . .

How could any one expect a court-martial to undo what a previous court-martial had done?

I do not even refer to the decision of the judges. Is not the ruling idea of discipline in the very blood of these soldiers strong enough to weaken their power of judgment? And when the Minister-of-War himself had asserted amid the acclamations of the two houses of parliament the irrevocability of the case to be judged, could you expect a court-martial to oppose a formal denial! They made their decision as they would have gone into battle, heads down, without reasoning. The fixed idea that they brought to the court-martial was clearly this: "Dreyfus was condemned by a court-martial; he is, therefore, guilty; we, a court-martial cannot declare him innocent. Now we know, moreover, that to recognize the guilt of Esterhazy would be to proclaim the innocence of Dreyfus." Nothing could enable them to get out of that charmed circle.

They have rendered an unjust verdict, one that will forever weigh upon our court-martials, and which from now on will cast the blot of suspicion upon all the decisions of military courts. The first court-martial might have been stupid, the second was necessarily criminal. Its excuse, I repeat is that the supreme chief had spoken, declaring the matter judged unimpeachable—holy and superior to men and reason, something that inferiors could not dare to question. They speak to us of the honor of the army, they want us to respect, to love it. Yes, by all means yes—that army which would rise at the first menace to defend French soil, which is in fact the whole people, and for which we have nothing but tenderness and reverence. But there is no question of such an army, whose dignity we justly desire in our longing for justice. It is a question of the sword, the master that we shall probably have forced upon us tomorrow. And as for kissing the hilt of the sword, piously—great God, no!

Dreyfus cannot be vindicated unless the whole General Staff is indicted. And the war-office through every possible expedient, through campaigns in the press, through pressure, influence, has sought to screen Esterhazy, in order to demolish Dreyfus once more. What a cleaning up the republican government must institute in that house of Jesuits, as General Billot himself called it. Where is there the truly powerful ministry, imbued with a just and wise patriotism, that would dare reform everything and restore everything? And how many citizens there are who, fearing an imminent war, tremble with alarm, knowing to whom supreme command of the national defense is entrusted! What a nest of low intrigue, corruption and dissipation that sacred precinct has become, where the fate of the nation is to be decided. Ah, what abominable measures have been resorted to in this affair of folly and stupidity, smacking of low police practice, of unbridled nightmares, of Spanish inquisition—all for the sweet pleasure of a few uniformed and accoutred personages who grind their heel into the nation, who hurl back into its throat the cry for truth and justice, under the lying guise of "reasons of state."

And it is still a greater crime to have used the yellow press, to have permitted all the rascals of Paris to come to their aid, so that now we have the rascals triumphing insolently in the defeat of right and honesty. And it is again a crime for them to accuse those who desire France, generous, liberal, at the head of free and just nations, of plotting her downfall. It is a crime to misdirect public opinion and to pervert it until it becomes delirious. It is a crime to poison small and simple minds, to arouse the passions of intolerance and reaction through the odium of that miserable anti-semitism of which great and liberal France with her rights of man, will expire if she is not soon cured. It is a crime to exploit patriotism for motives of hatred, and it is a crime, finally, to make of the sword the modern god when all human science is at work to bring about a future of truth and justice.

How pitiful that this truth, this justice we have so passionately desired, seems now more mutilated, punished, cast off than ever before!

I know what desolation there is in the heart of M. Scheurer-Kestner, and I firmly believe that he will deeply regret some day, not having acted in a more direct and revolutionary manner during his interpellation in the Senate, for not having opened up the whole business, flung down the gauntlet irrevocably. He thought that the truth itself would suffice; and what was the use of overturning everything? And it is for that serene faith that he is now being so cruelly tormented. And likewise for Colonel Picquart who through a sentiment of discipline and honor has been unwilling to publish the letters of General Gonse, while his superiors cover him with slime, and direct a trial of him in the most incredible and outrageous manner. These are two of the victims, two brave, open-hearted men who waited for God to act while the devil was frightfully busy.

Such then, Mr. President, is the simple truth. It is the fearful truth. It will persist as a great stain upon your administration. I suspect that you have no power in this matter, that you are the prisoner of the Constitution and of your situation. You have, none the less, your duty as a man, on which you will doubtless reflect and which you will fulfill. In any event, I do not despair in the least of ultimate triumph. I repeat with more intense conviction: the truth is on the march and nothing will stop her! It is only today that this affair has begun, since it is only now that sides have definitely been taken: on the one hand, the culprits who want no light at all on the business; on the other, lovers of justice who would lay down their lives for it. I have said elsewhere and I say again, when the truth is buried underground, it grows, it chokes, it gathers such an explosive force that on the day when it bursts out, it blows everything up with it. We shall soon see whether we have not laid the mines for a most far-reaching disaster of the near future.

But this letter is long, Mr. President, and it is time to conclude.

I ACCUSE COLONEL DU PATY DE CLAM of having been the diabolical agent of the judicial error, unconsciously, I prefer to believe, and of having continued to defend his deadly work during the past three years through the most absurd and revolting machinations.

I ACCUSE GENERAL MERCIER of having made himself an accomplice in one of the greatest crimes of history, probably through weak-mindedness.

I ACCUSE GENERAL BILLOT of having had in his hands the decisive proofs of the innocence of Dreyfus and of having concealed them, and of having rendered himself guilty of the crime of lèse humanity and lèse justice,

out of political motives and to save the face of the General Staff.
I ACCUSE GENERAL BOISDEFFRE AND GENERAL GONSE of being accomplices in the same crime, the former no doubt through religious prejudice, the latter out of esprit de corps.

I ACCUSE GENERAL DE PELLIEUX AND MAJOR RAVARY of having made a scoundrelly inquest, I mean an inquest of the most monstrous partiality, the complete report of which composes for us an imperishable monument of naïve effrontery.

I ACCUSE THE THREE HANDWRITING EXPERTS, MM. Belhomme, Varinard and Couard of having made lying and fraudulent reports, unless a medical examination will certify them to be deficient of sight and judgment.

I ACCUSE THE WAR-OFFICE of having led a vile campaign in the press, particularly in *l'Eclair* and in *l'Echo de Paris* in order to misdirect public opinion and cover up its sins.

I ACCUSE, LASTLY, THE FIRST COURT-MARTIAL of having violated all human right in condemning a prisoner on testimony kept secret from him, and I ACCUSE THE SECOND COURT-MARTIAL of having covered up this illegality by order, committing in turn the judicial crime of acquitting a guilty man with full knowledge of his guilt.

In making these accusations I am aware that I render myself liable to articles 30 and 31 of Libel Laws of July 29, 1881, which punish acts of defamation. I expose myself voluntarily.*

As to the men I accuse, I do not know them, I have never seen them, I feel neither resentment nor hatred against them. For me they are only entities, emblems of social malfeasance. The action I take here is simply a revolutionary step designed to hasten the explosion of truth and justice.

I have one passion only, for light, in the name of humanity which has borne so much and has a right to happiness. My burning protest is only the cry of my soul. Let them dare then to carry me to the court of appeals, and let there be an inquest in the full light of the day!

I am waiting.

Mr. President, I beg you to accept the assurances of my deepest respect.

* See pages 440-448 in this volume.

Morris Raphael Cohen

:

THE BERTRAND RUSSELL CASE

A Scandalous Denial of Justice

Nullius liber homo capiatur . . . aut aliquo modo distruatur . . . nisi per legale judicium parium. . . .

—MAGNA CHARTA, SEC. 39

The legal systems of all modern civilized people recognize the fallibility of judges of first instance, and therefore make provision for appeal and review. And our judicial statistics show that in a high proportion of cases the rulings of the first court have in fact been declared erroneous. The denial of the right of appeal is, therefore, a denial of justice. Such a denial is all the more grievous if it is due to pressure from a political or hierarchical source interfering with the due course of judicial proceedings.

In a number of famous instances, such as the Dreyfus case, enlightened public conscience was properly outraged by the fact that the accused did not receive a fair trial. For on the fairness of judicial procedure depends that security against baseless charges which is indispensable for dignified civilized life. But in the case of Bertrand Russell an internationally honored teacher, scholar, and philosopher was foully condemned, branded as a criminal, and ignominiously deprived of his position as a professor by a proceeding which had not the barest resemblance to a trial.

The reader will find in *The Harvard Law Review* of May 1940 a brief but incisive legal critique of the irregularity of Judge McGeehan's

239

procedure and the absurdity of the unprecedented doctrines on which his decision rested. But it does not require much legal learning to see that the most elementary requisite of just judicial procedure is violated when a man is condemned without being given a chance to be heard, to confront his accusers, and to offer evidence in refutation of their disingenuous charges.* If ever there was a case that called for the review for which higher courts are instituted, this was surely one. Yet such review was effectively prevented by a barrage of dubious technicalities. That such a thing can happen in a great American city is an ominous indication of how precarious are the constitutional rights of "due process" which are often supposed to go back to Magna Charta.

Let us look at the main facts of the record.

Bertrand Russell was, on the recommendation of its Philosophy Department, and of its Acting President, regularly appointed Professor of Philosophy at the City College and thereupon resigned his previous professorship at the University of California in Los Angeles. Soon thereafter a public clamor was raised by Bishop Manning (supported by various noneducational bodies) that Russell's appointment should be

---

* One does not expect perfect candor or a nice regard for truth in lawyers' briefs, and it is therefore not surprising to find the counsel for the complainant denying the public fact that Russell had been a teacher for most of his life, in England and China as well as in the United States. But one is taken aback to find gentlemen who are members of the Board of Higher Education telling the Appellate Division that "the post of Professor of Philosophy at City College is a brand-new position. It never existed previously and was never held by any prior incumbent. Indeed, the Department of Philosophy itself is a new department created by the Board in 1940." The fact—which any reader can verify—is that the Department of Philosophy has existed at the City College almost from its beginning. In my own lifetime Professors Newcomb, McNulty, Overstreet, and myself were officially designated as professors of philosophy. Can this have been unknown to Mr. Tuttle, who has been a member of the Board for more than thirty years and for a long time chairman of the Administrative Committee of the City College? It is rather the Department of Psychology, an offshoot of that of Philosophy, that was first established in 1940. And it was the post of Professor of Psychology, to which Dr. Murphy was appointed, that was then created. Russell was to fill the chair left vacant by Professor Overstreet's retirement. Acting President Mead in recommending Russell also mentioned the position still unfilled since my own retirement as professor of philosophy early in 1938.

It is also, I confess, hard to believe in the sincerity of these gentlemen's concern about Russell's acquiring permanent tenure after a year's service, when they knew that the whole term of Russell's service could not, because of the legal age limit, be more than a year and a half. Strange, how men zealous for public morality will so often be disdainful of honest truth in their arguments.

rescinded—i.e., in plain English, that he should be dismissed because of his views on religion and morals. Against this proposal Russell's fellow-teachers of philosophy throughout the country, and all the educational authorities of the institutions with which Russell had been connected, publicly protested and endorsed his qualifications. The Board of Higher Education then voted to stand by its original appointment.

The next day a complaint was brought in Judge McGeehan's court in Manhattan in the name of a Mrs. Kay of Brooklyn, asking that Russell's appointment be declared illegal because he was not a citizen and not a man of moral character. No evidence was brought to sustain the latter charge except the submission of several volumes of Russell's writings, published some years ago. The Corporation Counsel appeared on behalf of the Board of Higher Education (through an assistant, Mr. Bucci) and contended that the complaint should be dismissed. Mr. Bucci properly offered no evidence in refutation of the complaint, since proper judicial procedure required that the court first rule on his motion to dismiss the complaint as a legally insufficient cause of action. Within two days Judge McGeehan announced his decision disqualifying Russell in language which clearly showed the heat of a biased or partisan pleader eager to convict, rather than the careful judgment of a responsible judge who has, in conformity with the duty of his office, conscientiously considered the rights of both sides of the case. There were also a number of statements in his written opinions which are simply not true. Thus he said that "the Court had witnesses [note the plural] produced in court." The record shows this statement to be categorically false. No witnesses appeared in court. Mrs. Kay merely swore that she was the petitioner, on the judge's assurance to the Corporation Counsel that this was merely "so that her name will appear in the record." No one claimed that Mrs. Kay was a competent witness to testify as to Professor Russell's fitness for the position of professor. Nor can we accept as true the statement of the judge that the respondent "informed the Court that he would not serve an answer." Mr. Bucci denied it in a sworn affidavit which was never challenged. This was confirmed by a sworn affidavit by Mr. Fraenkel, who at no time was given a chance to produce evidence refuting the scurrilous and defamatory statements in the complaint and in the judge's written opinion. Judge McGeehan's reference to the proceedings as a trial has no support in fact or law. He pronounced judgment on Russell on the supposed ground of having read some of his books, but without asking Russell whether the views which he (the judge) read into these books were really there and if so whether Russell still adhered to those views.

Let us now consider the three alleged legal grounds for declaring Russell's appointment illegal.

The first point was that an alien may not teach in a New York college. The statute invoked clearly refers to public schools, which are directed to hold Arbor Day and other exercises that no one supposes to be obligatory in a college. It provides that teachers shall be graduates of normal schools and hold licenses, which no college professor is ever required to do. Even in the public schools the law allows an alien to teach if he declares his intention to become a citizen. Professor Russell had at least ten months in which to do so before qualifying for the active performance of his duties. Judge McGeehan tried to disregard this clear provision of the law by the arbitrary guess that the Federal courts would bar Russell from citizenship. If there were any real basis for this guess, the opponents of Russell would surely have tried to have him deported on the ground that a person of moral turpitude was not qualified to enter this country. But Judge McGeehan's mind was obviously not on the law. He himself declared that he would be writing for the legislature as well as the Court of Appeals, and it is not unfair to suspect that he also had in mind the daily newspapers. This is shown by his final appeal to a narrow local prejudice in the argument that "other universities and colleges both public and private seem to be able to find American citizens to employ." As an argument this is clearly worthless in law as well as in logic. Any implication that our institution of higher learning do not employ foreign scholars is patently false. Long lists can readily be compiled of foreign teachers in municipal and state institutions as well as in private Catholic, Protestant, and Jewish colleges. In New York City not only the city colleges, New York and Columbia Universities, but the institution which Judge McGeehan himself attended, have gladly availed themselves of the opportunity when a distinguished foreign scholar was available. This has long been considered an honored practice in New York as in other states. The laws of the United States have recognized its national advantage and have exempted such foreign teachers from the usual immigration quotas. To deprive our students of the best available teachers would obviously be to impoverish our country intellectually. Only petty ward politicians, ignorant of the essentially international character of all science and philosophy that seeks the truth, can ignore this. In any case, we surely have an issue here that should not be settled by the arbitrary whim of a judge of first instance who gave barely two days to the hearing of the case and to the writing of his opinion. Surely this should receive the careful consideration of the highest appellate courts.

The second ground on which Russell's appointment was declared illegal was even more unprecedented and revolutionary in its implication. It is that a professor in any public college in New York State must take a civil service examination (by whom?). This is a view so contrary to the experience of our institutions of higher learning that it is hard to believe that anyone in the smallest degree acquainted with the practices of modern colleges can in good faith maintain it. If this ground of the decision in the Russell case were sound law, every one of the professors in every one of our state-supported colleges would have to be dismissed and every member of the Boards of Trustees of Higher Education be penalized for the illegal appointments. Also, the Commissioner of Education of the State of New York would have to be punished for permitting so many to teach in violation of the law. The truth is that not even all the teachers in the public schools of New York State outside of two large cities are required to take examinations at all. The law clearly provides that examinations shall be held only when practicable, and the educational authorities in touch with actual conditions have never found examinations practicable in the appointment of professors in institutions of higher learning. Yet Judge McGeehan blandly asserts that the assumption by the Board of Higher Education that competitive examinations were impracticable was "unwarranted, arbitrary, and capricious." One might with more justice apply these epithets to the judge's own decision.

The third ground of the decision is of fateful significance not only to the independence of our educational system but for the general conception of the judicial function. That an individual judge may, on the basis of reading a number of passages in a scholar's works, set up his own judgment as to whether the author is fit for a professorship in a college, and venture to overrule the faculty and the educational authorities to whom such determination is expressly delegated by law and who have had more opportunity to study and competently to interpret these works, is a strange and ominous legal doctrine. Judges are not supposed to be endowed with superhuman wisdom or omniscience in all matters. They are therefore generally restricted to passing only on the question:

What has the law provided? Hence it has always been regarded as a sound and established legal principle that, where discretion is expressly conferred on administrative officials, no judge may interfere by simply setting up his own judgment as to the wisdom of what an administrative body did. He may act only if there can be no reasonable doubt that the administrators have gone beyond the power granted them. That this cannot possibly be so here is evidenced by the fact that almost all qualified educational authorities who expressed themselves in the case, including hundreds of American teachers of philosophy, regarded Professor Russell as eminently fit and urged the Board of Higher Education not to revoke his appointment.

The Western Philosophical Association, after the decision in the Russell Case was announced, unanimously adopted a resolution which in effect insisted that teachers of philosophy (as of other subjects) should be selected on the advice of those competent in their special field and not by judges after listening to arguments of lawyers. (What distinguished scholar will want to accept a professorship if thereby he subjects himself to having his name besmirched in a litigation in which he has not even a chance to appear in court to clear himself?) And Chancellor Chase of New York University won the reluctant approval even of the *New York Times* (which had been rather hostile to Russell) when he urged that, no matter how much one may disagree with Russell's views, the question whether a judge may overrule educational authority in passing on the fitness of a teacher (on the basis of the latter's *opinions*) had not been properly settled and needed to be reviewed by the higher courts.

The statement that the appointment of Professor Russell "is in effect establishing a chair of indecency" is a rather scurrilous way of referring to the several hundred eminent teachers of philosophy who endorsed his appointment to the Universities of Chicago and California and to Harvard, where he had served as professor of philosophy to the expressed satisfaction of students, fellow-teachers, and educational administrators. One had a right to expect that a court of law pronouncing judgment as to the possible influence of a certain teacher would take into account the testimony of actual pupils as distinguished as Dr. Marjorie Nicolson, Dean of Smith College (where Russell had lectured) and president of the national association of the United Chapters of Phi Beta Kappa. Dr. Nicolson had been a pupil of Bertrand Russell at the

British Institute of Philosophical Studies and wrote that both in a large popular course and in a small seminar "Mr. Russell never introduced into his discussions of philosophy any of the controversial questions which his opponents have raised. . . . Mr. Russell is first and foremost a philosopher, and in his teaching he always remembers that. I should have had no way of knowing Mr. Russell's opinions on marriage, divorce, theism, or atheism, had they not been given an exaggerated form in the newspapers."

Judge McGeehan condemned Russell as an immoral person because of his divorce record in England. This record was known to the authorities of the many colleges, including those for women and the co-educational ones, where Russell was invited to teach and gave a course of lectures. In a country where many leaders of our public life have been divorced, can it be said as a matter of law that teachers who have gone through such marital difficulties must be dismissed? * Many, perhaps a majority, of our people regard George Eliot as one of the noblest women of the nineteenth century, though she lived in what was legally an adulterous relation with George Henry Lewes.

It is not necessary to point out to any literate audience how forced and utterly unwarranted is the misinterpretation of Russell's writings adduced in justification of the monstrous charge that Russell's appointment would endanger the health and morals of New York through his inciting young people to masturbation or to the crimes of homosexuality and abduction. But the tolerance and even favorable comment which Judge McGeehan's rhetorical opinion received in parts of our public press show how urgent it is that those who know anything about the history and importance of freedom of thought should keep the public informed as to the necessity of the distinction between incitement to crime and the free expression of philosophic doubt as to the adequacy of our traditional or conventional morality. In defending society against crime we must not suppress the questioning mind, which has been the

---

* In this connection it is curious to note that while Judge McGeehan was District Attorney of Bronx County a large number of divorces were there granted on legally sufficient evidence of adultery. But though adultery is a crime in New York State, District Attorney McGeehan never prosecuted a single one of the parties whose guilt was thus officially recorded.

One is reminded of the story of the lady who congratulated Dr. Johnson on having left out all obscene words from his dictionary. "Madam," said the honest Doctor, "I am sorry you looked for them."

basis not only of democratic but of all liberal civilization, as distinguished from societies of robots that act either from habit or according to what others tell them.

Judge McGeehan himself publicly expressed his expectation that his decision would be appealed and reviewed by the higher courts. What prevented the important issue which he raised from receiving due consideration from any of our higher courts? The first obstacle was the technical ruling (unfortunately sustained by our Court of Appeals) that Mr. Russell could not be made a party in a suit in which his reputation and his position as a teacher were at stake. This is marvelously strange when we consider the interest of Mrs. Kay in the suit. None of her children could possibly have been able to take any of Russell's courses at the City College. In the first place they lived in Brooklyn, and if they went to college at all they would naturally go to Brooklyn College rather than to the City College, which is in upper Manhattan. In the second place her daughters could not be admitted to the City College, which in its regular classes does not admit women. And in the third place, as Russell would have to retire in 1942 because of the age limit, none of her children could possibly have managed to qualify for admission in Russell's classes. If she was really interested in keeping her children from contact with Russell's ideas she should have applied for an order restraining publishers from publishing Russell's books, booksellers from selling them, and public libraries from circulating them; for in fact Russell has had far more popular influence through his writings than through his classes, which have always been highly technical. I think it is important to bear in mind the fictitious character of Mrs. Kay's interest which the courts were so eager to protect that they refused to let Mr. Russell answer her complaint. The reason given was that she was suing the Board of Higher Education and should not, therefore, be compelled to litigate with Professor Russell, though in fact she was trying to deprive him of the right to pursue his calling, on which he and his children depended for their living. If this is law, then surely, in the language of Dickens, "the law is a ass."

An honest friend of the venerable doctrine of "due process" might have expected that it would operate against depriving a man of his property and reputation without ever giving him a chance to be heard. But such expectation would also have shown serious innocence as to the forces behind the scenes in this case.

Very significant is the part played in this unsavory case by the Corporation Counsel of New York City. At first he appeared (through his assistant, Mr. Bucci) as counsel for the Board of Higher Education and contended that there was no justification in law for the removal of Professor Russell from the position to which he had been appointed. But after Judge McGeehan's decision he not only refused to vindicate the law by appealing the case but actively and effectively opposed the effort of the Board to do so.

What reason did he give for this radical change of attitude? Clearly not that the judge's written opinion convinced him that the office of the Corporation Counsel had been mistaken as to the law in the case. On the contrary, in his letter to the Board of Higher Education he quite definitely intimated that Judge McGeehan's decision was not in conformity with the law. The reason alleged for his "advice" was a rather thinly veiled opinion that the higher courts could not in this case be trusted to decide the issues involved on their merits. He therefore urged the Board to obey a decision unwarranted by the law and break a contract entered into in good faith by both parties, thereby committing a serious injustice against Professor Russell, who had resigned his previous position in California in reliance on the honor and official action of the Board of Higher Education in New York City.

It is, frankly, hard to believe that an honorable legal official of a great municipality could thus be willing to participate in a grossly dishonorable (if not illegal) procedure, if he were not under some pressure not referred to in his letter to the Board. And indeed there is some evidence of intervention by the Mayor, who gave the identical advice to the Board. Two incidents point in this direction. The first is the haste of the Mayor in putting into the city budget a provision that no part of the money of the Board of Higher Education should be used to pay Russell's salary. This was an unprecedented move of no real legal force, for if anything is established in the Education Law of New York it is the complete freedom of a school board to control expenditures within its own budget. Certainly the Mayor and the Board of Estimate have no right to interfere in the appointment of a professor in our city colleges, nor have they the right to bring about the removal of anyone who has been appointed. The action of the Mayor was just "a play to the gallery" for political reasons, as was the action of the City Council.

The second indication is the Mayor's subsequent action in publicly directing the Corporation Counsel not to appeal a case where the Board of Education was involved. Now a city, like any other client, may instruct its counsel not to appeal a case if such appeal will not serve its best interests. But where an agency such as a Board of Education has by law been granted certain powers, with which the Mayor cannot interfere, then his preventing an appeal hamstrings by indirection that which he may not directly control. No Mayor will openly tell the Board of Higher Education to appoint Professor X or to dismiss Professor Y. Yet to prevent the college from using its funds to pay a given teacher is to all intents and purposes compelling it to discharge that teacher. The Mayor has not been provided with facilities, and the law certainly gives him no power, to deal thus with the employees of our educational institutions. But whatever the influence of the Mayor, there is no doubt that an effective judicial review of the issues raised by Judge McGeehan's decision was prevented (1) by the Corporation Counsel's refusal to appeal from an order the granting of which he had opposed on good legal grounds, and (2) by the Appellate Division's sustaining his power to prohibit the Board of Higher Education from appearing in court through any other lawyer. This extraordinary situation, by which an administrative body is prevented from defending in court the legality of the acts within its province, was sustained by the Appellate Division in an argument which, to say the least, begs the whole question. That court said: "There is no duty resting upon the Board to engage the services of Russell." But since this court refused to consider the merits of the contention that Russell's original appointment was illegal, the *prima facie* contract between the Board and Professor Russell could not be thus set aside. Even an Appellate Division cannot abrogate a contract while at the same time it refuses to consider the question of its legality.

Despite all technicalities, no one can deny the obvious fact that by a solemn official act the Board appointed Professor Russell and that he in reliance thereon gave up another position. In the minds of all honorable men, therefore, the Board of Higher Education incurred a contractual obligation to disregard which would be disgraceful to the fair name of any city.

Even more important is the larger significance of the unlimited power thus given to the Corporation Counsel. For by preventing the Board of Higher Education from appearing in court to defend what it regards as the proper interpretation of its duties, the Corporation Counsel thus becomes not its legal servant but its master, and this subjects it to all sorts of abuses without its having any legal recourse. The cherished independence of the educational system of New York from political interference, which has been built up through the years and has been recognized by the highest courts,* is thus completely destroyed. This is an ominous and sinister situation. The office of the Corporation Counsel is instituted so that the city and its various departments may have adequate legal advice and have their rights defended in the courts. The Corporation Counsel is a lawyer. He may advise his clients that they have a bad case in law, or perhaps even that they are likely to lose a good case because of his suspicion that the judges of last resort are prejudiced and will not decide according to the law. It may even be argued that he has a right to express his opinion that the Board of Higher Education would be wasting the city's money in litigating a given case. But this was not the situation in the Russell case, where the members of the Board of Higher Education, anxious to deal honorably with Professor Russell and to carry to the Court of Appeals the grave issues involved, generously agreed to pay for counsel at their own personal expense. Certainly there is no sound reason of public policy why the Corporation Counsel should be able, by his own arbitrary opinion, to prevent important issues from receiving the full consideration for which our courts are instituted.

* "If there be one public policy well established in this State it is that public education shall be beyond control by municipalities and politics."—Chief Judge Crane in Matter of Divisich v. Marshall, 281 N. Y. 170, 22 N.E. (2) 327 (1939).

Sybille Bedford

.

THE TRIAL OF DR. ADAMS

The First Day

"The trial began at the Central Criminal
Court yesterday. . . ."   *The Times*

The Judge came on swiftly. Out of the side-door, an ermined puppet
progressing weightless along the bench, head held at an angle, an arm
swinging, the other crooked under cloth and gloves, trailing a wake of
subtlety, of secret powers, age: an Elizabethan shadow gliding across
the arras.

The high-backed chair has been pulled, helped forward, the figure is
seated, has bowed, and the hundred or so people who had gathered
themselves at split notice to their feet rustle and subside into appor-
tioned place. And now the prisoner, the accused himself is here—how
had he come, how had one missed the instant of that other clockwork
entry?—standing in the front of the dock, spherical, adipose, uphol-
stered in blue serge, red-faced, bald, facing the Judge, facing this day.
And already the clerk, risen from below the Judge's seat, is addressing
him by full name.

There cannot be a man or woman in this court who has not heard it
before.

". . . You are charged with the murder . . ."

And that, too, is expected. It is what all is set for—nobody, today, is here by accident—yet, as they fall, the words in the colorless clerical voice consummate exposure.

"Do you plead Guilty or Not Guilty?"

There is the kind of pause that comes before a clock strikes, a nearly audible gathering of momentum, then, looking at the Judge who has not moved his eyes:

"I am not guilty, my Lord."

It did not come out loudly but it was heard, and it came out with a certain firmness and a certain dignity, and also possibly with a certain stubbornness, and it was said in a private, faintly non-conformist voice. It was also said in the greatest number of words anyone could manage to put into a plea of Not Guilty. A loquacious man, then, under evident pressure to make himself heard; and how many among those present who do not simply hope that the burden of his plea may be true.

Now what sounds like, but may not quite be, William Makepeace Leader, John Christian Henderson, James Frederick Wright, floats across the court. Men arise from back benches, scurry or shuffle into sight, get themselves into the jury box: two rows, one above the other, of six seated figures cheek by jowl and not a pin to drop between them. Two women are found to be there, side by side in the upper tier. One is in a red coat and hat, the other has jet black hair and a cast of features suggestive of having been reared perhaps under another law. Everybody in this box is, or appears to be, respectable, middle-aged.

The prisoner is still standing. His right to object to any member of his jury has been recited to him by the clerk and he has turned his large, blank, sagging face—a face designed to be jovial—to the jury box and stares at them with round, sad, solemn eyes. The jurors, one by one, are reading out the oath. It is an old form of words, and it is not couched in everyday syntax. Some approach the printed text with circumspection, some rush it, most come several mild croppers, inexorably corrected—each time—by the usher.

All of this has taken no time at all. A routine dispatched without irrelevancy or hitch between clerk and usher in the well of the court like a practiced sheep-herding, while bench and bar stayed aloof. Now counsel for the Crown is on his feet.

Outside in the street, the Old Bailey is sustaining a siege this morning. Police vans and press vans, cameras and cameramen, detective sergeants and C.I.D.s and hangers-on, comings and goings in closed limousines, young men in bowler hats bent double under the weight of papers nudging their way through the crowd, a line of special constables at every door and thirty extra quarts of milk left for the cafeteria. Here, inside the court, there is more than silence, there is quiet.

A male voice droning: "May it please your Lordship—" and the case is opened.

A trial is supposed to start from scratch, *ab ovo*. A tale is unfolded, step by step, link by link. Nothing is left unturned and nothing is taken for granted. The members of the jury listen. They hear the tale corroborated, and they hear it denied; they hear it pulled to pieces and they hear it put together again; they hear it puffed into thin air and they hear it back as good as new. They hear it from the middle, they hear it sideways and they hear it straight; they all but hear it backward again through a fine toothcomb. *But they should never have heard it before.* When they first walk into that court, sit down in that box, they are like people before the curtain has gone up. And this, one is conscious from the first, cannot be so in the present case.

The accused, a doctor, in his fifties, is charged with the murder of a patient six years ago. Leading counsel for the Crown is setting out the prosecution's tale in manageable, spare, slow facts. It is the Attorney-General in person. He is standing in his pew, sheaf of foolscap in hand, a somewhat massive figure, addressing the jury in a full voice. The beginning is a warning. They must try to dismiss from their minds all they may have read or heard of this before.

"This is a very unusual case. It is not often that a charge of murder is brought against a doctor. . . ."

Above on the dais the Judge is listening. Full face and immobile, the robed husk has taken on a measure of flesh and youth. The black cloth and the delicate pair of gloves have been deposited. The face is not the profile; gone is that hint of cunning. This is more than a supremely intelligent face, it is a face marked with intellectual fineness. The Judge sits quite still, in easy absorption. Startling Mandarin hands flower from wide sleeves.

"A word about this doctor. You will hear that he is a doctor of medicine and a bachelor of surgery, that he has a diploma in anesthetics, holds an appointment as anesthetist to a hospital and has practised anesthetics for many years. With his qualifications and experience, you may think perhaps it is safe to assume the Doctor was not ignorant of the effects of drugs on human beings. . . ."

It goes on in a sort of casual boom.

Now Mrs. Morell was an old woman. . . . A widow. . . . A wealthy woman. . . . She left £157,000. . . . She was eighty-one years old when she died in November 1950 in her house at Eastbourne. In 1948, she had a stroke and her left side became paralyzed. The Doctor was in charge. She was attended by four nurses; and these nurses will give evidence. They will say they never saw Mrs. Morell in any serious pain. The Crown will also call a Harley Street authority. This medical man will tell them that he has formed the opinion that Mrs. Morell was suffering from cerebral arteriosclerosis, in ordinary language [here the Attorney-General lowers his voice a confidential shade], hardening of the arteries. They will hear that for pain to accompany such a condition is most unusual.

"You will hear of large quantities of drugs prescribed for her by the Doctor in the course of months, and supplied to her. One of the questions to be considered in this case will be: why were they given? It is one thing to give an old lady something to help her to sleep, but quite another to prescribe for her large quantities of morphia and heroin. . . ."

Here come detailed figures. The listening mind is pulled up. Figures can be stumbling blocks. These are intended to sound large. They do sound large. Jotted down (roundly), they come to 1629 grains of barbiturates, 1928 grains of Sedormid, 164 grains of morphia and 139 grains of heroin, prescribed over a period of ten and a half months. One hundred and thirty-nine grains of heroin into ten months make how many grains, or what fraction of a grain, per day—? And how much is a grain of heroin in terms of what should or could be given—? To whom, and when, and for what—?

". . . You will hear that these drugs if administered over a period result in a serious degree of addiction to them, a craving for them, a dependence on them. . . . [With weight] The Doctor was the source of supply. Did not Mrs. Morell become dependent upon him? *Why* were these drugs prescribed to an old lady who was suffering from the effects of a stroke but who was not suffering from pain?"

Through all of this the Doctor has been sitting on his chair in the dock, warder on each side, like a contained explosive. He did not fidget and he did not move, but his face reflected that a remarkable degree of impassivity was maintained by will against an equally high degree of pressure from within. At certain assertions his mouth compressed slowly and hard, and he shook his head to and fro, almost swinging it, as if prompted by an inner vision that did not correspond to what he had to hear. This head-shaking, which the Doctor repeated throughout his trial, seemed to express sorrow, anger, primness and exasperation all at once. It was oddly convincing.

"Perhaps," a hint of complacency in the delivery, "perhaps you may think that the answer lies in the changes made in her *will*." Mrs. Morell's solicitor, Mr. Sogno, will tell them that she made three wills in 1947 and that in none of these wills was there any mention of the Doctor. Then in April 1949 when she had been getting morphia and heroin for some months, the Doctor telephoned to her solicitor saying that she was extremely anxious about her will and wanted to see Mr. Sogno that day. So Mr. Sogno went to see her and eventually she made another will in which she bequeathed to the Doctor an oak chest containing silver.

"Nearly a year later the Doctor called on Mr. Sogno without an appointment and a conversation took place," a sharp look over spectacles at the jury, "which you may think a very curious one. The Doctor told Mr. Sogno that Mrs. Morell had promised him her Rolls-Royce in her will and that she now remembered that she had forgotten this, and that she desired to leave him not only the Rolls-Royce car but also the contents of a locked box at the bank, a box which the Doctor said contained jewelry. The Doctor went on to say that though Mrs. Morell was very ill, her mind was perfectly clear and she was in a fit condition to execute a codicil. Mr. Sogno proposed that they might wait until Mrs. Morell's son came at the week-end, but the Doctor suggested that Mr. Sogno should prepare a codicil and that the codicil could be executed and later destroyed if it did not meet with Mrs. Morell's son's approval. Was not that," another swift look at the jury, "rather an astonishing suggestion? It showed—did it not?—a certain *keenness?*"

The Attorney-General appears to be an earnest pleader. When he poses a rhetorical question, as he frequently does, it has a dutiful rather than dramatic sound.

Once more Mr. Sogno went to see Mrs. Morell, and Mrs. Morell made another will leaving the Doctor the chest of silver and, if her son predeceased her, the Rolls-Royce and an Elizabethan cupboard. "Perhaps you might think it significant and sinister that during the period when he was prescribing for her these very substantial quantities of morphia and heroin the Doctor was concerning himself so much about her will and telephoning her solicitor."

In September of that year the Doctor went away on holiday and his partner looked after Mrs. Morell in his absence. She was annoyed with the Doctor for leaving her and executed a codicil revoking her bequests to him.

Here there is one of these pauses which in court are filled not with coughs but an immense rustling of papers. The first exhibit in this case, a photostat of a graph, is being passed round, one up to the Judge, half a dozen to the jury, another copy or two for counsel of the defense. The graph demonstrates the alleged prescriptions by the Doctor.

". . . You will see how the prescriptions increased in quantity . . ." During the last thirteen days of Mrs. Morell's life the rate of morphia was over three times higher than in any of the preceding months, and the rate of heroin seven and a half times. Why? What had happened to Mrs. Morell necessitating these tremendous increases? If she had been in acute pain, heavy doses might have been justified, but she was *not* in acute pain. "The nurses will tell you that during her last days she was comatose or semi-conscious. And that brings us back to the question— why did the Doctor prescribe such quantities, such fatal quantities for which there is no medical justification?" A pause. "The submission of the Crown is that he did so because he had decided that the time had come for her to die!

"He knew—did he not?—a lot about her will. Whether he knew of the codicil executed while he was on holiday and what happened to it, you may perhaps discover in the course of this trial. The Doctor may have thought she should have no further opportunity for altering her will!"

This leaves a sense of confusion. On the far back benches behind the dock, where the overflow of the irregular press sits squeezed, special correspondents scrawl on their pads and nudge their neighbors. "But he'd been *cut out—?*" "He didn't know." Someone says just under his breath, "Bet the old girl told him." "That wasn't what he said to the police at Eastbourne." "Shsh . . ." "Shshsh . . ."

The Crown must come now to the night of her death. Mrs. Morell was lying unconscious. "The night nurse will tell you she was very weak, except for occasional spasms. [Heavily] She was in a coma. At

10 P.M. the Doctor came and himself filled a 5 c.c. syringe with a preparation——"

The Attorney-General held up an object. It is always slightly startling when an actual utensil of the outside world, not a chart or a document or a photograph of one, appears in a court of law. It does in fact quite often, yet it brings with it a hint of lurid impropriety. It causes what is called a stir; people in the gallery try to stand up and are instantly suppressed.

"The Doctor gave this syringe to the night nurse and told her to inject it into the unconscious woman. [Tone of doom] She did so. The Doctor took the empty syringe and refilled it with a similar quantity —an unusually large quantity on each occasion—and told the nurse to give the second injection to the patient if she did not become quieter. The nurse did not like giving another large injection from this unusually large syringe and later in the evening she telephoned the Doctor. She received her instructions and it was her duty to obey them. She gave the second injection. Mrs. Morell gradually became quiet, and at 2 A.M. she died.

"Why were those large injections given to an unconscious woman on the Doctor's orders?

"The prosecution cannot tell you what they were. Mrs. Morell may indeed have been a dying woman when they were given. If she was, then the prosecution submits that she was dying from overdoses of morphia and heroin which the Doctor prescribed, and it was murder by him. If, on the other hand, these two injections accelerated her death, it was also murder. The prosecution will submit that the only possible conclusion to which the jury can come is that the Doctor killed her, deliberately and intentionally."

A slight pause; then before the court has been able to take stock:

"The case for the prosecution does not rest here. On the same day, November 13th, 1950, the Doctor filled in a form to secure Mrs. Morell's cremation. One question which he had to answer on this form was, 'Have you, as far as you are aware, any pecuniary interest in the death of the deceased?' The Doctor's answer in his own writing was, 'Not as far as I am aware.' Authority was given for Mrs. Morell to be cremated.

"Six years later when a detective superintendent from Scotland Yard was making inquiries, he asked the Doctor about this cremation certificate. The Doctor said, 'Oh, that was not done wickedly. God knows it wasn't. We always want cremations to go off smoothly for the dear relatives. If I had said I knew I was getting money under the will they might get suspicious, and I like cremations and burials to go off smoothly. There was nothing suspicious really. It was not deceitful.'

"But for this false answer on the form, there might not have been a cremation and the prosecution might have been in a position to say how much morphia and heroin there was in the body of Mrs. Morell at the time of her death!

". . . In November 1950, Detective-Superintendent Hannam, with two other detectives, went to the Doctor's house. They went into the surgery and the Doctor was told they had a warrant for a search of the premises for dangerous drugs . . . The superintendent said, 'Doctor, look at this list of your prescriptions for Mrs. Morell. There are a lot of dangerous drugs here.' Later he asked, 'Who administered them?' The Doctor answered, 'I did, nearly all. Perhaps the nurses gave some, but mostly me.' The superintendent asked, 'Were there any of them left over when she died?' and the Doctor replied, *'No, none. All was given to the patient.* Poor soul, she was in terrible agony.'

"So there you have the Doctor saying that she was in terrible agony, when the nurses will tell you she was comatose and had been comatose for days and had not been suffering real pain."

And when this had sunk in:

"You will hear that the maximum quantity of heroin which should be prescribed in a period of twenty-four hours is a quarter of a grain. Yet no less than eight grains were prescribed by the Doctor on a single day. The maximum dose of morphia is half a grain. There were ten grains prescribed on the 8th of November, twelve on the 9th and eighteen on the 11th. The prosecution will call medical authority who will tell you that in their view Mrs. Morell could not possibly have survived the administration of these drugs prescribed in her last five days."

From there the Attorney-General moves forward again to the near present, to 1956 and the inquiry six years after the death, a time-lag surely extraordinary in English justice, and about which we are told nothing.

". . . Last November the Doctor went to see Detective-Superintendent Hannam at police headquarters. He asked how the investigation was getting on. The superintendent said, 'I am still inquiring into the death of some of your patients, Doctor.' The Doctor said, 'Which?' and the superintendent answered, 'Mrs. Morell is certainly one.' The

Doctor said, 'Easing the passing of a dying person is not all that wicked. She wanted to die—that cannot be murder. It is impossible to accuse a doctor.' "

Half the court turned to look again at the accused.

"In December, the Doctor was arrested. He was told he would be taken to the police station and charged with the murder of Mrs. Morell. He said, 'Murder—can you prove it was murder?' Superintendent Hannam said, 'You are now charged with murder.' And the Doctor said, 'I do not think you could prove it was murder—she was dying in any event.' As he left the house he gripped the hand of his receptionist and said to her, 'I will see you in heaven.'

"She was dying in any event! [Decrescendo—businesslike] I submit to you that the evidence I and my learned friends will call before you will prove conclusively that this old lady was murdered." The Attorney-General sits down. The speech has lasted just under two hours.

Instantly a witness is on his way to the stand. A pharmaceutical chemist and what is called a formal witness. His name is given; his address. These will appear tomorrow in *The Times* and perhaps a half-dozen national and provincial newspapers. One of the three Crown counsel, a Q.C., swiftly extracts the relevant evidence—the drugs listed by the prosecution were in fact dispensed by Messrs. Browne, the chemists, from prescriptions by the Doctor. We learn—if we care to listen—how chemists' books are kept and drugs recorded; we learn how the prosecution's list has been compiled. This witness is followed by another chemist; then a third. The Judge courteously puts a question. It is the first time that we hear him speak, and at once he reveals both grasp and charm. Could it not be stated, he asks, how many grains a 5 c.c. syringe would hold? 12.5 grains, witness replies; that is, if the syringe is quite full. And so, openly, honestly, humbly, the first bare facts are made secure beyond *unnecessary* doubt. It may be dull, it may seem redundant, it certainly is expensive and exacting; it is also gallant and essential, this toiling care to train the light of sequence, truth and reason on the obvious and minute—justice here is not only seen, it is understood being done. Rigged accusation, fake evidence? a demagogue would meet short shrift. It is thanks to the law's patient production—quixotic almost in its extreme sesquipedalian way—of these routine witnesses: George Albert Church of Greenover Road, Teddington, ironmonger's assistant, who has nothing to gain and nothing to lose and little to fear, that people can rest stolid in their trust that if a man be accused of poisoning or stabbing it must be shown where the poison or a knife came from. It has not always been like this, it may one day be so no longer; even at this time it is not so everywhere. But here and now, while the fourth pharmaceutical chemist is testifying to a preparation of eyedrops, we can allow our minds the luxury to stray.

Court No. 1 at the Old Bailey is a large court as English courts go. It is all the same no more than a large room, and it is packed today. As an auditorium it boasts some drawbacks. For one thing it is cram-full of woodwork. Stained· oak obstructs foot and eye. Boxes, desks, tables, benches, fitted ingeniously enough, jut at all angles; they hold about two hundred people, and some of them can hear nearly everything and see one thing very well. The witness-box, at conversational distance from the dais, stands in something like the relation of the lectern to the altar; other items bear the stamp of the committee-room, while the benches of the press-box might have come from a Victorian school. The shorthand writer has his own small pen. The dock is something else again. It is like a capacious loose-box, the only space in court that is not jammed, and it is set up plumb in the middle of everything, blocking every view. Yet the sum of these arrangements achieves a satisfying sense of unity. The prisoner can look across the well at the Judge; the Judge sees him. Between them, below, in the small square pit, furrowed by advocates' benches, munitioned from the solicitors' table, the fray takes place.

The jury have the ringside view; but it is quite impossible for them to look a witness in the face. The public gallery proper is far and high beneath the roof. In court few members of the press or public can see the prisoner and none can see examining counsel *and* his witness at one time; and there are some low rows of seats behind the dock from which no one can see anything at all. All can see the Judge; which does not mean that he can be heard by everyone.

The purpose of a criminal trial is to determine whether a specific act, an event in time, took place or not, or took place in a certain way, to determine in short whether somebody has *done it*. The answer lies with the jury, twelve men and women selected at random within some, nowadays not very stringent, property qualifications. The facts connected with the alleged event are spread in open court by counsel and their witnesses, and re-assembled by the Judge; but it is the jury alone who must come to the conclusion, Yes or No, it was like this or it cannot have been; without their verdict no man in England can be punished for any of the great offenses, and their verdict, if it is acquittal, is irreversible.

We now have the bare bones of the prosecution's case. What do they amount to? A woman, eighty-one years old, half paralyzed by a stroke, has died. The prosecution says she did not die of age or illness but of drugs. Large doses of drugs, not given at any one time—no poisoner's moment—but drugs prescribed during the last five days of her life without a medical reason. Three questions—at this stage—leap to the mind.

Was the quantity of drugs prescribed actually administered? ("All given to the patient," the Doctor himself had volunteered, though at a moment when perhaps he hardly had his wits about.)

Was the dosage of these drugs actually fatal, or was it merely— however incomprehensibly or dangerously—very large?

Was there in fact no medical or other reason short of murder for their administration?

On these points, so far, would seem to rest the weight of the whole case, and not on the weak motive or the answer given on a form, or the Doctor's utterances to the police, wild though they may be.

The motive, as presented by the prosecution, is bewilderingly inadequate. Can they be suggesting that a—sane?—man in the Doctor's circumstances would commit murder for the chance of inheriting some silver and an ancient motor-car ironically enough no longer mentioned in the will? Unless some sense of strength can be infused into the motive it must become the sagging point of this unequal web. Yet in a way the motive has already drawn sustenance from an irregular but not secret source; it has waxed big by headlines, by printed innuendo, by items half remembered from the preliminary hearing. There have been published rumors of rich patients, mass poisonings, of legacy on legacy in solid sterling. . . . Everybody knows a bit too much and no one knows quite enough; there is a most disturbing element in this case, extra-mural half-knowledge that cannot be admitted and cannot be kept out.

And so there is a sense of flatness after the prosecution's speech. Was that all? At the very least a tighter case has been expected. There are also some ill-fitted points. The back benches mutter.

"You believe in the unknown quantity in the *unusually large syringe?*"

"Pelion on Ossa."

"Cheap. Not what you'd expect to get in a British court."

"Chap's got to put *something* in his case."

"Shsh . . ."

"Wouldn't you think he could have taken his pick? Widows dying like flies, corpses dug up all over the country . . ."

"Why Mrs. Morell?"

"No body."

"No reasonable gain."

"Stone cold."

"Shshsh."

"We'll see."

The fifth witness for the prosecution—called after the short adjournment: one hour and five minutes for luncheon—is a woman, and a good deal less peripheral. Suddenly the case is under way. Nurse Stronach—stocky, a face of blurred features except for a narrow mouth and strong jaw. By question fitted after question, counsel gets her to put the court in the picture; we have returned to the tortoise from the spectator's hare.

Nurse Stronach was relief nurse to Mrs. Morell (in Mrs. Morell's own house). Three weeks of night duty in June 1950, one of day duty. Another three weeks of day duty in October. On the Doctor's instructions, she is prompted to tell, Mrs. Morell was given a quarter of a grain of morphia every evening. The Doctor came every night.

Counsel [dead-pan, neutral voice] "Did you see him do anything with a syringe?"

Nurse Stronach [flatly] "He gave her injections."

"Did you see the Doctor give them?"

[Pursing her mouth] "We were not allowed in the room."

"Who forbade you to be in the room?"

"I think it was Mrs. Morell's wish that we were not in the room."

[Making his point] "You personally did not see the actual injection given, but you did see the Doctor prepare the syringe?"

[Pleased to have this offering] "Yes, but I could not tell you what it was."

[Gravely] "You do not know what the injections which the Doctor gave her were?"

"No, sir, I have no idea."

"Did the Doctor ever say anything to you about them?"

"He did not tell us."

[In half tones from the Judge] "Mr. Stevenson, is this perhaps a convenient moment to adjourn?" The usher takes it up; we are on our feet; the Judge has risen, he has his gloves, slides along the bench, is gone. The prisoner has vanished. The pattern is broken up, a crowd of people are making their way, talking, to the door.

Outside it is broad daylight. And one block away we are in London on a warm afternoon in March at 5 P.M.

[EDITOR'S NOTE: The trial of Dr. John Bodkin Adams in 1957 was the longest murder trial in the history of London's Old Bailey. After seventeen days in court, Dr. Adams was acquitted.]

Edgar Lustgarten

:

THE TRIAL OF LIZZIE BORDEN

from *Verdict in Dispute*

I

The charge against Lizzie Borden was inconceivable. That was the enduring strength of her defense. No matter how cogent the evidence, no matter how honest the witnesses, how could anyone credit the prosecution's case? That a woman, gently bred and delicately nurtured, should plan a murderous assault upon her stepmother; that she should execute it in the family home with such ferocious and demoniac force that the victim's head was smashed almost to pulp; that, having gazed upon her sickening handiwork, she should calmly wait an hour or more for her father to return; that she should then slaughter him with even greater violence so that hardened physicians shuddered at the sight; that neither loss of nerve nor pricking of remorse seemed to follow in the wake of such unnatural butchery—this was a tale that not merely challenged but defied belief. It was like asking one to accept the testimony of others that a horse recited Shakespeare or a dog had solved an anagram.

II

Everything combined to make this strain upon credence almost insupportable. At the eighteenth century's lowest moral ebb, some slatternly wanton such as Hogarth drew might have done these murders in a fetid slum, and still relied on incredulity giving the most unthinking jury

263

pause. But this was not the eighteenth century; it was 1892. It was no strumpet of the streets who faced her trial, but the well-respected daughter of a well-respected man. And the setting of the scene was not Gin Lane or Seven Dials but Fall River, Massachusetts, deep in the heart of puritan New England.

Fall River at that time was a pleasant enough place, about the size of modern Cambridge, and not unlike a University town in its strong sense of community. People took close interest in other people's business. The leading citizens and chief officials were known by sight to all. Town matters wagged more tongues than national politics, and Fall River natives recognised as aristocracy, not the remote Four Hundred of New York, but the old Yankee families dwelling in their midst.

To this local élite belonged the Bordens, with Andrew Jackson Borden at their head. He was a prosperous business man and banker who, through a union of acumen and avarice, steadily increased his considerable wealth. He chose to live, however, in rather modest style. His first wife having died when he was forty, he presently wedded one Miss Abby Gray and, with her and the two daughters of his former marriage, took up residence in a house on Second Street. It was a narrow house standing in a narrow garden, hemmed in by other houses on almost every side, with its front door only a few feet from the traffic and bustle of a much frequented thoroughfare. In a sense, nothing was lacking: downstairs had a sitting room, a dining room and a parlor; upstairs had a guest room and a dressing room for Mrs. Borden besides a separate bedroom for each of the two girls. But there was space without spaciousness, convenience without luxury, and both inside and out the house was unimposing if one remembered that this was the abode of a rich man.

In August 1892 the Bordens had been living there for about twenty years. Andrew was almost seventy. His wife was sixty-four. Miss Emma was forty-one. Miss Lizzie was thirty-two.

Before Miss Lizzie reached the age of thirty-three, this sedate and unexciting gentlewoman had made her name a lasting household word.

III

To all outward appearance the Borden house harbored a tranquil and contented household. But the façade was deceptive. Behind its look of blank correctitude lay deep antipathies and painful tensions.

The causes, though various, were intimately allied. There was the un-
attractive nature of the master; with his niggardly ways and autocratic
temper, old Andrew inspired dread rather than affection. There was the
classical aversion to the presence of a stepmother; the second Mrs. Borden, though amiable and harmless, could not engage the goodwill of
Andrew's daughters. And as the latter grew up, their bitterness developed in the shape of jealousy and squabbling over property—jealousy
that sprang from already strained relationships, squabbling that shad-
owed those relationships still more. The time came when Miss Lizzie, sharper-spoken of the sisters, pointedly dropped the appellation
"Mother" and adopted the formal "Mrs. Borden" in its stead.

The division in the family intensified and hardened. As years went
by, Miss Emma and Miss Lizzie evolved a technique to avoid their parents' company. Downstairs in the common rooms some contact was inevitable, but they contrived to reduce this to a satisfactory minimum by
altering the times at which they took their meals. Upstairs it was much
simpler. By bolting a single communicating door, the first floor could be
split up into independent parts, one served by the front stairs, the other
by the back.

On both sides of this door the bolts were permanently drawn.

IV

The Massachusetts summer is uncomfortably hot. That of 1892 was no
exception to the rule, and Fall River sweltered through those long July
days during which dogs are reputed to go mad.

Late in the month Miss Emma left for Fairhaven, where she had arranged to spend a holiday with friends. At the same time Miss Lizzie
paid a visit to New Bedford, but was back again at home before the
week was out. In the sultry, stifling nights that followed her return, four
people slept at the house on Second Street: Miss Lizzie, the old couple,
and the servant, Bridget Sullivan, who occupied a room on the attic floor
above.

On Wednesday, August 3rd, the four increased to five. Uncle Morse,
a brother of the late Mrs. Borden, arrived unexpectedly to stay a night
or two. He found Andrew and his wife a little out of sorts; whether
through the heat, or through some less obvious cause, in the previous
night both had been seized with vomiting, and, though better, were still

not free from physical malaise. Lizzie, too, they told him, had been similarly affected, but in that divided and dissevered house Uncle Morse was not to see his niece till nearly noon next day.

By then any thought of this mild indisposition had vanished in the stress of far more terrible events.

v

August 4th, 1892, is a memorable date in the history of crime.

At the Borden home, where the grisly drama was to be enacted, the morning opened normally enough. The older people were all early risers, and seven o'clock found them sitting down to breakfast, prepared and served by the young Irish maid. The sun climbed swiftly into a clear sky; the air was heavy with the heat of many weeks; all signs portended, rightly as it proved, that they were in for another scorching day. All the more reason to perform one's chores before the torrid blaze of afternoon.

By nine o'clock Uncle Morse had left the house to visit relatives elsewhere in the town. By nine fifteen Mr. Borden had set out on his round of business calls. Mrs. Borden had got a feather duster and was occupying herself with her household duties.

Meanwhile Miss Lizzie had made her first appearance. At nine o'clock she came into the kitchen where the servant Bridget was washing up the dishes. Bridget asked her what she fancied for her breakfast, but Miss Lizzie didn't seem to fancy very much. Having helped herself to a cup of coffee, she sat down to drink it at the kitchen table.

When the dishes were finished, Bridget took them to the dining room. There Mrs. Borden was assiduously dusting. She had noticed that the windows had got dirty and asked Bridget to wash them as her next domestic task.

Bridget decided to wash the outsides first. She got a brush and some cloths, filled a pail with water, and went out through the side door, which she left unlocked.

Mrs. Borden stayed inside. So did Miss Lizzie. The sun beat down with pitiless persistence and a drowsy silence fell upon the house.

VI

At the partition fence Bridget stopped for a gossip with the maid next door. Then she started on the window-cleaning, working her way methodically round the house. She naturally looked into each ground-floor room in turn. She saw nobody in any.

The outside washing took perhaps an hour. Bridget then went back into the house, carefully locking the side door behind her. The Bordens were fussy about things like that, being morbidly fearful of robbers and intruders.

Everything was quiet; no one was about. Upstairs, taking it easy, Bridget enviously thought; best thing to do, on a broiler such as this. Conscientiously she started on the inside of the windows. . . .

At a quarter to eleven there was a noise at the front door; fumbling with a key and rattling of the lock. Must be Mr. Borden. Bridget dropped her cloths and ran to let him in.

She found the front door not only locked but bolted. As she struggled to get it open so as not to keep the master waiting, somebody behind her laughed out loud.

Bridget glanced over her shoulder. Miss Lizzie was standing at the top of the staircase, a few feet from the open door of the guest room. What moved her to mirth at that particular moment must ever be a theme for speculation; whether it was the spectacle of a flustered Bridget, or whether it was some hilarious secret of her own. . . .

When Mr. Borden was finally admitted, Miss Lizzie came downstairs.

"Mrs. Borden has gone out," she volunteered. "She had a note from someone who is sick."

Her father made no comment. It was hotter than ever, and he had still not shaken off the after-effects of that mysterious illness. His walk round town had tired him more than usual. He went into the sitting room to rest.

Bridget was now doing the windows in the dining room. Miss Lizzie joined her there. She brought in an ironing board, put it on the table, produced some handkerchiefs and commenced to iron.

For a space the two women worked away in silence. Then Miss Lizzie asked a casual-sounding question.

"Are you going out?"

"I don't know," Bridget said, energetically polishing, "I might and I might not."

"If you go out," said Miss Lizzie, "be sure and lock the door, for Mrs. Borden has gone out on a sick call and I might go out too."

"Miss Lizzie, who is sick?" the maid inquired.

"I don't know. She had a note this morning; it must be in town."

The windows were finished. Bridget withdrew into the kitchen, where she washed out the cloths. Presently Miss Lizzie followed her.

"There's a cheap sale of dress goods on down town," she remarked. "They are selling some kind of cloth at eight cents a yard."

"Well," Bridget said, "I guess I'll have some."

But at the moment Bridget did not feel inclined for out-of-doors. She had been up since six and kept hard at it ever since. A lie on the bed would make a nice mid-morning break. . . .

In her attic box, Bridget yawned, stretched herself and relaxed. On the sitting room couch old Andrew, spent by his exertions, fell asleep. Once again the house lay in the stillness of that drowsy quiet.

VII

The alarm was given fifteen minutes later.

Bridget, day-dreaming beneath the baking roof, heard her name called somewhere far below. Even at that distance, though, she caught the note of urgency. She jumped up at once and called out to know what was the matter.

"Come down quick," Miss Lizzie's voice floated up through the house. "Come down quick; Father's dead; somebody came in and killed him."

Dumfounded and mistrusting her own ears, Bridget ran down the back stairs as fast as she could go.

Miss Lizzie was standing close to the side door. Bridget made as if to go into the sitting room, but Miss Lizzie checked her—perhaps to spare her feelings.

"Don't go in. I've got to have a doctor quick."

Doctor Bowen lived opposite. Bridget flew across the road, leaving Miss Lizzie sole guardian of the dead.

The doctor arrived and went straight into the sitting room. He was to describe what he saw there later on the witness stand. "Mr. Borden was lying on the lounge. His face was very badly cut, apparently with a sharp instrument; it was covered with blood. I felt of his pulse and satisfied myself that he was dead. I glanced about the room and saw there was nothing disturbed; neither the furniture nor anything at all. Mr. Borden was lying on his right side, apparently at ease, as if asleep. His face was hardly to be recognized by one who knew him."

VIII

The news spread like wildfire. As police and officials hurried to the house, a crowd of gapers packed the street outside, eager for any sight or sound connected with calamity.

Dr. Bowen had to force a passage through this throng when he came out of the gate. He had covered Andrew Borden's body with a sheet; there was no other service he could usefully perform; now, at Miss Lizzie's personal request, he was going to the post office to telegraph Miss Emma. Mrs. Borden, he had gathered, had gone upon some errand, and all they could do was wait for her return. Poor woman, Dr. Bowen thought, as he watched the gathering thicken; wherever she is, she'll hear the tidings soon enough.

He dispatched the telegram and gloomily made his way back towards the house. As he entered a neighbor of the Bordens caught his arm. Her face was gray and her hands shook uncontrollably.

"They have found Mrs. Borden," she said huskily.

"Where?" asked the doctor.

"Upstairs," said the neighbor. "In the front room."

It was Miss Lizzie's suggestion that had prompted them to search; "I'm almost positive," she said, "I heard her coming in." It was Bridget and the neighbor who discovered Mrs. Borden, lying lifeless and mangled on the guest room floor. Her body was growing cold, and the blood which enveloped her mutilated head had already become matted and practically dry.

The doctors concluded that when Andrew Borden died his wife had already been dead more than an hour.

IX

If the case had stopped short there, if no charge against anyone had ever been preferred, Massachusetts would still have gone through weeks of ferment. If some hobo, some outcast, had been taxed with the crimes, his trial and the verdict determining his fate would have furnished all America with months of keen discussion. But when, after seven days of correlating evidence, during which the incredible gradually took shape, Fall River police arrested Lizzie Borden, the case at once acquired an entirely different stamp. It transcended the limits of geography and fashion; its range in time was perpetuity, in space the globe.

X

The trial of Lizzie Borden, delayed by various formalities of the law, took place at New Bedford in June 1893. It lasted thirteen days.

English readers, recalling the farce at Monkeyville or the spirited court scenes filmed in Hollywood, might pardonably expect the Borden trial to yield its quota of slapstick and burlesque. On the contrary. From first to last, at all times and all levels, the proceedings were conducted with a native dignity seldom attained in any land or age.

Three judges sat upon the bench: Chief Justice Mason, Mr. Justice Blodgett and Mr. Justice Dewey. For the Commonwealth (equivalent of the Crown) was Hosea Knowlton, the District Attorney, aided and partnered by William Moody, a colleague imported from an adjacent area. George D. Robinson, a former Congressman and ex-Governor of the State, with Andrew Jennings and Melvin Adams made up the team engaged for the defense.

To the modern eye, which finds a whiskered barrister hardly less freakish than a bald musician, there would have been something richly comic in the fine display of fringe, mustache and beard visible on counsels' row at Lizzie Borden's trial. But the advocates who sported these adornments were far from comic figures. They were masters of their complicated craft: shrewd in tactics, dexterous in argument, keen in cross-questioning, eloquent in speech. The defense, while energetically contesting every point and seizing every benefit admitted by the rules, took care in doing so never to depart from the highest standard of forensic practice. The prosecution, while making no effort to conceal the reluctance and distaste with which they entered on the case, did not suffer this to influence or impede the effective discharge of their melancholy duty.

In contrast to the custom observed in English trials, junior counsel played a prominent part. They were not confined to calling a few unimportant witnesses; they shared the speeches, and sometimes the cross-examination. As Knowlton was reserving himself for later responsibilities, it fell to William Moody to open for the Commonwealth.

XI

Moody's speech was diffidently phrased, as befitted a naturally modest second string. He had frequent recourse to the protective "I believe" and to the half-apologetic "We fix that as well as we can." But there was no cause for diffidence in the evidence he outlined. Before he had finished it was clear to demonstration that the Commonwealth had only moved on very solid ground. Their case was widely as well as firmly based—on proof of motive, indications of design, circumstances pointing to exclusive opportunity, and acts by Miss Lizzie which (it could be argued) were only reconcilable with consciousness of guilt.

The motive broached, of course, was hatred of the stepmother, and concern for the destination of the father's substance. Counsel crystallized the bitterness that had inspired the former by referring to a slight but illuminating incident. It had occurred in the house on the morning of the murders while the bodies were still lying there in piteous quiescence. The Assistant City Marshal had arrived upon the scene, and in fulfilment of his office was questioning Miss Lizzie. "When did you last see your mother?" he had asked. "She is not my mother, sir," Miss Lizzie had replied. "She is my stepmother. My mother died when I was a child."

To support their second proposition, that the prisoner was plotting and contemplating murder, the Commonwealth relied upon a curious conversation which had taken place between Miss Lizzie and a friend. On the eve of the catastrophe, while old Andrew and his wife spent their last night on earth entertaining Uncle Morse, Miss Lizzie went across town to see Miss Alice Russell, with whom for some time she had been on familiar terms. Miss Russell soon observed that her companion was depressed, and apparently a prey to morbid fears and fancies. "I cannot help feeling," she said, "something's going to happen." Miss Russell tried to dissipate this mood by cheerful logic, but Miss Lizzie stubbornly declined to be persuaded. "Last night we were all sick," she said. "We are afraid we have been poisoned. . . . Father has so much trouble with men that come to see him, I am afraid that some of them will do something to him. I expect nothing but that the building will be burnt down over our heads. The barn has been broken into twice." "That," said Miss Russell soothingly, "was boys after pigeons." "All right," said Miss Lizzie, "but the house has been broken into in broad daylight, when Bridget and Emma and I were the only ones at home. I saw a man the other night lurking about the buildings, and as I came he jumped and ran away. Father had trouble with a man the other day; there were angry words, and he turned him out of the house."

Miss Lizzie's foreboding that "something" was going to happen might have been premonition or sheer coincidence. But the Commonwealth, taking the conversation as a whole, invited the jury to accept a different view—that she was cunningly diverting suspicion on to others in respect of crimes she herself meant to commit.

The prisoner's opportunity of accomplishing both murders was plain and incontestable on the admitted facts. But the Commonwealth were able to take this a step further. It was not only that *Miss Lizzie* had had ample opportunity; was there any opportunity for *anybody else?* The other members of the household were ruled out; Emma was in Fairhaven, Uncle Morse was with a niece more than a mile away, Bridget at the time of the second murder was upstairs. If it was not Miss Lizzie, then it must have been an intruder. There had been no entry by force. And, assuming for the moment that someone could get in and out completely unobserved, where were the signs that anyone had done so? Nothing was disturbed. No property was taken. No drawers had been ransacked. Mr. Borden's watch and money—more than eighty dollars —were left upon his person. What then was the motive prompting someone from outside? Was he perhaps one of those men Miss Lizzie spoke of to Miss Russell who had come to pay old Borden out after some angry clash? Then how came it that there was not the slightest evidence of a struggle? Old Andrew may have been asleep upon the sitting-room couch, but his wife would hardly go to sleep upon the guest-room floor. And yet, said Moody, "the assailant, whoever he or she may have been, was able to approach each victim, in broad daylight, and without a struggle or a murmur, to lay them low."

XII

Motive fixed; design set forth; opportunity established. But there still remains the weightiest part of the prosecution case: the *behavior* of Miss Lizzie that day and the days after. Upon three matters especially the Commonwealth pressed hard: one, the note from the unidentified sick person; two, the variations in Miss Lizzie's story; three, the burning of the light blue figured dress.

The business of the note is perhaps the most damning single point against the prisoner. "Mrs. Borden has gone out," says Miss Lizzie to her father, at the moment when he may go looking for her round the house. "She had a note from someone who is sick." There can be no denying that was what Miss Lizzie said; she admitted it herself when examined at the inquest. She had not, she deposed, seen the note with her own eyes, but Mrs. Borden told her of it, without naming the sender. Hence her own statement when her father returned home—a natural passing-on of domestic information. But the Commonwealth would have none of it. "That statement," declared Moody, "we put forward as a lie; it was intended for no purpose except to stifle enquiry into the whereabouts of Mrs. Borden."

It is the grave and awful fact that neither note nor sick person ever came to light. The implications for the prisoner are appalling, and, try as they would, the defense could not avoid them. The Commonwealth, not surprisingly, came to elevate the note to the most vital place of all, and it formed the subject matter of a powerful passage in the long speech which constituted Knowlton's winding up. "My learned associate said in opening that that statement was a lie. I reaffirm that serious charge. No note came; no note was written; nobody brought a note; nobody was sick. Mrs. Borden had not had a note. *I will stake the case,*" said the District Attorney, *"on your belief in the truth of that proposition.* . . . Little did it occur to Lizzie Borden when she told that lie to her father that there would be eighty thousand witnesses of its falsity. My distinguished friend has had the hardihood to suggest that somebody may have written that note and not come forward to say so. Why, Mr. Foreman, do you believe there exists in Fall River anybody so lost to all sense of humanity who would not have rushed forward without anything being said? But they have advertised for the writer of the note which was never written and which never came. . . . The whole falsehood of that note came from the woman in whose keeping Mrs. Borden was left by Andrew Borden, and it was false as the answer Cain gave to his Maker when He said to him, 'Where is thy brother Abel?' "

Cain had answered, "Am I my brother's keeper?" Lizzie Borden had not waited to be asked. "Mrs. Borden has gone out. She had a note from someone who is sick."

Maybe she was more free from sin than Cain. Maybe she was just smarter.

XIII

That morning of August 4th, as person after person—the maid, the neighbors, the doctor and the police—learnt from Miss Lizzie's lips that she had found her father killed, each in turn was moved to ask her: "Where were you?" It was not a query rooted in suspicion, but an instinctive reaction to something unexplained. Had she been out, had she repaired like Bridget to a remote part of the house, that she saw and heard nothing of the assault or the assailant?

Where were you? Miss Lizzie faced this question more than half a dozen times. Moody closely analyzed her answers. To Bridget she had said: "I was out in the backyard. I heard a groan, came in and found the door open and found my father." To Mrs. Churchill, first of the neighbors to arrive, she said: "I was out in the barn. I was going for a piece of iron when I heard a distress noise, came in and found the door open and found my father dead." To Dr. Bowen she said: "I was in the barn looking for some iron." To Miss Russell she said: "I went to the barn to get a piece of tin or iron." To one officer she said: "I was out in the barn for twenty minutes." To another she said: "I was upstairs in the barn for about half an hour." To a third she said: "I was in the barn and heard a noise like scraping."

Now hunting for what are called "discrepancies" is a favorite occupation of legal pettifoggers. Such gentry often may be heard to say that they have "been through the Statements with a fine tooth-comb," and they proudly point out the results of their tooth-combing—some trivial variation of emphasis or phrase. But statements made at different times by a really honest person hardly ever exactly correspond. Conformity is the offspring of deliberated art.

This consideration would not be ignored by able, upright men like Moody and his leader. Their criticism was thus not primarily directed at the variations catalogued above. They took a more effective point— that later, when the flurry of that day had passed and Miss Lizzie produced a full, detailed account, she departed in a genuinely essential particular from what she had said in her earlier replies. Three times at least in those first hours of confusion she had told of hearing some kind of a noise; a groan, a "distress noise," a noise like something scraping— but at any rate a sound that had attracted her attention, drew her back into the house, and so led to the discovery. But "as enquiry," Moody said, "begin to multiply upon her, another story came into view. . . . It is not, gentlemen, and I pray your attention to it, a difference of words here. In one case the statement is that she was alarmed by the noise of the homicide; in the other case the statement is that she came coolly, deliberately, about her business (from the barn), looking after her ironing, putting down her hat and *accidentally* discovered the homicide as she went upstairs."

However ingrained one's detestation of "discrepancies," one must concede the valid premise underlying this. In the upheaval following on the murders, the barn and the backyard may have seemed interchangeable and twenty minutes much the same as half an hour. But could you mistake how you had first made the discovery—whether a noise had sent you in already apprehensive or whether the hideous spectacle burst on you unawares? Could you forget whether the first alarm attracted eye or ear?

Unless Miss Lizzie was a liar and much worse, the answer is: you could.

XIV

The murders were committed on a Thursday. It was not till the next Sunday that Miss Lizzie burnt the dress.

There was no attempt at concealment or deception; no surreptitious happenings beneath the cloak of night. She acted quite openly, in daylight, before witnesses. For an innocent woman, her behavior was extraordinarily naïve; for a guilty one, it was extraordinarily stupid—or, as in the tales of G. K. Chesterton and Poe, extraordinarily clever in its very ostentation. For Miss Lizzie had been warned to pick her steps with care. On the Saturday evening the Mayor of Fall River had expressly informed her that she was now under suspicion.

It was the following day, a little before noon. Alice Russell, who at this time was staying in the house, came down from the upper floor and went into the kitchen. There she found both Miss Lizzie and Miss Emma. The latter was busy washing dishes at the sink. Miss Lizzie was standing at the far end by the stove. She had a dress over her arm.

As Miss Russell came in Miss Emma turned her head and said to her sister: "What are you going to do?" "I'm going to burn this old thing up," replied Miss Lizzie. "It's all covered with paint."

She proceeded forthwith to tear it into strips.

There were several policemen on duty in the yard who could easily see in any time they chose to look. Miss Russell was so conscious of the equivocal effect created by this scene that she urged her friend at least to stand back from the window. "I wouldn't do that," she said, "where people can see you." Perhaps this remark took Miss Lizzie by surprise. At any rate, she did step a little out of vision—and placidly went on with the destruction of the dress.

The police, as Moody pointed out, had already searched the house and examined every garment to see if it was stained. They had found none marked with paint.

If the Commonwealth could have proved beyond a peradventure that the dress Miss Lizzie burnt upon the stove was the dress she had worn on the morning of the murders, they would have pried loose the chief plank in her defense. *Not one who saw her on that convulsive morning had observed any blood upon her person or her clothes,* though—out of convention rather than necessity—neighbors had unhooked her dress, fanned her face and rubbed her hands. It was even more remarkable than in the case of Wallace. Wallace—on the assumption, for this purpose, of his guilt—had the house to himself while he washed and changed his clothes. He had to be quick, but he was safe from interruption. If Miss Lizzie committed these two sanguinary crimes ("the assailant would be spattered," said the prosecution expert) she would also presumably be bound to wash and change. But she must have done it *twice*—and each time at the risk of being come upon by Bridget before all the traces of blood had been removed. And even if she ran that risk and, by the yardstick of success, justified her daring, how did she dispose of the incriminating clothes? After the second death, when the time margin was so narrow, they could only have been hidden somewhere in the house.

There lay the significance of the light blue figured dress which the prosecution sought to prove was the robe of homicide. But this was precisely what they could not do. Their witnesses disagreed among themselves about the dress Miss Lizzie wore upon the crucial day. Mr. Churchill said one thing, Doctor Bowen said another, and neither Bridget nor Miss Russell could recall the dress at all.

None the less, and notwithstanding its contradictory features, the Sunday morning episode in the kitchen was not one calculated to allay suspicion.

x v

If, upon purely circumstantial evidence, you invite a jury to convict someone of murder, you must be ready with the answers to all their unspoken questions. Moody had dealt with "What for?" There still remained "What with?"

Murders like these are not done with bare hands, nor with any light and pocketable weapon. From some of the wounds on Andrew Borden's head the length of the inflicting blade could be accurately fixed. It was three and a half inches, and it had fallen with the weight of a hatchet or an axe.

Where was this fearsome and death-dealing instrument?

It had not been abandoned at the scene of the crime. The murderer, therefore, had taken it away. Was it likely, Moody asked, that an intruder would have done so—that he would have run out with his bloodstained weapon into the sunlit street? Or did probability point to an inmate of the house, acquainted with its resources for concealment and disposal?

In the cellar, in a box upon the chimney shelf, the police had discovered a hatchet's head. The handle had been broken off, and the fragment that remained was covered with a coarse white dust of ashes. The blade of this hatchet had been measured. It was exactly three and a half inches long. . . .

Here once again was deep suspicion that fell short of proof. The

Commonwealth were appropriately reserved. "We do not insist," said Moody, "that these homicides were committed with this hatchet. *It may* have been the weapon." He paused. "It may *well* have been the weapon."

X V I

With force, and yet with moderation, the case against Miss Lizzie had been placed before the court. Moody's was a sound professional performance, and his distinguished leader looked on with approval as he began a final recapitulation.

"Gentlemen, let me stop and see where we are. The Commonwealth will prove that there was an unkindly feeling between the prisoner and her stepmother; that on Wednesday, August 3rd, she was dwelling upon murder, predicting disaster and cataloguing defenses; that from the time when Mrs. Borden left the dining room to the time when the prisoner came downstairs an hour later from this hallway which led only to her chamber and that in which Mrs. Borden was found, there was no other human being present except the prisoner at the bar; that these acts were the acts of a person who, to have selected time and place as it was selected in this case, must have had a familiar knowledge of the interior of the premises and of the whereabouts and habits of those in occupation. We shall prove that the prisoner made contradictory statements. We shall prove that Mrs. Borden's was the prior death. Then we shall ask you to say whether any reasonable hypothesis except that of the prisoner's guilt can account for the sad occurrences on the morning of August 4th."

The opening was over and so was the morning session. The court did not sit that afternoon. Members of the jury were otherwise engaged, exercising a privilege coveted by millions. In State-provided transport and accompanied by officials, they went off to Fall River to inspect the Borden home.

X V I I

Next day the witnesses got into their stride, and defender Robinson got into his.

The ex-Governor was a jury advocate of natural talent and mature experience. He knew the world; he gauged people astutely; he had a flair for methods of approach. His mind was subtle, his expressions simple; he not merely understood others, he could make others understand.

In the Borden trial, his most important cross-examination was that of Bridget Sullivan, the Irish maid. It could hardly have been bettered.

Bridget was not by any means a vulnerable witness. She was neither fool nor knave. But, like most human beings, she was susceptible to suggestion and subject to mistake. Discreetly Robinson made his own suggestions; relentlessly he exploited her mistakes.

He began by seeking Bridget's help in challenging the idea that the Borden family was rent asunder by ill-feeling. How far he could go with this could hardly be foreseen, and it is worth observing how every question tests or prepares a foothold for the next.

"Did *you* have any trouble there?" he asked.

"I?" said Bridget. "No, sir."

"A pleasant *place* to live?"

"Yes, sir."

"A pleasant *family* to be in?"

"I don't know how the family was," said Bridget, "I got along all right."

This was a slight setback. It might even be a warning. Robinson explored with a sure but gentle touch, like a surgeon who comes upon some dubious obstruction.

"You never saw anything *out of the way?*"

"No, sir."

Good; if she never saw anything "out of the way" one might be a little bolder and more definite.

"You never saw any *conflict* in the family?"

"No, sir."

Excellent; one could go the whole hog now, and put it into terms the jury couldn't fail to grasp.

"Never saw any *quarrelling,* or anything of that kind?"

"No, sir," answered Bridget. "I did not."

Robinson's aim is clear. He achieves it with the last question of this sequence, when he gets Bridget to agree that she never saw any "quarrelling, or anything of that kind." But he dare not ask this baldly, without careful preparation, because he cannot foresee the terms of her reply. Supposing she says, in response to a blunt query, "Miss Lizzie and Mrs.

Borden quarrelled all day long." His cause will then be far worse off than if the matter had not been raised at all. So he needs to approach the question circumspectly, advancing only one step at a time, and at every stage leaving channels of escape which he can use without grave loss of face.

He starts with just one hard fact to work from. Bridget has been in the Bordens' service for close upon three years. That dictates the form of his first question.

"Did *you* have any trouble there?"

If Bridget says "Yes," Robinson can retort, without fear of contradiction, "But you *did* stay three years," and then, accepting the danger signal, ride off to some less inflammable topic with a specious air of having scored a point. If Bridget says "No"—as she does—he has strengthened his hand, improved his position, and gained a better sight of the ground ahead.

It does not take him very far. But it enables him to venture next on a question that appears superficially a mere rephrasing of his last. In fact, though, by an almost imperceptible change in stress, it is designed to bring him closer to his target.

"A pleasant *place* to live?" he asks.

This imports the idea that not only were things all right for Bridget personally, but the Borden household was all right in general. And yet he can be fairly certain that Bridget will say "Yes" to this after her affirmative reply to the previous question. The two sound so alike. If, surprisingly, she does say "No," Robinson's escape is open as before, but with additional virtue—"But you stayed there three years *and* you never had any trouble."

This, however, does not arise. Robinson safely collects another "Yes."

Now he comes to the most delicate point in the sequence. He must ask, however broadly, about the family themselves. He has, it is true, buttressed himself by the two preliminary questions, but this is the danger spot, and he knows it.

"It was a pleasant *family* to be in?"

Bridget's answer raises a problem. A downright "Yes" would have brought the advocate almost home. A downright "No" would have driven him from the trail; it would have been far too dangerous to press her further. Robinson would have made off under cover of a volley of safe questions. ("Pleasant enough to make the place pleasant, eh?" "Pleasant enough to stay three years with, eh?" etc.)

But Bridget's reply is enigmatic. "I don't know how the family was," she says. "I got along all right."

Is this to be taken at its face value? Or is she hinting that there were family dissensions and that she kept out of them? Robinson has gone a long way now; he does not want to withdraw without his prize. But the utmost care is called for.

The next question, so artless in appearance, packs into its small compass a lifetime's experience and skill.

"You never saw anything out of the way?"

"Out of the way" is exactly right. Respectable girls—and Bridget is a very respectable girl—do not describe places as "pleasant" where "out of the way" things occur—as Robinson will, if necessary, remind her. But Bridget gives no cause.

"No, sir," she says.

Now he is practically secure. If any quarrelling is mentioned, they are ordinary, everyday domestic quarrels, quarrels that could not be considered "out of the way." He can go straight forward.

"You never saw any conflict in the family?"

Even if, contrary to expectation, Bridget should say "Yes," Robinson is well protected. But Bridget says "No" and he reaches his goal.

"Never saw any quarrelling or anything of that kind?"

"No, sir." . . .

And few of the spectators are aware that they have heard a little gem of the cross-examiner's art.

So far so good. The girl had seen no open wrangles. But Robinson wishes to take it a stage further, and dispel any belief in a purely passive feud. He tackled Bridget about the allegation that Miss Emma and Miss Lizzie held aloof from family meals.

"Didn't they eat with the family?" he asked.

"Not all the time."

Robinson took this reply and turned it upside down.

"But they did from time to time, did they not?"

The meaning was the same but the effect had been changed. It was like substituting "half-full" for "half-empty."

"Yes, sir," Bridget said, somewhat doubtfully, and added, "Most of the time they didn't eat with their father and mother."

Counsel met her insistence with the utmost ingenuity.

"Did they get up as early as the father and mother?"

"No, sir."

"So they had their breakfast later?"

A logician would have jibbed at the word "so." But George D. Robinson had the measure of his audience. The Borden jurymen would not be conversant with the fallacy of *post hoc propter hoc*. Absences from breakfast were credibly accounted for.

"And how was it at dinner?"

"They were sometimes at dinner," Bridget said. "But a good many more times they were not."

"Sometimes they were out?" Robinson suggested.

"I don't know where they were; I could not tell."

Bridget was digging in her heels. A whole string of gains may be sacrificed by ill-timed importunity. Smoothly the advocate altered his direction.

"Did you ever hear Miss Lizzie talk with Mrs. Borden?"

"Yes, sir; she always spoke to Mrs. Borden when Mrs. Borden talked to her."

"Always did?" repeated Robinson, making certain they had caught it in the recesses of the jury box.

"Yes, sir."

"The conversation went on in the ordinary way, did it?"

"Yes, sir."

"How was it this Thursday morning after they came downstairs?"

Bridget wrinkled her forehead.

"I don't remember."

"Didn't they talk in the sitting room?"

"Yes."

"Who spoke?"

"Miss Lizzie and Mrs. Borden."

"Talking calmly, the same as anybody else?"

"Yes, sir."

This enabled Robinson to make a bigger throw.

"There was not, as far as you know, any trouble that morning?"

"No, sir," said Bridget. "I did not see any."

In this phase of the questioning relations were quite amicable. It would not have suited Robinson if they had been otherwise. But now a more acrimonious passage was impending.

The conception of a murderous intruder constituted a vital part of Robinson's defense. To account for the fact that between crimes One and Two an intruder must have remained upon the premises more than an hour, experiments had been carried out with the object of establishing that he could have concealed himself in a closet in the hall. But primarily he would have had to obtain access to the house; and this in practice was limited to periods during which the side door had been left unlocked. The more they were, and the longer, the better for Miss Lizzie.

Bridget, in direct examination, had fixed one; she owned to leaving the side door "off the hook" while she was cleaning the outside of the windows. She agreed, too, with Robinson that, while she was engaged upon the windows in the front and while she was chatting to the next door neighbors' maid, the side door would be hidden from her view and—Robinson's words—"the field pretty clear for a person to walk in."

All that was very well, but it was not enough. Robinson knew that a useful piece was missing. Earlier on the morning of the murders, Bridget had gone out, not to the front but to the yard; it would widen the scope for the conjectural intruder if she had left the door unhooked when she returned on that occasion. Many months before, at the inquest at Fall River, she had said she couldn't tell whether she did or not. With Miss Lizzie on trial for her life, Bridget had somehow recollected. "When I came back from the yard," she had asserted, "I hooked up the side door."

Robinson did not propose to let this matter pass. Every minute that the side door might have been unhooked was precious. Before she left the stand the girl was going to retract.

He picked up a bulky set of papers. It was a transcript of the evidence at the inquest.

"Do you think," he said, and there was the faintest undertone of menace in his drawl, "do you think you have told us today just as you told us before?"

"I have told all I know," said Bridget.

"I don't ask you that." The tone suddenly sharpened. "What I want to know is whether you have told it today just as you did before?"

"Well, I think I did," said Bridget, a shade taken aback. Mr. Robinson had seemed such an easy, pleasant man. "I think I did, as far as I remember."

"What did you do as to the side door when you came in from the yard?"

"I hooked it."

"Did you say so before at the other examination?"

"I think so."

"Do you *know* so?"

Bridget wavered.

"I'm not sure," she said.

"Let me read and see if you said this." He read aloud very slowly and distinctly. " 'Question: When you came in from the yard did you hook the side door? Answer: I don't know whether I did or not.' Did you say so?"

"Well, I *must* have hooked it because——"

"That isn't it." Robinson cut in without ceremony. *"Was* that the way you testified?"

"I testified the truth."

"I don't imply that you didn't." It was indeed Robinson's whole point that she did; that the truth about the hooking of the door had been given at the inquest and not at the trial. "I merely want to know if you recall testifying over there at Fall River that you couldn't tell whether you hooked the door or not?"

But it stuck in Bridget's gullet.

"It is *likely* I did hook it, for it was always kept hooked."

Robinson's face was very stern.

"Do you positively recollect one way or the other?"

"Well," said Bridget, scared but obstinate, "I *generally* hook the side door."

"That isn't what I asked." The ex-Governor was peremptory. "Did you hook it or did you not?"

"I know I *must* have hooked the door for I always——"

"That isn't it. Did you hook it or did you not?"

Bridget gave up.

"I don't know," she said. "I don't know whether I did or not."

The spectators took a deep breath. Ex-Governor Robinson's frown relaxed. He looked almost affable again as he passed on to the next question.

XVIII

At the luncheon breaks and afternoon adjournments jurymen poked each other in the ribs. That ole Guv'nor Robinson; he puts it across; there ain't no flies on him. But the jury were out of court when he put it across best and when the absence of flies was most conspicuous. For Robinson's triumphs at getting evidence in were surpassed by his triumphs at keeping evidence out.

There was, for example, Mr. Eli Bence.

Mr. Eli Bence had a simple tale to tell. He was a drug clerk at a Fall River Pharmacy. On August 3rd, sometime in the forenoon, Miss Lizzie, whom he knew, had come into the shop. She had asked for ten cents' worth of prussic acid—required, so she said, for cleaning sealskin furs. "Prussic acid, my good lady," Mr. Bence had replied, "is something we don't sell without a prescription from a doctor. It is a very dangerous thing to handle." Miss Lizzie had departed without her prussic acid.

The very name of this substance conjures up unnatural death; one might as well use the word "poison" and be done. A picture of Miss Lizzie trying, *without success,* to purchase prussic acid on the day before the murders might easily provoke a prejudicial train of thought. Had she turned from one method of killing to another—from the inaccessible poison to the handy household axe?

Her defenders could not afford to sit back unconcerned while the ground was prepared for this damaging idea. If there was any way of stifling it, stifled it must be. So Mr. Bence had barely settled on the stand, having got little further than announcing his full name, when George D. Robinson rose from his place with a general objection to the witness being heard.

This objection, argued of course in the absence of the jury, was based upon two points. First, that prussic acid had harmless as well as harmful uses; "it is an article," said Robinson, "which a person may legitimately buy." Second, that the attempted purchase could have no conceivable bearing upon murders with an axe—"and that is all we are enquiring about here."

Moody, for the Commonwealth, faced this submission squarely. (It might be thought that Moody, as Knowlton's junior colleague, was doing rather more than his fair share of the work. But it would seem that a rough division had been mutually agreed; Moody was to open the case and argue points of law, Knowlton was to cross-examine and make the final speech. And in the trial of Lizzie Borden, as will presently appear, the final speech on each side assumed paramount importance.)

The Commonwealth spokesman seized at once on Robinson's last point—that the prussic acid episode did not prove, or tend to prove, that the defendant committed two murders with an axe. Quite right, Moody said; the evidence is not being offered for that purpose. It is meant to show intent, to demonstrate premeditation, to cast a revealing beam of light upon the prisoner's state of mind.

For Robinson's other point, the Commonwealth were well armed. They had brought to court a furrier and an analytical chemist to say that prussic acid was not used for cleaning furs. "I can conceive," said Moody, "of no more significant act, nothing which tends to show more the purpose of doing mischief than the attempt, on an excuse which upon this proof was false, to obtain one of the most deadly poisons known to human kind."

The judges conferred. They agreed with the Commonwealth where a layman might have hesitated—that proof of attempts to procure an instrument of murder might be introduced as evidence of intent even though the murder charged was subsequently effected with an instrument of quite a different kind. But they were doubtful where a layman might have felt no doubt at all—whether prussic acid could not be put to uses neither noxious nor medical.

They decided to hear the furrier and the chemist. These experts duly testified, and, while the jury still kicked their heels outside, there followed a long and whispered consultation between judges and counsel, who moved forward to the bench. There was much wagging of expository fingers and skeptical shaking of celebrated heads. It was noted that those concerned for the Commonwealth looked grave, while those for the defense looked inwardly exultant.

When at last the advocates returned to their seats, the judges proceeded to give a joint decision. There was insufficient proof to satisy the court that the acid could not be used for an innocent purpose.

The poison evidence would therefore be excluded.

XIX

If Robinson had fought hard to keep out Eli Bence, he fought harder to keep out . . . Lizzie Borden.

Miss Lizzie had already given evidence on oath—at the inquest, to which she had been summoned by subpoena. There, under Knowlton's cross-examination, she had proved an obstinate but unconvincing witness. The contradictions in her story were rife and absolute; the explanations few and often incomplete. She had been downstairs in the kitchen when her father returned home; no, she had been upstairs, sewing on a piece of tape; no, she remembered, she had been downstairs after all. She had gone out to the barn to find a sinker for a fish line; she had not been to the barn before for possibly three months; she didn't know what made her choose that special, fateful moment; she had stayed up in the barn for a space of twenty minutes; it was a very hot day and the barn was dreadfully close; no, of course she wouldn't stay there any longer than she need. How long would it take to find the sinker—three minutes, or four? No, it took her ten. And the remaining ten, Miss Borden? She was just looking idly through the window of the barn, eating three pears she had brought in from the yard. . . .

These and a score of other jarring incongruities made Miss Lizzie's testimony a danger to herself. It had been the clinching factor that had led to her arrest, and now the Commonwealth were tendering it at trial to be read out to the jury as evidence of her guilt.

But again her leading advocate entered an objection. Miss Lizzie's inquest testimony, he claimed, was inadmissible.

The rule relating to and governing such matters rested on a long line of American authorities. All really depended on the status of Miss Lizzie when, in obedience to the fiat of the law, she appeared at the inquest and submitted herself to questions. Was she then a perfectly free agent, an ordinary citizen, called to help the coroner determine cause of death? If so, even though she may have been under suspicion, her testimony was "voluntary" and admissible. Or was she already in effect an accused person, called less to help the coroner than to answer for herself? If so, any statements made by her would not be "voluntary" and could not be employed against her at the trial.

The inquest concluded on August 11th. Miss Lizzie was arrested later the same day. Until that moment she was, by presumption, free, but Robinson argued that the contrary was the fact. For three days past the City Marshal of Fall River had had in his pocket a warrant for her arrest. During the whole of that period she was under observation by police detailed for the purpose and stationed round the house. She was not cautioned before she gave her evidence. Her request for counsel at the inquest was refused. "In other words, the practice that was resorted to was to put her really in the custody of the City Marshal, beyond the possibility of any retirement or release or freedom whatever; keeping her with a hand upon the shoulder, covering her at every second, surrounding her at every instant, empowered to take her at any moment, and under these circumstances taking her to that inquest to testify. Denied counsel, not told that she ought not to testify to anything that might tend to criminate herself, she stood alone, a defenseless woman, in that attitude. "If that is freedom," Robinson exclaimed, "then God save the Commonwealth of Massachusetts."

Moody's reply was vehement and scornful. How, he asked, could an undisclosed warrant, of which the woman had no suspicion whatsoever, bear upon the exercise of her will when she appeared as a witness at the inquest? Where was there a grain of evidence to show that her liberty was restrained for an instant until the end of her examination? What authority had been quoted, could be quoted, to justify exclusion of such testimony unless the person testifying was actually under arrest? Moody attacked Robinson with almost spiteful sarcasm. "I say of what my friend is pleased to call his argument: it is magnificent but it is not law."

Law or no law, Robinson gained the day. "The common law," said the Chief Justice, "regards substance more than form. It is plain that the prisoner at the time of her testimony was, so far as relates to this question, as effectively in custody as if the formal precept had been served. We are all of opinion that this is decisive, and the evidence is excluded."

This did not debar Miss Lizzie from telling her story to the jurymen afresh. In Massachusetts, unlike Britain at that period, prisoners were permitted to give evidence if they wished. But Miss Lizzie did not intend to avail herself of this privilege. One encounter with Mr. Knowlton was enough.

X X

With the acknowledged leading lady unwilling to perform, Miss Emma Borden became the star of the defense.

Here was indeed a most serviceable deputy. She could give much of Lizzie's story without running Lizzie's risk. She could tell the jury almost all her sister could have told about the prelude, the background, and the sequel to the crimes; but because on August 4th she had been away at Fairhaven, she could not be cross-questioned about the day itself. The substitution of the elder sister for the younger was a neat and effective tactical device.

According to the best theatrical tradition, Miss Emma's entrance was deliberately delayed. When at long last the Commonwealth rested (on the tenth day, in defiance of the scriptures) the defenders first released a little swarm of witnesses each of whom contributed some item of his own. One, who lived just behind the Borden home, had heard a curious "pounding" on the night of August 3rd. Another, who had passed the house early on the 4th, had seen a young fellow hanging round; he was pale and "acting strangely." A third, walking by a little later in the morning, observed an unknown man leaning up against the gate. Such evidence was flimsy, not to say remote, but shrewd George Robinson perceived a latent value in composing this sketch of an alternative assassin.

The jury spent some hours among these fanciful conjectures. When the big moment arrived, though, and Miss Emma took the stand, they were instantly plunged back into the cold harsh world of fact.

Miss Emma, whatever nervousness she felt, rose to the requirements of her exacting rôle. Her timing was precise. She described how her father always wore a single ring; how it had been given to him years ago by Lizzie; how it was the only jewelry he ever wore; how it was on his finger at the moment of his death and how it was still upon his finger in the grave. She described how thoroughly the police had searched the house and how Miss Lizzie never made the least objection. She described how her sister burnt the dress on Sunday morning, and said that *she, Miss Emma, had prompted her to do it.* "The dress got paint on it in May when the men painted the house. . . . On Saturday, the day of the search, I went to the clothes press to hang up my own dress. There was no vacant nail. I searched round to find a nail and noticed this dress. 'You've not destroyed that old dress yet,' I said to Lizzie. She said: 'I think I will,' and I said: 'I would if I were you.' "

Miss Lizzie would certainly have done it far less well. George Robinson himself could not have done it better. The telegraph systems tapped it out across the world; the sister has come out strongly on Lizzie Borden's side.

XXI

In a long trial for murder, as day follows day and witness follows witness, even the participants may temporarily forget the agony of decision that awaits them at the end. They may become so immersed in the interplay of advocates, the interpreting of laws, and the balancing of issues that these processs come to appear ends instead of means—means by which twelve can arrive at a conclusion which will spell for one either liberty or death.

The completion of the evidence reawakens apprehension. As the last of many witnesses passes from the stand, the minds of all in court are increasingly preoccupied by hopes or fears of the fast approaching verdict.

At this stage the verdict can sometimes be foreseen. Not so, however, in the case of Lizzie Borden. The clash was less one of *fact* than of *construction,* less a matter of which witness you accepted than which counsel. It was a battle of barristers for command over the jury, and the outcome of that battle had yet to be decided.

XXII

Other things being equal, recent impressions are bound to be the strongest. That is why advocates contend for the last word. In the Borden trial the last word lay with Knowlton, because of the evidence that had been called for the defense. Robinson had to precede his opponent, with all the disadvantages attached too that position.

In his introduction to the transcript of the trial—an essay that stands high in the literature of crime—Mr. Edmund Pearson compares Robinson with Knowlton, and does not conceal his preference for the latter. It is true that Knowlton was animated by the loftiest sentiments and the noblest ideals. It is true that he spoke majestic prose with a splendid rhythm and an almost biblical ring. It is true that Robinson, by contrast, was homespun and colloquial, with both feet firmly planted on the Massachusetts earth. None the less, I am convinced, he was the better advocate and had the astuter mind. He possessed what, for want of a better word, one may call courtcraft; he attuned himself exactly to the mental pitch prevailing; he neither preached to nor lectured nor apostrophized the jury, but *talked* to them about the case as a neighbor might at home.

Along these lines and within these limits, his final speech was a real forensic feat.

It is evident that throughout he kept in mind not only the logic of facts and of events, but the way the jury could be relied upon to *feel*. He began by playing on their natural reluctance to believe that a woman could have carried out these crimes; "it is physically and morally impossible." He traded on the human love of jeering at the police: "They make themselves ridiculous, insisting that a defendant shall know everything that was done on a particular time, shall account for every moment of that time, shall tell it three or four times alike, shall never waver or quiver, shall have tears or not have tears, shall make no mistakes."

Beside these matters of emotional propensity, he swept into place the one solid piece of evidence that told heavily and positively in favor of his client. "Blood speaks out, though it is voiceless. It speaks out against the criminal. Not a spot on her, from her hair to her feet, on dress or person anywhere. Think of it! Think of it for an instant."

Having laid this foundation of artistically commingled hypothesis and fact, Robinson turned to the prosecution's case. He took the points against him one by one, and in plain, familiar words, with nicely managed raillery, made all—or nearly all—appear paltry or fallacious.

"Why do they say she did it?" he enquired. "Well, in the first place, they say she was in the house." Already it sounded far less good a point than when it had been termed "exclusive opportunity." Robinson added to the ground so quickly gained. "She was in the house. Well, that may look to you like a very wrong place for her to be in. But . . . it is her own home. I don't know where I would want my daughter to be than at home, attending to the ordinary vocations of life, as a dutiful member of the household."

The jury pouted their lips sagely. No doubt about that; she had a right to be at home. No, sir; couldn't say she was to blame for being at home.

Next, the Commonwealth had talked about a motive. Why, Robinson demanded, did they set great store on this? "If a person commits a murder and we know it, there is no reason to enquire for what reason he did it. If he did it, then it does not make any difference whether he had any motive or not. . . . In this case the motive is only introduced to explain the evidence, and to bind her to the crimes." And what sort of motive had they ultimately proved? They had shown that, from five or six years ago, Lizzie did not call Mrs. Borden "Mother"—Lizzie, who was indeed her stepdaughter, and was now a woman thirty-two years old. They had stressed her correction of the Assistant City Marshal:

"She is not my mother, sir; she is my stepmother." Robinson's comment on this was superbly opportune. He recalled to the jury "a well-looking little girl" who had given some minor evidence on behalf of the defense. "Why, Martha Chagnon, that was here a day or two ago, stepped on the stand and began to talk about Mrs. Chagnon as her stepmother. Well, I advise the City Marshal to put a cordon around *her* house, so that there will not be another murder there. Right here, in your presence, she spoke of her stepmother, and Mrs. Chagnon herself came on the stand afterwards, and I believe the blood of neither of them has been spilled since."

It was the kind of illustration that a country jury loves: concrete, local, about people they had seen. They pouted again and shook their heads a little; didn't seem much in the stepmother business either.

The Wednesday evening talk between Miss Lizzie and Miss Russell —styled by the Commonwealth "evidence of design"—was dismissed by Robinson as hardly worthy of discussion. "There are a good many people who believe in premonitions. . . . Events often succeed predictions through a mere coincidence. . . . You all recollect that Miss Lizzie's monthly illness was then continuing and we know from sad experience that many a woman at such a time is unbalanced, her mind unsettled and everything is out of sorts and out of joint."

"We know from sad experience." It was another clever touch. The family men looked back into their own domestic lives, and the whole jury glowed with superior male strength.

The lawyers and reporters listening to the speech, who were well acquainted with George Robinson's quick wits, had never doubted his ability to score whenever circumstances offered the tiniest of openings. But they waited with deep interest to see how he would handle a matter in which they discerned no opening at all: the matter of the note "from someone who is sick."

The defender did not dodge the point; he could not if he would. And if it made the weakest part of a very powerful speech, no possible blame can be attributed to him.

"A person may say," he said: " 'Where is the note?' Well, we should be very glad to see it. Very glad." Nobody could doubt that this sentiment was sincere. If the note had materialized, it might have proved decisive. "Very likely Mrs. Borden burned it up. But then they say nobody has come forward to say they sent it. That is true. You will find men living perhaps in this county who do not know that this trial is going on, don't know anything about it, don't pay much attention to it; they are about their own business; don't consider it of consequence. Sometimes people don't *want* to get into a courtroom even if a life is in danger."

Robinson's manner was as confident as ever, but the content of his argument now wore a little thin. The jury looked puzzled. His grip on them was loosening. Up to now they had gone all the way with Guv'nor Robinson, but they didn't feel happy with this talk about the note. Did it make sense? They tried to imagine what they would have done themselves—the test that he was always asking them to apply. Would *they* not have known that the trial was going on? Would *they* have hung back, if it meant somebody's life? But there wasn't really time to think the problem out; Robinson was moving on to another, better point.

The Commonwealth had charged his client with inconsistent statements. "The others tell us she said she went out to the barn. It's the police that tell us how long she said she stayed there. It takes Assistant Marshal Fleet himself to get the thirty minutes. You see him. You see him." He pointed to this officer sitting there in court, stiff as a ramrod, haughty as a dowager, obsessed with his own distinction and importance. "You see him," said Robinson, like an enthusiastic teacher taking his pupils round a zoo, "you see the set of that mustache and the firmness of those lips." The mustache bristled, the firm lips set still tighter. "There he was in this young woman's room. . . . This man Fleet was troubled. He was on the scent for a job. He was ferreting out a crime. He had a theory. He was a detective. And so he says: 'You said this morning you were up in the barn for half an hour. Will you say that now?' Miss Lizzie said: 'I do not say half an hour. I said twenty minutes to half an hour.' 'Well,' says Assistant Marshal Fleet, 'we will call it twenty minutes.'" Robinson's voice grew higher in derision. "Much obliged to him. He was ready to call it twenty minutes, was he? What a favor that was! Now Lizzie has some sense of her own, and she says: 'I say from twenty minutes to half an hour, sir.' He had not awed her into silence. She still breathed, though he was there."

Assistant Marshal Fleet had no option but to listen, and the jury could savor his discomfiture in safety. They chuckled with delight at the slights he was enduring. That ole Guv'nor Robinson had them back again in thrall.

Robinson now ranged to and fro on ground that was congenial: the burning of the dress (where Miss Emma lent him strength), Miss Liz-

zie's supposed attempts to tempt Bridget to town ("If she had undertaken these deeds, think you not she would have sent Bridget out on
an errand?"), the Commonwealth's uncertainty about the murderer's
weapon. Nor did he forget to offer his own theory. "The side door,
gentlemen, was unfastened from about nine to eleven. . . . Bridget
was outside talking to the next-door girl; she couldn't see the side door
when she was there. Lizzie was about the house as usual. What was she
doing? The same as any decent woman does. Attending to her work,
ironing handkerchiefs, going up and down stairs. You say these things
are not all proved"—Knowlton had stirred restlessly—"but I am taking
you into the house just as I would into your own. What are your wives
doing now?"

The jury felt homesick. They were suddenly out of this oppressive,
crowded court; they had ceased to be the center of the waiting world;
they were back there on the farm, with a cool breeze blowing and the
missus putting on a good New England meal.

"What are your wives doing now?" Robinson's voice wound its way
into their thoughts. "Doing the ordinary work around the house, getting
the dinner. Well, where do they go? Down cellar for potatoes, into the
kitchen, here and there. You can see the whole thing. It was just the
same there.

"Now suppose the assassin came there and passed through. Where
could he go? He could go up into that bedchamber and secrete himself
to stay there—until he finds himself confronting Mrs. Borden. Now
what is going to be done? He is there for murder; not to murder her, but
to murder Mr. Borden. And he knows that he will be recognized, and
he must strike her down. A man that had in his mind the purpose to
kill Mr. Borden would not stop at the intervention of another person,
and Lizzie and Bridget and Mrs. Borden, all or any of them, would be
slaughtered if they came in that fellow's way.

"And when he had done his work, and Mr. Borden had come in, as
he could hear him, he could come down. Bridget was upstairs, Lizzie
outdoors. He could do his work quickly and securely, and pass out the
same door as he came in."

Robinson had very nearly finished, but, like most master advocates,
he had nursed and husbanded his most dramatic stroke.

Steadily he gazed upon the close-packed jury box. His tones were
level and imperative.

"To find her guilty, you must believe she is a fiend. *Gentlemen, does she look it?*"

The speech had gone full circle. "Is it possible?" "Does she look it?"

They looked, and saw Miss Lizzie with her high, severe collar; her modestly groomed hair; her long, slender hands and her sharp, patrician features; her unmistakable air of being, above all else, a lady.

They looked at her, and her advocate had played his strongest card.

XXIII

To Knowlton this was the most difficult and disagreeable case of his career. Having placed his own evidence squarely before the court, having closely cross-examined the opposition witnesses, he must have been tempted to exert himself no further. A short and colorless concluding speech, from which it would appear that he was loath to press the matter, presented itself as the least unpleasant course.

But Knowlton was a man of rectitude and principle; his personal inclinations did not influence his conduct. As a government official he owed a duty to the public. It was a primary part of that duty to ensure that criminals did not escape their just and proper punishment. He believed, with some reason, that he had a strong case, and that it would be a dereliction of his high responsibility to neglect any lawful means of capturing the jury.

As Robinson sat down, amid that buzz of tongues which bursts forth uncontrollably on the slackening of tension, Knowlton slowly rose, like a man oppressed with care, and resolutely started on his grim, ungrateful task.

He grappled at once with the greatest of his difficulties. "My distinguished friend says: 'Who could have done it?' The answer would have been: 'Nobody could have done it.' If you had read an account of these cold and heartless facts in any tale of fiction, you would have said: 'That will do for a story, but such things never happen. . . . It was an impossible crime.' But it was committed. Set any human being you can think of, put any degraded man or woman you ever heard of, at the bar, and say to them 'You did this thing,' and it would seem incredible. And yet—it was done; it was done."

He particularly deprecated Robinson's suggestion that the murders could not have been committed by a woman, and permitted himself a few general observations on the temperament and nature of the female sex. "They are no better than we; they are no worse than we. If they lack in strength and coarseness and vigor, they make up for it in cunning, in dispatch, in celerity, in ferocity. If their loves are stronger and more enduring than those of men, their hates are more undying, more unyielding, more persistent." In disdainful phrase he struck at a main obstacle to cool-headed decision. "We must face this case," he said, "as men, not as gallants."

Through the twelfth afternoon and through the thirteenth morning, Knowlton continued his remarkable address; gravely exhorting, patiently explaining, impeccable in literary style and moral tone. His thesis was twofold: that Miss Lizzie's story was in itself incredible; that anybody else could have done it was impossible. It was beyond credence, he declared, that on that sweltering day she went up to the barn, "the hottest place in Fall River," and there remained all the time that Bridget was upstairs. It was beyond credence that, upon discovering her father, she had not fled from the house to the safety of the street; "she did not know that the assassin was not there; she did not know that he had escaped." It was beyond credence that the murder of Mrs. Borden could take place without Miss Lizzie seeing or hearing anything unusual; "if she was downstairs she was in the path of the assassin, if she was upstairs only a thin deal door separated her from the crime." It was beyond credence that a dress that had been good enough to keep through May, through June, through July, and into August should, innocently and by sheer coincidence, be destroyed twelve hours after she had heard of the suspicions. It was beyond credence that a mysterious assassin should know he would find the side door open at the exact time he desired, should hide in closets where there was no blood found, should come out when there was no opportunity to come out without being seen by all the world, should know Bridget was going upstairs to rest when she didn't know herself, should know Lizzie was going to the barn when she couldn't have told it herself, should know that Mrs. Borden would be upstairs dusting when no one could have foreseen it. "What is the defense to our array of facts? Nothing; nothing. It is proven, Mr. Foreman; it is proven."

No passage in his speech was more impressive in its thoughtfulness and stunning in its horror than that in which he sought to analyze Miss

Lizzie's motives. The order of the crimes, he said, supplied their key. He reversed Robinson's theory that the woman met her death through coming upon and recognizing a murderous intruder who had got into the house to lie in wait for Mr. Borden. "No," said Knowlton, "it was Mrs. Borden whose life that wicked person sought, and all the motive we have to consider bears on her." And whatever might be said about old Andrew, except for Miss Lizzie (and the absent Miss Emma) his harmless wife had not a single foe. "There may be that in this case," said Knowlton very solemnly, "that saves us from the idea that Lizzie planned to kill her father. I hope she did not. I should be slow to believe she did. But it was not Lizzie Borden who came down those stairs, but a murderess, transformed from the daughter, transformed from the ties of affection, to the most consummate criminal we have read of in our history. She came down to meet that stern old man. That man who loved his daughter, but who loved his wife too, as the Bible commanded him. And, above all, the one man in this universe who would know who killed his wife. She had not thought of that. She had gone on. There is cunning in crime, but there is blindness in crime too. She had gone on with stealth and cunning, but she had forgotten the hereafter. They always do. And when the deed was done, she was coming downstairs to face Nemesis. There wouldn't be any question but that he would know the reason that woman lay in death. He knew who disliked her. He knew who couldn't tolerate her presence under that roof."

As a work of abstract art, this speech of Knowlton's has surpassing merit. The language is choice, the mood exalted, the reasoning taut and deep. It is excellent to read. But the study is one place, the courtroom is another, and the best advocacy seldom makes the best literature. The jury, simple folk that they were, may well have found George Robinson more comprehensible. They may have felt more at home with his less august style.

Before he ended, Knowlton made a brave attempt to lift the issue of the trial on to a spiritual plane. "Rise, gentlemen," he cried, "to the altitude of your duty. Act as you would be reported to act when you stand before the Great White Throne at the last day. . . . Only he who hears the voice of his inner consciousness—it is the voice of God Himself—saying to him 'Well done, good and faithful servant,' can enter into the reward and lay hold of eternal life."

This peroration has real grandeur. It puts to shame George Robinson's humble "Gentlemen, does she look it?" But one wonders which stood uppermost in the minds of the jury as they sat in their little private room deciding Lizzie's fate.

X X I V

By five o'clock that afternoon it was all over. Miss Lizzie had been acquitted in a tempest of applause. With her faithful sister Emma at her side, she was on her way home to celebrate her vindication. George D. Robinson, well pleased with himself, walked away from court amid the cheering of the crowds. Only in the office of the District Attorney Knowlton and Moody sat apart from the rejoicings. They alone, perhaps, were at that moment capable of beholding the Borden trial through the eye of history.

X X V

Miss Lizzie lived thereafter for four and thirty years, with every indication of an easy conscience. She had inherited a comfortable fortune which she placidly and soberly and decently enjoyed. She never married. She occupied herself—as she had formerly done—with a variety of charitable works, and in her will she left thirty thousand dollars to a society for the prevention of cruelty to animals.

Her death let loose in public a flood of speculation that had gone on in private ever since the trial. Students of crime and detection endlessly debate: was the Borden verdict right?

Others remember Lizzie for a different reason. A catchy little jingle, probably written before she was acquitted, has linked itself imperishably with folk and nursery lore.

> Lizzie Borden took an ax
> And gave her mother forty whacks,
> When she saw what she had done
> She gave her father forty-one.

Students may argue about her as they please. In the wide world that is her epitaph.

Rebecca West

:

ON THE NUREMBERG TRIAL

There rushed up towards the plane the astonishing face of the world's
enemy: pine woods on little hills, gray-green glossy lakes, too small
ever to be anything but smooth, gardens tall with red-tongued beans,
fields striped with copper wheat, russet-roofed villages with headlong
gables and pumpkin-steeple churches that no architect over seven
could have designed. Another minute and the plane dropped to the
heart of the world's enemy: Nuremberg. It took not many more minutes
to get to the courtroom where the world's enemy was being tried for his
sins; but immediately those sins were forgotten in wonder at a conflict
which was going on in that court, though it had nothing to do with the
indictments considered by it. The trial was then in its eleventh month,
and the courtroom was a citadel of boredom. Every person within its
walk was in the grip of extreme tedium. This is not to say that the
work in hand was being performed languidly. An iron discipline met
that tedium head on and did not yield an inch to it. But all the same the
most spectacular process in the court was by then a certain tug-of-war
concerning time. Some of those present were fiercely desiring that that
tedium should come to an end at the first possible moment, and the
others were as fiercely desiring that it should last for ever and ever.

The people in court who wanted the tedium to endure eternally were
the twenty-one defendants in the dock, who disconcerted the spectator
by presenting the blatant appearance that historical characters, particularly in distress, assume in bad pictures. They looked what they were as

crudely as Mary Queen of Scots at Fotheringay or Napoleon on St. Helena in a mid-Victorian Academy success. But it was, of course, an unusually ghastly picture. They were wreathed in suggestions of death. Not only were they in peril of the death sentence, there was constant talk about millions of dead and arguments whether these had died because of these men or not; knowing so well what death is, and experiencing it by anticipation, these men preferred the monotony of the trial to its cessation. So they clung to the procedure through their lawyers and stretched it to the limits of its texture; and thus they aroused in the rest of the court, the people who had a prospect of leaving Nuremberg and going back to life, a savage impatience. This the iron discipline of the court prevented from finding an expression for itself. But it made the air more tense.

It seemed ridiculous for the defendants to make any effort to stave off the end, for they admitted by their appearance that nothing was to go well with them again on this earth. These Nazi leaders, self-dedicated to the breaking of all rules, broke last of all the rule that the verdict of a court must not be foretold. Their appearance announced what they believed. The Russians had asked for the death penalty for all of them, and it was plain that the defendants thought that wish would be granted. Believing that they were to lose everything, they forgot what possession had been. Not the slightest trace of their power and their glory remained; none of them looked as if he could ever have exercised any valid authority. Göring still used imperial gestures, but they were so vulgar that they did not suggest that he had really filled any great position; it merely seemed probable that in certain bars the frequenters had called him by some such nickname as "The Emperor." These people were also surrendering physical characteristics which might have been thought inalienable during life, such as the color and texture of their skins and the molding of their features. Most of them, except Schacht, who was white-haired, and Speer, who was black like a monkey, were neither dark nor fair any more; and there was amongst them no leanness that did not sag and no plumpness that seemed more than inflation by some thin gas. So diminished were their personalities that it was hard to keep in mind which was which, even after one had sat and looked at them for days; and those who stood out defined themselves by oddity rather than character.

Hess was noticeable because he was so plainly mad: so plainly mad that it seemed shameful that he should be tried. His skin was ashen, and he had that odd faculty, peculiar to lunatics, of falling into strained positions which no normal person could maintain for more than a few minutes, and staying fixed in contortion for hours. He had the classless air characteristic of asylum inmates; evidently his distracted personality had torn up all clues to his past. He looked as if his mind had no surface, as if every part of it had been blasted away except the depth where the nightmares live. Schacht was as noticeable because he was so far from mad, so completely his ordinary self in these extraordinary circumstances. He sat twisted in his seat so that his tall body, stiff as a plank, was propped against the end of the dock, which ought to have been at his side. Thus he sat at right angles to his fellow defendants and looked past them and over their heads: it was always his argument that he was far superior to Hitler's gang. Thus, too, he sat at right angles to the judges on the bench confronting him: it was his argument that he was a leading international banker, a most respectable man, and no court on earth could have the right to try him. He was petrified by rage because this court was pretending to have this right. He might have been a corpse frozen by rigor mortis, a disagreeable corpse who had contrived to aggravate the process so that he should be specially difficult to fit into his coffin.

A few others were still individuals. Streicher was pitiable, because it was plainly the community and not he who was guilty of his sins. He was a dirty old man of the sort that gives trouble in parks, and a sane Germany would have sent him to an asylum long before. Baldur von Schirach, the Youth Leader, startled because he was like a woman in a way not common among men who looked like women. It was as if a neat and mousy governess sat there, not pretty, but with never a hair out of place, and always to be trusted never to intrude when there were visitors: as it might be Jane Eyre. And though one had read surprising news of Göring for years, he still surprised. He was so very soft. Sometimes he wore a German Air Force uniform, and sometimes a light beach suit in the worst of playful taste, and both hung loosely on him, giving him an air of pregnancy. He had thick brown young hair, the coarse bright skin of an actor who has used grease paint for decades, and the preternaturally deep wrinkles of the drug addict. It added up to something like the head of a ventriloquist's dummy. He looked infinitely corrupt, and acted naïvely. When the other defendants' lawyers came to the door to receive instructions, he often intervened and insisted on instructing them himself, in spite of the evident fury of the defendants, which, indeed, must have been poignant, since most of them might well have felt that, had it not been for him, they never would have had to employ these lawyers at all. One of these lawyers was a tiny little man of very Jewish appearance, and when he stood in front of the dock, his head hardly reaching to the top of it, and flapped his gown in annoyance because Göring's smiling wooden mask was bearing down between him and his client, it was as if a ventriloquist had staged a quarrel between two dummies.

Göring's appearance made a strong but obscure allusion to sex. It is a matter of history that his love affairs with women played a decisive part in the development of the Nazi party at various stages, but he looked as one who would never lift a hand against a woman save in something much more peculiar than kindness. He did not look like any recognized type of homosexual, yet he was feminine. Sometimes, particularly when his humor was good, he recalled the madam of a brothel. His like are to be seen in the late morning in doorways along the steep streets of Marseille, the professional mask of geniality still hard on their faces though they stand relaxed in leisure, their fat cats rubbing against their spread skirts. Certainly there had been a concentration on appetite, and on elaborate schemes for gratifying it; and yet there was a sense of desert thirst. No matter what aqueducts he had built to bring water to his encampment, some perversity in the architecture had let it run out and spill on the sands long before it reached him. Sometimes even now his wide lips smacked together as if he were a well-fed man who had heard no news as yet that his meals were to stop. He was the only one of all these defendants who, if he had the chance, would have walked out of the Palace of Justice and taken over Germany again, and turned it into the stage for the enactment of the private fantasy which had brought him to the dock.

As these men gave up the effort to be themselves, they joined to make a common pattern which simply reiterated the plea of not guilty. All the time they made quite unidiosyncratic gestures expressive of innocence and outraged common sense, and in the intervals they stood up and chatted among themselves, forming little protesting groups, each one of which, painted as a mural, would be instantly recognized as a holy band that had tried to save the world but had been frustrated by mistaken men. But this performance they rendered more weakly every day. They were visibly receding from the field of existence and were, perhaps, no longer conscious of the recession. It is possible that they never thought directly of death or even of imprisonment, and there was nothing positive in them at all except their desire to hold time still. They were all praying with their sharp-set nerves: "Let this trial never finish, let it go on for ever and ever, without end."

The nerves of all others present in the Palace of Justice were sending out a counter-prayer: the eight judges on the bench, who were plainly dragging the proceedings over the threshold of their consciousness by sheer force of will; the lawyers and the secretaries who sat sagged in their seats at the tables in the well of the court; the interpreters twittering unhappily in their glass box like cage-birds kept awake by a bright light, feeding the microphones with French and Russian and English versions of the proceedings for the spectators' earphones; the guards who stood with their arms gripping their white truncheons behind their backs, all still and hard as metal save their childish faces, which were puffy with boredom. All these people wanted to leave Nuremberg as urgently as a dental patient enduring the drill wants to up and leave the chair; and they would have had as much difficulty as the dental patient in explaining the cause of that urgency. Modern drills do not inflict real pain, only discomfort. But all the same the patients on whom they are used feel that they will go mad if that grinding does not stop. The people at Nuremberg were all well fed, well clothed, well housed, and well cared for by their organizations, on a standard well above their recent experience. This was obviously true of the soldiers who had campaigned in the war, and of the British and French civilians at work in the court; and it was, to an extent that would have surprised most Europeans, true of the American civilians. It never crossed the Atlantic, the news of just how uncomfortable life became in the United States during the war: what the gasoline shortage did to make life untenable in the pretty townships planned on the supposition that every householder had an automobile; how the titanic munitions program had often to plant factories in little towns that could not offer a room apiece to the incoming workers; what it was like to live in an all-electric house when electric equipment was impossible to replace or repair. By contrast, what Nuremberg gave was the life of Riley, but it was also the water-torture, boredom falling drop by drop on the same spot on the soul.

What irked was the isolation in a small area, cut off from normal life by the barbed wire of army regulations; the perpetual confrontation with the dreary details of an ugly chapter in history which the surrounding rubble seemed to prove to have been torn out of the book and to require no further discussion; the continued enslavement by the war machine. To live in Nuremberg was, even for the victors, in itself physical captivity. The old town had been destroyed. There was left the uninteresting new town, in which certain grubby hotels improvised accommodation for Allied personnel, and were the sole places in which they might sleep and eat and amuse themselves. On five days a week, from ten to five, and often on Saturday mornings, their duties compelled them to the Palace of Justice of Nuremberg, an extreme example of the German tendency to overbuild, which has done much to get them into the recurring financial troubles that make them look to war for release. Every German who wanted to prove himself a man of substance built himself a house with more rooms than he needed and put more bricks into it than it needed; and every German city put up municipal buildings that were as much demonstrations of solidity as for use. Even though the Nuremberg Palace of Justice housed various agencies we would not find in a British or American or French law court, such as a Labor Exchange, its mass could not be excused, for much of it was a mere waste of masonry and an expense of shame, in obese walls and distended corridors. It recalled Civil War architecture but lacked the homeliness; and it made the young American heart sicken with nostalgia for the clean-run concrete and glass and plastic of modern office buildings. From its clumsy tripes the personnel could escape at the end of the working day to the tennis courts and the swimming pools, provided that they were doing only routine work. Those who were more deeply involved had to go home and work on their papers, with little time for any recreation but dinner parties, which themselves, owing to the unique character of the Nuremberg event, were quite unrefreshing. For the guests at these parties had either to be co-workers grown deadly familiar with the passing months or VIPs come to see the show, who, as most were allowed to stay only two days, had nothing to bring to the occasion except the first superficial impressions, so apt to be the same in every case. The symbol of Nuremberg was a yawn.

The Allies reacted according to their histories. The French, many of whom had been in concentration camps, rested and read; no nation has endured more wars, or been more persistent in its creation of a culture, and it has been done this way. The British reconstituted an Indian hill station; anybody who wants to know what they were like in Nuremberg need only read the early works of Rudyard Kipling. In villas set among the Bavarian pines, amid German modernist furniture, each piece of which seemed to have an enormous behind, a triple feat of reconstitution was performed: people who were in Germany pretended they were people in the jungle who were pretending they were in England. The Americans gave those huge parties of which the type was fixed in pioneering days, when the folks of the scattered homesteads could meet so rarely that it would have been tiring out the horses for nothing not to let geniality go all up the scale; and for the rest they contended with disappointment. Do what you will with America, it remains vast, and it follows that most towns are small in a land where the people are enthralled by the conception of the big town. Here were children of that people, who had crossed a great ocean in the belief that they were going to see the prodigious, and were back in a small town smaller than any of the small towns they had fled.

For a small town is a place where there is nothing to buy with money; and in Nuremberg, as in all German towns at that time, purchase was a forgotten faculty. The Nurembergers went to work in shabby streetcars hooked three together; so presumably they paid their fares. They bought the few foodstuffs available to them in shops so bare that it was hard to associate them with the satisfaction of an appetite. They bought fuel, not much, as it was summer, but enough to cook by and give what they felt to be, much more urgently than might have been supposed, the necessity of light. In the old town a twisted tower leaned backward against the city wall, and of this the top floor had miraculously remained roofed and weather-tight. To get to it one had to walk a long way over the rubble, which exhaled the double stench of disinfectant and of that which was irredeemably infected, for it concealed thirty thousand dead; and then one had to walk up the sagging concave exterior of the tower, and go in through a window. It would seem that people who had to live in such a home would not care to stay awake when darkness fell; but at night a weak light burned in the canted window. Such minuscule extravagance was as far as expenditure could go, except for grubby peddling in the black market. One could not buy a new hat, a new kettle, a yard of ribbon, a baby's diaper. There was no money, there were only cigarettes. A judge's wife, come out for a visit, said to a woman staying in the same villa, who had said she was going into the town, "Will you buy me some silver paint? I want to touch up my evening shoes," and everyone in earshot, even the GI guards at the door, burst into laughter.

It was hysterical laughter. Merely to go into a shop and buy something is to exercise choice and to enjoy the freedom of the will; and when this is checked it hurts. True, the Allied personnel in Nuremberg could go into their own stores and buy what they wanted; but that was not the full healthy process, for they knew with a deadly particularity every item in their own stores, and the traveller does not feel he has made terms with the country he visits till the people have sold him their goods. Without that interchange he is like a ghost among the living. The Allied personnel were like ghosts, and it might have been that the story would have a supernatural ending. If Allah of the Arabian Nights had governed this dispensation an angel would have appeared and struck dead all the defendants, and would have cried out that the rest of the court might do what it willed, and they would have run towards the East, towards France, towards the Atlantic, and by its surf would have taken off from the ground and risen into the air on the force of their desire, and travelled in a black compact cloud across the ocean, back to America, back to peace, back to life.

It might seem that this is only to say that at Nuremberg people were bored. But this was boredom on a huge historic scale. A machine was running down, a great machine, the greatest machine that has ever been created: the war machine, by which mankind, in spite of its infirmity of purpose and its frequent desire for death, has defended its life. It was a hard machine to operate; it was the natural desire of all who served it, save those rare creatures, the born soldiers, that it should become scrap. There was another machine which was warming up: the peace machine, by which mankind lives its life. Since enjoyment is less urgent than defense it is more easily served. All over the world people were sick with impatience because they were bound to the machine that was running down, and they wanted to be among the operators of the machine that was warming up. They did not want to kill and be grimly immanent over conquered territory; they wanted to eat and drink and be merry and wise among their own kind. It maddened them further that some had succeeded in getting their desire and had made their transfer to peace. By what trickery did these lucky bastards get their priority of freedom? Those who asked themselves that bitter question grew frenzied in the asking, because their conditions became more and more exasperating. The prisoners who guarded the prisoners of Nuremberg were always finding themselves flaring up into rage because they were using equipment that had been worn out and could not be replaced because of the strain on the supply lines. It could not be credited how often, by 1946, the Allies' automobiles broke down on German roads. What was too old was enraging; and who was too new was exasperating too. The commonest sight in a Nuremberg office was a man lifting a telephone, giving a number, speaking a phrase with the slurred and confident ease that showed he had used it a thousand times before to set some routine in motion, and breaking off in a convulsion of impatience. "Smith isn't there? He's *gawn?* And you don't know anything about it? Too bad. . . ." All very inconvenient, and inconvenient too that it is impossible to imagine how, after any future war, just this will not happen—unless that war is so bad that after it nothing will happen any more.

The situation would have been more tolerable if these conquerors had taken the slightest interest in their conquest; but they did not. They were even embarrassed by it. "Pardon my mailed glove," they seemed to murmur as they drove in the American automobiles, which were all the Nuremberg roads then carried save for the few run by the British and French, past the crowds of Germans who waited for the streetcars beside the round black Nuremberg towers, which were hollow ruins; or on Sundays, as they timidly strolled about the villages, bearing themselves like polite people who find themselves intruding on a bereaved family, or as they informed their officers, if they were GIs, that such and such a garage proprietor or doorman was a decent fellow, really he was, though he was a kraut. Here were men who were wearing the laurels of the vastest and most improbable military victory in history, and all they wanted was to be back doing well where they came from, whether this was New York or the hick towns which comedians name to raise a laugh at the extreme of American provincialism. Lines on a young soldier's brow proclaimed that he did not care what decoration he won in the Ardennes; he wanted to go home and pretend Pearl Harbor had never been troubled and get in line for the partnership which should be open for the right man in a couple of years' time. A complexion beyond the resources of the normal bloodstream, an ambience of perfume amounting almost to a general anesthetic for the passer-by, showed that for the female the breaking of traditional shackles and participation in the male glory of military triumph cannot give the pleasure to be derived from standing under a bell of white flowers while the family friends file past.

Considering this huge and urgent epidemic of nostalgia, the behavior of these exiles was strangely sweet. They raged against things rather than against one another. At breakfast in the Grand Hotel they uttered such cries as, "Christ, am I allergic to powdered eggs with a hair in 'em!" with a passion that seemed excessive even for such ugly provocation; but there was very little spite. The nicknames were all good-humored, and were imparted to the stranger only on that understanding. When it was divulged that one of the most gifted of the interpreters, a handsome young person from Wisconsin, was known as the Passionate Haystack, care was taken to point out that no reflection on her was implied, but only a tribute to a remarkable hair-do. This kindliness could show itself as imaginative and quick-witted. The Russians in Nuremberg never mixed with their Allies except at large parties, which they attended in a state of smiling taciturnity. Once a young Russian officer, joyously drunk, walked into the ballroom of the Grand Hotel, which was crowded with American personnel, and walked up to a pretty stenographer and asked her to dance. The band was not playing, and there was a sudden hush. Someone told the band to strike up again, the floor was crowded with dancing couples, a group gathered round the Russian boy and rushed him away to safety, out of the hotel and into an automobile; and he was dumped on the sidewalk as soon as his captors found an empty street. It is encouraging that those men would take so much trouble to save from punishment a man of whom they knew nothing save that he belonged to a group which refused all intercourse with them.

This sweetness of atmosphere was due chiefly to the American tradition of pleasantness in superficial social relations, though many of the exiles were constrained to a special tenderness by their personal emotions. For some of them sex was here what it was anywhere else. There is an old story which describes a native of Cincinnati, returned from a trip to Europe, telling a fellow townsman of an encounter with a beautiful girl which had brightened a night he had spent in Paris. On and on the story goes, dwelling on the plush glories of the restaurant, the loveliness of the girl and her jewels and her dress, the magic of a drive in the Bois de Boulogne, the discreet luxury of the house to which she took him, till it rises to a climax in a bedroom carpeted with bear skins and lined with mirrors. "And then?" "Well—then it was very much like what it is in Cincinnati." To many, love in Nuremberg was just as they had known it in Cincinnati, but for others the life of the heart was lived, in this desolate place given over to ruin and retributive law, with a special poignancy.

Americans marry young. There was hardly a man in the town who had not a wife in the United States, who was not on the vigorous side of middle age, and who was not spiritually sick from a surfeit of war and exile. To the desire to embrace was added the desire to be comforted and to comfort; and the delights of gratification were heart-rending, like spring and sunset and the breaking wave, because they could not last. The illusion was strong that if these delights could go on for ever they would always remain perfect. It seemed to many lovers that whatever verdicts were passed on the Nazis at the end of the trial, much happiness that might have been immortal would then be put to death. Those wives who were four thousand miles away haunted Nuremberg like phantasms of the living and proved the sacredness of what was to be killed. "He loves me, but he is going back to her out of old affection and a sense of duty to his children. Ah, what I am losing in this man who can still keep a woman in his heart, when passion is gone, who is a good father." These temporary loves were often noble, though there were some who would not let them be so. There were men who said, "You are a good kid, but of course it is my wife I really love," when these terms were too perfunctory, considering his plight and the help he had been given. There were also women who despised the men who needed them. Through the Bavarian forests, on Saturdays and Sundays, there often drove one of the more exalted personalities of Nuremberg, accompanied by a lovely and odious female child, whom he believed, since he was among the more elderly exiles and was taking exile badly, not to be odious and to be kind. She seemed to be sucking a small jujube of contempt; by waving her eyelashes and sniffing as the automobile passed those likely to recognize its occupants, she sought to convey that she was in company that bored her.

Those who loved the trial for the law's sake also found the course of their love running not too smoothly. This was not because they were uncomfortably impressed by the arguments brought forward by the declared opponents of the Nuremberg prosecutions. None of these was really effective when set against the wholeness of the historical crisis which had provoked it. It was absurd to say that the defendants were being tried for *ex post facto* crimes when the Briand-Kellogg Pact of

1928 had made aggressive warfare a crime by renouncing the use of war as an instrument of policy; and it was notable that even those opponents who had a special insight into that pact because they had helped to frame it were unable to meet this point, save by pleading that it had not been designed to be used as a basis for the prosecution of war criminals. But that plea was invalid, for in 1928 the necessary conditions for such prosecutions did not exist. There was then no country that seemed likely to wage war which was not democratic in its government, since the only totalitarian powers in Europe, the Soviet Union and Italy, were still weak. It would not be logical to try the leaders of a democracy for their governmental crimes, since they had been elected by the people, who thereby took the responsibility for all their actions. If a democracy breaks the Briand-Kellogg Pact, it must pay by taxation and penalties that fall on the whole people. But the leaders of a totalitarian state seize political power and continually declare that they, and not the people, are responsible for all governmental acts, and if these be crimes according to international law, their claim to responsibility must make them subject to trial before what tribunal international law decrees. This argument is so much in accordance with reality that, in the courtroom itself, it was never doubted. All the defendants, with one exception, seemed to think that the Allies were right in indicting not the German people, but the officers and instruments of the Nazi Government, for conspiring together to commit crimes against peace and the rules of war and humanity; and in most cases their line of defense was that not they, but Hitler or some other members of the party, had taken the actual decisions which led to these crimes. This line of defense, by its references to Hitler alone, concedes the basis of the Nuremberg trials. The one dissenter who would not make this concession was Schacht, who behaved as if there had been a democratic state superimposed on the Nazi state, and that this had been the scene of his activities.

There was obviously more in the other argument used by the opponents of the trial: that even if it were right to persecute the Nazi leaders on charges of conspiracy to commit crimes against peace and the rules of war and humanity, it could not be right to have a Soviet judge on the bench, since the Soviet Union had convicted itself of these crimes by its public rape of Finland and Poland and the Baltic Provinces. Truly there was here often occasion for shame. The English judges sat without their wigs, in plain gowns like their American colleagues, as a sign that this was a tribunal above all local tribunals. The Russian judges sat in military uniform as a sign that this was no tribunal at all, and when Vishinsky visited Nuremberg in the early months of the trial, he attended a banquet at which the judges were present, and proposed a toast to the conviction of the accused, a cantrip which would have led to the quashing of the trial in any civilized country.

This incident appeared to recommend the obvious idealistic prescription of trying the Nazi leaders before a tribunal which should exclude all representatives of the belligerent powers and find all its judges in the neutral countries. But that prescription loses its appeal when it is considered with what a laggard step would, say, the Swedish judge have gone home from Nuremberg, after having concurred in a verdict displeasing to the Soviet Union. But that there had to be a trial cannot be doubted. It was not only that common sense could predict that if the Nazis were allowed to go free the Germans would not have believed in the genuineness of the Allies' expressed disapproval of them, and that the good Germans would have been cast down in spirit, while the bad Germans would have wondered how long they need wait for the fun and jobbery to start again. It was that, there in Germany, there was a call for punishment. This is something that no one who was not there in 1946 will ever know, and perhaps one had to be at Nuremberg to learn it fully. It was written on the tired, temporizing faces and the bodies, nearly dead with the desire for life, of the defendants in the dock. It was written also on the crowds that waited for the streetcars and never looked at the Allied personnel as they drove past, and it was written on Nuremberg itself, in many places: on the spot just within the walls of the old town, outside the shattered Museum of Gothic Art, where a vast stone head of Jehovah lay on the pavement. Instead of scrutinizing the faces of men, He stared up at the clouds, as if to ask what He himself could be about; and the voices of the German children, bathing in the chlorinated river that wound through the faintly stinking rubble, seemed to reproach Him, because they sounded the same as if they had been bathing in a clear river running between meadows. There was a strange pattern printed on this terrain; and somehow its meaning was that the people responsible for the concentration camps and the deportations and the attendant evocation of evil must be tried for their offenses.

It might seem possible that Britain and America might have limited their trials to the criminals they had found in the parts of Germany and Austria which they had conquered, and thus avoided the embarrassment of Soviet judges on the bench. But had they done so the Soviet Union would have represented them to its own people as dealing with the Nazi leaders too gently, to the Germans in the Eastern Zone as dealing with them too harshly. So there had to be an international tribunal at Nuremberg, and the Americans and the British and the French had to rub along with it as best they could. The Nuremberg judges realized the difficulty of the situation and believed that the imperfection could be remedied by strict adherence to a code of law, which they must force themselves to apply as if they were not victors but representatives of a neutral power. It was an idealistic effort, but the cost was immense. However much a man loved the law he could not love so much of it as wound its sluggish way through the Palace of Justice at Nuremberg. For all who were there, without exception, this was a place of sacrifice, of boredom, of headache, of homesickness.

Here was a paradox. In the courtroom these lawyers had to think day after day at the speed of whirling dervishes, yet were living slowly as snails, because of the boredom that pervaded all Nuremberg and was at its thickest in the Palace of Justice. They survived the strain. The effect on the defendants could be tested by their response to the cross-examinations of Göring. They were frightened when Sir David Maxwell Fyfe, the chief acting British prosecutor, cross-examined him and in a businesslike way got him against the wall and extorted from him admissions of vast crime; and they were amused when Mr. Justice Jackson, the chief American prosecutor, could not cross-examine Göring at all well, because he had a transatlantic prepossession that a rogue who had held high office would be a solemn and not a jolly rogue, and was disconcerted by his impudence. But to the Russian cross-examination of Göring neither they nor anyone else in the court could bend their attention, because it was childish; it might have been part of a mock trial organized by a civics teacher in a high school. This was perhaps a superficial impression. It might be that the Russians were pursuing a legal aim other than ours. "It seems to me, when I look back on the last few months," said one of the journalists who sat through the whole trial, "that again and again I have seen the Russians do the most mysterious things. I don't think I dreamed that one of the leading Russian lawyers, all togged up in his military uniform, stepped up to the rostrum and squared his shoulders as if he were going to do some weight-lifting and shouted at whatever defendant it was in the box, 'Did you conspire to wage an aggressive war against the peace-loving democracies? Answer yes or no.' When the defendant said 'No,' the Russian lawyer thought for a long time and said, 'I accept your answer.' I cannot work that one out." The men in the dock did not try.

But they were inert before the French. These were veiled from us by a misleading familiarity, an old and false association of images. They wore the round caps and white jabots and black gowns we have seen all our lives in Daumier drawings, and we expected them to be the wolves and sharks and alligators that Daumier drew. But they were civilized and gentle people, who gave a token of strength in their refusal to let what had happened to them of late years leave marks on their French surface. The judge, Monsieur Donnedieu de Vabres, was like many men that are to be seen all over France, and in many old French pictures, and in the plays of Molière and Marivaux: small and stocky, with a white mustache, and a brow kept wrinkled by the constant offenses against logic perpetrated by this chaotic universe; a man whom one might have suspected of being academic and limited and pedantic, though sensible and moderate; a man whom one would not have suspected of having been, only two years before, released from a term of imprisonment in a German jail, which would have left many of us incapable and fanatic. From the slightly too elegant speeches of all these French lawyers it could be divined that when they were little boys they were made to learn Lamartine's *Le Lac* by heart. From the speeches of none of them could it be divined that France had lately been shamed and starved and tortured. But they could not press their case so that the men in the dock found themselves forced to listen to it. They were too familiar with that case; they had known all about it before the Nazis ever existed, from the lips of their fathers and their grandfathers; they had been aware that if the Germans practiced habitually the brutalizing business of invasion they would strengthen the criminal element in their souls till they did such things as were now being proved against the men in the dock. Their apprehensions had been realized through their own agony. They had been so right that they had suffered wrongs for which no court could ever compensate them. The chief French prosecutor, Auguste Champetier de Ribes, had been the chief anti-Munich minister in Daladier's cabinet, and had followed his conscience before the war in full knowledge of what might happen to him after the war. The fire of their resentment was now burned to ashes. It did not seem worth while to say over again what they had said so often and so vainly; and the naïve element in the Nazis noted the nervelessness of their attack and wrote them off as weaklings. It was here that the Americans and the British found themselves possessed of an undeserved advantage. Through the decades they had refused to listen to the French point of view. Now they were like the sailor who was found beating a Jew because the Jews had crucified Christ. When he was reminded that that had happened a long time ago, he answered that that might be, but he had just heard about it.

So the Germans listened to the closing speeches made by Mr. Justice Jackson and Sir Hartley Shawcross, and were openly shamed by their new-minted indignation. When Mr. Justice Jackson brought his speech to an end by pointing a forefinger at each of the defendants in turn and denouncing his specific share in the Nazi crime, all of them winced, except old Streicher, who munched and mumbled away in some private and probably extremely objectionable dream, and Schacht, who became stiffer than ever, stiff as an iron stag in the garden of an old house. It was not surprising that all the rest were abashed, for the speech showed the civilized good sense against which they had conspired, and it was patently admirable, patently a pattern of the material necessary to the salvation of peoples. It is to be regretted that one phrase in it may be read by posterity as falling beneath the level of its context; for it has a particular significance to all those who attended the Nuremberg trial. "Göring," said Mr. Justice Jackson, "stuck a pudgy finger in every pie." The courtroom was not small, but it was full of Göring's fingers. His soft and white and spongy hands were forever smoothing his curiously abundant brown hair, or covering his wide mouth, while his plotting eyes looked facetiously around, or weaving impudent gestures of innocence in the air. The other men in the dock broke into sudden and relieved laughter at the phrase; Göring was plainly angered, though less by the phrase than by their laughter.

The next day, when Sir Hartley Shawcross closed the British case, there was no laughter at all. His speech was not so shapely and so decorative as Mr. Justice Jackson's,* for English rhetoric has crossed the Atlantic in this century and is now more at home in the United States than on its native ground, and he spoke at greater length and stopped more legal holes. But his words were full of a living pity, which gave the men in the box their worst hour. The feminine von Shirach achieved a gesture that was touching. He listened attentively to what Sir Hartley

* See page 467.

had to say of his activities as a Youth Leader; and when he heard him go on to speak of his responsibility for the deportation of forty thousand Soviet children he put up his delicate hand and lifted off the circlet of his headphones, laying it down very quietly on the ledge before him. It seemed possible that he had indeed the soul of a governess, that he was indeed Jane Eyre and had been perverted by a Mr. Rochester, who, disappearing into self-kindled flames, had left him disenchanted and the prey of a prim but inextinguishable remorse. And when Sir Hartley quoted the deposition of a witness who had described a Jewish father who, standing with his little son in front of a firing squad, "pointed to the sky, stroked his head, and seemed to explain something to the boy," all the defendants wriggled on their seats, like children rated by a schoolmaster, while their faces grew old.

There was a mystery there: that Mr. Prunes and Prisms should have committed such a huge, cold crime. But it was a mystery that girt all Nuremberg. It was most clearly defined in a sentence spoken by the custodian of the room in the Palace of Justice that housed all the exhibits relating to atrocities. Certain of these were unconvincing; some, though not all, of the photographs purporting to show people being shot and tortured had a posed and theatrical air. This need not have indicated conscious fraud. It might well have been that these photographs represented attempts to reconstruct incidents which had really occurred, made at the instigation of officials as explanatory glosses to evidence provided by eyewitnesses, and that they had found their way into the record by error. But there was much stuff that was authentic. Somebody had been collecting tattooed human skin, and it is hard to think where such a connoisseur could find his pieces unless he had power over a concentration camp. Some of these pelts were infinitely pathetic, because of their obscenity. Through the years came the memory of the inconveniently high-pitched voice of an English child among a crowd of tourists watching a tournament of water-jousting in a French port: "Mummy, come and look, there's a sailor who's got no shirt on, and he has the funniest picture on his back—there's a lady with no clothes on upside down on a St. Andrew's Cross, and there's a snake crawling all over her and somebody with a whip." There had been men who had thought they could make a pet of cruelty, and the grown beast had flayed them.

But it was astonishing that there had been so much sadism. The French doctor in charge of these exhibits pondered, turning in his hand a lampshade made of tattooed human skin, "These people where I live send me in my breakfast tray strewn with pansies, beautiful pansies. I have never seen more beautiful pansies, arranged with exquisite taste. I have to remind myself that they belong to the same race that supplied me with my exhibits, the same race that tortured me month after month, year after year, at Mauthausen." And, indeed, flowers were the visible sign of that mystery, flowers that were not only lovely but beloved. In the windowboxes of the high-gabled houses the pink and purple petunias were bright like lamps. In the gardens of the cottages bordering a road which was no longer there, which was a torn trench, the phloxes shone white and clear pink and mauve, as under harsh heat they will not do, unless they are well watered. It is tedious work, training clematis over low posts, so that its beauty does not stravaig up the walls but lies open under the eye; but on the edge of the town many gardeners grew it thus. The countryside beyond continued this protestation of innocence. A path might mount the hillside, through the lacework of light and shadow the pine trees cast over the soft reddish bed of the pine needles, to the upland farm where the wedding party poured out of the door, riotous with honest laughter, but freezing before a camera into honest solemnity; it might fall to the valley and follow the trout stream, where the dragonflies drew iridescent patterns just above the cloudy green water, to the edge of the millpond, where the miller's flax-haired little son played with the gray kittens among the meadowsweet; it would not lead to any place where it seemed other than plain that Germany was a beautiful country, inhabited by a people who loved all pleasant things and meant no harm.

Yet the accusations that were made against the leaders in the Palace of Justice at Nuremberg were true. They were proved true because the accusers did not want to make them. They would much rather have gone home. That could be seen by those who shamefully evaded the rules of the court and found a way into one of the offices in the Palace of Justice which overlooked the orchard which served as exercise ground of the jail behind it. There, at certain hours, the minor Nazi prisoners not yet brought to trial padded up and down, sullen and puffy, with a look of fierceness, as if they were missing the opportunity for cruelty as much as the company of women or whatever their fancy might be. They were watched by American military guards, who stood with their young chins dropped and their hands clasped behind them, slowly switching their white truncheons back-

wards and forwards, in the very rhythm of boredom itself. If an apple
fell from the tree beside them they did not bend to pick it up. Nothing
that happened there could interest them. It was not easy to tell that
these guards were not the prisoners, so much did they want to go
home. Never before can conquerors in charge of their captives have
been less furious, more innocent of vengeance. A history book opened
in the mind; there stirred a memory that Alexander the Great had had
to turn back on the Hydaspes because his soldiers were homesick.

. . . .

Monday, September 30, 1946, was one of those glorious days that
autumn brings to Germany, heavy and golden, yet iced, like an iced
drink. By eight o'clock a fleet of Allied automobiles, collected from
all over Western Germany, was out in the countryside picking up the
legal personnel and the visitors from their billets and bringing them back
to the Palace of Justice. The Germans working in the fields among
the early mists did not raise their heads to look at the unaccustomed
traffic, though the legal personnel, which had throughout the trial gone
about their business unattended, now had armed military police with
screaming sirens in jeeps as outriders.

This solemn calm ended on the doorstep of the Palace of Justice.
Within there was turbulence. The administration of the court had always aroused doubts, by a certain tendency towards the bizarre, which
manifested itself especially in the directions given to the military police
in charge of the gallery where the VIPs sat. The ventilation of the
court was bad, and the warm air rose to the gallery, so in the afternoon the VIPs were apt to doze. This struck the commandant,
Colonel Andrus, as disrespectful to the court, though the gallery was
so high that what went on there was unlikely to be noticed. Elderly
persons of distinction, therefore, enjoyed the new experience of being
shaken awake by young military policemen under a circle of amused
stares. If they were sitting in the front row of the gallery, an even odder
experience might overtake them. The commandant had once looked up
at the gallery and noted a woman who had crossed her ankles and was
showing her shins and a line of petticoat, and he conceived that this
might upset the sex-starved defendants, thus underestimating both the
length of time it takes for a woman to become a VIP and the degree
of the defendants' preoccupations. But, out of a further complication of
delicacy, he forbade both men and women to cross their ankles. Thus
it happened that one of the most venerable of English judges found him-

self, one hot summer afternoon, being tapped on the shoulder with a white club by a young military policeman and told to wake up, stay awake, and uncross his legs.

These rules were the subject of general mirth in Nuremberg, but the higher American authorities neither put an end to them nor took their existence as a warning that perhaps the court should be controlled on more sensible lines. An eccentricity prevailed which came to its climax in the security arrangements for these two final days. There was a need for caution. Certainly in Berlin nobody would have lifted a finger to avenge the Nazis, but here in Bavaria there were still some people who had never had any reason to feel that the Nazi regime had been a bad thing for them, and among them there must have been some boys who had been too young for military service and had enjoyed their time with Hitler Youth. It might also have been that Martin Bormann, who at the end of the war had replaced Göring, and who was said to have been killed by Russian fire after escaping from the Chancellery, and who was being indicted *in absentia* at this trial, might now choose to reappear.

It therefore seemed obvious that there would be stringent precautions to see that no unauthorized person entered the Palace of Justice, and we had imagined that we would have to queue up before a turnstile, by which competent persons would sit and examine our passes under a strong light. There was a rumor that there was a mark on the passes which would show only under X-rays. But, instead, authority jammed the vast corridors of the Palace of Justice with a mass of military police, who, again and again, demanded the passes of the entrants and peered at them in a half-light. It was extremely unlikely that these confused male children could have detected the grossest forgery, but the question was never posed, for the corridor was so dark that it was difficult to read large print. No attempt had been made to clarify the situation by posting at strategic points men who could recognize the legal personnel; and thus it happened that, outside the judges' entrance to the courtroom, a military policeman, switching his white club, savagely demanded, "And how the hell did you get in here?" of a person who was in fact one of the judges. In the midst of this muddle certain precautionary measures were taken which were at once not strict enough and too strict and quite ineffectual.

Men were forbidden to take briefcases into court, and women were forbidden to carry handbags or wear long coats. These prohibitions were undignified and futile. Women's suits are not made with pockets large enough to hold passes, script, fountain pens, notebooks, and spectacle cases, and few women went into court without a certain amount of their possessions packed away inside their brassieres or stocking tops. One French woman journalist, obedient to the ban on long coats, came in a padded jacket which she had last worn on an assignment in the Asiatic theater of war, and when she was sitting in court discovered that in the holster pocket over her ribs she had left a small loaded revolver. It may look on paper as if those responsible for the security arrangements at Nuremberg could justify themselves by pointing to the fact that the Palace of Justice was not blown up. But those who were there know that there was just one reason for this: nobody wanted to blow it up. But although the problem raised by Nuremberg security need not have been approached so eccentrically, it never could have been brought to a satisfactory solution. There were no persons qualified by experience to take control at a high level, for there had never been a like occasion; and there was not such a superfluity of customs officials and police workers that a large number of them could have been abstracted from their usual duties and seconded to special duties without harm; and if there had been, the business of transporting them and housing them would have created fresh problems. This was a business badly done, but it could have been done no better.

It seemed natural enough that nobody should have been very anxious to blow up the Palace of Justice when the defendants came into the dock that Monday. The court had not sat for a month, while the judges were considering their verdicts, and during that time the disease of uniformity which had attacked the prisoners during the trial had overcome them. Their pale and lined faces all looked alike; their bodies sagged inside their clothes, which seemed more alive than they were. They were gone. They were finished. It seemed strange that they could ever have excited loyalty; it was plainly impossible that they should ever attract it again. It was their funeral which the Germans were attending as they looked down on the ground when they walked in the streets of the city. Those Germans thought of them as dead.

They were not abject. These ghosts gathered about them the rags of what had been good in them during their lives. They listened with decent composure to the reading of the judgments, and, as on any other day, they found amusement in the judges' pronunciation of the

German names. That is something pitiable which those who do not attend trials never see: the eagerness with which people in the dock snatch at any occasion for laughter. Sometimes it seems from the newspaper reports that a judge has been too facetious when trying a serious case, and the fastidious shudder. But it can be taken for granted that the accused person did not shudder, he welcomed the little joke, the small tear in the tent of grimness that enclosed him. These defendants laughed when they could, and retained their composure when it might well have cracked. On Monday afternoon the darkened mind of Hess passed through some dreadful crisis. He ran his hands over his brows again and again as if he were trying to brush away cobwebs, but the blackness covered him. All humanity left his face; it became an agonized muzzle. He began to swing backwards and forwards on his seat with the regularity of a pendulum. His head swung forward almost to his knees. His skin became blue. If one could pity Ribbentrop and Göring, then was the time. They had to sit listening to the judgment upon them while a lunatic swayed and experienced a nameless evil in the seat beside them. He was taken away soon, but it was as if the door of hell had swung ajar. It was apparent now, as on many occasions during the trial, that the judges found it repulsive to try a man in such a state; but the majority of the psychiatrists consulted by the court had pronounced him sane.

The first part of the judgment did not refer to the defendants but to bodies they had formed. It had been argued by the prosecution that the seven Nazi organizations—the Gestapo, SD, SS, Reich Cabinet, Corps of Political Leaders, General Staff and OKW, and Storm Troops—should be declared criminal in nature and that membership in them should by itself be the subject of a criminal charge. The judges admitted this in the cases of the first three, on the grounds that at an early date these organizations had so openly aimed at the commission of violence and the preaching of race hatred that no man could have joined them without criminal intent. The image of a rat in a trap often crossed the mind at Nuremberg, and it was evoked then. No man who had ever been an SS member could deny it. The initials and the number of his blood group were tattooed under his arm. But, of course, that trap did not spring. There were too many SS men, too many armpits, for any occupying force to inspect. The Storm Troopers were not put in the same category, because they were assessed as mere hooligans and bullies, too brutish to be even criminals. Of the others it was recognized that many persons must have joined them or consented to remain within them without realizing what Hitler was going to make of them. This was reasonable enough, for it meant that members of this organization could still be prosecuted if there was reason to believe they had committed crimes as a result of their membership.

But the refusal to condemn all the seven organizations was greatly resented by some of the spectators. It was felt to be a sign that the tribunal was soft and not genuinely anti-Nazi. This was partly due to temperamental and juristic differences among the nations. The four judges took turns at reading the judgment, and this section was read by the English member judge, Lord Oaksey. His father before him was a judge, who was Lord Chief Justice in the twenties; and he had the advantage which the offspring of an old theatrical family have over other actors. He had inherited the technique and he refined on it, and could get his effects economically. He read this passage of the judgment in a silver voice untarnished by passion, with exquisite point; but to a spectator who was not English it might have seemed that this was just one of the committee of an English club explaining to his colleagues that it was necessary to expel a member. The resemblance need not have been disquieting. People who misbehave in such clubs really do get expelled by their committees, and they remain expelled; whereas the larger gestures and rhetoric of history have often been less effective. But this was not understood by those whose national habit it is to cross breed their judges with prosecutors or to think that the law should have its last say with a moralist twang.

There was, in other quarters, a like unease about the verdicts on the Service defendants, on Field Marshal Keitel and General Jodl and Admirals Doenitz and Raeder. Keitel and Jodl were found guilty on all four counts of the indictment: first, of conspiracy to commit the crimes alleged in the other counts, which were crimes against peace, crimes in war, and crimes against humanity. Raeder was found guilty on the three counts, and Doenitz was found guilty on the second. There was some feeling among those who attended only the end of the trial, and a very great deal of strong feeling among people all over the world who did not attend the court, that these defendants had been put into the dock for carrying out orders as soldiers and sailors must. But there is a great deal in the court's argument that the only orders a soldier or a sailor is bound to obey are those which are recognized practice in the Services of the time. It is obvious that if an admiral were ordered by a demented First Sea Lord to serve broiled babies in the officers' mess he ought to disobey; and it was shown that these generals and admirals had exhibited very little reluctance to carry out orders of Hitler which tended toward baby-broiling. Here was another point at which there was a split between the people who had attended the trial, or long stints of it, and the people who had not. Much evidence came up during the hearings which proved these men very different from what the products of Sandhurst and Dartmouth, West Point and Annapolis, are hoped to be. Doenitz, for example, exhorted his officers to be inspired by the example of some of their comrades who, confined in a camp in Australia, found that there were a few Communists among the other captured troops, managed to distract the attention of the guards, and murdered these wretched men.

But it was in the case of the admirals that the court made a decision which proved Nuremberg to be a step farther on the road to civilization. They were charged with violating the Naval Protocol of 1936, which reaffirmed the rules of submarine warfare laid down in the London Naval Agreement of 1930. They had, and there was no doubt about it, ordered their submarines to attack all merchant ships without warning and not stop to save the survivors. But the tribunal acquitted them on this charge on the grounds that the British and the Americans had committed precisely the same offense. On May 8, 1940, the British Admiralty ordered all vessels in the Skagerrak to be sunk on sight. Also Admiral Nimitz stated in answer to interrogatories that unrestricted submarine warfare had been carried on by the American Navy in the Pacific Ocean from the first day that the campaign opened. The fact was that we and the Germans alike had found the protocol unworkable. Submarines cannot be used at all if they are to be obliged to hang about after they have made a killing and throw away their own security. The Allies admitted this by acquitting the admirals, and the acquittal was not only fair dealing between victors and vanquished, it was a step towards honesty. It was written down forever that submarine warfare cannot be carried on without inhumanity, and that we have found ourselves able to be inhumane. We have to admit that we are in this trap before we can get out of it. This *nostra culpa* of the conquerors might well be considered the most important thing that happened at Nuremberg. But it evoked no response at the time, and it has been forgotten.

But in this court nothing could be clear-cut, and nothing could have a massive effect, because it was international, and international law, as soon as it escapes from the sphere of merchandise (in which, were men good, it would alone need to be busy), is a mist with the power to make solids as misty as itself. It was true that the Nazi crimes of cruelty demanded punishment. There in Nuremberg the Germans, pale among the rubble, were waiting for that punishment as a purification, after which they might regain their strength and rebuild their world; and it was obvious that the tribunal must sit to disprove Job's lament that the houses of the wicked are safe from fear. A tyrant had suspended the rule of law in his country and no citizen could seek legal protection from personal assault, theft, or imprisonment; and he had created so absolute a state of anarchy that when he fell from power the courts themselves had disappeared and could not be reconstituted to do justice on him and his instruments. Finally he had invaded other territories and reproduced this ruin there. Plainly some sort of emergency tribunal had to take over the work of the vanished tribunals when it was possible, if the Nazis were not to enjoy a monstrous immunity simply because they had included among their crimes the destruction of the criminal courts. It was only just that the Nazis should pay the due penalty for the offenses they had committed against the laws of their own land, the millions of murders, kidnappings and wrongful imprisonments, and thefts. "Of course," people said then and still say, "it was right that the Nazis should have been punished for what they did to the Jews. To the left wing. To the religious dissidents. To the Poles. To the Czechs. To the French deportees. To half Europe. But aggressive war, that was a new crime, invented for the occasion, which had never been written on the statute books before." They spoke the very reverse of truth. The condemnation of aggressive war as a crime was inherent in the Kellogg-Briand Pact; whereas no international body has ever given its sanction to a mechanism by which crimes committed in one nation which had gone unpunished because of a collapse of civil order could subsequently be punished by other nations. It is to be doubted whether the most speculative mind had ever drawn up the specification for such a mechanism.

Here one sees the dangers of international law. It would seem entirely reasonable to give nations which had remained at the common level of civilization the right to exercise judicial powers in nations which have temporarily fallen below that level and are unable to guarantee their citizens justice. But we can all remember how Hitler prefaced his invasions by pretenses that civil order had been destroyed wherever there was a German minority, how it was roared at the world over the radio that Germans in Czechoslovakia and Poland and Yugoslavia were being beaten in the streets and driven out of their houses and farms and were denied all police protection. Such an article of international law would give both knight-errantry and tyranny their marching orders. This, at Nuremberg, was not a remote consideration, though Germany seemed to lie dead around us. Each of the judges read some part of the judgment; and when the Russian had his turn there was a temptation not to give the earphones the right switch to the English version, for the Russian language rolled forth from the firm fleshy lips of this strong man like a river of life, a river of genius, inexhaustible and unpredictable genius. To listen to Slav oratory is to feel that Aksakov and Dostoevski and Bishop Peter Nyegosh had half their great work done for them by the language they used. But soon the desire to know what he was talking about proved irresistible. It turned out that the Russian was reading the part of the judgment that condemned the Germans for their deportations: for taking men and women away from their homes and sending them to distant camps where they worked as slave labor in conditions of great discomfort, and were often unable to communicate with their families. There was here a certain irony, and a certain warning.

The trouble about Nuremberg was that it was so manifestly a part of life as it is lived; the trial had not sufficiently detached itself from the oddity of the world. It was of a piece with the odd things that happened on its periphery; and these were odd enough. Some visitors to the trial were strolling through a village outside Nuremberg after the Monday session had ended, to freshen their brains with the evening air, when a frizzled and grizzled head was popped over a garden fence. There are women whom age makes look not like old women but immature apes, and this was one of them. She was not unlikable, she was simply like an ape. She demanded, in English, to know whether we were English. Two of us were. "I shot your King Edward," she assured us, her bright eyes winking among her wrinkles, her teeth clacking at a different rate from her speech. In view of the occasion that had brought us to Nuremberg this seemed a not unlikely fantasy to vex a failing mind grounded in its environs, and there was the coo of "Yes, yes, yes," of which lunatics must grow weary. But she stepped through her garden gate into the road, and one of the party, a devoted student of the text and illustrations in such books as the autobiographical works of the sixth Duke of Portland, recognized a familiar accent in the drainpipe tweed coat, the thin ankles and high-arched feet turned outwards at an angle of forty-five degrees. "You mean you went shooting with King Edward?" she suggested. "Yes, yes, in your Norfolk!" Chattering like the monkeys in Gibraltar at sundown, she cried out the names of great English houses, of great English families, but briefly, for she had a more passionate preoccupation. "Well, have you sentenced all the scoundrels? What have they done to them?" She stamped her little foot on the ground. "What have they done to Sauckel? To Sauckel? That, that is what I wish to know."

It was explained to her that that day the judges had delivered judgment only on the Nazi organizations and the validity and significance of the indictment, and that the verdicts and sentences on the Nazi leaders would not be pronounced till tomorrow. She was disappointed. "I wanted to hear from you that Sauckel is to be hanged. I hope that I might have that good news. I shall not sleep happy till I have heard that that scoundrel pays for his crimes. Never," she cried, standing on tiptoe as if she were about to spring into the branches above us, "never will we undo the harm he did by bringing these wretched foreign laborers into our Germany. I had a nice house, *a home,* yes, *a home,* inherited from my family, in the village that is ten miles along the road, and what did this Sauckel do but send two thousand foreign workers to the factories in the district, two thousand wretches, cannibals, scum of the earth, Russians, Balks, Balts, Slavs—Slavs, I tell you. What did they do when our armies were defeated but break loose? For three days they kept carnival; they looted and they ate and drank of our goods. I had to hide with my neighbors in their cellar, and they slept in my bed and they ate in my kitchen and there was not a potato left, and they took all my good china and my linen and all they could carry, the brutes, the beasts!"

Somebody murmured that the foreign workers would have preferred to stay at home, and she glittered agreement. "Yes, yes, of course they should have been left at home, the place for a pig is in the sty. Oh, hanging will be too good for Sauckel, I could kill him with my own hands. You are doing very well at that trial. You English do all things well; we Germans should never have had a war with you. I am glad that you are giving"—she laughed— *"what for* to the Nazis. They were *canaille,* all of them. Not one had one known before, in the old days. But there is one quarrel I have with you. I am not against the Jews—of course it was terrible what Hitler did to the Jews, and none of us had any idea of what was going on in the camps—but to have a Jew as your chief prosecutor—really, really now, was that quite *gentleman?*" She looked from face to face in coquettish challenge. Nobody said anything, she was so very old. After a pause she pressed, "Was it now?" and shook her forefinger at us, showing a palm embarrassing to the sight, because it was tiny and plum-colored and pulpy like the inside of a monkey's paw. Someone said sadly, "But Sir David Maxwell Fyfe is not a Jew." She gave a trill of kind but derisive laughter. "Oh, but I have seen him." "All the same, he is not a Jew. Some dark types of Scotsmen are very difficult to tell from Jews." "But how, how, can you be so simple?" she gasped into her handkerchief. "Think, you dear people, of the name. The name. David. Who would call his son David but a Jew?" "Many Englishmen, many Scotsmen, and a great many more Welshmen," she was told. She could not contain her laughter; it blew away from her in a trail of shrillness. "Oh, you English are so simple; it is because you are aristocrats. A man who called his son David might tell you that he was English or Scotch or Welsh, because he would know that you would believe him. But we Germans understand a little better about such things, and he would not dare to pretend to us that he was not a Jew."

. . . .

The next day, the last day of the trial, there was something like hatred to be seen on the faces of many Germans in the street. The Palace of Justice was even fuller than before, the confusion engendered in the corridors by the inefficient scrutiny system was still more turbulent. There were some bad officials at Nuremberg, and that day they got completely out of hand. One of them, an American, male and a colonel, had always been remarkable for having the drooping bosom and resentful expression of a nursing mother who has had a difficult parturition, and for having throughout the trial nagged at the correspondents as if they were the staff of the maternity ward that had failed him. Hitherto he had not been arresting; the mind had simply noted him as infringing a feminine patent. But standing this day at the entrance of the gallery, staring at obviously valid passes, minute after minute, with the moonish look of a stupid woman trying to memorize the pattern of a baby's bootee, he was strangely revolting in his epicene distress.

The defendants were, however, quiet and cool. They were feeling the relief that many of us had known in little, when we had waited all through an evening for an air raid and at last heard the sirens, and, ironically, they even looked better in health. In the morning session they learned which of them the court considered guilty and which innocent, and why; and they listened to the verdicts with features decently blank except when they laughed. And, miraculously enough, they found the standing joke of the judges' pronunciation of German names just as funny today as before; and the acquittals amused them no end. Three of the defendants were found not guilty. One of these was a negative matter which caused no reaction except comradely satisfaction: that Hans Fritzsche, the radio chief of Goebbels' Propaganda Ministry, should have been found innocent recalled the case of poor Elmer in the classic American comedy, *Three Men on a Horse*. Elmer, it may be remembered, was a gentle creature, who neither smoked nor drank nor used rough words, and when he was found in a compromising attitude with a gangster's moll, and the gangster was wroth, one of the gang inquired, "But even if the worst was true, what would that amount to, in the case of Elmer?"

But the acquittals of von Papen and Schacht were richly positive. The two old foxes had got away again. They had tricked and turned and doubled on their tracks and lain doggo at the right time all their lives, which their white hairs showed had not been brief; and they had done it this time too. And it was absolutely right that they should have been acquitted. It would only have been possible to get them by stretching the law, and it is better to let foxes go and leave the law unstretched. Von Papen had never performed an official act, not even to the initialing of a faintly dubious memorandum, which could be connected with the commission of a war crime or a crime against humanity. He had intrigued and bullied his way through artificially provoked diplomatic crises with the weaker powers, he had turned the German Embassy in Vienna into a thieves' kitchen where the downfall of Schuschnigg was planned and executed; but this skulduggery could not be related to the planning of aggressive warfare, and if he had been found guilty there would have been grounds for a comparison, which would have been quite unfair but very difficult to attack on logical grounds, with Sir Neville Henderson. As for Schacht, he had indeed found the money for the Nazis' rearmament program, but rearmament itself had never been pronounced a crime; and it is impossible to conceive an article of international law which would have made him a criminal for his doings and not given grounds for a comparison with Lord Keynes. Indeed, the particular jiggery-pokery he had invented to make Germany's foreign trade a profitable racket, particularly in the Balkans, was so gloriously successful, and would have produced such staggering returns if it had been uninterrupted, that he cannot have wished for war.

But, all the same, these were not children of light, and the association of innocence with their names was entertaining. When the verdict on von Papen was pronounced, the other defendants gave him good-natured, rallying glances of congratulation; and he looked just as any Foreign Office man would look on acquittal, modest and humorous and restrained. But when the defendants heard that Schacht was to go free, Göring laughed, but all the rest looked grim. A glance at Schacht showed that in this they were showing no unpardonable malice. He was sitting in his customary twisted attitude, to show that he had nothing to do with the defendants sitting beside him and was paying no attention to the proceedings of the court, his long neck stretched up as if to give him the chance to breathe the purer upper air, his face red with indignation. As he heard the verdict of not guilty he looked more indignant than ever, and he tossed his white hairs. Had anyone gone to him and congratulated him on his acquittal he would certainly have replied that he considered it insulting to suppose that any other verdict could have been passed on him, and that he was meditating an action for wrongful imprisonment. There was, to be sure, nothing unnatural or illogical in his attitude. The court had cleared him with no compliments but with no qualifications, and the charges which had been brought against him were definitely part of the more experimental side of Nuremberg. Why should he feel grateful for the acquittal that was his right? There was no reason at all. But it must have been trying to be incarcerated over months in the company of one whose reason was quite so net and dry, who was capable of such strictly logical behavior as Schacht was to show over the affair of the orange.

This was quite a famous affair, for it amused the other defendants, who laughed at it as they had not been able to laugh at his acquittal, and told their wives. That was how it got known, long before one of the court psychiatrists told it in his book. Each defendant was given an orange with his lunch; and of the three acquitted men two had the same inspiration to perform a symbolic act of sympathy with their doomed comrades by giving their oranges away. Von Papen sent his to von Neurath, and Fritzsche sent his to von Schirach. But Schacht ate his own orange. And why not? Why should a man give up an orange which he had a perfect right to eat and send it to somebody else, just because he had been acquitted of crimes that he had not committed and the other man had been found guilty of crimes that he had committed? The laughter of his fellow prisoners was manifestly unjust. But surely they earned the right to be a little unjust, to laugh illogically, by what happened to them later at the afternoon session.

Something had happened to the architecture of the court which might happen in a dream. It had always appeared that the panelled wall behind the dock was solid. But one of the panels was really a door. It opened, and the convicted men came out one by one to stand between two guards and hear what they had earned. Göring, in his loose suit, which through the months had grown looser and looser, came through that door and looked surprised, like a man in pajamas who opens a door out of his hotel room in the belief that it leads to his bathroom and finds that he has walked out into a public room. Earphones were handed to him by the guard and he put them on, but at once made a gesture to show that they were not carrying the sound. They had had to put on a longer flex to reach from the ground to the ear of a standing man, and the adjustment had been faulty. His guards knelt down and worked on them. On the faces of all the judges there was written the thought, "Yes, this is a nightmare. This failure of the earphones proves it," and it was written on his face too. But he bent down and spoke to them and took a hand in the repair. This man of fifty-three could see the fine wires without spectacles. When the earphones were repaired he put them on with a steady hand and learned that this was not a nightmare, he was not dreaming. He took them off with something like a kingly gesture and went out, renouncing the multitudinous words and gestures that must have occurred to him at this moment. He was an inventive man and could not have had to look far for a comment which, poetic, patriotic, sardonic, or obscene, would certainly have held the ear of the court and sounded in history; and he was a man without taste. Yet at this moment he had taste enough to know that the idea of his death was more impressive than any of his own ideas.

A great mercy was conferred upon him. At this last moment that he would be seen by his fellow men it was not evident that he was among the most evil of human beings that have ever been born. He simply appeared as a man bravely sustaining the burden of fear. This mercy was extended to all the prisoners. It must be recorded that there was not a coward among them. Even Ribbentrop, who was white as stone because of his terror, showed a hard dignity, and Kaltenbrunner, who looked like a vicious horse and gave no promise of restraint, bowed quietly to the bench. Frank, the governor of Poland, he who had repented and become a good Catholic and wore black glasses more constantly than any of the others, gave an odd proof of his complete perturbation. He lost his sense of direction and stood with his back to the bench until he was spun round by the guards. But then he listened courageously enough to his sentence of death.

There was a deep unity in their behavior as there was a unity in their appearance. The only diversion was the mad little slap Hess gave the guards when they tried to hand him his earphones. He would not wear them, so he did not hear his sentence. The Service defendants, too, were distinct in their bearing, for they had experience of courts-martial and knew the protocol, and bowed and went out when their sentences were delivered. The others seemed to believe that the judge would add to their sentences some phrase of commination, and waited for it, looking straight in front of them; and, curiously enough, they seemed to be disappointed when the commination did not come. Perhaps they hoped that it would also be an explanation. That was what all in the court required: an explanation. We were going to hang eleven of these eighteen men, and imprison the other seven for ten, fifteen, twenty years, or for life; but we had no idea why they had done what they did. All but Streicher had Intelligence Quotients far above the average, and most of them had not been unfavored in their circumstances. We had learned what they did, beyond all doubt, and that is the great achievment of the Nuremberg trial. No literate person can now pretend that these men were anything but abscesses of cruelty. But we learned nothing about them that we did not know before, except that they were capable of heroism to which they had no moral right, and that there is nothing in the legend that a bully is always a coward.

Then the court rose. It did so in the strict physical sense of the word. Usually when a court rises it never enjoys a foot of real elevation; the judge stalks from the bench, the lawyers and spectators debouch through the corridors, their steps heavy by reason of what they have just heard. But this court rose as a plane takes off, as gulls wheel off the sea when a siren sounds, as if it were going to fly out of the window, to soar off the roof. The courtroom was empty in a minute or two, and the staff hurried along the corridors into one another's offices, saying good-bye, good-bye to each other, good-bye to the trial, good-bye to the feeling of autumn that had grown so melancholy in these latter days, because of the reddening creepers and the ice in the sunshine, and these foreseen sentences of death.

The great left at once, that very day, if they were great enough, and so did some who were not so very great, but who, avid for home, had plotted for precedence as addicts plot to get drugs. The less great and the less farseeing had to wait their turn, for again transport could not meet the demands of the occasion, and the going was worse than the coming. Fog took a hand, and it was usually noon before the planes could leave the ground. Visitors and correspondents waited at the airport for days, some of them for a week, and more and more people tried to go away by train, and some who succeeded ran into awkward currency difficulties. And in the Palace of Justice there were packing cases on the floor of every office: the typewriters had to go home, the files had to go home, the stationery had to go home. Those who had finished and were free ran in and bent down beaming to say good-bye to those still on their knees beside these packing cases, who beamed up at them because they were to be free themselves quite soon, and cried happy things for the parting gift, which if they were to remain any time was often a pot of those prodigious cyclamens grown by the one-legged gardener in the greenhouse at the press camp. It was a party, it was like going off for a cruise, only instead of leaving home, you were going home, going home, going home.

TESTIMONY AND ARGUMENT AS LITERATURE

Joan of Arc

:

TESTIMONY GIVEN AT HER TRIAL
FOR HERESY AND WITCHCRAFT

George Bernard Shaw said there were two opinions about Joan of Arc, "one that she was miraculous; the other that she was unbearable." Both opinions were justified. Her leadership of the army of the Dauphin, Prince Charles of France, to victory when it was threatened with overwhelming defeat was miraculous in the sense that an act of genius is a miracle. She was unbearable because, convinced that she was divinely inspired, she refused to yield to the authority of those who considered themselves her superiors.

At the time Joan appeared, Orleans, the last stronghold of the Dauphin's forces, was besieged by the armies of the French Duke of Burgundy and the English Duke of Bedford. Burgundy and Bedford sought to establish the right of the infant King Henry VI of England to the throne of France. The Dauphin, son of the mad Charles VI of France, claimed he was the rightful heir to the throne. Joan of Arc, believing herself instructed by the Archangel Michael and the Saints Catherine and Margaret to lift the siege of Orleans and to lead the Dauphin to Rheims, the ancient coronation city of France, presented herself to the Dauphin and asked to be placed in command of his troops. As it was believed that only a miracle could save the French—and no other miracle was in the offing—the Dauphin was persuaded. Every school boy knows what followed. Joan, though she was only 18 or 19 at the time, and without any knowledge of warfare, was an exceptional military commander and inspired all who followed her. The siege of Orleans was

335

broken and the Dauphin was crowned King Charles VII of France at Rheims. Joan continued to lead the French troops until her capture by the Burgundians at Compiegne in May, 1430.

As Joan had been a great inspiration to the French and many of the English feared her as an emissary from God, Bedford was determined to attaint her in some manner. He paid the Duke of Burgundy a sum equivalent to more than $50,000 for Joan's transfer to the English. To demonstrate that Joan was diabolically inspired,—and therefore, that the French resistance and spirit of French nationalism that she had awakened was unholy—a condemnation by Church authority was necessary. The center of Ecclesiastical learning and power in France was the University of Paris. The University was pro-English, or Burgundian in its sympathies, and was chosen therefore to determine whether Joan was in fact a sorceress. The leader or Chief Judge in the inquiry was Peter Cauchon, Bishop of Beauvais, within whose diocese Joan had been captured.

Joan was questioned for fifteen days by sixty judges or Assessors from the faculty of the University. The interrogations and Joan's answers were carefully transcribed, and five Latin translations, three of which still exist, were made by her Judges. The examiners were masters and doctors of theology and French law, and Joan, unlettered and untutored, had no counsel. Yet they could not confound her. Her answers reflect her honesty, boldness, simplicity and greatness of heart.

The purpose of the examinations was to show that Joan's visions were not from God, but were evil spirits of corporeal substance (as all churchmen knew, real saints were ethereal); that Joan practised witchcraft, using emblems, such as her banner, as articles of sorcery; that she had, in pride and presumption, caused herself to be venerated and adored; that she refused obedience to the Church.

In the following transcription, the questions and answers have been rearranged, to give the interrogation greater coherence, but no liberties have been taken with the text.

Q: Asked her name, surname, place of birth, father, mother, etc.

A: In my own country they call me Jeannette; since I came into France I have been called Jeanne. Of my surname I know nothing. I was born in the village of Domremy . . . My father is called Jacques d'Arc; my mother, Ysabelle . . . I am, I should say, about nineteen years of age. From my mother I learned my Pater, my Ave Maria, and my Credo. I believe I learned all this from my mother.

Q: In your youth, did you learn any trade?

A: Yes, I learnt to spin and to sew; in sewing and spinning I fear no woman in Rouen.

Q (*Not recorded*):

A: I was thirteen when I had a Voice from God for my help and guidance. The first time that I heard this Voice, I was very much frightened; it was mid-day, in the summer, in my father's garden . . . I heard this Voice to my right, towards the Church; rarely do I hear it without its being accompanied also by a light. This light comes from the same side as the voice. Generally it is a great light . . .

Q: How long is it since you heard your Voices?

A: I heard them yesterday and today.

Q: What were you doing yesterday morning when the voice came to you?

A: I was asleep: the Voice awoke me.

Q: Was it by touching you on the arm?

A: It awoke me without touching me.

Q: Was it in your room?

A: Not so far as I know, but in the Castle.

Q: Did you thank it? and did you go on your knees?

A: I did thank it. I was sitting on the bed; I joined my hands; I implored its help. The Voice said to me: "Answer boldly; God will help thee." . . . (*Addressing herself to the Bishop of Beauvais:*) You say you are my judge. Take care what you are doing; for in truth I am sent by God, and you place yourself in great danger.

Q: Has this Voice sometimes varied its counsel?

A: I have never found it give two contrary opinions.

Q: This Voice that speaks to you, is it that of an Angel, or of a Saint, or from God direct?

A: It is the Voice of Saint Catherine and Saint Margaret. Their faces are adorned with beautiful crowns, very rich and precious.

Q: How do you know if these were the two Saints? How do you distinguish one from the other?

A: I know quite well it is they; and I can easily distinguish one from the other.

Q: How do you distinguish them?

A: By the greeting they give me. It is seven years now since they have undertaken to guide me. I know them well because they were named to me.

Q: What was the first Voice that came to you when you were about thirteen?

A: It was Saint Michael; I saw him before my eyes; he was not alone, but quite surrounded by the Angels of Heaven . . .

Q: Did you see Saint Michael and these Angels bodily and in reality?

A: I saw them with my bodily eyes as well as I see you; when they went from me, I wept. I should have liked to be taken away with them.

Q: And what was Saint Michael like?

A: You will have no more answer from me; and I am not yet free to tell you . . . There is a saying among children that, "Sometimes one is hanged for speaking the truth."

Q: How do you know whether the object that appears to you is male or female?

A: I know well enough. I recognize them by their voices, as they revealed themselves to me; I know nothing but by the revelation and order of God.

Q: What part of their heads do you see?

A: The face.

Q: These saints who show themselves to you, have they any hair?

A: It is well to know they have.

Q: Is there anything between their crowns and their hair?

A: No.

Q: Is their hair long and hanging down?

A: I know nothing about it. I do not know if they have arms or other members. They speak very well and in very good language; I hear them very well.

Q: How do they speak if they have no members?

A: I refer me to God. The voice is beautiful, sweet and low; it speaks the French tongue.

Q: Does not Saint Margaret speak English?

A: Why should she speak English if she is not on the English side?

Q: In what likeness did Saint Michael appear to you?

A: I did not see a crown: I know nothing of his dress.

Q: Was he naked?

A: Do you think God has not wherewithal to clothe him?

Q: Had he hair?

A: Why should it have been cut off? I have not seen Saint Michael since I left the Castle of Crotoy. I do not see him often. I do not know if he has hair.

Q: Had he scales?

A: I do not know. I feel great joy when I see him. I think that, when I see him, I am not in mortal sin.

Q: When you confess, do you believe that you are in mortal sin?

A: I do not know if I have been in mortal sin; I do not believe that I have done the works thereof. Please God I shall not do, and that I have not done, things by which my soul will be burdened.

Q: What sign did you give to your King (*the Dauphin when she saw him for the first time*) that you came from God?

A: . . . The sign was that an Angel assured my King, in bringing him the crown, that he should have the whole realm of France, by the means of God's help and my labors; that he was to set me to work— that is to say, to give me soldiers; and that otherwise he would not be so soon crowned and consecrated.

Q: Of what material was the said crown?

A: It is well to know it was of fine gold; it was so rich that I do not know how to count its riches or to appreciate its beauty. The crown signified that my King should possess the Kingdom of France.

Q: Were there stones in it?

A: I have told you what I know about it.

Q: Did you touch or kiss it?

A: No.

Q: Did the Angel who brought it come from above, or along the ground?

A: He came from above,—I mean, he came at our Lord's bidding. He entered by the door of the chamber.

Q: Did he move along the ground from the door of the chamber?

A: When he came into the king's presence, he did him reverence, bowing before him and speaking the words I have told you about the sign. Then he reminded him of the beautiful patience he had shown in the face of the great tribulations which had come to him. And from the door of the chamber he stepped and moved along the ground as he came to the king. When the Angel came I accompanied him and went with him up the steps to the King's chamber, and the Angel went in first. And then I said to the King, "Sire, there is your sign—take it."

Q: This crown, did it smell well and had it a good odor? did it glitter?

A: I do not remember about it; I will think it over. Yes, it smelt good, and will smell good always, if it be well guarded, as it should be . . .

Q: Did the Angel write you a letter?

A: No.

Q: What sign had your King and the people who were with him and yourself, to believe that it was an Angel?

A: The King believed it by the teaching of the Clergy who were there, and by the sign of the crown.

Q: But how did the Clergy know it was an Angel?

A: By their knowledge and because they were clerics.

Q: If the devil were to put himself in the form or likeness of an angel, how would you know if it were a good or an evil angel?

A: I should know quite well if it were Saint Michael or a counterfeit. The first time I was in great doubt if it were Saint Michael; and I was much afraid. I had seen him many times before I knew it was Saint Michael.

Q: Why did you recognize him sooner that time, when you say you believed it was he, than the first time he appeared to you?

A: The first time I was a young child, and I was much afraid; afterwards, he had taught me so well, and it was so clear to me, that I believed firmly it was he.

Q: What doctrine did he teach you?

A: Above all things he told me to be a good child, and that God would help me,—to come to the help of the King of France, among other things. The greater part of what he taught me is already in the book in which you are writing: (*the trial record*) he told me of the great misery there was in the Kingdom of France.

Q: Did you ever kiss or embrace Saint Catherine or Saint Margaret?

A: I have embraced them both.

Q: Did they smell good?

A: It is well to know, they smelled good.

Q: In embracing them, did you feel any heat or anything else?

A: I could not have embraced them without feeling and touching them.

Q: What part did you kiss—face or feet?

A: It is more proper and respectful to kiss their feet.

Q: Do you know if you are in the Grace of God?

A: If I am not, may God place me there; if I am, may God so keep me. I should be the saddest in all the world if I knew that I were not in the grace of God.* But if I were in a state of sin, do you think the Voice would come to me? I would that every one could hear the Voice as I hear it. . . .

Q: Do you know if Saint Catherine and Saint Margaret hate the English?

A: They love what God loves; they hate what God hates.

Q: Does God hate the English?

A: Of the love or hate God may have for the English or of what he will do for their souls, I know nothing; but I know quite well that they will be put out of France, except those who shall die there, and that God will send victory to the French against the English.

Q: Was God for the English when they were prospering in France?

A: I do not know if God hated the French; but I believe that He wished them to be defeated for their sins, if they were in sin.

Q: Do the people of Domremy (*where Joan was born*) side with the Burgundians or with the opposite party.

A: I knew only one Burgundian at Domremy: I should have been quite willing for them to cut off his head—always had it pleased God.

Q: Had you in your youth any intention of fighting the Burgundians?

A: I had a great will and desire that my King should have his own Kingdom.

Q: Is it for any merit of yours that God sent you this Angel?

A: He came for a great purpose: I was in hopes that the King would believe the sign, and that they would cease to argue with me, and would aid the good people of Orleans. The Angel came for the merits of the King and of the good Duke d'Orleans.

Q: Why to you rather than to another?

A: It has pleased God so to do by a simple maiden, in order to drive back the enemies of the King.

Q: When you were at Orleans, had you a standard, or banner; and of what color was it?

A: I had a banner of which the field was sprinkled with lilies; the world was painted there, with an angel at each side; it was white, of the white cloth called "bocassin"; there was written above, I believe, "Jhesus Maria"; it was fringed with silk.

---

* "Was there ever a better answer on cross-examination? If Joan had said, Yes, I am in a state of grace, it would have been a presumption of her own salvation. If she said, No, that would have been a confession."

—Charles Curtis

Q: The words "Jhesus Maria" were they written above, below, or on the side?

A: At the side, I believe.

Q: Which did you care for most, your banner or your sword?

A: Better, forty times better, my banner than my sword!

Q: Who made you get this painting done upon your banner?

A: I have told you often enough, that I had nothing done but by the command of God. It was I, myself, who bore this banner, when I attacked the enemy, to save killing any one, for I have never killed any one.

Q: Do you not know that the people of your party had services, masses, and prayers offered for you?

A: I know nothing of it; if they had any service, it was not by my order; but if they prayed for me, my opinion is they did not do ill.

Q: In what spirit did the people of your party kiss your hands and your garments?

A: Many came to see me willingly, but they kissed my hands as little as I could help. The poor folk came to me readily, because I never did them any unkindness; on the contrary, I loved to help them.

Q: Do you always do, always accomplish, what your Voices command you?

A: With all my power I accomplish the command that Our Lord sends me through my Voices, in so far as I understand them. My Voices command nothing but by the good pleasure of Our Lord.

Q: In warfare, have you done nothing without counsel of your voices?

A: I have already answered you thereon: read your book again well, and you will find it. At the request of the men-at-arms, there was an assault made before Paris, and, at the request of the King himself, one also before La Charité. These were neither against nor by the order of my Voices.

Q: Would you like to have a woman's dress?

A: Give me one, if I may take it and leave; otherwise, no. I am content with what I have, since it pleases God that I wear it.

Q: Was it God who prescribed to you the dress of a man?

A: What concerns this dress is a small thing—less than nothing. I did not take it by advice of any man in the world. I did not take this dress or do anything but by the command of Our Lord and of the Angels.

Q: Did it appear to you that this command to take man's dress was lawful?

A: All I have done is by Our Lord's command. If I had been told to take some other, I should have done it; because it would have been His command.

Q: What warrant and what help do you expect to have from Our Lord for wearing this man's dress?

A: For this dress and for other things that I have done, I wish to have no other recompense than the salvation of my soul.

Q: When you asked to hear Mass, did it not seem to you that it would be more proper to be in female dress? Which would you like best, to have a woman's dress to hear Mass, or to remain in a man's dress and not hear it?

A: Give me assurance beforehand that I shall hear Mass if I am in female attire, and I will answer you this.

Q: Very well, I give you assurance of it: you shall hear Mass if you put on female attire.

A: And what say you, if I have sworn and promised to our King my Master, not to put off this dress? Well, I will answer you this: Have made for me a long dress down to the ground, without a train; give it to me to go to Mass, and then on my return I will put on again the dress I have.

Q: You have asserted that, for speaking the truth, men were sometimes hanged: do you, then, know any crime or fault in yourself for which you should die, if you confessed it?

A: I know none.

Q: Will you refer yourself to the decision of the Church?

A: I refer myself to God Who sent me, to Our Lady, and to all the Saints in Paradise. And in my opinion it is all one, God and the Church; and one should make no difficulty about it. Why do you make a difficulty?

Q: There is a Church Triumphant in which are God and the Saints, the Angels, and the Souls of the Saved. There is another Church, the Church Militant, in which are the Pope, the Vicar of God on earth, the Cardinals, Prelates of the Church, the Clergy and all good Christians and Catholics: this Church, regularly assembled, cannot err, being ruled by the Holy Spirit. Will you refer yourself to this Church which we have thus just defined to you?

A: I came to the King of France from God, from the Blessed Virgin Mary, from all the Saints of Paradise, and the Church Victorious above, and by their command. To this Church I submit all my good deeds, all that I have done or will do. As to saying whether I will submit myself to the Church Militant, I will not now answer anything more.

Q: Will you refer yourself to the judgment of the Church on earth for all you have said or done, be it good or bad? Especially will you refer to the Church the cases, crimes, and offenses which are imputed to you everything which touches on this Trial?

A: On all that I am asked I will refer to the Church Militant, provided they do not command anything impossible. And I hold as a thing impossible to declare that my actions and my words and all that I have answered on the subject of my visions and revelations I have not done and said by the order of God: This, I will not declare for anything in the world. And that which God hath made me do, hath commanded or shall command, I will not fail to do for any man alive. It would be impossible for me to revoke it. And in case the Church should wish me to do anything contrary to the command which has been given me of God, I will not consent to it, whatever it may be.

Q: If the Church Militant tells you that your revelations are illusions, or diabolical things, will you defer to the Church?

A: I will defer to God, Whose Commandment I always do. . . . In case the Church should prescribe the contrary, I should not refer to any one in the world, but to God alone, Whose Commandment I always follow.

Q: Do you not then believe you are subject to the Church of God which is on earth, that is to say to our Lord the Pope, to the Cardinals, the Archbishops, Bishops, and other prelates of the Church?

A: Yes, I believe myself to be subject to them; but God must be served first.

Q: Have you then command from your Voices not to submit yourself to the Church Militant, which is on earth, not to its decision?

A: I answer nothing from my own head; what I answer is by command of my Voices; they do not order me to disobey the Church, but God must be served first.

Joan was condemned by her judges as a witch, as an heretic and an apostate who flouted the authority of the Church, and as an immoral woman who wore men's outer and under garments, against the laws of modesty and decency. She was at first also accused of sexual immorality, but physical examinations conducted by a number of women,—among them the Duchess of Bedford—proved her unquestionably virgin. It was ordered that unless she recanted her heresies she was to be burned alive. Joan refused to recant.

On the day set for her execution, she was placed upon a scaffold in a public square and then once again publicly exhorted to abandon her heresies—to confess that she had been led by evil spirits—and to yield obedience to the Church. The text of the exhortation was the words of St. John, "The branch cannot bear fruit of itself, except it abide in the vine." Joan was admonished that if she wished to be considered a true Catholic and not be excommunicated, she would have to abide in the vine of the Church.

Before the torch was put to her pyre Joan, overcome by fear, declared that her visions had forsaken her, that she revoked her heresies and promised to obey the Church in all things, including the direction to resume a woman's dress. She was then taken from the scaffold and returned to prison. The man's clothing she had put off was left with her in the cell. Three days later she put it on again. She said then that she would rather die than be in irons, that she had done wrong in denying her Voices. "I would rather," she declared, "do penance once for all—that is to die—than endure any longer the suffering of a prison. I have done nothing against God or the Faith, in spite of all they have made me revoke."

Joan was then formally denounced as a relapsed heretic and on May 30, 1431, she was burned to death.

As Joan predicted, the English were finally driven out of France. In 1455 the Borgia Pope, Calixtus, ordered a reexamination of her trial. After the reexamination it was adjudged that she had been falsely accused and unjustly condemned. The body of Peter Cauchon, Bishop of Beauvais, was exhumed and cast into the sewers. Finally in 1920, Joan was canonized a Saint, and placed in the company of her beloved Saints Catherine and Margaret.

Clarence Darrow

:

SUMMATION IN THE SWEET CASE

Housing segregation by the mob was the issue in the Sweet trial in Detroit in 1926.

The Negro population of the city had jumped from about 6,000 in 1910 to about 70,000 at the time of the Sweet case sixteen years later. Most of the increase came during the war when Detroit was in the midst of an unprecedented boom in the automobile industry.

The manufacturers brought Negro laborers from the South into the city. However, neither the manufacturers nor the city made any provisions for housing, and the newcomers were jammed into an already overcrowded area.

The Negro workmen could stay in the automobile factories in the daytime, but they had no place to stay at night, so they expanded the Negro section and some of them moved out to what was called the white district.

This set the stage for the Sweet case.

Dr. Ossian H. Sweet was a successful gynecologist. He had received his M.D. degree from Howard University. He had worked under Madame Curie and was interested in the effects of radium, particularly on cancer. Later he was to study in Vienna.

Returning from Europe, the Sweets first stayed with the parents of Dr. Sweet's wife until they purchased a home. This new home was located at Garland and Charlevoix, a lower-middle-class white neighborhood. In September of 1925, Dr. Sweet, his wife and their two-year-old baby girl moved into this home.

But Dr. Sweet anticipated trouble. Other Negroes moving into homes in white neighborhoods had been intimidated by so-called Improvement Associations and were forced to move out. So with the Sweets' belongings went ten guns and a supply of ammunition.

A white crowd gathered around the house the first night, September 8, but it was relatively quiet. The second night a larger crowd—estimated at several hundred—gathered in the neighborhood of the Sweet home. About eight policemen were on duty to prevent disorder. But now cries of "Niggers!" rumbled through the street.

Dr. Sweet's two brothers, Otis, a dentist, and Henry, a student, together with seven friends, were in the house on the second night with Dr. and Mrs. Sweet. The baby was at her grandmother's home.

The police testified at the trial that all was quiet on the street when suddenly shots were fired from the windows of the Sweet house. A white man, Leon Breiner, sitting nearby smoking his pipe, was killed, and another white man wounded.

The eleven Negroes in the house were immediately arrested and charged with first-degree murder. Arthur Garfield Hays, one of the attorneys for the defense, later commented in court that if the baby had been home she, too, probably would have been arrested.

Darrow became chief counsel for the Sweet case, and with him to Detroit went Hays. The trial of the eleven Negroes began October 30, 1925, before Judge Frank Murphy of Recorder's Court. Judge Murphy later became a justice of the United States Supreme Court.

Robert M. Toms was prosecuting attorney and Lester S. Moll was his assistant. Darrow throughout the trial referred to Toms as "a nice fellow."

In her pamphlet, "Clarence Darrow's Two Great Trials," Marcet Haldeman-Julius reported that in Detroit Darrow was in a more formal mood than in Dayton, Tennessee, at the Scopes trial. "The famous galluses were safely hidden under well-pressed vest and coat. Almost invariably his gray hair was neatly brushed."

Selection of the jury was long and difficult. When the panel was called, only one colored person was on it and he was peremptorily dismissed.

The defense contended during the trial that the eleven Negroes had used their constitutional rights of self-defense. It was important for the defense to prove that there had been anti-Negro agitation.

The prosecution, on the other hand, contended that there had been no such agitation and that there was no mob around the Sweet home at the time of the killing.

While State witnesses testified they were in the neighborhood of the Sweet home merely because of curiosity, Darrow sat slouched in his chair working a crossword puzzle.

The defense charged that when the neighborhood heard a colored family had bought a home in the area, a "Water Works Improvement Association" had been formed.

Darrow in his cross-examination tried to prove that the purpose of the Association was to keep Negroes out of the neighborhood. Typical was his questioning of State witness Eben E. Draper. Darrow asked Draper whether his joining the Association was prompted by the Sweets' purchasing a home in the area. Draper answered, "Possibly."

DARROW: Did it?

DRAPER: Yes.

DARROW: You joined that club to aid in keeping that a white district?

DRAPER: Yes.

DARROW: At the meeting in the school, was any reference made to keeping the district free from colored people?

DRAPER: Yes.

A youngster of fifteen, a witness for the State, gave the defense the break it was looking for.

Darrow asked him how many people were in the neighborhood.

WITNESS: There was a great crowd—no, I won't say a great crowd, a large crowd—well, there were a few people and the officers were keeping them moving.

DARROW: Have you talked with anyone about the case?

WITNESS: Lieutenant Johnson [the police detective].

DARROW: And when you started to answer the question you forgot to say "a few people," didn't you?

WITNESS: Yes, sir.

Darrow in his plea asked for a verdict of Not Guilty. He pointed out: "The Sweets spent their first night in their first home afraid to go to bed. The next night they spent in jail. Now the State wants them to spend the rest of their lives in the penitentiary. The State claims there was no mob there that night. Gentlemen, the State has put on enough witnesses who said they were there, to make a mob.

"There are persons in the North and South who say a black man is inferior to a white and should be controlled by the whites. There are those who recognize his rights and say he should try and enjoy them. To me this case is a cross-section of human history. It involves the future, and the hope of some of us that the future shall be better than the past."

The jury was out forty-six hours. No decision could be reached. Judge Murphy declared a mistrial. The jury was dismissed. That was November 27, 1925.

The defense asked that if there were to be any more trials, each defendant be tried separately.

About five months later, in April 1926, the trial of Henry Sweet, younger brother of Dr. Sweet, opened, again in Judge Murphy's court. This time with Darrow appeared Mr. Perry and Thomas W. Chawke.

It took a week to impanel the jury; 165 prospective jurors were questioned. Most were dismissed for cause; peremptory challenges were used against twenty.

When the jury was finally impaneled, it was made up of a retired steamship steward, locomotive engineer, pharmacist, machinist, electrician, electroplater, grocery store manager, a former army man who was at the time of the trial a Water Board employee, a steamship line executive, a retired lumberman, an electrical engineer and contractor, and a watchman. They ranged in age from 24 to 82 years.

The trial was practically identical to the first except for Darrow's plea.

The ex-army man on the jury many times dozed off during the examination and the remark was often heard in the courtroom that "Number eight is asleep again." But he was wide awake during Darrow's final arguments which lasted for seven hours.

INTRODUCTORY NOTES BY ARTHUR WEINBERG

"The life of the Negro race has been a life of tragedy, of injustice, of oppression. The law has made him equal, but man has not. And, after all, the last analysis is, what has man done?— and not what has the law done?"

If the Court please, gentlemen of the jury: You have listened so long and patiently that I do not know whether you are able to stand much more. I want to say, however, that while I have tried a good many cases in the forty-seven or forty-eight years that I have lived in courthouses, that in one way this has been one of the pleasantest trials I have ever been in. The kindness and the consideration of the Court is such as to make it easy for everybody, and I have seldom found as courteous, gentlemanly and kindly opponents as I have had in this case. I appreciate their friendship. Lawyers are apt to look at cases from different standpoints, and I sometimes find it difficult to understand how a lawyer on the other side can think as he thinks and say what he says; I, being an extremely reasonable man and entirely free from all kinds of prejudices myself, find this hard to comprehend.

My friend Mr. Moll says, gentlemen, that this isn't a race question. This is a murder case. We don't want any prejudice; we don't want the other side to have any. Race and color have nothing to do with this case. This is a case of murder.

I insist that there is nothing but prejudice in this case; that if it was reversed and eleven white men had shot and killed a black while protecting their home and their lives against a mob of blacks, nobody would have dreamed of having them indicted. I know what I am talking about, and so do you. They would have been given medals instead. Ten colored men and one woman are in this indictment, tried by twelve jurors, gentlemen. Every one of you are white, aren't you? At least you all think so. We haven't one colored man on this jury. We couldn't get one. One was called and he was disqualified. You twelve white men are trying a colored man on race prejudice.

Now, let me ask you whether you are not prejudiced. I want to put this square to you, gentlemen. I haven't any doubt but that every one of you is prejudiced against colored people. I want you to guard against it. I want you to do all you can to be fair in this case, and I believe you will. A number of you have answered the question that you are acquainted with colored people. One juror I have in mind, who is sitting here, said there were two or three families living on the street in the block where he lives, and he had lived there for a year or more, but he didn't know their names and had never met them. Some of the rest of you said that you had employed colored people to work for you, are even employing them now. All right. You have seen some colored people in this case. They have been so far above the white people that live at the corner of Garland and Charlevoix that they can't be compared, intellectually, morally and physically, and you know it. How many of you jurors, gentlemen, have ever had a colored person visit you in your home? How many of you have ever visited in their homes? How many of you have invited them to dinner at your house? Probably not one of you. Now, why, gentlemen? There isn't one of you men who doesn't know just from the witnesses you have seen in this case that there are colored people who are intellectually the equal of all of you. Am I right? Colored people living right here in the city of Detroit are intellectually the equals and some of them superior to most of us. Is that true? Some of them are people of more character and learning than most of us.

Now, why don't you individually, and why don't I, and why doesn't every white person whose chances have been greater and whose wealth is larger, associate with them? There is only one reason, and that is prejudice. Can you give any other reason for it? They would be intellectual companions. They have good manners. They are clean. They are all of them clean enough to wait on us, but not clean enough to associate with. Is there any reason in the world why we don't associate with them excepting prejudice? I think not one man of this jury wants to be prejudiced. It is forced into us almost from our youth, until somehow or other we feel we are superior to these people who have black faces.

Now, gentlemen, I say you are prejudiced. I fancy everyone of you is, otherwise you would have some companions amongst these colored people. You will overcome it, I believe, in the trial of this case. But they tell me there is no race prejudice, and it is plain nonsense, and nothing else.

Who are we, anyway? A child is born into this world without any knowledge of any sort. He has a brain which is a piece of putty; he inherits nothing in the way of knowledge or of ideas. If he is white, he knows nothing about color. He has no antipathy to the black. The black and the white both will live together and play together, but as soon as the baby is born we begin giving him ideas. We begin planting seeds in his mind. We begin telling him he must do this and he must not do that. We tell him about race and social equality and the thousands of things that men talk about until he grows up. It has been trained into us, and you, gentlemen, bring that feeling into this jury box.

You need not tell me you are not prejudiced. I know better. We are not very much but a bundle of prejudices anyhow. We are prejudiced against other people's color. Prejudiced against other men's religions; prejudiced against other people's politics. Prejudiced against people's looks. Prejudiced about the way they dress. We are full of prejudices. You can teach a man anything beginning with the child; you can make anything out of him, and we are not responsible for it. Here and there some of us haven't any prejudices on some questions, but if you look deep enough you will find them; and we all know it.

All I hope for, gentlemen of the jury, is this: that you are strong enough, and honest enough, and decent enough to lay it aside in this case and decide it as you ought to. And I say, there is no man in Detroit that doesn't know that these defendants, every one of them, did right. There isn't a man in Detroit who doesn't know that the defendant did his duty, and that this case is an attempt to send him and his companions to prison because they defended their constitutional rights. It is a wicked attempt, and you are asked to be a party to it. You know it. I don't need to talk to this jury about the facts in this case. There is no man who can read or can understand that does not know the facts. Is there prejudice in it?

Now, let's see. I don't want to lean very much on your intelligence. I don't need much. I just need a little. Would this case be in this court if these defendants were not black? Would we be standing in front of you if these defendants were not black? Would anybody be asking you to send a boy to prison for life for defending his brother's home and protecting his own life, if his face wasn't black? What were the people in the neighborhood of Charlevoix and Garland Streets doing on that fatal night? There isn't a child that doesn't know. Have you any doubt as to why they were there? Was Mr. Moll right when he said that color has nothing to do with the case? There is nothing else in this case but the feeling of prejudice which has been carefully nourished by the white man until he doesn't know that he has it himself. While I admire and like my friend Moll very much, I can't help criticizing his argument. I suppose I may say what old men are apt to say, in a sort of patronizing way. that his zeal is due to youth and inexperience. That is about all we have to brag about as we get older, so we ought to be permitted to do that. Let us look at this case.

Mr. Moll took particular pains to say to you, gentlemen, that these eleven people here are guilty of murder; he calls this a cold-blooded, deliberate and premeditated murder; that is, they were there to kill. That was their purpose. Eleven, he said. I am not going to discuss the case of all of them just now, but I am starting where he started. He doesn't want any misunderstanding. Amongst that eleven is Mrs. Sweet, the wife of Dr. Sweet. She is a murderer, gentlemen? The state's attorney said so, and the assistant state's attorney said so. The state's attorney would have to endorse it because he himself stands by what his assistant says. Pray, tell me what has Mrs. Sweet done to make her a murderer? She is the wife of Dr. Sweet. She is the mother of his little baby. She left the child at her mother's home while she moved into this highly cultured community near Goethe Street. Anyway, the baby was to be safe; but she took her own chance, and she didn't have a gun; none was provided for her. Brother Toms drew from the witnesses that there were ten guns, and ten men. He didn't leave any for her. Maybe she had a penknife, but there is no evidence on that question. What did she do, gentlemen? She is put down here as a murderer. She wasn't even upstairs. She didn't even look out of a window. She was down in the back kitchen cooking a ham to feed her family and friends, and a white mob came to drive them out of their home before the ham was served for dinner. She is a murderer, and all of these defendants who were driven out of their home must go to the penitentiary for life if you can find twelve jurors somewhere who have enough prejudice in their hearts, and hatred in their minds.

Now, that is this case, gentlemen, and that is all there is to this case. Take the hatred away, and you have nothing left. Mr. Moll says that this is a case between Breiner and Henry Sweet.

MOLL: No, I did not say any such thing.

DARROW: Well, let me correct it. He says that he holds a brief for Breiner. That is right; isn't it?

MOLL: That is right.

DARROW: Well, I will put it just as it is, he holds a brief for Breiner, this prosecuting attorney. He is wrong. If he holds a brief for Breiner, he should throw it in the stove. It has no place in a court of justice. The question here is whether these defendants or this defendant is guilty of murder. It has nothing to do with Breiner. He says that I wiggled and squirmed every time they mentioned Breiner. Well, now, I don't know. Did I? Maybe I did. I didn't know it. I have been around courtrooms so long that I fancy I could listen to anything without moving a hair. Maybe I couldn't.

I rather think my friend is pretty wise. He said that I don't like to hear them talk about Breiner. I don't, gentlemen, and I might have shown it. This isn't the first case I was ever in. I don't like to hear the state's attorney talk about the blood of a victim. It has such a mussy sound. I wish they would leave it out. I will be frank with you about it. I don't think it has any place in a case. I think it tends to create prejudice and feeling and it has no place, and it is always dangerous. And perhaps—whether I showed it or not, my friend read my mind. I don't like it.

Now, gentlemen, as he talked about Breiner, I am going to talk about him, and it isn't easy, either. It isn't easy to talk about the dead, unless you "slobber" over them and I am not going to "slobber" over Breiner. I am going to tell you the truth about it. Why did he say that he held a brief for Breiner, and ask you to judge between Breiner and Henry Sweet? You know why he said it. To get a verdict, gentlemen. That is why he said it. Had it any place in this case? Henry Sweet never knew that such a man lived as Breiner. Did he? He didn't shoot at him. Somebody shot into that crowd and Breiner got it. Nobody had any feeling against him. But who was Breiner, anyway? I will tell you who he was. I am going to measure my words when I state it, and I am going to make good before I am through in what I say.

Who was he? He was a conspirator in as foul a conspiracy as was ever hatched in a community; in a conspiracy to drive from their homes a little family of black people. Not only that, but to destroy these blacks and their home. Now, let me see whether I am right. What do we know of Breiner? He lived two blocks from the Sweet home. On the fourteenth day of July, seven hundred people met at the schoolhouse and the schoolhouse was too small, and they went out into the yard. This schoolhouse was right across the street from the Sweet house.

Every man in that community knew all about it. Every man in that community understood it. And in that schoolhouse a man rose and told what they had done in his community; that by main force they had driven Negro families from their homes, and that when a Negro moved to Garland Street, their people would be present to help. That is why Mr. Breiner came early to the circus on September 9, 1925. He went past that house, back and forth, two or three times that night. What was he doing? "Smoking his pipe." What were the rest of them doing? They were a part of a mob and they had no rights, and the Court will tell you so, I think. And, if he does, gentlemen, it is your duty to accept it.

Gentlemen, it is a reflection upon anybody's intelligence to say that everyone did not know why this mob was there. You know! Every one of you know why. They came early to take their seats at the ringside. Didn't they? And Breiner sat at one point where the stones were thrown, didn't he? Was he a member of that mob? Gentlemen, that mob was bent not only on making an assault upon the rights of the owners of that house, not only making an assault upon their persons and their property, but they were making an assault on the constitution and the laws of the nation and the state under which they live.

Gentlemen, my friend said that he wasn't going to mince matters. I think I will, because I know the prejudice is the other way. You can pick twelve men in these black faces that are watching your deliberations and have throughout all these weary days, and with them I would not need to mince matters; but I must be very careful not to shock your sensibilities. I must state just as much or as near the facts as I dare to state without shocking you and be fair to my client.

It was bad enough for a mob, by force and violation of law, to attempt to drive these people from their house but, gentlemen, it is worse to send them to prison for life for defending their home. Think of it. That is this case. Are we human? Hardly.

Did the witnesses for the State appearing here tell the truth? You know they did not. I am not going to analyze the testimony of every one of them. But they did not tell the truth and they did not mean to tell the truth. Let me ask you this question, gentlemen: Mr. Moll says that these colored people had a perfect right to live in that house. He did not say it was an outrage to molest them. Oh, no, he said they had a perfect right to live in that house. But the mob met there to drive them out. That is exactly what they did, and they have lied and lied and lied to send these defendants to the penitentiary for life, so that they will not go back to their home.

Now, you know that the mob met there for that purpose. They violated the Constitution and the law; they violated every human feeling, and threw justice and mercy and humanity to the winds, and they made a murderous attack upon their neighbor because his face was black. Which is the worse, to do that or lie about it? In describing this mob, I heard the word "few" from the State's witnesses so many times that I could hear it in my sleep, and I presume that when I am dying I will hear that "few," "few," "few" stuff that I heard in Detroit from people who lied and lied and lied. What was this "few?" And who were they, and how did they come there?

I can't tell you about every one of these witnesses, but I can tell you about some of them. Too many. I can't even carry all of their names in my mind and I don't want to. There are other things more interesting—bugs, for instance. Anything is more interesting to carry in your mind than the names of that bunch, and yet I am going to say something for them, too, because I know something about human nature and life; and I want to be fair, and if I did not want to, I think perhaps it would pay me to be.

Are the people who live around the corner of Charlevoix and Garland worse than other people? There isn't one of you who doesn't know that they lied. There isn't one of you who does not know that they tried to drive those people out and now are trying to send them to the penitentiary so that they can't move back; all in violation of the law, and are trying to get you to do the job. Are they worse than other people? I don't know as they are. How much do you know about prejudice? Race prejudice. Religious prejudice. These feelings that have divided men and caused them to do the most terrible things. Prejudices have burned men at the stake, broken them on the rack, torn every joint apart, destroyed people by the million. Men have done this on account of some terrible prejudice which even now is reaching out to undermine this republic of ours and to destroy the freedom that has been the most cherished part of our institutions. These witnesses honestly believe that they are better than blacks. I do not. They honestly believe that it is their duty to keep colored people out. They honestly believe that blacks are an inferior race and yet if they look at themselves, I don't know how they can.

Gentlemen, lawyers are very intemperate in their statements. My friend, Moll, said that my client here was a coward. A coward, gentlemen. Here, he says, were a gang of gunmen, and cowards—shot Breiner through the back. Nobody saw Breiner, of course. If he had his face turned toward the house, while he was smoking there, waiting for the shooting to begin, it wasn't our fault. It wouldn't make any difference which way he turned. I suppose the bullet would have killed him just the same, if he had been in the way of it. If he had been at home, it would not have happened. Who are the cowards in this case? Cowards, gentlemen! Eleven people with black skins, eleven people, gentlemen, whose ancestors did not come to America because they wanted to, but were brought here in slave ships, to toil for nothing, for the whites—whose lives have been taken in nearly every state in the Union—they have been victims of riots all over this land of the free. They have had to take what is left after everybody else had grabbed what he wanted. The only place where he has been put in front is on the battlefield. When we are fighting we give him a chance to die, and the best chance. But, everywhere else, he has been food for the flames, and the ropes, and the knives, and the guns and the hate of the white, regardless of law and liberty, and the common sentiments of justice that should move men. Were they cowards?

No, gentlemen, they may have been gunmen. They may have tried to murder. But they were not cowards. Eleven people, knowing what it meant, with the history of the race behind them, with the knowledge of shootings and killings and insult and injury without end, eleven of them go into a house, gentlemen, with no police protection, in the face of a mob, and the hatred of a community, and take guns and ammunition and fight for their rights, and for your rights and for mine, and for the rights of every being that lives. They went in and faced a mob seeking to tear them to bits. Call them something besides cowards. The cowardly curs were in the mob gathered there with the backing of the law. A lot of children went in front and threw the stones. They stayed for two days and two nights in front of this home, and by their threats and assault were trying to drive the Negroes out. Those were the cowardly curs, and you know it. I suppose there isn't any ten of them that would come out in the open daylight against those ten. Oh no, gentlemen, their blood is too pure for that. They can only act like a band of coyotes baying some victim who has no chance. And then my clients are called cowards.

All right, gentlemen, call them something else. These blacks have been called many names along down through the ages, but there have been those through the sad years who believed in justice and mercy and charity and love and kindliness, and there have been those who believed that a black man should have some rights, even in a country where he was brought in chains. There are those even crazy enough to hope and to dream that sometime he will come from under this cloud and take his place amongst the people of the world. If he does, it will be through his courage and his culture. It will be by his intelligence and his scholarship and his effort, and I say, gentlemen of the jury, no honest, right-feeling man, whether on a jury or anywhere else, would place anything in his way in this great struggle behind him and before him.

What are you, gentlemen? And what am I? I don't know. I can only go a little way toward the source of my own being. I know my father and I know my mother. I know my grandmothers and my grandfathers on both sides, but I didn't know my great-grandfathers and great-grandmothers on either side, and I don't know who they were. All that a man can do in this direction is but little. He can only slightly raise the veil that hangs over all the past. He can peer into the darkness just a little way and that is all. I know that somewhere around 1600, as the record goes, some of my ancestors came from England. Some of them. I don't know where all of them came from, and I don't think any human being knows where all his ancestors came from. But back of that, I can say nothing. What do you know of yours? I will tell you what I know, or what I think I know, gentlemen. I will try to speak as modestly as I can, knowing the uncertainty of human knowledge, because it is uncertain. The best I can do is to go a little way back. I know that back of us all and each of us is the blood of all the world. I know that it courses in your veins and mine. It has all come out of the infinite past, and I can't pick out mine and you can't pick out yours, and it is only the ignorant who know, and I believe that back of that—back of that—is what we call the lower order of life; back of that there lurks the instinct of the distant serpent, of the carnivorous tiger. All the elements have been gathered together to make the mixture that is you and I and all the race, and nobody knows anything about his own. Gentlemen, I wonder who we are anyhow, to be so proud about our ancestry? We had better try to do something to be proud of ourselves; we had better try to do something kindly, something humane, to some human being, than to brag about our ancestry, of which none of us know anything.

Now, let us go back to the street again. I don't know. Perhaps I weary you. Perhaps these things that seem important to me are unimportant, but they are all a part of the great human tragedy that stands before us. And if I could do something, which I can't, to make the world better, I would try to have it more tolerant, more kindly, more understanding; could I do that and nothing else, I would be glad.

The police department went up there on the morning of the eighth, in the city of Detroit, in the state of Michigan, U.S.A., to see that a family were permitted to move into a home that they owned without getting their throats cut by the noble Nordics who inhabit that jungle. Fine, isn't it? No race question in this? Oh, no, this is a murder case, and yet, in the forenoon of the eighth, they sent four policemen there, to protect a man and his wife, with two little truckloads of household furniture, who were moving into that place. Pretty tough, isn't it? Aren't you glad you are not black? You deserve a lot of credit for it, don't you, because you didn't choose black ancestry? People ought to be killed who chose black ancestry. The policemen went there to protect the lives and the small belongings of these humble folks who moved into their home. What are these black people to do?

I seem to wander from one thing to another without much sequence. I must get back again to the colored man. You don't want him. Perhaps you don't want him next to you. Suppose you were colored. Did any of you ever dream that you were colored? Did you ever wake up out of a nightmare when you dreamed that you were colored? Would you be willing to have my client's skin? Why? Just because somebody is prejudiced! Imagine yourselves colored, gentlemen. Imagine yourselves back in the Sweet house on that fatal night. That is the only right way to treat this case, and the Court will tell you so. Would you move there? Where would you move? Dancy says there were six or seven thousand colored people here sixteen years ago. And seventy-one thousand five years ago. Gentlemen, why are they here? They came here as you came here, under the laws of trade and business, under the instincts to live; both the white and the colored, just the same; the instincts of all animals to propagate their kind, the feelings back of life and on which life depends. They came here to live. Your factories were open for them. Mr. Ford hired them. The automobile companies hired them. Everybody hired them. They were all willing to give them work, weren't they? Every one of them. You and I are willing to give them work, too. We are willing to have them in our houses to take care of the children and do the rough work that we shun ourselves. They are not offensive, either. We invited them; pretty nearly all the colored population has come to Detroit in the last fifteen years; most of them, anyhow. They have always had a corner on the meanest jobs. The city must grow, or you couldn't brag about it. The colored people must live somewhere. Everybody is willing to have them live somewhere else. The people at the corner of Garland and Charlevoix would be willing to have them go to some other section. Everybody would be willing to have them go somewhere else.

Somewhere they must live. Are you going to kill them? Are you going to say that they can work, but they can't get a place to sleep? They can toil in the mill, but can't eat their dinner at home. We want them to build automobiles for us, don't we? We even let them become our chauffeurs. Oh, gentlemen, what is the use! You know it is wrong. Every one of you knows it is wrong. You know that no man in conscience could blame a Negro for almost anything. Can you think of these people without shouldering your own responsibility? Don't make it harder for them, I beg you.

They sent four policemen in the morning to help this little family move in. They had a bedstead, a stove and some bedding, ten guns and some ammunition, and they had food to last them through a siege. I feel that they should have taken less furniture and more food and guns.

Gentlemen, nature works in a queer way. I don't know how this question of color will ever be solved, or whether it will be solved. Nature has a way of doing things. There is one thing about nature, she has plenty of time. She would make broad prairies so that we can raise wheat and corn to feed men. How does she do it? She sends a glacier plowing across a continent, and takes fifty thousand years to harrow it and make it fit to till and support human life. She makes a man. She tries endless experiments before the man is done. She wants to make a race and it takes an infinite mixture to make it. She wants to give us some conception of human rights, and some kindness and charity, and she makes pain and suffering and sorrow and death. It all counts. That is a rough way, but it is the only way. It all counts in the great, long, broad scheme of things. I look on a trial like this with a feeling of disgust and shame. I can't help it now. It will be after we have learned in the terrible and expensive school of human experience that we will be willing to find each other and understand each other.

Now, let us get to the bare facts of this case. The city of Detroit had the police force there to help these people move into their home. When they unloaded their goods, men and women on the street began going from house to house. They went from house to house to sound the alarm, "the Negroes are coming," as if a foreign army was invading their homes; as if a wild beast had come down out of the mountains in the olden times. Can you imagine those colored people? They didn't dare move without thinking of their color. Where we go into a hotel unconsciously, or a church, if we choose, they do not. Of course, colored people belong to a church, and they have a YMCA. That is, a Jim Crow YMCA. The black Christians cannot mix with the white Christians. They will probably have a Jim Crow Heaven where the white angels will not be obliged to meet the black angels, except as servants.

Gentlemen, they say there is nothing to justify this shooting; it was an orderly, neighborly crowd; an orderly, neighborly crowd. They came there for a purpose and intended to carry it out. How long, pray, would these men wait penned up in that house? How long would you wait? The very presence of the crowd was a mob, as I believe the Court will tell you. Suppose a crowd gathers around your house; a crowd which doesn't want you there; a hostile crowd, for a part of two days and two nights, until the police force of this city is called in to protect you. How long, tell me, are you going to live in that condition with a mob surrounding your house and the police force standing in front of it? How long should these men have waited? You wouldn't have waited. Counsel say they had just as good reason to shoot on the eighth as on the ninth. Concede it. They did not shoot. They waited and hoped and prayed that in some way this crowd would pass them by and grant them the right to live. The mob came back the next night and the colored people waited while they were gathering; they waited while they were coming from every street and every corner, and while the officers were supine and helpless and doing nothing. And they waited until dozens of stones were thrown against the house on the roof, probably—I don't know how many. Nobody knows how many. They waited until the windows were broken before they shot. Why did they wait so long? I think I know. How much chance had these people for their lives after they shot, surrounded by a crowd as they were? They would never take a chance unless they thought it was necessary to take the chance. Eleven black people penned up in the face of a mob. What chance did they have?

Suppose they shot before they should. What is the theory of counsel in this case? Nobody pretends there is anything in this case to prove that our client Henry fired the fatal shot. There isn't the slightest. It wasn't a shot that would fit the gun he had. The theory of this case is that he was part of a combination to do something. Now, what was that combination, gentlemen? Your own sense will tell you what it was. Did they combine to go there and kill somebody? Were they looking for somebody to murder? Dr. Sweet scraped together his small earnings by his industry and put himself through college, and he scraped together his small earnings of three thousand dollars to buy that home because he wanted to kill somebody?

It is silly to talk about it. He bought that home just as you buy yours, because he wanted a home to live in, to take his wife and to raise his family. There is no difference between the love of a black man for his offspring and the love of a white. He and his wife had the same feeling of fatherly and motherly affection for their child that you gentlemen have for yours, and that your father and mother had for you. They bought that home for that purpose; not to kill somebody. They might have feared trouble, as they probably did, and as the evidence shows that every man with a black face fears it, when he moves into a home that is fit for a dog to live in. It is part of the curse that, for some inscrutable reason, has followed the race—if you call it a race—and which curse, let us hope, sometime the world will be wise enough and decent enough and human enough to wipe out.

They went there to live. They knew the dangers. Why do you suppose they took these guns and this ammunition and these men there? Because they wanted to kill somebody? It is utterly absurd and crazy. They took them there because they thought it might be necessary to defend their home with their lives and they were determined to do it. They took guns there that in case of need they might fight, fight even to death for their home, and for each other, for their people, for their race, for their rights under the Constitution and the laws under which all of us live; and unless men and women will do that, we will soon be a race of slaves, whether we are black or white. "Eternal vigilance is the price of liberty," and it has always been so and always will be. Do you suppose they were in there for any other purpose?

Gentlemen, there isn't a chance that they took arms there for anything else. They did go there knowing their rights, feeling their responsibility, and determined to maintain those rights if it meant death to the last man and the last woman, and no one could do more. No man lived a better life or died a better death than fighting for his home and his children, for himself, and for the eternal principles upon which life depends. Instead of being here under indictment, for murder, they should be honored for the brave stand they made for their rights and ours. Some day, both white and black, irrespective of color, will honor the memory of these men, whether they are inside prison walls or outside, and will recognize that they fought not only for themselves, but for every man who wishes to be free.

Did they shoot too quick? Tell me just how long a man needs wait for a mob? The Court, I know, will instruct you on that. How long do you need to wait for a mob? We have been told that because a person trespasses on your home or on your ground you have no right to shoot him. Is that true? If I go up to your home in a peaceable way, and go on your ground, or on your porch, you have no right to shoot me. You have a right to use force to put me off if I refuse to go, even to the extent of killing me. That isn't this case, gentlemen. That isn't the case of a neighbor who went up to the yard of a neighbor without permission and was shot to death. Oh, no. The Court will tell you the difference, unless I am mistaken, and I am sure I am not; unless I mistake the law, and I am sure I do not. This isn't a case of a man who trespasses upon the ground of some other man and is killed. It is the case of an unlawful mob, which in itself is a crime; a mob bent on mischief; a mob that has no rights. They are too dangerous. It is like a fire. One man may do something. Two will do much more; three will do more than three times as much; a crowd will do something that no man ever dreamed of doing. The law recognizes it. It is the duty of every man—I don't care who he is—to disperse a mob. It is the duty of the officers to disperse them. It was the duty of the inmates of the house, even though they had to kill somebody to do it.

Now, gentlemen, I wouldn't ask you to take the law on my statement. The Court will tell you the law. A mob is a criminal combination of itself. Their presence is enough. You need not wait until it spreads. It is there, and that is enough. There is no other law; there hasn't been for years, and it is the law which will govern this case.

Now, gentlemen, how long did they need to wait? Why, it is silly. How long would you wait? How long do you suppose ten white men would be waiting? Would they have waited as long? I will tell you how long they needed to wait. I will tell you what the law is, and the Court will confirm me, I am sure. Every man may act upon appearances as they seem to him. Every man may protect his own life. Every man has the right to protect his own property. Every man is bound under the law to disperse a mob even to the extent of taking life. It is his duty to do it, but back of that he has the human right to go to the extent of killing to defend his life. He has a right to defend the life of his kinsman, servant, his friends, or those about him, and he has a right to defend, gentlemen, not from real danger, but from what seems to him real danger at the time.

Here is Henry Sweet, the defendant in this case, a boy. How many of you know why you are trying him? What had he to do with it? Why is he in this case? A boy, twenty-one years old, working his way through college, and he is just as good a boy as the boy of any juror in this box; just as good a boy as you people were when you were boys, and I submit to you, he did nothing whatever that was wrong. Of course, we lawyers talk and talk and talk, as if we feared results. I don't mean to trifle with you. I always fear results. When life or liberty is in the hands of a lawyer, he realizes the terrible responsibility that is on him, and he fears that some word will be left unspoken, or some thought will be forgotten. I would not be telling you the truth if I told you that I did not fear the result of this important case; and when my judgment and my reason come to my aid and take counsel with my fears, I know, and I feel perfectly well that no twelve American jurors, especially in any Northern land, could be brought together who would dream of taking a boy's life or liberty under circumstances like this. That is what my judgment tells me, but my fears perhaps cause me to go further and to say more when I should not have said as much.

Now, let me tell you when a man has the right to shoot in self-defense, and in defense of his home; not when these vital things in life are in danger, but when he thinks they are. These despised blacks did not need to wait until the house was beaten down above their heads. They didn't need to wait until every window was broken. They didn't need to wait longer for that mob to grow more inflamed. There is nothing so danger- ous as ignorance and bigotry when it is unleashed as it was here. The Court will tell you that these inmates of this house had the right to decide upon appearances, and if they did, even though they were mistaken, they are not guilty. I don't know but they could safely have stayed a little longer. I don't know but it would have been well enough to let this mob break a few more windowpanes. I don't know but it would have been better and been safe to let them batter down the house before they shot. I don't know. How am I to tell, and how are you to tell?

You are twelve white men, gentlemen. You are twelve men sitting here eight months after all this occurred, listening to the evidence, perjured and otherwise, in this court, to tell whether they acted too quickly or too slowly. A man may be running an engine on the railroad. He may stop too quickly or too slowly. In an emergency he is bound to do one or the other, and the jury a year after, sitting in cold blood, may listen to the evidence and say that he acted too quickly. What do they know about it? You must sit out there upon a moving engine with your hand on the throttle and facing danger and must decide and act quickly. Then you can tell.

Cases often occur in the courts, which doesn't speak very well for the decency of courts, but they have happened, where men have been ship- wrecked at sea, a number of the men having left the ship and gone into a small boat to save their lives; they have floated around for hours and tossed on the wild waves of an angry sea; their food disappearing, the boat heavy and likely to sink and no friendly sail in sight . . . What are they to do? Will they throw some of their companions off the boat and save the rest? Will they eat some to save the others? If they kill anybody, it is because they want to live. Every living thing wants to live. The strongest instinct in life is to keep going. You have seen a tree upon a rock send a shoot down for ten or fifteen or twenty feet, to search for water, to draw it up, that it may still survive; it is a strong instinct with animals and with plants, with all sentient things, to keep alive. Men are out in a boat, in an angry sea, with little food, and less water. No hope in sight. What will they do? They throw a companion overboard to save themselves, or they kill somebody to save themselves. Juries have come into court and passed on the question of whether they should have waited longer, or not. Later, the survivors were picked up by a ship and perhaps, if they had waited longer, all would have been saved. Yet a jury, months after it was over, sitting safely in their jury box, pass upon the question of whether they acted too quickly or not. Can they tell? No. To decide that case, you must be in a small boat, with little food and water; in a wild sea, with no sail in sight, and drifting around for hours or days in the face of the deep, beset by hunger and darkness and fear and hope. Then you can tell; but, no man can tell without it. It can't be done, gentlemen, and the law says so, and this Court will tell you so.

Let me tell you what you must do, gentlemen. It is fine for lawyers to say, naïvely, that nothing happened. No foot was set upon that ground; as if you had to put your foot on the premises. You might put your hand on. The foot isn't sacred. No foot was set upon their home. No shot was fired, nothing except that the house was stoned and windows broken, and an angry crowd was outside seeking their destruction. That is all. That is all, gentlemen. I say that no American citizen, unless he is black, need wait until an angry mob sets foot upon his premises before he kills. I say that no free man need wait to see just how far an aggressor will go before he takes life. The first instinct a man has is to save his life. He doesn't need to experiment. He hasn't time to experiment. When he thinks it is time to save his life, he has the right to act. There isn't any question about it. It has been the law of every English-speaking country so long as we have had law. Every man's home is his castle, which even the king may not enter. Every man has a right to kill, to defend himself or his family, or others, either in the defense of the home or in the defense of themselves. So far as that branch of the case is concerned, there is only one thing that this jury has a right to consider, and that is whether the defendants acted in honest fear of danger. That is all. Perhaps they could have safely waited longer. I know a little about psychology. If I could talk to a man long enough, and not too long, and he talk to me a little, I could guess fairly well what is going on in his head, but I can't understand the psychology of a mob, and neither can anybody else. We know it is unreasoning. We know it is filled with hatred. We know it is cruel. We know it has no heart, no soul, and no pity. We know it is as cruel as the grave. No man has a right to stop and dicker while waiting for a mob.

Now, let us look at these fellows. Here were eleven colored men, penned up in the house. Put yourselves in their place. Make yourselves colored for a little while. It won't hurt, you can wash it off. They can't, but you can; just make yourself black for a little while; long enough, gentlemen, to judge them, and before any of you would want to be judged, you would want your juror to put himself in your place. That is all I ask in this case, gentlemen. They were black, and they knew the history of the black. Our friend makes fun of Dr. Sweet and Henry Sweet talking these things all over in the short space of two months. Well, gentlemen, let me tell you something, that isn't evidence. This is just theory. This is just theory, and nothing else. I should imagine that the only thing that two or three colored people talk of when they get together is race. I imagine that they can't rub color off their faces or rub it out of their minds. I imagine that it is with them always. I imagine that the stories of lynchings, the stories of murders, the stories of oppression is a topic of constant conversation. I imagine that everything that appears in the newspapers on this subject is carried from one to another until every man knows what others know, upon the topic which is the most important of all to their lives.

What do you think about it? Suppose you were black. Do you think you would forget it even in your dreams? Or would you have black dreams? Suppose you had to watch every point of contact with your neighbor and remember your color, and you knew your children were growing up under this handicap. Do you suppose you would think of anything else? Do you suppose this boy coming in here didn't know all about the conditions, and did not learn all about them? Did he not know about Detroit? Do you suppose he hadn't read the story of his race? He is intelligent. He goes to school. He would have been a graduate now, except for this long hesitation, when he is waiting to see whether he goes back to college or goes to jail. Do you suppose that black students and teachers are discussing it? Anyhow, gentlemen, what is the use? The jury isn't supposed to be entirely ignorant. They are supposed to know something. These black people were in the house with the black man's psychology, and with the black man's fear, based on what they had heard and what they had read and what they knew. I don't need to go far. I don't need to travel to Florida. I don't even need to talk about the Chicago riots. The testimony showed that in Chicago a colored boy on a raft had been washed to a white bathing beach, and men and boys of my race stoned him to death. A riot began, and some hundred and twenty were killed. I don't need to go to Washington or to St. Louis. Let us take Detroit. I don't need to go far either in space or time. Let us take this city. Now, gentlemen, I am not saying that the white people of Detroit are different from the white people of any other city. I know what has been done in Chicago. I know what prejudice growing out of race and religion has done the world over, and all through time. I am not blaming Detroit. I am stating what has happened, that is all. And I appeal to you, gentlemen, to do your part to save the honor of this city, to save its reputation, to save yours, to save its name, and to save the poor colored people who cannot save themselves.

I was told there had not been a lynching of a colored man in thirty years or more in Michigan. All right. Why, I can remember when the early statesmen of Michigan cared for the colored man and when they embodied the rights of the colored men in the constitution and statutes. I can remember when they laid the foundation that made it possible for a man of any color or any religion, or any creed, to own his home wherever he could find a man to sell it. I remember when civil rights laws were passed that gave the Negro the right to go where the white man went and as he went. There are some men who seem to think those laws were wrong. I do not. Wrong or not, it is the law, and if you were black you would protest with every fiber of your body your right to live. Michigan used to protect the rights of colored people. There were not many of them here, but they have come in the last few years, and with them has come prejudice. Then, too, the Southern white man has followed his black slave. But that isn't all. Black labor has come in competition with white. Prejudices have been created where there was no prejudice before. We have listened to the siren song that we are a superior race and have superior rights, and that the black man has none. It is a new idea in Detroit that a colored man's home can be torn down about his head because he is black. There are some eighty thousand blacks here now, and they are bound to reach out. They have reached out in the past, and they will reach out in the future. Do not make any mistake, gentlemen. I am making no promises. I know the instinct for life. I know it reaches black and white alike. I know that you cannot confine any body of people to any particular place; and, as the population grows, the colored people will go farther. I know it, and you must change the law or you must take it as it is, or you must invoke the primal law of nature and get back to clubs and fists, and if you are ready for that, gentlemen, all right, but do it with your eyes open. That is all I care for. You must have a government of law or blind force, and if you are ready to let blind force take the place of law, the responsibility is on you, not on me.

Now, let us see what has happened here. So far as I know, there had been nothing of the sort happened when Dr. Sweet bought his home. He took an option on it in May, and got his deed in June; and in July, in that one month, while he was deliberating on moving, there were three cases of driving Negro families out of their homes in Detroit. This was accomplished by stones, clubs, guns and mobs. Suppose one of you were colored and had bought a house on Garland Avenue. Take this just exactly as it is. You bought it in June, intending to move in July, and you read and heard about what happened in another part of the city. Would you have waited? Would you have waited a month, as Sweet did?

Remember, these men didn't have any too much money. Dr. Sweet paid three thousand dollars on his home, leaving a loan on it of sixteen thousand dollars more. He had to scrape together some money to buy his furniture, and he bought fourteen hundred dollars' worth the day after he moved in and paid two hundred dollars down. Gentlemen, it is only right to consider Dr. Sweet and his family. He has a little child. He has a wife. They must live somewhere. If they could not, it would be better to take them out and kill them, and kill them decently and quickly. Had he any right to be free? They determined to move in and to take nine men with them. What would you have done, gentlemen? If you had courage, you would have done as Dr. Sweet did. You would have been crazy or a coward if you hadn't. Would you have moved in alone? No, you would not have gone alone. You would have taken your wife. If you had a brother or two, you would have taken them because you would know that you could rely on them, and you would have taken those nearest to you. And you would have moved in just as Dr. Sweet did. Wouldn't you? He didn't shoot the first night. He didn't look for trouble. He kept his house dark so that the neighbors wouldn't see him. He didn't dare have a light in his house, gentlemen, for fear of the neighbors. Noble neighbors, who were to have a colored family in their neighborhood. He had the light put out in the front part of the house, so as not to tempt any of the mob to violence.

Now, let us go back a little. What happened before this? I don't need to go over the history of the case. Everybody who wants to understand knows it, and many who don't want to understand it. As soon as Dr. Sweet bought this house, the neighbors organized the "Water Works Park Improvement Association." They were going to aid the police. They didn't get a chance to try to aid them until that night. They were going to regulate automobile traffic. They didn't get any chance to regulate automobile traffic until that night. They were going to protect the homes and make them safe for children. The purpose was clear, and every single member reluctantly said that they joined it to keep colored people out of the district. They might have said it first as well as last. People, even in a wealthy and aristocratic neighborhood like Garland and Charlevoix, don't give up a dollar without expecting some profit; not a whole dollar. Sometimes two in one family, the husband and wife, joined. They got in quick. The woods were on fire. Something had to be done, as quick as they heard that Dr. Sweet was coming; Dr. Sweet, who had been a bellhop on a boat, and a bellhop in hotels, and fired furnaces and sold popcorn and worked his way with his great handicap through school and through college, and graduated as a doctor, and gone to Europe and taken another degree; Dr. Sweet, who knew more than any man in the neighborhood ever would know or ever want to know. He deserved more for all he had done. When they heard he was coming, then it was time to act, and act together, for the sake of their homes, their families and their firesides, and so they got together.

I shall not talk to you much longer. I am sorry I talked so long. But this case is close to my heart.

Gentlemen, who are these people who were in this house? Were they people of character? Were they people of standing? Were they people of intelligence?

First, there was Dr. Sweet. Gentlemen, a white man does pretty well when he does what Dr. Sweet did. A white boy who can start in with nothing, and put himself through college, study medicine, taking post-graduate work in Europe, earning every penny of it as he goes along, shoveling snow and coal, and working as a bellhop on boats, working at every kind of employment that he can get to make his way; is some fellow. But Dr. Sweet has the handicap of the color of his face. And there is no handicap more terrible than that. Supposing you had your choice, right here this minute, would you rather lose your eyesight or become colored? Would you rather lose your hearing or be a Negro? Would you rather go out there on the street and have your leg cut off by a streetcar, or have a black skin?

I don't like to speak of it; I do not like to speak of it in the presence of these colored people, whom I have always urged to be as happy as they can. But it is true. Life is a hard game anyhow. But, when the cards are stacked against you, it is terribly hard. And they are stacked against a race for no reason but that they are black.

Who are these men who were in this house? There was Dr. Sweet. There was his brother, who was a dentist. There was this young boy who worked his way for three years through college, with a little aid from his brother, and who was on his way to graduate. Henry's future is now in your hands. There was his companion, who was working his way through college—all gathered in that house. Were they hoodlums? Were they criminals? Were they anything except men who asked for a chance to live; who asked for a chance to breathe the free air and make their own way, earn their own living, and get their bread by the sweat of their brow?

Gentlemen, these black men shot. Whether any bullets from their guns hit Breiner, I do not care. I will not discuss it. It is passing strange that the bullet that went through him, went directly through, not as if it were shot from some higher place. It was not the bullet that came from Henry Sweet's rifle; that is plain. It might have come from the house; I do not know, gentlemen, and I do not care. There are bigger issues in this case than that. The right to defend your home, the right to defend your person, is as sacred a right as any human being could fight for, and as sacred a cause as any jury could sustain.

That issue not only involves the defendants in this case, but it involves every man who wants to live, every one who wants freedom to work and to breathe; it is an issue worth fighting for, and worth dying for, it is an issue worth the attention of this jury, who have a chance that is given few juries to pass upon a real case that will mean something in the history of a race.

These men were taken to the police station. Gentlemen, there was never a time that these black men's rights were protected in the least;

never once. They had no rights—they are black. They were to be driven out of their home under the law's protection. When they defended their home, they were arrested and charged with murder. They were taken to a police station, manacled. And they asked for a lawyer. And, every man, if he has any brains at all, asks for a lawyer when he is in the hands of the police. If he does not want to have a web woven around him, to entangle or ensnare him, he will ask for a lawyer. And, the lawyer's first aid to the injured always is, "Keep your mouth shut." It is not a case of whether you are guilty or not guilty. That makes no difference. "Keep your mouth shut." The police grabbed them, as is their habit. They got the county attorney to ask questions. What did they do? They did what everybody does, helpless, alone, and unadvised. They did not know, even, that anybody was killed. At least there is no evidence that they knew. But, they knew that they had been arrested for defending their own rights to live; and they were there in the hands of their enemies; and they told the best story they could think of at the time—just as ninety-nine men out of a hundred always do. Whether they are guilty or not guilty makes no difference. But lawyers and even policemen should have protected their rights.

Some things that these defendants said were not true, as is always the case. The prosecutor read a statement from this boy, which is conflicting. In two places he says that he shot "over them." In another he said that he shot "at them." He probably said it in each place but the reporter probably got one of them wrong. But Henry makes it perfectly explicit, and when you go to your jury room and read it all, you will find that he does. In another place he said he shot to defend his brother's home and family. He says that in two or three places. You can also find he said that he shot so that they would run away and leave them to eat their dinner. They are both there. These conflicting statements you will find in all cases of this sort. You always find them, where men have been sweated, without help, without a lawyer, groping around blindly, in the hands of the enemy, without the aid of anybody to protect their rights. Gentlemen, from the first to the last, there has not been a substantial right of these defendants that was not violated.

We come now to lay this man's case in the hands of a jury of our peers—the first defense and the last defense is the protection of home and life as provided by our law. We are willing to leave it here. I feel, as I look at you, that we will be treated fairly and decently, even understandingly and kindly. You know what this case is. You know why it is. You know that if white men had been fighting their way against colored men, nobody would ever have dreamed of a prosecution. And you know that, from the beginning of this case to the end, up to the time you write your verdict, the prosecution is based on race prejudice and nothing else.

Gentlemen, I feel deeply on this subject; I cannot help it. Let us take a little glance at the history of the Negro race. It only needs a minute. It seems to me that the story would melt hearts of stone. I was born in America. I could have left it if I had wanted to go away. Some other men, reading about this land of freedom that we brag about on the Fourth of July, came voluntarily to America. These men, the defendants, are here because they could not help it. Their ancestors were captured in the jungles and on the plains of Africa, captured as you capture wild beasts, torn from their homes and their kindred; loaded into slave ships, packed like sardines in a box, half of them dying on the ocean passage; some jumping into the sea in their frenzy, when they had a chance to choose death in place of slavery. They were captured and brought here. They could not help it. They were bought and sold as slaves, to work without pay, because they were black. They were subjected to all this for generations, until finally they were given their liberty, so far as the law goes—and that is only a little way, because, after all, every human being's life in this world is inevitably mixed with every other life and, no matter what laws we pass, no matter what precautions we take, unless the people we meet are kindly and decent and human and liberty-loving, then there is no liberty. Freedom comes from human beings, rather than from laws and institutions.

Now, that is their history. These people are the children of slavery. If the race that we belong to owes anything to any human being, or to any power in this universe, it owes it to these black men. Above all other men, they owe an obligation and a duty to these black men which can never be repaid. I never see one of them, that I do not feel I ought to pay part of the debt of my race—and if you gentlemen feel as you should feel in this case, your emotions will be like mine.

Gentlemen, you were called into this case by chance. It took us a week to find you, a week of culling out prejudice and hatred. Probably we did not cull it all out at that; but we took the best and the fairest that we could find. It is up to you.

Your verdict means something in this case. It means something more than the fate of this boy. It is not often that a case is submitted to twelve men where the decision may mean a milestone in the progress of the human race. But this case does. And I hope and I trust that you have a feeling of responsibility that will make you take it and do your duty as citizens of a great nation, and, as members of the human family, which is better still.

Let me say just a parting word for Henry Sweet, who has well nigh been forgotten. I am serious, but it seems almost like a reflection upon this jury to talk as if I doubted your verdict. What has this boy done? This one boy now that I am culling out from all of the rest, and whose fate is in your hands—can you tell me what he has done? Can I believe myself? Am I standing in a court of justice, where twelve men on their oaths are asked to take away the liberty of a boy twenty-one years of age, who has done nothing more than what Henry Sweet has done?

Gentlemen, you may think he shot too quick; you may think he erred in judgment; you may think that Dr. Sweet should not have gone there, prepared to defend his home. But, what of this case of Henry Sweet? What has he done? I want to put it up to you, each of you, individually. Dr. Sweet was his elder brother. He had helped Henry through school. He loved him. He had taken him into his home. Henry had lived with him and his wife; he had fondled his baby. The doctor had promised Henry money to go through school. Henry was getting his education, to take his place in the world, gentlemen—and this is a hard job. With his brother's help, he had worked himself through college up to the last year. The doctor had bought a home. He feared danger. He moved in with his wife and he asked this boy to go with him. And this boy went to help defend his brother and his brother's wife and his child and his home.

Do you think more of him or less of him for that? I never saw twelve men in my life—and I have looked at a good many faces of a good many juries—I never saw twelve men in my life, that, if you could get them to understand a human case, were not true and right.

Should this boy have gone along and helped his brother? Or should he have stayed away? What would you have done? And yet, gentlemen, here is a boy, and the president of his college came all the way here from Ohio to tell you what he thinks of him. His teachers have come here, from Ohio, to tell you what they think of him. The Methodist bishop has come here to tell you what he thinks of him.

So, gentlemen, I am justified in saying that this boy is as kindly, as well disposed, as decent a man as any one of you twelve. Do you think he ought to be taken out of his school and sent to the penitentiary? All right, gentlemen, if you think so, do it. It is your job, not mine. If you think so, do it. But if you do, gentlemen, if you should ever look into the face of your own boy, or your own brother, or look into your own heart, you will regret it in sackcloth and ashes. You know, if he committed any offense, it was being loyal and true to his brother whom he loved. I know where you will send him, and it will not be to the penitentiary.

Now, gentlemen, just one more word, and I am through with this case. I do not live in Detroit. But I have no feeling against this city. In fact, I shall always have the kindest remembrance of it, especially if this case results as I think and feel that it will. I am the last one to come here and stir up race hatred, or any other hatred. I do not believe in the law of hate. I may not be true to my ideals always, but I believe in the law of love, and I believe you can do nothing with hatred. I would like to see a time when man loves his fellow-man, and forgets his color or his creed. We will never be civilized until that time comes. I know the Negro race has a long road to go. I believe the life of the Negro race has been a life of tragedy, of injustice, of oppression. The law has made him equal, but man has not. And, after all, the last analysis is, what has man done?—and not what has the law done? I know there is a long road ahead of him, before he can take the place which I believe he should take. I know that before him there is suffering, sorrow, tribulation and death among the blacks, and perhaps the whites. I am sorry. I would do what I could to avert it. I would advise patience; I would advise toleration; I would advise understanding; I would advise all of those things which are necessary for men who live together.

Gentlemen, what do you think is your duty in this case? I have watched day after day, these black, tense faces that have crowded this court. These black faces that now are looking to you twelve whites, feeling that the hopes and fears of a race are in your keeping.

This case is about to end, gentlemen. To them, it is life. Not one of their color sits on this jury. Their fate is in the hands of twelve whites. Their eyes are fixed on you, their hearts go out to you, and their hopes hang on your verdict.

This is all. I ask you, on behalf of this defendant, on behalf of these helpless ones who turn to you, and more than that—on behalf of this great state, and this great city which must face this problem, and face it fairly—I ask you, in the name of progress and of the human race, to return a verdict of Not Guilty in this case!

The jury returned its verdict the following day, May 19, 1926: Not Guilty. None of the other cases was tried.

The Sweets never moved back into the house. For a long time their house at Garland and Charlevoix streets remained vacant. Today, thirty-one years later, both white and colored live in the neighborhood.

Oscar Wilde

:

TESTIMONY GIVEN AGAINST THE MARQUIS OF QUEENSBERRY

The most notorious cases of the 1890's were those in which Oscar Wilde was involved. The first was a criminal complaint brought by Wilde against the Marquis of Queensberry, originator of the Queensberry Rules. Wilde had been intimate with Queensberry's son, Lord Alfred Douglas. Queensberry attempted, without success, to end the association. He then announced he would ruin Wilde, and his son, and proceeded to do so by publicizing the nature of their relationship. On February 18, 1895, Queensberry delivered an inscribed card to the porter of a club of which Wilde was a member. The card bore the inscription, "To Oscar Wilde, posing as a somdomite (sic.)." The card was delivered without an envelope so that it might be read by others in the club.

Wilde secured a criminal warrant charging Queensberry with libel. Queensberry entered a plea of justification—that is, that the statement was true; and he proved it. When it became clear after several days of trial that his case would be lost, Wilde withdrew the charge.

Although he failed in his purpose Wilde was superb on the witness stand. There is no more severe test of one's wit and conversational gifts than intensive cross-examination. Wilde was more than equal to the test. The following are extracts from the cross-examination of Wilde by Mr. Edward Carson, counsel for Queensberry at the trial of Wilde's complaint against Queensberry.

In an attempt to show that Wilde's writings were immoral, Carson read several extracts from Wilde's published works into the record. The passages immediately following were from an article written by Wilde for the Saturday Review entitled, "Phrases and Philosophies for the Use of the Young."

CARSON (*Reading*): "Religions die when they are proved to be true." Is that true?

WILDE: Yes; I hold that. It is a suggestion towards a philosophy of the absorption of religions by science, but it is too big a question to go into now.

CARSON: Do you think that was a safe axiom to put forward for the philosophy of the young?

WILDE: Most stimulating.

CARSON: "If one tells the truth one is sure, sooner or later, to be found out?"

WILDE: That is a pleasing paradox, but I do not set very high store on it as an axiom.

CARSON: Is that good for the young?

WILDE: Anything is good for the young that stimulates thought, in what-ever age.

CARSON: Whether moral or immoral?

WILDE: There is no such thing as morality or immorality in thought. There is immoral emotion.

CARSON: "Pleasure is the only thing one should live for?"

WILDE: I think that the realization of oneself is the prime aim of life, and to realize oneself through pleasure is finer than to do so through pain. I am, on that point, entirely on the side of the ancients—the Greeks. It is a pagan idea.

CARSON: "A truth ceases to be true when more than one person believes in it?"

WILDE: Perfectly. That would be my metaphysical definition of truth; something so personal that the same truth could never be appreciated by two minds.

CARSON: "The condition of perfection is idleness?"

WILDE: Oh, yes, I think so. Half of it is true. The life of contemplation is the highest life.

CARSON: "There is something tragic about the enormous number of young men there are in England at the present moment who start life with perfect profiles, and end by adopting some useful profession?"

WILDE: I should think that the young have enough sense of humor.

The examination then turned to letters written by Wilde to Lord Alfred Douglas:

CARSON: Did any one say that he had found letters of yours?

WILDE: Yes. A man . . . saw me at the rooms of Mr. Alfred Taylor and told me that he had found some letters in a suit of clothes which Lord Alfred Douglas had been good enough to give him.

CARSON: Did he ask for anything?—

WILDE: I don't think he made a direct demand.

CARSON: What happened at that interview?

WILDE: I felt that this was the man who wanted money from me. I said, "I suppose you have come about my beautiful letter to Lord Alfred Douglas. If you had not been so foolish as to send a copy of it to Mr. Beerbohm Tree, I would gladly have paid you a very large sum of money for the letter, as I consider it to be a work of art." He said "A very curious construction can be put on that letter." I said in reply, "Art is rarely intelligible to the criminal classes." He said, "A man has offered me £60 for it." I said to him, "If you will take my advice you will go to that man and sell my letter to him for £60. I myself have never received so large a sum for any prose work of that length; but I am glad to find that there is some one in England who considers a letter of mine worth £60." He was somewhat taken aback by my manner, perhaps, and said, "The man is out of town." I replied, "He is sure to come back," and I advised him to get the £60. He then changed his manner a little, saying that he had not a single penny, and that he had been on many occasions trying to find me. I said that I could not guarantee his cab expenses, but that I would gladly give him half-a-sovereign. He took the money. . . .

CARSON: Did Allen then go away?

WILDE: Yes, and in about five minutes Cliburn came to the house. I went out to him and said, "I cannot bother any more about this matter." He produced the letter out of his pocket, saying, "Allen has asked me to give it back to you." I did not take it immediately, but asked: "Why does Allen give me back this letter?" He said, "Well, he says that you were kind to him, and that there is no use trying to 'rent' you as you only laugh at us." I took the letter and said, "I will accept it back, and you can thank Allen from me for all the anxiety he has shown about it." I looked at the letter, and saw that it was extremely soiled. I said to him, "I think it is quite unpardonable that better care was not taken of this original manuscript of mine" . . . He said he was very sorry, but it had been in so many hands. I gave him half-a-sovereign for his trouble, and then said, "I am afraid you are leading a wonderfully wicked life." He said, "There is good and bad in every one of us." I told him he was a born philosopher, and he then left.

CARSON: Was anything said about a sonnet?

WILDE: Yes. I said, "The letter, which is a prose poem, will shortly be published in sonnet form in a delightful magazine, and I will send you a copy of it."

CARSON: As a matter of fact, the letter was the basis of a French poem that was published in "The Spirit Lamp?"

WILDE: Yes.

CARSON: Suppose a man who was not an artist had written this letter, would you say it was a proper letter?

WILDE: A man who was not an artist could not have written that letter.

CARSON: Why?

WILDE: Because nobody but an artist could write it. He certainly could not write the language unless he were a man of letters.

CARSON: I can suggest, for the sake of your reputation, that there is nothing very wonderful in this "red rose-leaf lips of yours?"

WILDE: A great deal depends on the way it is read.

CARSON: "Your slim gilt soul walks between passion and poetry." Is that a beautiful phrase?

WILDE: Not as you read it, Mr. Carson. You read it very badly.

CARSON: Have you often written in the same style as this?

WILDE: I don't repeat myself in style.

CARSON: Did you ever have any of your beautiful letters, except the one found out, turned into a sonnet?

WILDE: I require to read a great deal of modern poetry before I can say.

CARSON: Did any of these men who visited you at the Savoy have whiskies and sodas and iced champagne?

WILDE: I can't say what they had.

CARSON: Did you drink champagne yourself?

WILDE: Yes; iced champagne is a favorite drink of mine—strongly against my doctor's orders.

CARSON: Never mind your doctor's orders, sir.

WILDE: I never do.

CARSON: He (*Alphonse Conway*) sold newspapers at the kiosque on the pier?

WILDE: It is the first I heard of his connection with literature.

CARSON: Was his conversation literary?

WILDE: On the contrary, quite simple and easily understood. He had been to school, where naturally he had not learned much.

After the charge against Queensberry was dropped, Wilde was himself arrested on a charge that "He did on divers dates unlawfully commit divers acts of gross indecency with another male person." The first jury to hear the charge disagreed. During that trial that Wilde made the often quoted statement justifying his relationship with Lord Alfred Douglas:

MR. C. F. GILL (*counsel for the Public Prosecutor*) [referring to a phrase *in a published poem of Lord Alfred Douglas*]: What is the "Love that dare not speak its name"?

WILDE: The "Love that dare not speak its name" in this century is such a great affection of an elder for a younger man as there was between David and Jonathan, such as Plato made the very basis of his philosophy, and such as you find in the sonnets of Michael Angelo and Shakespeare. It is that deep, spiritual affection that is as pure as it is perfect. It dictates and pervades great works of art like those of Shakespeare and Michael Angelo, and those two letters of mine, such as they are. It is in this century misunderstood, so much misunderstood that it may be described as the "Love that dare not speak its name," and on account of it I am placed where I am now. It is beautiful, it is fine, it is the noblest form of affection. There is nothing unnatural about it. It is intellectual, and it repeatedly exists between an elder and a younger man, where the elder man has intellect, and the younger man has all the joy, hope and glamour of life before him. That it should be so the world does not understand. The world mocks at it, and sometimes puts one in the pillory for it.

After the first jury's disagreement, Wilde was again tried. On the retrial the jury rendered a verdict of guilty. Wilde was sentenced and served two years of hard labor. The pietic held the conviction a vindication of justice; others condemned it as hypocritical, cruel and senseless. To paraphrase Frank Harris, some said *"that* is what they *do* to their poets in England," and others said, *"that* is what the poets in England *do."*

Plato

.

APOLOGY

*An Account of Socrates' Defense Against the Charge
of Impiety and Corrupting the Young*

In 399 B.C. the seventy-year-old Socrates was tried before the judges and
citizens of Athens on charges of impiety and corrupting the young. He was
found guilty and sentenced to death. Plato was present at the trial, and the
Apology is his account, written some years after, of Socrates' three speeches
in defense of himself. Although it is not to be taken as an exact transcript of
the trial, the *Apology* probably does represent the general line of argument
that Socrates followed; in this sense it is the most historical in intent of Plato's
writings.

The citizens who advanced the charges against Socrates and served as his
prosecutors were Anytus, a politician of the restored democratic government,
the poet Meletus, and the rhetorician Lycon. It is clear that the particular
charges against Socrates were merely a mask for a general animosity. A non-
conformist and advocate of the voice of the wise rather than the voice of the
many, Socrates must have represented a threat to the new regime.

In his speeches Socrates seems less interested in refuting the charges, which
he easily shows to be trumped up and inconsistent, than in explaining the
animosity towards him and defending his "philosopher's mission of searching
into myself and other people." He has been a gadfly to the state, urging its
citizens to self-improvement, and in his search for wisdom he has exposed
their ignorance. His true enemies, he realizes, are not his prosecutors but all
those who oppose the life of reason and virtue, who shrink before his conviction that "the unexamined life is not worth living."

Socrates is found guilty of the charges and is allowed to propose a penalty.
Refusing to betray his mission, he suggests that he ought rather to be rewarded as a benefactor of the state. He does, however, propose a fine of

381

money for most of which his friends, among them Plato, will serve as security.

In his last speech, after the sentence of death has been passed, he implies that he has made the court's decision inevitable. He cannot beg to be forgive for a crime which he has not committed, and, carrying his belief in his religious function to its final logic, he prefers to sacrifice his life rather than to take upon him in any way the unrighteousness of his accusers. He has, in effect, forced his judges to martyr a man whom they wished merely to intimidate into silence.

—INTRODUCTORY NOTE BY JUSTIN KAPLAN

APOLOGY

Persons of the Dialogue

Socrates, Meletus

Scene

In the court

Socrates speaks: How you, O Athenians, have been affected by my accusers, I cannot tell; but I know that they almost made me forget who I was—so persuasively did they speak; and yet they have hardly uttered a word of truth. But of the many falsehoods told by them, there was one which quite amazed me;—I mean when they said that you should be upon your guard and not allow yourselves to be deceived by the force of my eloquence. To say this, when they were certain to be detected as soon as I opened my lips and proved myself to be anything but a great speaker, did indeed appear to me most shameless—unless by the force of eloquence they mean the force of truth; for if such is their meaning, I admit that I am eloquent. But in how different a way from theirs! Well, as I was saying, they have scarcely spoken the truth at all; but from me you shall hear the whole truth: not, however, delivered after their manner in a set oration duly ornamented with words and phrases. No, by heaven! but I shall use the words and arguments which occur to me at the moment; for I am confident in the justice of my cause:* at my time of life I ought not to be appearing before you, O men of Athens, in the character of a juven le orator—let no one expect it of me. And I must beg of you to grant ɪ a favor:—If I defend myself in my accustomed manner, and you he: me using the words which I have been in the habit of using in the agora. at the tables of the money-changers, or anywhere else, I would ask you not to be surprised, and not to interrupt me on this account. For I aɪn more than seventy years of age, and appearing now for the first time in a court of law, I am quite a stranger to the language of the place; and therefore I would have you regard me as if I were really a stranger, whom you would excuse if he spoke in his native tongue, and after the fashion of his country:—Am I making an unfair request of you? Never mind the manner, which may or may not be good; but think only of the truth of my words, and give heed to that: let the speaker speak truly and the judge decide justly.

And first, I have to reply to the older charges and to my first accusers, and then I will go on to the later ones. For of old I have had many accusers, who have accused me falsely to you during many years; and I am more afraid of them than of Anytus and his associates, who are dangerous, too, in their own way. But far more dangerous are the others, who began when you were children, and took possession of your minds with their falsehoods, telling of one Socrates, a wise man, who speculated about the heaven above, and searched into the earth beneath, and made the worse appear the better cause. The disseminators of this tale are the accusers whom I dread; for their hearers are apt to fancy that such enquirers do not believe in the existence of the gods. And they are many, and their charges against me are of ancient date, and they were made by them in the days when you were more impressible than you are now—in childhood, or it may have been in youth—and the cause when heard went by default, for there was none to answer. And hardest of all, I do not know and cannot tell the names of my accusers; unless in the chance case of a comic poet. All who from envy and malice have persuaded you—

* Or, I am certain that I am right in taking this course.

some of them having first convinced themselves—all this class of men are most difficult to deal with; for I cannot have them up here, and cross-examine them, and therefore I must simply fight with shadows in my own defense, and argue when there is no one who answers. I will ask you then to assume with me, as I was saying, that my opponents are of two kinds; one recent, the other ancient: and I hope that you will see the propriety of my answering the latter first, for these accusations you heard long before the others, and much oftener.

Well, then, I must make my defense, and endeavor to clear away in a short time a slander which has lasted a long time. May I succeed, if to succeed be for my good and yours, or likely to avail me in my cause! The task is not an easy one; I quite understand the nature of it. And so leaving the event with God, in obedience to the law I will now make my defense.

I will begin at the beginning, and ask what is the accusation which has given rise to the slander of me, and in fact has encouraged Meletus to prefer this charge against me. Well, what do the slanderers say? They shall be my prosecutors, and I will sum up their words in an affidavit: "Socrates is an evildoer, and a curious person, who searches into things under the earth and in heaven, and he makes the worse appear the better cause; and he teaches the aforesaid doctrines to others." Such is the nature of the accusation: it is just what you have yourselves seen in the comedy of Aristophanes,* who has introduced a man whom he calls Socrates, going about and saying that he walks in air, and talking a deal of nonsense concerning matters of which I do not pretend to know either much or little—not that I mean to speak disparagingly of any one who is a student of natural philosophy. I should be very sorry if Meletus could bring so grave a charge against me. But the simple truth is, O Athenians, that I have nothing to do with physical speculations. Very many of those here present are witnesses to the truth of this, and to them I appeal. Speak then, you who have heard me, and tell your neighbors whether any of you have ever known me hold forth in few words or in many upon such matters. . . . You hear their answer. And from what they say of this part of the charge you will be able to judge of the truth of the rest.

As little foundation is there for the report that I am a teacher, and take money; this accusation has no more truth in it than the other. Although, if a man were really able to instruct mankind, to receive money for giving instruction would, in my opinion, be an honor to him. There is Gorgias

* Aristoph., *Clouds,* 225 ff.

of Leontium, and Prodicus of Ceos, and Hippias of Elis, who go the round of the cities, and are able to persuade the young men to leave their own citizens by whom they might be taught for nothing, and come to them whom they not only pay, but are thankful if they may be allowed to pay them. There is at this time a Parian philosopher residing in Athens, of whom I have heard; and I came to hear of him in this way:—I came across a man who has spent a world of money on the Sophists, Callias, the son of Hipponicus, and knowing that he had sons, I asked him: "Callias," I said, "if your two sons were foals or calves, there would be no difficulty in finding some one to put over them; we should hire a trainer of horses, or a farmer, probably, who would improve and perfect them in their own proper virtue and excellence; but as they are human beings, whom are you thinking of placing over them? Is there any one who understands human and political virtue? You must have thought about the matter, for you have sons; is there any one?" "There is," he said. "Who is he?" said I; "and of what country? and what does he charge?" "Evenus the Parian," he replied; "he is the man, and his charge is five minae." Happy is Evenus, I said to myself, if he really has this wisdom, and teaches at such a moderate charge. Had I the same, I should have been very proud and conceited; but the truth is that I have no knowledge of the kind.

I dare say, Athenians, that some one among you will reply, "Yes, Socrates, but what is the origin of these accusations which are brought against you; there must have been something strange which you have been doing? All these rumors and this talk about you would never have arisen if you had been like other men: tell us, then, what is the cause of them, for we should be sorry to judge hastily of you." Now, I regard this as a fair challenge, and I will endeavor to explain to you the reason why I am called wise and have such an evil fame. Please to attend then. And although some of you may think I am joking, I declare that I will tell you the entire truth. Men of Athens, this reputation of mine has come of a certain sort of wisdom which I possess. If you ask me what kind of wisdom, I reply, wisdom such as may perhaps be attained by man, for to that extent I am inclined to believe that I am wise; whereas the persons of whom I was speaking have a superhuman wisdom, which I may fail to describe, because I have it not myself; and he who says that I have, speaks falsely, and is taking away my character. And here, O men of Athens, I must beg you not to interrupt me, even if I seem to say something extravagant. For the word which I will speak is not mine. I will refer you to a witness who is worthy of credit; that witness shall be the God of Delphi—he will tell you about my wisdom, if I have any, and of what sort it is. You must have known Chaerephon; he was early a friend of mine, and also a friend of yours, for he shared in the recent exile of the people, and returned with you. Well, Chaerephon, as you know, was very impetuous in all his doings, and he went to Delphi and boldly asked the oracle to tell him whether—as I was saying, I must beg you not to interrupt—he asked the oracle to tell him whether any one was wiser than I was, and the Pythian prophetess answered, that there was no man wiser. Chaerephon is dead himself; but his brother, who is in court, will confirm the truth of what I am saying.

Why do I mention this? Because I am going to explain to you why I have such an evil name. When I heard the answer, I said to myself, What can the God mean? and what is the interpretation of his riddle? for I know that I have no wisdom, small or great. What then can he mean when he says that I am the wisest of men? And yet he is a god, and cannot lie; that would be against his nature. After long consideration, I thought of a method of trying the question. I reflected that if I could only find a man wiser than myself, then I might go to the god with a refutation in my hand. I should say to him, "Here is a man who is wiser than I am; but you said that I was the wisest." Accordingly I went to one who had the reputation of wisdom, and observed him—his name I need not mention; he was a politician whom I selected for examination—and the result was as follows: When I began to talk with him, I could not help thinking that he was not really wise, although he was thought wise by many, and still wiser by himself; and thereupon I tried to explain to him that he thought himself wise, but was not really wise; and the consequence was that he hated me, and his enmity was shared by several who were present and heard me. So I left him, saying to myself, as I went away: Well, although I do not suppose that either of us knows anything really beautiful and good, I am better off than he is,—for he knows nothing, and thinks that he knows; I neither know nor think that I know. In this latter particular, then, I seem to have slightly the advantage of him. Then I went to another who had still higher pretensions to wisdom, and my conclusion was exactly the same. Whereupon I made another enemy of him, and of many others besides him.

Then I went to one man after another, being not unconscious of the enmity which I provoked, and I lamented and feared this: but necessity was laid upon me,—the word of God, I thought, ought to be considered first. And I said to myself, Go I must to all who appear to know, and find out the meaning of the oracle. And I swear to you, Athenians, by the dog I swear!—for I must tell you the truth—the result of my mission was just this: I found that the men most in repute were all but the most foolish; and that others less esteemed were really wiser and better. I will tell you the tale of my wanderings and of the "Herculean" labors, as I may call them, which I endured only to find at last the oracle irrefutable. After the politicians, I went to the poets; tragic, dithyrambic, and all sorts. And there, I said to myself, you will be instantly detected; now you will find out that you are more ignorant than they are. Accordingly I took them some of the most elaborate passages in their own writings, and asked what was the meaning of them—thinking that they would teach me something. Will you believe me? I am almost ashamed to confess the truth, but I must say that there is hardly a person present who would not have talked better about their poetry than they did themselves. Then I knew that not by wisdom do poets write poetry, but by a sort of genius and inspiration; they are like diviners or soothsayers who also say many fine things, but do not understand the meaning of them. The poets appeared to me to be much in the same case; and I further observed that upon the strength of their poetry they believed themselves to be the wisest of men in other things in which they were not wise. So I departed, conceiving myself to be superior to them for the same reason that I was superior to the politicians.

At last I went to the artisans, I was conscious that I knew nothing at all, as I may say, and I was sure that they knew many fine things; and here I was not mistaken, for they did know many things of which I was ignorant, and in this they certainly were wiser than I was. But I observed that even the good artisans fell into the same error as the poets;—because they were good workmen they thought that they also knew all sorts of high matters, and this defect in them overshadowed their wisdom; and therefore I asked myself on behalf of the oracle, whether I would like to be as I was, neither having their knowledge nor their ignorance, or like them in both; and I made answer to myself and to the oracle that I was better off as I was.

This inquisition has led to my having many enemies of the worst and most dangerous kind, and has given occasion also to many calumnies. And I am called wise, for my hearers always imagine that I myself possess the wisdom which I find wanting in others: but the truth is, O men of Athens, that God only is wise; and by his answer he intends to show that the wisdom of men is worth little or nothing; he is not speaking of Socrates, he is only using my name by way of illustration, as if he said, He, O men, is the wisest, who, like Socrates, knows that his wisdom is in truth worth nothing. And so I go about the world obedient to the god, and search and make enquiry into the wisdom of any one, whether citizen or stranger, who appears to be wise; and if he is not wise, then in vindication of the oracle I show him that he is not wise; and my occupation quite absorbs me, and I have no time to give either to any public matter of interest or to any concern of my own, but I am in utter poverty by reason of my devotion to the god.

There is another thing:—young men of the richer classes, who have not much to do, come about me of their own accord; they like to hear the pretenders examined, and they often imitate me, and proceed to examine others; there are plenty of persons, as they quickly discover, who think that they know something, but really know little or nothing; and then those who are examined by them instead of being angry with themselves are angry with me: This confounded Socrates, they say; this villainous misleader of youth!—and then if somebody asks them, Why, what evil does he practise or teach? they do not know, and cannot tell; but in order that they may not appear to be at a loss, they repeat the ready-made charges which are used against all philosophers about teaching things up in the clouds and under the earth, and having no gods, and making the worse appear the better cause; for they do not like to confess that their pretense of knowledge has been detected—which is the truth; and as they are numerous and ambitious and energetic, and are drawn up in battle array and have persuasive tongues, they have filled your ears with their loud and inveterate calumnies. And this is the reason why my three accusers, Meletus and Anytus and Lycon, have set upon me; Meletus, who has a quarrel with me on behalf of the poets; Anytus, on behalf of the craftsmen and politicians; Lycon, on behalf of the rhetoricians: and, as I said at the beginning, I cannot expect to get rid of such a mass of calumny all in a moment. And this, O men of Athens, is the truth and the whole truth; I have concealed nothing, I have dissembled nothing. And yet, I know that my plainness of speech makes them hate me, and what is their hatred but a proof that I am speaking the truth? Hence has arisen the prejudice against me; and this is the reason of it, as you will find out either in this or in any future enquiry.

I have said enough in my defense against the first class of my accusers; I turn to the second class. They are headed by Meletus, that good man and true lover of his country, as he calls himself. Against these, too, I must try to make a defense:—Let their affidavit be read: it contains something of this kind: It says that Socrates is a doer of evil, who corrupts the youth; and who does not believe in the gods of the State, but has other new divinities of his own. Such is the charge; and now let us examine the particular counts. He says that I am a doer of evil, and corrupt the youth; but I say, O men of Athens, that Meletus is a doer of evil, in that he pretends to be in earnest when he is only in jest, and is so eager to bring men to trial from a pretended zeal and interest about matters in which he really never had the smallest interest. And the truth of this I will endeavor to prove to you.

Come hither, Meletus, and let me ask a question of you. You think a great deal about the improvement of youth?

Yes, I do.

Tell the judges, then, who is their improver; for you must know, as you have taken the pains to discover their corrupter, and are citing and accusing me before them. Speak, then, and tell the judges who their improver is.—Observe, Meletus, that you are silent, and have nothing to say. But is not this rather disgraceful, and a very considerable proof of what I was saying, that you have no interest in the matter? Speak up, friend, and tell us who their improver is.

The laws.

But that, my good sir, is not my meaning. I want to know who the person is, who, in the first place, knows the laws.

The judges, Socrates, who are present in court.

What, do you mean to say, Meletus, that they are able to instruct and improve youth?

Certainly they are.

What, all of them, or some only and not others?

All of them.

By the goddess Here, that is good news! There are plenty of improvers, then. And what do you say of the audience,—do they improve them?

Yes, they do.

And the senators?

Yes, the senators improve them.

But perhaps the members of the assembly corrupt them?—or do they improve them?

They improve them.

Then every Athenian improves and elevates them; all with the exception of myself; and I alone am their corrupter? Is that what you affirm?

That is what I stoutly affirm.

I am very unfortunate if you are right. But suppose I ask you a question: How about horses? Does one man do them harm and all the world good? Is not the exact opposite the truth? One man is able to do them good, or at least not many;—the trainer of horses, that is to say, does them good, and others who have to do with them rather injure them? Is not that true, Meletus, of horses, or of any other animals? Most assuredly it is; whether you and Anytus say yes or no. Happy indeed would be the condition of youth if they had one corrupter only, and all the rest of the world were their improvers. But you, Meletus, have sufficiently shown that you never had a thought about the young: your carelessness is seen in your not caring about the very things which you bring against me.

And now, Meletus, I will ask you another question—by Zeus I will: Which is better, to live among bad citizens, or among good ones? Answer, friend, I say; the question is one which may be easily answered. Do not the good do their neighbors good, and the bad do them evil?

Certainly.

And is there any one who would rather be injured than benefited by those who live with him? Answer, my good friend, the law requires you to answer—does any one like to be injured?

Certainly not.

And when you accuse me of corrupting and deteriorating the youth, do you allege that I corrupt them intentionally or unintentionally?

Intentionally, I say.

But you have just admitted that the good do their neighbors good, and the evil do them evil. Now, is that a truth which your superior wisdom has recognized thus early in life, and am I, at my age, in such darkness and ignorance as not to know that if a man with whom I have to live is corrupted by me, I am very likely to be harmed by him; and yet I corrupt him, and intentionally, too—so you say, although neither I nor any other human being is ever likely to be convinced by you. But either I do not corrupt them, or I corrupt them unintentionally; and on either view of the case you lie. If my offense is unintentional, the law has no cognizance of unintentional offenses: you ought to have taken me privately, and warned and admonished me; for if I had been better advised, I should have left off doing what I only did unintentionally—no doubt

I should; but you would have nothing to say to me and refused to teach me. And now you bring me up in this court, which is a place not of instruction, but of punishment.

It will be very clear to you, Athenians, as I was saying, that Meletus has no care at all, great or small, about the matter. But still I should like to know, Meletus, in what I am affirmed to corrupt the young. I suppose you mean, as I infer from your indictment, that I teach them not to acknowledge the gods which the State acknowledges, but some other new divinities or spiritual agencies in their stead. These are lessons by which I corrupt the youth, as you say.

Yes, that I say emphatically.

Then, by the gods, Meletus, of whom we are speaking, tell me and the court, in somewhat plainer terms, what you mean! For I do not as yet understand whether you affirm that I teach other men to acknowledge some gods, and therefore that I do believe in gods, and am not an entire atheist—this you do not lay to my charge,—but only you say that they are not the same gods which the city recognizes—the charge is that they are different gods. Or, do you mean that I am an atheist simply, and a teacher of atheism?

I mean the latter—that you are a complete atheist.

What an extraordinary statement! Why do you think so, Meletus? Do you mean that I do not believe in the godhead of the sun or moon, like other men?

I assure you, judges, that he does not: for he says that the sun is stone, and the moon is earth.

Friend Meletus, you think that you are accusing Anaxagoras: and you have but a bad opinion of the judges, if you fancy them illiterate to such a degree as not to know that these doctrines are found in the books of Anaxagoras the Clazomenian, which are full of them. And so, forsooth, the youth are said to be taught them by Socrates, when there are not infrequently exhibitions of them at the theater* (price of admission one drachma at the most); and they might pay their money, and laugh at Socrates if he pretends to father these extraordinary views. And so, Meletus, you really think that I do not believe in any god?

I swear by Zeus that you believe absolutely in none at all.

Nobody will believe you, Meletus, and I am pretty sure that you do not believe yourself. I cannot help thinking, men of Athens, that Meletus

---

* Probably in allusion to Aristophanes who caricatured, and to Euripides who borrowed the notions of Anaxagoras, as well as to other dramatic poets.

is reckless and impudent, and that he has written this indictment in a spirit of mere wantonness and youthful bravado. Has he not compounded a riddle, thinking to try me? He said to himself:—I shall see whether the wise Socrates will discover my facetious contradiction, or whether I shall be able to deceive him and the rest of them. For he certainly does appear to me to contradict himself in the indictment as much as if he said that Socrates is guilty of not believing in the gods, and yet of believing in them—but this is not like a person who is in earnest.

I should like you, O men of Athens, to join me in examining what I conceive to be his inconsistency; and do you, Meletus, answer. And I must remind the audience of my request that they would not make a disturbance if I speak in my accustomed manner:

Did ever man, Meletus, believe in the existence of human things, and not of human beings? . . . I wish, men of Athens, that he would answer, and not be always trying to get up an interruption. Did ever any man believe in horsemanship, and not in horses? or in fluteplaying, and not in flute-players? No, my friend; I will answer to you and to the court, as you refuse to answer for yourself. There is no man who ever did. But now please to answer the next question: Can a man believe in spiritual and divine agencies, and not in spirits or demigods?

He cannot.

How lucky I am to have extracted that answer, by the assistance of the court! But then you swear in the indictment that I teach and believe in divine or spiritual agencies (new or old, no matter for that); at any rate, I believe in spiritual agencies,—so you say and swear in the affidavit; and yet if I believe in divine beings, how can I help believing in spirits or demigods;—must I not? To be sure I must; and therefore I may assume that your silence gives consent. Now what are spirits or demigods? are they not either gods or the sons of gods?

Certainly they are.

But this is what I call the facetious riddle invented by you: the demigods or spirits are gods, and you say first that I do not believe in gods, and then again that I do believe in gods; that is, if I believe in demigods. For if the demigods are the illegitimate sons of gods, whether by the nymphs or by any other mothers, of whom they are said to be the sons— what human being will ever believe that there are no gods if they are the sons of gods? You might as well affirm the existence of mules, and deny that of horses and asses. Such nonsense, Meletus, could only have been intended by you to make trial of me. You have put this into the indictment because you had nothing real of which to accuse me. But no one who has a particle of understanding will ever be convinced by you that the same men can believe in divine and superhuman things, and yet not believe that there are gods and demigods and heroes.

I have said enough in answer to the charge of Meletus: any elaborate defense is unnecessary; but I know only too well how many are the enmities which I have incurred, and this is what will be my destruction if I am destroyed;—not Meletus, nor yet Anytus, but the envy and detraction of the world, which has been the death of many good men, and will probably be the death of many more; there is no danger of my being the last of them.

Some one will say: And are you not ashamed, Socrates, of a course of life which is likely to bring you to an untimely end? To him I may fairly answer: There you are mistaken: a man who is good for anything ought not to calculate the chance of living or dying; he ought only to consider whether in doing anything he is doing right or wrong—acting the part of a good man or of a bad. Whereas, upon your view, the heroes who fell at Troy were not good for much, and the son of Thetis above all, who altogether despised danger in comparison with disgrace; and when he was so eager to slay Hector, his goddess mother said to him, that if he avenged his companion Patroclus, and slew Hector, he would die himself—"Fate," she said, in these or the like words, "waits for you next after Hector"; he, receiving this warning, utterly despised danger and death, and instead of fearing them, feared rather to live in dishonor, and not to avenge his friend. "Let me die forthwith," he replies, "and be avenged of my enemy, rather than abide here by the beaked ships, a laughing-stock and a burden of the earth." Had Achilles any thought of death and danger? For wherever a man's place is, whether the place which he has chosen or that in which he has been placed by a commander, there he ought to remain in the hour of danger; he should not think of death or of anything but of disgrace. And this, O men of Athens, is a true saying.

Strange, indeed, would be my conduct, O men of Athens, if I, who, when I was ordered by the generals whom you chose to command me at Potidaea and Amphipolis and Delium, remained where they placed me, like any other man, facing death—if now, when, as I conceive and imagine, God orders me to fulfil the philosopher's mission of searching into myself and other men, I were to desert my post through fear of death, or any other fear; that would indeed be strange, and I might justly

be arraigned in court for denying the existence of the gods, if I disobeyed
the oracle because I was afraid of death, fancying that I was wise when
I was not wise. For the fear of death is indeed the pretense of wisdom,
and not real wisdom, being a pretense of knowing the unknown; and no
one knows whether death, which men in their fear apprehend to be the
greatest evil, may not be the greatest good. Is not this ignorance of a
disgraceful sort, the ignorance which is the conceit that a man knows
what he does not know? And in this respect only I believe myself to differ
from men in general, and may perhaps claim to be wiser than they are:—
that whereas I know but little of the world below, I do not suppose that
I know: but I do know that injustice and disobedience to a better,
whether God or man, is evil and dishonorable, and I will never fear or
avoid a possible good rather than a certain evil. And therefore if you
let me go now, and are not convinced by Anytus, who said that since I
had been prosecuted I must be put to death; (or if not that I ought never
to have been prosecuted at all); and that if I escape now, your sons will
all be utterly ruined by listening to my words—if you say to me, Socrates, this time we will not mind Anytus, and you shall be let off, but
upon one condition, that you are not to inquire and speculate in this way
any more, and that if you are caught doing so again you shall die;—if
this was the condition on which you let me go, I should reply: Men of
Athens, I honor and love you; but I shall obey God rather than you, and
while I have life and strength I shall never cease from the practice and
teaching of philosophy, exhorting any one whom I meet and saying to
him after my manner: You, my friend,—a citizen of the great and mighty
and wise city of Athens,—are you not ashamed of heaping up the greatest amount of money and honor and reputation, and caring so little about
wisdom and truth and the greatest improvement of the soul, which you
never regard or heed at all? And if the person with whom I am arguing,
says: Yes, but I do care; then I do not leave him or let him go at once;
but I proceed to interrogate and examine and cross-examine him, and if
I think that he has no virtue in him, but only says that he has, I reproach him with undervaluing the greater, and overvaluing the less. And
I shall repeat the same words to every one whom I meet, young and old,
citizen and alien, but especially to the citizens, inasmuch as they are my
brethren. For know that this is the command of God; and I believe that
no greater good has ever happened in the State than my service to God.
For I do nothing but go about persuading you all, old and young alike,
not to take thought for your persons or your properties, but first and

chiefly to care about the greatest improvement of the soul. I tell you that virtue is not given by money, but that from virtue comes money and every other good of man, public as well as private. This is my teaching, and if this is the doctrine which corrupts the youth, I am a mischievous person. But if any one says that this is not my teaching, he is speaking an untruth. Wherefore, O men of Athens, I say to you, do as Anytus bids or not as Anytus bids, and either acquit me or not; but whichever you do, understand that I shall never alter my ways, not even if I have to die many times.

Men of Athens, do not interrupt, but hear me; there was an understanding between us that you should hear me to the end: I have something more to say, at which you may be inclined to cry out; but I believe that to hear me will be good for you, and therefore I beg that you will not cry out. I would have you know, that if you kill such an one as I am, you will injure yourselves more than you will injure me. Nothing will injure me, not Meletus nor yet Anytus—they cannot, for a bad man is not permitted to injure a better than himself. I do not deny that Anytus may, perhaps, kill him, or drive him into exile, or deprive him of civil rights; and he may imagine, and others may imagine, that he is inflicting a great injury upon him: but there I do not agree. For the evil of doing as he is doing—the evil of unjustly taking away the life of another—is greater far.

And now, Athenians, I am not going to argue for my own sake, as you may think, but for yours, that you may not sin against the God by condemning me, who am his gift to you. For if you kill me you will not easily find a successor to me, who, if I may use such a ludicrous figure of speech, am a sort of gadfly, given to the State by God; and the State is a great and noble steed who is tardy in his motions owing to his very size, and requires to be stirred into life. I am that gadfly which God has attached to the State, and all day long and in all places am always fastening upon you, arousing and persuading and reproaching you. You will not easily find another like me, and therefore I would advise you to spare me. I dare say that you may feel out of temper (like a person who is suddenly awakened from sleep), and you think that you might easily strike me dead as Anytus advises, and then you would sleep on for the remainder of your lives, unless God in his care of you sent you another gadfly. When I say that I am given to you by God, the proof of my mission is this:—if I had been like other men, I should not have neglected all my own concerns or patiently seen the neglect of them during all these years, and have been doing yours, coming to you individually like a father or elder brother, exhorting you to regard virtue; such conduct, I say, would be unlike human nature. If I had gained anything, or if my exhortations had been paid, there would have been some sense in my doing so; but now, as you will perceive, not even the impudence of my accusers dares to say that I have ever exacted or sought pay of any one; of that they have no witness. And I have a sufficient witness to the truth of what I say—my poverty.

Some one may wonder why I go about in private giving advice and busying myself with the concerns of others, but do not venture to come forward in public and advise the State. I will tell you why. You have heard me speak at sundry times and in divers places of an oracle or sign which comes to me, and is the divinity which Meletus ridicules in the indictment. This sign, which is a kind of voice, first began to come to me when I was a child; it always forbids but never commands me to do anything which I am going to do. This is what deters me from being a politician. And rightly, as I think. For I am certain, O men of Athens, that if I had engaged in politics, I should have perished long ago, and done no good either to you or to myself. And do not be offended at my telling you the truth: for the truth is, that no man who goes to war with you or any other multitude, honestly striving against the many lawless and unrighteous deeds which are done in a state, will save his life; he who will fight for the right, if he would live even for a brief space, must have a private station and not a public one.

I can give you convincing evidence of what I say, not words only, but what you value far more—actions. Let me relate to you a passage of my own life which will prove to you that I should never have yielded to injustice from any fear of death and that "as I should have refused to yield" I must have died at once. I will tell you a tale of the courts, not very interesting perhaps, but nevertheless true. The only office of State which I ever held, O men of Athens, was that of senator: the tribe Antiochis, which is my tribe, had the presidency at the trial of the generals who had not taken up the bodies of the slain after the battle of Arginusae; and you proposed to try them in a body, contrary to law, as you all thought afterwards; but at the time I was the only one of the Prytanes who was opposed to the illegality, and I gave my vote against you; and when the orators threatened to impeach and arrest me, and you called and shouted, I made up my mind that I would run the risk, having law and justice with me, rather than take part in your injustice because I feared imprisonment and death. This happened in the days of the democracy. But when the oligarchy of the Thirty was in power, they sent for me and four others into the rotunda, and bade us bring Leon the Salaminian from Salamis, as they wanted to put him to death. This was a specimen of the sort of commands which they were always giving with the view of implicating as many as possible in their crimes; and then I showed, not in word only but in deed, that, if I may be allowed to use such an expression, I cared not a straw for death, and that my great and only care was lest I should do an unrighteous or unholy thing. For the strong arm of that oppressive power did not frighten me into doing wrong; and when we came out of the rotunda the other four went to Salamis and fetched Leon, but I went quietly home. For which I might have lost my life, had not the power of the Thirty shortly afterwards come to an end. And many will witness to my words.

Now, do you really imagine that I could have survived all these years, if I had led a public life, supposing that like a good man I had always maintained the right and had made justice, as I ought, the first thing? No, indeed, men of Athens, neither I nor any other man. But I have been always the same in all my actions, public as well as private, and never have I yielded any base compliance to those who are slanderously termed my disciples, or to any other. Not that I have any regular disciples. But if any one likes to come and hear me while I am pursuing my mission, whether he be young or old, he is not excluded. Nor do I converse only with those who pay; but any one, whether he be rich or poor, may ask and answer me and listen to my words; and whether he turns out to be a bad man or a good one, neither result can be justly imputed to me; for I never taught or professed to teach him anything. And if any one says that he has ever learned or heard anything from me in private which all the world has not heard, let me tell you that he is lying.

But I shall be asked, Why do people delight in continually conversing with you? I have told you already, Athenians, the whole truth about this matter: they like to hear the cross-examination of the pretenders to wisdom; there is amusement in it. Now, this duty of cross-examining other men has been imposed upon me by God; and has been signified to me by oracles, visions, and in every way in which the will of divine power was ever intimated to any one. This is true, O Athenians; or, if not true, would be soon refuted. If I am or have been corrupting the youth, those of them who are now grown up and have become sensible that I gave them bad advice in the days of their youth should come forward as accusers, and take their revenge; or if they do not like to come themselves, some of their relatives, fathers, brothers, or other kinsmen, should say what evil their families have suffered at my hands. Now is their time. Many of them I see in the court. There is Crito, who is of the same age and of the same deme with myself, and there is Critobulus his son, whom I also see. Then again there is Lysanias of Sphettus, who is the father of Aeschines—he is present; and also there is Antiphon of Cephisus, who is the father of Epigenes; and there are the brothers of several who have associated with me. There is Nicostratus the son of Theosdotides, and the brother of Theodotus (now Theodotus himself is dead, and therefore he, at any rate, will not seek to stop him); and there is Paralus the son of Demodocus, who had a brother Theages; and Adeimantus the son of Ariston, whose brother Plato is present; and Aeantodorus, who is the brother of Apollodorus, whom I also see. I might mention a great many others, some of whom Meletus should have produced as witnesses in the course of his speech; and let him still produce them, if he has forgotten —I will make way for him. And let him say, if he has any testimony of the sort which he can produce. Nay, Athenians, the very opposite is the truth. For all these are ready to witness on behalf of the corrupter, of the injurer of their kindred, as Meletus and Anytus call me; not the corrupted youth only—there might have been a motive for that—but their uncorrupted elder relatives. Why should they too support me with their testimony? Why, indeed, except for the sake of truth and justice, and because they know that I am speaking the truth, and that Meletus is a liar.

Well, Athenians, this and the like of this is all the defense which I have to offer. Yet a word more. Perhaps there may be some one who is offended at me, when he calls to mind how he himself on a similar, or even a less serious occasion, prayed and entreated the judges with many tears, and how he produced his children in court, which was a moving spectacle, together with a host of relations and friends; whereas I, who am probably in danger of my life, will do none of these things. The contrast may occur to his mind, and he may be set against me, and vote in anger because he is displeased at me on this account. Now, if there be such a person among you,—mind, I do not say that there is,—to him I may fairly reply: My friend, I am a man, and like other men, a creature of flesh and blood, and not "of wood or stone," as Homer says; and I have a family, yes, and sons, O Athenians, three in number, one almost a man, and two others who are still young; and yet I will not bring any of them hither in order to petition you for an acquittal. And why not? Not from any self-assertion or want of respect for you. Whether I am or am not afraid of death is another question, of which I will not now speak. But, having regard to public opinion, I feel that such conduct would be discreditable to myself, and to you, and to the whole State. One who has reached my years, and who has a name for wisdom, ought not to demean himself. Whether this opinion of me be deserved or not, at any rate the world has decided that Socrates is in some way superior to other men. And if those among you who are said to be superior in wisdom and courage, and any other virtue, demean themselves in this way, how shameful is their conduct! I have seen men of reputation, when they have been condemned, behaving in the strangest manner: they seemed to fancy that they were going to suffer something dreadful if they died, and that they could be immortal if you only allowed them to live; and I think that such are a dishonor to the State, and that any stranger coming in would have said of them that the most eminent men of Athens, to whom the Athenians themselves give honor and command, are no better than women. And I say that these things ought not to be done by those of us who have a reputation; and if they are done, you ought not to permit them; you ought rather to show that you are far more disposed to condemn the man who gets up a doleful scene and makes the city ridiculous, than him who holds his peace.

But, setting aside the question of public opinion, there seems to be something wrong in asking a favor of a judge, and thus procuring an acquittal, instead of informing and convincing him. For his duty is, not to make a present of justice, but to give judgment; and he has sworn that he will judge according to the laws, and not according to his own good pleasure; and we ought not to encourage you, nor should you allow yourselves to be encouraged, in this habit of perjury—there can be no piety in that. Do not then require me to do what I consider dishonorable and impious and wrong, especially now, when I am being tried for impiety on the indictment of Meletus. For if, O men of Athens, by force of persuasion and entreaty I could overpower your oaths, then I should be teaching you to believe that there are no gods, and in defending should simply convict myself of the charge of not believing in them. But that is not so—far otherwise. For I do believe that there are gods, and in a sense higher than that in which any of my accusers believe in them. And to you and to God I commit my cause, to be determined by you as is best for you and me.

*

There are many reasons why I am not grieved, O men of Athens, at the vote of condemnation. I expected it, and am only surprised that the votes are so nearly equal; for I had thought that the majority against me would have been far larger; but now, had thirty votes gone over to the other side, I should have been acquitted. And I may say, I think, that I have escaped Meletus. I may say more; for without the assistance of Anytus and Lycon, any one may see that he would not have had a fifth part of the votes, as the law requires, in which case he would have incurred a fine of a thousand drachmae.

And so he proposes death as the penalty. And what shall I propose on my part, O men of Athens? Clearly that which is my due. And what is my due? What returns shall be made to a man who has never had the wit to be idle during his whole life; but has been careless of what the many care for—wealth, and family interests, and military offices, and speaking in the assembly, and magistracies, and plots, and parties. Reflecting that I was really too honest a man to be a politician and live, I did not go where I could do no good to you or to myself; but where I could do the greatest good privately to every one of you, thither I went, and sought to persuade every man among you that he must look to himself, and seek virtue and wisdom before he looks to his private interests, and look to the State before he looks to the interests of the State; and that this should be the order which he observes in all his actions. What shall be done to such an one? Doubtless some good thing, O men of Athens, if he has his reward; and the good should be of a kind suitable to him. What would be a reward suitable to a poor man who is your benefactor, and who desires leisure that he may instruct you? There can be no reward so fitting as maintenance in the Prytaneum, O men of Athens, a reward which he deserves far more than the citizen who has won the prize at Olympia in the horse or chariot race, whether the chariots were drawn by two horses or by many. For I am in want, and he has enough; and he only gives you the appearance of happiness, and I give you the reality. And if I am to estimate the penalty fairly, I should say that maintenance in the Prytaneum is the just return.

Perhaps you think that I am braving you in what I am saying now, as in what I said before about the tears and prayers. But this is not so. I speak rather because I am convinced that I never intentionally wronged any one, although I cannot convince you—the time has been too short; if there were a law at Athens, as there is in other cities, that a capital cause should not be decided in one day, then I believe that I should have convinced you. But I cannot in a moment refute great slanders; and, as I am convinced that I never wronged another, I will assuredly not wrong myself. I will not say to myself that I deserve any evil, or propose any penalty. Why should I? Because I am afraid of the penalty of death which Meletus proposes? When I do not know whether death is a good or an evil, why should I propose a penalty which would certainly be an evil? Shall I say imprisonment? And why should I live in prison, and be the slave of the magistrate of the year—of the Eleven? Or shall the penalty be a fine, and imprisonment until the fine is paid? There is the same objection. I should have to lie in prison, for money I have none, and cannot pay. And if I say exile (and this may possibly be the penalty which you will affix), I must indeed be blinded by the love of life, if I am so irrational as to expect that when you, who are my own citizens, cannot endure my discourses and words, and have found them so grievous and odious that you will have no more of them, others are likely to endure me. No, indeed, men of Athens, that is not very likely. And what a life should I lead, at my age, wandering from city to city, ever changing my place of exile, and always being driven out! For I am quite sure that wherever I go, that, as here, the young men will flock to me; and if I drive them away, their elders will drive me out at their request; and if I let them come, their fathers and friends will drive me out for their sakes.

Some one will say: Yes, Socrates, but cannot you hold your tongue, and then you may go into a foreign city, and no one will interfere with you? Now, I have great difficulty in making you understand my answer to this. For if I tell you that to do as you say would be a disobedience to the God, and therefore that I cannot hold my tongue, you will not believe that I am serious; and if I say again that daily to discourse about virtue, and of those other things about which you hear me examining myself and others, is the greatest good of man, and that the unexamined life is not worth living, you are still less likely to believe me. Yet I say what is true, although a thing of which it is hard for me to persuade you. Also, I have never been accustomed to think that I deserve to suffer any harm. Had I money I might have estimated the offense at what I was able to pay, and not have been much the worse. But I have none, and therefore I must ask you to proportion the fine to my means. Well, perhaps I could afford a mina, and therefore I propose that penalty: Plato, Crito, Critobulus, and Apollodorus, my friends here, bid me say thirty minae, and they will be the sureties. Let thirty minae be the penalty; for which sum they will be ample security to you.

Not much time will be gained, O Athenians, in return for the evil name which you will get from the detractors of the city, who will say that you killed Socrates, a wise man; for they will call me wise, even although I am not wise, when they want to reproach you. If you had waited a little while, your desire would have been fulfilled in the course of nature. For I am far advanced in years, as you may perceive, and not far from death. I am speaking now not to all of you, but only to those who have condemned me to death. And I have another thing to say to them: You think that I was convicted because I had no words of the sort which would have procured my acquittal—I mean, if I had thought fit to leave nothing undone or unsaid. Not so; the deficiency which led to my conviction was not of words—certainly not. But I had not the boldness or impudence or inclination to address you as you would have liked me to do, weeping and wailing and lamenting, and saying and doing many things which you have been accustomed to hear from others, and which, as I maintain, are unworthy of me. I thought at the time that I ought not to do anything common or mean when in danger: nor do I now repent of the style of my defense; I would rather die having spoken after my manner, than speak in your manner and live. For neither in war nor yet at law ought I or any man use every way of escaping death. Often in battle there can be no doubt that if a man will throw away his arms, and fall on his knees before his pursuers, he may escape death; and in other dangers there are other ways of escaping death, if a man is willing to say and do anything. The difficulty, my friends, is not to avoid death, but to avoid unrighteousness; for that runs faster than death. I am old and move slowly, and the slower runner has overtaken me, and my accusers are keen and quick, and the faster runner, who is unrighteousness, has overtaken them. And now I depart hence condemned by you to suffer the penalty of death,—they too go their ways condemned by the truth to suffer the penalty of villainy and wrong; and I must abide by my award—let them abide by theirs. I suppose that these things may be regarded as fated,—and I think that they are well.

And now, O men who have condemned me, I would fain prophesy to you; for I am about to die, and in the hour of death men are gifted with prophetic power. And I prophesy to you who are my murderers, that immediately after my departure punishment far heavier than you have inflicted on me will surely await you. Me you have killed because you wanted to escape the accuser, and not to give an account of your lives. But that will not be as you suppose: far otherwise. For I say that there will be more accusers of you than there are now; accusers whom hitherto I have restrained: and as they are younger they will be more inconsiderate with you, and you will be more offended at them. If you think that by killing men you can prevent some one from censuring your evil lives, you are mistaken; that is not a way of escape which is either possible or honorable; the easiest and the noblest way is not to be disabling others, but to be improving yourselves. This is the prophecy which I utter before my departure to the judges who have condemned me.

Friends, who would have acquitted me, I would like also to talk with you about the thing which has come to pass, while the magistrates are busy, and before I go to the place at which I must die. Stay then a little, for we may as well talk with one another while there is time. You are my friends, and I should like to show you the meaning of this event which has happened to me. O my judges—for you I may truly call judges—I should like to tell you of a wonderful circumstance. Hitherto the divine faculty of which the internal oracle is the source has constantly been in the habit of opposing me even about trifles, if I was going to make a slip or error in any matter; and now as you see there has come upon me that which may be thought, and is generally believed to be, the last and worst evil. But the oracle made no sign of opposition, either when I was leaving my house in the morning, or when I was on my way to the court, or while I was speaking, at anything which I was going to say; and yet I have often been stopped in the middle of a speech, but now in nothing I either said or did touching the matter in hand has the oracle opposed me. What do I take to be the explanation of this silence? I will tell you. It is an intimation that what has happened to me is a good, and that those of us who think that death is an evil are in error. For the customary sign would surely have opposed me had I been going to evil and not to good.

Let us reflect in another way, and we shall see that there is great reason to hope that death is a good; for one of two things—either death is a state of nothingness and utter unconsciousness, or, as men say, there is a change and migration of the soul from this world to another. Now, if you suppose that there is no consciousness, but a sleep like the sleep of him who is undisturbed even by dreams, death will be an unspeakable gain. For if a person were to select the night in which his sleep was undisturbed even by dreams, and were to compare with this the other days and nights of his life, and then were to tell us how many days and nights he had passed in the course of his life better and more pleasantly than this one, I think that any man, I will not say a private man, but even the great king will not find many such days or nights, when compared with the others. Now, if death be of such a nature, I say that to die is gain; for eternity is then only a single night. But if death is the journey to another place, and there, as men say, all the dead abide, what good, O my friends and judges, can be greater than this? If, indeed, when the pilgrim arrives in the world below, he is delivered from the professors of justice in this world, and finds the true judges who are said to give judgment there, Minos and Rhadamanthus and Aeacus and Triptolemus, and other sons of God who were righteous in their own life, that pilgrimage will be worth making. What would not a man give if he might converse with Orpheus and Musaeus and Hesiod and Homer? Nay, if this be true, let me die again and again. I myself, too, shall have a wonderful interest in there meeting and conversing with Palamedes, and Ajax the son of Telamon, and any other ancient hero who has suffered death through an unjust judgment; and there will be no small pleasure, as I think, in comparing my own sufferings with theirs. Above all, I shall then be able to continue my search into true and false knowledge; as in this world, so also in the next; and I shall find out who is wise, and who pretends to be wise, and is not. What would not a man give, O judges, to be able to examine the leader of the great Trojan expedition; or Odysseus or Sisyphus, or numberless others, men and women too! What infinite delight would there be in conversing with them and asking them questions! In another world they do not put a man to death for asking questions: assuredly not. For besides being happier than we are, they will be immortal, if what is said is true.

Wherefore, O judges, be of good cheer about death, and know of a certainty, that no evil can happen to a good man, either in life or after death. He and his are not neglected by the gods; nor has my own approaching end happened by mere chance. But I see clearly that the time had arrived when it was better for me to die and be released from trouble; wherefore the oracle gave no sign. For which reason, also, I am not angry with my condemners, or with my accusers; they have done me no harm, although they did not mean to do me any good; and for this I may gently blame them.

Still, I have a favor to ask of them. When my sons are grown up, I would ask you, O my friends, to punish them; and I would have you trouble them, as I have troubled you, if they seem to care about riches, or anything, more than about virtue; or if they pretend to be something when they are really nothing—then reprove them, as I have reproved you, for not caring about that for which they ought to care, and thinking that they are something when they are really nothing. And if you do this, both I and my sons will have received justice at your hands.

The hour of departure has arrived, and we go our ways—I to die, and you to live. Which is better God only knows.

Daniel Webster

:

SUMMATION IN THE TRIAL OF JOHN FRANCIS KNAPP FOR THE MURDER OF JOSEPH WHITE

Daniel Webster's skill and power as a trial lawyer are legendary, and his summation in the case against John Francis Knapp is one of his most celebrated. John Francis Knapp was charged with the murder of Captain Joseph White, a rich merchant of Salem, Massachusetts. White was 82 at the time of his death. One evening in April, 1830, shortly after he retired, Mr. White was struck with a blunt instrument and then stabbed to death.

The murder was committed by Richard Crowninshield, but it was committed at the instance of Joseph Knapp, Jr., whose mother-in-law, Mrs. Beckford, was the victim's niece and one of his principal heirs. Shortly before his death, White had drawn a will reducing the amount bequeathed to Mrs. Beckford. Joseph Jr. hoped, by killing White and destroying his will, to expedite and enlarge Mrs. Beckford's inheritance.

The people of the area were greatly excited and alarmed by the news of the crime. A Committee of Vigilance was formed to apprehend the murderer, and rewards were offered for his arrest and conviction. During the period of the investigation, Joseph Knapp, Sr., a respected shipmaster who knew nothing of his sons' part in the crime, received a letter addressed to "Joseph Knapp," but intended for Joseph Knapp, Jr. The letter, bearing the forged signature "Charles Grant," was sent from Belfast, Mass., by a man named Palmer. The letter requested a loan of $300, and threatened Knapp with ruin if the money was not advanced. Palmer was a friend of Richard Crowninshield, and had learned the particulars of the murder from him. After Joseph Knapp, Sr., received the letter, he showed it to his son Joseph Jr. who denied that it was intended for him. The shipmaster then turned the letter over to the Vigilance Committee.

Joseph Knapp, Jr., then mailed another letter to the Vigilance Committee signed with the name "Grant." In that letter, Joseph, Jr., hoping to divert suspicion, accused Steven White, one of the murder victim's nephews, of the crime. The letter sent by Joseph, Jr. was mailed at Salem, and it resulted in his indictment. It evidenced familiarity with circumstances of the crime that were not generally known. The signature "Grant" directed suspicion to the Knapps, for they were the only persons other than the Vigilance Committee and the sender of the first letter who knew of the first "Grant" letter.

Joseph Knapp, Jr., was arrested and confessed to his minister Coleman the roles that he and John Francis played in the crime. In his confession Joseph Jr. revealed the place where one of the murder weapons was concealed, and where it was later found. However, he retracted the confession before his trial. Richard Crowninshield was also arrested, and committed suicide by hanging himself from the bars of his cell.

John Francis Knapp was the first of the accused to be tried. He was defended by Franklin Dexter, a prominent Massachusetts lawyer. Daniel Webster was called in as special prosecutor.

One of the issues in the case was whether John Francis Knapp, who protested his innocence throughout and who concededly was not with the murderer at the time White was killed, could be charged with first degree murder as one who aided, abetted and participated in the crime. Webster contended that John Francis, by standing ready to assist the murderer, furnished all the aid that was needed, and that although physically in the street below, he was constructively present in the room when the crime was committed.

WEBSTER'S SUMMATION

I am little accustomed, gentlemen, to the part which I am now attempting to perform. Hardly more than once or twice has it happened to me to be concerned on the side of the government in any criminal prosecution whatever, and never, until the present occasion, in any case affecting life. But I very much regret that it should have been thought necessary to suggest to you that I am brought here to "hurry you against the law and beyond the evidence." I hope I have too much regard for justice, and too much respect for my own character, to attempt either; and were I to make such attempt, I am sure that in this court nothing can be carried against the law, and that gentlemen intelligent and just as you are, are not, by any power, to be hurried beyond the evidence. Though I could well have wished to shun this occasion, I have not felt at liberty to withhold my professional assistance, when it is supposed that I may be in some degree useful in investigating and discovering the truth respecting this most extraordinary murder. It has seemed to be a duty incumbent on me, as on every other citizen, to do my best and my utmost to bring to light the perpetrators of this crime. Against the prisoner at the bar, as an individual, I cannot have the slightest prejudice. I would not do him the smallest injury or injustice. But I do not affect to be indifferent to the discovery and the punishment of this deep guilt. I cheerfully share in the opprobrium, how great soever it may be, which is cast on those who feel and manifest an anxious concern that all who had a part in planning, or a hand in executing, this deed of midnight assassination, may be brought to answer for their enormous crime at the bar of public justice.

Gentlemen, it is a most extraordinary case. In some respects it has hardly a precedent anywhere; certainly none in our New England history. This bloody drama exhibited no suddenly excited, ungovernable rage. The actors in it were not surprised by any lion-like temptation springing upon their virtue, and overcoming it, before resistance could begin. Nor did they do the deed to glut savage vengeance, or satiate long-settled and deadly hate. It was a cool, calculating, money-making murder. It was all "hire and salary, not revenge." It was the weighing of money against life; the counting out of so many pieces of silver against so many ounces of blood.

An aged man, without an enemy in the world, in his own house, and in his own bed, is made the victim of a butcherly murder for mere pay. Truly, here is a new lesson for painters and poets. Whosoever shall hereafter draw the portrait of murder, if he will show it as it has been exhibited where such example was last to have been looked for,—in the very bosom of our New England society,—let him not give it the grim visage of Moloch, the brow knitted by revenge, the face black with settled hate, and the bloodshot eye emitting livid fires of malice. Let him draw, rather, a decorous, smooth-faced, bloodless demon; a picture in repose, rather than in action; not so much an example of human nature in its depravity, and in its paroxysms of crime, as an infernal being, a fiend, in the ordinary display and development of his character.

The deed was executed with a degree of self-possession and steadiness equal to the wickedness with which it was planned. The circumstances now clearly in evidence spread out the whole scene before us. Deep sleep had fallen on the destined victim, and on all beneath his roof. A healthful old man, to whom sleep was sweet, the first sound slumbers of the night held him in their soft but strong embrace. The assassin enters, through the window already prepared, into an unoccupied apartment. With noiseless foot he paces the lonely hall, half lighted by the moon. He winds up the ascent of the stairs, and reaches the door of the chamber. Of this he moves the lock, by soft and continued pressure, till it turns on its hinges without noise, and he enters, and beholds his victim before him. The room is uncommonly open to the admission of light. The face of the innocent sleeper is turned from the murderer, and the beams of the moon, resting on the gray locks of his aged temple, show him where to strike. The fatal blow is given, and the victim passes, without a struggle or a motion, from the repose of sleep to the repose of death! It is the assassin's purpose to make sure work; and he plies the dagger, though it is obvious that life has been destroyed by the blow of the bludgeon. He even raises the aged arm, that he may not fail in his aim at the heart, and replaces it again over the wounds of the poniard! To finish the picture, he explores the wrist for the pulse! He feels for it, and ascertains that it beats no longer! It is accomplished. The deed is done. He retreats, retraces his steps to the window, passes out through it as he came in, and escapes. He has done the murder. No eye has seen him; no ear has heard him. The secret is his own, and it is safe! Ah, gentlemen, that was a dreadful mistake! Such a secret can be safe nowhere. The whole creation of God has neither nook nor corner where the guilty can bestow it and say it is safe. Not to speak of the eye which pierces through all disguises, and beholds everything as in the splendor of noon, such secrets of guilt are never safe from detection, even by men. True it is, generally speaking, that "murder will out." True it is that Providence hath so ordained, and doth so govern things, that those who break the great law of Heaven by shedding man's blood seldom succeed in avoiding discovery. Especially in a case exciting so much attention as this, discovery must come, and will come, sooner or later. A thousand eyes turn at once to explore every man, every thing, every circumstance connected with the time and place; a thousand ears catch every whisper; a thousand excited minds intensely dwell on the scene, shedding all their light, and ready to kindle the slightest circumstance into a blaze of discovery. Meantime the guilty soul cannot keep its own secret. It is false to itself, or, rather, it feels an irresistible impulse of conscience to be true to itself. It labors under its guilty possession, and knows not what to do with it. The human heart was not made for the residence of such an inhabitant. It finds itself preyed on by a torment which it dares not acknowledge to God or man. A vulture is devouring it, and it can ask no sympathy or assistance, either from heaven or earth. The secret which the murderer possesses soon comes to possess him, and, like the evil spirits of which we read, it overcomes him, and leads him whither-soever it will. He feels it beating at his heart, rising to his throat, and demanding disclosure. He thinks the whole world sees it in his face, reads it in his eyes, and almost hears its workings in the very silence of his thoughts. It has become his master. It betrays his discretion, it breaks down his courage, it conquers his prudence. When suspicions from with-out begin to embarrass him, and the net of circumstance to entangle him, the fatal secret struggles with still greater violence to burst forth. It must be confessed, it will be confessed; there is no refuge from confession but suicide, and suicide is confession.

Much has been said, on this occasion, of the excitement which has existed and still exists, and of the extraordinary measures taken to dis-cover and punish the guilty. No doubt there has been, and is, much excitement, and strange, indeed, it would be had it been otherwise. Should not all the peaceable and well-disposed naturally feel concerned, and naturally exert themseves to bring to punishment the authors of this secret assassination? Was it a thing to be slept upon or forgotten? Did you, gentlemen, sleep quite as quietly in your beds after this murder as before? Was it not a case for rewards, for meetings, for committees, for the united efforts of all the good to find out a band of murderous con-spirators, of midnight ruffians, and to bring them to the bar of justice and law? If this be excitement, is it an unnatural or an improper excitement?

It seems to me, gentlemen, that there are appearances of another feeling, of a very different nature and character, not very extensive, I would hope, but still there is too much evidence of its existence. Such is human nature that some persons lose their abhorrence of crime in their admiration of its magnificent exhibitions. Ordinary vice is reprobated by them; but extraordinary guilt, exquisite wickedness, the high flights and poetry of crime seize on the imagination, and lead them to forget the depths of the guilt in admiration of the excellence of the performance, or the unequaled atrocity of the purpose. There are those in our day who have made great use of this infirmity of our nature, and by means of it done infinite injury to the cause of good morals. They have affected not only the taste, but I fear also the principles, of the young, the heedless, and the imaginative, by the exhibition of interesting and beautiful monsters. They render depravity attractive, sometimes by the polish of its manners, and sometimes by its very extravagance, and study to show off crime under all the advantages of cleverness and dexterity. Gentlemen, this is an extraordinary murder, but it is still a murder. We are not to lose ourselves in wonder at its origin, or in gazing on its cool and skillful execution. We are to detect and to punish it; and while we proceed with caution against the prisoner, and are to be sure that we do not visit on his head the offenses of others, we are yet to consider that we are dealing with a case of most atrocious crime, which has not the slightest circumstance about it to soften its enormity. It is murder; deliberate, concerted, malicious murder. Although the interest of this case may have diminished by the repeated investigation of the facts, still the additional labor which it imposes upon all concerned is not to be regretted if it should result in removing all doubts of the guilt of the prisoner.

The learned counsel for the prisoner has said truly that it is your individual duty to judge the prisoner; that it is your individual duty to determine his guilt or innocence; and that you are to weigh the testimony with candor and fairness. But much, at the same time, has been said, which, although it would seem to have no distinct bearing on the trial, cannot be passed over without some notice. A tone of complaint so peculiar has been indulged as would almost lead us to doubt whether the prisoner at the bar, or the managers of this prosecution, are now on trial. Great pains have been taken to complain of the manner of the prosecution. We hear of getting up a case; of setting in motion trains of machinery; of foul testimony; of combinations to overwhelm the prisoner; of private prosecutors; that the prisoner is hunted, persecuted, driven to his trial; that everybody is against him; and various other complaints, as if those who would bring to punishment the authors of this murder were almost as bad as they who committed it. In the course of my whole life, I have never heard before so much said about the particular counsel who happen to be employed; as if it were extraordinary that other counsel than the usual officers of the government should assist in the management of a case on the part of the government. In one of the last criminal trials in this county, that of Jackman for the "Goodridge robbery" (so called), I remember that the learned head of the Suffolk bar, Mr. Prescott, came down in aid of the officers of the government. This was regarded as neither strange nor improper. The counsel for the prisoner in that case contented themselves with answering his arguments, as far as they were able, instead of carping at his presence.

Complaint is made that rewards were offered in this case, and temptations held out, to obtain testimony. Are not rewards always offered when great and secret offenses are committed? Rewards were offered in the case to which I have alluded, and every other means taken to discover the offenders that ingenuity or the most persevering vigilance could suggest. The learned counsel have suffered their zeal to lead them into a strain of complaint at the manner in which the perpetrators of this crime were detected, almost indicating that they regard it as a positive injury to them to have found out their guilt. Since no man witnessed it, since they do not now confess it, attempts to discover it are half esteemed as officious intermeddling and impertinent inquiry. It is said that here even a committee of vigilance was appointed. This is a subject of reiterated remark. This committee are pointed at as though they had been officiously intermeddling with the administration of justice. They are said to have been "laboring for months" against the prisoner. Gentlemen, what must we do in such a case? Are people to be dumb and still, through fear of overdoing? Is it come to this: that an effort cannot be made, a hand cannot be lifted, to discover the guilty, without its being said there is a combination to overwhelm innocence? Has the community lost all moral sense? Certainly, a community that would not be roused to action upon an occasion such as this was—a community which should not deny sleep to their eyes, and slumber to their eyelids, till they had exhausted all the means of discovery and detection—must indeed be lost to all moral sense, and would scarcely deserve protection from the laws. The learned counsel have endeavored to persuade you that there exists a prejudice against the persons accused of this murder. They would have you understand that it is not confined to this vicinity alone, but that even the legislature have caught this spirit; that, through the procurement of the gentleman here styled "private prosecutor," who is a member of the senate, a special session of this court was appointed for the trial of these offenders; that the ordinary movements of the wheels of justice were too slow for the purposes devised. But does not everybody see and know that it was matter of absolute necessity to have a special session of the court? When or how could the prisoners have been tried without a special session? In the ordinary arrangement of the courts, but one week in a year is allotted for the whole court to sit in this county. In the trial of all capital offenses, a majority of the court, at least, is required to be present. In the trial of the present case alone, three weeks have already been taken up. Without such special session, then, three years would not have been sufficient for the purpose. It is answer sufficient to all complaints on this subject to say that the law was drawn by the late chief justice himself, to enable the court to accomplish its duties, and to afford the persons accused an opportunity for trial without delay.

Again, it is said that it was not thought of making Francis Knapp, the prisoner at the bar, a principal till after the death of Richard Crowninshield, Jr.; that the present indictment is an afterthought; that "testimony was got up" for the occasion. It is not so. There is no authority for this suggestion. The case of the Knapps had not then been before the grand jury. The officers of the government did not know what the testimony would be against them. They could not, therefore, have determined what course they should pursue. They intended to arraign all as principals who should appear to have been principals, and all as accessories who should appear to have been accessories. All this could be known only when the evidence should be produced.

But the learned counsel for the defendant take a somewhat loftier flight still. They are more concerned, they assure us, for the law itself, than even for their client. Your decision in this case, they say, will stand as a precedent. Gentlemen, we hope it will. We hope it will be a precedent both of candor and intelligence, of fairness and of firmness; a precedent of good sense and honest purpose pursuing their investigation discreetly, rejecting loose generalities, exploring all the circumstances, weighing each, in search of truth, and embracing and declaring the truth when found. It is said that "laws are made, not for the punishment of the guilty, but for the protection of the innocent." This is not quite accurate, perhaps, but, if so, we hope they will be so administered as to give that protection. But who are the innocent whom the law would protect? Gentlemen, Joseph White was innocent. They are innocent who, having lived in the fear of God through the day, wish to sleep in His peace through the night, in their own beds. The law is established that those who live quietly may sleep quietly; that they who do no harm may feel none. The gentleman can think of none that are innocent except the prisoner at the bar, not yet convicted. Is a proved conspirator to murder innocent? Are the Crowninshields and the Knapps innocent? What is innocence? How deep stained with blood, how reckless in crime, how deep in depravity may it be, and yet retain innocence? The law is made, if we would speak with entire accuracy, to protect the innocent by punishing the guilty. But there are those innocent out of a court, as well as in; innocent citizens not suspected of crime, as well as innocent prisoners at the bar.

The criminal law is not founded in a principle of vengeance. It does not punish that it may inflict suffering. The humanity of the law feels and regrets every pain it causes, every hour of restraint it imposes, and, more deeply still, every life it forfeits. But it uses evil as the means of preventing greater evil. It seeks to deter from crime by the example of punishment. This is its true, and only true, main object. It restrains the liberty of the few offenders, that the many who do not offend may enjoy their liberty. It takes the life of the murderer, that other murders may not be committed. The law might open the jails, and at once set free all persons accused of offenses, and it ought to do so if it could be made certain that no other offenses would hereafter be committed; because it punishes, not to satisfy any desire to inflict pain, but simply to prevent the repetition of crimes. When the guilty, therefore, are not punished, the law has so far failed of its purpose; the safety of the innocent is so far endangered. Every unpunished murder takes away something from the security of every man's life. Whenever a jury, through whimsical and ill-founded scruples, suffer the guilty to escape, they make themselves answerable for the augmented danger of the innocent.

We wish nothing to be strained against this defendant. Why, then, all this alarm? Why all this complaint against the manner in which the crime is discovered? The prisoner's counsel catch at supposed flaws of evidence, or bad character of witnesses, without meeting the case. Do they mean to deny the conspiracy? Do they mean to deny that the two Crowninshields and the two Knapps were conspirators? Why do they rail against Palmer, while they do not disprove, and hardly dispute, the truth of any one fact sworn to by him? Instead of this, it is made matter of sentimentality that Palmer has been prevailed upon to betray his bosom companions, and to violate the sanctity of friendship. Again I ask, why do they not meet the case? If the fact is out, why not meet it? Do they mean to deny that Captain White is dead? One would have almost supposed even that, from some remarks that have been made. Do they mean to deny the conspiracy? Or, admitting a conspiracy, do they mean to deny only that Frank Knapp, the prisoner at the bar, was abetting in the murder, being present, and so deny that he was a principal? If a conspiracy is proved, it bears closely upon every subsequent subject of inquiry. Why do they not come to the fact? Here the defense is wholly indistinct. The counsel neither take the ground nor abandon it. They neither fly nor light,—they hover. But they must come to a closer mode of contest. They must meet the facts, and either deny or admit them. Had the prisoner at the bar, then, a knowledge of this conspiracy or not? This is the question. Instead of laying out their strength in complaining of the manner in which the deed is discovered, of the extraordinary pains taken to bring the prisoner's guilt to light, would it not be better to show there was no guilt? Would it not be better to show his innocence? They say, and they complain, that the community feel a great desire that he should be punished for his crimes. Would it not be better to convince you that he has committed no crime?

Gentlemen, let us now come to the case. Your first inquiry on the evidence will be, was Captain White murdered in pursuance of a conspiracy, and was the defendant one of this conspiracy? If so, the second inquiry is, was he so connected with the murder itself as that he is liable to be convicted as a principal? The defendant is indicted as a principal. If not guilty as such, you cannot convict him. The indictment contains three distinct classes of counts. In the first, he is charged as having done the deed with his own hand; in the second, as an aider and abettor to Richard Crowninshield, Jr., who did the deed; in the third, as an aider and abettor to some person unknown. If you believe him guilty on either of these counts, or in either of these ways, you must convict him. It may be proper to say, as a preliminary remark, that there are two extraordinary circumstances attending this trial. One is that Richard Crowninshield, Jr., the supposed immediate perpetrator of the murder, since his arrest, has committed suicide. He has gone to answer before a tribunal of perfect infallibility. The other is that Joseph Knapp, the supposed originator and planner of the murder, having once made a full disclosure of the facts under a promise of indemnity, is, nevertheless, not now a witness. Notwithstanding his disclosure and his promise of indemnity, he now refuses to testify. He chooses to return to his original state, and now stands answerable himself when the time shall come for his trial. These circumstances it is fit you should remember in your investigation of the case. Your decision may affect more than the life of this defendant. If he be not convicted as principal, no one can be. Nor can any one be convicted of a participation in the crime as accessory. The Knapps and George Crowninshield will be again on the community. This shows the importance of the duty you have to perform, and serves to remind you of the care and wisdom necessary to be exercised in its performance. But certainly these considerations do not render the prisoner's guilt any clearer, nor enhance the weight of the evidence against him. No one desires you to regard consequences in that light. No one wishes anything to be strained or too far pressed against the prisoner. Still, it is fit you should see the full importance of the duty which devolves upon you.

And now, gentlemen, in examining this evidence, let us begin at the beginning, and see, first, what we know independent of the disputed testimony. This is a case of circumstantial evidence; and these circumstances, we think, are full and satisfactory. The case mainly depends upon them, and it is common that offenses of this kind must be proved in this way. Midnight assassins take no witnesses. The evidence of the facts relied on has been somewhat sneeringly denominated by the learned counsel "circumstantial stuff," but it is not such stuff as dreams are made of. Why does he not rend this stuff? Why does he not scatter it to the winds? He dismisses it a little too summarily. It shall be my business to examine this stuff, and try its cohesion.

It is necessary, gentlemen, to settle now, at the commencement, the great question of a conspiracy. If there was none, or the defendant was not a party, then there is no evidence here to convict him. If there was a conspiracy, and he is proved to have been a party, then these two facts have a strong bearing on others, and all the great points of inquiry. The defendant's counsel take no distinct ground, as I have already said, on this point, either to admit or to deny. They choose to confine themselves to a hypothetical mode of speech. They say, supposing there was a conspiracy, *non sequitur* that the prisoner is guilty as principal. Be it so. But still, if there was a conspiracy, and if he was a conspirator, and helped to plan the murder, this may shed much light on the evidence which goes to charge him with the execution of that plan. We mean to make out the conspiracy, and that the defendant was a party to it, and then to draw all just inferences from these facts. Let me ask your attention, then, in the first place, to those appearances, on the morning after the murder, which have a tendency to show that it was done in pursuance of a preconcerted plan of operation. What are they? A man was found murdered in his bed. No stranger had done the deed; no one unacquainted with the house had done it. It was apparent that somebody within had opened, and that somebody without had entered. There had obviously and certainly been concert and co-operation. The inmates of the house were not alarmed when the murder was perpetrated. The assassin had entered without any riot or any violence. He had found the way prepared before him. The house had been previously opened. The window was unbarred from within, and its fastening unscrewed. There was a lock on the door of the chamber in which Mr. White slept, but the key was gone. It had been taken away and secreted. The footsteps of the murderer were visible, out doors, tending towards the window. The plank by which he entered the window still remained. The road he pursued had been thus prepared for him. The victim was slain, and the murderer had escaped. Everything indicated that somebody within had co-operated with somebody without. Everything proclaimed that some of the inmates, or somebody having access to the house, had had a hand in the murder. On the face of the circumstances, it was apparent, therefore, that this was a premeditated, concerted murder; that there had been a conspiracy to commit it. Who, then, were the conspirators? If not now found out, we are still groping in the dark, and the whole tragedy is still a mystery. If the Knapps and the Crowninshields were not the conspirators in this murder, then there is a whole set of conspirators not yet discovered. . . . We know, from uncontroverted facts, that this murder was, and must have been, the result of concert and co-operation between two or more. We know it was not done without plan and deliberation. We see that whoever entered the house to strike the blow was favored and aided by some one who had been previously in the house, without suspicion, and who had prepared the way. This is concert; this is co-operation; this is conspiracy. If the Knapps and the Crowninshields, then, were not the conspirators, who were? Joseph Knapp had a motive to desire the death of Mr. White, and that motive has been shown. He was connected by marriage with the family of Mr. White. His wife was the daughter of Mrs. Beckford, who was the only child of a sister of the deceased. The deceased was more than eighty years old, and had no children. His only heirs were nephews and nieces. He was supposed to be possessed of a very large fortune . . . According to this idea, Mrs. Beckford, on Mr. White's death without a will, would have been entitled to one-half of his ample fortune, and Joseph Knapp had married one of her three children. There was a will, and this will gave the bulk of the property to others; and we learn from Palmer that one part of the design was to destroy the will before the murder was committed. There had been a previous will, and that previous will was known or believed to have been more favorable than the other to the Beckford family; so that, by destroying the last will, and destroying the life of the testator at the same time, either the first and more favorable will would be set up, or the deceased would have no will, which would be, as was supposed, still more favorable. But the conspirators not having succeeded in obtaining and destroying the last will, though they accomplished the murder, that will being found in existence and safe, and that will bequeathing the mass of the property to others, it seemed at the time impossible for Joseph Knapp, as for any one else, indeed, but the principal devisee, to have any motive which should lead to the murder. The key which unlocks the whole mystery is the knowledge of the intention of the conspirators to steal the will. This is derived from Palmer, and it explains all. It solves the whole marvel. It shows the motive which actuated those against whom there is much evidence, but who, without the knowledge of this intention, were not seen to have had a motive. This intention is proved, as I have said, by Palmer; and it is so congruous with all the rest of the case—it agrees so well with all facts and circumstances—that no man could well withhold his belief, though the facts were stated by a still less credible witness. If one desirous of opening a lock turns over and tries a bunch of keys till he finds one that will open it, he naturally supposes he has found the key of that lock. So, in explaining circumstances of evidence which are apparently irreconcilable or unaccountable, if a fact be suggested which at once accounts for all, and reconciles all, by whomsoever it may be stated, it is still difficult not to believe that such fact is the true fact belonging to the case. In this respect, Palmer's testimony is singularly confirmed. If it were false, his ingenuity could not furnish us such clear exposition of strange appearing circumstances. Some truth not before known can alone do that.

When we look back, then, to the state of things immediately on the discovery of the murder, we see that suspicion would naturally turn at once, not to the heirs at law, but to those principally benefited by the will. They, and they alone, would be supposed or seem to have a direct object for wishing Mr. White's life to be terminated. And, strange as it may seem, we find counsel now insisting that, if no apology, it is yet mitigation of the atrocity of the Knapps' conduct in attempting to charge this foul murder on Mr. White, the nephew and principal devisee, that public suspicion was already so directed! As if assassination of character were excusable in proportion as circumstances may render it easy! Their endeavors, when they knew they were suspected themselves, to fix the charge on others, by foul means and by falsehood, are fair and strong proof of their own guilt. But more of that hereafter.

. . . .

The acts of the parties themselves furnish strong presumption of their guilt. What was done on the receipt of the letter from Maine? This letter was signed by Charles Grant, Jr., a person not known to either of the Knapps, nor was it known to them that any other person besides the Crowninshields knew of the conspiracy. This letter, by the accidental omission of the word "Jr.," fell into the hands of the father, when intended for the son. The father carried it to Wenham, where both the sons were. They both read it. Fix your eye steadily on this part of the "circumstantial stuff" which is in the case, and see what can be made of it. This was shown to the two brothers on Saturday, the 15th of May. Neither of them knew Palmer, and, if they had known him, they could not have known him to have been the writer of this letter. It was mysterious to them how any one at Belfast could have had knowledge of this affair. Their conscious guilt prevented due circumspection. They did not see the bearing of its publication. They advised their father to carry it to the Committee of Vigilance, and it was so carried. On the Sunday following, Joseph began to think there might be something in it. Perhaps, in the meantime, he had seen one of the Crowninshields. He was apprehensive that they might be suspected. He was anxious to turn attention from their family. What course did he adopt to effect this? He addressed one letter, with a false name, to Mr. White, and another to the committee, and, to complete the climax of his folly, he signed the letter addressed to the committee "Grant," the same name as that which was signed to the letter received from Belfast. It was in the knowledge of the committee that no person but the Knapps had seen this letter from Belfast, and that no other person knew its signature. It therefore must have been irresistibly plain to them that one of the Knapps was the writer of the letter received by the committee, charging the murder on Mr. White. Add to this the fact of its having been dated at Lynn, and mailed at Salem four days after it was dated, and who could doubt respecting it? Have you ever read or known of folly equal to this? Can you conceive of crime more odious and abominable? Merely to explain the apparent mysteries of the letter from Palmer, they excite the basest suspicions against a man whom, if they were innocent, they had no reason to believe guilty, and whom, if they were guilty, they most certainly knew to be innocent. Could they have adopted a more direct method of exposing their own infamy? The letter to the committee has intrinsic marks of a knowledge of this transaction. It tells the time and the manner in which the murder was committed. Every line speaks the writer's condemnation. In attempting to divert attention from his family, and to charge the guilt upon another, he indelibly fixes it upon himself. Joseph Knapp requested Allen to put these letters into the post office, because, said he, "I wish to nip this silly affair in the bud." If this were not the order of an overruling Providence, I should say that it was the silliest piece of folly that was ever practiced. Mark the destiny of crime. It is ever obliged to resort to subterfuges; it trembles in the broad light; it betrays itself in seeking concealment. He alone walks safely who walks uprightly. Who for a moment can read these letters and doubt of Joseph Knapp's guilt? The constitution of nature is made to inform against him. There is no corner dark enough to conceal him. There is no turnpike road broad enough or smooth enough for a man so guilty to walk in without stumbling. Every step proclaims his secret to every passenger. His own acts come out to fix his guilt. In attempting to charge another with his own crime, he writes his own confession. To do away the effect of Palmer's letter, signed "Grant," he writes a letter himself, and affixes to it the name of Grant. He writes in a disguised hand. But how could it happen that the same Grant should be in Salem that was at Belfast? This has brought the whole thing out. Evidently he did it, because he has adopted the same style. Evidently he did it, because he speaks of the price of blood, and of other circumstances connected with the murder, that no one but a conspirator could have known.

.   .   .   .

The second and the material inquiry is, was the prisoner present at the murder, aiding and abetting therein? This leads to the legal question in the case. What does the law mean when it says that, in order to charge him as a principal, "he must be present, aiding and abetting in the murder?" In the language of the late chief justice: "It is not required that the abettor shall be actually upon the spot when the murder is committed, or even in sight of the more immediate perpetrator of the victim, to make him a principal. If he be at a distance, co-operating in the act, by watching to prevent relief, or to give an alarm, or to assist his confederate in escape, having knowledge of the purpose and object of the assassin, this, in the eye of the law, is being present, aiding and abetting, so as to make him a principal in the murder." "If he be at a distance, co-operating." This is not a distance to be measured by feet or rods. If the intent to lend aid combine with a knowledge that the murder is to be committed, and the person so intending be so situate that he can by any possibility lend this aid in any manner, then he is present in legal contemplation. He need not lend any actual aid,—to be ready to assist is assisting.

There are two sorts of murder. The distinction between them it is of essential importance to bear in mind: (1) Murder in an affray, or upon sudden and unexpected provocation; (2) murder secretly, with a deliberate, predetermined intention to commit the crime. Under the first class, the question usually is whether the offense be murder or manslaughter in the person who commits the deed. Under the second class, it is often a question whether others than he who actually did the deed were present, aiding and assisting therein. Offenses of this kind ordinarily happen when there is nobody present except those who go on the same design. If a riot should happen in the courthouse, and one should kill another, this may be murder, or it may not, according to the intention with which it was done, which is always matter of fact, to be collected from the circumstances at the time. But in secret murders, premeditated and determined on, there can be no doubt of the murderous intention. There can be no doubt, if a person be present, knowing a murder is to be done, of his concurring in the act. His being there is a proof of his intent to aid and abet, else why is he there? It has been contended that proof must be given that the person accused did actually afford aid,—did lend a hand in the murder itself,—and without this proof, although he may be near by, he may be presumed to be there for an innocent purpose; he may have crept silently there to hear the news, or from mere curiosity to see what was going on. Preposterous! Absurd! Such an idea shocks all common sense. A man is found to be a conspirator to commit a murder; he has planned it; he has assisted in arranging the time, the place, and the means; and he is found in the place, and at the time, and yet it is suggested that he might have been there, not for co-operation and concurrence, but from curiosity! Such an argument deserves no answer. It would be difficult to give it one in decorous terms. Is it not to be taken for granted that a man seeks to accomplish his own purposes? When he has planned a murder, and is present at its execution, is he there to forward or to thwart his own design? Is he there to assist, or there to prevent? But "curiosity"! He may be there from mere "curiosity"! Curiosity to witness the success of the execution of his own plan of murder! The very walls of a court house ought not to stand, the ploughshare should run through the ground it stands on, where such an argument could find toleration. It is not necessary that the abettor should actually lend a hand,—that he should take a part in the act itself. If he be present ready to assist, that is assisting. Some of the doctrines advanced would acquit the defendant, though he had gone to the bedchamber of the deceased, though he had been standing by when the assassin gave the blow. This is the argument we have heard to-day. No doubt the law is, that being ready to assist is assisting, if the party has the power to assist, in case of need. It is so stated by Foster, who is a high authority. "If A. happeneth to be present at a murder, for instance, and taketh no part in it, nor endeavoreth to prevent it, nor apprehendeth the murderer, nor levyeth hue and cry after him, this strange behavior of his, though highly criminal, will not of itself render him either principal or accessory." "But if a fact amounting to murder should be committed in prosecution of some unlawful purpose, though it were but a bare trespass, to which A., in the case last stated, had consented, and he had gone in order to give assistance, if need were, for carrying it into execution, this would have amounted to murder in him, and in every person present and joining with him." "If the fact was committed in prosecution of the original purpose, which was unlawful, the whole party will be involved in the guilt of him who gave the blow; for in combinations of this kind, the mortal stroke, though given by one of the party, is considered in the eye of the law, and of sound reason too, as given by every individual present and abetting. The person actually giving the stroke is no more than the hand or instrument by which the others strike." The author, in speaking of being present, means actual presence; not actual in opposition to constructive, for the law knows no such distinction. There is but one presence, and this is the situation from which aid, or supposed aid, may be rendered. The law does not say where the person is to go, or how near he is to go, but that he must be where he may give assistance, or where the perpetrator may believe that he may be assisted by him. Suppose that he is acquainted with the design of the murderer, and has a knowledge of the time when it is to be carried into effect, and goes out with a view to render assistance, if need be; why, then, even though the murderer does not know of this, the person so going out will be an abettor in the murder.

It is contended that the prisoner at the bar could not be a principal, he being in Brown street, because he could not there render assistance; and you are called upon to determine this case, according as you may be of opinion whether Brown street was or was not a suitable, convenient, well-chosen place to aid in this murder. This is not the true question. The inquiry is not whether you would have selected this place in preference to all others, or whether you would have selected it at all. If the parties chose it, why should we doubt about it? How do we know the use they intended to make of it, or the kind of aid that he was to afford by being there? The question for you to consider is, did the defendant go into Brown street in aid of this murder? Did he go there by agreement,—by appointment with the perpetrator? If so, everything else follows. The main thing—indeed the only thing—is to inquire whether he was in Brown street by appointment with Richard Crowninshield. It might be to keep general watch; to observe the lights, and advise as to time of access; to meet the murderer on his return, to advise him as to his escape; to examine his clothes, to see if any marks of blood were upon them; to furnish exchange of clothes, or new disguise, if necessary; to tell him through what streets he could safely retreat, or whether he could deposit the club in the place designed; or it might be without any distinct object, but merely to afford that encouragement which would proceed from Richard Crowninshield's consciousness that he was near. It is of no consequence whether, in your opinion, the place was well chosen, or not, to afford aid. If it was so chosen— if it was by appointment that he was there—it is enough. Suppose Richard Crowninshield, when applied to to commit the murder, had said: "I won't do it unless there can be some one near by to favor my escape. I won't go unless you will stay in Brown street." Upon the gentleman's argument, he would not be an aider and abettor in the murder, because the place was not well chosen, though it is apparent that the being in the place chosen was a condition without which the murder should never have happened.

You are to consider the defendant as one in the league, in the combination, to commit the murder. If he was there by appointment with the perpetrator, he is an abettor. The concurrence of the perpetrator in his being there is proved by the previous evidence of the conspiracy. If Richard Crowninshield, for any purpose whatsoever, made it a condition of the agreement that Frank Knapp should stand as backer, then Frank Knapp was an aider and abettor, no matter what the aid was, or what sort it was or degree, be it ever so little, even if it were to judge of the hour when it was best to go, or to see when the lights were extinguished, or to give an alarm if any one approached. Who better calculated to judge of these things than the murderer himself? And, if he so determined them, that is sufficient.

Now as to the facts. Frank Knapp knew that the murder was that night to be committed. He was one of the conspirators; he knew the object; he knew the time. . . . The hour was come, and he knew it. If so, and he was in Brown street without explaining why he was there, can the jury for a moment doubt whether he was there to countenance, aid, or support, or for curiosity alone, or to learn how the wages of sin and death were earned by the perpetrator? [Here Mr. Webster read the law from Hawkins,—1 Hawk. 204, lib. 1, c. 32, § 7.] The perpetrator would derive courage and strength and confidence from the knowledge that one of his associates was near by. If he was in Brown street, he could have been there for no other purpose. If there for this purpose, then he was, in the language of the law, present, aiding and abetting in the murder. His interest lay in being somewhere else. If he had nothing to do with the murder, no part to act, why not stay at home? Why should he jeopard his own life if it was not agreed that he should be there? He would not voluntarily go where the very place would cause him to swing if detected. He would not voluntarily assume the place of danger. His taking this place proves that he went to give aid. His staying away would have made an *alibi*. If he had nothing to do with the murder, he would be at home, where he could prove his *alibi*. He knew he was in danger, because he was guilty of the conspiracy, and, if he had nothing to do, would not expose himself to suspicion of detection. Did the prisoner at the bar countenance this murder? Did he concur, or did he nonconcur, in what the perpetrator was about to do? Would he have tried to shield him? Would he have furnished his cloak for protection? Would he have pointed out a safe way of retreat? As you would answer these questions, so you should answer the general question whether he was there consenting to the murder, or whether he was there as a spectator only.

One word more on this presence, called "constructive presence." What aid is to be rendered? Where is the line to be drawn between acting and omitting to act? Suppose he had been in the house, suppose he had followed the perpetrator to the chamber, what could he have done? This was to be a murder by stealth. It was to be a secret assassination. It was not their purpoose to have an open combat; they were to approach their victim unawares, and silently give the fatal blow. But if he had been in the chamber, no one can doubt that he would have been an abettor, because of his presence and ability to render services, if needed. What service could he have rendered if there? Could he have helped him to fly? Could he have aided the silence of his movements? Could he have facilitated his retreat on the first alarm? Surely this was a case where there was more of safety in going alone than with another; where company would only embarrass. Richard Crowninshield would prefer to go alone. He knew his errand too well. His nerves needed no collateral support. He was not the man to take with him a trembling companion. He would prefer to have his aid at a distance. He would not wish to be incumbered by his presence. He would prefer to have him out of the house. He would prefer that he should be in Brown street. But whether in the chamber, in the house, in the garden, or in the street, whatsoever is aiding in actual presence is aiding in constructive presence; anything that is aid in one case is aid in the other. If, then, the aid be anywhere, so as to embolden the perpetrator, to afford him hope or confidence in his enterprise, it is the same as though the person stood at his elbow with his sword drawn. His being there ready to act, with the power to act, is what makes him an abettor. . . . The prisoner has attempted to prove an *alibi* in two ways: In the first place, by four young men with whom he says he was in company, on the evening of the murder, from seven o'clock till near ten o'clock. This depends upon the certainty of the night. In the second place, by his family, from ten o'clock afterwards. This depends upon the certainty of the time of the night. These two classes of proof have no connection with each other. One may be true, and the other false; or they may both be true, or both be false. I shall examine this testimony with some attention, because, on a former trial, it made more impression on the minds of the court than on my own mind. I think, when carefully sifted and compared, it will be found to have in it more of plausibility than reality.

Mr. Page testifies that, on the evening of the 6th of April, he was in company with Burchmore, Balch, and Forrester, and that he met the defendant about seven o'clock, near the Salem Hotel; that he afterwards met him at Remond's, about nine o'clock, and that he was in company with him a considerable part of the evening. This young gentleman is a member of college, and says that he came to town the Saturday evening previous; that he is now able to say that it was the night of the murder when he walked with Frank Knapp, from the recollection of the fact that he called himself to an account, on the morning after the murder, as it is natural for men to do when an extraordinary occurrence happens. Gentlemen, this kind of evidence is not satisfactory; general impressions as to time are not to be relied on. If I were called on to state the particular day on which any witness testified in this cause, I could not do it. Every man will notice the same thing in his own mind. There is no one of these young men that could give an account of himself for any other day in the month of April. They are made to remember the fact, and then they think they remember the time. The witness has no means of knowing it was Tuesday, rather than any other time. He did not know it at first; he could not know it afterwards. He says he called himself to an account. This has no more to do with the murder than with the man in the moon. Such testimony is not worthy to be relied on in any forty-shilling cause. What occasion had he to call himself to an account? Did he suppose that he should be suspected? Had he any intimation of this conspiracy?

Suppose, gentlemen, you were either of you asked where you were, or what you were doing, on the fifteenth day of June. You could not answer this question without calling to mind some events to make it certain. Just as well may you remember on what you dined each day of the year past. Time is identical. Its subdivisions are all alike. No man knows one day from another, or one hour from another, but by some fact connected with it. Days and hours are not visible to the senses, nor to be apprehended and distinguished by the understanding. The flow of time is known only by something which marks it; and he who speaks of the date of occurrences with nothing to guide his recollection speaks at random, and is not to be relied on. . . .

Now, what does the testimony of these four young men amount to? The only circumstance by which they approximate to an identifying of the night is that three of them say it was cloudy. They think their walk was either on Monday or Tuesday evening, and it is admitted that Monday evening was clear, whence they draw the inference that it must have been Tuesday. But, fortunately, there is one fact disclosed in their testimony that settles the question. Balch says that on the evening, whenever it was, he saw the prisoner. The prisoner told him he was going out of town on horseback for a distance of about twenty minutes' drive, and that he was going to get a horse at Osborn's. This was about seven o'clock. At about nine, Balch says he saw the prisoner again, and was then told by him that he had had his ride, and had returned. Now, it appears by Osborn's books that the prisoner had a saddle horse from his stable, not on Tuesday evening, the night of the murder, but on the Saturday evening previous. This fixes the time about which these young men testify, and is a complete answer and refutation of the attempted *alibi* on Tuesday evening.

I come now to speak of the testimony adduced by the defendant to explain where he was after ten o'clock on the night of the murder. This comes chiefly from members of the family,—from his father and brothers.

.　.　.　.　.　.　.　.　.　.　.　.　.

I come to the testimony of the father. I find myself incapable of speaking of him or his testimony with severity. Unfortunate old man! Another Lear, in the conduct of his children; another Lear, I apprehend, in the effect of his distress upon his mind and understanding. He is brought here to testify, under circumstances that disarm severity, and call loudly for sympathy. Though it is impossible not to see that his story cannot be credited, yet I am unable to speak of him otherwise than in sorrow and grief. Unhappy father! he strives to remember, perhaps persuades himself that he does remember, that on the evening of the murder he was himself at home at ten o'clock. He thinks, or seems to think, that his son came in at about five minutes past ten. He fancies that he remembers his conversation; he thinks he spoke of bolting the door; he thinks he asked the time of night; he seems to remember his then going to his bed. Alas! these are but the swimming fancies of an agitated and distressed mind. Alas! they are but the dreams of hope, its uncertain lights, flickering on the thick darkness of parental distress. Alas! the miserable father knows nothing, in reality, of all these things. . . .

But, gentlemen, let us now consider what is the evidence produced on the part of the government to prove that John Francis Knapp, the prisoner at the bar, was in Brown street on the night of the murder. This is a point of vital importance in this cause. Unless this be made out, beyond reasonable doubt, the law of presence does not apply to the case. The government undertakes to prove that he was present, aiding in the murder, by proving that he was in Brown street for this purpose. Now, what are the undoubted facts? They are that two persons were seen in that street, several times during that evening, under suspicious circumstances,—under such circumstances as induced those who saw them to watch their movements. Of this there can be no doubt. Mirick saw a man standing at the post opposite his store from fifteen minutes before nine until twenty minutes after, dressed in a full frock-coat, glazed cap, and so forth, in size and general appearance answering to the prisoner at the bar. This person was waiting there, and, whenever any one approached him, he moved to and from the corner, as though he would avoid being suspected or recognized. Afterwards, two persons were seen by Webster walking in Howard street with a slow, deliberate movement that attracted his attention. This was about half-past nine. One of these he took to be the prisoner at the bar; the other he did not know. About half-past ten a person is seen sitting on the rope-walk steps, wrapped in a cloak. He drops his head when passed, to avoid being known. Shortly after, two persons are seen to meet in this street, without ceremony or salutation, and in a hurried manner to converse for a short time, then to separate, and run off with great speed. Now, on this same night, a gentleman is slain,—murdered in his bed,—his house being entered by stealth from without, and his house situated within three hundred feet of this street. The windows of his chamber were in plain sight from this street. A weapon of death is afterwards found in a place where these persons were seen to pass, in a retired place, around which they had been seen lingering. It is now known that this murder was committed by four persons, conspiring together for this purpose. No account is given who these suspected persons thus seen in Brown street and its neighborhood were. Now I ask, gentlemen, whether you or any man can doubt that this murder was committed by the persons who were thus in and about Brown street. Can any person doubt that they were there for purposes connected with this murder? If not for this purpose, what were they there for? When there is a cause so near at hand, why wander into conjecture for an explanation? Common sense requires you to take the nearest adequate cause for a known effect. Who were these suspicious persons in Brown street? There was something extraordinary about them; something noticeable, and noticed at the time; something in their appearance that aroused suspicion. And a man is found the next morning murdered in the near vicinity. Now, so long as no other account shall be given of those suspicious persons, so long the inference must remain irresistible that they were the murderers. Let it be remembered that it is already shown that this murder was the result of conspiracy and of concert; let it be remembered that the house, having been opened from within, was entered by stealth from without; let it be remembered that Brown street, where these persons were repeatedly seen under such suspicious circumstances, was a place from which every occupied room in Mr. White's house is clearly seen; let it be remembered that the place, though thus very near to Mr. White's house, is a retired and lonely place; and let it be remembered that the instrument of death was afterwards found concealed very near the same spot. Must not every man come to the conclusion that these persons thus seen in Brown street were the murderers? Every man's own judgment, I think, must satisfy him that this must be so. It is a plain deduction of common sense. It is a point on which each one of you may reason like a Hale or a Mansfield. The two occurrences explain each other. The murder shows why these persons were thus lurking, at that hour, in Brown street, and their lurking in Brown street shows who committed the murder. If, then, the persons in and about Brown street were the plotters and executors of the murder of Captain White, we know who they were, and you know that there is one of them. This fearful concatenation of circumstances puts him to an account. He was a conspirator. He had entered into this plan of murder. The murder is committed, and he is known to have been within three minutes' walk of the place. He must account for himself. He has attempted this, and failed. Then, with all these general reasons to show he was actually in Brown street, and his failures in his *alibi,* let us seem what is the direct proof of his being there. . . .

Now as to the proof of his identity with one of the persons seen in Brown street. Mr. Mirick, a cautious witness, examined the person he saw closely, in a light night, and says that he thinks the prisoner at the bar is the person, and that he should not hesitate at all if he were seen in the same dress. His opinion is formed partly from his own observation, and partly from the description of others; but this description turns out to be only in regard to the dress. It is said that he is now more confident than on the former trial. If he has varied in his testimony, make such allowance as you may think proper. I do not perceive any material variance. He thought him the same person when he was first brought to court, and as he saw him get out of the chaise. This is one of the cases in which a witness is permitted to give an opinion. This witness is as honest as yourselves,—neither willing nor swift; but he says he believes it was the man. His words are, "This is my opinion," and this opinion it is proper for him to give. If partly founded on what he has heard, then this opinion is not to be taken; but if on what he saw, then you can have no better evidence. I lay no stress on similarity of dress. No man will ever lose his life by my voice on such evidence. But then it is proper to notice that no inferences drawn from any dissimilarity of dress can be given in the prisoner's favor, because, in fact, the person seen by Mirick was dressed like the prisoner. The description of the person seen by Mirick answers to that of the prisoner at the bar. In regard to the supposed discrepancy of statements, before and now, there would be no end to such minute inquiries. It would not be strange if witnesses should vary. I do not think much of slight shades of variation. If I believe the witness is honest, that is enough. If he has expressed himself more strongly now than then, this does not prove him false. . . . Mr. Southwick swears all that a man can swear. He has the best means of judging that could be had at the time. He tells you that he left his father's house at half-past ten o'clock, and, as he passed to his own house in Brown street, he saw a man sitting on the steps of the ropewalk; that he passed him three times, and each time he held down his head, so that he did not see his face; that the man had on a cloak, which was not wrapped around him, and a glazed cap; that he took the man to be Frank Knapp at the time; that, when he went into his house, he told his wife that he thought it was Frank Knapp; that he knew him well, having known him from a boy. And his wife swears that he did so tell her when he came home. What could mislead this witness at the time? He was not then suspecting Frank Knapp of anything. He could not then be influenced by any prejudice. If you believe that the witness saw Frank Knapp in this position at this time, it proves the case. Whether you believe it or not depends upon the credit of the witness. He swears it. If true, it is solid evidence. Mrs. Southwick supports her husband. Are they true? Are they worthy of belief? If he deserves the epithets applied to him, then he ought not to be believed. In this fact they cannot be mistaken; they are right, or they are perjured. As to his not speaking to Frank Knapp, that depends upon their intimacy. But a very good reason is, Frank chose to disguise himself. This makes nothing against his credit. . . .

I think you will be of opinion that Brown street was a probable place for the conspirators to assemble, and for an aid to be stationed. If we knew their whole plan, and if we were skilled to judge in such a case, then we could perhaps determine on this point better. But it is a retired place, and still commands a full view of the house; a lonely place, but still a place of observation; not so lonely that a person woud excite suspicion to be seen walking there in an ordinary manner; not so public as to be noticed by many. It is near enough to the scene of action in point of law. It was their point of centrality. The club was found near the spot, in a place provided for it, in a place that had been previously hunted out, in a concerted place of concealment. Here was their point of rendezvous; here might the lights be seen; here might an aid be secreted; here was he within call; here might he be aroused by the sound of the whistle; here might he carry the weapon; here might he receive the murderer after the murder.

Then, gentlemen, the general question occurs, is it satisfactorily proved, by all these facts and circumstances, that the defendant was in and about Brown street on the night of the murder? Considering that the murder was effected by a conspiracy; considering that he was one of the four conspirators; considering that two of the conspirators have accounted for themselves on the night of the murder, and were not in Brown street; considering that the prisoner does not account for himself, nor show where he was; considering that Richard Crowninshield, the other conspirator and the perpetrator, is not accounted for, nor shown to be elsewhere; considering that it is now past all doubt that two persons were seen lurking in and about Brown street at different times, avoiding observation, and exciting so much suspicion that the neighbors actually watched them; considering that, if these persons thus lurking in Brown street at that hour were not the murderers, it remains to this day wholly unknown who they were or what their business was; considering the testimony of Miss Jaqueth, and that the club was afterwards found near this place; considering, finally, that Webster and Southwick saw these persons, and then took one of them for the defendant, and that Southwick then told his wife so, . . .

By the counsel for the prisoner, much stress has been laid upon the question whether Brown street was a place in which aid could be given, —a place in which actual assistance could be rendered in this transaction. This must be mainly decided by their own opinion who selected the place; by what they thought at the time, according to their plan of operation. If it was agreed that the prisoner should be there to assist, it is enough. If they thought the place proper for their purpose, according to their plan, it is sufficient. Suppose we could prove expressly that they agreed that Frank should be there, and he was there, and you should think it not a well-chosen place for aiding and abetting, must he be acquitted? No! It is not what I think or you think of the appropriateness of the place; it is what they thought at the time. If the prisoner was in Brown street by appointment and agreement with the perpetrator, for the purpose of giving assistance if assistance should be needed, it may safely be presumed that the place was suited to such assistance as it was supposed by the parties might chance to become requisite. If in Brown street, was he there by appointment? Was he there to aid, if aid were necessary? Was he there for or against the murderer? to concur, or to oppose? to favor, or to thwart? Did the perpetrator know he was there,—there waiting? If so, then it follows that he was there by appointment. He was at the post half an hour. He was waiting for somebody. This proves appointment, arrangement, previous agreement; then it follows that he was there to aid, to encourage, to embolden the perpetrator, and that is enough. If he were in such a situation as to afford aid, or that he was relied upon for aid, then he was aiding and abetting. It is enough that the conspirator desired to have him there. Besides, it may be well said that he could afford just as much aid there as if he had been in Essex street,—as if he had been standing even at the gate or at the window. It was not an act of power against power that was to be done; it was a secret act, to be done by stealth. The aid was to be placed in a position secure from observation. It was important to the security of both that he should be in a lonely place. Now, it is obvious that there are many purposes for which he might be in Brown street: (1) Richard Crowninshield might have been secreted in the garden, and waiting for a signal; (2) or he might be in Brown street to advise him as to the time of making his entry into the house; (3) or to favor his escape; (4) or to see if the street was clear when he came out; (5) or to conceal the weapon or the clothes; (6) to be ready for any unforeseen contingency. Richard Crowninshield lived in Danvers. He would retire by the most secret way. Brown street is that way. If you find him there, can you doubt why he was there? If, gentlemen, the prisoner went into Brown street, by appointment with the perpetrator, to render aid or encouragement in any of these ways, he was present, in legal contemplation, aiding and abetting in this murder. It is not necessary that he should have done anything; it is enough that he was ready to act, and in a place to act. If his being in Brown street, by appointment, at the time of the murder, emboldened the purpose and encouraged the heart of the murderer by the hope of instant aid if aid should become necessary, then, without doubt, he was present, aiding and abetting, and was a principal in the murder.

I now proceed, gentlemen, to the consideration of the testimony of Mr. Colman. Although this evidence bears on every material part of the cause, I have purposely avoided every comment on it till the present moment, when I have done with the other evidence in the case. As to the admission of this evidence, there has been a great struggle, and its importance demanded it. The general rule of law is that confessions are to be received as evidence. They are entitled to great or to little consideration, according to the circumstances under which they are made. Voluntary, deliberate confessions are the most important and satisfactory evidence; but confessions hastily made, or improperly obtained, are entitled to little or no consideration. It is always to be inquired whether they were purely voluntary, or were made under any undue influence of hope or fear; for, in general, if any influence were exerted on the mind of the person confessing, such confessions are not to be submitted to a jury. Who is Mr. Colman? He is an intelligent, accurate, and cautious witness; a gentleman of high and well-known character, and of unquestionable veracity; as a clergyman, highly respectable; as a man, of fair name and fame. Why was Mr. Colman with the prisoner? Joseph J. Knapp was his parishioner; he was the head of a family, and had been married by Mr. Colman. The interests of that family were dear to him. He felt for their afflictions, and was anxious to alleviate their sufferings. He went from the purest and best of motives to visit Joseph Knapp. He came to save, not to destroy; to rescue, not to take away life. In this family he thought there might be a chance to save one. It is a misconstruction of Mr. Colman's motives, at once the most strange and the most uncharitable,—a perversion of all just views of his conduct and intentions the most unaccountable,—to represent him as acting, on this occasion, in hostility to any one, or as desirous of injuring or endangering any one. He has stated his own motives and his own conduct in a manner to command universal belief and universal respect. For intelligence, for consistency, for accuracy, for caution, for candor, never did witness acquit himself better, or stand fairer. In all that he did as a man, and all he has said as a witness, he has shown himself worthy of entire regard.

Now, gentlemen, very important confessions made by the prisoner are sworn to by Mr. Colman. They were made in the prisoner's cell, where Mr. Colman had gone with the prisoner's brother, N. Phippen Knapp. Whatever conversation took place was in the presence of N. P. Knapp. Now, on the part of the prisoner, two things are asserted: First, that such inducements were suggested to the prisoner, in this interview, that no confessions made by him ought to be received; second, that, in point of fact, he made no such confessions as Mr. Colman testifies to, nor, indeed, any confessions at all. These two propositions are attempted to be supported by the testimony of N. P. Knapp. These two witnesses, Mr. Colman and N. P. Knapp, differ entirely. There is no possibility of reconciling them. No charity can cover both. One or the other has sworn falsely. If N. P. Knapp be believed, Mr. Colman's testimony must be wholly disregarded. It is, then, a question of credit,—a question of belief between the two witnesses. As you decide between these, so you will decide on all this part of the case. Mr. Colman has given you a plain narrative, a consistent account, and has uniformly stated the same things. He is not contradicted, except by the testimony of Phippen Knapp. He is influenced, as far as we can see, by no bias or prejudice, any more than other men, except so far as his character is now at stake. He has feelings on this point, doubtless, and ought to have. If what he has stated be not true, I cannot see any ground for his escape. If he be a true man, he must have heard what he testifies. No treachery of memory brings to memory things that never took place. There is no reconciling his evidence with good intention if the facts in it are not as he states them. He is on trial as to his veracity. The relation in which the other witness stands deserves your careful consideration. He is a member of the family. He has the lives of two brothers depending, as he may think, on the effect of his evidence; depending on every word he speaks. I hope he has not another responsibility resting upon him. By the advice of a friend, and that friend Mr. Colman, J. Knapp made a full and free confession, and obtained a promise of pardon. He has since, as you know, probably by the advice of other friends, retracted that confession, and rejected the offered pardon. Events will show who of these friends and advisers advised him best and befriended him most. In the meantime, if this brother, the witness, be one of these advisers, and advised the retraction, he has, most emphatically, the lives of his brothers resting upon his evidence and upon his conduct. Compare the situation of these two witnesses. Do you not see mighty motive enough on the one side, and want of all motive on the other? I would gladly find an apology for that witness in his agonized feelings, in his distressed situation; in the agitation of that hour, or of this. I would gladly impute it to error, or to want of recollection, to confusion of mind, or disturbance of feeling. I would gladly impute to any pardonable source that which cannot be reconciled to facts and to truth; but, even in a case calling for so much sympathy, justice must yet prevail, and we must come to the conclusion, however reluctantly, which that demands from us. It is said Phippen Knapp was probably correct, because he knew he should probably be called as a witness. Witness to what? When he says there was no confession, what could he expect to bear witness of? But I do not put it on the ground that he did not hear. I am compelled to put it on the other ground, that he did hear, and does not now truly tell what he heard. If Mr. Colman were out of the case, there are other reasons why the story of Phippen Knapp should not be believed. It has in it inherent improbabilities. It is unnatural, and inconsistent with the accompanying circumstances. He tells you that they went "to the cell of Frank, to see if he had any objection to taking a trial, and suffering his brother to accept the offer of pardon,"—in other words, to obtain Frank's consent to Joseph's making a confession,—and, in case this consent was not obtained, that the pardon would be offered to Frank. Did they bandy about the chance of life, between these two, in this way? Did Mr. Colman, after having given this pledge to Joseph, and after having received a disclosure from Joseph, go to the cell of Frank for such a purpose as this? It is impossible; it cannot be so. Again, we know that Mr. Colman found the club the next day; that he went directly to the place of deposit, and found it at the first attempt, exactly where he says he had been informed it was. Now, Phippen Knapp says that Frank had stated nothing respecting the club; that it was not mentioned in that conversation. He says, also, that he was present in the cell of Joseph all the time that Mr. Colman was there; that he believes he heard all that was said in Joseph's cell; and that he did not himself know where the club was, and never had known where it was, until he heard it stated in court. Now, it is certain that Mr. Colman says he did not learn the particular place of deposit of the club from Joseph; that he only learned from him that it was deposited under the steps of the Howard street meeting house, without defining the particular steps. It is certain, also, that he had more knowledge of the position of the club than this; else how could he have placed his hand on it so readily? and where else could he have obtained this knowledge, except from Frank? . . .

. . . Is not Mr. Colman's testimony credible, natural, and proper? To judge of this, you must go back to that scene. The murder had been committed. The two Knapps were now arrested. Four persons were already in jail supposed to be concerned in it, . . . It was important to learn the facts. To do this, some one of those suspected must be admitted to turn state's witness. The contest was, who should have this privilege? It was understood that it was about to be offered to Palmer, then in Maine. There was no good reason why he should have the preference. Mr. Colman felt interested for the family of the Knapps, and particularly for Joseph. He was a young man who had hitherto maintained a fair standing in society. He was a husband. Mr. Colman was particularly intimate with his family. With these views he went to the prison. He believed that he might safely converse with the prisoner, because he thought confessions made to a clergyman were sacred, and that he could not be called upon to disclose them. He went, the first time, in the morning, and was requested to come again. He went again at three o'clock, and was requested to call again at five o'clock. In the meantime he saw the father and Phippen, and they wished he would not go again, because it would be said the prisoners were making confession. He said he had engaged to go again at five o'clock, but would not, if Phippen would excuse him to Joseph. Phippen engaged to do this, and to meet him at his office at five o'clock. Mr. Colman went to the office at the time, and waited; but, as Phippen was not there, he walked down street, and saw him coming from the jail. He met him, and while in conversation near the church, he saw Mrs. Beckford and Mrs. Knapp going in a chaise towards the jail. He hastened to meet them, as he thought it not proper for them to go in at that time. While conversing with them near the jail, he received two distinct messages from Joseph that he wished to see him. He thought it proper to go, and, accordingly, went to Joseph's cell, and it was while there that the disclosures were made. Before Joseph had finished his statement, Phippen came to the door. He was soon after admitted. A short interval ensued, and they went together to the cell of Frank. Mr. Colman went in by invitation of Phippen. He had come directly from the cell of Joseph, where he had for the first time learned the incidents of the tragedy. He was incredulous as to some of the facts which he had learned, they were so different from his previous impressions. He was desirous of knowing whether he could place confidence in what Joseph had told him. He therefore put the questions to Frank as he has testified before you, in answer to which Frank Knapp informed him: (1) That the murder took place between ten and eleven o'clock; (2) that Richard Crowninshield was alone in the house; (3) that he, Frank Knapp, went home afterwards; (4) that the club was deposited under the steps of the Howard street meeting house, and under the part nearest the burying ground, in a rat hole; (5) that the dagger or daggers had been worked up at the factory. It is said that these five answers just fit the case; that they are just what was wanted, and neither more nor less. True, they are; but the reason is because truth always fits. Truth is always congruous, and agrees with itself. Every truth in the universe agrees with every other truth in the universe; whereas falsehoods not only disagree with truths, but usually quarrel among themselves. Surely Mr. Colman is influenced by no bias, no prejudice. He has no feelings to warp him, except, now that he is contradicted, he may feel an interest to be believed. If you believe Mr. Colman, then the evidence is fairly in the case.

I shall now proceed on the ground that you do believe Mr. Colman. When told that Joseph had determined to confess, the defendant said: "It is hard or unfair that Joseph should have the benefit of confessing, since the thing was done for his benefit." What thing was done for his benefit? Does not this carry an implication of the guilt of the defendant? Does it not show that he had a knowledge of the object and history of the murder? The defendant said: "I told Joseph, when he proposed it, that it was a silly business, and would get us into trouble." He knew, then, what this business was. He knew that Joseph proposed it, and that he agreed to it, else he could not get us into trouble. He understood its bearing and its consequences. Thus much was said, under circumstances that make it clearly evidence against him, before there is any pretense of an inducement held out. And does not this prove him to have had a knowledge of the conspiracy? He knew the daggers had been destroyed, and he knew who committed the murder. How could he have innocently known these facts? Why, if by Richard's story, this shows him guilty of a knowledge of the murder and of the conspiracy. More than all, he knew when the deed was done, and that he went home afterwards. This shows his participation in that deed. "Went home afterwards!" Home from what scene? home from what fact? home from what transaction? home from what place? This confirms the supposition that the prisoner was in Brown street for the purposes ascribed to him. These questions were directly put, and directly answered. He does not intimate that he received the information from another. Now, if he knows the time, and went home afterwards, and does not excuse himself, is not this an admission that he had a hand in this murder? Already proved to be a conspirator in the murder, he now confesses that he knew who did it, at what time it was done, that he was himself out of his own house at the time, and went home afterwards. Is not this conclusive, if not explained? Then comes the club. He told where it was. This is like possession of stolen goods. He is charged with the guilty knowledge of this concealment. He must show, not say, how he came by this knowledge. If a man be found with stolen goods, he must prove how he came by them. The place of deposit of the club was premeditated and selected, and he knew where it was.

Joseph Knapp was an accessory, and an accessory only; he knew only what was told him. But the prisoner knew the particular spot in which the club might be found. This shows his knowledge something more than that of an accessory. This presumption must be rebutted by evidence, or it stands strong against him. He has too much knowledge of this transaction to have come innocently by it. It must stand against him until he explains it.

This testimony of Mr. Colman is represented as new matter, and therefore an attempt has been made to excite a prejudice against it. It is not so. How little is there in it, after all, that did not appear from other sources? It is mainly confirmatory. Compare what you learn from this confession with what you before knew: As to its being proposed by Joseph, was not that known? As to Richard's being alone in the house, was not that known? As to the daggers, was not that known? As to the time of the murder, was not that known? As to his being out that night, was not that known? As to his returning afterwards, was not that known? As to the club, was not that known? So this information concerns what was known before, and fully confirms it.

. . . .

Gentlemen, I have gone through with the evidence in this case, and have endeavored to state it plainly and fairly before you. I think there are conclusions to be drawn from it, the accuracy of which you cannot doubt. I think you cannot doubt that there was a conspiracy formed for the purpose of committing this murder, and who the conspirators were; that you cannot doubt that the Crowninshields and the Knapps were the parties in this conspiracy; that you cannot doubt that the prisoner at the bar knew that the murder was to be done on the night of the 6th of April; that you cannot doubt that the murderers of Captain White were the suspicious persons seen in and about Brown street on that night; that you cannot doubt that Richard Crowninshield was the perpetrator of that crime; that you cannot doubt that the prisoner at the bar was in Brown street on that night. If there, then it must be by agreement, to countenance, to aid, the perpetrator, and, if so, then he is guilty as principal.

Gentlemen, your whole concern should be to do your duty, and leave consequences to take care of themselves. You will receive the law from the court. Your verdict, it is true, may endanger the prisoner's life, but then it is to save other lives. If the prisoner's guilt has been shown and proved beyond all reasonable doubt, you will convict him. If such reasonable doubts of guilt still remain, you will acquit him. You are the judges of the whole case. You owe a duty to the public, as well as to the prisoner at the bar. You cannot presume to be wiser than the law. Your duty is a plain, straightforward one. Doubtless we would all judge him in mercy. Towards him, as an individual, the law inculcates no hostility; but towards him, if proved to be a murderer, the law, and the oaths you have taken, and public justice demand that you do your duty. With consciences satisfied with the discharge of duty, no consequences can harm you. There is no evil that we cannot either face or fly from but the consciousness of duty disregarded. A sense of duty pursues us ever. It is omnipresent, like the Deity. If we take to ourselves the wings of the morning, and dwell in the uttermost parts of the sea, duty performed or duty violated is still with us, for our happiness or our misery. If we say the darkness shall cover us, in the darkness, as in the light, our obligations are yet with us. We cannot escape their power, nor fly from their presence. They are with us in this life, will be with us at its close; and in that scene of inconceivable solemnity, which lies yet farther onward, we shall still find ourselves surrounded by the consciousness of duty, to pain us wherever it has been violated, and to console us so far as God may have given us grace to perform it.

[EDITOR'S NOTE: John Francis Knapp was found guilty by the jury and was convicted and hanged. His brother, Joseph Knapp, Jr., met the same fate.]

Emile Zola

:

ADDRESS TO THE JURY AT HIS
TRIAL FOR LIBEL

"Anti-Semitism really burst into prominence in the Third Republic with the publication of Édouard Drumont's two-volume, twelve-hundred-page *La France juive* on April 14, 1886," says Robert F. Byrnes in his recent study of this tragic problem. A gifted but embittered journalist, Drumont poured everything that was ever said or rumored against the Jews into his seething caldron which became the source for countless other books and pamphlets. In 1892 he started a daily anti-Semitic newspaper, *Libre Parole,* which also met with immediate success. Yet by the fall of 1894 anti-Semitism in France reached its lowest ebb and Drumont was on the point of selling his paper.

Then suddenly Captain Alfred Dreyfus, a comparatively unknown Jewish member of the French General Staff, was found guilty of selling military secrets to the German General Staff and sentenced to life imprisonment on Devil's Island. Now France flamed with anti-Semitism, and even such men as Clemenceau thought that Dreyfus should have been executed. But the Captain's brother, Mathieu Dreyfus, got to work and learned through the venerable vice-president of the Senate, Scheurer-Kestner, that Colonel Picquart of the General Staff had traced the only incriminating evidence against Captain Dreyfus to Major Esterhazy, a Hungarian-born member of the General Staff and a man of scandalous character. Picquart had been rewarded for his investigation with exile to a dangerous army post in Africa.

The little Dreyfus group stubbornly pressed the investigation month after month, for nearly three years, in the face of every conservative and reactionary element in France, for the issue was no longer the innocence of Dreyfus but the honor of the army. Clemenceau and Zola joined in the clamor for the trial of Esterhazy. On January 9, 1898, he was quickly tried by his fellow officers and found not guilty, while Colonel Picquart was dismissed from the army.

Émile Zola (1840-1902) at this time was fifty-eight and entitled to a rest. He had completed the twenty massive volumes of the Rougon-Macquart series and was about to complete his city trilogy—*Lourdes, Rome,* and *Paris.* But he had been following the Dreyfus affair for months and late in 1897 he published three fearless articles, one in praise of the valiant Scheurer-Kestner, one against the legend of a Jewish "syndicate," and one against the obscurantist tactics of the General Staff. Outraged by the exoneration of Esterhazy, he dashed off an open letter to Félix Faure, President of the French Republic, and took it to his friend Georges Clemenceau in his office at the newspaper *L'Aurore.* Clemenceau, who had already decided that something must be done, simply scribbled Zola's opening word, *"J'accuse,"* at the head of the article and printed it with Zola's signature in his own column on January 13, 1898.*

Zola's crescendo of charges against generals, judges, editors, and handwriting experts recalled Cicero's terrible charges against Catiline and Mark Antony. The explosion was tremendous, and tens of thousands of extra copies of the letter had to be reprinted. Zola expected to be prosecuted and he was prosecuted promptly—the honor of the army demanded that.

Defended by Fernand Labori before a prejudiced court, an intimidated jury, and an infuriated country, Zola could hardly have counted on much justice. He could hardly have counted on escaping with his life from the angry crowds that surrounded the courthouse. But he did not cringe when he read his declaration before those twelve bewildered men. He did not forget that only a few months before Prime Minister Méline had announced that "No Dreyfus Affair exists."

February 21, 1898

In the chamber at the sitting of January 22, M. Méline, the Prime Minister, declared, amid the frantic applause of his complaisant majority, that he had confidence in the twelve citizens to whose hands he entrusted the defense of the army. It was of you, gentlemen, that he spoke. And just as General Billot dictated its decision to the court-martial entrusted with the acquittal of Major Esterhazy, by appealing from the tribune for respect for the *chose jugée,* so likewise M. Méline wished to give you the order to condemn me "out of respect for the army," which he accuses me of having insulted!

I denounce to the conscience of honest men this pressure brought to bear by the constituted authorities upon the justice of the country.

* The letter is printed on page 229.

These are abominable political practices, which dishonor a free nation. We shall see, gentlemen, whether you will obey.

But it is not true that I am here in your presence by the will of M. Méline. He yielded to the necessity of prosecuting me only in great trouble, in terror of the new step which the advancing truth was about to take. This everybody knew. If I am before you, it is because I wished it. I alone decided that this obscure, this abominable affair, should be brought before your jurisdiction, and it is I alone of my free will who chose you, you, the loftiest, the most direct emanation of French justice, in order that France, at last, may know all, and give her decision. My act had no other object, and my person is of no account. I have sacrificed it in order to place in your hands, not only the honor of the army, but the imperiled honor of the nation.

It appears that I was cherishing a dream in wishing to offer you all the proofs, considering you to be the sole worthy, the sole competent judge. They have begun by depriving you with the left hand of what they seemed to give you with the right. They pretended, indeed, to accept your jurisdiction, but if they had confidence in you to avenge the members of the court-martial, there were still other officers who remained superior even to your jurisdiction. Let who can understand. It is absurdity doubled with hypocrisy, and it shows clearly that they dreaded your good sense—that they dared not run the risk of letting us tell all and of letting you judge the whole matter. They pretend that they wished to limit the scandal. What do you think of this scandal— of my act, which consisted in bringing the matter before you—in wishing the people, incarnate in you, to be the judge? They pretend also that they could not accept a revision in disguise, thus confessing that in reality they have but one fear, that of your sovereign control. The law has in you its complete representation, and it is this chosen law of the people that I have wished for—this law which, as a good citizen, I hold in profound respect, and not the suspicious procedure by which they hoped to make you a laughingstock.

I am thus excused, gentlemen, for having brought you here from your private affairs without being able to inundate you with the full flood of light of which I dreamed. The light, the whole light—this was my sole, my passionate desire! And this trial has just proved it. We have had to fight step by step against an extraordinarily obstinate desire for darkness. A battle has been necessary to obtain every atom of truth. Everything has been refused us. Our witnesses have been terrorized in the hope of preventing us from proving our case. And it is on your behalf alone that we have fought, that this proof might be put before you in its entirety, so that you might give your opinion on your consciences without remorse. I am certain, therefore, that you will give us credit for our efforts, and I feel sure too that sufficient light has been thrown upon the affair.

You have heard the witnesses; you are about to hear my counsel, who will tell you the true story, the story that maddens everybody and that everybody knows. I am, therefore, at my ease. You have the truth at last, and it will do its work. M. Méline thought to dictate your decision by entrusting to you the honor of the army. And it is in the name of the honor of the army that I too appeal to your justice.

I give M. Méline the most direct contradiction. Never have I insulted the army. I spoke, on the contrary, of my sympathy, my respect for the nation in arms, for our dear soldiers of France, who would rise at the first menace to defend the soil of France. And it is just as false that I attacked the chiefs, the generals who would lead them to victory. If certain persons at the War Office have compromised the army itself by their acts, is it to insult the whole army to say so? Is it not rather to act as a good citizen to separate it from all that compromises it, to give the alarm, so that the blunders that alone have been the cause of our defeat shall not occur again and shall not lead us to fresh disaster.

I am not defending myself, moreover. I leave history to judge my act, which was a necessary one; but I affirm that the army is dishonored when gendarmes are allowed to embrace Major Esterhazy after the abominable letters written by him. I affirm that that valiant army is insulted daily by the bandits who, on the plea of defending it, sully it by their degrading championship—who trail in the mud all that France still honors as good and great. I affirm that those who dishonor that great national army are those who mingle cries of *"Vive l'armée!"* with those of *"À bas les juifs!"* and *"Vive* Esterhazy!" *Grand Dieu!* The people of St. Louis, of Bayard, of Condé, and of Hoche, the people which counts a hundred great victories, the people of the great wars of the Republic and the Empire, the people whose power, grace, and generosity have dazzled the world, crying *"Vive* Esterhazy!" It is a shame the stain of which our efforts on behalf of truth and justice can alone wipe out!

You know the legend that has grown up: Dreyfus was condemned justly and legally by seven infallible officers, whom it is impossible even to suspect of a blunder without insulting the whole army. Dreyfus expiates in merited torments his abominable crime, and as he is a Jew, a Jewish syndicate is formed, an international *sans patrie* syndicate disposing of hundreds of millions, the object of which is to save the traitor at any price, even by the most shameless intrigues. And thereupon this syndicate began to heap crime on crime, buying consciences, precipitating France into a disastrous tumult, resolved on selling her to the enemy, willing even to drive all Europe into a general war rather than renounce its terrible plan.

It is very simple, nay childish, if not imbecile. But it is with this poisoned bread that the unclean press has been nourishing our poor people now for months. And it is not surprising if we are witnessing a dangerous crisis; for when folly and lies are thus sown broadcast, you necessarily reap insanity.

Gentlemen, I would not insult you by supposing that you have yourselves been duped by this nursery tale. I know you; I know who you are. You are the heart and the reason of Paris, of my great Paris, where I was born, which I love with an infinite tenderness, which I have been studying and writing of now for forty years. And I know likewise what is now passing in your brains; for, before coming to sit here as defendant, I sat there on the bench where you are now. You represent there the average opinion; you try to illustrate prudence and justice in the mass. Soon I shall be in thought with you in the room where you deliberate, and I am convinced that your effort will be to safeguard your interests as citizens, which are, of course, the interests of the whole nation. You may make a mistake, but you will do so in the thought that while securing your own weal you are securing the weal of all.

I see you at your homes at evening under the lamp; I hear you talk with your friends; I accompany you into your factories and shops. You are all workers—some tradesmen, others manufacturers, some professional men; and your very legitimate anxiety is the deplorable state into which business has fallen. Everywhere the present crisis threatens to become a disaster. The receipts fall off; transactions become more and more difficult. So that the idea which you have brought here, the thought that I read in your countenances, is that there has been enough of this and that it must be ended. You have not gone the length of saying, like many: "What matters it that an innocent man is at the Île du Diable? Is the interest of a single man worth disturbing a great country?" But you say, nevertheless, that the agitation which we are carrying on, we who hunger for truth and justice, costs too dearly! And if you condemn me, gentlemen, it is that thought which will be at the bottom of your verdict. You desire tranquillity for your homes, you wish for the revival of business, and you may think that by punishing me you will stop a campaign that is injurious to the interests of France.

Well, gentlemen, if that is your idea, you are entirely mistaken. Do me the honor of believing that I am not defending my liberty. By punishing me you would only magnify me. Whoever suffers for truth and justice becomes august and sacred. Look at me. Have I the look of a hireling, of a liar, and a traitor? Why should I be playing a part? I have behind me neither political ambition nor sectarian passion. I am a free writer, who has given his life to labor; who tomorrow will go back to the ranks and resume his interrupted task. And how stupid those who call me an Italian—me, born of a French mother, brought up by grandparents in the Beauce, peasants of that vigorous soil; me, who lost my father at seven years of age, who never went to Italy till I was fifty-four. And yet I am proud that my father was from Venice—the resplendent city whose ancient glory sings in all memories. And even if I were not French, would not the forty volumes in the French language, which I have sent by millions of copies throughout the world, suffice to make me a Frenchman?

So I do not defend myself. But what a blunder would be yours if you were convinced that by striking me you would re-establish order in our unfortunate country! Do you not understand now that what the nation is dying of is the darkness in which there is such an obstinate determination to leave her? The blunders of those in authority are being heaped upon those of others; one lie necessitates another, so that the mass is becoming formidable. A judicial blunder was committed, and then to hide it, it has been necessary to commit every day fresh crimes against good sense and equity! The condemnation of an innocent man has involved the acquittal of a guilty man, and now today you are asked in turn to condemn me because I have cried out in my anguish on beholding our country embarked on this terrible course. Condemn me, then! But it will be one more error added to the others— a fault the burden of which you will hear in history. And my condemnation, instead of restoring the peace for which you long, and which we all of us desire, will be only a fresh seed of passion and disorder. The cup, I tell you, is full; do not make it run over!

Why do you not judge justly the terrible crisis through which the country is passing? They say that we are the authors of the scandal, that we who are lovers of truth and justice are leading the nation astray and urging it to violence. Surely this is a mockery! To speak only of General Billot—was he not warned eighteen months ago? Did not Colonel Picquart insist that he should take up the matter of revision, if he did not wish the storm to burst and destroy everything? Did not M. Scheurer-Kestner, with tears in his eyes, beg him to think of France, and save her such a calamity? No! Our desire has been to make peace, to allay discontent, and, if the country is now in trouble, the responsibility lies with the power which, to cover the guilty, and in the furtherance of political ends, has denied everything, hoping to be strong enough to prevent the truth from being revealed. It has maneuvered in behalf of darkness, and it alone is responsible for the present distraction of the public conscience!

The Dreyfus case, gentlemen, has now become a very small affair. It is lost in view of the formidable questions to which it has given rise. There is no longer a Dreyfus case. The question now is whether France is still the France of the rights of man, the France that gave freedom to the world, and ought to give it justice. Are we still the most noble, the most fraternal, the most generous of nations? Shall we preserve our reputation in Europe for justice and humanity? Are not all the victories that we have won called in question? Open your eyes, and understand that, to be in such confusion, the French soul must have been stirred to its depths in face of a terrible danger. A nation cannot be thus moved without imperiling its moral existence. This is an exceptionally serious hour; the safety of the nation is at stake.

When you have understood that, gentlemen, you will feel that but one remedy is possible—to tell the truth, to do justice. Anything that keeps back the light, anything that adds darkness to darkness, will only prolong and aggravate the crisis. The duty of good citizens, of all who feel it to be imperatively necessary to put an end to this matter, is to demand broad daylight. There are already many who think so. The men of literature, philosophy, and science are rising in the name of intelligence and reason. And I do not speak of the foreigner, of the shudder that has run through all Europe. Yet the foreigner is not necessarily the enemy. Let us not speak of the nations that may be our opponents tomorrow. But great Russia, our ally; little and generous Holland; all the sympathetic nations of the north; those countries of the French language, Switzerland and Belgium—why are their hearts so heavy, so overflowing with sympathetic suffering? Do you dream, then, of an isolated France? Do you prefer, when you pass the frontier, not to meet the smile of approval for your historic reputation for equity and humanity?

Alas, gentlemen, like so many others, you expect the thunderbolt to descend from heaven in proof of the innocence of Dreyfus. Truth does not come thus. It requires research and knowledge. We know well where the truth is, or where it might be found. But we dream of that only in the recesses of our souls, and we feel patriotic anguish lest we expose ourselves to the danger of having this proof someday cast in our face after having involved the honor of the army in a falsehood. I wish also to declare positively that, though, in the official notice of our list of witnesses, we included certain ambassadors, we had decided in advance not to call them. Our boldness has provoked smiles. But I do not think that there was any real smiling in our Foreign Office, for there they must have understood! We intended to say to those who know the whole truth that we also know it. This truth is gossiped about at the embassies; tomorrow it will be known to all, and, if it is now impossible for us to seek it where it is concealed by official red tape, the government, which is not ignorant—the government, which is convinced as we are—of the innocence of Dreyfus, will be able, whenever it likes and without risk, to find witnesses who will demonstrate everything.

Dreyfus is innocent. I swear it! I stake my life on it—my honor! At this solemn moment, in the presence of this tribunal which is the representative of human justice, before you, gentlemen, who are the very incarnation of the country, before the whole of France, before the whole world, I swear that Dreyfus is innocent. By my forty years of work, by the authority that this toil may have given me, I swear that Dreyfus is innocent. By all I have now, by the name I have made for myself, by my works, which have helped for the expansion of French literature, I swear that Dreyfus is innocent. May all that melt away, may my works perish, if Dreyfus be not innocent! He is innocent. All seems against me—the two Chambers, the civil authority, the most widely circulated journals, the public opinion they have poisoned. And I have for me only an ideal of truth and justice. But I am quite calm; I shall conquer. I was determined that my country should not remain the victim of lies and injustice. I may be condemned here. The day will come when France will thank me for having helped to save her honor.

Zola received no ovation in that hostile courtroom, nor did his attorney, Labori, who spoke with fearless eloquence for nearly three tense days. Zola was found guilty by a vote of seven to five and condemned to a year's imprisonment, with a fine of three thousand francs.

After various appeals and delays, Zola, against his wishes, was forced by his supporters to flee to England while new evidence for Dreyfus turned up. The 1894 decision against Dreyfus was annulled, and he was returned to Paris to be tried again and found "guilty of treason—under extenuating circumstances"! To put an end to the horrible farce (and make it even more farcical) President Loubet "pardoned" him. Complete exoneration was delayed, until 1906, when the Supreme Court of Appeals cleared Dreyfus. During World War I, he was made a general.

Meanwhile Zola returned to France, a hero to millions, and went on with his writing. When he died in 1902 of accidental asphyxiation, thirty thousand people attended the funeral. Of the tributes paid to Zola, the noblest was by Anatole France, who concluded with these words: "Gentlemen, there is only one country in the world in which this great thing could be accomplished. How admirable is the genius of our country! How beautiful is the soul of France, which since centuries past has taught right and justice to Europe and to the world! France is again the land of golden reason and benevolent thoughts, the soil of equitable magistrature, the country of Turgot, of Montesquieu, of Voltaire, of Malesherbes. Zola has merited well of his country in not despairing of justice in France.

"Let us not sorrow for him because he endured and suffered. Let us envy him.

"Envy him! He has honored his country and the world through an immense work and through a great action. Envy him his destiny and his heart, which made his lot that of the greatest: he was a moment of the conscience of man."

—NOTES BY HOUSTON PETERSON

Sir Charles Russell

.

CROSS-EXAMINATION OF PIGOTT BEFORE
THE PARNELL COMMISSION

from Wellman's *The Art of Cross-Examination*

Probably one of the most dramatic and successful of the more celebrated cross-examinations in the history of the English courts is Sir Charles Russell's cross-examination of Pigott, the chief witness in the investigation growing out of the attack upon Charles S. Parnell and sixty-five Irish members of Parliament, by name, for belonging to a lawless and even murderous organization, whose aim was the overthrow of English rule. . . .

The case is an admirable illustration of the importance of so using a damaging letter that a dishonest witness cannot escape its effect by ready and ingenious explanations, when given an opportunity, as is often done by an unskilful cross-examiner. The cross-examination of Pigott shows that Sir Charles Russell thoroughly understood this branch of the art, for he read to Pigott only a portion of his damaging letter, and then mercilessly impaled him upon the sharp points of his questions before dragging him forward in a bleeding condition to face other portions of his letter, and repeated the process until Pigott was cut to pieces.

The principal charge against Parnell, and the only one that interests us in the cross-examination of the witness Pigott, was the writing of a letter by Parnell which the *Times* claimed to have obtained and published in facsimile, in which he excused the murderer of Lord Frederick Cavendish, Chief Secretary for Ireland, and of Mr. Burke, Under Secretary, in Phoenix Park, Dublin, on May 6, 1882. One particular sentence in the letter read, "I cannot refuse to admit that Burke got no more than his deserts."

The publication of this letter naturally made a great stir in Parliament and in the country at large. Parnell stated in the House of Commons that the letter was a forgery, and later asked for the appointment of a select committee to inquire whether the facsimile letter was a forgery. The Government refused this request, but appointed a special committee, composed of three judges, to investigate all the charges made by the *Times*.

In order to undertake this defense of Parnell, Russell returned to the *Times* the retainer he had enjoyed from them for many previous years. It was known that the *Times* had bought the letter from Mr. Houston, the secretary of the Irish Loyal and Patriotic Union, and that Mr. Houston had bought it from Pigott. But how did Pigott come by it? That was the question of the hour, and people looked forward to the day when Pigott should go into the box and tell his story, and when Sir Charles Russell should rise to cross-examine him. Pigott's evidence in chief, so far as the letter was concerned, came practically to this: he had been employed by the Irish Loyal and Patriotic Union to hunt up documents which might incriminate Parnell, and he had bought the facsimile letter, with other letters, in Paris from an agent of the Clan-na-Gael, who had no objection to injuring Parnell for a valuable consideration.

Addressing the witness with much courtesy, while a profound silence fell upon the crowded court, Lord Russell began his cross-examination: "Mr. Pigott, would you be good enough, with my Lords' permission, to write some words on that sheet of paper for me? Perhaps you will sit down in order to do so?" A sheet of paper was then handed to the witness. I thought he looked for a moment surprised. This clearly was not the beginning that he had expected. He hesitated, seemed confused. Perhaps Russell observed it. At all events he added quickly:

"Would you like to sit down?"

"Oh, no, thanks," replied Pigott, a little flurried.

THE PRESIDENT: Well, but I think it is better that you should sit down. Here is a table upon which you can write in the ordinary way—the course you always pursue.

RUSSELL: Will you write the word "livelihood"?

Pigott wrote.

RUSSELL: Just leave a space. Will you write the word "likelihood"?

Pigott wrote.

RUSSELL: Will you write your own name? Will you write the word "proselytism," and finally (I think I will not trouble you at present with any more) "Patrick Egan" and "P. Egan"?

He uttered these last words with emphasis, as if they imported something of great importance. Then, when Pigott had written, he added carelessly, "There is one word I had forgotten. Lower down, please, leaving spaces, write the word 'hesitancy.'" Then, as Pigott was about to write, he added, as if this were the vital point, "with a small 'h.'" Pigott wrote and looked relieved.

RUSSELL: Will you kindly give me the sheet?

Pigott took up a bit of blotting paper to lay on the sheet, when Russell, with a sharp ring in his voice, said rapidly, "Don't blot it, please." It seemed to me that the sharp ring in Russell's voice startled Pigott. While writing he had looked composed; now again he looked flurried, and nervously handed back the sheet. The attorney general looked keenly at it, and then said, with the air of a man who had himself scored, "My Lords, I suggest that had better be photographed, if your Lordships see no objection."

RUSSELL (*Turning sharply toward the attorney general, and with an angry glance and an Ulster accent, which sometimes broke out when he felt irritated*): Do not interrupt my cross-examination with that request.

Little did the attorney general at the moment know that, in the ten minutes or quarter of an hour which it had taken to ask these questions, Russell had gained a decisive advantage. Pigott had in one of his letters to Pat Egan spelt "hesitancy" thus, "hesitency." In one of the incriminatory letters "hesitancy" was so spelt; and in the sheet now handed back to Russell, Pigott had written "hesitency," too. In fact it was Pigott's spelling of this word that had put the Irish members on his scent. Pat Egan, seeing the word spelt with an "e" in one of the incriminatory letters, had written to Parnell, saying in effect, "Pigott is the forger. In the letter ascribed to you 'hesitancy' is spelt 'hesitency.' That is the way Pigott always spells the word." These things were not dreamt of in the philosophy of the attorney general when he interrupted Russell's cross-examination with the request that the sheet "had better be photographed." So closed the first round of the combat.

Russell went on in his former courteous manner, and Pigott, who had now completely recovered confidence, looked once more like a man determined to stand to his guns.

Russell, having disposed of some preliminary points at length (and after he had been perhaps about half an hour on his feet), closed with the witness.

RUSSELL: The first publication of the articles "Parnellism and Crime" was on the 7th March, 1887?

PIGOTT (*Sturdily*): I do not know.

RUSSELL (*Amiably*): Well, you may assume that is the date.

PIGOTT (*Carelessly*): I suppose so.

RUSSELL: And you were aware of the intended publication of the correspondence, the incriminatory letters?

PIGOTT (*Firmly*): No, I was not at all aware of it.

RUSSELL (*Sharply, and with the Ulster ring in his voice*): What?

PIGOTT (*Boldly*): No, certainly not.

RUSSELL: Were you not aware that there were grave charges to be made against Mr. Parnell and the leading members of the Land League?

PIGOTT: I was not aware of it until they actually commenced.

RUSSELL: What?

PIGOTT: I was not aware of it until the publication actually commenced.

RUSSELL: Do you swear that?

PIGOTT: I do.

RUSSELL (*Making a gesture with both hands, and looking toward the bench*): Very good, there is no mistake about that.

Then there was a pause; Russell placed his hands beneath the shelf in front of him, and drew from it some papers—Pigott, the attorney general, the judges, every one in court looking intently at him the while. There was not a breath, not a movement. I think it was the most dramatic scene in the whole cross-examination, abounding as it did in dramatic scenes. Then, handing Pigott a letter, Russell said calmly:

"Is that your letter? Do not trouble to read it; tell me if it is your letter."

Pigott took the letter, and held it close to his eyes as if reading it.

RUSSELL: Do not trouble to read it.

PIGOTT: Yes, I think it is.

RUSSELL: Have you any doubt of it?

PIGOTT: No.

RUSSELL (*Addressing the judges*): My Lords, it is from Anderton's Hotel, and it is addressed by the witness to Archbishop Walsh. The date, my Lords, is the 4th of March, three days before the first appearance of the first of the articles, "Parnellism and Crime."

He then read:

"Private and confidential."

"My Lord: The importance of the matter about which I write will doubtless excuse this intrusion on your Grace's attention. Briefly, I wish to say that I have been made aware of the details of certain proceedings that are in preparation with the object of destroying the influence of the Parnellite party in Parliament."

Having read this much Russell turned to Pigott and said:

"What were the certain proceedings that were in preparation?"

PIGOTT: I do not recollect.

RUSSELL: Turn to my Lords and repeat the answer.

PIGOTT: I do not recollect.

RUSSELL: You swear that—writing on the 4th of March, less than two years ago?

PIGOTT: Yes.

RUSSELL: You do not know what that referred to?

PIGOTT: I do not really.

RUSSELL: May I suggest to you?

PIGOTT: Yes, you may.

RUSSELL: Did it refer to the incriminatory letters among other things?

PIGOTT: Oh, at that date? No, the letters had not been obtained, I think, at that date, had they, two years ago?

RUSSELL (*Quietly and courteously*): I do not want to confuse you at all, Mr. Pigott.

PIGOTT: Would you mind giving me the date of that letter?

RUSSELL: The 4th of March.

PIGOTT: The 4th of March.

RUSSELL: Is it your impression that the letters had not been obtained at that date?

PIGOTT: Oh, yes, some of the letters had been obtained before that date.

RUSSELL: Then, reminding you that some of the letters had been obtained before that date, did that passage that I have read to you in that letter refer to these letters among other things?

PIGOTT: No, I rather fancy they had reference to the forthcoming articles in the *Times*.

RUSSELL: I thought you told us you did not know anything about the forthcoming articles.

PIGOTT: Yes, I did. I find now I am mistaken—that I must have heard something about them.

RUSSELL: Then try not to make the same mistake again, Mr. Pigott. "Now," you go on (*continuing to read from Pigott's letter to the archbishop*), "I cannot enter more fully into details than to state that the proceedings referred to consist in the publication of certain statements purporting to prove the complicity of Mr. Parnell himself, and some of his supporters, with murders and outrages in Ireland, to be followed, in all probability, by the institution of criminal proceedings against these parties by the Government."

Having finished the reading, Russell laid down the letter and said (turning toward the witness), "Who told you that?"

PIGOTT: I have no idea.

RUSSELL (*Striking the paper energetically with his fingers*): But that refers, among other things, to the incriminatory letters.

PIGOTT: I do not recollect that it did.

RUSSELL: Do you swear that it did not?

PIGOTT: I will not swear that it did not.

RUSSELL: Do you think it did?

PIGOTT: No, I do not think it did.

RUSSELL: Do you think that these letters, if genuine, would prove or would not prove Parnell's complicity in crime?

PIGOTT: I thought they would be very likely to prove it.

RUSSELL: Now, reminding you of that opinion, I ask you whether you did not intend to refer—not solely, I suggest, but among other things —to the letters as being the matter which would prove complicity or purport to prove complicity?

PIGOTT: Yes, I may have had that in my mind.

RUSSELL: You could have had hardly any doubt that you had?

PIGOTT: I suppose so.

RUSSELL: You suppose you may have had?

PIGOTT: Yes.

RUSSELL: There is the letter and the statement (*reading*), "Your Grace may be assured that I speak with full knowledge, and am in a position to prove, beyond all doubt and question, the truth of what I say." Was that true?

PIGOTT: It could hardly be true.

RUSSELL: Then did you write that which was false?

PIGOTT: I suppose it was in order to give strength to what I said. I do not think it was warranted by what I knew.

RUSSELL: You added the untrue statement in order to add strength to what you said?

PIGOTT: Yes.

RUSSELL: You believe these letters to be genuine?

PIGOTT: I do.

RUSSELL: And did at this time?

PIGOTT: Yes.

RUSSELL (*Reading*): "And I will further assure your Grace that I am also able to point out how these designs may be successfully combated and finally defeated." How, if these documents were genuine documents, and you believed them to be such, how were you able to assure his Grace that you were able to point out how the design might be successfully combated and finally defeated?

PIGOTT: Well, as I say, I had not the letters actually in my mind at that time. So far as I can gather, I do not recollect the letter to Archbishop Walsh at all. My memory is really a blank on the circumstance.

RUSSELL: You told me a moment ago, after great deliberation and consideration, you had both the incriminatory letters and the letter to Archbishop Walsh in your mind.

PIGOTT: I said it was probable I did; but I say the thing has completely faded out of my mind.

RUSSELL (*Resolutely*): I must press you. Assuming the letters to be genuine, what were the means by which you were able to assure his Grace that you could point out how the design might be successfully combated and finally defeated?

PIGOTT (*Helplessly*): I cannot conceive, really.

RUSSELL: Oh, try. You must really try.

PIGOTT (*In manifest confusion and distress*): I cannot.

RUSSELL (*Looking fixedly at the witness*): Try.

PIGOTT: I cannot.

RUSSELL: Try.

PIGOTT: It is no use.

RUSSELL (*Emphatically*): May I take it, then, your answer to my Lords is that you cannot give any explanation?

PIGOTT: I really cannot absolutely.

RUSSELL (*Reading*): "I assure your Grace that I have no other motive except to respectfully suggest that your Grace would communicate the substance to some one or other of the parties concerned, to whom I could furnish details, exhibit proofs, and suggest how the coming blow may be effectually met." What do you say to that, Mr. Pigott?

PIGOTT: I have nothing to say except that I do not recollect anything about it absolutely.

RUSSELL: What was the coming blow?

PIGOTT: I suppose the coming publication.

RUSSELL: How was it to be effectively met?

PIGOTT: I have not the slightest idea.

RUSSELL: Assuming the letters to be genuine, does it not even now occur to your mind how it could be effectively met?

PIGOTT: No.

Pigott now looked like a man, after the sixth round in a prize fight, who had been knocked down in every round. But Russell showed him no mercy. I shall take another extract.

RUSSELL: Whatever the charges in "Parnellism and Crime," including the letters, were, did you believe them to be true or not?

PIGOTT: How can I say that when I say I do not know what the charges were? I say I do not recollect that letter to the archbishop at all, or any of the circumstances it refers to.

RUSSELL: First of all you knew this: that you procured and paid for a number of letters?

PIGOTT: Yes.

RUSSELL: Which, if genuine, you have already told me, would gravely implicate the parties from whom these were supposed to come.

PIGOTT: Yes, gravely implicate.

RUSSELL: You would regard that, I suppose, as a serious charge?

PIGOTT: Yes.

RUSSELL: Did you believe that charge to be true or false?

PIGOTT: I believed that charge to be true.

RUSSELL: You believed that to be true?

PIGOTT: I do.

RUSSELL: Now I will read this passage [from Pigott's letter to the archbishop], "I need hardly add that, did I consider the parties really guilty of the things charged against them, I should not dream of suggesting that your Grace should take part in an effort to shield them; I only wish to impress on your Grace that the evidence is apparently convincing, and would probably be sufficient to secure conviction if submitted to an English jury." What do you say to that, Mr. Pigott?

PIGOTT (*Bewildered*): I say nothing, except that I am sure I could not have had the letters in my mind when I said that, because I do not think the letters conveyed a sufficiently serious charge to cause me to write in that way.

RUSSELL: But you know that was the only part of the charge, so far as you have yet told us, that you had anything to do in getting up?

PIGOTT: Yes, that is what I say; I must have had something else in my mind which I cannot at present recollect—that I must have had other charges.

RUSSELL: What charges?

PIGOTT: I do not know. That is what I cannot tell you.

RUSSELL: Well, let me remind you that that particular part of the charges —the incriminatory letters—were letters that you yourself knew all about.

PIGOTT: Yes, of course.

RUSSELL (*Reading from another letter of* PIGOTT'S *to the archbishop*): "I was somewhat disappointed in not having a line from your Grace, as I ventured to expect I might have been so far honored. I can assure your Grace that I have no other motive in writing save to avert, if possible, a great danger to people with whom your Grace is known to be in strong sympathy. At the same time, should your Grace not desire to interfere in the matter, or should you consider that they would refuse me a hearing, I am well content, having acquitted myself of what I conceived to be my duty in the circumstances. I will not further trouble your Grace save to again beg that you will not allow my name to transpire, seeing that to do so would interfere injuriously with my prospects, without any compensating advantage to any one. I make the request all the more confidently because I have had no part in what is being done to the prejudice of the Parnellite party, though I was enabled to become acquainted with all the details."

PIGOTT: Yes.

RUSSELL: What do you say to that?

PIGOTT: That it appears to me clearly that I had not the letters in my mind.

RUSSELL: Then if it appears to you clearly that you had not the letters in your mind, what had you in your mind?

PIGOTT: It must have been something far more serious.

RUSSELL: What was it?

PIGOTT: I cannot tell you. I have no idea.

RUSSELL: It must have been something far more serious than the letters?

PIGOTT: Far more serious.

RUSSELL: Can you give my Lords any clue of the most indirect kind to what it was?

PIGOTT: I cannot.

RUSSELL: Or from whom you heard it?

PIGOTT: No.

RUSSELL: Or when you heard it?

PIGOTT: Or when I heard it.

RUSSELL: Or where you heard it?

PIGOTT: Or where I heard it.

RUSSELL: Have you ever mentioned this fearful matter—whatever it is—to anybody?

PIGOTT: No.

RUSSELL: Still locked up, hermetically sealed in your own bosom?

PIGOTT: No, because it has gone away out of my bosom, whatever it was.

Pigott's cross-examination was finished the following day, and the second day he disappeared entirely, and later sent back from Paris a confession of his guilt, admitting his perjury, and giving the details of how he had forged the alleged Parnell letter by tracing words and phrases from genuine Parnell letters, placed against the window pane, and admitting that he had sold the forged letter for £605. After the confession was read, the Commission "found" that it was a forgery, and the *Times* withdrew the facsimile letter.

A warrant was issued for Pigott's arrest on the charge of perjury, but when he was tracked by the police to a hotel in Madrid, he asked to be given time enough to collect his belongings, and, retiring to his room, blew out his brains.

Gandhi

:

A PLEA FOR THE SEVEREST PENALTY, UPON HIS CONVICTION FOR SEDITION

March 23, 1922

While the Peace Conference was getting underway in Paris early in 1919, a new kind of conflict was beginning in India, a conflict that was to hasten the dismemberment of the British Empire. For it was then that Gandhi began to take an active part in the Indian nationalist movement. Hundreds of eloquent men had preceded him in the struggle. "But this voice was somehow different from the others," Nehru afterward wrote from prison to his daughter. "It was quiet and low, and yet it could be heard above the shouting of the multitude; it was soft and gentle, and yet there seemed to be steel hidden away somewhere in it; it was courteous and full of appeal, and yet there was something grim and frightening in it; every word used was full of meaning and seemed to carry a deadly earnestness. Behind the language of peace and friendship there was power and the quivering shadow of action."

Mohandas Karamchand Gandhi (1869-1948) was born into a middle-class, middle-caste family. After a general education in India he studied law in London, passed the bar examination, and returned home for two years of unpromising practice. In 1893 he went to South Africa to work on a single case, but a few days after landing at Durban, Natal, he was thrown out of a first-class train compartment and thus quickly learned about discrimination against Indians in that part of the world. Instead of leaving after completing his case, he remained in South Africa almost continuously for twenty years. Although he now flourished in his profession, he gave it up entirely about 1900 to devote all his attention to fighting the unjust laws against his countrymen. But it was a new kind of fighting—*Satyagraha.*

"The term *Satyagraha* was coined by me in South Africa," said Gandhi, "to express the force that the Indians there used for full eight years, and it was coined in order to distinguish it from the movement then going on in the United Kingdom and South Africa under the name of Passive Resistance.

"Its root meaning is 'holding on to truth,' hence truth-force. I have also called it love-force or soul-force. In the application of *Satyagraha,* I discovered in the earliest stages that pursuit of truth did not admit of violence being inflicted on one's opponent, but that he must be weaned from error by patience and sympathy. For what appears to be truth to the one may appear to be error to the other. And patience means self-suffering. So the doctrine came to mean vindication of truth, not by the infliction of suffering on the opponent, but on one's self."

The prolonged application of *Satyagraha,* or nonviolent non-co-operation, did not by any means remove all of the legal discrimination against Indians in South Africa, but it enabled them to live and move with more freedom and dignity. So many concessions had been wrung from General Smuts and his white supporters by 1914 that Gandhi could leave for India with a quiet sense of moral victory.

After settling in India with a small colony of disciples, he began his long crusade against untouchability; he improved the lot of the indigo share-croppers and supported striking textile workers. But as late as July, 1918, he urged Indians to take up arms in defense of the Empire, for he thought such loyalty would ensure for his people more liberty and participation in the government after the war.

The fateful shock came with the passage of the Rowlatt Acts which "gave great powers to the government and the police to arrest, keep in prison without trial, or to have a secret trial of, any person they disapproved of or suspected." In protest Gandhi at once called a nation-wide *hartal,* a complete cessation of work and business—his first overt act against the British government of India. It spread throughout the country and paralyzed activity, but violence broke out here and there. Realizing that the people were not yet ready for such mass movements, that he had committed a "Himalayan miscalculation," Gandhi suspended the *hartal* on April 6, 1919. But in Amritsar, a week later, a crowd of some ten or twenty thousand was fired upon by General Dyer's troops, and nearly four hundred were killed, over a thousand wounded. Most of the crowd apparently did not realize that public processions and assemblies had been prohibited. In any case the "lesson" had been unduly severe, and coming immediately after the enactment of the Rowlatt Acts, it was doubly indelible.

Against this dark background Gandhi now moved forward with infectious self-confidence, drawing more and more determined people to him and taking over the leadership of the Indian National Congress. In 1920 the Congress adopted his program of nonviolent, non-co-operation, *Satyagraha,* on a far wider scale than ever attempted in South Africa. In support of the program Gandhi traveled up and down the frenzied country for seven months, making hundreds of speeches, sometimes to mass meetings of a hundred thousand or more. He was always under the shadow of the police, but in 1922 he was arrested, charged with sedition for three of his articles in his magazine, *Young India.* At the conclusion of "the great trial" in the crowded little courtroom of Ahmadabad, Gandhi was asked by the judge if he wished to make a statement before receiving sentence.

"Nonviolence is the first article of my faith."

Before I read this statement, I would like to state that I entirely endorse the learned Advocate General's remarks in connection with my humble self. I think that he was entirely fair to me in all the statements that he has made, because it is very true and I have no desire whatsoever to conceal from this court the fact that to preach disaffection toward the existing system of government has become almost a passion with me; and the learned Advocate General is also entirely in the right when he says that my preaching of disaffection did not commence with my connection with *Young India,* but that it commenced much earlier; and in the statement that I am about to read, it will be my painful duty to admit before this court that it commenced much earlier than the period stated by the Advocate General. It is the most painful duty with me, but I have to discharge that duty knowing the responsibility that rests upon my shoulders, and I wish to endorse all the blame that the learned Advocate General has thrown on my shoulders, in connection with the Bombay occurrences, Madras occurrences, and the Chauri Chaura occurrences. Thinking over these deeply and sleeping over them night after night, it is impossible for me to dissociate myself from the diabolical crimes of Chauri Chaura or the mad outrages of Bombay. He is quite right when he says that as a man of responsibility, a man having received a fair share of education, having had a fair share of experience of this world, I should have known the consequences of every one of my acts. I know that I was playing with fire. I ran the risk, and if I was set free, I would still do the same. I have felt it this morning that I would have failed in my duty, if I did not say what I said here just now.

I wanted to avoid violence, I want to avoid violence. Nonviolence is the first article of my faith. It is also the last article of my creed. But

I had to make my choice. I had either to submit to a system which I considered had done an irreparable harm to my country, or incur the risk of the mad fury of my people bursting forth, when they understood the truth from my lips. I know that my people have sometimes gone mad. I am deeply sorry for it and I am therefore here to submit not to a light penalty but to the highest penalty. I do not ask for mercy. I do not plead any extenuating act. I am here, therefore, to invite and cheerfully submit to the highest penalty that can be inflicted upon me for what in law is a deliberate crime and what appears to me to be the highest duty of a citizen. The only course open to you, the judge, is, as I am just going to say in my statement, either to resign your post or inflict on me the severest penalty, if you believe that the system and law you are assisting to administer are good for the people. I do not expect that kind of conversion, but by the time I have finished with my statement, you will perhaps have a glimpse of what is raging within my breast to run this maddest risk which a sane man can run.

[The following statement was then read.]

I owe it perhaps to the Indian public and to the public in England to placate which this prosecution is mainly taken up that I should explain why from a stanch loyalist and co-operator I have become an uncompromising disaffectionist and non-co-operator. To the court too I should say why I plead guilty to the charge of promoting disaffection toward the government established by law in India.

My public life began in 1893 in South Africa in troubled weather. My first contact with British authority in that country was not of a happy character. I discovered that as a man and as an Indian I had no rights. More correctly, I discovered that I had no rights as a man because I was an Indian.

But I was not baffled. I thought that this treatment of Indians was an excrescence upon a system that was intrinsically and mainly good. I gave the government my voluntary and hearty co-operation, criticizing it freely where I felt it was faulty but never wishing its destruction.

Consequently, when the existence of the Empire was threatened in 1899 by the Boer challenge, I offered my services to it, raised a volunteer ambulance corps, and served at several actions that took place for the relief of Ladysmith. Similarly in 1906, at the time of the Zulu revolt, I raised a stretcher-bearer party and served till the end of the "rebellion." On both these occasions I received medals and was even mentioned in dispatches. For my work in South Africa I was given by Lord Hardinge a Kaiser-i-Hind Gold Medal. When the war broke out in 1914 between England and Germany, I raised a volunteer ambulance corps in London consisting of the then resident Indians in London, chiefly students. Its work was acknowledged by the authorities to be valuable. Lastly, in India, when a special appeal was made at the War Conference in Delhi in 1918 by Lord Chelmsford for recruits, I struggled at the cost of my health to raise a corps in Kheda, and the response was being made when the hostilities ceased and orders were received that no more recruits were wanted. In all these efforts at service I was actuated by the belief that it was possible by such services to gain a status of full equality in the Empire for my countrymen.

The first shock came in the shape of the Rowlatt Act, a law designed to rob the people of all real freedom. I felt called upon to lead an intensive agitation against it. Then followed the Punjab horrors beginning with the massacre at Jallianwala Bagh and culminating in crawling orders, public floggings, and other indescribable humiliations. I discovered too that the plighted word of the Prime Minister to the Mussulmans of India regarding the integrity of Turkey and the holy places of Islam was not likely to be fulfilled. But in spite of the forebodings and the grave warnings of friends, at the Amritsar Congress in 1919, I fought for co-operation and working with the Montagu-Chelmsford reforms, hoping that the Prime Minister would redeem his promise to the Indian Mussulmans, that the Punjab wound would be healed, and that the reforms, inadequate and unsatisfactory though they were, marked a new era of hope in the life of India.

But all that hope was shattered. The Khilafat promise was not to be redeemed. The Punjab crime was whitewashed and most culprits went not only unpunished but remained in service and in some cases continued to draw pensions from the Indian revenue, and in some cases were even rewarded. I saw too that not only did the reforms not mark a change of heart, but they were only a method of further draining India of her wealth and of prolonging her servitude.

I came reluctantly to the conclusion that the British connection had made India more helpless than she ever was before, politically and economically. A disarmed India has no power of resistance against any aggressor if she wanted to engage in an armed conflict with him. So much is this the case that some of our best men consider that India must take generations before she can achieve the Dominion status. She has become so poor that she has little power of resisting famines. Before the British advent, India spun and wove in her millions of cottages just the supplement she needed for adding to her meager agricultural resources. This cottage industry, so vital for India's existence, has been ruined by incredibly heartless and inhuman processes as described by English witnesses. Little do town dwellers know how the semistarved masses of India are slowly sinking to lifelessness. Little do they know that their miserable comfort represents the brokerage they get for the work they do for the foreign exploiter, that the profits and the brokerage are sucked from the masses. Little do they realize that the government established by law in British India is carried on for this exploitation of the masses. No sophistry, no jugglery in figures can explain away the evidence that the skeletons in many villages present to the naked eye. I have no doubt whatsoever that both England and the town dwellers of India will have to answer, if there is a God above, for this crime against humanity which is perhaps unequaled in history. The law itself in this country has been used to serve the foreign exploiter. My unbiased examination of the Punjab Martial Law cases has led me to believe that at least ninety-five per cent of convictions were wholly bad. My experience of political cases in India leads me to the conclusion that in nine out of every ten the condemned men were totally innocent. Their crime consisted in the love of their country. In ninety-nine cases out of a hundred justice has been denied to Indians as against Europeans in the courts of India. This is not an exaggerated picture. It is the experience of almost every Indian who has had anything to do with such cases. In my opinion, the administration of the law is thus prostituted consciously or unconsciously for the benefit of the exploiter.

The greatest misfortune is that Englishmen and their Indian associates in the administration of the country do not know that they are engaged in the crime I have attempted to describe. I am satisfied that many Englishmen and Indian officials honestly believe that they are administering one of the best systems devised in the world and that India is making steady though slow progress. They do not know that a subtle but effective system of terrorism and an organized display of force on the one hand, and the deprivation of all powers of retaliation or self-defense on the other, have emasculated the people and induced in them the habit of simulation. This awful habit has added to the ignorance and the self-deception of the administrators. Section 124-A, under which I am happily charged, is perhaps the prince among the political sections of the Indian Penal Code designed to suppress the liberty of the citizen. Affection cannot be manufactured or regulated by law. If one has an affection for a person or system, one should be free to give the fullest expression to his disaffection, so long as he does not contemplate, promote, or incite to violence. But the section under which Mr. Banker [a colleague in nonviolence] and I are charged is one under which mere promotion of disaffection is a crime. I have studied some of the cases tried under it, and I know that some of the most loved of India's patriots have been convicted under it. I consider it a privilege, therefore, to be charged under that section. I have endeavored to give in their briefest outline the reasons for my disaffection. I have no personal ill will against any single administrator, much less can I have any disaffection toward the King's person. But I hold it to be a virtue to be disaffected toward a government which in its totality has done more harm to India than any previous system. India is less manly under the British rule than she ever was before. Holding such a belief, I consider it to be a sin to have affection for the system. And it has been a precious privilege for me to be able to write what I have in the various articles, tendered in evidence against me.

In fact, I believe that I have rendered a service to India and England by showing in non-co-operation the way out of the unnatural state in which both are living. In my humble opinion, non-co-operation with evil is as much a duty as is co-operation with good. But in the past, non-co-operation has been deliberately expressed in violence to the evildoer. I am endeavoring to show to my countrymen that violent non-co-operation only multiplies evil and that as evil can only be sustained by violence, withdrawal of support of evil requires complete abstention from violence. Nonviolence implies voluntary submission to the penalty for non-co-operation with evil. I am here, therefore, to invite and submit cheerfully to the highest penalty that can be inflicted upon me for what in law is a deliberate crime and what appears to me to be the highest duty of a citizen. The only course open to you, the judge, is either to resign your post, and thus dissociate yourself from evil if you feel that the law you are called upon to administer is an evil and that in reality I am innocent, or to inflict on me the severest penalty if you believe that the system and the law you are assisting to administer are good for the people of this country and that my activity is therefore injurious to the public weal.

Passing sentence on Gandhi, his judge confessed, presented a problem of the utmost difficulty. Though Gandhi was evidently of a noble and even saintly character, quite different "from any person I have ever tried or am likely to have to try," it was his painful task, since the law is no respecter of persons, to consider him solely in the character of a criminal. In attempting to balance what was due to Gandhi and what was in public interest, he imposed a sentence of six years' imprisonment, two years for each count of the charge. When the sentence was passed, Gandhi said it was as light as any judge would inflict on him, and thanked the court for its courtesy. Then the people moved forward and fell at Gandhi's feet, sobbing. Calm and smiling, he looked over their heads, giving encouragement, and, when his friends had left the court, he was led away to Sabarmati jail.

—NOTES BY HOUSTON PETERSON

Robert H. Jackson

:

CLOSING ADDRESS IN THE
NUREMBERG TRIAL

MR. PRESIDENT AND MEMBERS OF THE TRIBUNAL:
An advocate can be confronted with few more formidable tasks than
to select his closing arguments where there is great disparity between
his appropriate time and his available material. In eight months—
a short time as state trials go—we have introduced evidence which
embraces as vast and varied a panorama of events as ever has been
compressed within the framework of a litigation. It is impossible in
summation to do more than outline with bold strokes the vitals of this
trial's mad and melancholy record, which will live as the historical text
of the twentieth century's shame and depravity.

It is common to think of our own time as standing at the apex of
civilization, from which the deficiencies of preceding ages may patron-
izingly be viewed in the light of what is assumed to be "progress." The
reality is that in the long perspective of history the present century will
not hold an admirable position, unless its second half is to redeem its
first. These two-score years in this twentieth century will be recorded
in the book of years as one of the most bloody in all annals. Two
World Wars have left a legacy of dead which number more than all
the armies engaged in any war that made ancient or medieval history.
No half-century ever witnessed slaughter on such a scale, such cruelties
and inhumanities, such wholesale deportations of peoples into slavery, such annihilations of minorities. The terror of Torquemada pales
before the Nazi inquisition. These deeds are the overshadowing histori-

cal facts by which generations to come will remember this decade. If we cannot eliminate the causes and prevent the repetition of these barbaric events, it is not an irresponsible prophecy to say that this twentieth century may yet succeed in bringing the doom of civilization.

Goaded by these facts, we have moved to redress the blight on the record of our era. The defendants complain that our pace is too fast. In drawing the Charter of this Tribunal, we thought we were recording an accomplished advance in International Law. But they say that we have outrun our times, that we have anticipated an advance that should be, but has not yet been made. The Agreement of London, whether it originates or merely records, at all events marks a transition in International Law which roughly corresponds to that in the evolution in local law when men ceased to punish local crime by "hue and cry," and began to let reason and inquiry govern punishment. The society of nations has emerged from the primitive "hue and cry," the law of "catch and kill." It seeks to apply sanctions to enforce International Law, but to guide their application by evidence, law, and reason instead of outcry. The defendants denounce the law under which their accounting is asked. Their dislike for the law which condemns them is not original. It has been remarked before that

> No man e'er felt the halter draw
> With good opinion of the law.

I shall not labor the law of this case. The position of the United States was explained in my opening statement. My distinguished colleague, the Attorney General of Great Britain, will reply on behalf of all the Chief Prosecutors to the defendants' legal attack. At this stage of the proceedings, I shall rest upon the law of these crimes as laid down in the Charter. The defendants, who except for the Charter would have no right to be heard at all, now ask that the legal basis of this trial be nullified. This Tribunal, of course, is given no power to set aside or to modify the Agreement between the Four Powers, to which eighteen other nations have adhered. The terms of the Charter are conclusive upon every party to these proceedings.

In interpreting the Charter, however, we should not overlook the unique and emergent character of this body as an International Military Tribunal. It is no part of the constitutional mechanism of internal justice of any of the Signatory nations. Germany has unconditionally surrendered, but no peace treaty has been signed or agreed upon. The

Allies are still technically in a state of war with Germany, although the enemy's political and military institutions have collapsed. As a Military Tribunal, it is a continuation of the war effort of the Allied nations. As an International Tribunal, it is not bound by the procedural and sub- stantive refinements of our respective judicial or constitutional systems, nor will its rulings introduce precedents into any country's internal civil system of justice. As an International Military Tribunal, it rises above the provincial and transient and seeks guidance not only from International Law but also from the basic principles of jurisprudence which are assumptions of civilization and which long have found em- bodiment in the codes of all nations.

Of one thing we may be sure. The future will never have to ask, with misgiving: "What could the Nazis have said in their favor?" His- tory will know that whatever could be said, they were allowed to say. They have been given the kind of a trial which they, in the days of their pomp and power, never gave to any man.

But fairness is not weakness. The extraordinary fairness of these hearings is an attribute of our strength. The prosecution's case, at its close, seemed inherently unassailable because it rested so heavily on German documents of unquestioned authenticity. But it was the weeks upon weeks of pecking at this case by one after another of the defendants that has demonstrated its true strength. The fact is that the testimony of the defendants has removed any doubts of guilt which, because of the extraordinary nature and magnitude of these crimes, may have existed before they spoke. They have helped write their own judgment of condemnation.

But justice in this case has nothing to do with some of the arguments put forth by the defendants or their counsel. We have not previously and we need not now discuss the merits of all their obscure and tor- tuous philosophy. We are not trying them for possession of ob- noxious ideas. It is their right, if they choose, to renounce the Hebraic heritage in the civilization of which Germany was once a part. Nor is it our affair that they repudiated the Hellenic influence as well. The intellectual bankruptcy and moral perversion of the Nazi regime might have been no concern of International Law had it not been utilized to goose-step the *Herrenvolk* across international frontiers. It is not their thoughts, it is their overt acts which we charge to be crimes. Their creed and teachings are important only as evidence of motive, purpose, knowledge, and intent.

We charge unlawful aggression but we are not trying the motives, hopes, or frustrations which may have led Germany to resort to aggressive war as an instrument of policy. The law, unlike politics, does not concern itself with the good or evil in the *status quo,* nor with the merits of grievances against it. It merely requires that the *status quo* be not attacked by violent means and that policies be not advanced by war. We may admit that overlapping ethnological and cultural groups, economic barriers, and conflicting national ambitions created in the 1930s, as they will continue to create, grave problems for Germany as well as for the other peoples of Europe. We may admit too that the world had failed to provide political or legal remedies which would be honorable and acceptable alternatives to war. We do not underwrite either the ethics or the wisdom of any country, including my own, in the face of these problems. But we do say that it is now, as it was for sometime prior to 1939, illegal and criminal for Germany or any other nation to redress grievances or seek expansion by resort to aggressive war.

Let me emphasize one cardinal point. The United States has no interest which would be advanced by the conviction of any defendant if we have not proved him guilty on at least one of the counts charged against him in the Indictment. Any result that the calm and critical judgment of posterity would pronounce unjust would not be a victory for any of the countries associated in this prosecution. But in summation we now have before us the tested evidences of criminality and have heard the flimsy excuses and paltry evasions of the defendants. The suspended judgment with which we opened this case is no longer appropriate. The time has come for final judgment and if the case I present seems hard and uncompromising, it is because the evidence makes it so.

I perhaps can do no better service than to try to lift this case out of the morass of detail with which the record is full and put before you only the bold outlines of a case that is impressive in its simplicity. True, its thousands of documents and more thousands of pages of testimony deal with an epoch, and cover a continent, and touch almost every branch of human endeavor. They illuminate specialties, such as diplomacy, naval development and warfare, land warfare, the genesis of air warfare, the politics of the Nazi rise to power, the finance and economics of totalitarian war, sociology, penology, mass psychology, and mass pathology. I must leave it to experts to comb the evidence and write volumes on their specialties, while I picture in broad strokes the offenses whose acceptance as lawful would threaten the continuity of civilization. I must, as Kipling put it, "splash at a ten-league canvas with brushes of comet's hair."

THE CRIMES OF THE NAZI REGIME

The strength of the case against these defendants under the conspiracy count, which it is the duty of the United States to argue, is in its simplicity. It involves but three ultimate inquiries: first, have the acts defined by the Charter as crimes been committed; second, were they committed pursuant to a common plan or conspiracy; third, are these defendants among those who are criminally responsible?

The charge requires examination of a criminal policy, not of a multitude of isolated, unplanned, or disputed crimes. The substantive crimes upon which we rely, either as goals of a common plan or as means for its accomplishment, are admitted. The pillars which uphold the conspiracy charge may be found in five groups of overt acts, whose character and magnitude are important considerations in appraising the proof of conspiracy.

I. THE SEIZURE OF POWER AND SUBJUGATION OF GERMANY TO A POLICE STATE

The Nazi Party seized control of the German state in 1933. "Seizure of power" is a characterization used by defendants and defense witnesses, and so apt that it has passed into both history and everyday speech.

The Nazi junta in the early days lived in constant fear of overthrow. Göring, in 1934, pointed out that its enemies were legion and said:

Therefore the concentration camps have been created, where we have first confined thousands of Communists and Social Democrat functionaries.

In 1933 Göring forecast the whole program of purposeful cruelty and oppression when he publicly announced:

Whoever in the future raises a hand against a representative of the National Socialist movement or of the state, must know that he will lose his life in a very short while.

New political crimes were created to this end. It was made a treason, punishable with death, to organize or support a political party other than the Nazi Party. Circulating a false or exaggerated statement, or one which would harm the state or even the Party, was made a crime. Laws were enacted of such ambiguity that they could be used to punish almost any innocent act. It was, for example, made a crime to provoke "any act contrary to the public welfare."

The doctrine of punishment by analogy was introduced to enable conviction for acts which no statute forbade. Minister of Justice Gürtner explained that National Socialism considered every violation of the goals of life which the community set up for itself to be a wrong *per se,* and that the act could be punished even though it was not contrary to existing "formal" law.

The Gestapo and the SD were instrumentalities of an espionage system which penetrated public and private life. Göring controlled a personal wire-tapping unit. All privacy of communication was abolished. Party Blockleiters, appointed over every fifty households, continuously spied on all within their ken. Upon the strength of this spying, individuals were dragged off to "protective custody" and to concentration camps, without legal proceedings of any kind, and without statement of any reason therefor. The partisan political police were exempted from effective legal responsibility for their acts.

With all administrative offices in Nazi control and with the Reichstag reduced to impotence, the judiciary remained the last obstacle to this reign of terror. But its independence was soon overcome and it was reorganized to dispense a venal justice. Judges were ousted for political or racial reasons and were spied upon and put under pressure to join the Nazi Party. After the Supreme Court had acquitted three of the four men whom the Nazis accused of setting the Reichstag fire, its jurisdiction over treason cases was transferred to a newly established "People's Court" consisting of two judges and five Party officials. The German film of this "People's Court" in operation, which we showed in this chamber, revealed its presiding judge pouring partisan abuse upon speechless defendants. Special courts were created to try political crimes, only Party members were appointed judges, and "Judges Letters" instructed the puppet judges as to the "general lines" they must follow.

The result was the removal of all peaceable means either to resist or to change the government. Having sneaked through the portals of power, the Nazis slammed the gate in the face of all others who might also aspire to enter. Since the law was what the Nazis said it was, every form of opposition was rooted out, and every dissenting voice throttled. Germany was in the clutch of a police state, which used the fear of the concentration camp as a means to enforce nonresistance. The Party was the state, the state was the Party, and terror by day and death by night were the policy of both.

II. THE PREPARATION AND WAGING OF WARS OF AGGRESSION

From the moment the Nazis seized power, they set about by feverish but stealthy efforts, in defiance of the Versailles Treaty, to arm for war. In 1933 they found no air force. By 1939 they had 21 squadrons, consisting of 240 echelons or about 2,400 first-line planes, together with trainers and transports. In 1933 they found an army of 3 infantry and 3 cavalry divisions. By 1939 they had raised and equipped an army of 51 divisions, 4 of which were fully motorized and 4 of which were panzer divisions. In 1933 they found a navy of 1 cruiser and 6 light cruisers. By 1939 they had built a navy of 4 battleships, 1 aircraft carrier, 6 cruisers, 22 destroyers, and 54 submarines. They had also built up in that period an armament industry as efficient as that of any country in the world.

These new weapons were put to use, commencing in September 1939, in a series of undeclared wars against nations with which Germany had arbitration and nonaggression treaties, and in violation of repeated assurances. On September 1, 1939 this rearmed Germany attacked Poland. The following April witnessed the invasion and occupation of Denmark and Norway, and May saw the overrunning of Belgium, the Netherlands, and Luxembourg. Another spring found Yugoslavia and Greece under attack, and in June 1941 came the invasion of Soviet Russia. Then Japan, which Germany had embraced as a partner, struck without warning at Pearl Harbor in December 1941 and four days later Germany declared war on the United States.

We need not trouble ourselves about the many abstract difficulties that can be conjured up about what constitutes aggression in doubtful cases. I shall show you, in discussing the conspiracy, that by any test ever put forward by any responsible authority, by all the canons of plain sense, these were unlawful wars of aggression in breach of treaties and in violation of assurances.

III. WARFARE IN DISREGARD OF INTER-NATIONAL LAW

It is unnecessary to labor this point on the facts. Göring asserts that the Rules of Land Warfare were obsolete, that no nation could fight a total war within their limits. He testified that the Nazis would have denounced the Conventions to which Germany was a party, but that General Jodl wanted captured German soldiers to continue to benefit from their observance by the Allies.

It was, however, against the Soviet people and Soviet prisoners that Teutonic fury knew no bounds, in spite of a warning by Admiral Canaris that the treatment was in violation of International Law.

We need not, therefore, for purposes of the conspiracy count, recite the revolting details of starving, beating, murdering, freezing, and mass extermination admittedly used against the eastern soldiery. Also, we may take as established or admitted that the lawless conduct such as shooting British and American airmen, mistreatment of western prisoners of war, forcing French prisoners of war into German war work, and other deliberate violations of the Hague and Geneva Conventions, did occur, and in obedience to highest levels of authority.

IV. ENSLAVEMENT AND PLUNDER OF POPULATIONS IN OCCUPIED COUNTRIES

The defendant Sauckel, Plenipotentiary General for the Utilization of Labor, is authority for the statement that "out of five million foreign workers who arrived in Germany, not even 200,000 came voluntarily." It was officially reported to defendant Rosenberg that in his territory "recruiting methods were used which probably have their origin in the blackest period of the slave trade." Sauckel himself reported that male and female agents went hunting for men, got them drunk, and "shanghaied" them to Germany. These captives were shipped in trains without heat, food, or sanitary facilities. The dead were thrown out at stations, and the newborn were thrown out the windows of moving trains.

Sauckel ordered that "all the men must be fed, sheltered, and treated in such a way as to exploit them to the highest possible extent at the lowest conceivable degree of expenditure." About two million of these were employed directly in the manufacture of armaments and munitions. The director of the Krupp locomotive factory in Essen complained to the company that Russian forced laborers were so underfed that they were too weakened to do their work, and the Krupp doctor confirmed their pitiable condition. Soviet workers were put in camps under Gestapo guards, who were allowed to punish disobedience by confinement in a concentration camp or by hanging on the spot.

Populations of occupied countries were otherwise exploited and oppressed unmercifully. Terrorism was the order of the day. Civilians were arrested without charges, committed without counsel, executed without hearing. Villages were destroyed, the male inhabitants shot or sent to concentration camps, the women sent to forced labor, and the children scattered abroad. The extent of the slaughter in Poland alone was indicated by Frank, who reported:

If I wanted to have a poster put up for every seven Poles who were shot, the forests of Poland would not suffice for producing the paper for such posters.

Those who will enslave men cannot be expected to refrain from plundering them. Boastful reports show how thoroughly and scientifically the resources of occupied lands were sucked into the German war economy, inflicting shortage, hunger, and inflation upon the inhabitants. Besides this grand plan to aid the German war effort there were the sordid activities of the Rosenberg *Einsatzstab,* which pillaged art treasures for Göring and his fellow bandits. It is hard to say whether the spectacle of Germany's number two leader urging his people to give up every comfort and strain every sinew on essential war work while he rushed around confiscating art by the trainload should be cast as tragedy or comedy. In either case it was a crime.

International Law at all times before and during this war spoke with precision and authority respecting the protection due civilians of an occupied country, and the slave trade and plunder of occupied countries were at all times flagrantly unlawful.

V. PERSECUTION AND EXTERMINATION
OF JEWS AND CHRISTIANS

The Nazi movement will be of evil memory in history because of its persecution of the Jews, the most far-flung and terrible racial persecution of all time. Although the Nazi Party neither invented nor monopolized anti-Semitism, its leaders from the very beginning embraced it, incited it, and exploited it. They used it as "the psychological spark that ignites the mob." After the seizure of power, it became an official state policy. The persecution began in a series of discriminatory laws eliminating the Jews from the civil service, the professions, and economic life. As it became more intense it included segregation of Jews in ghettos and exile. Riots were organized by Party leaders to loot Jewish business places and to burn synagogues. Jewish property was confiscated and a collective fine of a billion marks was imposed upon German Jewry. The program progressed in fury and irresponsibility to the "final solution." This consisted of sending all Jews who were fit to work to concentration camps as slave laborers, and all who were not fit, which included children under twelve and people over fifty, as well as any others judged unfit by an SS doctor, to concentration camps for extermination.

Adolf Eichmann, the sinister figure who had charge of the extermination program, has estimated that the anti-Jewish activities resulted in the killing of six million Jews. Of these, four million were killed in extermination institutions, and two million were killed by *Einsatzgruppen,* mobile units of the Security Police and SD which pursued Jews in the ghettos and in their homes and slaughtered them by gas wagons, by mass shooting in anti-tank ditches, and by every device which Nazi ingenuity could conceive. So thorough and uncompromising was this program that the Jews of Europe as a race no longer exist, thus fulfilling the diabolic "prophecy" of Adolf Hitler at the beginning of the war.

Of course, any such program must reckon with the opposition of the Christian church. This was recognized from the very beginning. Defendant Bormann wrote all Gauleiters in 1941 that "National Socialism and Christian concepts are irreconcilable," and that the people must be separated from the churches and the influence of the churches totally removed. Defendant Rosenberg even wrote dreary treatises advocating a new and weird Nazi religion.

The Gestapo appointed "church specialists" who were instructed that the ultimate aim was "destruction of the confessional churches." The record is full of specific instances of the persecution of clergymen, the confiscation of church property, interference with religious publications, disruption of religious education, and suppression of religious organizations.

The chief instrumentality for persecution and extermination was the concentration camp, sired by defendant Göring and nurtured under the over-all authority of defendants Frick and Kaltenbrunner.

The horrors of these iniquitous places have been vividly disclosed by documents and testified to by witnesses. The Tribunal must be satiated with ghastly verbal and pictorial portrayals. From your records it is clear that the concentration camps were the first and worst weapon of oppression used by the National Socialist state, and that they were the primary means utilized for the persecution of the Christian church and the extermination of the Jewish race. This has been admitted to you by some of the defendants from the witness stand. In the words of defendant Frank:

A thousand years will pass and this guilt of Germany will still not be erased.

These, then, were the five great substantive crimes of the Nazi regime. Their commission, which cannot be denied, stands admitted. The defendant Keitel, who is in a position to know the facts, has given the Tribunal what seems to be a fair summation of the case on these facts:

The defendant has declared that he admits the contents of the general Indictment to be proved from the objective and factual point of view (that is to say, not every individual case) and this in consideration of the law of procedure governing this trial. It would be senseless, despite the possibility of refuting several documents or individual facts to attempt to shake the Indictment as a whole.

I pass now to the inquiry whether these groups of criminal acts were integrated in a common plan or conspiracy.

THE COMMON PLAN OR CONSPIRACY

The prosecution submits that these five categories of premeditated crimes were not separate and independent phenomena but that all were committed pursuant to a common plan or conspiracy. The defense admits that these classes of crimes were committed but denies that they are connected one with another as parts of a single program.

The central crime in this pattern of crime, the kingpin which holds them all together, is the plot for aggressive war. The chief reason for international cognizance of these crimes lies in this fact. Have we established the plan or conspiracy to make aggressive war?

Certain admitted or clearly proven facts help answer that question. First is the fact that such war of aggression did take place. Second, it is admitted that from the moment the Nazis came to power, every one of them and every one of the defendants worked like beavers to prepare for *some* war. The question therefore comes to this: were they preparing for the war which did occur, or were they preparing for some war which never has happened? It is probably true that in the early days none of them had in mind what month of what year war would begin, the exact dispute which would precipitate it, or whether its first impact would be Austria, Czechoslovakia, or Poland. But I submit that the defendants either knew or are chargeable with knowledge that the war for which they were making ready would be a war of German aggression. This is partly because there was no real expectation that any power or combination of powers would attack Germany. But it is chiefly because the inherent nature of the German plans was such that they were certain sooner or later to meet resistance and that they could then be accomplished only by aggression.

The plans of Adolf Hitler for aggression were just as secret as *Mein Kampf,* of which over six million copies were published in Germany. He not only openly advocated overthrowing the Treaty of Versailles, but made demands which went far beyond a mere rectification of its alleged injustices. He avowed an intention to attack neighboring states and seize their lands, which he said would have to be won with "the power of a triumphant sword." Here, for every German to hearken to, were the "ancestral voices prophesying war."

Göring has testified in this courtroom that at his first meeting with Hitler, long before the seizure of power:

I noted that Hitler had a definite view of the impotency of protest and, as a second point, that he was of the opinion that Germany should be freed of the peace of Versailles. . . . We did not say we shall have to have a war and defeat our enemies; this was the aim and the methods had to be adapted to the political situation.

When asked if this goal were to be accomplished by war if necessary, Göring did not deny that eventuality but evaded a direct answer by saying: "We did not even debate about those things at that time." He went on to say that the aim to overthrow the Treaty of Versailles was open and notorious and that "Every German in my opinion was for its modification, and there was no doubt that this was a strong inducement for joining the Party." Thus, there can be no possible excuse for any person who aided Hitler to get absolute power over the German people, or took a part in his regime, to fail to know the nature of the demands he would make on Germany's neighbors.

Immediately after the seizure of power the Nazis went to work to implement these aggressive intentions by preparing for war. They first enlisted German industrialists in a secret rearmament program. Twenty days after the seizure of power Schacht was host to Hitler, Göring, and some twenty leading industrialists. Among them were Krupp von Bohlen of the great Krupp armament works and representatives of I. G. Farben and other Ruhr heavy industries. Hitler and Göring explained their program to the industrialists, who became so enthusiastic that they set about to raise three million Reichsmarks to strengthen and confirm the Nazi Party in power. Two months later Krupp was working to bring a reorganized association of German industry into agreement with the political aims of the Nazi government. Krupp later boasted of the success in keeping the German war industries secretly alive and in readiness despite the disarmament clauses of the Versailles Treaty, and recalled the industrialists' enthusiastic acceptance of "the great intentions of the Führer in the rearmament period of 1933-39."

Some two months after Schacht had sponsored this first meeting to gain the support of the industrialists, the Nazis moved to harness industrial labor to their aggressive plans. In April 1933 Hitler ordered Dr. Ley "to take over the trade unions," numbering some six million members. By Party directive Ley seized the unions, their property, and their funds. Union leaders, taken into "protective custody" by the SS and SA, were put into concentration camps. The free labor unions were then replaced by a Nazi organization known as the German Labor Front, with Dr. Ley as its head. It was expanded until it controlled over twenty-three million members. Collective bargaining was eliminated, the voice of labor could no longer be heard as to working conditions, and the labor contract was prescribed by "trustees of labor" appointed by Hitler. The war purpose of this labor program was clearly acknowledged by Robert Ley five days after war broke out, when he declared in a speech that:

We National Socialists have monopolized all resources and all our energies during the past seven years so as to be able to be equipped for the supreme effort of battle.

The Nazis also proceeded at once to adapt the government to the needs of war. In April 1935 the Cabinet formed a Defense Council, the working committee of which met frequently thereafter. In the meeting of May 23, 1933, at which defendant Keitel presided, the members were instructed that

No document must be lost since otherwise the enemy propaganda would make use of it. Matters communicated orally cannot be proven; they can be denied by us in Geneva.

In January 1934, with defendant Jodl present, the Council planned a mobilization calendar and mobilization order for some 240,000 industrial plants. Again it was agreed that nothing should be in writing so that "the military purpose may not be traceable."

On May 21, 1933, the top secret Reich Defense Law was enacted. Defendant Schacht was appointed Plenipotentiary General for War Economy with the task of secretly preparing all economic forces for war and, in the event of mobilization, of financing the war. Schacht's secret efforts were supplemented in October 1936 by the appointment of defendant Göring as Commissioner of the Four Year Plan, with the duty of putting the entire economy in a state of readiness for war within four years.

A secret program for the accumulation of the raw materials and foreign credits necessary for extensive rearmament was also set on foot immediately upon seizure of power. In September 1934 the Minister of Economics was already complaining that:

The task of stockpiling is being hampered by the lack of foreign currency; the need for secrecy and camouflage also is a retarding influence.

Foreign currency controls were at once established. Financing was delegated to the wizard Schacht, who conjured up the MEFO bill to serve the dual objectives of tapping the short-term money market for rearmament purposes while concealing the amount of these expenditures.

The spirit of the whole Nazi administration was summed up by Göring at a meeting of the Council of Ministers, which included Schacht, on May 27, 1936, when he said,

All measures are to be considered from the standpoint of an assured waging of war.

The General Staff, of course, also had to be enlisted in the war plans. Most of the Generals, attracted by the prospect of rebuilding their armies, became willing accomplices. The hold-over Minister of War von Blomberg and the Chief of Staff General von Fritsch, however, were not cordial to the increasingly belligerent policy of the Hitler regime, and by vicious and obscene plotting they were discredited and removed in January 1938. Thereupon, Hitler assumed for himself Supreme Command of the Armed Forces, and the positions of von Blomberg and von Fritsch were filled by others who became, as Blomberg said of Keitel, "a willing tool in Hitler's hands for every one of his decisions." The Generals did not confine their participation to merely military matters. They participated in all major diplomatic and political maneuvers, such as the Obersalzburg meeting where Hitler, flanked by Keitel and other top Generals, issued his virtual ultimatum to Schuschnigg.

As early as November 5, 1937, the plan to attack had begun to take definiteness as to time and victim. In a meeting which included defendants Raeder, Göring, and von Neurath, Hitler stated the cynical objective:

The question for Germany is where the greatest possible conquest could be made at the lowest possible cost.

He discussed various plans for the invasion of Austria and Czechoslovakia, indicating clearly that he was thinking of these territories not as ends in themselves, but as means for further conquest. He pointed out that considerable military and political assistance would be afforded by possession of these lands and discussed the possibility of constituting from them new armies up to a strength of about twelve divisions. The aim he stated boldly and baldly as the acquisition of additional living space in Europe, and recognized that "the German question can be solved only by way of force."

Six months later, emboldened by the bloodless Austrian conquest, Hitler, in a secret directive to Keitel, stated his "unalterable decision to smash Czechoslovakia by military action in the near future." On the same day, Jodl noted in his diary that the Führer had stated his final decision to destroy Czechoslovakia soon and had initiated military preparations all along the line. By April the plan had been perfected to attack Czechoslovakia "with lightning-swift action as the result of an 'incident.' "

All along the line preparations became more definite for a war of expansion, on the assumption that it would result in world-wide conflict. In September 1938 Admiral Carls officially commented on a "Draft Study of Naval Warfare Against England":

There is full agreement with the main theme of the study.

1. If according to the Führer's decision Germany is to acquire a position as a world power, she needs not only sufficient colonial possessions but also secure naval communications and secure access to the ocean.

2. Both requirements can only be fulfilled in opposition to Anglo-French interests and will limit their position as world powers. It is unlikely that they can be achieved by peaceful means. The decision to make Germany a world power therefore forces upon us the necessity of making the corresponding preparations for war.

3. War against England means at the same time war against the Empire, against France, probably against Russia as well, and a large number of countries overseas; in fact, against one-half to one-third of the whole world.

It can only be justified and have a chance of success if it is prepared economically as well as politically and militarily and waged with the aim of conquering for Germany an outlet to the ocean.

This Tribunal knows what categorical assurances were given to an alarmed world after the *Anschluss,* after Munich, and after the occupation of Bohemia and Moravia, that German ambitions were realized and that Hitler had "no further territorial demands to make in Europe." The record of this trial shows that those promises were calculated deceptions and that those high in the bloody brotherhood of Nazidom knew it.

As early as April 15, 1938, Göring pointed out to Mussolini and Ciano that the possession of those territories would make possible an attack on Poland. Ribbentrop's Ministry wrote on August 26, 1938, that:

After the liquidation of the Czechoslovakian question, it will be generally assumed that Poland will be next in turn.

Hitler, after the Polish invasion, boasted that it was the Austrian and Czechoslovakian triumphs by which "the basis for the action against Poland was laid." Göring suited the act to the purpose and gave immediate instructions to exploit for the further strengthening of Germany the war potential, first of the Sudetenland, and then of the whole Protectorate.

By May 1939 the Nazi preparations had ripened to the point that Hitler confided to defendants Göring, Raeder, Keitel, and others, his readiness "to attack Poland at the first suitable opportunity," even though he recognized that "further successes cannot be attained without the shedding of blood." The larcenous motives behind this decision he made plain in words that echoed the covetous theme of *Mein Kampf:*

Circumstances must be adapted to aims. This is impossible without invasion of foreign states or attacks upon foreign property. Living space, in proportion to the magnitude of the state, is the basis of all power—further successes cannot be attained without expanding our living space in the east. . . .

While a credulous world slumbered, snugly blanketed with perfidious assurances of peaceful intentions, the Nazis prepared not merely as before for *a* war, but now for *the* war. The defendants Göring, Keitel, Raeder, Frick, and Funk, with others, met as the Reich Defense Council in June 1939. The minutes, authenticated by Göring, are revealing evidence of the way in which each step of Nazi planning dovetailed with every other. These five key defendants, three months before the first Panzer unit had knifed into Poland, were laying plans for "employment of the *population* in wartime," and had gone so far as to classify industry for priority in labor supply "after five million servicemen had been called up." They decided upon measures to avoid "confusion when mobilization takes place," and declared a purpose "to gain and maintain the lead in the decisive initial weeks of a war." They then planned to use in production prisoners of war, criminal prisoners, and concentration camp inmates. They then decided on "compulsory work for women in wartime." They had already passed on applications from 1,172,000 specialist workmen for classification as indispensable, and had approved 727,000 of them. They boasted that orders to workers to report for duty "are ready and tied up in bundles at the labor offices." And they resolved to increase the industrial manpower supply by bringing into Germany "hundreds of thousands of workers" from the Protectorate to be "housed together in hutments."

It is the minutes of this significant conclave of many key defendants which disclose how the plan to start the war was coupled with the plan to wage the war through the use of illegal sources of labor to maintain production. Hitler, in announcing his plan to attack Poland, had already foreshadowed the slave-labor program as one of its corollaries when he cryptically pointed out to defendants Göring, Raeder, Keitel, and others that the Polish population "will be available as a source of labor." This was the part of the plan made good by Frank, who, as Governor General notified Göring that he would supply "at least one million male and female agricultural and industrial workers to the Reich," and by Sauckel, whose impressments throughout occupied territory aggregated numbers equal to the total population of some of the smaller nations of Europe.

Here also comes to the surface the link between war labor and concentration camps, a manpower source that was increasingly used and with increasing cruelty. An agreement between Himmler and the Minister of Justice Thierack in 1942 provided for "the delivery of anti-social elements from the execution of their sentence to the Reichsführer SS to be worked to death." An SS directive provided that bedridden prisoners be drafted for work to be performed in bed. The Gestapo ordered forty-five thousand Jews arrested to increase the "recruitment of manpower into the concentration camps." One hundred thousand Jews were brought from Hungary to augment the camps' manpower. On the initiative of the defendant Dönitz, concentration-camp labor was used in the construction of submarines. Concentration camps were thus geared into war production on the one hand, and into the administration of justice and the political aims of the Nazis on the other.

The use of prisoner-of-war labor as here planned also grew with German needs. At a time when every German soldier was needed at the front and forces were not available at home, Russian prisoners of war were forced to man antiaircraft guns against Allied planes. Field Marshal Milch reflected the Nazi merriment at this flagrant violation of International Law, saying,

This is an amusing thing, that the Russians must work the guns.

The orders for the treatment of Soviet prisoners of war were so ruthless that Admiral Canaris, pointing out that they would "result in arbitrary mistreatments and killings," protested to the OKW against them as breaches of International Law. The reply of Keitel was unambiguous:

The objections arise from the military conception of chivalrous warfare! This is the destruction of an ideology! Therefore I approve and back the measures.

The Geneva Convention would have been thrown overboard openly except that Jodl objected because he wanted the benefits of Allied observance of it while it was not being allowed to hamper the Germans in any way.

Other crimes in the conduct of warfare were planned with equal thoroughness as a means of insuring the victory of German arms. In October 1938, almost a year before the start of the war, the large-scale violation of the established rules of warfare was contemplated as a policy, and the Supreme Command circulated a most secret list of devious explanations to be given by the Propaganda Minister in such cases. Even before this time commanders of the armed forces were instructed to employ any means of warfare so long as it facilitated victory. After the war was in progress the orders increased in savagery. A typical Keitel order, demanding use of the "most brutal means," provided that:

It is the duty of the troops to use all means without restriction, even against women and children, so long as it insures success.

The German naval forces were no more immune from the infection than the land forces. Raeder ordered violations of the accepted rules of warfare wherever necessary to gain strategic successes. Dönitz urged his submarine crews not to rescue survivors of torpedoed enemy ships in order to cripple merchant shipping of the Allied nations by decimating their crews.

Thus, the war crimes against Allied forces and the crimes against humanity committed in occupied territories are incontestably part of the program of making the war because, in the German calculations, they were indispensable to its hope of success.

Similarly, the whole group of pre-war crimes, including the persecutions within Germany, fall into place around the plan for aggressive war like stones in a finely wrought mosaic. Nowhere is the whole catalogue of crimes of Nazi oppression and terrorism within Germany so well integrated with the crime of war as in that strange mixture of wind and wisdom which makes up the testimony of Hermann Göring. In describing the aims of the Nazi program before the seizure of power, Göring said:

> The first question was to achieve and establish a different political structure for Germany which would enable Germany to obtain against the Dictate [of Versailles], and not only a protest, but an objection of such a nature that it would actually be considered.

With these purposes, Göring admitted that the plan was made to over-throw the Weimar Republic, to seize power, and to carry out the Nazi program by whatever means were necessary, whether legal or illegal.

From Göring's cross-examination we learn how necessarily the whole program of crime followed. Because they considered a strong state nec-essary to get rid of the Versailles Treaty, they adopted the *Führer-prinzip*. Having seized power, the Nazis thought it necessary to protect it by abolishing parliamentary government and suppressing all organ-ized opposition from political parties. This was reflected in the philoso-phy of Göring that the opera was more important than the Reichstag. Even the "opposition of each individual person was not tolerated un-less it was a matter of unimportance." To insure the suppression of opposition a secret political police was necessary. In order to eliminate incorrigible opponents, it was necessary to establish concentration camps and to resort to the device of protective custody. Protective custody, Göring testified, meant that

> People were arrested and taken into protective custody who had committed no crime but who one might expect, if they remained in freedom, would do all sorts of things to damage the German state.

The same purpose was dominant in the persecution of the Jews. In the beginning, fanaticism and political opportunism played a princi-pal part, for anti-Semitism and its allied scapegoat mythology were a vehicle on which the Nazis rode to power. It was for this reason that the filthy Streicher and the blasphemous Rosenberg were welcomed to a place at Party rallies and made leaders and officials of the state or Party. But the Nazis soon regarded the Jews as foremost amongst the opposition to the police state with which they planned to put forward their plans of military aggression. Fear of their pacifism and their op-position to strident nationalism was given as the reason that the Jews had to be driven from the political and economic life of Germany. Accordingly, they were transported like cattle to the concentration camps, where they were utilized as a source of forced labor for war purposes.

At a meeting held on November 12, 1938, two days after the violent anti-Jewish pogroms instigated by Goebbels and carried out by the Party Leadership Corps and the SA, the program for the elimination of the Jews from the German economy was mapped out by Göring, Funk, Heydrich, Goebbels, and other top Nazis. The measures adopted included confinement of the Jews in ghettos, cutting off their food supply, "aryanizing" their shops, and restricting their freedom of movement. Here another purpose behind the Jewish persecutions crept in, for it was the wholesale confiscation of their property which helped finance German rearmament. Although Schacht's plan to have foreign money ransom the entire race within Germany was not adopted, the Jews were stripped to the point where Göring was able to advise the Reich Defense Council that the critical situation of the Reich exchequer, due to rearmament, had been relieved "through the billion Reichsmark fine imposed on Jewry, and through profits accrued to the Reich in the aryanization of Jewish enterprises."

A glance over the dock will show that, despite quarrels among themselves, each defendant played a part which fitted in with every other, and that all advanced the common plan. It contradicts experience that men of such diverse backgrounds and talents should so forward each other's aims by coincidence.

The large and varied role of Göring was half militarist and half gangster. He stuck a pudgy finger in every pie. He used his SA musclemen to help bring the gang into power. In order to entrench that power he contrived to have the Reichstag burned, established the Gestapo, and created the concentration camps. He was equally adept at massacring opponents and at framing scandals to get rid of stubborn generals. He built up the Luftwaffe and hurled it at his defenseless neighbors. He was among the foremost in harrying the Jews out of the land. By mobilizing the total economic resources of Germany he made possible the waging of the war which he had taken a large part in planning. He was, next to Hitler, the man who tied the activities of all the defendants together in a common effort.

The parts played by the other defendants, although less comprehensive and less spectacular than that of the Reichsmarshal, were nevertheless integral and necessary contributions to the joint undertaking, without any one of which the success of the common enterprise would have been in jeopardy. There are many specific deeds of which these men have been proven guilty. No purpose would be served—nor indeed is time available—to review all the crimes which the evidence has charged up to their names. Nevertheless, in viewing the conspiracy as a whole and as an operating mechanism it may be well to recall briefly the outstanding services which each of the men in the dock rendered to the common cause.

The zealot HESS, before succumbing to wanderlust, was the engineer tending the Party machinery, passing orders and propaganda down to the Leadership Corps, supervising every aspect of Party activities, and maintaining the organization as a loyal and ready instrument of power. When apprehensions abroad threatened the success of the Nazi scheme for conquest, it was the duplicitous RIBBENTROP, the salesman of deception, who was detailed to pour wine on the troubled waters of suspicion by preaching the gospel of limited and peaceful intentions. KEITEL, weak and willing too, delivered the armed forces, the instrument of aggression, over to the Party and directed them in executing its felonious designs.

KALTENBRUNNER, the grand inquisitor, took up the bloody mantle of Heydrich to stifle opposition and terrorize compliance, and buttressed the power of National Socialism on a foundation of guiltless corpses. It was ROSENBERG, the intellectual high priest of the "master race," who provided the doctrine of hatred which gave the impetus for the annihilation of Jewry, and who put his infidel theories into practice against the eastern occupied territories. His woolly philosophy also added boredom to the long list of Nazi atrocities. The fanatical FRANK, who solidified Nazi control by establishing the new order of authority without law, so that the will of the Party was the only test of legality, proceeded to export his lawlessness to Poland, which he governed with the lash of Caesar and whose population he reduced to sorrowing remnants. FRICK, the ruthless organizer, helped the Party to seize power, supervised the police agencies to insure that it stayed in power, and chained the economy of Bohemia and Moravia to the German war machine.

STREICHER, the venomous vulgarian, manufactured and distributed obscene racial libels which incited the populace to accept and assist the progressively savage operations of "race purification." As Minister of Economics FUNK accelerated the pace of rearmament, and as Reichsbank President banked for the SS the gold teeth fillings of concentration camp victims—probably the most ghoulish collateral in banking history. It was SCHACHT, the façade of starched respectability, who in the early days provided the window-dressing, the bait for the hesitant, and whose wizardry later made it possible for Hitler to finance the colossal rearmament program, and to do it secretly.

DÖNITZ, Hitler's legatee of defeat, promoted the success of the Nazi aggressions by instructing his pack of submarine killers to conduct warfare at sea with the illegal ferocity of the jungle. RAEDER, the political admiral, stealthily built up the German navy in defiance of the Versailles Treaty, and then put it to use in a series of aggressions which he had taken a large part in planning. VON SCHIRACH, poisoner of a generation, initiated the German youth in Nazi doctrine, trained them in legions for service in the SS and Wehrmacht, and delivered them up to the Party as fanatic, unquestioning executors of its will.

SAUCKEL, the greatest and cruelest slaver since the Pharaohs of Egypt, produced desperately needed manpower by driving foreign peoples into the land of bondage on a scale unknown even in the ancient days of tyranny in the kingdom of the Nile. JODL, betrayer of the traditions of his profession, led the Wehrmacht in violating its own code of military honor in order to carry out the barbarous aims of Nazi policy. VON PAPEN, pious agent of an infidel regime, held the stirrup while Hitler vaulted into the saddle, lubricated the Austrian annexation, and devoted his diplomatic cunning to the service of Nazi objectives abroad.

SEYSS-INQUART, spearhead of the Austrian fifth column, took over the government of his own country only to make a present of it to Hitler, and then, moving north, brought terror and oppression to the Netherlands and pillaged its economy for the benefit of the German juggernaut. VON NEURATH, the old-school diplomat, who cast the pearls of his experience before Nazis, guided Nazi diplomacy in the early years, soothed the fears of prospective victims, and as Reich Protector of Bohemia and Moravia, strengthened the German position for the coming attack on Poland. SPEER, as Minister of Armaments and War Production, joined in planning and executing the program to dragoon prisoners of war and foreign workers into German war industries, which waxed in output while the laborers waned in starvation. FRITZSCHE, radio propaganda chief, by manipulation of the truth goaded

German public opinion into frenzied support of the regime and anesthetized the independent judgment of the population so that they did without question their masters' bidding. And BORMANN, who has not accepted our invitation to this reunion, sat at the throttle of the vast and powerful engine of the Party, guiding it in the ruthless execution of Nazi policies, from the scourging of the Christian church to the lynching of captive Allied airmen.

The activities of all these defendants, despite their varied backgrounds and talents, were joined with the efforts of other conspirators not now in the dock, who played still other essential roles. They blend together into one consistent and militant pattern animated by a common objective to reshape the map of Europe by force of arms. Some of these defendants were ardent members of the Nazi movement from its birth. Others, less fanatical, joined the common enterprise later, after successes had made participation attractive by the promise of rewards. This group of latter-day converts remedied a crucial defect in the ranks of the original true believers, for as Dr. Seimers has pointed out in his summation:

There were no specialists among the National Socialists for the particular tasks. Most of the National Socialist collaborators did not previously follow a trade requiring technical education.

It was the fatal weakness of the early Nazi band that it lacked technical competence. It could not from among its own ranks make up a government capable of carrying out all the projects necessary to realize its aims. Therein lies the special crime and betrayal of men like Schacht and von Neurath, Speer and von Papen, Raeder and Dönitz, Keitel and Jodl. It is doubtful whether the Nazi master plan could have succeeded without their specialized intelligence which they so willingly put at its command. They did so with knowledge of its announced aims and methods, and continued their services after practice had confirmed the direction in which they were tending. Their superiority to the average run of Nazi mediocrity is not their excuse. It is their condemnation.

The dominant fact which stands out from all the thousands of pages of the record of this trial is that the central crime of the whole group of Nazi crimes—the attack on the peace of the world—was clearly and deliberately planned. The beginning of these wars of aggression was not an unprepared and spontaneous springing to arms by a population excited by some current indignation. A week before the invasion of Poland Hitler told his military commanders:

I shall give a propagandist cause for starting war—never mind whether it be plausible or not. The victor shall not be asked later on whether we told the truth or not. In starting and making a war, not the right is what matters, but victory.

The propagandist incident was duly provided by dressing concentration camp inmates in Polish uniforms, in order to create the appearance of a Polish attack on a German frontier radio station. The plan to occupy Belgium, Holland, and Luxembourg first appeared as early as August 1938 in connection with the plan for attack on Czechoslovakia. The intention to attack became a program in May 1939, when Hitler told his commanders that:

The Dutch and Belgian air bases must be occupied by armed forces. Declarations of neutrality must be ignored.

Thus, the follow-up wars were planned before the first was launched. These were the most carefully plotted wars in all history. Scarcely a step in their terrifying succession and progress failed to move according to the master blueprint or the subsidiary schedules and timetables until long after the crimes of aggression were consummated.

Nor were the war crimes and the crimes against humanity unplanned, isolated, or spontaneous offenses. Aside from our undeniable evidence of their plotting, it is sufficient to ask whether six million people could be separated from the population of several nations on the basis of their blood and birth, could be destroyed and their bodies disposed of, except that the operation fitted into the general scheme of government. Could the enslavement of five millions of laborers, their impressment into service, their transportation to Germany, their allocation to work where they would be most useful, their maintenance—if slow starvation can be called maintenance—and their guarding have been accomplished if it did not fit into the common plan? Could hundreds of concentration camps located throughout Germany, built to accommodate hundreds of thousands of victims, and each requiring labor and materials for construction, manpower to operate and supervise, and close gearing into the economy—could such efforts have been expended under German autocracy if they had not suited the plan? Has the Teutonic passion for organization become famous for its toleration of nonconforming activity? Each part of the plan fitted into every other.

The slave-labor program meshed with the needs of industry and agriculture, and these in turn synchronized with the military machine. The elaborate propaganda apparatus geared with the program to dominate the people and incite them to a war their sons would have to fight. The armament industries were fed by the concentration camps. The concentration camps were fed by the Gestapo. The Gestapo was fed by the spy system of the Nazi Party. Nothing was permitted under the Nazi iron rule that was not in accordance with the program. Everything of consequence that took place in this regimented society was but a manifestation of a premeditated and unfolding purpose to secure the Nazi state a place in the sun by casting all others into darkness.

COMMON DEFENSES AGAINST THE CHARGE OF COMMON RESPONSIBILITY

The defendants meet this overwhelming case, some by admitting a limited responsibility, some by putting the blame on others, and some by taking the position, in effect, that while there have been enormous crimes there are no criminals. Time will not permit me to examine each individual and peculiar defense, but there are certain lines of defense common to so many cases that they deserve some consideration.

Counsel for many of the defendants seek to dismiss the conspiracy or common-planning charge on the ground that the pattern of the Nazi plan does not fit the concept of conspiracy applicable in German law to the plotting of a highway robbery or a burglary. Their concept of conspiracy is in the terms of a stealthy meeting in the dead of night, in a secluded hideout, in which a group of felons plot every detail of a specific crime. The Charter forestalls resort to such parochial and narrow concepts of conspiracy taken from local law by using the additional and nontechnical term, "common plan." Omitting entirely the alternative term of "conspiracy," the Charter reads that "leaders, organizers, instigators, and accomplices participating in the formulation or execution of a common plan to commit" any of the described crimes "are responsible for all acts performed by any persons in execution of such plan."

The Charter concept of a common plan really represents the conspiracy principle in an international context. A common plan or conspiracy to seize the machinery of a state, to commit crimes against the peace of the world, to blot a race out of existence, to enslave millions, and to subjugate and loot whole nations cannot be thought of in the same terms as the plotting of petty crimes, although the same underlying principles are applicable. Little gangsters may plan which will carry a pistol and which a stiletto, who will approach a victim from the front and who from behind, and where they will waylay him. But in planning a war the pistol becomes a Wehrmacht, the stiletto a Luftwaffe. Where to strike is not a choice of dark alleys, but a matter of world geography.

The operation involves the manipulation of public opinion, the law of the state, the police power, industry, and finance. The baits and bluffs must be translated into a nation's foreign policy. Likewise, the degree of stealth which points to a guilty purpose in a conspiracy will depend upon its object. The clandestine preparations of a state against international society, although camouflaged to those abroad, might be quite open and notorious among its own people. But stealth is not an essential ingredient of such planning. Parts of the common plan may be proclaimed from the housetops, as anti-Semitism was, and parts of it kept undercover, as rearmament for a long time was. It is a matter of strategy how much of the preparation shall be made public, as was Göring's announcement in 1935 of the creation of an air force, and how much shall be kept covert, as in the case of the Nazis' use of shovels to teach "labor corps" the manual of arms. The forms of this grand type of conspiracy are amorphous, the means are opportunistic, and neither can divert the law from getting at the substance of things.

The defendants contend, however, that there could be no conspiracy involving aggressive war because: (1) none of the Nazis wanted war; (2) rearmament was only intended to provide the strength to make Germany's voice heard in the family of nations; and (3) the wars were not in fact aggressive wars but were defensive against a "Bolshevik menace."

When we analyze the argument that the Nazis did not want war it comes down, in substance, to this: "The record looks bad indeed—objectively—but when you consider the state of my mind—subjectively I hated war. I knew the horrors of war. I wanted peace." I am not so sure of this. I am even less willing to accept Göring's description of the General Staff as pacifist. However, it will not injure our case to admit that as an abstract proposition none of these defendants liked war. But they wanted things which they knew they could not get without war. They wanted their neighbors' lands and goods. Their philosophy seems to be that if the neighbors would not acquiesce, then they are the aggressors and are to blame for the war. The fact is, however, that war never became terrible to the Nazis until it came home to them, until it exposed their deceptive assurances to the German people that German cities, like the ruined one in whcih we meet, would be invulnerable. From then on war was terrible.

But again the defendants claim: "To be sure we were building guns. But not to shoot. They were only to give us weight in negotiating." At its best this argument amounts to a contention that the military forces were intended for blackmail, not for battle. The threat of military invasion which forced the Austrian *Anschluss,* the threats which preceded Munich, and Göring's threat to bomb the beautiful city of Prague if the President of Czechoslovakia did not consent to the Protectorate, are examples of what the defendants have in mind when they talk of arming to back negotiation.

But from the very nature of German demands, the day was bound to come when some country would refuse to buy its peace, would refuse to pay Danegeld—

> For the end of that game is oppression and shame,
> And the nation that plays it is lost.

Did these defendants then intend to withdraw German demands, or was Germany to enforce them and manipulate propaganda so as to place the blame for the war on the nation so unreasonable as to resist? Events have answered that question, and documents such as Admiral Carls's memorandum, quoted earlier, leave no doubt that the events occurred as anticipated.

But some of the defendants argue that the wars were not aggressive and were only intended to protect Germany against some eventual danger from the "menace of Communism," which was something of an obsession with many Nazis.

At the outset this argument of self-defense falls because it completely ignores this damning combination of facts clearly established in the record: first, the enormous and rapid German preparations for war; second, the repeatedly avowed intentions of the German leaders to attack, which I have previously cited; and third, the fact that a series of wars occurred in which German forces struck the first blows, without warning, across the borders of other nations.

Even if it could be shown—which it cannot be—that the Russian war was really defensive, such is demonstrably not the case with those wars which preceded it.

It may also be pointed out that even those who would have you believe that Germany was menaced by Communism also compete with each other in describing their opposition to the disastrous Russian venture. Is it reasonable that they would have opposed that war if it were undertaken in good-faith self-defense?

The frivolous character of the self-defense theory on the facts it is sought to compensate, as advocates often do, by resort to a theory of law. Dr. Jahrreiss, in his scholarly argument for the defense, rightly points out that no treaty provision and no principle of law denied Germany, as a sovereign nation, the right of self-defense. He follows with the assertion, for which there is authority in classic International Law, that:

. . . every state is alone judge of whether in a given case it is waging a war of self-defense.

It is not necessary to examine the validity of an abstract principle which does not apply to the facts of our case. I do not doubt that if a nation arrived at a judgment that it must resort to war in self-defense, because of conditions affording reasonable grounds for such an honest judgment, any tribunal would accord it great and perhaps conclusive weight, even if later events proved that judgment mistaken.

But the facts in this case call for no such deference to honest judgment because no such judgment was even pretended, much less honestly made.

In all the documents which disclose the planning and rationalization of these attacks, not one sentence has been or can be cited to show a good-faith fear of attack. It may be that statesmen of other nations lacked the courage forthrightly and fully to disarm. Perhaps they suspected the secret rearmament of Germany. But if they hesitated to abandon arms, they did not hesitate to neglect them. Germany well knew that her former enemies had allowed their armaments to fall into decay, so little did they contemplate another war. Germany faced a Europe that not only was unwilling to attack, but was too weak and pacifist even adequately to defend, and went to the very verge of dishonor, if not beyond, to buy its peace. The minutes we have shown you of the Nazis' secret conclaves identify no potential attacker. They bristle with the spirit of aggression and not of defense. They contemplate always territorial expansion, not the maintenance of territorial integrity.

Minister of War von Blomberg, in his 1937 directive prescribing general principles for the preparation for war of the armed forces, has given the lie to these feeble claims of self-defense. He stated at that time:

> The general political situation justifies the supposition that Germany need not consider an attack on any side. Grounds for this are, in addition to the lack of desire for war in almost all nations, particularly the Western Powers, the deficiencies in the preparedness for war in a number of states and of Russia in particular.

Nevertheless, he recommended

> . . . a continuous preparedness for war in order to (a) counterattack at any time, and (b) to enable the military exploitation of politically favorable opportunities should they occur.

If these defendants may now cynically plead self-defense, although no good-faith need of self-defense was asserted or contemplated by any responsible leader at the time, it reduces nonaggression treaties to a legal absurdity. They become only additional instruments of deception in the hands of the aggressor, and traps for well-meaning nations. If there be in nonaggression pacts an implied condition that each nation may make a *bona fide* judgment as to the necessity for self-defense against imminent, threatened attack, they certainly cannot be invoked to shelter those who never made any such judgment at all.

In opening this case I ventured to predict that there would be no serious denial that the crimes charged were committed, and that the issue would concern the responsibility of particular defendants. The defendants have fulfilled that prophecy. Generally, they do not deny that these things happened, but it is contended that they "just happened," and that they were not the result of a common plan or conspiracy.

One of the chief reasons the defendants say there was no conspiracy is the argument that conspiracy was impossible with a dictator. The argument runs that they all had to obey Hitler's orders, which had the force of law in the German state, and hence obedience cannot be made the basis of a criminal charge. In this way it is explained that while there have been wholesale killings, there have been no murderers.

This argument is an effort to evade Article 8 of the Charter, which provides that the order of the government or of a superior shall not free a defendant from responsibility but can only be considered in mitigation. This provision of the Charter corresponds with the justice and with the realities of the situation, as indicated in defendant Speer's description of what he considered to be the common responsibility of the leaders of the German nation:

. . . with reference to utterly decisive matters, there is total responsibility. There must be total responsibility insofar as a person is one of the leaders, because who else could assume responsibility for the development of events, if not the immediate associates who work with and around the head of the state?

And again he told the Tribunal:

. . . it is impossible after the catastrophe to evade this total responsibility. If the war had been won, the leaders would also have assumed total responsibility.

Like much of the defense counsel's abstract arguments, the contention that the absolute power of Hitler precluded a conspiracy crumbles in face of the facts of record. The *Führerprinzip* of absolutism was itself a part of the common plan, as Göring has pointed out. The defendants may have become slaves of a dictator, but he was *their* dictator. To make him such was, as Göring has testified, the object of the Nazi movement from the beginning. Every Nazi took this oath:

I pledge eternal allegiance to Adolf Hitler. I pledge unconditional obedience to him and the Führers appointed by him.

Moreover, they forced everybody else in their power to take it. This oath was illegal under German law, which made it criminal to become a member of an organization in which obedience to "unknown superiors or unconditional obedience to known superiors is pledged." These men destroyed free government in Germany and now plead to be excused from responsibility because they became slaves. They are in the position of the fictional boy who murdered his father and mother and then pleaded for leniency because he was an orphan.

What these men have overlooked is that Adolf Hitler's acts are their acts. It was these men among millions of others, and it was these men leading millions of others, who built up Adolf Hitler and vested in his psychopathic personality not only innumerable lesser decisions but the supreme issue of war or peace. They intoxicated him with power and adulation. They fed his hates and aroused his fears. They put a loaded gun in his eager hands. It was left to Hitler to pull the trigger, and when he did they all at that time approved. His guilt stands admitted, by some defendants reluctantly, by some vindictively. But his guilt is the guilt of the whole dock, and of every man in it.

But it is urged that these defendants could not be in agreement on a common plan or in a conspiracy because they were fighting among themselves or belonged to different factions or cliques. Of course, it is not necessary that men should agree on everything in order to agree on enough things to make them liable for a criminal conspiracy. Unquestionably there were conspiracies within the conspiracy, and intrigues and rivalries and battles for power. Schacht and Göring disagreed, but over which of them should control the economy, not over whether the economy should be regimented for war. Göring claims to have departed from the plan because through Dahlerus he conducted some negotiations with men of influence in England just before the Polish war. But it is perfectly clear that this was not an effort to prevent aggression against Poland but to make that aggression successful and safe by obtaining English neutrality. Rosenberg and Göring may have had some differences as to how stolen art should be distributed but they had none about how it should be stolen. Jodl and Goebbels may have disagreed about whether to denounce the Geneva Convention, but they never disagreed about violating it. And so it goes through the whole long and sordid story. Nowhere do we find an instance where any one of the defendants stood up against the rest and said: "This thing is wrong and I will not go along with it." Wherever they differed, their differences were as to method or disputes over jurisdiction, but always within the framework of the common plan.

Some of the defendants also contend that in any event there was no conspiracy to commit war crimes or crimes against humanity because cabinet members never met with the military to plan these acts. But these crimes were only the inevitable and incidental results of the plan to commit the aggression for *Lebensraum* purposes. Hitler stated, at a conference with his commanders, that:

The main objective in Poland is the destruction of the enemy and not the reaching of a certain geographical line.

Frank picked up the tune and suggested that when their usefulness was exhausted,

. . . then, for all I care, mincemeat can be made of the Poles and Ukrainians and all the others who run around here—it does not matter what happens.

Reichskommissar Koch in the Ukraine echoed the refrain:

I will draw the very last out of this country. I did not come to spread bliss. . . .

This was *Lebensraum* on its seamy side. Could men of their practical intelligence expect to get neighboring lands free from the claims of their tenants without committing crimes against humanity?

The last stand of each defendant is that even if there was a conspiracy, he was not in it. It is therefore important in examining their attempts at avoidance of responsibility to know, first of all, just what it is that a conspiracy charge comprehends and punishes.

In conspiracy we do not punish one man for another man's crime. We seek to punish each for his own crime of joining a common criminal plan in which others also participated. The measure of the criminality of the plan and therefore of the guilt of each participant is, of course, the sum total of crimes committed by all in executing the plan. But the gist of the offense is participation in the formulation or execution of the plan. These are rules which every society has found necessary in order to reach men, like these defendants, who never get blood on their own hands but who lay plans that result in the shedding of blood. All over Germany today, in every zone of occupation, little men who carried out these criminal policies under orders are being convicted and punished. It would present a vast and unforgivable caricature of justice if the men who planned these policies and directed these little men should escape all penalty.

These men in this dock, on the face of the record, were not strangers to this program of crime, nor was their connection with it remote or obscure. We find them in the very heart of it. The positions they held show that we have chosen defendants of self-evident responsibility. They are the very top surviving authorities in their respective fields and in the Nazi state. No one lives who, at least until the very last moments of the war, outranked Göring in position, power, and influence. No soldier stood above Keitel and Jodl, and no sailor above Raeder and Dönitz. Who can be responsible for the duplicitous diplomacy if not the Foreign Ministers, von Neurath and Ribbentrop, and the diplomatic handy man, von Papen? Who should be answerable for the oppressive administration of occupied countries if Gauleiters, Protectors, Governors, and Commissars such as Frank, Seyss-Inquart, Frick, von Schirach, von Neurath, and Rosenberg are not? Where shall we look for those who mobilized the economy for total war if we overlook Schacht, and Speer, and Funk? Who was the master of the great slaving enterprise if it was not Sauckel? Where shall we find the hand that ran the concentration camps if it is not the hand of Kaltenbrunner? And who whipped up the hates and fears of the public, and manipulated the Party organizations to incite these crimes, if not Hess, von Schirach, Fritzsche, Bormann, and the unspeakable Julius Streicher? The list of defendants is made up of men who played indispensable and reciprocal parts in this tragedy. The photographs and the films show them again and again together on important occasions. The documents show them agreed on policies and on methods, and all working aggressively for the expansion of Germany by force of arms.

Each of these men made a real contribution to the Nazi plan. Every man had a key part. Deprive the Nazi regime of the functions performed by a Schacht, a Sauckel, a von Papen, or a Göring, and you have a different regime. Look down the rows of fallen men and picture them as the photographic and documentary evidence shows them to have been in their days of power. Is there one whose work did not substantially advance the conspiracy along its bloody path towards its bloody goal? Can we assume that the great effort of these men's lives was directed towards ends they never suspected?

To escape the implications of their positions and the inference of guilt from their activities, the defendants are almost unanimous in one defense. The refrain is heard time and again: these men were without authority, without knowledge, without influence, indeed without importance. Funk summed up the general self-abasement of the dock in his plaintive lament that,

I always, so to speak, came up to the door. But I was not permitted to enter.

In the testimony of each defendant, at some point there was reached the familiar blank wall: nobody knew anything about what was going on. Time after time we have heard the chorus from the dock:

I only heard about these things here for the first time.

These men saw no evil, spoke none, and none was uttered in their presence. This claim might sound very plausible if made by one defendant. But when we put all their stories together, the impression which emerges of the Third Reich, which was to last a thousand years, is ludicrous. If we combine only the stories from the front bench, this is the ridiculous composite picture of Hitler's government that emerges. It was composed of:

A number two man who knew nothing of the excesses of the Gestapo which he created, and never suspected the Jewish extermination program although he was the signer of over a score of decrees which instituted the persecutions of that race;

A number three man who was merely an innocent middleman transmitting Hitler's orders without even reading them, like a postman or delivery boy;

A Foreign Minister who knew little of foreign affairs and nothing of foreign policy;

A Field Marshal who issued orders to the armed forces but had no idea of the results they would have in practice;

A security chief who was of the impression that the policing functions of his Gestapo and SD were somewhat on the order of directing traffic;

A Party philosopher who was interested in historical research, and had no idea of the violence which his philosophy was inciting in the twentieth century;

A Governor General of Poland who reigned but did not rule;

A Gauleiter of Franconia whose occupation was to pour forth filthy writings about the Jews, but who had no idea that anybody would read them;

A Minister of the Interior who knew not even what went on in the interior of his own office, much less the interior of his own department, and nothing at all about the interior of Germany;

A Reichsbank President who was totally ignorant of what went in and out of the vaults of his bank;

And a Plenipotentiary for the War Economy who secretly marshaled the entire economy for armament, but had no idea it had anything to do with war.

This may seem like a fantastic exaggeration, but this is what you would actually be obliged to conclude if you were to acquit these defendants.

They do protest too much. They deny knowing what was common knowledge. They deny knowing plans and programs that were as public as *Mein Kampf* and the Party program. They deny even knowing the contents of documents they received and acted upon.

Nearly all the defendants take two or more conflicting positions. Let us illustrate the inconsistencies of their positions by the record of one defendant—one who, if pressed, would himself concede that he is the most intelligent, honorable, and innocent man in the dock. That is Schacht. And this is the effect of his own testimony—but let us not forget that I recite it not against him alone, but because most of its self-contradictions are found in the testimony of several defendants:

Schacht did not openly join the Nazi movement until it had won, nor openly desert it until it had lost. He admits that he never gave it public opposition, but asserts that he never gave it private loyalty. When we demand of him why he did not stop the criminal course of the regime in which he was a minister, he says he had not a bit of influence. When we ask why he remained a member of the criminal regime, he tells us that by sticking on he expected to moderate its program. Like a Brahmin among untouchables, he could not bear to mingle with the Nazis socially, but never could he afford to separate from them politically. Of all the Nazi aggressions by which he now claims to have been shocked, there is not one that he did not support before the world with the weight of his name and prestige. Having armed Hitler to blackmail a continent, his answer now is to blame England and France for yielding.

Schacht always fought for his position in a regime he now affects to despise. He sometimes disagreed with his Nazi confederates about what was expedient in reaching their goal, but he never dissented from the goal itself. When he did break with them in the twilight of the regime, it was over tactics, not principles. From then on he never ceased to urge others to risk their positions and their necks to forward his plots, but never on any occasion did he hazard either of his own. He now boasts that he personally would have shot Hitler if he had had the opportunity, but the German newsreel shows that even after the fall of France, when he faced the living Hitler, he stepped out of line to grasp the hand he now claims to loath and hung upon the words of the man he now says he thought unworthy of belief. Schacht says he steadily "sabotaged" the Hitler government. Yet, the most relentless secret service in the world never detected him doing the regime any harm until long after he knew the war to be lost and the Nazis doomed. Schacht, who dealt in hedges all his life, always kept himself in a position to claim that he was in either camp. The plea for him is as specious on analysis as it is persuasive on first sight. Schacht represents the most dangerous and reprehensible type of opportunism—that of the man of influential position who is ready to join a movement that he knows to be wrong because he thinks it is winning.

These defendants, unable to deny that they were the men in the very top ranks of power, and unable to deny that the crimes I have outlined actually happened, know that their own denials are incredible unless they can suggest someone who is guilty.

The defendants have been unanimous, when pressed, in shifting the blame on other men, sometimes on one and sometimes on another. But the names they have repeatedly picked are Hitler, Himmler, Heydrich, Goebbels, and Bormann. All of these are dead or missing. No matter how hard we have pressed the defendants on the stand, they have never pointed the finger at a living man as guilty. It is a temptation to ponder the wondrous workings of a fate which has left only the guilty dead and only the innocent alive. It is almost too remarkable.

The chief villain on whom blame is placed—some of the defendants vie with each other in producing appropriate epithets—is Hitler. He is the man at whom nearly every defendant has pointed an accusing finger.

I shall not dissent from this consensus, nor do I deny that all these dead or missing men shared the guilt. In crimes so reprehensible that degrees of guilt have lost their significance they may have played the most evil parts. But their guilt cannot exculpate the defendants. Hitler did not carry all responsibility to the grave with him. All the guilt is not wrapped in Himmler's shroud. It was these dead whom these living chose to be their partners in this great conspiratorial brotherhood, and the crimes that they did together they must pay for one by one.

It may well be said that Hitler's final crime was against the land that he had ruled. He was a mad Messiah who started the war without cause and prolonged it without reason. If he could not rule he cared not what happened to Germany. As Fritzsche has told us from the stand, Hitler tried to use the defeat of Germany for the self-destruction of the German people. He continued the fight when he knew it could not be won, and continuance meant only ruin. Speer, in this courtroom, has described it as follows:

The sacrifices which were made on both sides after January 1945 were without sense. The dead of this period will be the accusers of the man responsible for the continuation of that fight, Adolf Hitler, just as much as the destroyed cities, destroyed in that last phase, who had lost tremendous cultural values and tremendous numbers of dwellings. . . . The German people remained faithful to Adolf Hitler until the end. He has betrayed them knowingly. He has tried to throw it into the abyss. . . .

Hitler ordered everyone else to fight to the last and then retreated into death by his own hand. But he left life as he lived it, a deceiver; he left the official report that he had died in battle. This was the man whom these defendants exalted to a Führer. It was they who conspired to get him absolute authority over all of Germany. And in the end he and the system they created for him brought the ruin of them all. As stated by Speer on cross-examination:

. . . the tremendous danger, however, contained in this totalitarian system only became abundantly clear at the moment when we were approaching the end. It was then that one could see what the meaning of the principle was, namely, that every order should be carried out without any criticism. Everything . . . you have seen in the way of orders which were carried out without any consideration, did after all turn out to be mistakes. . . . This system —let me put it like this—to the end of the system it has become clear what tremendous dangers are contained in any such system, as such, quite apart from Hitler's principle. The combination of Hitler and this system, then, brought about this tremendous catastrophe to this world.

But let me for a moment turn devil's advocate. I admit that Hitler was the chief villain. But for the defendants to put all blame on him is neither manly nor true. We know that even the head of a state has the same limits to his senses and to the hours of his day as do lesser men. He must rely on others to be his eyes and ears as to most that goes on in a great empire. Other legs must run his errands; other hands must execute his plans. On whom did Hitler rely for such things more than upon these men in the dock? Who led him to believe he had an invincible air armada if not Göring? Who kept disagreeable facts from him? Did not Göring forbid Field Marshal Milch to warn Hitler that in his opinion Germany was not equal to the war upon Russia? Did not Göring, according to Speer, relieve General Gallant of his air force command for speaking of the weaknesses and bungling of the air force? Who led Hitler, utterly untraveled himself, to believe in the indecision and timidity of democratic peoples if not Ribbentrop, von Neurath, and von Papen? Who fed his illusion of German invincibility if not Keitel, Jodl, Raeder and Dönitz? Who kept his hatred of the Jew inflamed more than Streicher and Rosenberg? Who would Hitler say deceived him about conditions in concentration camps if not Kaltenbrunner, even as he would deceive us? These men had access to Hitler, and often could control the information that reached him and on which he must base his policy and his orders. They were the Praetorian Guard, and while they were under Caesar's orders, Caesar was always in their hands.

If these dead men could take the witness stand and answer what has been said against them, we might have a less distorted picture of the parts played by these defendants. Imagine the stir that would occur in the dock if it should behold Adolf Hitler advancing to the witness box, or Himmler with an armful of dossiers, or Goebbels, or Bormann with the reports of his Party spies, or the murdered Röhm or Canaris. The ghoulish defense that the world is entitled to retribution only from the cadavers, is an argument worthy of the crimes at which it is directed.

We have presented to this Tribunal an affirmative case based on incriminating documents which are sufficient, if unexplained, to require a finding of guilt on Count One against each defendant. In the final analysis, the only question is whether the defendants' own testimony is to be credited as against the documents and other evidence of their guilt. What, then, is their testimony worth?

The fact is that the Nazi habit of economizing in the use of truth pulls the foundations out from under their own defenses. Lying has always been a highly approved Nazi technique. Hitler, in *Mein Kampf,* advocated mendacity as a policy. Von Ribbentrop admits the use of the "diplomatic lie." Keitel advised that the facts of rearmament be kept secret so that they could be denied at Geneva. Raeder deceived about rebuilding the German navy in violation of Versailles. Göring urged Ribbentrop to tell a "legal lie" to the British Foreign Office about the *Anschluss,* and in so doing only marshaled him the way he was going. Göring gave his word of honor to the Czechs and proceeded to break it. Even Speer proposed to deceive the French into revealing the specially trained among their prisoners.

Nor is the lie direct the only means of falsehood. They all speak with a Nazi doubletalk with which to deceive the unwary. In the Nazi dictionary of sardonic euphemisms "final solution" of the Jewish problem was a phrase which meant extermination; "special treatment" of prisoners of war meant killing; "protective custody" meant concentration camp; "duty labor" meant slave labor; and an order to "take a firm attitude" or "take positive measures" meant to act with unrestrained savagery. Before we accept their word at what seems to be its face, we must always look for hidden meanings. Göring assured us, on his oath, that the Reich Defense Council never met "as such." When we produced the stenographic minutes of a meeting at which he presided and did most of the talking, he reminded us of the "as such" and explained this was not a meeting of the Council "as such" because other persons were present. Göring denies "threatening" Czechoslovakia—he only told President Hácha that he would "hate to bomb the beautiful city of Prague."

Besides outright false statements and doubletalk, there are also other circumventions of truth in the nature of fantastic explanations and absurd professions. Streicher has solemnly maintained that his only thought with respect to the Jews was to resettle them on the island of Madagascar. His reason for destroying synagogues, he blandly said, was only because they were architecturally offensive. Rosenberg was stated by his counsel to have always had in mind a "chivalrous solution" to the Jewish problem. When it was necessary to remove Schuschnigg after the *Anschluss,* Ribbentrop would have had us believe that the Austrian Chancellor was resting at a "villa." It was left to cross-examination to reveal that the "villa" was Buchenwald Concentration Camp. The record is full of other examples of dissimulations and evasions. Even Schacht showed that he, too, had adopted the Nazi attitude that truth is any story which succeeds. Confronted on cross-examination with a long record of broken vows and false words, he declared in justification:

I think you can score many more successes when you want to lead someone if you don't tell them the truth than if you tell them the truth.

This was the philosophy of the National Socialists. When for years they have deceived the world, and masked falsehood with plausibilities, can anyone be surprised that they continue the habits of a lifetime in this dock? Credibility is one of the main issues of this trial. Only those who have failed to learn the bitter lessons of the last decade can doubt that men who have always played on the unsuspecting credulity of generous opponents would not hesitate to do the same now.

It is against such a background that these defendants now ask this Tribunal to say that they are not guilty of planning, executing, or conspiring to commit this long list of crimes and wrongs. They stand before the record of this trial as bloodstained Gloucester stood by the body of his slain King. He begged of the widow, as they beg of you: "Say I slew them not." And the Queen replied, "Then say they were not slain. But dead they are. . . ." If you were to say of these men that they are not guilty, it would be as true to say there has been no war, there are no slain, there has been no crime.

JUDGMENTS,
OBSERVATIONS AND
REFLECTIONS
ON THE LAW

George Bernard Shaw

·

ON THE ENTIRELY REASONABLE MURDER
OF A POLICE CONSTABLE

From The Sunday Express, 13 *May* 1928

I have been asked to give my opinion "on the popular point of view that a particularly brutal and callous murder of this kind [the reference is to the murder of Police Constable Gutteridge] is one of the cases in which capital punishment is justified."

Now the first thing I have to observe is that the adjectives "brutal and callous" are wildly inappropriate, and represent simply the popular loss of temper over the murder, and the customary English resort to vituperation to relieve the strain.

The murder of Constable Gutteridge was an entirely reasonable one; the work, apparently, of an out-and-out Rationalist. Further, the person who committed it was one of those sensitive people to whom the condition of a criminal under punishment is unbearable.

Also it was the work of someone who was credulous as to "the marvels of science," which take the same place in modern life as miracles did in that of the Ages of Faith.

Reasonable murders practically all fall into the same class: they are murders committed by criminals to escape detection and capture. The reasoning is simple. Our police statistics show the number of murders committed every year, and the proportion of them that are never brought to justice. That is, they show the odds for and against impunity for the murderer.

A robber surprised in the act by a police officer or a householder has to consider that if he surrenders he will certainly spend several years in penal servitude. If he shoots, this certainty is replaced by a risk of being hanged, and a chance of escape.

Such was the situation created by the encounter with the unfortunate

509

Constable Gutteridge, who, though very likely an amiable and humane person, confronted his murderer not as a man, but as a representative of all the terrors and cruelties of the law. The criminal was rational enough to decide to shoot. There is no ground for suspecting him of any animosity to the man: he shot the law.

He had a sufficient smattering of physiology to know that the last picture that was focused on the constable's retina was a picture of himself; and his modern superstitious credulity as to the possibility of this picture, or rather these two co-ordinated pictures, being photographed in the laboratory and used to identify him led him to destroy the dead man's eyes with two more careful shots.

These shots were not an outrage: they were a precautionary operation. They complete the impression of the murderer's character. He (or she) was most certainly not the Bill Sikes of the popular imagination.

He (I will assume the male sex) was a murderer not from malice, but solely in the way of business, and therefore conceivably a good husband and a kind father. He was sensitive and imaginative, because only sensitive and imaginative people risk hanging to avoid penal servitude.

He had brains enough to be able to calculate his chances, and strength of mind enough to act on his calculation. He was an habitual criminal, because such calculations are not made on the spur of the moment: he must have thought it all out before he armed himself with a loaded revolver.

He had lost the ordinary squeamishness about bloodshed and death that disables the man of peace in such emergencies; but this gives no special clue to him, because the war has left millions of men in that condition.

These reasonable murders are very dangerous, partly because they serve us right for making our criminal law more "brutal and callous" (if we must sling adjectives) than any criminal ever was or could ever possibly be; so that the criminal feels a natural right to do his worst to us to prevent us from doing our worst to him; and partly because they threaten not only the police force, but the whole body of citizens whose only resource when confronted with a criminal is to call in the police.

Their peculiarity has also an important bearing on the question of the death penalty. There is only one excuse for the official slaughter of a man (or woman) in cold blood; and that is that he gives more trouble to the community than he is worth. The same excuse, that is, that we have for killing a tiger or a mad dog.

If we could get this into our heads, and get the wicked and stupid idea of retaliative punishment (murdering the murderer) and the superstitious idea of expiatory punishment (the blood sacrifice) out of them, we should spare some murderers and kill quite a number of intolerable nuisances whom we now only torment in a cowardly and spiteful way, because, let us say, instead of murdering women they pass their lives in entrapping them into bogus marriages and deserting them after spending all their money.

In Scotland they hang people very properly for throwing vitriol: in England the vitriol thrower is sacred because vitriol blinds but does not kill. Such a distinction is absurd. We should calculate as coolly as the murderer of Constable Gutteridge, and refuse to sacrifice the lives of useful people to caging and guarding mischievous ones, simply turning on our convenient domestic gas when it becomes apparent that any individual is not suited for life in a civilized community. There should be no vindictiveness nor punishment nor any other sort of sentimentality in the matter: our attitude at the execution should be apologetic and regretful.

Now a criminal who shoots to escape detection as a matter of business may be no more homicidal by nature than any soldier. The remedy in his case may be to give up our cruel punishments, and to give him a better chance for the honest employment of his talents than our present system offers.

I have dealt with the general subject pretty fully elsewhere, and must leave it at this. But as somebody is pretty sure to fall back on the official theory that punishment is deterrent—I call it official because it is the judicial theory, and the recent impudent attempts to revive the vindictive theory have not yet had any judicial confirmation—I may as well remind my readers that there are two conclusive objections to it.

The first is that no severity of punishment deters when detection is uncertain, as it must always be.

When pickpockets were hanged, pockets were picked under the gallows. Now that the penalty is comparatively trifling, pockets are still picked, but never when a policeman is looking on.

The second is that the deterrence theory leads to the conclusion that somebody must be punished for every crime to deter others from committing it. Whether that somebody has committed the crime or not is of no consequence: an innocent person will do as well as a guilty one for the purpose.

As the gentleman in Bleak House said, "Much better hang wrong feller than hang no feller."

Albert Camus

:

REFLECTIONS ON THE GUILLOTINE

Shortly before World War I, a murderer whose crime was particularly shocking (he had killed a family of farmers, children and all) was condemned to death in Algiers. He was an agricultural worker who had slaughtered in a bloody delirium, and had rendered his offense still more serious by robbing his victims. The case was widely publicized, and it was generally agreed that decapitation was altogether too mild a punishment for such a monster. I have been told this was the opinion of my father, who was particularly outraged by the murder of the children. One of the few things I know about him is that this was the first time in his life he wanted to attend an execution. He got up while it was still dark, for the place where the guillotine was set up was at the other end of the city, and once there, found himself among a great crowd of spectators. He never told what he saw that morning. My mother could only report that he rushed wildly into the house, refused to speak, threw himself on the bed, and suddenly began to vomit. He had just discovered the reality concealed beneath the great formulas that ordinarily serve to mask it. Instead of thinking of the murdered children, he could recall only the trembling body he had seen thrown on a board to have its head chopped off.

This ritual act must indeed be horrible if it can subvert the indignation of a simple, upright man; if the punishment which he regarded as deserved a hundred times over had no other effect on him than to turn his stomach. When the supreme act of justice merely nauseates the honest citizen it is supposed to protect, it seems difficult to maintain that this act is intended—as its proper functioning *should* intend it—to confer a greater degree of peace and order upon the city. Justice of this kind is obviously no less shocking than the crime itself, and the new "official" murder, far from offering redress for the offense committed against society, adds instead a second defilement to the first. This is so apparent that no one dares speak openly of the ritual act itself. The officials and the journalists whose responsibility it is to speak of it, as if conscious of the simultaneously provocative and shameful aspects of such justice, have devised a kind of ceremonial language for dealing with it, a language reduced to the most stereotyped formulas. Over breakfast we may read, on some back page of our newspaper, that the condemned man "paid his debt to society," that he "expiated his crime," or that "at five o'clock this morning justice was done." Officials deal with this man as "the accused," "the patient," or merely refer to him as the C.A.M. (*Condamné à mort*). Capital punishment, one might say, is written about only in whispers. In a highly organized society such as ours we acknowledge a disease is serious by the fact that we do not dare speak of it openly. In middle-class families, it was long the rule to say that the oldest daughter had a "weak chest," or that Papa suffered from a "growth": to have tuberculosis or cancer was regarded as something of a disgrace. This is even more certainly true in the case of capital punishment: everyone does his best to speak of it only in euphemisms. The death penalty is to the body politic what cancer is to the individual body, with perhaps the single difference that no one has ever spoken of the necessity of cancer. Yet we do not usually hesitate to describe the death penalty as a *regrettable necessity,* justifying the fact that we are killing someone because it is "necessary," and then not speaking of what we are doing because it is "regrettable."

My intention, on the contrary, is to speak of it crudely. Not out of a taste for scandal, and not, I think, because I am morbidly inclined. As a writer I have always abhorred a certain eagerness to please, and as a man I believe that the repulsive aspects of our condition, if they are inevitable, must be confronted in silence. But since silence, or the casuistry of speech, is now contributing to the support of an abuse that must be reformed, or of a misery that can be relieved, there is no other solution than to speak out, to expose the obscenity hiding beneath our cloak of words. France shares with Spain and England the splendid distinction of being among the last countries on this side of the Iron

Curtain to retain the death penalty in its arsenal of repression. This primitive rite survives in our country only because an ignorant and unconcerned public opinion has no other way to express itself than by using the same ceremonial phrases with which it has been indoctrinated: when the imagination is not functioning, words lack the resonance of their meanings and a deaf public scarcely registers a man's condemnation to death. But expose the machinery, make people touch the wood and the iron, let them hear the thud of heads falling, and a suddenly aroused public imagination will repudiate both vocabulary and punishment alike.

When the Nazis staged public executions of hostages in Poland, they first gagged their prisoners with rags soaked in plaster so they could not cry out some final word of liberty or rebellion. It may seem an effrontery to compare the fate of these innocent victims with that of our condemned criminals, but apart from the fact that it is not only criminals who are guillotined in France, the method is the same: we gag our guilty with a stuffing of words, though we cannot justly affirm the legitimacy of their punishment unless we have first considered its reality. Instead of saying, as we always have, that the death penalty is first of all a necessity, and afterwards that it is not advisable to talk about it, we should first speak of what the death penalty really is, and only then decide if, *being what it is,* it is necessary.

Speaking for myself, I believe the death penalty is not only useless but profoundly harmful, and I must record this conviction here before proceeding to the subject itself. It would not be honest to allow it to appear as if I had arrived at this conclusion solely as a result of the weeks of inquiry and investigation I have just devoted to the question. But it would be equally dishonest to attribute my conviction to sentimentality alone. I stand as far as possible from that position of spineless pity in which our humanitarians take such pride, in which values and responsibilities change places, all crimes become equal, and innocence ultimately forfeits all rights. I do not believe, contrary to many of my illustrious contemporaries, that man is by nature a social animal; the opposite, I think, is probably nearer the truth. I believe only that man cannot now live outside a society whose laws are necessary to his physical survival, which is a very different thing. I believe that responsibility must be established according to a reasonable and effective scale of values by society itself. But the law finds its final justification in the benefit it provides, or does not provide, the society of a given place and time. For years I have not been able to regard the death penalty as anything but a punishment intolerable to the imagination: a public sin of sloth which my reason utterly condemns. I was nevertheless prepared to believe that my imagination influenced my judgment. But during these weeks of research, I have found nothing which has modified my reasoning, nothing which has not, in all honesty, reinforced my original conviction. On the contrary. I have found new arguments to add to those I already possessed; today I share Arthur Koestler's conclusion without qualification: capital punishment is a disgrace to our society which its partisans cannot reasonably justify.

It is well known that the major argument of those who support capital punishment is its value as an *example*. We do not chop off heads merely to punish their former owners, but to intimidate, by a terrifying example, those who might be tempted to imitate their actions. Society does not take revenge—society merely protects itself. We brandish the newly severed head so that the next prospective murderer may therein read his future and renounce his intentions. All of which would indeed be an impressive argument if one were not obliged to remark: (1) That society itself does not believe in the value of this much advertised example. (2) That it has not been ascertained whether capital punishment ever made a single determined murderer renounce his intentions, while it is certain that its effect has been one of fascination upon thousands of criminals. (3) That the death penalty constitutes, from other points of view, a loathsome example of which the consequences are unforeseeable.

First of all, then, society does not believe its own words. If it did, we would be shown the heads. Executions would be given the same promotional campaign ordinarily reserved for government loans or a new brand of *apéritif*. Yet it is well known on the contrary, that in France executions no longer take place in public—they are perpetrated in prison yards before an audience limited to specialists. It is less well known why this should be so, and since when it has been so. The last public execution took place in 1939—the guillotining of Weidmann, a murderer several times over whose exploits had brought him much notoriety. On the morning of his execution, a huge crowd rushed to Versailles; many photographers attended the ceremony and were permitted to take photographs from the time Weidmann was exposed to the crowd until the moment he was decapitated. A few hours later

Paris-Soir published a full page of pictures of this appetizing event, and the good people of Paris were able to discover that the lightweight precision instrument used by their executioner was as different from the scaffold of their history books as a Jaguar is from an old de Dion-Bouton. The officials connected with the event and the government itself, contrary to every hope, regarded this excellent publicity in a very dim light, declaring that the press had only appealed to the most sadistic impulses of its readers. It was therefore decided that the public would no longer be permitted to witness executions, an arrangement which, shortly afterwards, made the work of the Occupation authorities considerably easier.

Logic, in this case, was not on the side of the lawmakers. Logically, in fact, they should have voted a medal to the editor of *Paris-Soir* and encouraged his staff to do still better next time. If punishment is to be exemplary, then the number of newspaper photographs must be multiplied, the instrument in question must be set up on a platform in the Place de la Concorde at two in the afternoon, the entire population of the city must be invited, and the ceremony must be televised for those unable to attend. Either do this, or stop talking about the value of an example. How can a furtive murder committed by night in a prison yard serve as an example? At best it can periodically admonish the citizenry that they will die if they commit murder; a fate which can also be assured them if they do not. For punishment to be truly exemplary, it must be terrifying. Tuaut de la Bouverie, representative of the people in 1791 and a partisan of public execution, spoke more logically when he declared to the National Assembly: "There must be terrible spectacles in order to control the people."

Today there is no spectacle at all—only a penalty known to everyone by hearsay and, at long intervals, the announcement of an execution couched in soothing formulas. How shall a future criminal, in the very act of committing his crime, keep in mind a threat which has been made increasingly abstract by every possible effort? And if it is really desirable that the incipient murderer preserve a vision of his ultimate fate that might counterbalance and ultimately reverse his criminal intent, then why do we not burn the reality of that fate into his sensibility by every means of language and image within our power?

Instead of vaguely evoking a debt that someone has paid to society this morning, would it not be more politic—if we are interested in setting an example—to profit by this excellent opportunity to remind each taxpayer in detail just what sort of punishment he can expect? Instead of saying, "If you kill someone you will pay for it on the scaffold," would it not be more politic—if we are interested in setting an example—to say instead: "If you kill someone, you will be thrown into prison for months or even years, torn between an impossible despair and a constantly renewed fear, until one morning we will sneak into your cell, having taken off our shoes in order to surprise you in your sleep, which has at last overcome you after the night's anguish. We will throw ourselves upon you, tie your wrists behind your back, and with a pair of scissors cut away your shirt collar and your hair, if it should be in the way. Because we are perfectionists we will lash your arms together with a strap so that your body will be arched to offer unhampered access to the back of your neck. Then we will carry you, one man holding you up under each arm, your feet dragging behind you, down the long corridors, until, under the night sky, one of the executioners will at last take hold of the back of your trousers and throw you down on a board, another will make sure your head is in the lunette, and a third one will drop, from a height of two meters twenty centimeters, a blade weighing sixty kilograms that will slice through your neck like a razor." *

For the example to be even better, for the terror it breeds to become in each of us a force blind enough and powerful enough to balance, at the right moment, our irresistible desire to kill, we must go still further. Instead of bragging, with our characteristic pretentious ignorance, that we have invented a swift and humane† means of killing those condemned to death, we should publish in millions of copies, read out in every school and college, the eyewitness accounts and medical reports that describe the state of the body after execution. We should particularly recommend the printing and circulation of a recent communication made to the Academy of Medicine by Doctors Piedelièvre and Fournier. These courageous physicians, having examined, in the interests of science, the bodies of the condemned after execution, have considered it their duty to sum up their terrible observations thus: "If we may be permitted to present our opinion on this subject, such spectacles are horribly painful. The blood rushes from the vessels according to the rhythm of the severed carotids, then coagulates. The

---

* A description of the actual procedure in French prisons. Cf. the movie *We Are All Murderers*.—Translator.

† According to the optimistic Dr. Guillotine, the condemned man would feel nothing at all—at most a "slight coolness at the back of his neck."

muscles contract and their fibrillation is stupefying. The intestine undulates and the heart produces a series of irregular, incomplete, and convulsive movements. The mouth tightens, at certain moments, into a dreadful grimace. It is true that the eyes of a decapitated head are immobile, the pupils dilated; fortunately, they cannot see, and if they exhibit no signs of disturbance, none of the characteristic opalescence of a cadaver, they at least have no capacity for movement: their transparency is that of life, but their fixity is mortal. All this may last minutes, even hours, in a healthy subject: death is not immediate. . . . Thus each vital element survives decapitation to some extent. There remains, for the physician, the impression of a hideous experiment, a murderous vivisection followed by a premature burial." *

I doubt that many readers can read this dreadful report without blanching. We can, in fact, count on its power as an example, its capacity to intimidate. What is to prevent us from adding to it the reports of witnesses that further authenticate the observations of medical men? If the severed head of Charlotte Corday is supposed to have blushed under the executioner's hand, we shall hardly be surprised after examining the accounts of more recent observers. Here is how one assistant executioner, hardly likely to cultivate the sentimental or romantic aspects of his trade, describes what he has been obliged to see: "There was one wild man, suffering from a real fit of delirium tremens, whom we had to throw under the knife. The head died right away. But the body literally sprang into the basket, where it lay struggling against the cords that bound it. Twenty minutes later, in the cemetery, it was still shuddering." † The present chaplain of La Santé, the reverend father Devoyod, who does not appear to be opposed to the death penalty, tells, nevertheless, the following remarkable story in his book *Les Délinquants*‡ (which renews the famous episode of a man named Languille whose severed head answered to its name§): "The morning of the execution, the condemned man was in a very bad humor, and refused to receive the succor of religion. Knowing the depths of his heart and his true regard for his wife, whose sentiments were genuinely Christian, we said to him, 'For the love of this woman, commune with

---

* *Justice sans bourreau*, No. 2, June, 1956.
† Published by Roger Grenier, in *Les Monstres*, Gallimard.
‡ Editions Matot-Braine, Reims.
§ In 1905, in Loiret.

yourself a moment before you die.' And the condemned man consented, communing at length before the crucifix, and afterwards scarcely seemed to notice our presence. When he was executed, we were not far from him; his head fell onto the trough in front of the guillotine, and the body was immediately put into the basket. But contrary to custom, the basket was closed before the head could be put in. The assistant carrying the head had to wait a moment until the basket was opened again. And during that brief space of time, we were able to see the two eyes of the condemned man fixed on us in a gaze of supplication, as if to ask our forgiveness. Instinctively we traced a sign of the cross in order to bless the head, and then the eyelids blinked, the look in the eyes became gentle again, and then the gaze, which had remained expressive, was gone. . . ." The reader will accept or reject the explanation proposed by the priest according to his faith. But at least those eyes that "remained expressive" need no interpretation.

I could cite many other eyewitness accounts as hallucinatory as these. But as for myself, I hardly need or know how to go further. After all, I make no claim that the death penalty is exemplary: indeed, this torture affects me only as what it is—a crude surgery practiced in conditions that deprive it of any edifying character whatsoever. Society, on the other hand, and the State (which has seen other tortures) can easily bear such details; and since they favor preaching examples, they might as well make them universally known so that a perpetually terrorized populace can become Franciscan to a man. For who is it we think we are frightening by this example constantly screened from view; by the threat of a punishment described as painless, expedient, and on the whole less disagreeable than cancer; by a torture crowned with all the flowers of rhetoric? Certainly not those who pass for honest (and some are) because they are asleep at such an hour, to whom the *great example* has not been revealed, and who drink their morning coffee at the hour of the premature burial, informed of the operation of justice, if they happen to read the newspapers, by a mealy-mouthed bulletin that dissolves like sugar in their memory. Yet these same peaceful creatures furnish society with the largest percentage of its homicides. Many of these honest men are criminals without knowing it. According to one magistrate, the overwhelming majority of the murderers he had tried did not know, when they shaved themselves that morning, that they were going to kill someone that night. For the sake of example and security alike, we should brandish rather than disguise the agonized face of our victim before the eyes of every man as he shaves himself in the morning.

This is not done. The State conceals the circumstances and even the existence of its executions, keeps silent about such reports and such accounts. It does not concern itself with the exemplary value of punishment save by tradition, nor does it trouble to consider the present meaning of its act. The criminal is killed because he has been killed for centuries, and furthermore he is killed according to a procedure established at the end of the eighteenth century. The same arguments that have served as legal tender for centuries are perpetuated as a matter of routine, contradicted only by those measures which the evolution of public sensibility renders inevitable. The law is applied without consideration of its significance, and our condemned criminals die by rote in the name of a theory in which their executioners no longer believe. If they believed in it, it would be known, and above all it would be seen. But such publicity, beyond the fact that it arouses sadistic instincts of which the repercussions are incalculable and which end, one day or another, by satisfying themselves with yet another murder, also risks provoking the disgust and revolt of public opinion itself. It would become more difficult to execute by assembly line, as we do in France at this moment, if such executions were translated into the bold images of popular fantasy. The very man who enjoys his morning coffee while reading that justice has been done would certainly choke on it at the slightest of such details. And the texts I have quoted may go far toward supporting the position of certain professors of criminal law who, in their evident incapacity to justify the anachronism of capital punishment, console themselves by declaring with the sociologist Tarde that it is better to kill without causing suffering than it is to cause suffering without killing. Which is why we can only approve the position of Gambetta, who as an adversary of the death penalty nevertheless voted against a bill proposing the exclusion of the public from executions, asserting: "If you do away with the horror of the spectacle, if you perform executions in the prison yards, you will also do away with the public reaction of revolt which has shown itself in recent years, and thereby establish the death penalty all the more firmly."

We must either kill publicly, or admit we do not feel authorized to kill. If society justifies the death penalty as a necessary example, then it must justify itself by providing the publicity necessary to *make* an example. Society must display the executioner's hands on each occasion, and require the most squeamish citizens to look at them, as well as those who, directly or remotely, have supported the work of those hands from the first. Otherwise society confesses that it kills without consciousness of what it does or what it says; or that it kills yet knows, too, that far from intimidating belief, these disgusting ceremonies can only awaken a sense of criminality, and thoroughly undermine public morale. Who could be more explicit than a judge at the end of his career?—Counselor Falco's courageous confession deserves careful attention: "On only one occasion during my years on the bench I recommended a verdict in favor of execution of the accused and against the commutation of his punishment; I decided that despite my position I would attend the ceremony—with complete objectivity, of course. The man in question was not at all sympathetic, not even interesting: he had brutally murdered his little daughter and then thrown her body down a well. Nevertheless, after his execution, for weeks, and even for months, my nights were haunted by this memory. . . . I served in the war like everyone else, and I saw an innocent generation killed before my eyes; yet confronted with the memory of that dreadful spectacle, I still can say I never once experienced the same kind of bad conscience I felt as I watched the kind of administrative assassination known as capital punishment." *

But after all, why should society believe in the value of such an example, since it does not affect the incidence of crime, and since its effects, if they exist at all, are invisible? For capital punishment cannot intimidate a man who does not know he is going to commit murder, who decides on it in an instant and prepares his action in the heat of passion or an *idée fixe;* cannot intimidate a man who starts off for an assignation carrying with him a weapon to frighten his faithless mistress or his rival and then, at the last minute, makes use of it, although without any such intention—or without thinking he had any such intention. In short, capital punishment cannot intimidate the man who throws himself upon crime as one throws oneself into misery. Which is to say that it is ineffective in the majority of cases. It is only fair to point out that in France, at least, capital punishment is rarely applied in cases of "crimes of passion." Yet even "rarely" is enough to make one shudder.

* The magazine *Réalités,* No. 105, October, 1954.

But does the death penalty act as a deterrent, at least, upon that "race" of criminals it claims to affect—those who live by crime? Nothing is less certain. Arthur Koestler reminds us that in the period when pickpockets were punished by hanging in England, other thieves exercised their talents in the crowds surrounding the scaffold where their fellow was being hanged. Statistics compiled during the past fifty years in England show that out of 250 men hanged, 170 had previously attended one or even two public executions. Even as late as 1886, out of 167 men condemned to death in the Bristol prison, 164 had attended at least one execution. Figures corresponding to these cannot be ascertained in France because of the secrecy which surrounds executions here. But those we have remind us that in that crowd my father stood among to watch a public execution, there must have been a considerable number of future criminals who did not run home and vomit. The power of intimidation operates only on those timid souls who are not dedicated to crime, and gives way before precisely those incorrigibles whom it is concerned to correct.

Yet it cannot be denied that men fear death. The deprivation of life is certainly the supreme punishment, and arouses in each of us his decisive fear. The fear of death, rising from the obscurest depths, ravages the self; the instinct for life, when threatened, panics and flounders among the most dreadful agonies. The legislator may with some justice assume that his law affects one of the most mysterious and powerful motives of human nature. But the law is always simpler than nature. When, in its attempt to establish its sovereignty, the law ventures into the blind realms of being, it runs a terrible risk of being impotent to control the very complexity it attempts to set in order.

Indeed if the fear of death is one kind of evidence, the fact that this same fear, no matter how great it may be, has never sufficed to discourage human passions, is still another. Bacon was right: no passion is so weak that it cannot confront and master the fear of death. Vengeance, love, honor, grief, even fear of something else—all are victorious over the fear of death in one circumstance or another. And shall cupidity, hatred, or jealousy not accomplish all that love or patriotism or the human passion for liberty are able to achieve? For centuries the death penalty, often accompanied by various barbarous refinements, has tried to restrain the incidence of crime; yet crime persists. Why? Because the instincts which confront and war against each other within man are not, as the law would have them, constant forces in a state of equilibrium. They are variable forces that die and triumph one after another, whose successive imbalances nourish the life of the mind in the same way that electrical oscillations, occurring with sufficient frequency, establish a current. Consider the series of oscillations passing from desire to satiation, from decision to renunciation, which all of us experience in a single day and then multiply these variations to infinity and we may form an idea of the extent of our psychological proliferation. These imbalances, these disequilibriums are generally too fugitive to permit any one force to gain control of the entire self. Yet it sometimes happens that a single element of the soul's resources can break free and occupy the entire field of consciousness; no instinct, even that of self-preservation, can then oppose the tyranny of this irresistible force. In order that the death penalty be really intimidating, human nature itself would have to be different from what it is, would have to be as stable and serene as the law itself. It would no longer be life, but still-life.

But life is not still-life, is not stable, not serene. Which is why, surprising as it may seem to those who have not observed or experienced in themselves the complexity of the human situation, the murderer for the most part considers himself innocent when he commits his crime. Before being judged, the criminal acquits *himself.* He feels he is—if not entirely within his rights—at least extenuated by circumstances. He does not reflect; he does not foresee; or if he does, it is only to foresee that he will be pardoned—altogether or in part. Why should he fear what he regards as highly unlikely? He will fear death after being judged, not before his crime. Therefore, in order to intimidate effectively, the law must permit the murderer *no escape,* must be implacable *in advance,* must admit no possibility of an extenuating circumstance. Who among us would dare to demand this?

And even if we did, there is still another paradox of human nature to consider. The instinct of self-preservation, if it is a fundamental one, is no more so than that other instinct less often discussed by academic psychologists: the death instinct which at certain times demands the destruction of the self or of others. It is probable that the desire to kill frequently coincides with the desire to die or to kill oneself.* The instinct of self-preservation thus finds itself confronted in variable proportions by the instinct for self-destruction. The latter is the only means

* One can read week after week in our press about criminals who wavered between killing others and killing themselves.

by which we can altogether explain the numerous perversions which—from alcoholism to drug addiction—lead the self to a destruction of which it cannot long remain ignorant. Man desires to live, but it is vain to hope that this desire can control all his actions. He desires to be annihilated as well—he wills the irreparable, death for its own sake. It so happens that the criminal desires not only his crime, but the misery that accompanies it, especially if this misery is unbounded and inordinate. When this perverse desire grows until it gains control of the self, the prospect of being put to death is not only impotent to restrain the criminal, but probably deepens even further the abyss into which he plunges: there are situations in which one kills in order to die.

Such singularities suffice to explain how a punishment that seems calculated to intimidate the normal mind has in reality nothing whatever to do with ordinary psychological processes. All statistics show, without exception—in the countries which have abolished it, as well as in others—that there is no connection between the death penalty and the incidence of crime.* This incidence, in fact, neither rises nor falls. The guillotine exists; crime exists; between them there is no other apparent connection than that of the law. All we are entitled to conclude from the figures provided by statisticians is this: for centuries crimes other than murder were punished by death, and this supreme punishment, deliberately repeated, caused none of these crimes to disappear. For several centuries these crimes have no longer been punished by death, yet they have not increased in number, and the incidence of some has even diminished. Similarly, murder has been punished by capital punishment for centuries, yet the race of Cain has not disappeared from the earth. In the thirty-three nations that have abolished the death penalty or no longer impose it, the number of murders has not increased. How can we therefore conclude that the death penalty is really intimidating?

Its partisans can deny neither these facts nor these figures. Their only and ultimate reply is significant; it explains the paradoxical attitude of a society which so carefully conceals the executions it claims as exemplary: "It is true that nothing proves that the death penalty is ex-

* *Vide* the report of the English Select Committee of 1930 and of the Royal commission which has continued this study recently: "All the figures that we have examined confirm our statement that the abolition of the death penalty has provoked no increase in the number of crimes committed."

emplary; it is even certain that thousands of murderers have not been intimidated by it. But we cannot know who *has* been intimidated by such a penalty; consequently, nothing proves that it does not serve as an example." Thus the greatest of all punishments, the penalty that involves the ultimate forfeiture of the condemned man and concedes the supreme privilege to society, rests on nothing more than an unverifiable possibility. Death, however, does not admit of degrees of likelihood; it fixes all things—blame and body alike—in its definitive rigidity. Yet it is administered in our country in the name of a possibility, a calculation of likelihood. And even if this possibility should be reasonable, would it not have to be certitude itself to authorize certain and absolute extinction? Yet the man we condemn to die is cut in two not so much for the crime he has committed as for the sake of all the crimes that might have happened, but which *have not* happened—which could occur, but somehow *will not* occur. Hence, the greatest possible uncertainty appears to authorize the most implacable certitude of all.

I am not the only one to be astonished by this dangerous contradiction. The State itself disapproves, and its bad conscience explains in turn all the contradictions of the official attitude. This attitude suppresses the publicity of executions because it cannot affirm, faced with the facts, that they have ever served to intimidate criminals. It cannot escape the dilemma which Beccaria had already pointed to when he wrote: "If it is important to show the people frequent proof of power, then executions must be frequent; but in that case crimes must be frequent too, which will prove that the death penalty is far from making the desired impression; thus this penalty is at the same time useless and necessary." What can the State do about a punishment both useless and necessary, except conceal it without abolishing it? And so it will be preserved in obscurity, continued with perplexity and hesitation, in the blind hope that one man at least, one day at least, will be intimidated by consideration of the punishment that lies ahead, and will abandon his murderous intent, thereby justifying, though no one will ever know it, a law which has no support in reason or experience. To persist in its claim that the guillotine is exemplary, the State must raise the incidence of real murders in order to avoid an unknown murder of which it cannot be sure (will never be sure) that it would ever have been committed at all. Is it not a strange law, that recognizes the murder it commits, and remains forever ignorant of the crime it prevents?

But what will remain of this power of example, if it is proved that capital punishment has another power, this one quite real, which degrades men to the worst excesses of shame, madness, and murder?

The exemplary effects of these ceremonies can readily be traced in public opinion—the manifestations of sadism they reveal, the terrible notoriety they arouse in the case of certain criminals. Instead of an operatic nobility of attitude at the foot of the scaffold, we find nothing but disgust, contempt, or perverse pleasure. The effects are well known. Propriety too has had its share in effecting the removal of the scaffold from the square in front of the city hall to the city walls, and from the walls to the prison yard. We are less well informed about the sentiments of those whose business it is to attend this kind of spectacle. Let us listen to the words of the director of an English prison, who speaks of "an acute sense of personal shame," of a prison chaplain who speaks of "horror, shame, and humiliation";* and let us consider especially the feelings of the man who kills because it is his trade—I mean the executioner. What shall we think of these civil servants of ours, who refer to the guillotine as "the bike," the condemned man as "the client" or "luggage," except, in the words of the priest Bela Just, who served as prison chaplain for more than thirty executions, that "The idiom of the executors of justice yields nothing in point of cynicism or vulgarity to that of its violators." † Here, furthermore, are the reflections of one of our assistant executioners on his official travels across the country: "When it came time for our trips to the provinces, the real fun began: taxis, good restaurants, everything we wanted!" ‡ The same man, boasting of the executioner's skill in releasing the knife, says: "One can *indulge oneself in the luxury* of pulling the client's hair." The depravity expressed here has other, more profound aspects. The clothing of the condemned man belongs, by custom, to the executioner. We learn that old father Deibler hung all the clothing he had collected in a shack and that he used *to go look at his collection from time to time.* There are more serious examples. Here is our assistant executioner again: "The new executioner has guillotine fever. Sometimes he stays at home

---

* Report of the Select Committee, 1930.
† Bela Just, *La Potence et la croix,* Fasquelle.
‡ Roger Grenier, *op. cit.*

for days at a time, sitting in a chair, ready to go, his hat on his head, his overcoat on, waiting for a summons from the public prosecutor." *

And this is the man of whom Joseph de Maistre said that his very existence was accorded by a special decree of divine power and that without him, "order gives way to chaos, thrones collapse, and society disappears." This is the man by means of whom society gets rid of its culprit, and once the executioner signs the prison release, he is permitted to walk out, a free man. The honorable and solemn example, as conceived by our legislation, has had one certain effect, at least—it perverts or destroys the human quality and reason of all who participate in it directly. It will be objected that we are discussing only a few exceptional creatures who make a living out of such degradation. There might be fewer protests if it were known that there are hundreds of men who offer their services as executioner *without pay.* Men of my generation, who have survived the history of our times, will not be surprised to learn this. They know that behind the most familiar, the most peaceful face lies the instinct to torture and to kill. The punishment which claims to intimidate an unknown murderer unquestionably provides a number of known monsters with their vocation as killers. Since we are not above justifying our cruelest laws by considerations of probability, let us not hesitate to admit that out of these hundreds of men whose services are refused, one, at least, has satisfied in some other way the bloody impulses which the guillotine awakened within him.

If we are to maintain the death penalty, let us at least be spared the hypocrisy of justification by example. Let us call by its right name this penalty about which all publicity is suppressed, this intimidation which does not operate upon honest men to the degree that they are honest, which fascinates those who have ceased to be honest, and which degrades and disorders those who lend their hands to it. It is a punishment, certainly, a dreadful physical and moral torture, but one offering no certain example save that of demoralization. It forbids, but it prevents nothing—when it does not in fact arouse the will to murder itself. It is *as if it were not,* except for the man who suffers it—in his soul for months or years, and in his body during the desperate and violent moment when he is cut in two without being altogether deprived of life. Let us call it by a name which, lacking all patents of nobility, at

* *Ibid.*

least provides that of truth—let us recognize it for what it ultimately is: a revenge.

Punishment, penalizing rather than preventing, is a form of revenge; society's semiarithmetical answer to violation of its primordial law. This answer is as old as man himself, and usually goes by the name of *retaliation*. He who hurts me must be hurt; who blinds me in one eye must himself lose an eye; who takes a life must die. It is a feeling, and a particularly violent one, which is involved here, not a principle. Retaliation belongs to the order of nature, of instinct, not to the order of law. The law by definition cannot abide by the same rules as nature. If murder is part of man's nature, the law is not made to imitate or reproduce such nature. We have all known the impulse to retaliate, often to our shame, and we know its power: the power of the primeval forests. In this regard, we live—as Frenchmen who grow justifiably indignant at seeing the oil king of Saudi Arabia preach international democracy while entrusting his butcher with the task of cutting off a thief's hand—in a kind of middle ages ourselves, without even the consolations of faith. Yet if we still define our justice according to the calculations of a crude arithmetic,* can we at least affirm that this arithmetic is correct, and that even such elementary justice, limited as it is to a form of legal revenge, is *safeguarded* by the death penalty? The answer must again be: No.

We scarcely need to point out how inapplicable the law of retaliation has become in our society: it is as excessive to punish the pyromaniac by setting his house on fire as it is insufficient to punish the thief by deducting from his bank account a sum equivalent to the amount he has stolen. Let us admit instead that it is just and even necessary to compensate the murder of the victim by the death of the murderer. But capital punishment is not merely death. It is as different,

* Several years ago I urged the reprieve of six Tunisians who had been condemned to death for the murder of three French policemen in a riot: the circumstances during which the killing had occurred made responsibility difficult to determine. A note from the office of the President of the Republic informed me that my petition was being considered by the appropriate authorities. Unfortunately, by the time this note was in the mail I had already read that the sentence had been carried out two weeks before. Three of the condemned men had been put to death, the other three reprieved. The reasons for reprieving the latter rather than those who were executed had not been decisive. I conclude that because there were three victims there had to be three death penalties.

in its essence, from the suppression of life as a concentration camp from a prison. It is undeniably a murder which arithmetically cancels out the murder already committed; but it also adds a regularization of death, a public premeditation of which its future victims are informed, an *organization* which in itself is a source of moral suffering more terrible than death. There is thus no real compensation, no equivalence. Many systems of law regard a premeditated crime as more serious than a crime of pure violence. But what is capital punishment if not the most premeditated of murders, to which no criminal act, no matter how calculated, can be compared? If there were to be a real equivalence, the death penalty would have to be pronounced upon a criminal who had forewarned his victim of the very moment he would put him to a horrible death, and who, from that time on, had kept him confined at his own discretion for a period of months. It is not in private life that one meets such monsters.

Here again, when our official jurists speak of death without suffering, they do not know what they are talking about, and furthermore they betray a remarkable lack of imagination. The devastating, degrading fear imposed on the condemned man for months or even years* is a punishment more terrible than death itself, and one that has not been imposed on his victim. A murdered man is generally rushed to his death, even at the height of his terror of the mortal violence being done to him, without knowing what is happening: the period of his horror is only that of his life itself, and his hope of escaping whatever madness has pounced upon him probably never deserts him. For the man condemned to death, on the other hand, the horror of his situation is served up to him at every moment for months on end. Torture by hope alternates only with the pangs of animal despair. His lawyer and his confessor, out of simple humanity, and his guards, to keep him docile, unanimously assure him that he will be reprieved. He believes them with all his heart, yet he cannot believe them at all. He hopes by day,

---

* Roemen, condemned to death at the time of the Liberation, remained in chains 700 days before being executed: a scandal. Those condemned by common law wait, as a general rule, three to six months until the morning of their death. Yet if one wishes to preserve their chances of reprieve, it is not advisable to shorten the delay. I can bear witness, moreover, that the examination leading to a recommendation of mercy is conducted in France with a gravity that does not exclude an evident willingness to reprieve to the full extent that law and public opinion will allow.

despairs by night.* And as the weeks pass, his hope and despair increase proportionately, until they become equally insupportable. According to all accounts, the color of his skin changes: fear acts like an acid. "It's nothing to know you're going to die," one such man in the Fresnes prison said, "but not to know if you're going to live is the real torture." At the moment of his execution Cartouche remarked, "Bah! a nasty quarter of an hour and it's all over." But it takes months, not minutes. The condemned man knows long in advance that he is going to be killed and that all that can save him is a reprieve which operates, so far as he is concerned, like the will of heaven itself. In any case he cannot intervene, plead for himself: he is no longer a man, but a thing waiting to be manipulated by the executioners. He is kept in a state of absolute necessity, the condition of inert matter, yet within him is the consciousness that is his principal enemy.

When the officials whose trade is to kill such a man refer to him as "luggage," they know what they are saying: to be unable to react to the hand that moves you, holds you, or lets you drop—is that not the condition of some package, some *thing,* or better still, some trapped animal? Yet an animal in a trap can starve itself to death; the man condemned to death cannot. He is provided with a special diet (at Fresnes, diet No. 4 with *extras* of milk, wine, sugar, preserves, and butter); he is encouraged to eat well—if necessary he is forced to eat. The animal must be in good condition for the kill. The thing—the animal—has a right only to those corrupted privileges known as caprices. "You'd be surprised how sensitive they are!" declared one sergeant at Fresnes without a trace of irony. Sensitive? Unquestionably—how else recover the freedom and dignity of will that man cannot live without? Sensitive or not, from the moment the death sentence is pronounced, the condemned man becomes part of an imperturbable mechanism. He spends several weeks within the cogs and gears of a machine that controls his every gesture, ultimately delivering him to the hands that will lay him out on the last device of all. The luggage is no longer subjected to the operations of chance, the hazards that dominate the existence of a living being, but to mechanical laws that permit him to foresee in the minutest perspective the day of his decapitation.

His condition as an object comes to an end on this day. During the three-quarters of an hour that separates him from his extinction, the

* Since there are no executions on Sunday, Saturday night is always a good night in death row.

certainty of his futile death overcomes everything: the fettered, utterly submissive creature experiences a hell that makes a mockery of the one with which he is threatened. For all their hemlock, the Greeks were humane: they provided their criminals a relative liberty at least, the possibility of postponing or advancing the hour of their own death; and of choosing between suicide and execution. For reasons of security, we carry out our justice by ourselves. Yet there could not be real justice in such cases unless the murderer, having made known his decision months in advance, had entered his victim's house, tied him up securely, informed him he would be put to death in the next hour, and then used this hour to set up the apparatus by which his victim would be dispatched. What criminal has ever reduced his victim to a condition so desperate, so hopeless, and so powerless?

This doubtless explains the strange quality of submission that is so often observed in the condemned man at the moment of his execution. After all, those who have nothing to lose by it might make a last desperate effort, preferring to die by a stray bullet or to be guillotined in a violent struggle that would numb every sense: it would be a kind of freedom in dying. And yet, with very few exceptions, the condemned man walks quite docilely to his death in dismal impassivity. Which must be what our journalists mean when they tell us the condemned man died courageously. What they *really* mean, of course, is that the condemned man made no trouble, no attempt to abandon his status as luggage, and that we are all grateful to him for his good behavior. In so disgraceful a business the accused has shown a commendable sense of propriety in allowing the disgrace to be disposed of as soon as possible. But the compliments and character references are just another part of the general mystification that surrounds the death penalty. For the condemned man often behaves "properly" only to the degree that he is afraid, and deserves the eulogies of our press only if his fear or his despair are sufficiently great to sterilize him altogether. Let me not be misunderstood: some men—political prisoners or not—die heroically, and we must speak of them with the admiration and respect they deserve. But the majority of those condemned to death know no other silence than that of fear, no other impassivity than that of horror, and it seems to me that the silence of fear and horror deserves still more respect than the other. When the priest Bela Just offered to write to the relatives of one young criminal only a few minutes before he was to be hung, and received these words in answer: "I don't have the courage, not even for that," one wonders how a priest, at such a confession of weakness, could keep from falling on his knees before what is most miserable and most sacred in man. As for those who do not talk, those who show us what they have gone through only by the puddle they leave in the place they are dragged from, who would dare say they died as cowards? And by what name shall we call those who have brought these men to their "cowardice"? After all, each murderer, at the moment of his crime, runs the risk of the most terrible death, while those who execute him risk nothing, except perhaps a promotion.

No—what the condemned man experiences at this moment is beyond all morality. Neither virtue, nor courage, nor intelligence, not even innocence has a share in his condition at that moment. Society is reduced at one blow to that condition of primitive terror in which nothing can be judged and all equity, all dignity, have vanished. "The sense of his own innocence does not immunize the executed man against the cruelty of his death. . . . I have seen terrible criminals die courageously, and innocent men walk to the knife trembling in every limb." *
When the same witness adds that, in his experience, such failures of nerve are more frequent among intellectuals, he does not mean that this category of men has less courage than any other, but that they have more imagination. Confronted with an inescapable death, a man, no matter what his convictions, is devastated throughout his entire system.† The sense of powerlessness and solitude of the fettered prisoner, confronted by the public coalition which has *willed* his death, is in itself an unimaginable punishment. In this regard, too, it would be far better if the execution were held in public: the actor that is in every man could then come to the aid of the stricken animal, could help him keep up a front, even in his own eyes. But the darkness and the secrecy of the ceremony are without appeal: in such a disaster, courage, the soul's consistency, faith itself—all are merely matters of chance. As a general rule, the man is destroyed by waiting for his execution long before he is actually killed. Two deaths are imposed, and the first is worst than the second, though the culprit has killed but once. Compared to this torture, the law of retaliation seems like a civil-

---

* Bela Just, *op. cit.*

† A great surgeon, himself a Catholic, told me that he had learned never to tell his patients, even when they were believers, that they were suffering from an incurable cancer. The shock, he believed, was too dangerous, and even risked jeopardizing their faith.

ized principle. For that law, at least, has never claimed that a man must be blinded in both eyes to pay for having blinded his brother in one.

This fundamental injustice, moreover, has its repercussions among the relatives of the man who is executed. The victim has his relatives too, whose sufferings are generally infinite and who, for the most part, wish to be revenged. They *are* revenged, in the manner I have described, but the relatives of the executed man thereby experience a misery that punishes them beyond the bounds of all justice. A mother's or a father's expectation during the endless months, the prison parlor, the awkward conversations which fill the brief minutes they are allowed to spend with the condemned man, the images of the execution itself —all are tortures that have not been inflicted on the relatives of the victim. Whatever the feelings of the latter, they cannot require their revenge to exceed the crime to such an extent, and torment those who violently share their own grief. "I have been reprieved, Father," writes one man condemned to death, "and I still don't really believe in my good luck. The reprieve was signed April 30, and they told me Wednesday, on my way back from the parlor. I sent them to tell Papa and Mama, who had not yet left the prison. You can imagine their happiness." * We can imagine their happiness only to the degree that we can imagine their unceasing misery until the moment of the reprieve, and the utter despair of those who receive another kind of news, the kind that unjustly punishes their innocence and their misery.

As for the law of retaliation, it must be admitted that even in its primitive form it is legitimate only between two individuals of whom one is absolutely innocent and the other absolutely guilty. Certainly the victim is innocent. But can society, which is supposed to represent the victim, claim a comparable innocence? Is it not responsible, at least in part, for the crime which it represses with such severity? This theme has been frequently developed elsewhere, and I need not continue a line of argument which the most varied minds have elaborated since the eighteenth century. Its principal features can be summed up, in any case, by observing that every society has the criminals it deserves. As far as France is concerned, however, it is impossible not to draw attention to circumstances which might make our legislators more mod-

---

* Devoyod, *op. cit.* It is impossible to read objectively the petitions for reprieve presented by fathers and mothers who evidently cannot comprehend the punishment that has suddenly fallen upon them.

est. Answering a questionnaire on capital punishment in *Figaro* in 1952, a colonel declared that the establishment of perpetual forced labor as the supreme penalty amounted to the same thing as the establishment of schools of crime. This superior officer seems to be unaware —and I am happy for his sake—that we already have our schools of crime, which differ in one particular from our reformatories—that fact that one can leave them at any hour of the day or night: they are our bars and our slums, the glories of our republic. And on this point, at least, it is impossible to express oneself with moderation.

According to statistics, there are 64,000 overcrowded living accommodations (three to five persons to a room) in the city of Paris alone. Now of course the man who murders children is a particularly unspeakable creature, scarcely worth working up much pity over. It is probable, too (I say probable), that none of my readers, placed in the same promiscuous living conditions, would go so far as to murder children: there is no question of reducing the guilt of such monsters. But would such monsters, in decent living conditions, have an occasion to go so far? The least one can say is that they are not the only guilty parties: it is difficult to account for the fact that the right to punish these criminals is given to the very men who prefer to subsidize sugar beets rather than new construction.*

But alcohol makes this scandal all the more striking. It is well known that the French nation has been systematically intoxicated by its parliamentary majority for generally disgraceful reasons. Yet even with such knowledge in our grasp, the determined responsibility of alcohol for crimes of blood is still astounding. One lawyer (Guillon) has estimated that it is a factor in 60 per cent of all such cases. Dr. Lagriffe sets the rate somewhere between 41.7 and 72 per cent. An investigation conducted in 1951 at the distribution center of the Fresnes prison, among inmates guilty of breaches of common law, revealed 29 per cent were chronic alcoholics and 24 per cent had alcoholic backgrounds. Finally, 95 per cent of all murderers of children have been alcoholics. These are all fine figures, but there is one we must consider which is still finer: that of the *apéritif* manufacturer who declared a profit of 410,-000,000 francs in 1953. A comparison of these figures authorizes us to inform the stockholders of this company, and the assemblymen who voted for sugar beets rather than for buildings, that they have certainly

* France ranks ahead of all other nations in consumption of alcohol, fifteenth in construction.

killed more children than they suspect. As an adversary of capital punishment, I am far from demanding the death penalty for these individuals. But to begin with, it seems to me an indispensable and urgent duty to conduct them under military escort to the next execution of the murderer of a child, and at the conclusion of the ceremony to present them with a table of statistics which will include the figures I have been discussing.

When the state sows alcohol, it cannot be surprised if it reaps crime.* And it is *not* surprised, after all—it merely restricts itself to chopping off the same heads for which it poured out so much alcohol. It imperturbably executes its justice and sets itself up as a creditor: its good conscience is not affected. Hence we have one representative of the interests of alcohol indignantly answering the *Figaro* questionnaire: "I know what the most outspoken abolitionist of capital punishment would do if he were suddenly to discover assassins on the point of killing his mother, his father, his children, or his best friend . . . *Alors!*" This "*Alors!*" seems a little drunk already. Naturally the most outspoken abolitionist of capital punishment would fire, and with every justification, at the assassins, and without affecting in the slightest his reasons for outspokenly urging the abolition of capital punishment. But if his ideas led to consequences of any value, and if the same assassins smelled a little too much of alcohol, would he not subsequently turn his attentions to those who make it their business to intoxicate our future criminals? It is even a little surprising that the parents of victims of alcoholic crimes have never had the notion of requesting a few elucidations from the floor of the Assembly itself. But the contrary is the rule, and the State, armed with the confidence of all, with the full support of public opinion, continues to punish murderers, even and especially when they are alcoholics, somewhat the way a pimp punishes the hard-working creatures who provide his livelihood. But the pimp doesn't preach about his business. The State does. Its jurisprudence, if it admits that drunkenness occasionally constitutes an extenuating circumstance, is unaware of chronic alcoholism. Drunkenness, however, accompanies only crimes of violence, which are not punishable by death, whereas the chronic alcoholic is also capable of premeditated

* At the end of the last century, the partisans of capital punishment made much of an increase in the incidence of crime after 1880, which seemed to parallel a diminution in the application of the death penalty. It was in 1880, however, that the law permitting retail liquor establishments to set up shop without previous authorization was promulgated. Such facts are not difficult to interpret!

crimes, which gain him the death penalty. The State thus maintains the right to punish in the very case in which its own responsibility is profoundly involved.

Does this come down to saying that every alcoholic must be declared nonresponsible by a State which will strike its breast in horror until the entire populace drinks nothing but fruit juice? Certainly not. No more than it comes down to saying that the facts of heredity eliminate responsibility and guilt. A criminal's real responsibility cannot be determined exactly. All calculation is powerless to take into account the total number of our ancestors, alcoholic or not. At the other end of time, such a number would be 10^{22} times greater than the number of inhabitants of the earth at present. The total of diseased or morbid tendencies which could be transmitted is thus incalculable. We enter the world burdened with the weight of an infinite necessity, and according to logic must agree on a situation of a general nonresponsibility. Logically, neither punishment nor reward can be distributed accurately, and therefore all society becomes impossible. Yet the instinct of self-preservation, in societies and individuals alike, requires, on the contrary, the postulate of individual responsibility; a responsibility that must be accepted, without daydreaming of an absolute indulgence which would coincide with the death and disappearance of any society whatsoever. But the same line of reasoning that compels us to abandon a general nonresponsibility must also lead us to conclude that there is never, on the other hand, a situation of total responsibility, and consequently no such thing as absolute punishment or absolute reward. No one can be rewarded absolutely, not even by the Nobel prize. But no one must be punished absolutely if he is found guilty, and with all the more reason if there is a chance he might be innocent. The death penalty, which neither serves as an example nor satisfies the conditions of retaliative justice, usurps in addition an exorbitant privilege by claiming the right to punish a necessarily relative guilt by an absolute and irreparable penalty.

If, in fact, the death penalty serves as a questionable example of our gimcrack justice, one must agree with its supporters that it is eliminative: capital punishment definitively eliminates the condemned man. This fact alone, actually, ought to exclude, especially for its partisans, the discussion of all the other dangerous arguments which, as we have seen, can be ceaselessly contested. It would be more honest to say that capital punishment is definitive because it must be, to point out that certain men are socially irrecoverable, constituting a permanent danger to each citizen and to the social order as a whole, so that, before anything else, they must be suppressed. No one, at least, will question the existence of certain beasts in our society, creatures of incorrigible energy and brutality that nothing seems capable of subduing. And although the death penalty certainly does not solve the problem they present, let us at least agree that it goes a long way toward eliminating it.

I will return to these men. But first, is capital punishment confined only to them? Can we be absolutely certain that not one man of all those executed is recoverable? Can we even swear that one or another may not be *innocent?* In both cases, must we not admit that capital punishment is eliminative only to the degree that it is irreparable? Yesterday, March 15, 1957, Burton Abbott, condemned to death for the murder of a 14-year-old girl, was executed in California: it was certainly the kind of crime that I imagine would class him among the irrecoverables. Although Abbott had constantly protested his innocence, he was condemned. His execution was scheduled for March 15 at 10:00 in the morning. At 9:10 a reprieve was granted to allow the defense to present an appeal.* At 11 o'clock the appeal was rejected. At 11:15 Abbott entered the gas chamber. At 11:18 he began to breathe the first fumes of gas. At 11:20 the secretary of the reprieve board telephoned the prison: the board had changed its decision. The governor had been called first, but he had gone sailing, and they had called the prison directly. Abbott was removed from the gas chamber: it was too late. If the weather had been bad the day before, the governor of California would not have gone sailing. He would have telephoned two minutes earlier: Abbott would be alive today and would perhaps see his innocence proved. Any other punishment, even the most severe, would have permitted this chance. Capital punishment, however, permitted him none.

It may be thought that this case is exceptional. Our lives are exceptional too, and yet, in the fugitive existence we have been granted, this exception occurred not ten hours by plane from where I am writing. Abbott's misfortune is not so much an exception as it is one news item among many others, an error which is not at all isolated, if we examine our newspapers (for example, the Deshay case, to instance only the

* It should be pointed out that it is the custom in American prisons to conduct the condemned man to a new cell on the eve of his execution, thus informing him of the ceremony that awaits him.

most recent). The jurist Olivecroix, applying a calculus of probabilities to the chance of judiciary error, concluded in 1860 that approximately one innocent man was condemned out of every 257 cases. The proportion seems low, but only in relation to moderate punishment. In relation to capital punishment, the proportion is infinitely high. When Hugo wrote that he preferred to call the guillotine Lesurques,* he did not mean that every man who was decapitated was a Lesurques, but that one Lesurques was enough to wipe out the value of capital punishment forever. It is understandable that Belgium definitely abjured pronouncing capital punishment after one such judiciary error, and that England brought up the question of its abolition after the Hayes case. We can readily sympathize with the conclusions of that attorney general who, consulted on the petition for reprieve of a criminal who was most probably guilty but whose victim's body had not been recovered, wrote as follows: "The survival of X assures the authorities the possibility of effectively examining at their leisure every new sign that may subsequently be discovered of the existence of his wife [the victim, whose body had not been recovered]. . . . On the other hand, his execution, eliminating this hypothetical possibility of examination, would give, I fear, to the slightest evidence of her still being alive a theoretical value, a pressure of regret which I consider it inopportune to create." The man's feeling for both justice and truth are admirably expressed, and it would be advisable to cite as often as possible in our assize courts that "pressure of regret" which sums up so steadfastly the danger with which every juryman is confronted. Once the innocent man is dead, nothing more can be done for him except to re-establish his good name, if someone is still interested in asking for such a service. His innocence is restored—actually he had never lost it in the first place. But the persecution of which he has been the victim, his dreadful sufferings, and his hideous death have been acquired forever. There is nothing left to do but consider the innocent men of the future, in order to spare them such torments. It has been done in Belgium; but in France, apparently, there are no bad consciences.

Why should our consciences be bad if they are based on our conception of justice: has not this conception made great progress, does it not follow in the footsteps of science itself? When the learned expert gives his opinion in the assize courts, it is as if a priest had spoken, and

* The name of an innocent man guillotined in the *Courrier de Lyon* case.

the jury, raised in the religion of science—the jury nods. Nevertheless several recent cases—particularly the Besnard affair—have given us a good idea of the comedy such expertise can provide. Guilt is not better established because it can be demonstrated in a test tube. Another test tube can prove the contrary, and the personal equation will thereby maintain all its old significance in such perilous mathematics as these. The proportion of scientists who are really experts is the same as that of judges who are really psychologists—scarcely more than that of juries that are really serious and objective. Today, as yesterday, the chance of error remains. Tomorrow another expert's report will proclaim the innocence of another Abbott. But Abbott will be dead, scientifically enough, and science, which claims to prove innocence as well as guilt, has not yet succeeded in restoring the life it has taken.

And among the guilty themselves, can we also be sure of having killed only "irrecoverables"? Those who like myself have had to attend hearings in our assize courts know that a number of elements of sheer accident enter into a sentence, even a death sentence. The looks of the accused; his background (adultery is often regarded as an incriminating circumstance by some jurors: I have never been able to believe that all are completely faithful to their wives and husbands); his attitude (which is only regarded as being in his favor if it is as conventional as possible, which usually means as near play-acting as possible); even his elocution (one must neither stutter nor speak too well) and the incidents of the hearing sentimentally evaluated (the truth, unfortunately, is not always moving)—all these are so many accidents that influence the final decision of a jury. At the moment the verdict recommending the death penalty is pronounced, one can be sure that this most certain of punishments has only been arrived at by a great conjunction of uncertainties. When one realizes that the verdict of death depends on the jury's estimation of the extenuating circumstances, particularly since the reforms of 1832 gave our juries the power to admit *undetermined* extenuating circumstances, one can appreciate the margin left to the momentary humors of the jurors. It is no longer the law which establishes with any precision those cases in which the death penalty is recommended, but the jury which, after the event, estimates its suitability by guesswork, to say the least. As there are no two juries alike, the man who is executed might as well have been spared. Irrecoverable in the eyes of the honest citizens of

Île-et-Vilaine, he might well be granted the shadow of an excuse by the good people of Var. Unfortunately, the same knife falls in both departments. And it is not concerned with such details.

The accidents of the times combine with those of geography to reinforce the general absurdity. The Communist French worker who was just guillotined in Algeria for having planted a bomb, discovered before it could explode, in the cloakroom of a factory was condemned as much by his act as by the times, for in the Algerian situation at present, Arab public opinion was to be shown that the guillotine was made for French necks too, and French public opinion, outraged by terrorist activities, was to be given satisfaction at the same time. Nevertheless, the minister in charge of the execution counted many Communist votes in his constituency, and if the circumstances had been slightly different, the accused would have got off lightly and perhaps one day, as his party's deputy, might have found himself drinking at the same bar as the minister. Such thoughts are bitter and one might wish they remained fresh a little longer in the minds of our governors. These gentlemen should be aware that times and manners change; a day comes along when the criminal who was executed too quickly no longer seems quite so guilty. By then it is too late, and what can you do but repent or forget? Naturally, one forgets. But society is nonetheless affected: one unpunished crime, according to the Greeks, infects the whole city. Innocence condemned to death, or crime excessively punished, leaves a stain no less hideous in the long run. We know it, in France.

Such is the nature of human justice, it will be said, and despite its imperfections, after all, even human justice is better than the operation of despotism or chance. But this rueful preference is tolerable only in relation to moderate punishment. Confronted by death sentences, it is a scandal. A classic work on French law excuses the death penalty from being subject to degree in the following words: "Human justice has not the slightest ambition to insure proportion of this nature. Why? Because it knows itself to be imperfect." Must we therefore conclude that this imperfection authorizes us to pronounce an absolute judgment, and that society, uncertain of realizing justice in its pure state, must rush headlong with every likelihood of error, upon the supreme injustice? If human justice knows itself to be imperfect, might not that knowledge be more suitably and modestly demonstrated by leaving a sufficient margin around our condemnations for the eventual reparation of error? * This very weakness in which human justice finds extenuating circumstances for itself in every case and on every occasion —is it not to be accorded to the criminal himself as well? Can the jury in all decency say, "If we condemn you to death by mistake, you will surely forgive us in consideration of the weaknesses of the human nature we all share. But we nevertheless condemn you to death without the slightest consideration of these weaknesses or of this common nature"? All men have a community in error and in aberration. Yet must this community operate in behalf of the tribunal and be denied to the accused? No, for if justice has any meaning in this world, it is none other than the recognition of this very community: it cannot, in its very essence, be separated from compassion. Let it be understood that by compassion I mean only the consciousness of a common suffering, not a frivolous indulgence that takes no account of the sufferings and rights of the victim. Compassion does not exclude punishment, but it withholds an ultimate condemnation. It is revolted by the definitive, irreparable measure that does injustice to man in general since it does not recognize his share in the misery of the common condition.

As a matter of fact, certain juries know this well enough, and often admit the extenuating circumstances of a crime which nothing can extenuate. This is because they regard the death penalty as too extreme and prefer to punish insufficiently rather than to excess. In such cases, the extreme severity of the punishment tends to sanction crime instead of penalizing it. There is scarcely one session of the assize courts of which one cannot read in our press that a verdict is incoherent, that in the face of the facts it appears either insufficient or excessive. The jurors are not unaware of this. They simply prefer, as we should do ourselves, when confronted with the enormity of capital punishment, to appear confused, rather than compromise their sleep for nights to come. Knowing themselves imperfect, at least they draw the appropriate consequences. And true justice is on their side, precisely to the degree that logic is not.

There are, however, great criminals that every jury will condemn, no matter where and when they are tried. Their crimes are certain, and the

---

* Satisfaction was expressed over the recent reprieve of Sillon, who killed his four-year-old daughter in order to keep her from her mother, who had asked for a divorce. During his detention it was discovered that Sillon was suffering from a brain tumor that could account for the insanity of his action.

proofs elicited by the prosecution correspond with the admissions of the defense. What is abnormal and even monstrous in their crimes unquestionably determines their category as pathological, though in the majority of such cases psychiatrists affirm the criminal's responsibility. Recently, in Paris, a young man of rather weak character, but known for the sweetness and affection of his nature and his extreme devotion to his family, described himself as being annoyed by his father's remarks on the lateness of the hours he had been keeping. The father was reading at the dining-room table. The young man took an axe and struck his father several mortal blows with it from behind. Then, in the same fashion, he struck down his mother, who was in the kitchen. He removed his bloody trousers and hid them in the closet, changed his clothes, and after paying a visit to the family of his fiancée without revealing the slightest discomposure, returned to his own house and informed the police his parents had been murdered. The police immediately discovered the bloody trousers, and easily obtained the parricide's unperturbed confession. The psychiatrists agreed on his responsibility for these "murders by irritation." The young man's strange indifference, of which he gave other indications in prison (rejoicing that his parents' funeral had been so well attended: "Everyone liked them," he said to his lawyers), can nevertheless scarcely be considered as normal. But his reason was apparently intact.

Many "monsters" offer a countenance just as impenetrable. They are therefore eliminated upon consideration of the facts alone. Because of the nature or the degree of their crimes it is inconceivable that they would repent or even wish to change their ways. In their case, a recurrence is what must be avoided, and there is no other solution than to eliminate them. On this—and only this—aspect of the question is the discussion of the death penalty legitimate. In all other cases the arguments of its partisans cannot withstand the criticism of its opponents. At this point, in fact, at our present level of ignorance, a kind of wager is established: no expertise, no exercise of reason can give the deciding vote between those who think a last chance must always be granted to even the last of men and those who consider this chance as entirely illusory. But it is perhaps possible, at this very point, to override the *eternal* opposition between the partisans and opponents of the death penalty, by determining the advisability of such a penalty *at this time, and in Europe*. With considerably less competence, I shall attempt to parallel the efforts of professor Jean Graven, a Swiss jurist who writes, in his remarkable study of the problems of capital punishment: ". . . Regarding the problem that once again confronts our conscience and our reason, it is our opinion that the solution must be based not upon the conceptions, the problems, and the arguments of the past, nor on the theoretical hopes and promises of the future, but on the ideas, the given circumstances, and the necessities of today." * One could, in fact, argue forever about the advantages or devastations of the death penalty as it has been through the ages or as it might be contemplated in some eternity of ideas. But the death penalty plays its part here and now, and we must determine here and now where we stand in relation to a contemporary executioner. What does the death penalty mean for us, halfway through the twentieth century?

For the sake of simplification, let us say that our civilization has lost the only values that, to a certain degree, could justify the death penalty, and that it suffers, on the contrary, from every evil that necessitates its suppression. In other words, the abolition of the death penalty should be demanded by the conscious members of our society on grounds of both logic and fidelity to the facts.

Of logic, first of all. To decide that a man must be definitively punished is to deny him any further opportunity whatsoever to make reparation for his acts. It is at this juncture, we repeat, that the arguments for and against capital punishment confront one another blindly, eventuating in a fruitless checkmate. Yet it is exactly here that none of us can afford to be positive, for we are all judges, all party to the dispute. Hence our uncertainty about our right to kill and our impotence to convince others on either side. Unless there is absolute innocence, there can be no supreme judge. Now we have all committed some transgression in our lives, even if this transgression has not put us within the power of the law and has remained an unknown crime: there are no just men, only hearts more or less poor in justice. The mere fact of living permits us to know this, and to add to the sum of our actions a little of the good that might partially compensate for the evil we have brought into the world. This right to live that coincides with the opportunity for reparation is the natural right of every man, even the worst. The most abandoned criminal and the worthiest judge here find themselves side by side, equally miserable and jointly responsible. Without this right, the moral life is strictly impossible. None among us, in par-

* *Revue de Criminologie et de Police technique*, Geneva, special number, 1952.

ticular, is entitled to despair of a single man, unless it be after his death, which transforms his life into destiny and admits of a final judgment. But to pronounce this final judgment before death, to decree the closing of accounts when the creditor is still alive, is the privilege of no man. On these grounds, at least, he who judges absolutely condemns himself absolutely.

Barnard Fallot of the Masuy gang, who worked for the Gestapo, confessed to the entire list of terrible crimes of which he was accused, and later went to his death with great courage, declaring himself beyond hope of reprieve: "My hands are too red with blood," he said to one of his fellow prisoners.* Public opinion and that of his judges certainly classified him among the irrecoverables, and I would have been tempted to put him in that category myself, had I not read one astonishing piece of evidence: after having declared that he wanted to die bravely, Fallot told the same prisoner: "Do you know what I regret most of all? Not having known sooner about the Bible they gave me here. If I had, I wouldn't be where I am now." It is not a question of surrendering to the sentimentality of conventional imagery and conjuring up Victor Hugo's good convicts. The age of enlightenment, as it is called, wished to abolish the death penalty under the pretext that man was fundamentally good. We know, of course, that he is not (he is simply better or worse). After the last twenty years of our splendid history we know it very well. But it is because man is not fundamentally good that no one among us can set himself up as an absolute judge, for no one among us can pretend to absolute innocence. The verdict of capital punishment destroys the only indisputable human community there is, the community in the face of death, and such a judgment can only be legitimated by a truth or a principle that takes its place above all men, beyond the human condition.

Capital punishment, in fact, throughout history has always been a religious punishment. When imposed in the name of the king, representative of God on earth, or by priests, or in the name of a society considered as a sacred body, it is not the human community that is destroyed but the functioning of the guilty man as a member of the divine community which alone can give him his life. Such a man is certainly deprived of his earthly life, yet his opportunity for reparation is preserved. The real judgment is not pronounced in this world, but in the next. Religious values, especially the belief in an eternal life,

* Jean Bobognano, *Quartier des fauves, prison de Fresnes,* Édition du Fuseau.

are thus the only ones on which the death penalty can be based since according to their own logic they prevent that penalty from being final and irreparable: it is justified only insofar as it is not supreme.

The Catholic Church, for example, has always admitted the neccessity of the death penalty. It has imposed the penalty itself, without avarice, at other periods. Today, its doctrines still justify capital punishment, and concede the State the right to apply it. No matter how subtle this doctrine may be, there is at its core a profound feeling which was directly expressed by a Swiss councilor from Fribourg during a discussion of capital punishment by the national council in 1937; according to M. Grand, even the worst criminal examines his own conscience when faced with the actuality of execution. "He repents, and his preparation for death is made easier. The Church has saved one of its members, has accomplished its divine mission. This is why the Church has steadfastly countenanced capital punishment, not only as a means of legitimate protection, but *as a powerful means of salvation*. . . . [My italics.] Without becoming precisely a matter of doctrine, the death penalty, like war itself, can be justified by its quasi-divine efficacity."

By virtue of the same reasoning, no doubt, one can read on the executioner's sword in Fribourg the motto "Lord Jesus, thou art the Judge." The executioner is thereby invested with a divine function. He is the man who destroys the body in order to deliver the soul to its divine judgment, which no man on earth can foresee. It will perhaps be considered that such mottos imply rather outrageous confusions, and certainly those who confine themselves to the actual teachings of Jesus will see this handsome sword as yet another outrage to the body of Christ. In this light can be understood the terrible words of a Russian prisoner whom the executioners of the Tsar were about to hang in 1905, when he turned to the priest who was about to console him with the image of Christ and said: "Stand back, lest you commit a sacrilege." An unbeliever will not fail to remark that those who have placed in the very center of their faith the overwhelming victim of a judicial error should appear more reticent, to say the least, when confronted by cases of legal murder. One might also remind the believer that the emperor Julian, before his conversion, refused to give official posts to Christians because they systematically refused to pronounce the death sentence or to aid in administering it. For five centuries Christians believed that the strict moral teaching of their master forbade them to kill. But the Catholic faith is derived not only from the teachings of Christ, it is nourished by the Old Testament, by Saint Paul, and by the Fathers as well. In particular the immortality of the soul and the universal resurrection of the body are articles of dogma. Hence, capital punishment, for the believer, can be regarded as a provisional punishment which does not in the least affect the definite sentence, but remains a disposition necessary to the terrestrial order, an administrative measure which, far from making an end of the guilty man, can promote, on the contrary, his redemption in heaven. I do not say that all believers follow this reasoning, and I can imagine without much difficulty that most Catholics stand closer to Christ than to Moses or Saint Paul. I say only that the belief in the immortality of the soul has permitted Catholicism to formulate the problem of capital punishment in very different terms, and to justify it.

But what does such a justification mean to the society we live in, a society which in its institutions and manners alike has become almost entirely secular? When an atheist—or skeptic—or agnostic judge imposes the death penalty on an unbelieving criminal, he is pronouncing a definitive punishment that cannot be revised. He sits upon God's throne,* but without possessing God's powers and, moreover, without believing in them. He condemns to death, in fact, because his ancestors believed in eternal punishment. Yet the society which he claims to represent pronounces, in reality, a purely eliminative measure, destroys the human community united against death, and sets itself up as an absolute value because it pretends to absolute power. Of course society traditionally assigns a priest to the condemned man, and the priest may legitimately hope that fear of punishment will help effect the condemned man's conversion. Yet who will accept this casuistry as the justification of a punishment so often inflicted and so often received in an entirely different spirit? It is one thing to believe and "therefore know not fear," and another to find one's faith through fear. Conversion by fire or the knife will always be suspect, and one can well understand why the Church renounced a triumph by terror over infidel hearts. In any case, a secularized society has nothing to gain from a conversion concerning which it professes complete disinterest: it enacts a consecrated punishment, and at the same time deprives that punishment of its justification and its utility alike. Delirious in its own behalf,

---

* The decision of the jury is preceded by the formula "before God and my conscience. . . ."

society plucks the wicked from its bosom as if it were virtue personified. In the same way, an honorable man might kill his son who had strayed from the path of duty, saying, "Really, I didn't know what else I could do!" Society thus usurps the right of selection, as if it were nature, and adds a terrible suffering to the eliminative process, as if it were a redeeming god.

To assert, in any case, that a man must be absolutely cut off from society because he is absolutely wicked is the same as saying that society is absolutely good, which no sensible person will believe today. It will not be believed—in fact, it is easier to believe the contrary. Our society has become as diseased and criminal as it is only because it has set itself up as its own final justification, and has had no concern but its own preservation and success in history. Certainly it is a secularized society, yet during the nineteenth century it began to fashion a kind of ersatz religion by proposing itself as an object of adoration. The doctrines of evolution, and the theories of selection that accompanied such doctrines, have proposed the future of society as its final end. The political utopias grafted onto these doctrines have proposed, at the end of time, a Golden Age that justifies in advance all intermediary enterprises. Society has grown accustomed to legalizing whatever can minister to its future, and consequently to usurping the supreme punishment in an absolute fashion: it has regarded as a crime and a sacrilege everything that contradicts its own intentions and temporal dogmas. In other words, the executioner, formerly a priest, has become a civil servant. The results surround us. Halfway through the century, our society, which has forfeited the logical right to pronounce the death penalty, must now abolish it for reasons of realism.

Confronted with crime, how does our civilization in fact define itself? The answer is easy: for thirty years crimes of State have vastly exceeded crimes of individuals. I shall not even mention wars—general or local—although blood is a kind of alcohol that eventually intoxicates like the strongest wine. I am referring here to the number of individuals killed directly by the State, a number that has grown to astronomic proportions and infinitely exceeds that of "private" murders. There are fewer and fewer men condemned by common law, and more and more men executed for political reasons. The proof of this fact is that each of us, no matter how honorable he is, can now envisage the *possibility* of someday being put to death, whereas such an eventuality at the beginning of the century would have appeared farcical at best. Alphonse

Karr's famous remark, "Let my lords the assassins begin," no longer has any meaning: those who spill the most blood are also those who believe they have right, logic, and history on their side.

It is not so much against the individual killer that our society must protect itself then, as against the State. Perhaps this equation will be reversed in another thirty years. But for the present, a legitimate defense must be made against the State, before all else. Justice and the most realistic sense of our time require that the law protect the individual against a State given over to the follies of sectarianism and pride. "Let the State begin by abolishing the death penalty" must be our rallying cry today.

Bloody laws, it has been said, make bloody deeds. But it is also possible for a society to suffer that state of ignominy in which public behavior, no matter how disorderly, comes nowhere near being so bloody as the laws. Half of Europe knows this state. We have known it in France and we risk knowing it again. The executed of the Occupation produced the executed of the Liberation whose friends still dream of revenge. Elsewhere, governments charged with too many crimes are preparing to drown their guilt in still greater massacres. We kill for a nation or for a deified social class. We kill for a future society, likewise deified. He who believes in omniscience can conceive of omnipotence. Temporal idols that demand absolute faith tirelessly mete out absolute punishments. And religions without transcendence murder those they condemn en masse and without hope.

How can European society in the twentieth century survive if it does not defend the individual by every means within its power against the oppression of the State? To forbid putting a man to death is one means of publicly proclaiming that society and the State are not absolute values, one means of demonstrating that nothing authorizes them to legislate definitively, to bring to pass the irreparable. Without the death penalty, Gabriel Péri and Brasillach would perhaps be among us still; we could then judge them, according to our lights, and proudly speak out our judgment, instead of which they now judge us, and it is we who must remain silent. Without the death penalty the corpse of Rajk would not still be poisoning Hungary, a less guilty Germany would be received with better grace by the nations of Europe, the Russian Revolution would not still be writhing in its shame, and the blood of Algeria would weigh less heavily upon us here in France. Without the death penalty, Europe itself would not be infected by the corpses accumulated in its exhausted earth for the last twenty years. Upon our continent all values have been overturned by fear and hatred among individuals as among nations. The war of ideas is waged by rope and knife. It is no longer the natural human society that exercises its rights of repression, but a ruling ideology that demands its human sacrifices. "The lesson the scaffold always provides," Francart wrote, "is that human life ceases to be sacred when it is considered useful to suppress it." Apparently it has been considered increasingly useful, the lesson has found apt pupils, and the contagion is spreading everywhere. And with it, the disorders of nihilism. A spectacular counter-blow is required: it must be proclaimed, in institutions and as a matter of principle, that the human person is above and beyond the State. Every measure which will diminish the pressure of social forces on the individual will also aid in the decongestion of a Europe suffering from an afflux of blood, will permit us to think more clearly, and to make our way toward recovery. The disease of Europe is to believe in nothing and to claim to know everything. But Europe does not know everything, far from it, and to judge by the rebellion and the hope in which we find ourselves today, Europe does believe in something: Europe believes that the supreme misery of man, at its mysterious limit, borders on his supreme greatness. For the majority of Europeans faith is lost, and with it the justifications faith conferred upon the order of punishment. But the majority of Europeans are also sickened by that idolatry of the State which has claimed to replace their lost faith. From now on, with divided goals, certain and uncertain, determined never to submit and never to oppress, we must recognize both our hope and our ignorance, renounce all absolute law, all irreparable institutions. We know enough to be able to say that this or that great criminal deserves a sentence of perpetual forced labor. But we do not know enough to say that he can be deprived of his own future, which is to say, of our common opportunity for reparation. In tomorrow's united Europe, on whose behalf I write, the solemn abolition of the death penalty must be the first article of that European Code for which we all hope.

From the humanitarian idylls of the eighteenth century to its bloody scaffolds the road runs straight and is easily followed; we all know today's executioners are humanists. And therefore we cannot be too suspicious of humanitarian ideologies applied to a problem like that of capital punishment. I should like to repeat, by way of conclusion, that my opposition to the death penalty derives from no illusions as to the natural goodness of the human creature, and from no faith in a Golden Age to come. On the contrary, the abolition of capital punishment seems necessary to me for reasons of qualified pessimism, reasons I have attempted to explain in terms of logic and the most realistic considerations. Not that the heart has not made its contribution to what I have been saying: for anyone who has spent several weeks among these texts, these memories, and these men—all, intimately or remotely, connected with the scaffold—there can be no question of leaving their dreadful ranks unaffected by what one has seen and heard. Nevertheless, I do not believe there is no responsibility in this world for what I have found, or that one should submit to our modern propensity for absolving victim and killer in the same moral confusion. This purely sentimental confusion involves more cowardice than generosity, and ends up by justifying whatever is worst in this world: if everything is blessed, then slave camps are blessed, and organized murder, and the cynicism of the great political bosses—and ultimately, blessing everything alike, one betrays one's own brothers. We can see this happening all around us. But indeed, with the world in its present condition the man of the twentieth century asks for laws and institutions of *convalescence* that will check without crushing, lead without hampering. Hurled into the unregulated dynamism of history, man needs a new physics, new laws of equilibrium. He needs, most of all, a reasonable society, not the anarchy into which his own pride and the State's inordinate powers have plunged him.

It is my conviction that the abolition of the death penalty will help us advance toward that society. In taking this initiative, France could propose its extension on either side of the Iron Curtain; in any case she could set an example. Capital punishment would be replaced by a sentence of perpetual forced labor for criminals judged incorrigible, and by shorter terms for others. As for those who believe that such punishment is still more cruel than capital punishment itself, I wonder why, in that case, they do not reserve it for Landru and his like and relegate capital punishment to secondary offenders. One might also add that such forced labor leaves the condemned man the possibility of choosing his death, whereas the guillotine is a point of no return. On the other hand, I would answer those who believe that a sentence of perpetual forced labor is too mild a punishment by remarking first on their lack of imagination and then by pointing out that the privation of liberty could seem to them a mild punishment only to the degree that contemporary society has taught them to despise what liberty they have.*

That Cain was not killed, but bore in the sight of all men a mark of reprobation is, in any case, the lesson we should draw from the Old Testament, not to mention the Gospels, rather than taking our inspiration from the cruel examples of the Mosaic law. There is no reason why at least a limited version of such an experiment should not be attempted in France (say for a ten-year period), if our government is still capable of redeeming its vote for alcohol by the great measure in behalf of civilization which total abolition would represent. And if public opinion and its representatives cannot renounce our slothful law which confines itself to eliminating what it cannot amend, at least, while waiting for a day of regeneration and of truth, let us not preserve as it is this "solemn shambles" (in Tarde's expression) which continues to disgrace our society. The death penalty, as it is imposed, even as rarely as it is imposed, is a disgusting butchery, an outrage inflicted on the spirit and body of man. This truncation, this living severed head, these long gouts of blood, belong to a barbarous epoch that believed it could subdue the people by offering them degrading spectacles. Today, when this ignoble death is secretly administered, what meaning can such torture have? The truth is that in an atomic age we kill as we did in the age of steelyards: where is the man of normal sensibility whose stomach is not turned at the mere idea of such clumsy surgery? If the French state is incapable of overcoming its worst impulses to this degree, and of furnishing Europe with one of the remedies it needs most, let it at least reform its means of administering capital punishment. Science, which has taught us so much about killing, could at least teach us to kill decently. An anesthetic which would permit the accused to pass from a state of sleep to death, which would remain within his reach for at least a day so that he could make free

---

* See also the report on the death penalty made by Representative Dupont to the National Assembly on May 31, 1791: "He [*the assassin*] is consumed by a bitter, burning temper; what he fears above all is repose, a state that leaves him to himself, and to escape it he continually faces death and seeks to inflict it; solitude and his conscience are his real tortures. Does this not tell us what kind of punishment we should impose, to what agonies he is most sensitive? *Is it not in the very nature of the disease that we must seek the remedy which can cure it?*" I italicize this last sentence, which makes this little-known Representative a real precursor of our modern psychological theories.

use of it, and which in cases of refusal or failure of nerve could then be administered to him, would assure the elimination of the criminal, if that is what we require, but would also provide a little decency where today there is nothing but a sordid and obscene exhibition.

I indicate these compromises only to the degree that one must sometimes despair of seeing wisdom and the principles of civilization impose themselves upon those responsible for our future. For certain men, more numerous than is supposed, knowing what the death penalty really is and being unable to prevent its application is physically insupportable. In their own way, they suffer this penalty too, and without any justification. If we at least lighten the weight of the hideous images that burden these men, society will lose nothing by our actions. But ultimately even such measures will be insufficient. Neither in the hearts of men nor in the manners of society will there be a lasting peace until we outlaw death.

A. P. Herbert

:

ON THE LAW PROHIBITING BUSINESS
ON THE LORD'S DAY;
ON THE REASONABLE MAN;
AND THE GRAMOPHONE LIBEL CASE

from *Misleading Cases in the Common Law*

REX *v.* GARVIN, RIDDLE, JOHNSTON, THOMAS, ROBINSON, BEETLE, PULBOROUGH, AND OTHERS

The hearing of this case was concluded today in the Court of Criminal Appeal.

The Lord Chief Justice, delivering judgment, said: In this painful case the defendants are the proprietors and editors of certain Sunday newspapers. They were charged at the Old Bailey, on an information laid by the Sunday Society, with certain offenses under the Sunday Observance Act, 1677—an Act of the reign of Charles II, which has never been repealed. All the defendants were found guilty, and they were sentenced to fines ranging from five hundred thousand to two million pounds, or in the alternative to imprisonment for a very long time; and they have now appealed on the ground that these sentences are excessive.

That the offenses were committed is not seriously disputed. By the Act it is laid down that

> *No tradesmen, artificers, workmen, laborers, or other person whatsoever shall do or exercise any worldly labor, business, or work of their ordinary callings upon the Lord's Day, or any part thereof.*

It was proved to the satisfaction of the judge and jury that the accused persons have for many years distributed, sold, and in some cases printed their newspaper upon the Lord's Day, or some part thereof. And

553

it is only necessary for this Court to consider the facts of the case so far as they may affect the measure of punishment.

It was urged in evidence by the very able Secretary of the informing Society, Mr. Haddock, that the dissemination of what is called "news" is always an anti-social and disturbing act; that "news" consists, as to ninety per cent, of the records of human misfortune, unhappiness, and wrongdoing, as to nine percent of personal advertisement, and as to one per cent of constructive and improving matter; that the study of the newspaper is harmful to the citizen because (*a*) by their insistence upon railway accidents, floods, divorces, murders, fires, successful robberies, the rates of taxation and other evils, and (*b*) by the prominence which they give to exceptionally good fortune, the winners of large sweepstakes, the salaries and faces of beautiful actresses, and the occasional success of what are known, it appears, as "outsiders," he is led to the conclusion that industry, thrift and virtue are not worth pursuing in a world so much governed by incalculable chances; and, in general, that the conditions of mind most fostered by the news of the day are curiosity, cupidity, envy, indignation, horror, and fear.

Now, whatever may be desirable or permitted upon a weekday, it is argued by Mr. Haddock that to influence great numbers of the citizens in this way for pecuniary gain on the morning of the Sabbath is clearly contrary to the intention of the Act. But evidence was called to show that there are large masses of the population who because of the existence of the defendants' journals ignore the news of the world throughout the week, and only begin to consider it at about that time on Sunday morning when the bells are summoning them to matins, from which hour until the midday meal they remain, as one witness put it, "embedded" in the news. And numerous divines swore that they expect their largest congregations upon Christmas Day, which is one of the only two holy days in the year on which no newspapers appear to seduce their flock with the activities of racehorses or the contents of trunks.

These are grave charges. And it is necessary to consider the particular character of the various journals in question. The defendant Garvin, who appears to possess an unusual command of language, maintained that his paper, *The Observer,* was in a class by itself and deliberately designed for the special needs of the Sabbath reader; but this defense was put forward by several others, though on different grounds. He was asked to say whether in his opinion a man of average powers could in the same morning give proper attention to bodily cleanliness, to divine service, and to one of his leading articles. The witness replied that his leading articles were half-way between a cold bath and a religious exercise, and that this was the place which they occupied, very fitly, in the life of the nation. I have here four or five columns extracted from one of these articles (Exhibit A). It is headed "THE CATACLYSM—SANITY OR SURRENDER? —DISRAELI, THE DIE-HARD AND THE DELUGE." It begins:

> *This week the chiaroscuro of human affairs is colored full-blooded in the tones of madness. After Mesopotamia—Manchester. After Clynes—Catastrophe. After Baldwin—what? In this journal we have never concealed our opinion, etc.*

It was argued by Mr. Haddock, I think with some force, that on Sunday morning at eleven o'clock no Christian Englishman should be thinking about Mesopotamia or chiaroscuro. Yet this writer has at least the intention of elevating, however depressing his messages in fact may be. But what is to be said of the witnesses Ervine and Agate, who have admitted in evidence that every Sunday morning, in two columns or more, they direct the attention of their numerous followers to the performance of stage-plays, the personal appearance of actresses, the material rewards of playwrights and managers, the problems of sex, and other matters which are without doubt "worldly" within the meaning of the Act?

And these unfortunately are not the worst. There are other papers represented in that dock which devote a considerable space to accounts of crime and criminal proceedings, the past conduct of pugilists, and the future behavior of horses; and it was argued for the prosecution that the same law which forbids the subject to witness a play by the poet Shakespeare on Sunday evening should, *a fortiori,* protect him in the morning from the more sensational dramas of the underworld. There are papers published on Sunday morning, it appears, which many Britons are compelled to conceal from their wives; while in other households two copies are purchased in order that the reading of neither spouse may be interrupted. In these papers an importance is attached to the crimes of passion which neither their number nor their moral teaching would seem to justify; and no governess is unwillingly caressed but some representative will be at hand to report the proceedings. I am satisfied that the purveying of these reports for money has not the educational or religious purpose which might excuse it, and that it is a "worldly business" within the meaning of the Act.

I see no reason why any of the sentences should be reduced. These papers are not poor papers. On the contrary, they make no secret of their large circulation and extensive influence; and many of them go so far as to publish statistical records of their sales, glorying in the fact that every Sabbath they distract greater numbers of His Majesty's subjects from holy thoughts than this or that other paper. It is in the power of this Court to vary sentences either in a downward or an upward direction, and the sentences of certain of the defendants will be increased to penal servitude for terms of years calculated *pro rata* according to circulation. The defendant claiming the largest circulation will be boiled alive, and an order will be made to that effect.

These papers must not be printed again. It has been urged that this order will deprive many citizens of their weekly entertainment; but I am satisfied that the needs of the people are amply supplied by certain papers which are published during the week and especially on Wednesdays. The appeal must be dismissed.

Frog, J., and *Batter, J.,* concurred.

ON THE REASONABLE MAN

FARDELL *v.* POTTS

The Court of Appeal today delivered judgment in the case of *Fardell* v. *Potts*.

Lord Justice Morrow said: In this case the appellant was a Mrs. Fardell, a woman, who, while navigating a motor-launch on the River Thames, collided with the respondent, who was navigating a punt, as a result of which the respondent was immersed and caught cold. The respondent brought an action for damages, in which it was alleged that the collision and subsequent immersion were caused by the negligent navigation of the appellant. In the Court below the learned judge decided that there was evidence on which the jury might find that the defendant had not taken reasonable care, and, being of that opinion, very properly left to the jury the question whether in fact she had failed to use reasonable care or not. The jury found for the plaintiff and awarded him two hundred and fifty pounds damages. This verdict we are asked to set aside on the ground of misdirection by the learned judge, the contention being that the case should never have been allowed to go to the jury; and this contention is supported by a somewhat novel proposition, which has been ably, but tediously, argued by Sir Ethelred Rutt.

The Common Law of England has been laboriously built about a mythical figure—the figure of "The Reasonable Man." In the field of jurisprudence this legendary individual occupies the place which in another science is held by the Economic Man, and in social and political discussions by the Average or Plain Man. He is an ideal, a standard, the embodiment of all those qualities which we demand of the good citizen. No matter what may be the particular department of human life which falls to be considered in these Courts, sooner or later we have to face the question: Was this or was it not the conduct of a reasonable man? Did the defendant take such care to avoid shooting the plaintiff in the stomach as might reasonably be expected of a reasonable man? (*Moocat* v. *Radley* (1883), 2 Q.B.). Did the plaintiff take such precautions to inform himself of the circumstances as any reasonable man would expect of an ordinary person having the ordinary knowledge of an ordinary person of the habits of wild bulls when goaded with garden-forks and the persistent agitation of red flags? (*Williams* v. *Dogbody,* (1841), 2 A.C.).

I need not multiply examples. It is impossible to travel anywhere or to travel for long in that confusing forest of learned judgments which constitutes the Common Law of England without encountering the Reasonable Man. He is at every turn, an ever-present help in time of trouble, and his apparitions mark the road to equity and right. There has never been a problem, however difficult, which His Majesty's judges have not in the end been able to resolve by asking themselves the simple question, "Was this or was it not the conduct of a reasonable man?" and leaving that question to be answered by the jury.

This noble creature stands in singular contrast to his kinsmen the Economic Man, whose every action is prompted by the single spur of selfish advantage, and directed to the single end of monetary gain. The Reasonable Man is always thinking of others; prudence is his guide, and "Safety First," if I may borrow a contemporary catchword, is his rule of life. All solid virtues are his, save only that peculiar quality by which the affection of other men is won. For it will not be pretended that socially he is much less objectionable than the Economic Man. While any given example of his behavior must command our admiration, when taken in the mass his acts create a very different set of impressions. He is one who invariably looks where he is going, and is careful to examine the immediate foreground before he executes a leap or a bound; who neither star-gazes nor is lost in meditation when approaching trapdoors or the margin of a dock; who records in every case upon the counterfoils of checks such ample details as are desirable, scrupulously substitutes the word "Order" for the word "Bearer," crosses the instrument "a/c Payee only," and registers the package in which it is dispatched; who never mounts a moving omnibus and does not alight from any car while the train is in motion; who investigates exhaustively the *bona fides* of every mendicant before distributing alms, and will inform himself of the history and habits of a dog before administering a caress; who believes no gossip, nor repeats it, without firm basis for believing it to be true; who never drives his ball till those in front of him have definitely vacated the putting-green which is his own objective; who never from one year's end to another makes an excessive demand upon his wife, his neighbors, his servants, his ox, or his ass; who in the way of business looks only for that narrow margin of profit which twelve men such as himself would reckon to be "fair," and contemplates his fellow-merchants, their agents, and their goods, with that degree of suspicion and distrust which the law deems admirable; who never swears, gambles, or loses his temper; who uses nothing except in moderation, and even while he flogs his child is meditating only on the golden mean. Devoid, in short, of any human weakness, with not one single saving vice, sans prejudice, procrastination, ill-nature, avarice, and absence of mind, as careful for his own safety as he is for that of others, this excellent but odious character stands like a monument in our Courts of Justice, vainly appealing to his fellow-citizens to order their lives after his own example.

I have called him a myth; and, in so far as there are few, if any, of his mind and temperament to be found in the ranks of living men, the title is well chosen. But it is a myth which rests upon solid and even, it may be, upon permanent foundations. The Reasonable Man is fed and kept alive by the most valued and enduring of our juridical institutions—the common jury. Hateful as he must necessarily be to any ordinary citizen who privately considers him, it is a curious paradox that where two or three are gathered together in one place they will with one accord pretend an admiration for him, and, when they are gathered together in the formidable surroundings of a British jury, they are easily persuaded that they themselves are, each and generally, reasonable men. And without stopping to consider how strange a chance it must have been that has picked fortuitously from a whole people no fewer than twelve examples of a species so rare, they immediately invest themselves with the attributes of the Reasonable Man, and are therefore at one with the Courts in their anxiety to support the tradition that such a being in fact exists. Thus it is that while the Economic Man has under the stress of modern conditions almost wholly disappeared from view, his Reasonable cousin has gained in power with every case in which he has figured.

To return, however, as every judge must ultimately return, to the case which is before us—it has been urged for the appellant, and my own researches incline me to agree, that in all that mass of authorities which bears upon this branch of the law *there is no single mention of a reasonable woman*. It was ably insisted before us that such an omission, extending over a century and more of judicial pronouncements, must be something more than a coincidence; that among the innumerable tributes to the reasonable man there might be expected at least some passing reference to a reasonable person of the opposite sex; that no such reference is found, for the simple reason that no such being is contemplated by the law; that legally at least there *is* no reasonable woman, and that therefore in this case the learned judge should have directed the jury that, while there was evidence on which they might find that the defendant had not come up to the standard required of a reasonable man, her conduct was only what was to be expected of a woman, as such.

It must be conceded at once that there is merit in this contention, however unpalatable it may at first appear. The appellant relies largely on *Baxter's Case,* 1639 (2 Bole, at p. 100), in which it was held that for the purposes of *estover* the wife of a tenant by the mesne was at law in the same position as an ox or other *cattle demenant* (to which a modern parallel may perhaps be found in the statutory regulations of many railway companies, whereby, for the purposes of freight, a typewriter is counted as a musical instrument). And it is probably no mere chance that in our legal textbooks the problems relating to married women are usually considered immediately after the pages devoted to idiots and lunatics. Indeed, there is respectable authority for saying that at Common Law this was the status of a woman. Recent legislation has whittled away a great part of this venerable conception, but so far as concerns the law of negligence, which is our present consideration, I am persuaded that it remains intact. It is no bad thing that the law of the land should here and there conform with the known facts of everyday experience. The view that there exists a class of beings, illogical, impulsive, careless, irresponsible, extravagant, prejudiced, and vain, free for the most part from those worthy and repellent excellences which distinguish the Reasonable Man, and devoted to the irrational arts of pleasure and attraction, is one which should be as welcome and as well accepted in our Courts as it is in our drawing-rooms. I find therefore that at Common Law a reasonable woman does not exist. The contention of the respondent fails and the appeal must be allowed. Costs to be costs in the action, above and below, but not costs in the case.

Bungay, L. J., and *Blow, L. J.* concurred.

THE GRAMOPHONE LIBEL CASE

CHICKEN *v.* HAM

The House of Lords today delivered judgment in the notorious Gramophone Libel Case.

The *Lord Chancellor* said: My Lords, this case may well go down to history as "The Lawyers' Dream." From first to last it has occupied the attention of the Courts for more than four years. Two juries have disagreed about it and one was imprisoned; there have been two trials of the action in the King's Bench and two appeals to the Court of Appeal, while for the past fourteen days it has monopolized the attention of your lordships' House. Twenty-five King's Counsel have been from time to time concerned in the case, each of them accompanied by a member of the Junior Bar, which juniors have received by custom a remuneration equal to two-thirds of their leaders' fees. These fees have with few exceptions been a thousand guineas marked on each brief, plus a daily payment by way of stimulus of one hundred guineas or more; and there are present at the moment no fewer than eight learned counsel who will receive between them a sum of about six hundred and fifty pounds for sitting quietly in their places today and listening as attentively as they are able to your lordships' learned judgments. These judgments are five in number, and each of these, therefore, lasting an hour or less, will cost somebody about one hundred and fifty pounds, a figure for which it is possible to engage the most expensive variety artist for a week.

It is not therefore astonishing that the costs of this case are estimated already at a figure between two and three hundred thousand pounds. But it would be very wrong to suppose that this sum has not been expended for the benefit of the community. The point which your lordships are required to decide has never been decided before, and, if your lordships are able to decide it now, it need never be decided again, nor can it be decided otherwise. It is never likely to arise again, but that is another matter. Your lordships' House is almost the only authority in this mortal world whose word on any subject is the last word forever. Your pronouncements have the unalterable force of a law of nature; and if we are able by taking pains to add a single grain of certitude to the shifting sands of human affairs, is there anyone who is prepared pedantically to count the cost? "It is something," as Lord Mildew said in *Rex* v. *Badger* "to dot an 'i' in perpetuity."

This is an appeal by one Ham against a decision of the Court of Appeal sitting *in ludo,* reversing a judgment by the Divisional Court (Adder, J., and Mudd, J.), reversing a decision by Judge Brewer in the Shepherd's Bush County Court. The facts are these. The man Ham made a gramophone record, which consisted of a number of uncomplimentary statements, composed and uttered by himself, concerning the private life and personal appearance of Mr. Ebenezer Chicken, the head and father of the well-known multiple stores. This record he sent as a Christmas present to Mr. Chicken, who, at a gathering of his friends and relations, put the record on his own gramophone, when there issued from the instrument, to the astonishment, horror, and satisfaction of the company, a series of defamatory and abusive expressions directed unmistakably against the head of the household. Mr. Chicken, therefore, brought a suit for defamation against Mr. Ham. Now, my lords, you are aware that by the mysterious provisions of the English law a defamatory statement may be either a slander or a libel, a slander being, shortly, a defamation by word of mouth, and a libel by the written or printed word; and the legal consequences are in the two cases very different. A layman, with the narrow outlook of a layman on these affairs, might rashly suppose that it is equally injurious to say at a public meeting, "Mr. Chicken is a toad," and to write upon a post card, "Mr. Chicken is a toad." But the unselfish labors of generations of British jurists have discovered between the two some profound and curious distinctions; for example, in order to succeed in an action for slander the injured party must prove that he has suffered some actual and special damage, whereas the victim of a written defamation need not; so that we have this curious result, that in practice it is safer to insult a man at a public meeting than to insult him on a post card, and that which is written in the corner of a letter is in law more deadly than that which is shouted from the house-tops. My lords, it is not for us to boggle at the wisdom of our ancestors, and this is only one of a great body of juridical refinements handed down to us by them, without which few of our profession would be able to keep body and soul together. *Jus varium, judix opulentus.*

Now in this case it was held by the County Court judge that Mr. Ham's utterance through the gramophone was a verbal slander, and that therefore the plaintiff must prove that he has suffered some special and material damage. This he was unable to do, for, on the contrary, his friends have visited him with even greater persistency, and as a result of the publicity which the case received the business of Chicken's stores was actually augmented. Mr. Chicken, therefore, appealed to the Divisional Court, which held that the utterance complained of was libel and not slander; but the Court of Appeal by a majority reversed this decision and held that it was slander and not libel; but, for reasons which I am wholly unable to follow, a new trial was ordered; and Mr. Chicken added a new wing to his stores.

With the proceedings of the next few years we need not concern ourselves in detail; they culminated in a second hearing by the Court of Appeal, which held on this occasion that Mr. Ham's action was libel and not slander. Mr. Ham appealed. Mr. Chicken added another wing to his stores, and a large new issue of capital was made.

Now, my lords, we are called upon to decide whether the words complained of, which are without doubt defamatory, and have so been found, are in the nature of a libel or a slander. I have myself no doubt as to the answer. The law is that the spoken word, if defamatory, is a slander, and I do not follow the Master of the Rolls when he says that by "spoken" we are to understand "spoken" in the sense in which the word was understood at the date when "spoken" became the essential element in the definition of slander, that is, spoken by the vocal organs of the human frame without the intervention or assistance of a machine. It is clear that these words were spoken by Mr. Ham through this instrument, and the absurdity of any suggestion that they were not is apparent if we accept the only other alternative and say they were *written* through the gramophone. The law is clear. The appeal must be allowed.

Lord Lick said: I do not agree. This is a libel and not a slander. The law is clear. *Potts* v. *The Metropolitan Water Board* shows that the distinction in law is not between the spoken and the written insult, but between that which is uttered once, and once only, and that which is uttered in such a form that it is capable of indefinite repetition or publication at the will of others than the original utterer. A statute is not a slander, neither is it written (*Fish* v. *Mulligan*). There is nothing absurd in speaking of writing on a gramophone. Indeed, the first half of the word is derived from a Greek word meaning "I write." In *Silvertop* v. *The Stepney Guardians* a man trained a parrot to say three times after meals, "Councillor Ward has not washed today." It was held that this was libel. The appeal must be dismissed.

Lord Arrowroot said: I do not agree. The law is clear. The appeal must be allowed.

Lord Sheep said: I do not agree. In my judgment this case has been from the first a brilliant and elaborate advertising maneuver for the advancement of Mr. Chicken's stores, which this year, I notice, declared a dividend of fifty-six per cent. It is clear to me that the man Ham is in this case the tool and servant of the man Chicken; that the defamatory utterances of Ham were made at Chicken's own instigation and in a manner ingeniously calculated to provoke prolonged discussion and disagreement among His Majesty's judges; that this object having been attained, to the great notoriety and advantage of Mr. Chicken's business, Mr. Chicken in any event will cheerfully pay the costs of the entire proceedings; and that your lordships' House has for the first time been employed as an advertising agent for a multiple store. But as to the point ostensibly at issue, I concur with my learned brother Lord Lick. The law is clear. This is a libel and the appeal must be dismissed.

Lord Goat said: The law is clear——(At this point, however, his lordship suffered a heart attack, and succumbed.)

The *Lord Chancellor* said: Our learned brother's unexpected demise is particularly unfortunate at the present time, two of your lordships having held for the appellant and two for the respondent. Opinion therefore is equally divided, and this House is unable to say whether the words complained of are a libel or a slander, and the judgment of the Court of Appeal must stand.

The House then adjourned.

[NOTE.—But *quaere*—in view of the fact that the two decisions of the Court of Appeal are contradictory it is doubtful whether it can be taken that the point is definitely settled.]

[EDITOR'S NOTE: In HARTMANN v. WINCHELL, 296 N.Y. 276, the New York Court of Appeals ruled that a defamation broadcast over the radio was libel not slander, because the defamatory remarks were read from a script; and in OSTROWE v. LEE, 256 N.Y. 36, Judge CARDOZO held that the dictating of a defamatory letter to a stenographer was a libel not a slander, because "a stenographer does not grasp the meaning of dictated words till the dictation is over and the symbols have been read."]

Francis Bacon

:

OF JUDICATURE

Judges ought to remember that their office is *jus dicere,* and not *jus dare;* to interpret law, and not to make law, or give law. Else will it be like the authority claimed by the church of Rome, which under pretext of exposition of Scripture doth not stick to add and alter; and to pronounce that which they do not find; and by shew of antiquity to introduce novelty. Judges ought to be more learned than witty, more reverend than plausible, and more advised than confident. Above all things, integrity is their portion and proper virtue. *Cursed* (saith the law) *is he that removeth the landmark.* The mislayer of a mere-stone is to blame. But it is the unjust judge that is the capital remover of landmarks, when he defineth amiss of lands and property. One foul sentence doth more hurt than many foul examples. For these do but corrupt the stream, the other corrupteth the fountain. So saith Solomon, *Fons turbatus, et vena corrupta, est justus cadens in causâ suâ coram adversario:* [A righteous man falling down before the wicked is as a troubled fountain or a corrupt spring.] The office of judges may have reference unto the parties that sue, unto the advocates that plead, unto the clerks and ministers of justice underneath them, and to the sovereign or state above them.

First, for the causes or parties that sue. *There be* (saith the Scripture) *that turn judgment into wormwood;* and surely there be also that turn it into vinegar; for injustice maketh it bitter, and delays make it sour. The principal duty of a judge is to suppress force and fraud;

whereof force is the more pernicious when it is open, and fraud when it is close and disguised. Add thereto contentious suits, which ought to be spewed out, as the surfeit of courts. A judge ought to prepare his way to a just sentence, as God useth to prepare his way, by raising valleys and taking down hills: so when there appeareth on either side an high hand, violent prosecution, cunning advantages taken, combination, power, great counsel, then is the virtue of a judge seen, to make inequality equal; that he may plant his judgment as upon an even ground. *Qui fortiter emungit, elicit sanguinem;* [Violent blowing makes the nose bleed;] and where the wine-press is hard wrought, it yields a harsh wine, that tastes of the grape-stone. Judges must beware of hard constructions and strained inferences; for there is no worse torture than the torture of laws. Specially in case of laws penal, they ought to have care that that which was meant for terror be not turned into rigour; and that they bring not upon the people that shower whereof the Scripture speaketh, *Pluet super eos laqueos* [He shall rain snares upon them]; for penal laws pressed are a *shower of snares* upon the people. Therefore let penal laws, if they have been sleepers of long, or if they be grown unfit for the present time, be by wise judges confined in the execution: *Judicis officium est, ut res, ita tempora rerum, &c.* [A judge must have regard to the time as well as to the matter.] In causes of life and death, judges ought (as far as the law permitteth) in justice to remember mercy; and to cast a severe eye upon the example, but a merciful eye upon the person.

Secondly, for the advocates and counsel that plead. Patience and gravity of hearing is an essential part of justice; and an overspeaking judge is no well-tuned cymbal. It is no grace to a judge first to find that which he might have heard in due time from the bar; or to show quickness of conceit in cutting off evidence or counsel too short; or to prevent information by questions, though pertinent. The parts of a judge in hearing are four: to direct the evidence; to moderate length, repetition, or impertinency of speech; to recapitulate, select, and collate the material points of that which hath been said; and to give the rule or sentence. Whatsoever is above these is too much; and proceedeth either of glory and willingness to speak, or of impatience to hear, or of shortness of memory, or of want of a staid and equal attention. It is a strange thing to see that the boldness of advocates should prevail with judges; whereas they should imitate God, in whose seat they sit; who *represseth the presumptuous, and giveth grace to the modest.* But it is more strange, that judges should have noted favorites; which cannot but cause multiplication of fees, and suspicion of bye-ways. There is due from the judge to the advocate some commendation and gracing, where causes are well handled and fair pleaded; especially towards the side which obtaineth not; for that upholds in the client the reputation of his counsel, and beats down in him the conceit of his cause. There is likewise due to the public a civil reprehension of advocates, where there appeareth cunning counsel, gross neglect, slight information, indiscreet pressing, or an over-bold defense. And let not the counsel at the bar chop with the judge, nor wind himself into the handling of the cause anew after the judge hath declared his sentence; but on the other side, let not the judge meet the cause half way, nor give occasion for the party to say his counsel or proofs were not heard.

Thirdly, for that that concerns clerks and ministers. The place of justice is an hallowed place; and therefore not only the bench, but the foot-pace and precincts and purprise thereof, ought to be preserved without scandal and corruption. For certainly *Grapes* (as the Scripture saith) *will not be gathered of thorns or thistles;* neither can justice yield her fruit with sweetness amongst the briars and brambles of catching and polling clerks and ministers. The attendance of courts is subject to four bad instruments. First, certain persons that are sowers of suits; which make the court swell, and the country pine. The second sort is of those that engage courts in quarrels of jurisdiction, and are not truly *amici curiae,* [friends of the court] but *parasiti curiae* [parasites of the court] in putting a court up beyond her bounds, for their own scraps and advantage. The third sort is of those that may be accounted the left hands of courts; persons that are full of nimble and sinister tricks and shifts, whereby they pervert the plain and direct course of courts, and bring justice into oblique lines and labyrinths. And the fourth is the poller and exacter of fees; which justifies the common resemblance of the courts of justice to the bush whereunto while the sheep flies for defence in weather, he is sure to lose part of his fleece. On the other side, an ancient clerk, skilful in precedents, wary in proceeding, and understanding in the business of the court, is an excellent finger of a court; and doth many times point the way to the judge himself.

Fourthly, for that which may concern the sovereign and estate. Judges ought above all to remember the conclusion of the Roman Twelve Tables; *Salus populi suprema lex;* [The supreme law of all is the weal of the people;] and to know that laws, except they be in order to that end, are but things captious, and oracles not well inspired. Therefore it is an happy thing in a state when kings and states do often consult with judges; and again when judges do often consult with the king and state: the one, when there is matter of law intervenient in business of state; the other, when there is some consideration of state intervenient in matter of law. For many times the things deduced to judgment may be *meum* and *tuum,* when the reason and consequence thereof may trench to point of estate: I call matter of estate, not only the parts of sovereignty, but whatsoever introduceth any great alteration or dangerous precedent; or concerneth manifestly any great portion of people. And let no man weakly conceive that just laws and true policy have any antipathy; for they are like the spirits and sinews, that one moves with the other. Let judges also remember, that Solomon's throne was supported by lions on both sides: let them be lions, but yet lions under the throne; being circumspect that they do not check or oppose any points of sovereignty. Let not judges also be so ignorant of their own right, as to think there is not left to them, as a principal part of their office, a wise use and application of laws. For they may remember what the apostle saith of a greater law than theirs; *Nos scimus quia lex bona est, modo quis eâ utatur legitime.* [We know that the law is good, if a man use it lawfully.]

Francis Bacon

:

I hold every man a debtor to his profession; from the which, as men of course do seek to receive countenance and profit, so ought they of duty to endeavour themselves, by way of amends, to be a help and ornament thereunto. This is performed in some degree by the honest and liberal practice of a profession, when men shall carry a respect not to descend into any course that is corrupt and unworthy thereof, and preserve themselves free from the abuses wherewith the same profession is noted to be infected; but much more is this performed if a man be able to visit and strengthen the roots and foundation of the science itself; thereby not only gracing it in reputation and dignity, but also amplifying it in perfection and substance. Having, therefore, from the beginning, come to the study of the laws of this realm, with a desire no less, if I could attain unto it, that the same laws should be the better for my industry, than that myself should be the better for the knowledge of them; I do not find that, by mine own travel, without the help of authority, I can in any kind confer so profitable an addition unto that science, as by collecting the rules and grounds dispersed throughout the body of the same laws; for hereby no small light will be given in new cases, wherein the authorities do square and vary, to confirm the law, and to make it received one way; and in cases wherein the law is cleared by authority, yet, nevertheless, to see more profoundly into the reason of such judgments and ruled cases, and thereby to make more use of them for the decision of other cases more doubtful; so that the uncertainty of law, which is the principal and most just challenge that is made to the laws of our nation at this time, will, by this new strength laid to the foundation, be somewhat the more settled and corrected. Neither will the use hereof be only in deciding of doubts, and helping soundness of judgment, but further in gracing of argument, in correcting unprofitable subtlety, and reducing the same to a more sound and substantial sense of law; in reclaiming vulgar errors, and generally the amendment in some measure of the very nature and complexion of the whole law: and, therefore, the conclusions of reason of this kind are worthily and aptly called by a great civilian *legum leges,* laws of laws, for that many *placita legum,* that is, particular and positive learnings of laws, do easily decline from a good temper of justice, if they be not rectified and governed by such rules.

Now for the manner of setting down of them, I have in all points, to the best of my understanding and foresight, applied myself not to that which might seem most for the ostentation of mine own wit or knowledge, but to that which may yield most use and profit to the students and professors of our laws.

And, therefore, whereas these rules are some of them ordinary and vulgar, that now serve but for grounds and plain songs to the more shallow and impertinent sort of arguments; other of them are gathered and extracted out of the harmony and congruity of cases, and are such as the wisest and deepest sort of lawyers have in judgment and use, though they be not able many times to express and set them down.

For the former sort, which a man that should rather write to raise a high opinion of himself, than to instruct others, would have omitted, as trite and within every man's compass; yet, nevertheless, I have not affected to neglect them, but have chosen out of them such as I thought good: I have reduced them to a true application, limiting and defining their bounds, that they may not be read upon at large, but restrained to point of difference; for as, both in the law and other sciences, the handling of questions by commonplace, without aim or application, is the weakest; so yet, nevertheless, many common principles and generalities are not to be contemned, if they be well derived and reduced into particulars, and their limits and exclusions duly assigned; for there be two contrary faults and extremities in the debating and sifting out of the law, which may be best noted in two several manner of arguments. Some argue upon general grounds, and come not near the point in question: others, without laying any foundation of a ground or difference, do loosely put cases, which, though they go near the point, yet, being put so scattered, prove not, but rather serve to make the law appear more doubtful than to make it more plain.

Secondly, Whereas some of these rules have a concurrence with the civil Roman law, and some others a diversity, and many times an opposition, such grounds which are common to our law and theirs, I have not affected to disguise into other words than the civilians use, to the end they might seem invented by me, and not borrowed or translated from them: no, but I took hold of it as a matter of great authority and majesty, to see and consider the concordance between the laws penned, and as it were dictated *verbatim,* by the same reason. On the other side, the diversities between the civil Roman rules of law and ours, happening either when there is such an indifferency of reason so equally balanced, as the one law embraceth one course, and the other the contrary, and both just, after either is once positive and certain, or where the laws vary in regard of accommodating the law to the different considerations of estate, I have not omitted to set down.

Thirdly, Whereas I could have digested these rules into a certain method or order, which, I know, would have been more admired, as that which would have made every particular rule, through coherence and relation unto other rules, seem more cunning and deep; yet I have avoided so to do, because this delivering of knowledge in distinct and disjoined aphorisms doth leave the wit of man more free to turn and toss, and to make use of that which is so delivered to more several purposes and applications; for we see that all the ancient wisdom and science was wont to be delivered in that form, as may be seen by the parables of Solomon, and by the aphorisms of Hippocrates, and the moral verses of Theognes and Phocylides; but chiefly the precedent of the civil law, which hath taken the same course with their rules, did confirm me in my opinion.

Fourthly, Whereas I know very well it would have been more plausible and more current, if the rules, with the expositions of them, had been set down either in Latin or in English; that the harshness of the language might not have disgraced the matter; and that civilians, statesmen, scholars, and other sensible men might not have been barred from them; yet I have forsaken that grace and ornament of them, and only taken this course: the rules themselves I have put in Latin, not purified further than the property of the terms of the law would permit; but Latin, which language I chose, as the briefest to contrive the rules compendiously, the aptest for memory, and of the greatest authority and majesty to be avouched and alleged in argument: and for the expositions and distinctions, I have retained the peculiar language of our law, because it should not be singular among the books of the same science, and because it is most familiar to the students and professors thereof, and because that it is most significant to express conceits of law; and to conclude, it is a language wherein a man shall not be enticed to hunt after words but matter; and for the excluding of any other than professed lawyers, it was better manners to exclude them by the strangeness of the language, than by the obscurity of the conceit; which is as though it had been written in no private and retired language, yet by those that are not lawyers would for the most part not have been understood, or, which is worse, mistaken.

Fifthly, Whereas I might have made more flourish and ostentation of reading, to have vouched the authorities, and sometimes to have enforced or noted upon them, yet I have abstained from that also; and the reason is, because I judged it a matter undue and preposterous to prove rules and maxims; wherein I had the example of Mr. Littleton and Mr. Fitzherbert, whose writings are the institutions of the laws of England; whereof the one forbeareth to vouch any authority altogether; the other never reciteth a book, but when he thinketh the case so weak of credit in itself as it needs a surety; and these two I did far more esteem than Mr. Perkins or Mr. Standford, that have done the contrary. Well will it appear to those that are learned in the laws, that many of the cases are judged cases, either within the books or of fresh report, and most of them fortified by judged cases and similitude of reason; though, in some few cases, I did intend expressly to weigh down the authority by evidence of reason, and therein rather to correct the law, than either to soothe a received error, or by unprofitable subtlety, which corrupteth the sense of law, to reconcile contrarieties. For these reasons I resolved not to derogate from the authority of the rules, by vouching of any of the authority of the cases, though in mine own copy I had them quoted: for, although the meanness of mine own person may now at first extenuate the authority of this collection, and that every man is adventurous to control; yet, surely, according to Gamaliel's reason, if it be of weight, time will settle and authorize it; if it be light and weak, time will reprove it. So that, to conclude, you have here a work without any glory of affected novelty, or of method, or of language, or of quotations and authorities, dedicated only to use, and submitted only to the censure of the learned, and chiefly of time.

Lastly, there is one point above all the rest I account the most material for making these reasons indeed profitable and instructing; which is, that they be not set down alone, like short, dark oracles, which every man will be content still to allow to be true, but in the mean time they give little light or direction; but I have attended them, a matter not practised, no, not in the civil law, to any purpose, and for want whereof, indeed, the rules are but as proverbs, and many times plain fallacies, with a clear and perspicuous exposition, breaking them into cases, and opening them with distinctions, and sometimes shewing the reasons above, whereupon they depend, and the affinity they have with other rules. And though I have thus, with as good discretion and foresight as I could, ordered this work, and, as I might say, without all colours or shews, husbanded it best to profit; yet, nevertheless, not wholly trusting to mine own judgment; having collected three hundred of them, I thought good, before I brought them all into form, to publish some few, that, by the taste of other men's opinions in this first, I might receive either approbation in mine own course, or better advice for the altering of the other which remain; for it is a great reason that that which is intended to the profit of others should be guided by the conceits of others.

Edmond Cahn

:

THE CONSUMERS OF INJUSTICE

There was an incident in 1781 that symbolized the beginning of a new age for government and law. The Revolutionary War had been going on since 1775, and the final battle was fought at Yorktown on the coast of Virginia during the month of October 1781. The British army, sent to subdue the colonists, found itself hopelessly wedged between a formidable French fleet on one side and the American forces under General Washington on the other. The British commander decided that capitulation was inevitable, and General Washington granted him generous and honorable terms. The last great body of imperial troops paraded on the Yorktown plain in surrender to a threadbare and despised collection of amateur soldiers, who had resolved to pursue their national destiny under a free, republican government. As the brilliant ranks of redcoated soldiers filed across the plateau, the British bandmaster signaled to his band and they began playing a popular English tune of the time. It was to this tune that the defeated army marched stiffly away from the scene of battle. Though no one knows even now whether the bandmaster selected the tune purposely or by chance, the name of the tune furnished an inspired commentary. It was "The World Turned Upside Down."

I

The Consumer Perspective

Ever since that time philosophers have been attempting either to ignore or to build upon the historic fact which the British band acknowl-

574

edged so candidly. Some have perceived quite clearly, others have refused to perceive, that the world of political and legal relations had been turned upside down and the old systems and perspectives would never be adequate again. Henceforth, though a philosopher looking at the legal world would see all the established and familiar elements which his predecessors had been describing since ancient times, everything could look different to him, for he could see all the concepts and phenomena of the institution in a radically new perspective. Everything had turned 180 degrees. What had once looked trivial now became important, and what had previously dominated the stage shifted now to the deep background.

The new factor is the power and the responsibility of the citizen entitled to a free vote in a representative democracy. As the right to vote has expanded, group by group and class by class, it has revolutionized the functions of law in the democratic countries. In one form or another the scene at Yorktown has been re-enacted again and again in other lands and on other shores all over the world, and we may safely predict there will be other Yorktown surrenders until there is no further occasion for them. In the emancipated countries (including, of course, Britain itself, which was emancipated by Yorktown only slightly less than America), the right to vote spread slowly and tediously as parliaments gradually eroded the old barriers of religion, property, race, and sex. Though the process is incomplete, we know that every impulse and current in human affairs operates to favor it. More and more, men realize that there is no hope of genuine enfranchisement unless they have the franchise.

What then is this new perspective that is based on the vantage-point of the voting citizen, and how does it differ from the old, pre-democratic perspective? The new perspective is the perspective of the democratic citizen in the role of consumer of the law. The old perspective, developed while observing an empire, a kingdom, a landed aristocracy, or an oligarchy, was essentially a ruler's or at best an official's perspective; what democratic legal theory has been trying to attain since 1781 is a consumer's perspective.

How does a person become a consumer of the law? The most obvious way consists in being safeguarded and regulated from day to day by official rules or becoming involved directly with the legal mechanism—for example, being charged with a crime or engaging in a law suit. A second way, which representative government makes available to its citizens, is to influence the shape and form of law, as by voting, by advocating reforms, by asserting group interests. Then there is the third way, which is perhaps the most characteristically democratic. It is the way of assuming and shouldering responsibility for those acts that our representatives do in our name and by force of our authority, the evil acts as well as the good, the oppressive and unjust and the foolish, too.

This is the way that is new. The philosophy that does not reckon with it is talking a pre-democratic language and addressing us in terms that are fit for powdered wigs and knee breeches. To cope with the problem of our democratic era we need to reassess all the familiar, accepted doctrines. We need to ascertain how suitable they are for the specific, homely experiences of individual human beings. This alone is the genuinely democratic perspective. And when we do adopt it and do concern ourselves with the individual human being as consumer of the law, what will we think about the traditional notions of law and justice? How adequate are they for the new age of representative government?

Let me put a concrete instance. Not long ago a couple of masked bandits entered a store in one of our largest cities, pointed their guns at the woman who owned the store, and demanded the contents of the cash register. It happened that a policeman was visiting her at the time. When the bandits saw the policeman, they shot and killed him, took the money and disappeared. Incensed by the murder of one of their comrades, the police rounded up a number of unemployed young men of the neighborhood. The woman identified two of them as the burglars. Although they protested their innocence and offered credible evidence that they were elsewhere at the time of the crime, the district attorney prosecuted them zealously, the jury believed the woman's testimony, and on their conviction for the robbery and killing, the judge sentenced them to ninety-nine years in the penitentiary.

One of the young men, whom I shall call only by his first name, Joe, had come from Poland to America as a baby in the arms of his mother, Tillie. After Joe's conviction was affirmed on appeal and all hope of legal redress had been abandoned, it was Tillie, a simple scrubwoman, who caused the truth to come to light. She posted a newspaper advertisement offering a reward of 5,000 dollars which represented eleven years of savings from scrubbing floors. The advertisement intrigued newspaper reporters, who began investigating and soon discovered that the entire prosecution had been baseless.

The prosecution's key witness, the woman who owned the store, had originally refused to identify the two defendants. She had changed her testimony and identified them only because the police, knowing that she had been selling liquor illegally, had threatened to send her to jail if she did not lie as they demanded. But the conspiracy was not confined to the police; at its apex stood the district attorney. Why had he been so eager for a conviction and so ruthless in securing one? Because, at the time of the crime, a great international exposition was about to open in the city and visitors and customers had to be reassured that the prosecutor and police were efficient and that the streets of the city were entirely safe.

After these facts were disclosed in the newspaper, public clamor brought it about that the two young men were pardoned and released. By then, of course, the exposition was long since over, and the district attorney had been honored at many community meetings and lawyers' banquets, had received the usual certificates, tributes, resolutions, and diplomas, had eaten and digested his meals, smoked and enjoyed his cigars, and delivered various solemn speeches at his church.

II

The New Democratic Involvement

What shall we say is new about this case in terms of the theory of justice? Surely men have been imprisoned, tortured, and executed for crimes they did not commit as far back as we can trace the history of law to the very dawn of politically organized society. In innumerable instances where a crime was actually committed, the wrong person has been punished; in innumerable other instances, a person has been punished though no crime at all was committed and the judicial authorities were either deceived or chose to be deceived in upholding a baseless accusation. Here is the testimony of Michel de Montaigne, who was an experienced lawyer and magistrate as well as a very great essayist:

How many innocent people we have known to be punished, I mean without the fault of the judges; and how many are there that we have not known of! This happened in my time: Certain men are condemned to death for murder; the sentence, if not pronounced, is at least decided and fixed. At that point the judges are informed, by the officers of an inferior court near by, that they hold several men in custody who openly confess to that murder, and are able to throw a light on the whole business that admits of no doubt. And yet they deliberate whether they shall interrupt and defer the execution of the sentence passed upon the first accused. They consider the novelty of the case, and its consequence for suspending judgements; that the sentence is juridically passed, and the judges have no reason to repent of it. To sum up, those poor devils are sacrificed to the forms of justice. . . . How many condemnations I have witnessed more criminal than the crime!

The disaster befell Joe and his mother Tillie because it was convenient for the city and its merchants that someone, almost anyone, be found, identified, and convicted. We must concede that most of the pattern is very old, older than the Bible. It is older than the death that came to Uriah the Hittite because a king desired to possess Uriah's wife, or the death that came to Naboth because another king desired to possess Naboth's vineyard, and there is no comforting reason to assert that any city or state is today immune from incidents of the kind.

Certainly, there was little novelty in Joe's position. In all probability, no one—not even the district attorney—hated Joe personally, at least at the start. True, Joe's catastrophe did have some special aspects, which he may have considered rather important. It happened that at the time when Joe was accused of the crime his wife was expecting a child, which was born during the course of the prosecution. After Joe had been convicted and the conviction affirmed by the highest court, and after a long period had passed during which he remained in the penitentiary, he and his wife had agreed that she should divorce him and marry a friend of theirs, so that the child might have a normal home and family. All this was carried out before Tillie had saved enough money to offer a reward. But though Joe may have attached special importance to the circumstances, it is improbable that they were in any sense unusual in the annals of legal systems.

Who will contend that there was anything novel about Tillie's behavior? Mothers have always defended their sons, on every continent and in every age, and if the case is exceptional at all, it must be because Joe happened to be as innocent as Tillie believed him. In all probability, all she needed was his unsupported assertion that he was innocent. She could not have been influenced by mountains of evidence to the contrary. Moreover, being completely unacquainted with the shibboleths and slogans of popular psychology, she did not even have to fear that she was yielding to an Oedipus complex.

As all the factors in Joe's or Tillie's predicament were old and familiar, so are most of the factors in our own. It has always been possible for the members of a society to project themselves imaginatively—as we do now—into the place of a victim of legal oppression and share the impact of his experience. This capacity to identify ourselves with him has great survival value for all concerned. Our personal impulse for self-preservation becomes active the moment we realize that what happened to him might readily happen to us if we were caught in the toils of a similar mischance.

In some instances there is also a higher, more unselfish level that our identification may reach. On this level we become eager to save Joe not because of any collateral or contingent threat to our own safety but because any harm to Joe, as a specimen of the *genus homo* inflicts immediate harm on all mankind, and as our larger self encompasses Joe, his injury automatically becomes ours. On this level we are not so much preoccupied with the possibility that we may some day stand in the prisoner's dock. We are more preoccupied with the fact that we already stand there—in Joe's person.

Yet, all these things were true before 1781, and were known to the wise men of ancient times. The new factor is quite different. It is not that we find ourselves identified with either Joe or Tillie. It is that, progressively since the beginning of the modern period, we citizens find ourselves identified with the *district attorney*. This is the new factor. Representative government has implicated us. We are participants—accomplices, if you will—in the deeds that are done in our name and by our authority. We are the principals whom the district attorney represents as agent, and though no one contends that we are accountable as moral sureties for anything and everything he may do, we feel somehow and to some degree linked and tied to the consequences of his behavior. Without intending anything of the sort, we have wandered into the circle of responsibility. As human beings, it has always been possible to connect ourselves with the victim of wrong; as citizens, the new, democratic experience is that we find ourselves unexpectedly connected with the inflicter of wrong. What can this experience do but tighten and intensify our involvement in Joe's mistreatment at the hands of the law?

Though this new burden has become a feature of our citizenship, there is sadly little in the traditional theories of justice to assist in coping with it. The reason is all too evident. Like general philosophy, the philosophy of law had brilliant beginnings in ancient Greece. Aristotle clearly intimated that he sensed some of the significance of cases like

Joe's. Even he did not go beyond the threshold of the problem, perhaps because he was primarily concerned with a pattern of distributive, hence political justice, perhaps because the ancients were unacquainted with our notions of representative government, or perhaps because he could not quite throw off the dream of an all-wise, benevolent despot. Be that as it may, the curtain of history fell immediately on the Athenian democratic experiment, and when in the course of time it rose again, the new scene would be composed in the Latin language and would be played in the vicinity of the Roman forum. And while general philosophy may have remained more or less true to its Hellenic sources, the philosophy of government and law has for two thousand years carried the marks and reflected the values of the Roman empire. It has remained a view of law from the perspective of the emperor, or prince, or ruler, sometimes an ecclesiastical ruler but a ruler nonetheless. This is the perspective that has continued to dominate the philosophy of law even in modern England and America, though Jeremy Bentham, John Stuart Mill, Louis D. Brandeis, Benjamin N. Cardozo, and Jerome Frank attempted in diverse ways to revise and democratize it.

What support or understanding can the traditions of legal philosophy offer to either Joe or Tillie, or for that matter to us in our modern democratic predicament? If we consult the principal currents of natural-law theory, whether derived from Thomas Aquinas on the one hand or John Locke on the other, we find no more than the political systems of their times would have led us to expect; that is, they assume that their utmost task is to declare, on some ground or other, at what final point and in what extreme circumstances the people of a country may be justified in disregarding a royal statute or in opposing and dethroning their prince. In the various traditions there are philosophic formulas for decapitating a statute, and other philosophic formulas for decapitating a monarch, but there are no formulas to meet the needs of Joe's case, where no one questioned the propriety or justness of the criminal statute. Joe would not think of overthrowing the government; for that matter, he would not even attempt to nullify the laws against holdups and murders. Approving completely of these laws, he desired only to be acquitted of violating them.

What John Locke said in the seventeenth century about the inalienable rights of the citizenry makes good doctrine for revolutionary purposes, and it may be needed on future occasions in one country or another. The difficulty is not its falseness but its inadequacy. It is something like the constitution of the Russian empire under the Romanovs, which was defined as consisting of "despotism tempered by assassination." In an ongoing democracy, solutions are not so simple, and the central problems of justice cannot be removed by assassinating or overthrowing the sovereign. There are times when they can be solved by assassinating or repealing a particular statute, such as one providing for racial segregation. Nevertheless, in the overwhelming majority of cases everything of human import depends on how the general, abstract rules are adapted and applied to the circumstances of the specific transaction. This is philosophy's greatest challenge in a modern democratic society.

Yet we live still under the shadow of imperial Rome, and some of our ablest jurists continue to employ the pre-democratic perspective. In the twentieth century we find Professor Hans Kelsen saying:

> If, according to a legal norm, a sanction has to be executed against a murderer, this does not mean that the fact of murder is "in itself" the condition of the sanction. There is no fact "in itself" that A has killed B, there is only my or somebody else's belief or knowledge that A has killed B. A himself may either acquiesce or deny. From the point of view of law, however, all these are no more than private opinions without relevance.

What Kelsen says is quite adequate if one looks at law only from the perspective of the ruler, legislator, or executive. It is in the consumer's perspective that it becomes radically inadequate. Fancy trying to convince Joe or Tillie that the fact of Joe's innocence was "no more than a private opinion without relevance"!

The old perspectives and traditions are tenacious, and I suppose that none of us has thrown them off entirely. Perhaps there are some who fear to turn the juristic world upside down and adopt the new democratic perspective because they confuse the consumer's point of view with obsolete economic individualism. Perhaps they believe, or pretend to believe, that concern with individual human beings is some sort of casuistic cloak for a gospel of unregulated private enterprise. Of course, they are entirely mistaken. The consumer perspective—or "anthropocentric" view of law (as I have called it)—is not welded to any specific tenure system or mode of social organization. It is determined by our changing needs, claims, and aspirations as human beings and citizens living under a representative government. For us, many of the old ways of thought no longer suffice, and we insist, in Horace Kallen's words,

The ultimate consumer is the basic social reality. He is the *natural* terminus of any chain of change in human life. He is the end for whose sake things are not merely used but used up. He is the topmost turn of any economy, the seat of value, the individual in whom the processes of life, whatever their course, begin and end and find their meaning.

III

Trusting the Averages

The ugliest sign of our thralldom to the old outlook is that it tends to desensitize men of fine intellect and good will. Somehow they learn not to notice what happens to people like Joe, and even to suppress, though they cannot entirely forget, their own inevitable involvement. As it was customary for an emperor, king, or despot to think of the people in large quantitative terms, as raw material for programs or convenient fodder for cannon, a view of law conceived in the old imperial perspective will almost inevitably adopt the same wholesale approach. Fancying himself a ruler of the destinies of men, or perhaps a species of pagan god, the old-style philosopher assumed a post of lofty remoteness where he could look down on the scurryings of the populace as one might watch a swarm of interesting but not very important insects. If curiosity happened to draw him closer to the scene, they might appear somewhat larger to his eye and then, instead of assimilating them to a beehive or an anthill, he might call them "the herd."

This is what mere quantity or numerical mass or preoccupation with arithmetic can do to blunt the moral sensibilities of intelligent men. Perplexed by the marvelous variety of human personalities and transactions, the modern professional theorist gropes for some reassuring formula or other, consisting if possible of arithmetical measurements and statistics. The rage to quantify that we witness today goes back to ancient times, as we know from the example of King Solomon, who smugly recorded that he possessed a total of 700 wives and 300 concubines. Solomon's maxim of procedure is extremely popular today in sociology, opinion research, and communication theory. It is "If you cannot understand them, you can at least contrive to count them."

If they are properly organized and interpreted, statistical studies have genuine utility, and modern society cannot operate without them. For one thing, they may serve to condense and recapitulate the experience of the past, which they preserve for the benefit of the present and future, and thus they may constitute a major factor in the transmission of a cultural heritage. How, indeed, could anyone learn to exercise the faculty of judgment unless he could take into account the averages established by previous social experience and use them to build his expectations of his neighbors' behavior?

Yet how far can we trust a mere average? To a reflective observer, an average may indicate much or nothing. Standing by itself, it does not reveal any sufficient reason for our approving or disapproving. The "average man" who emerges from scientific statistical studies should not be confused with the "reasonable man" whom the law uses as a conceptual model of behavior that it will approve or disapprove. Neither of them is a very attractive fellow. The "reasonable man" concocted by legal theory never violates the law or gets into trouble with government officials. How can he? He is too careful, too prompt, too foresighted, too prudent, too obedient—in point of fact, just too dull. I have never met a completely "reasonable man," and I doubt that one exists. Nor have I ever met the "average man" of scientific statistics: that quaint person who owns 2.6 suits of clothes, marries 1.2 times, and is blessed with 2.8 children. The world either does not know or does not heed what the lawyers and statisticians have prescribed for it, and continues to behave in ways that startle and shock them.

Consequently, averages can furnish only the beginning of understanding. The register and range of the items, their scope and peculiarities of distribution—these speak much more revealingly to a sensitive mind, which never allows collectives or averages to dull its interest in concrete particulars. The man who stops at averages and feels no concern with particulars is rather like one who refuses to read novels, short stories, poems, essays, dramas, and epics, yet keeps demanding "literature."

Once we examine law and government from the consumer perspective, we are less likely to be beguiled by averages. If one-half of the statutes passed at a legislative session are too lavish and extravagant with the people's money, and the other half too scant and niggardly, it is not probable that an intelligent electorate will be satisfied just because the averages come out well. If a foreign office is too aggressive and bellicose in certain affairs, can it gain public confidence by being too backward and diffident in others? And if an innocent man named Joe is wrongfully convicted of a crime, who will have the impudence to solace him by pointing out how many guilty men escape altogether from punishment? In the anthropocentric view, the quality of government and law is to be tested and approved or found wanting, case by case. While the particular case may involve a whole nation, a class or group within the nation, or a single individual, it is by what they do here—in this case—that the legislators, executives, or judges must vindicate themselves. In matters of political and administrative discretion it is reasonable to evaluate the whole record and set failures off against successes; but in a matter like Joe's, any such policy of indulgence is impossible, for there can be only one outcome—success or failure, right or wrong—in which we, the citizens, have been implicated.

Somehow the old imperial perspective still continues to sway men's thinking. Let us take an example that is directly pertinent to Joe's unjust conviction: the general problem of "police lawlessness" in the United States. Whenever popular protests are raised against police lawlessness or whenever the Supreme Court endeavors to require lawful methods of the police, some very conscientious lawyers will protest that efficiency in punishing crime is the more important consideration and that the "third degree" and like horrors are not used frequently—or, at least, are not exposed frequently. Here is a typical rationalization in a recent book: "The dangers of encouraging police lawlessness are not to be minimized; but surely there is a good deal of hyperbole, if not nonsense, in the current judicial apprehension. It leaves out of account the question of the scale of police lawlessness. The danger to civil liberties is not great so long as the misconduct of the police is no more than occasional."

I shall not tarry with this passage, the fallacies of which seem apparent as soon as one considers that the so-called "occasional" case was in fact Joe's, and may readily become one's own. Let me rather present a less obvious instance of the error, taken from the pen of no less a figure than Benjamin N. Cardozo. Justice Cardozo may rightly be regarded as a paragon of moral insight on the American bench. If, therefore, the fallacy of averaging types of judges or philosophies or litigants or their cases, one against the other, could influence a mind like Cardozo's, surely no one else has the right to feel immune from it. I believe it did infect these passages, which I quote from his most celebrated work, *The Nature of the Judicial Process:*

The eccentricities of judges balance one another. One judge looks at problems from the point of view of history, another from that of philosophy, another from that of social utility, one is a formalist, another a latitudinarian, one is timorous of change, another dissatisfied with the present; out of the attrition of diverse minds there is beaten something which has a constancy and uniformity and average value greater than its component elements. . . .

Ever in the making, as law develops through the centuries, is this new faith which silently and steadily effaces our mistakes and eccentricities. I sometimes think that we worry ourselves overmuch about the enduring consequences of our errors. They may work a little confusion for a time. In the end, they will be modified or corrected or their teachings ignored. The future takes care of such things.

Lawyers have a way of hailing these fine paragraphs and drawing comfort from the assurance that "the eccentricities . . . balance one another" and "the future takes care of such things." But if we are candid with ourselves we must recognize that the comfort is sorely insufficient. Revere Cardozo as we may, we cannot help retorting that averages in the administration of justice do not avail the person who is wronged grievously in his own, particular case. The appeal to time and patience may assist in evolving better concepts and techniques for future use of the profession, but it cannot excuse or exonerate our sending an innocent man to the penitentiary here and now. Enlightenment tomorrow or elsewhere will not serve, for his destiny rests in our hands today, and our sense of injustice (for that is what I call it) forbids us to be patient at his cost.

IV

Graded Pragmatism

Why do I propose we speak of the "sense of injustice" rather than the "sense of justice"? There are various reasons, each of them related in one way or another to our taking a consumer's or anthropocentric perspective. When we adopt this perspective we investigate the meaning of a concept by observing the occasions when it becomes relevant to the common, earthy experiences of individual human beings. When then does the concept of "justice" achieve this relevance? In the existential sense, when is a citizen in a democratic society disposed to invoke the name of justice?

I believe he invokes it when, personally or vicariously, he experiences the impact of an act of injustice. It is not his custom to meditate in his study and search for self-evident juristic propositions or tidy utopian diagrams about abstract justice. If justice were only an ideal mode or state or condition, our response as human beings would be merely contemplative, and—as we all know—contemplation bakes no loaves. But the response with which men meet a real or imagined instance of injustice is entirely different; it is alive with warmth and movement that courses through the entire human organism. How often when we are faced with a social problem and cannot determine which of many alternative solutions would be just, we find ourselves certain and unanimous that one particular solution would be utterly unjust!

If it is preferable to speak of the "sense of injustice," what shall we mean when we find occasion to use the term "justice"? We cannot be satisfied to employ it in the traditional ideal or static sense because, in that sense, justice—like goodness—is a hopelessly ambiguous concept. Since the time of Immanuel Kant philosophers have reiterated that justice is a term too ambiguous and multivalent to convey a definable meaning in human relations and social arrangements. The most they are disposed to grant is that justice may be regarded as a quality of the human will or, in other words, a type of good motive or volition.

This is indeed a sad demotion for a concept as sublime and inspiring as justice. To treat justice as a mere quality of the will and nothing more is to trivialize it and impoverish ourselves unnecessarily. In the context of our consumer's or anthropocentric view, which focuses on the "sense of injustice," the word "justice" can bear a much more estimable meaning. For us, justice will mean neither a static diagram on the one hand nor a mere quality of will on the other; it will mean the active process of remedying or preventing what would arouse the "sense of injustice." It will be taken not as a condition or a quality but as a species of human activity.

In conducting this activity or process, while there is no single, orthodox formula to prescribe for universal application, we generally obtain the worthiest results when we use the methods of pragmatism as James, Dewey, Peirce, and Kallen have outlined them. But with a certain difference or refinement, for the pragmatism that serves us best in practicing justice is a *graded* pragmatism. I call it "graded" because it classifies and grades the beliefs that we happen to possess at any given moment. It insists that our beliefs, judgments, prehensions, meanings, and warranted assertions are not created equal and cannot be rendered equal in terms of either verification or verifiability. Weak verification and weak verifiability are not equal to strong verification and strong verifiability. Therefore beliefs must be ranked and graded according to the conceived cost that may follow from proceeding to act on them. What is clearly a warranted assertion for a low price in prospective human consequences may not be warranted at all if the prospective price is raised.

A graded pragmatism is concerned with two main centers of cost: cost to the human subject of the conceived action, and cost to the human object. The subject inquires what will be the initial cost, what the prospective upkeep and maintenance that the idea offered to him may require him to assume, and his belief will be graded according to the highest cost-level he feels willing and able to maintain. For example, people may believe quite sincerely in the idea of education at one cost-level and not believe in it at another. Some may believe sincerely in secular public education, but not at the cost of sending their own children to certain public schools in New York City. Judges may believe sincerely in the idea of speedy justice at the cost-level of opening court at ten o'clock, but not at the cost-level of nine o'clock.

Then there is the factor of conceived cost to the human object of the action. Here all our experience in the law endorses the wisdom of using a graded pragmatism. If a charge against a man amounts to mere gossip or hearsay, we refuse to predicate any sort of liability on it. We do not impose liability for money damages unless our belief is based on a preponderance of credible evidence; we do not impose civil liability for the commission of fraud unless our belief is verified further and is based on clear and convincing proof; and we do not impose a prison sentence for crime unless our belief is entirely firm and is based on proof beyond a reasonable doubt. Thus by consciously and critically grading our beliefs according to their prospective costs and human concussions, we enlist the teachings of pragmatism in the service of the sense of injustice.*

* In a rather neglected passage, Kant recognized our need to grade beliefs when they lack—as almost all of them do—absolute and necessary correctness. He said:

"Once an end is accepted, the conditions of its attainment are hypothetically necessary. . . . The physician must do something for a patient in danger, but does not know the nature of his illness. He observes the symptoms, and if he can find no more likely alternative, judges it to be a case of phthisis. Now even in his own estimation his belief is contingent only; another observer might perhaps come to a sounder conclusion. Such contingent belief, which yet forms the ground for the actual employment of means to certain actions, I entitle *pragmatic belief*.

"The usual test, whether that which someone asserts is merely his persuasion— or at least his subjective conviction, that is, his firm belief—is *betting*. It often happens that someone propounds his views with such positive and uncompromising assurance that he seems to have entirely set aside all thought of possible error. A bet disconcerts him. Sometimes it turns out that he has a conviction which can be estimated at a value of one ducat, but not of ten. For he is very willing to

v

The Public Sense of Injustice

When do men experience the "sense of injustice"? Typically, when officials violate or threaten to violate their demands for equality, for recognition of desert, for respect of human dignity, for conscientious adjudication, for the confinement of government to its proper functions, and for the fulfillment of the common expectations of the society. These are the circumstances that arouse the sense of injustice and summon it into operation. For example, whenever officials misuse their power, or oppress the innocent and unoffending, they provoke our sense of injustice.

When we see or hear or read about this sort of conduct we feel that sympathetic reaction of outrage, resentment, and anger and those affections of the viscera and adrenal secretions that prepare human beings to resist attack, for our physiology has equipped us to regard an act of injustice to another as a personal aggression against ourselves. Empathy or imaginative interchange projects us into the place of the one who is wronged, not merely to pity or compassionate him but to resist and defend. The sense of injustice transmutes the wrong into an act of assault, and prepares our psychic organs for measures of self-defense.

This is the way justice can acquire a public meaning. Through mutual communication and discussion the men who live in a particular ethos may perceive the same threat and experience the same bodily reactions. The fact that they are roused individually and jointly gives us sufficient warrant to speak of "justice" without utter relativism or subjectivism or solipsism. Anyone who desires empirical proof can observe and verify

---

venture one ducat, but when it is a question of ten he becomes aware, as he had not previously been, that it may very well be that he is in error. If, in a given case, we represent ourselves as staking the happiness of our whole life, the triumphant tone of our judgment is greatly abated; we become extremely diffident, and discover for the first time that our belief does not reach so far. Thus pragmatic belief always exists in some specific degree, which, according to differences in the interests at stake, may be large or may be small."

Kant's paragraphs—from *Critique of Pure Reason*—are most perspicacious and I regret not having come upon them earlier. Nevertheless, the analogy to betting, gallant though it sounds, does not provide us with a very satisfactory tool of valuation. I prefer the analogy to cost (or appropriation), which may seem a bit prosaic but at least permits one to distinguish between initial outlay and continual maintenance when projecting the conceived consequences of a belief. In dealing with social problems the best conceptual tools are those that grip the dimension of duration.

this interchangeability for himself. It is real and demonstrable. It is also indispensable to the preservation of society. If man did not have the capacity to recognize oppression of another as a species of attack on himself, he would be unprepared—in the glandular sense—for survival as a political being. In short, the human animal as we know him is equipped and predisposed to fight injustice.

This predisposition, like other natural capacities, being designed to end in action, is finite and limited. Each of us is bound by the perspective predicament to his own brief time and narrow place, and though the sense of injustice gives him a lengthening tether to enable him to wander some distance away from self and its immediate setting, he does remain tethered. Since he lives a finite existence in a finite world, his survival does not require that the sense of injustice encompass infinitude; nor need he wait for assurance that what it admonishes him to do would be universally right and valid, for when he faces any particular crisis of his own he does not feel compelled to legislate for the universe. If we were to ask him whether the voice of his sense of injustice is right in all times and all places he would reply—quite reasonably—that the injustices he needs to subdue arise invariably in particular times and particular places. Injustice does not threaten him *semper et ubique* but here and now. He can safely assume that he will never be called to combat it in all times and all places.

Nevertheless, the tether that holds us is a rather elastic one. If the circumstances of the specific case permit us to engage in imaginative interchange, we can respond to an injustice despite great disparities of time, place, culture, law, and ethical tradition. For example, the trial and condemnation of Socrates will stir men's sense of injustice as long as they can conceive the danger of corrupt judges and mob passions.

Here, then, is the sense of injustice at work within men and the law. Is it nothing more than a reasonless compound of glandular secretions and angry emotions, a mere syndrome of outraged feelings, a "sense," as it were, that is completely without sense? Clearly not. While the sense of injustice uses empathy, projection, and emotion, it simultaneously summons perception, reasoning, intelligence, and judgment—all the capacities that make for understanding and the application of sense. In the experience of the sense of injustice, thinking and feeling suffuse each other reciprocally, reason and empathy blend together indissociably, and the rational directs the emotional while the emotional impels the rational. The combined process enables men to develop and communities to advance. Without reason the sense of injustice could not serve the purposes of social utility, which only observation, analysis, and science can discern, while without empathy it would lose its warm sensibility and cogent drive. Compounded indissolubly of both reason and impulsion, it is an active, spontaneous source of law. It makes a practical, working difference in courts, legislatures, and administrative tribunals.

In this compound the democratic citizen and the democratic state find their best, eventual hope of cohesion and survival. The public experience of the sense of injustice can work the greatest of social transformations, because it incites men to join one another and participate—first in recognizing a jeopardy, then in resisting it, and finally in exulting side by side whenever they have practiced justice successfully. All of these are public acts of solidarity, which weld a people together and fill them with a patriotism of irresistible power. There is no established interest, no sinister influence, no outworn institution or superstition that can stand against it. If, by way of metaphor, we imagine the ancient stronghold of Jericho as a citadel of injustice, then no wonder its walls collapsed—not, however, as some have thought, when the priests blew their trumpets but, as the Scripture makes clear, when the people shouted in unison with a great and mighty voice. In less dramatic circumstances the public sense of injustice is equally solidary. Though like any other human capacity it is finite and fallible, it can create its own cumulative rewards by addressing the weak, the insecure, and the deviant ones of the community with a promise of mutual support and confidence.

In public life or private, the sense of injustice offers us no categorical warranty; how amid the ways of this world should we ever come to expect one? What it does offer should supply hope and certainty enough for the responsible citizens of a free land. It promises men that, if they only will, they can close ranks in mutual defense, collaborate with their neighbors in the enterprises of justice, and from day to day become increasingly secure. It promises that persuasion and free assent can triumph over brute force and build the foundations of a happier commonwealth.

Justice Oliver Wendell Holmes, Jr.

:

DISSENTING OPINION IN
UNITED STATES v. SCHWIMMER

The applicant seems to be a woman of superior character and intelligence, obviously more than ordinarily desirable as a citizen of the United States. It is agreed that she is qualified for citizenship except so far as the views set forth in a statement of facts "may show that the applicant is not attached to the principles of the Constitution of the United States and well disposed to the good order and happiness of the same, and except in so far as the same may show that she cannot take the oath of allegiance without a mental reservation." The views referred to are an extreme opinion in favor of pacifism and a statement that she would not bear arms to defend the Constitution. So far as the adequacy of her oath is concerned, I hardly can see how that is affected by the statement, inasmuch as she is a woman over fifty years of age, and would not be allowed to bear arms if she wanted to. And as to the opinion the whole examination of the applicant shows that she holds none of the now-dreaded creeds, but thoroughly believes in organized government and prefers that of the United States to any other in the world. Surely it cannot show lack of attachment to the principles of the Constitution that she thinks that it can be improved. I suppose that most intelligent people think that it might be. Her particular improvement looking to the abolition of war seems to me not materially different in its bearing on this case from a wish to establish cabinet government as in England, or a single house, or one term of seven years for the President. To touch a more burning ques-

591

tion, only a judge mad with partisanship would exclude because the applicant thought that the 18th Amendment should be repealed.

Of course, the fear is that if a war came the applicant would exert activities such as were dealt with in Schenck v. United States. But that seems to me unfounded. Her position and motives are wholly different from those of Schenck. She is an optimist and states in strong and, I do not doubt, sincere words her belief that war will disappear and that the impending destiny of mankind is to unite in peaceful leagues. I do not share that optimism nor do I think that a philosophic view of the world would regard war as absurd. But most people who have known it regard it with horror, as a last resort, and, even if not yet ready for cosmopolitan efforts, would welcome any practicable combinations that would increase the power on the side of peace. The notion that the applicant's optimistic anticipations would make her a worse citizen is sufficiently answered by her examination, which seems to me a better argument for her admission than any that I can offer. Some of her answers might excite popular prejudice, but if there is any principle of the Constitution that more imperatively calls for attachment than any other it is the principle of free thought—not free thought for those who agree with us but freedom for the thought that we hate. I think that we should adhere to that principle with regard to admission into, as well as to life within, this country. And, recurring to the opinion that bars this applicant's way, I would suggest that the Quakers have done their share to make the country what it is, that many citizens agree with the applicant's belief, and that I had not supposed hitherto that we regretted our inability to expel them because they believe more than some of us do in the teachings of the Sermon on the Mount.

Justice Louis D. Brandeis

:

CONCURRING OPINION IN
WHITNEY v. CALIFORNIA

Miss Whitney was convicted of the felony of assisting in organizing, in the year 1919, the Communist Labor Party of California, of being a member of it, and of assembling with it. These acts are held to constitute a crime, because the party was formed to teach criminal syndicalism. The statute which made these acts a crime restricted the right of free speech and of assembly theretofore existing. The claim is that the statute, as applied, denied to Miss Whitney the liberty guaranteed by the 14th Amendment.

The felony which the statute created is a crime very unlike the old felony of conspiracy or the old misdemeanor of unlawful assembly. The mere act of assisting in forming a society for teaching syndicalism, of becoming a member of it, or of assembling with others for that purpose is given the dynamic quality of crime. There is guilt although the society may not contemplate immediate promulgation of the doctrine. Thus the accused is to be punished, not for attempt, incitement or conspiracy, but for a step in preparation, which, if it threatens the public order at all, does so only remotely. The novelty in the prohibition introduced is that the statute aims, not at the practice of criminal syndicalism, nor even directly at the preaching of it, but at association with those who propose to preach it.

Despite arguments to the contrary which had seemed to me persuasive, it is settled that the due process clause of the 14th Amendment applies to matters of substantive law as well as to matters of procedure. Thus all

fundamental rights comprised within the term "liberty" are protected by
the Federal Constitution from invasion by the states. The right of free
speech, the right to teach, and the right of assembly are, of course, fundamental rights. These may not be denied or abridged. But, although the
rights of free speech and assembly are fundamental, they are not in their
nature absolute. Their exercise is subject to restriction, if the particular
restriction proposed is required in order to protect the state from destruction or from serious injury, political, economic or moral. That the necessity which is essential to a valid restriction does not exist unless speech
would produce, or is intended to produce, a clear and imminent danger
of some substantive evil which the state constitutionally may seek to prevent has been settled.

It is said to be the function of the legislature to determine whether at a
particular time and under the particular circumstances the formation of,
or assembly with, a society organized to advocate criminal syndicalism
constitutes a clear and present danger of substantive evil; and that by
enacting the law here in question the legislature of California determined
that question in the affirmative. The legislature must obviously decide,
in the first instance, whether a danger exists which calls for a particular
protective measure. But where a statute is valid only in case certain conditions exist, the enactment of the statute cannot alone establish the facts
which are essential to its validity. Prohibitory legislation has repeatedly
been held invalid, because unnecessary, where the denial of liberty involved was that of engaging in a particular business. The power of the
courts to strike down an offending law are no less when the interests
involved are not property rights, but the fundamental personal rights of
free speech and assembly.

This court has not yet fixed the standard by which to determine when
a danger shall be deemed clear; how remote the danger may be and yet
be deemed present; and what degree of evil shall be deemed sufficiently
substantial to justify resort to abridgment of free speech and assembly
as the means of protection. To reach sound conclusions on these matters,
we must bear in mind why a state is, ordinarily, denied the power to
prohibit dissemination of social, economic and political doctrine which
a vast majority of its citizens believes to be false and fraught with evil
consequence.

Those who won our independence believed that the final end of the
state was to make men free to develop their faculties; and that in its
government the deliberative forces should prevail over the arbitrary.

They valued liberty both as an end and as a means. They believed liberty to be the secret of happiness and courage to be the secret of liberty. They believed that freedom to think as you will and to speak as you think are means indispensable to the discovery and spread of political truth; that without free speech and assembly discussion would be futile; that with them, discussion affords ordinarily adequate protection against the dissemination of noxious doctrine; that the greatest menace to freedom is an inert people; that public discussion is a political duty; and that this should be a fundamental principle of the American government.* They recognized the risks to which all human institutions are subject. But they knew that order cannot be secured merely through fear of punishment for its infraction; that it is hazardous to discourage thought, hope and imagination; that fear breeds repression; that repression breeds hate; that hate menaces stable government; that the path of safety lies in the opportunity to discuss freely supposed grievances and proposed remedies; and that the fitting remedy for evil counsels is good ones. Believing in the power of reason as applied through public discussion, they eschewed silence coerced by law—the argument of force in its worst form. Recognizing the occasional tyrannies of governing majorities, they amended the Constitution so that free speech and assembly should be guaranteed.

Fear of serious injury cannot alone justify suppression of free speech and assembly. Men feared witches and burned women. It is the function of speech to free men from the bondage of irrational fears. To justify suppression of free speech there must be reasonable ground to fear that serious evil will result if free speech is practiced. There must be reasonable ground to believe that the danger apprehended is imminent. There must be reasonable ground to believe that the evil to be prevented is a serious one. Every denunciation of existing law tends in some measure to increase the probability that there will be violation of it. Condonation of a breach enhances the probability. Expressions of approval add to the probability. Propagation of the criminal state of mind by teaching syndicalism increases it. Advocacy of lawbreaking heightens it still fur-

---

* Compare Thomas Jefferson: "We have nothing to fear from the demoralizing reasonings of some, if others are left free to demonstrate their errors and especially when the law stands ready to punish the first criminal act produced by the false reasoning; these are safer corrections than the conscience of the judge." Also in first Inaugural Address: "If there be any among us who would wish to dissolve this union or change its republican form, let them stand undisturbed as monuments of the safety with which error of opinion may be tolerated where reason is left free to combat it."

ther. But even advocacy of violation, however reprehensible morally, is not a justification for denying free speech where the advocacy falls short of incitement and there is nothing to indicate that the advocacy would be immediately acted on. The wide difference between advocacy and incitement, between preparation and attempt, between assembling and conspiracy, must be borne in mind. In order to support a finding of clear and present danger it must be shown either that immediate serious violence was to be expected or was advocated, or that the past conduct furnished reason to believe that such advocacy was then contemplated.

Those who won our independence by revolution were not cowards. They did not fear political change. They did not exalt order at the cost of liberty. To courageous, self-reliant men, with confidence in the power of free and fearless reasoning applied through the processes of popular government, no danger flowing from speech can be deemed clear and present, unless the incidence of the evil apprehended is so imminent that it may befall before there is opportunity for full discussion. If there be time to expose through discussion the falsehood and fallacies, to avert the evil by the processes of education, the remedy to be applied is more speech, not enforced silence. Only an emergency can justify repression. Such must be the rule if authority is to be reconciled with freedom. Such, in my opinion, is the command of the Constitution. It is, therefore, always open to Americans to challenge a law abridging free speech and assembly by showing that there was no emergency justifying it.

Moreover, even imminent danger cannot justify resort to prohibition of these functions essential to effective democracy, unless the evil apprehended is relatively serious. Prohibition of free speech and assembly is a measure so stringent that it would be inappropriate as the means for averting a relatively trivial harm to society. A police measure may be unconstitutional merely because the remedy, although effective as means of protection, is unduly harsh or oppressive. Thus, a state might, in the exercise of its police power, make any trespass upon the land of another a crime, regardless of the results or of the intent or purpose of the trespasser. It might, also, punish an attempt, a conspiracy, or an incitement to commit the trespass. But it is hardly conceivable that this court would hold constitutional a statute which punished as a felony the mere voluntary assembly with a society formed to teach that pedestrians had the moral right to cross unenclosed, unposted, waste lands and to advocate their doing so, even if there was imminent danger that advocacy would lead to a trespass. The fact that speech is likely to result in some violence or in destruction of property is not enough to justify its suppression. There must be the probability of serious injury to the state. Among free-men, the deterrents ordinarily to be applied to prevent crime are educa-tion and punishment for violations of the law, not abridgment of the rights of free speech and assembly.

The California Syndicalism Act recites, in § 4:

"Inasmuch as this act concerns and is necessary to the immediate preservation of the public peace and safety, for the reason that at the present time large numbers of persons are going from place to place in this state advocating, teaching and practicing criminal syndicalism, this act shall take effect upon approval by the governor."

This legislative declaration satisfies the requirement of the Constitution of the state concerning emergency legislation. But it does not preclude inquiry into the question whether, at the time and under the circum-stances, the conditions existed which are essential to validity under the Federal Constitution. As a statute, even if not void on its face, may be challenged because invalid as applied, the result of such an inquiry may depend upon the specific facts of the particular case. Whenever the fundamental rights of free speech and assembly are alleged to have been invaded, it must remain open to a defendant to present the issue whether there actually did exist at the time a clear danger; whether the danger, if any, was imminent; and whether the evil apprehended was one so sub-stantial as to justify the stringent restriction interposed by the legislature. The legislative declaration, like the fact that the statute was passed and was sustained by the highest court of the state, creates merely a rebut-table presumption that these conditions have been satisfied.

Whether, in 1919, when Miss Whitney did the things complained of, there was in California such clear and present danger of serious evil, might have been made the important issue in the case. She might have required that the issue be determined either by the court or the jury. She claimed below that the statute as applied to her violated the Federal Constitution; but she did not claim that it was void because there was no clear and present danger of serious evil, nor did she request that the existence of these conditions of a valid measure thus restricting the rights of free speech and assembly be passed upon by the court or a jury. On the other hand, there was evidence on which the court or jury might have found that such danger existed. I am unable to assent to the sugges-tion in the opinion of the court that assembling with a political party, formed to advocate the desirability of a proletarian revolution by mass action at some date necessarily far in the future, is not a right within the protection of the 14th Amendment. In the present case, however, there was other testimony which tended to establish the existence of a conspiracy, on the part of members of the International Workers of the World, to commit present serious crimes; and likewise to show that such a conspiracy would be furthered by the activity of the society of which Miss Whitney was a member. Under these circumstances the judgment of the state court cannot be disturbed.

Our power of review in this case is limited not only to the question whether a right guaranteed by the Federal Constitution was denied but to the particular claims duly made below, and denied. We lack here the power occasionally exercised on review of judgments of lower federal courts to correct in criminal cases vital errors, although the objection was not taken in the trial court. This is a writ of error to a state court. Because we may not inquire into the errors now alleged, I concur in affirming the judgment of the state court.

Herman Melville

.

FAST-FISH AND LOOSE-FISH

from *Moby Dick*

The allusion to the waifs and waif-poles in the last chapter but one, necessitates some account of the laws and regulations of the whale fishery, of which the waif may be deemed the grand symbol and badge.

It frequently happens that when several ships are cruising in company, a whale may be struck by one vessel, then escape, and be finally killed and captured by another vessel; and herein are indirectly comprised many minor contingencies, all partaking of this one grand feature. For example—after a weary and perilous chase and capture of a whale, the body may get loose from the ship by reason of a violent storm; and drifting far away to leeward, be retaken by a second whaler, who, in a calm, snugly tows it alongside, without risk of life or line. Thus the most vexatious and violent disputes would often arise between the fishermen, were there not some written or unwritten, universal, undisputed law applicable to all cases.

Perhaps the only formal whaling code authorized by legislative enactment was that of Holland. It was decreed by the States-General in A.D. 1695. But though no other nation has ever had any written whaling law, yet the American fishermen have been their own legislators and lawyers in this matter. They have provided a system which for terse comprehensiveness surpasses Justinian's Pandects and the By-laws of the Chinese Society for the Suppression of Meddling with other People's Business. Yes; these laws might be engraven on a Queen Anne's farthing, or the barb of a harpoon, and worn round the neck, so small are they.

I. A Fast-Fish belongs to the party fast to it.

II. A Loose-Fish is fair game for anybody who can soonest catch it.

But what plays the mischief with this masterly code is the admirable brevity of it, which necessitates a vast volume of commentaries to expound it.

First: What is a Fast-Fish? Alive or dead a fish is technically fast, when it is connected with an occupied ship or boat, by any medium at all controllable by the occupant or occupants—a mast, an oar, a nine-inch cable, a telegraph wire, or a strand of cobweb, it is all the same. Likewise a fish is technically fast when it bears a waif, or any other recognized symbol of possession; so long as the party waifing it plainly evince their ability at any time to take it alongside, as well as their intention so to do.

These are scientific commentaries; but the commentaries of the whalemen themselves sometimes consist in hard words and harder knocks—the Coke-upon-Littleton of the fist. True, among the more upright and honorable whalemen allowances are always made for peculiar cases, where it would be an outrageous moral injustice for one party to claim possession of a whale previously chased or killed by another party. But others are by no means so scrupulous.

Some fifty years ago there was a curious case of whale-trover litigated in England, wherein the plaintiffs set forth that after a hard chase of a whale in the Northern seas; and when indeed they (the plaintiffs) had succeeded in harpooning the fish; they were at last, through peril of their lives, obliged to forsake not only their lines, but their boat itself. Ultimately the defendants (the crew of another ship) came up with the whale, struck, killed, seized, and finally appropriated it before the very eyes of the plaintiffs. And when those defendants were remonstrated with, their captain snapped his fingers in the plaintiffs' teeth, and assured them that by way of doxology to the deed he had done, he would now retain their line, harpoons, and boat, which had remained attached to the whale at the time of the seizure. Wherefore the plaintiffs now sued for the recovery of the value of their whale, line, harpoons, and boat.

Mr. Erskine was counsel for the defendants; Lord Ellenborough was the judge. In the course of the defense, the witty Erskine went on to illustrate his position, by alluding to a recent crim. con. case, wherein a gentleman, after in vain trying to bridle his wife's viciousness, had at last abandoned her upon the seas of life; but in the course of years, repenting of that step, he instituted an action to recover possession of her. He then proceeded to say that, though the gentleman had originally harpooned the lady, and at once had her fast, and only by reason of the great stress of her plunging viciousness, had at last abandoned her; yet abandon her he did, so that she became a loose-fish; and therefore when a subsequent gentleman re-harpooned her, the lady then became that subsequent gentleman's property, along with whatever harpoon might have been found sticking in her.

Now in the present case Erskine contended that the examples of the whale and the lady were reciprocally illustrative of each other.

These pleadings, and the counter-pleadings, being duly heard, the very learned judge in set terms decided, to wit—That as for the boat, he awarded it to the plaintiffs, because they had merely abandoned it to save their lives; but that with regard to the controverted whale harpoons, and line, they belonged to the defendant; the whale, because it was a Loose-Fish at the time of the final capture; and the harpoons and line because when the fish made off with them, it (the fish) acquired a property in those articles; and hence anybody who afterwards took the fish had a right to them. Now the plaintiffs afterwards took the fish; ergo, the aforesaid articles were theirs.

A common man looking at this decision of the very learned judge might possibly object to it. But ploughed up to the primary rock of the matter, the two great principles laid down in the twin whaling laws previously quoted, and applied and elucidated by Lord Ellenborough in the above cited case; these two laws touching Fast-Fish and Loose-Fish, I say, will, on reflection, be found the fundamentals of all human jurisprudence; for notwithstanding its complicated tracery of sculpture, the Temple of the Law, like the Temple of the Philistines, has but two props to stand on.

Is it not a saying in everyone's mouth, Possession is half of the law: that is, regardless of how the thing came into possession? But often possession is the whole of the law. What are the sinews and souls of Russian serfs and Republican slaves but Fast-Fish, whereof possession is the whole of the law? What to the rapacious landlord is the widow's last mite but a Fast-Fish? What is yonder undetected villain's marble mansion with a door-plate for a waif; what is that but a Fast-Fish? What is the ruinous discount which Mordecai, the broker, gets from poor Woebegone, the bankrupt, on a loan to keep Woebegone's family from starvation; what is that ruinous discount but a Fast-Fish? What is the Archbishop of Savesoul's income of £100,000 seized from the scant bread and cheese of hundreds of thousands of broken-backed laborers; what is that globular £100,000 but a Fast-Fish? What are the Duke of Dunder's hereditary towns and hamlets but Fast-Fish? What to that redoubted harpooneer, John Bull, is poor Ireland, but a Fast-Fish? What to that apostolic lancer, Brother Jonathan, is Texas but a Fast-Fish? And concerning all these, is not Possession the whole of the law?

But if the doctrine of Fast-Fish be pretty generally applicable, the kindred doctrine of Loose-Fish is still more widely so. That is internationally and universally applicable.

What was America in 1492 but a Loose-Fish, in which Columbus struck the Spanish standard by way of waifing it for his royal master and mistress? What was Poland to the Czar? What Greece to the Turk? What India to England? What at last will Mexico be to the United States? All Loose-Fish.

What are the Rights of Man and the Liberties of the World but Loose-Fish? What all men's minds and opinions but Loose-Fish? What is the principle of religious belief in them but a Loose-Fish? What to the ostentatious smuggling verbalists are the thoughts of thinkers but Loose-Fish? What is the great globe itself but a Loose-Fish! And what are you, reader, but a Loose-Fish and a Fast-Fish, too?

HEADS OR TAILS

De balena vero sufficit, si rex habeat caput, et regina caudam.
Bracton, l. 3, c. 3.

Latin from the books of the Laws of England, which taken along with the context, means, that of all whales captured by anybody on the coast of that land, the King, as Honorary Grand Harpooneer, must have the head, and the Queen be respectfully presented with the tail —a division which, in the whale, is much like halving an apple; there is no intermediate remainder. Now as this law, under a modified form, is to this day in force in England; and as it offers in various respects a strange anomaly touching the general law of Fast- and Loose-Fish, it is here treated of in a separate chapter, on the same courteous principle that prompts the English railways to be at the expense of a separate car, specially reserved for the accommodation of royalty. In the first place, in curious proof of the fact that the above-mentioned law is still in force, I proceed to lay before you a circumstance that happened within the last two years.

It seems that some honest mariners of Dover, or Sandwich, or some one of the Cinque Ports, had after a hard chase succeeded in killing and beaching a fine whale which they had originally descried afar off from the shore. Now the Cinque Ports are partially or somehow under the jurisdiction of a sort of policeman or beadle, called a Lord Warden. Holding the office directly from the crown, I believe, all the royal emoluments incident to the Cinque Port territories become by assignment his. By some writers this office is called a *sinecure*. But not so. Because the Lord Warden is busily employed at times in fobbing his perquisites; which are his chiefly by virtue of that same fobbing of them.

Now when these poor sunburnt mariners bare-footed and with their trousers rolled high up on their eely legs, had wearily hauled their fat fish high and dry, promising themselves a good £150 from the precious oil and bone; and in fantasy sipping rare tea with their wives, and good ale with their cronies, upon the strength of their respective shares; up steps a very learned and most Christian and charitable gentleman, with a copy of Blackstone under his arm; and laying it upon the whale's head, he says—"Hands off! This fish, my masters, is a Fast-Fish. I seize it as the Lord Warden's." Upon this the poor mariners in their respectful consternation—so truly English—knowing not what to say, fall to vigorously scratching their heads all round; meanwhile ruefully glancing from the whale to the stranger. But that did in nowise mend the matter, or at all soften the hard heart of the learned gentleman with the copy of Blackstone. At length one of them, after long scratching about for his ideas, made bold to speak.

"Please, sir, who is the Lord Warden?"

"The Duke."

"But the Duke had nothing to do with taking this fish."

"It is his."

"We have been at great trouble, and peril, and some expense, and is all that to go to the Duke's benefit; we getting nothing at all for our pains but our blisters?"

"It is his."

"Is the Duke so very poor as to be forced to this desperate mode of getting a livelihood?"

"It is his."

"I thought to relieve my old bedridden mother by part of my share of this whale."

"It is his."

"Won't the Duke be content with a quarter or a half?"

"It is his."

In a word, the whale was seized and sold, and his Grace the Duke of Wellington received the money. Thinking that viewed in some particular lights, the case might by a bare possibility in some small degree be deemed, under the circumstances, a rather hard one, an honest clergyman of the town respectfully addressed a note to his Grace, begging him to take the case of those unfortunate mariners into full consideration. To which my Lord Duke in substance replied (both letters were published) that he had already done so, and received the money, and would be obliged to the reverend gentleman if for the future he (the reverend gentleman) would decline meddling with other people's business. Is this the still militant old man, standing at the corners of the three kingdoms, on all hands coercing alms of beggars?

It will readily be seen that in this case the alleged right of the Duke to the whale was a delegated one from the Sovereign. We must needs inquire then on what principle the Sovereign is originally invested with that right. The law itself has already been set forth. But Plowden gives us the reason for it. Says Plowden, the whale so caught belongs to the King and Queen, "because of its superior excellence." And by the soundest commentators this has ever been held a cogent argument in such matters.

But why should the King have the head, and the Queen the tail? A reason for that, ye lawyers?

In his treaties on "Queen-Gold," or Queen-pinmoney, an old King's Bench author, one William Prynne, thus discourseth: "Ye tail is ye Queen's, that ye Queen's wardrobe may be supplied with ye whale-bone." Now this was written at a time when the black limber bone of the Greenland or Right Whale was largely used in ladies' bodices. But this same bone is not in the tail; it is in the head, which is a sad mistake for a sagacious lawyer like Prynne. But is the Queen a mermaid, to be presented with a tail? An allegorical meaning may lurk here.

There are two royal fish so styled by the English law writers—the whale and the sturgeon; both royal property under certain limitations, and nominally supplying the tenth branch of the crown's ordinary revenue. I know not that any other author has hinted of the matter; but by inference it seems to me that the sturgeon must be divided in the same way as the whale, the King receiving the highly dense and elastic head peculiar to that fish, which symbolically regarded, may possibly be humorously grounded upon some presumed congeniality. And thus there seems a reason in all things, even in law.

Henry Miller

:

A LETTER DEFENDING THE
FREEDOM TO READ

On May 10th, 1957, the book *Sexus* (*The Rosy Crucifixion*), by the world-famous American author, Henry Miller, was ordered by the Attorney General [of Norway] to be confiscated on the grounds that it was "obscene writing."

Volume I of the Danish edition of the book had at this stage been available for over eight months on the Norwegian market, and was on sale in a considerable number of the most reputable bookshops in the country.

Copies of the book were confiscated in a total of 9 bookshops. Proceedings were instituted against two of these booksellers, chosen at random. . . .

In a judgment pronounced by the Oslo Town Court on June 17th, 1958, the two booksellers were found guilty of having "offered for sale, exhibited, or in other ways endeavored to disseminate obscene writing," and this judgment has now been appealed to the Supreme Court.

It is and has been my pleasure and privilege to act as defending counsel. As a result of my official association with this case I have enjoyed a certain measure of personal contact, through the medium of correspondence, with that eminent author and warmhearted and talented fellow human, Henry Miller.

The letter addressed to myself which is reproduced in this document, and which constitutes Henry Miller's ardent appeal to the tribunal of the Norwegian Supreme Court, is intended by him to assist in the defense of the most important bastion of freedom, democracy, and humanism: the freedom to read.

Trygve Hirsch
Barrister-at-Law

Mr. Trygve Hirsch
Oslo, Norway

Dear Mr. Hirsch:

To answer your letter of January 19th requesting a statement of me which might be used in the Supreme Court trial to be conducted in March or April of this year. . . . It is difficult to be more explicit than I was in my letter of September 19th, 1957, when the case against my book *Sexus* was being tried in the lower courts of Oslo. However, here are some further reflections which I trust will be found à propos.

When I read the decision of the Oslo Town Court, which you sent me some months ago, I did so with mingled feelings. If occasionally I was obliged to roll with laughter—partly because of the inept translation, partly because of the nature and the number of infractions listed —I trust no one will take offense. Taking the world for what it is, and the men who make and execute the laws for what they are, I thought the decision as fair and honest as any theorem of Euclid's. Nor was I unaware of, or indifferent to, the efforts made by the Court to render an interpretation beyond the strict letter of the law. (An impossible task, I would say, for if laws are made for men and not men for laws, it is also true that certain individuals are made for the law and can only see things through the eyes of the law.)

I failed to be impressed, I must confess, by the weighty, often pompous or hypocritical, opinions adduced by scholars, literary pundits, psychologists, medicos and such like. How could I be when it is precisely such single-minded individuals, so often wholly devoid of humor, at whom I so frequently aim my shafts?

Re-reading this lengthy document today, I am more than ever aware of the absurdity of the whole procedure. (How lucky I am not to be indicted as a "pervert" or "degenerate," but simply as one who makes sex pleasurable and innocent!) Why, it is often asked, when he has so much else to give, did he have to introduce these disturbing, controversial scenes dealing with sex? To answer that properly, one would have to go back to the womb—with or without the analyst's guiding hand. Each one—priest, analyst, barrister, judge—has his own answer, usually a ready-made one. But none go far enough, none are deep enough, inclusive enough. The divine answer, of course, is—first remove the mote from your own eye!

If I were there, in the dock, my answer would probably be— "Guilty! Guilty on all ninety-seven counts! To the gallows!" For when I take the short, myopic view, I realize that I was guilty even before I wrote the book. Guilty, in other words, because I am the way I am. The marvel is that I am walking about as a free man. I should have been condemned the moment I stepped out of my mother's womb.

In that heart-rending account of my return to the bosom of the family which is given in *Reunion in Brooklyn,* I concluded with these words, and I meant them, each and every one of them: "I regard the entire world as my home. I inhabit the earth, not a particular portion of it labeled America, France, Germany, Russia. . . . I owe allegiance to mankind, not to a particular country, race, or people. I answer to God, not to the Chief Executive, whoever he may happen to be. I am here on earth to work out my own private destiny. My destiny is linked with that of every other living creature inhabiting this planet— perhaps with those on other planets too, who knows? I refuse to jeopardize my destiny by regarding life within the narrow rules which are laid down to circumscribe it. I dissent from the current view of things, as regards murder, as regards religion, as regards society, as regards our well-being. I will try to live my life in accordance with the vision I have of things eternal. I say 'Peace to you all!' and if you don't find it, it's because you haven't looked for it."

It is curious, and **not** irrelevant, I hope, to mention at this point the reaction I had upon reading Homer recently. At the request of the publisher, Gallimard, who is bringing out a new edition of *The Odyssey,* I wrote a short introduction to this work. I had never read *The Odyssey* before, only *The Iliad,* and that but a few months ago. What I wish to say is that, after waiting sixty-seven years to read these universally esteemed classics, I found much to disparage in them. In *The Iliad,* or "the butcher's manual," as I call it, more than in *The Odyssey.* But it would never occur to me to request that they be banned or burned. Nor did I fear, on finishing them, that I would leap outdoors, axe in hand, and run amok. My boy, who was only nine when he read *The Iliad* (in a child's version), my boy who confesses to "liking murder once in a while," told me he was fed up with Homer, with all the killing and all the nonsense about the gods. But I have never feared that this son of mine, now going on eleven, still an avid reader of our detestable "Comics," a devotee of Walt Disney (who is not to my taste at all), an ardent movie fan, particularly of the "Westerns," I have never feared, I say, that he will grow up to be a killer. (Not even if the Army claims him!) I would rather see his mind absorbed by other interests and I do my best to provide them, but, like all of us, he is a product of the age. No need, I trust, for me to elaborate on the dangers which confront us all, youth especially, in *this* age. The point is that with each age the menace varies. Whether it be witchcraft, idolatry, leprosy, cancer, schizophrenia, communism, fascism, or what, we have ever to do battle. Seldom do we really vanquish the enemy, in whatever guise he presents himself. At best we become immunized. But we never know, nor are we able to prevent in advance, the dangers which lurk around the corner. No matter how knowledgeable, no matter how wise, no matter how prudent and cautious, we all have an Achilles' heel. Security is not the lot of man. Readiness, alertness, responsiveness—these are the sole defenses against the blows of fate.

I smile to myself in putting the following to the honorable members of the Court, prompted as I am to take the bull by the horns. Would it please the Court to know that by common opinion I pass for a sane, healthy, normal individual? That I am not regarded as a "sex addict," a pervert, or even a neurotic? Nor as a writer who is ready to sell his soul for money? That, as a husband, a father, a neighbor, I am looked upon as "an asset" to the community? Sounds a trifle ludicrous, does it not? Is this the same *enfant terrible,* it might be asked, who wrote the unmentionable *Tropics, The Rosy Crucifixion, The World of Sex, Quiet Days in Clichy?* Has he reformed? Or is he simply in his dotage now?

To be precise, the question is—are the author of these questionable works and the man who goes by the name of Henry Miller one and the same person? My answer is yes. And I am also one with the protagonist of these "autobiographical romances." That is perhaps harder to swallow. But why? Because I have been "utterly shameless" in revealing every aspect of my life? I am not the first author to have adopted the confessional approach, to have revealed life nakedly, or to have used language supposedly unfit for the ears of school girls. Were I a saint recounting his life of sin, perhaps these bald statements relating to my sex habits would be found enlightening, particularly by priests and medicos. They might even be found instructive.

But I am not a saint, and probably never will be one. Though it occurs to me, as I make this assertion, that I have been called that more than once, and by individuals whom the Court would never suspect capable of holding such an opinion. No, I am not a saint, thank heavens! Nor even a propagandist of a new order. I am simply a man, a man born to write, who has taken as his theme the story of his life. A man who has made it clear, in the telling, that it was a good life, a rich life, a merry life, despite the ups and downs, despite the barriers and obstacles (many of his own making), despite the handicaps imposed by stupid codes and conventions. Indeed, I hope that I have made more than that clear, because whatever I may say about my own life, which is only *a* life, is merely a means of talking about life itself, and what I have tried, desperately sometimes, to make clear is this, that I look upon life itself as good, good no matter on what terms, that I believe it is *we* who make it unlivable, *we,* not the gods, not fate, not circumstance.

Speaking thus, I am reminded of certain passages in the Court's decision which reflect on my sincerity as well as on my ability to think straight. These passages contain the implication that I am often deliberately obscure as well as pretentious in my "metaphysical and surrealistic" flights. I am only too well aware of the diversity of opinion which these "excursi" elicit in the minds of my readers. But how am I to answer such accusations, touching as they do the very marrow of my literary being? Am I to say "You don't know what you are talking about"? Ought I to muster impressive names—"authorities"—to counterbalance these judgments? Or would it not be simpler to say, as I have before—"Guilty! Guilty on all counts, your Honor!"

Believe me, it is not impish, roguish perversity which leads me to pronounce, even quasi-humorously, this word "guilty." As one who thoroughly and sincerely believes in what he says and does, even when wrong, is it not more becoming on my part to admit "guilt" than attempt to defend myself against those who use this word so glibly? Let us be honest. Do those who judge and condemn me—not in Oslo necessarily, but the world over—do these individuals truly believe me to be a culprit, to be "the enemy of society," as they often blandly assert? What is it that disturbs them so? Is it the existence, the prevalence, of immoral, amoral, or unsocial behavior, such as is described in my works, or is it the exposure of such behavior in print? Do people of our day and age really behave in this "vile" manner or are these actions merely the product of a "diseased" mind? (Does one refer to such authors as

Petronius, Rabelais, Rousseau, Sade, to mention but a few, as "diseased minds"?) Surely some of you must have friends or neighbors, in good standing too, who have indulged in this questionable behavior, or worse. As a man of the world, I know only too well that the appanage of a priest's frock, a judicial robe, a teacher's uniform provides no guarantee of immunity to the temptations of the flesh. We are all in the same pot, we are all guilty, or innocent, depending on whether we take the frog's view or the Olympian view. For the nonce I shall refrain from pretending to measure or apportion guilt, to say, for example, that a criminal is more guilty, or less, than a hypocrite. We do not have crime, we do not have war, revolution, crusades, inquisitions, persecution and intolerance because some among us are wicked, mean-spirited, or murderers at heart; we have this malignant condition of human affairs because all of us, the righteous as well as the ignorant and the malicious lack true forbearance, true compassion, true knowledge and understanding of human nature.

To put it as succinctly and simply as possible, here is my basic attitude toward life, my prayer, in other words: "Let us stop thwarting one another, stop judging and condemning, stop slaughtering one another." I do not implore you to suspend or withhold judgment of me or my work. Neither I nor my work is that important. (One cometh, another goeth.) What concerns me is the harm you are doing to yourselves. I mean by perpetuating this talk of guilt and punishment, of banning and proscribing, of whitewashing, and blackballing, of closing your eyes when convenient, of making scapegoats when there is no other way out. I ask you pointblank—does the pursuance of your limited role enable you to get the most out of life? When you write me off the books, so to speak, will you find your food and wine more palatable, will you sleep better, will you be a better man, a better husband, a better father than before? Those are the things that matter—what happens to *you,* not what you do to *me.*

I know that the man in the dock is not supposed to ask questions; he is there to answer. But I am unable to regard myself as a culprit. I am simply "out of line." Yet I am in the tradition, so to say. A list of my precursors would make an impressive roster. This trial has been going on since the days of Prometheus. Since before that. Since the days of the Archangel Michael. In the not too distant past there was one who was given the cup of hemlock for being "the corrupter of youth." Today he is regarded as one of the sanest, most lucid minds that ever was. We who are always being arraigned before the bar can do no better than to resort to the celebrated Socratic method. Our only answer is to return the question.

There are so many questions one could put to the Court, to any Court. But would one get a response? Can the Court of the Land ever be put in question? I am afraid not. The judicial body is a sacrosanct body. This is unfortunate, as I see it, for when issues of grave import arise, the last Court of reference, in my opinion, should be the public. When justice is at stake, responsibility cannot be shifted to an elect few without injustice resulting. No Court could function if it did not follow the steel rails of precedent, taboo, and prejudice.

I come back to the lengthy document representing the decision of the Oslo Town Court, to the tabulation of all the infractions of the moral code therein listed. There is something frightening as well as disheartening about such an indictment. It has a medieval aspect. And it has nothing to do with justice. Law itself is made to look ridiculous. Once again let me say that it is not the courts of Oslo or the laws and codes of Norway which I inveigh against; everywhere in the civilized world there is this mummery and flummery manifesting as the Voice of Inertia. The offender who stands before the Court is not being tried by his peers but by his dead ancestors. The moral codes, operative only if they are in conformance with natural or divine laws, are not safeguarded by these flimsy dikes; on the contrary, they are exposed as weak and ineffectual barriers.

Finally, here is the crux of the matter. Will an adverse decision by this Court or any other Court effectively hinder the further circulation of this book? The history of similar cases does not substantiate such an eventuality. If anything, an unfavorable verdict will only add more fuel to the flames. Proscription only leads to resistance; the fight goes on underground, becomes more insidious therefore, more difficult to cope with. If only one man in Norway reads the book and believes with the author that one has the right to express himself freely, the battle is won. You cannot eliminate an idea by suppressing it, and the idea which is linked with this issue is one of freedom to read what one chooses. Freedom, in other words, to read what is bad for one as well as what is good for one—or, what is simply innocuous. How can one guard against evil, in short, if one does not know what evil is?

But it is not something evil, not something poisonous, which this book *Sexus* offers the Norwegian reader. It is a dose of life which I administered to myself first, and which I not only survived but thrived on. Certainly I would not recommend it to infants, but then neither would I offer a child a bottle of *aqua vite*. I can say one thing for it unblushingly—compared to the atom bomb, it is full of lifegiving qualities.

HENRY MILLER

[EDITOR'S NOTE: The final decision of the Norwegian Supreme Court found the defendants not guilty, but upheld the ban on the book.]

Justice Oliver Wendell Holmes, Jr.

.

THE PATH OF THE LAW

An Address delivered by Mr. Justice Holmes, then of the Supreme Court of Massachusetts, on January 8, 1897.

When we study law we are not studying a mystery but a well-known profession. We are studying what we shall want in order to appear before judges, or to advise people in such a way as to keep them out of court. The reason why it is a profession, why people will pay lawyers to argue for them or to advise them, is that in societies like ours the command of the public force is entrusted to the judges in certain cases, and the whole power of the state will be put forth, if necessary, to carry out their judgments and decrees. People want to know under what circumstances and how far they will run the risk of coming against what is so much stronger than themselves, and hence it becomes a business to find out when this danger is to be feared. The object of our study, then, is prediction, the prediction of the incidence of the public force through the instrumentality of the courts.

The means of the study are a body of reports, of treatises and of statutes, in this country and in England, extending back for six hundred years, and now increasing annually by hundreds. In these sibylline leaves are gathered the scattered prophecies of the past upon the cases in which the axe will fall. These are what properly have been called the oracles of the law. Far the most important and pretty nearly the whole meaning of every new effort of legal thought is to make these

614

prophecies more precise, and to generalize them into a thoroughly connected system. The process is one, from a lawyer's statement of a case, eliminating as it does all the dramatic elements with which his client's story has clothed it, and retaining only the facts of legal import up to the final analyses and abstract universals of theoretic jurisprudence. The reason why a lawyer does not mention that his client wore a white hat when he made a contract, while Mrs. Quickly would be sure to dwell upon it along with the parcel gilt goblet and the sea-coal fire, is that he foresees that the public force will act in the same way whatever his client had upon his head. It is to make the prophecies easier to be remembered and to be understood that the teachings of the decisions of the past are put into general propositions and gathered into textbooks, or that statutes are passed in a general form. The primary rights and duties with which jurisprudence busies itself again are nothing but prophecies. One of the many evil effects of the confusion between legal and moral ideas, about which I shall have something to say in a moment, is that theory is apt to get the cart before the horse, and to consider the right or the duty as something existing apart from and independent of the consequences of its breach, to which certain sanctions are added afterward. But, as I shall try to show, a legal duty so called is nothing but a prediction that if a man does or omits certain things he will be made to suffer in this or that way by judgment of the court; and so of a legal right.

The number of our predictions when generalized and reduced to a system is not unmanageably large. They present themselves as a finite body of dogma which may be mastered within a reasonable time. It is a great mistake to be frightened by the ever increasing number of reports. The reports of a given jurisdiction in the course of a generation take up pretty much the whole body of the law, and restate it from the present point of view. We could reconstruct the corpus from them if all that went before were burned. The use of the earlier reports is mainly historical, a use about which I shall have something to say before I have finished.

I wish, if I can, to lay down some first principles for the study of this body of dogma or systematized prediction which we call the law, for men who want to use it as the instrument of their business to enable them to prophesy in their turn, and, as bearing upon the study, I wish to point out an ideal which as yet our law has not attained.

The first thing for a businesslike understanding of the matter is to understand its limits, and therefore I think it desirable at once to point out and dispel a confusion between morality and law, which sometimes rises to the height of conscious theory, and more often and indeed constantly is making trouble in detail without reaching the point of consciousness. You can see very plainly that a bad man has as much reason as a good one for wishing to avoid an encounter with the public force, and therefore you can see the practical importance of the distinction between morality and law. A man who cares nothing for an ethical rule which is believed and practiced by his neighbors is likely nevertheless to care a good deal to avoid being made to pay money, and will want to keep out of jail if he can.

I take it for granted that no hearer of mine will misinterpret what I have to say as the language of cynicism. The law is the witness and external deposit of our moral life. Its history is the history of the moral development of the race. The practice of it, in spite of popular jests, tends to make good citizens and good men. When I emphasize the difference between law and morals I do so with reference to a single end, that of learning and understanding the law. For that purpose you must definitely master its specific marks, and it is for that I ask you for the moment to imagine yourselves indifferent to other and greater things.

I do not say that there is not a wider point of view from which the distinction between law and morals becomes of secondary or no importance, as all mathematical distinctions vanish in presence of the infinite. But I do say that that distinction is of the first importance for the object which we are here to consider—a right study and mastery of the law was a business with well-understood limits, a body of dogma enclosed within definite lines. I have just shown the practical reason for saying so. If you want to know the law and nothing else, you must look at it as a bad man, who cares only for the material consequences which such knowledge enables him to predict, not as a good one, who finds his reasons for conduct, whether inside the law or outside of it, in the vaguer sanctions of conscience. The theoretical importance of the distinction is no less, if you would reason on your subject aright. The law is full of phraseology drawn from morals, and by the mere force of language continually invites us to pass from one domain to the other without perceiving it, as we are sure to do unless we have the boundary constantly before our minds. The law talks about rights, and duties, and malice, and intent, and negligence, and so forth, and nothing is easier, or, I may say, more common in legal reasoning, than to take these words in their moral sense, at some stage of the argument, and so to drop into fallacy. For instance, when we speak of the rights of man in a moral sense, we mean to mark the limits of interference with individual freedom which we think are prescribed by conscience, or by our ideal, however reached. Yet it is certain that many laws have been enforced in the past, and it is likely that some are enforced now, which are condemned by the most enlightened opinion of the time, or which at all events pass the limit of interference as many consciences would draw it. Manifestly, therefore, nothing but confusion of thought can result from assuming that the rights of man in a moral sense are equally rights in the sense of the Constitution and the law. No doubt simple and extreme cases can be put of imaginable laws which the statute-making power would not dare to enact, even in the absence of written constitutional prohibitions, because the community would rise in rebellion and fight; and this gives some plausibility to the proposition that the law, if not a part of morality, is limited by it. But this limit of power is not coextensive with any system of morals. For the most part it falls far within the lines of any such system, and in some cases may extend beyond them, for reasons drawn from the habits of a particular people at a particular time. I once heard the late Professor Agassiz say that a German population would rise if you added two cents to the price of a glass of beer. A statute in such a case would be empty words, not because it was wrong, but because it could not be enforced. No one will deny that wrong statutes can be and are enforced, and we should not all agree as to which were the wrong ones.

The confusion with which I am dealing besets confessedly legal conceptions. Take the fundamental question, What constitutes the law? You will find some text writers telling you that it is something different from what is decided by the courts of Massachusetts or England, that it is a system of reason, that it is a deduction from principles of ethics or admitted axioms or what not, which may or may not coincide with the decisions. But if we take the view of our friend the bad man we shall find that he does not care two straws for the axioms or deductions, but that he does want to know what the Massachusetts or English courts are likely to do in fact. I am much of his mind. The prophecies of what the courts will do in fact, and nothing more pretentious, are what I mean by the law.

Take again a notion which as popularly understood is the widest conception which the law contains—the notion of legal duty, to which already I have referred. We fill the word with all the content which we draw from morals. But what does it mean to a bad man? Mainly, and in the first place, a prophecy that if he does certain things he will be subjected to disagreeable consequences by way of imprisonment or compulsory payment of money. But from his point of view, what is the difference between being fined and being taxed a certain sum for doing a certain thing? That his point of view is the test of legal principles is shown by the many discussions which have arisen in the courts on the very question whether a given statutory liability is a penalty or a tax. On the answer to this question depends the decision whether conduct is legally wrong or right, and also whether a man is under compulsion or free. Leaving the criminal law on one side, what is the difference between the liability under the mill acts or statutes authorizing a taking by eminent domain and the liability for what we call a wrongful conversion of property where restoration is out of the question. In both cases the party taking another man's property has to pay its fair value as assessed by a jury, and no more. What significance is there in calling one taking right and another wrong from the point of view of the law? It does not matter, so far as the given consequence, the compulsory payment, is concerned, whether the act to which it is attached is described in terms of praise or in terms of blame, or whether the law purports to prohibit it or to allow it. If it matters at all, still speaking from the bad man's point of view, it must be because in one case and not in the other some further disadvantages, or at least some further consequences, are attached to the act by the law. The only other disadvantages thus attached to it which I ever have been able to think of are to be found in two somewhat insignificant legal doctrines, both of which might be abolished without disturbance. One is, that a contract to do a prohibited act is unlawful, and the other, that, if one of two or more joint wrongdoers has to pay all the damages, he cannot recover contribution from his fellows. And that I believe is all. You see how the vague circumference of the notion of duty shrinks and at the same time grows more precise when we wash it with cynical acid and expel everything except the object of our study, the operations of the law.

Nowhere is the confusion between legal and moral ideas more manifest than in the law of contract. Among other things, here again the so-called primary rights and duties are invested with a mystic significance beyond what can be assigned and explained. The duty to keep a contract at common law means a prediction that you must pay damages if you do not keep it—and nothing else. If you commit a tort, you are liable to pay a compensatory sum. If you commit a contract, you are liable to pay a compensatory sum unless the promised event comes to pass, and that is all the difference. But such a mode of looking at the matter stinks in the nostrils of those who think it advantageous to get as much ethics into the law as they can. It was good enough for Lord Coke, however, and here, as in many other cases, I am content to abide with him. In *Bromage v. Genning,** a prohibition was sought in the King's Bench against a suit in the marches of Wales for the specific performance of a covenant to grant a lease, and Coke said that it would subvert the intention of the covenantor, since he intends it to be at his election either to lose the damages or to make the lease. Sergeant Harris for the plaintiff confessed that he moved the matter against his conscience, and a prohibition was granted. This goes further than we should go now, but it shows what I venture to say has been the common law point of view from the beginning, although Mr. Harriman, in his very able little book upon Contracts has been misled, as I humbly think, to a different conclusion.

I have spoken only of the common law, because there are some cases in which a logical justification can be found for speaking of civil liabilities as imposing duties in an intelligible sense. These are the relatively few in which equity will grant an injunction, and will enforce it by putting the defendant in prison or otherwise punishing him unless he complies with the order of the court. But I hardly think it advisable to shape general theory from the exception, and I think it would be better to cease troubling ourselves about primary rights and sanctions altogether, than to describe our prophecies concerning the liabilities commonly imposed by the law in those inappropriate terms.

I mentioned, as other examples of the use by the law of words drawn from morals, malice, intent, and negligence. It is enough to take malice as it is used in the law of civil liability for wrongs—what we lawyers call the law of torts—to show that it means something different in law from what it means in morals, and also to show how the difference has been obscured by giving to principles which have little or nothing to do with each other the same name. Three hundred years ago a parson preached a sermon and told a story out of Fox's *Book of Martyrs* of a man who had assisted at the torture of one of the

* Roll. Rep. 368.

saints, and afterward died, suffering compensatory inward torment. It happened that Fox was wrong. The man was alive and chanced to hear the sermon, and thereupon he sued the parson. Chief Justice Wray instructed the jury that the defendant was not liable, because the story was told innocently, without malice. He took malice in the moral sense, as importing a malevolent motive. But nowadays no one doubts that a man may be liable, without any malevolent motive at all, for false statements manifestly calculated to inflict temporal damage. In stating the case in pleading, we still should call the defendant's conduct malicious; but, in my opinion at least, the word means nothing about motives, or even about the defendant's attitude toward the future, but only signifies that the tendency of his conduct under the known circumstances was very plainly to cause the plaintiff temporal harm.*

In the law of contract the use of moral phraseology has led to equal confusion, as I have shown in part already, but only in part. Morals deal with the actual internal state of the individual's mind, what he actually intends. From the time of the Romans down to now, this mode of dealing has affected the language of the law as to contract, and the language used has reacted upon the thought. We talk about a contract as a meeting of the minds of the parties, and thence it is inferred in various cases that there is no contract because their minds have not met; that is, because they have intended different things or because one party has not known of the assent of the other. Yet nothing is more certain than that parties may be bound by a contract to things which neither of them intended, and when one does not know of the other's assent. Suppose a contract is executed in due form and in writing to deliver a lecture, mentioning no time. One of the parties thinks that the promise will be construed to mean at once, within a week. The other thinks that it means when he is ready. The court says that it means within a reasonable time. The parties are bound by the contract as it is interpreted by the court, yet neither of them meant what the court declares that they have said. In my opinion no one will understand the true theory of contract or be able even to discuss some fundamental questions intelligently until he has understood that all contracts are formal, that the making of a contract depends not on the agreement of two minds in one intention, but on the agreement of two sets of external signs—not on the parties' having *meant* the same thing but on their having *said*

* See Hanson *v.* Globe Newspaper Co., 159 Mass. 293, 302.

the same thing. Furthermore, as the signs may be addressed to one sense or another—to sight or to hearing—on the nature of the sign will depend the moment when the contract is made. If the sign is tangible, for instance, a letter, the contract is made when the letter of acceptance is delivered. If it is necessary that the minds of the parties meet, there will be no contract until the acceptance can be read— none, for example, if the acceptance be snatched from the hand of the offerer by a third person.

This is not the time to work out a theory in detail, or to answer many obvious doubts and questions which are suggested by these general views. I know of none which are not easy to answer, but what I am trying to do now is only by a series of hints to throw some light on the narrow path of legal doctrine, and upon two pitfalls which, as it seems to me, lie perilously near to it. Of the first of these I have said enough. I hope that my illustrations have shown the danger, both to speculation and to practice, of confounding morality with law, and the trap which legal language lays for us on that side of our way. For my own part, I often doubt whether it would not be a gain if every word of moral significance could be banished from the law altogether, and other words adopted which should convey legal ideas uncolored by anything outside the law. We should lose the fossil records of a good deal of history and the majesty got from ethical associations, but by ridding ourselves of an unnecessary confusion we should gain very much in the clearness of our thought.

So much for the limits of the law. The next thing which I wish to consider is what are the forces which determine its content and its growth. You may assume, with Hobbes and Bentham and Austin, that all law emanates from the sovereign, even when the first human beings to enunciate it are the judges, or you may think that law is the voice of the Zeitgeist, or what you like. It is all one to my present purpose. Even if every decision required the sanction of an emperor with despotic power and a whimsical turn of mind, we should be interested none the less, still with a view to prediction, in discovering some order, some rational explanation, and some principle of growth for the rules which he laid down. In every system there are such explanations and principles to be found. It is with regard to them that a second fallacy comes in, which I think it important to expose.

The fallacy to which I refer is the notion that the only force at work in the development of the law is logic. In the broadest sense, indeed, that notion would be true. The postulate on which we think about the universe is that there is a fixed quantitative relation between every phenomenon and its antecedents and consequents. If there is such a thing as a phenomenon without these fixed quantitative relations, it is a miracle. It is outside the law of cause and effect, and as such transcends our power of thought, or at least is something to or from which we cannot reason. The condition of our thinking about the universe is that it is capable of being thought about rationally, or, in other words, that every part of it is effect and cause in the same sense in which those parts are with which we are most familiar. So in the broadest sense it is true that the law is a logical development, like everything else. The danger of which I speak is not the admission that the principles governing other phenomena also govern the law, but the notion that a given system, ours, for instance, can be worked out like mathematics from some general axioms of conduct. This is the natural error of the schools, but it is not confined to them. I once heard a very eminent judge say that he never let a decision go until he was absolutely sure that it was right. So judicial dissent often is blamed, as if it meant simply that one side or the other were not doing their sums right, and, if they would take more trouble, agreement inevitably would come.

This mode of thinking is entirely natural. The training of lawyers is a training in logic. The processes of analogy, discrimination, and deduction are those in which they are most at home. The language of judicial decision is mainly the language of logic. And the logical method and form flatter that longing for certainty and for repose which is in every human mind. But certainty generally is illusion, and repose is not the destiny of man. Behind the logical form lies a judgment as to the relative worth and importance of competing legislative grounds, often an inarticulate and unconscious judgment, it is true, and yet the very root and nerve of the whole proceeding. You can give any conclusion a logical form. You always can imply a condition in a contract. But why do you imply it? It is because of some belief as to the practice of the community or of a class, or because of some opinion as to policy, or, in short, because of some attitude of yours upon a matter not capable of exact quantitative measurement, and therefore not capable of founding exact logical conclusions. Such matters really are battlegrounds where the means do not exist for determinations that shall be good for all time, and where the decision can do no more than embody the preference of a given body in a given time and place. We do not realize how large a part of our law is open to reconsideration upon a slight change in the habit of the public mind. No concrete proposition is self-evident, no matter how ready we may be to accept it, not even Mr. Herbert Spencer's "Every man has a right to do what he wills, provided he interferes not with a like right on the part of his neighbors."

Why is a false and injurious statement privileged, if it is made honestly in giving information about a servant? It is because it has been thought more important that information should be given freely, than that a man should be protected from what under other circumstances would be an actionable wrong. Why is a man at liberty to set up a business which he knows will ruin his neighbor? It is because the public good is supposed to be best subserved by free competition. Obviously such judgments of relative importance may vary in different times and places. Why does a judge instruct a jury that an employer is not liable to an employee for an injury received in the course of his employment unless he is negligent, and why do the jury generally find for the plaintiff if the case is allowed to go to them? It is because the traditional policy of our law is to confine liability to cases where a prudent man might have foreseen the injury, or at least the danger, while the inclination of a very large part of the community is to make certain classes of persons insure the safety of those with whom they deal. Since the last words were written, I have seen the requirement of such insurance put forth as part of the program of one of the best known labor organizations. There is a concealed, half conscious battle on the question of legislative policy, and if anyone thinks that it can be settled deductively, or once for all, I only can say that I think he is theoretically wrong, and that I am certain that his conclusion will not be accepted in practice *semper ubique et ab omnibus.*

Indeed, I think that even now our theory upon this matter is open to reconsideration, although I am not prepared to say how I should decide if a reconsideration were proposed. Our law of torts comes from the old days of isolated, ungeneralized wrongs, assaults, slanders, and the like, where the damages might be taken to lie where they fell by legal judgment. But the torts with which our courts are kept busy today are mainly the incidents of certain well-known businesses. They are injuries to person or property by railroads, factories, and the like. The liability for them is estimated, and sooner or later goes into the price paid by the public. The public really pays the damages, and the question of liability, if pressed far enough, is really the question how far it is desirable that the public should insure the safety of those whose work it uses. It might be said that in such cases the chance of a jury finding for the defendant is merely a chance, once in a while rather arbitrarily interrupting the regular course of recovery, most likely in the case of an unusually conscientious plaintiff, and therefore better done away with. On the other hand, the economic value even of a life to the community can be estimated, and no recovery, it may be said, ought to go beyond that amount. It is conceivable that some day in certain cases we may find ourselves imitating, on a higher plane, the tariff for life and limb which we see in the *Leges Barbarorum*.

I think that the judges themselves have failed adequately to recognize their duty of weighing considerations of social advantage. The duty is inevitable, and the result of the often proclaimed judicial aversion to deal with such considerations is simply to leave the very ground and foundation of judgments inarticulate, and often unconscious, as I have said. When socialism first began to be talked about, the comfortable classes of the community were a good deal frightened. I suspect that this fear has influenced judicial action both here and in England, yet it is certain that it is not a conscious factor in the decisions to which I refer. I think that something similar has led people who no longer hope to control the legislatures to look to the courts as expounders of the Constitutions, and that in some courts new principles have been discovered outside the bodies of those instruments, which may be generalized into acceptance of the economic doctrines which prevailed about fifty years ago, and a wholesale prohibition of what a tribunal of lawyers does not think about right. I cannot but believe that if the training of lawyers led them habitually to consider more definitely and explicitly the social advantage on which the rule they lay down must be justified, they sometimes would hesitate where now they are confident, and see that really they were taking sides upon debatable and often burning questions.

So much for the fallacy of logical form. Now let us consider the present condition of the law as a subject for study, and the ideal toward which it tends. We still are far from the point of view which I desire to see reached. No one has reached it or can reach it as yet. We are only at the beginning of a philosophical reaction, and of a reconsideration of the worth of doctrines which for the most part still are taken for granted without any deliberate, conscious, and systematic questioning of their grounds. The development of our law has gone on for nearly a thousand years, like the development of a plant, each generation taking the inevitable next step, mind, like matter, simply obeying a law of spontaneous growth. It is perfectly natural and right that it should have been so. Imitation is a necessity of human nature, as has been illustrated by a remarkable French writer, M. Tarde, in an admirable book, *Les Lois de l'Imitation.* Most of the things we do, we do for no better reason than that our fathers have done them or that our neighbors do them, and the same is true of a larger part than we suspect of what we think. The reason is a good one, because our short life gives us no time for a better, but it is not the best. It does not follow, because we all are compelled to take on faith at second hand most of the rules on which we base our action and our thought, that each of us may not try to set some corner of his world in the order of reason, or that all of us collectively should not aspire to carry reason as far as it will go throughout the whole domain. In regard to the law, it is true, no doubt, that an evolutionist will hesitate to affirm universal validity for his social ideals, or for the principles which he thinks should be embodied in legislation. He is content if he can prove them best for here and now. He may be ready to admit that he knows nothing about an absolute best in the cosmos, and even that he knows next to nothing about a permanent best for men. Still it is true that a body of law is more rational and more civilized when every rule it contains is referred articulately and definitely to an end which it subserves, and when the grounds for desiring that end are stated or are ready to be stated in words.

At present, in very many cases, if we want to know why a rule of law has taken its particular shape, and more or less if we want to know why it exists at all, we go to tradition. We follow it into the Year Books, and perhaps beyond them to the customs of the Salian Franks, and somewhere in the past, in the German forests, in the needs of Norman kings, in the assumptions of a dominant class, in the absence of generalized ideas, we find out the practical motive for what now best is justified by the mere fact of its acceptance and that men are accustomed to it. The rational study of law is still to a large extent the study of history. History must be a part of the study, because without it we cannot know the precise scope of rules which it is our business to know. It is a part of the rational study, because it is the first step toward an enlightened skepticism, that is, toward a deliberate reconsideration of the worth of those rules. When you get the dragon out of his cave on to the plain and in the daylight, you can count his teeth and claws, and see just what is his strength. But to get him out is only the first step. The next is either to kill him, or to tame him and make him a useful animal. For the rational study of the law the black-letter man may be the man of the present, but the man of the future is the man of statistics and the master of economics. It is revolting to have no better reason for a rule of law than that so it was laid down in the time of Henry IV. It is still more revolting if the grounds upon which it was laid down have vanished long since, and the rule simply persists from blind imitation of the past. I am thinking of the technical rule as to trespass *ab initio,* as it is called, which I attempted to explain in a recent Massachusetts case.*

Let me take an illustration, which can be stated in a few words, to show how the social end which is aimed at by a rule of law is obscured and only partially attained in consequence of the fact that the rule owes its form to a gradual historical development, instead of being reshaped as a whole, with conscious articulate reference to the end in view. We think it desirable to prevent one man's property being misappropriated by another, and so we make larceny a crime. The evil is the same whether the misappropriation is made by a man into whose hands the owner has put the property, or by one who wrongfully takes it away. But primitive law in its weakness did not get much beyond an effort to prevent violence, and very naturally made a wrongful taking, a trespass, part of its definition of the crime. In modern times the judges enlarged the definition a little by holding that, if the wrongdoer gets possession by a trick or device, the crime is committed. This really was giving up the requirement of a trespass, and it would have been more logical, as well as truer to the present object of the law, to abandon the requirement altogether. That, however, would have seemed too bold, and was left to statute. Statutes were passed making embezzlement a crime. But the force of tradition caused the crime of embezzlement to be regarded as so far distinct from larceny that to this day, in some jurisdictions at least, a slip corner is kept open for thieves to contend, if indicted for larceny, that they should have been indicted for embezzlement, and if indicted for embezzlement, that they should have been indicted for larceny, and to escape on that ground.

Far more fundamental questions still await a better answer than that

* Commonwealth *v.* Rubin, 165 Mass. 453.

we do as our fathers have done. What have we better than a blind guess to show that the criminal law in its present form does more good than harm? I do not stop to refer to the effect which it has had in degrading prisoners and in plunging them further into crime, or to the question whether fine and imprisonment do not fall more heavily on a criminal's wife and children than on himself. I have in mind more far-reaching questions. Does punishment deter? Do we deal with criminals on proper principles? A modern school of Continental criminalists plumes itself on the formula, first suggested, it is said, by Gall, that we must consider the criminal rather than the crime. The formula does not carry us very far, but the inquiries which have been started look toward an answer of my questions based on science for the first time. If the typical criminal is a degenerate, bound to swindle or to murder by as deep-seated an organic necessity as that which makes the rattlesnake bite, it is idle to talk of deterring him by the classical method of imprisonment. He must be got rid of; he cannot be improved, or frightened out of his structural reaction. If, on the other hand, crime, like normal human conduct, is mainly a matter of imitation, punishment fairly may be expected to help to keep it out of fashion. The study of criminals has been thought by some well-known men of science to sustain the former hypothesis. The statistics of the relative increase of crime in crowded places like large cities where example has the greatest chance to work, and in less populated parts, where the contagion spreads more slowly, have been used with great force in favor of the latter view. But there is weighty authority for the belief that, however this may be, "not the nature of the crime, but the dangerousness of the criminal, constitutes the only reasonable legal criterion to guide the inevitable social reaction against the criminal." *

The impediments to rational generalization, which I illustrated from the law of larceny, are shown in the other branches of the law, as well as in that of crime. Take the law of tort or civil liability for damages apart from contract and the like. Is there any general theory of such liability, or are the cases in which it exists simply to be enumerated, and to be explained each on its special ground, as is easy to believe from the fact that the right of action for certain well-known classes of wrongs like trespass or slander has its special history for each class? I think that there is a general theory to be discovered, although resting in

* Havelock Ellis, *The Criminal*, 41, citing Garofalo. See also Ferri, *Sociologie Criminelle, passim.* Compare Tarde, *La Philosophie Pénale.*

tendency rather than established and accepted. I think that the law regards the infliction of temporal damage by a responsible person as actionable, if under the circumstances known to him the danger of his act is manifest according to common experience, or according to his own experience if it is more than common, except in cases where upon special grounds of policy the law refuses to protect the plaintiff or grants a privilege to the defendant.* I think that commonly malice, intent, and negligence mean only that the danger was manifest to a greater or less degree, under the circumstances known to the actor, although in some cases of privilege malice may mean an actual malevolent motive, and such a motive may take away a permission knowingly to inflict harm, which otherwise would be granted on this or that ground of dominant public good. But when I stated my view to a very eminent English judge the other day, he said: "You are discussing what the law ought to be; as the law is, you must show a right. A man is not liable for negligence unless he is subject to a duty." If our difference was more than a difference in words, or with regard to the proportion between the exceptions and the rule, then, in his opinion, liability for an act cannot be referred to the manifest tendency of the act to cause temporal damage in general as a sufficient explanation, but must be referred to the special nature of the damage, or must be derived from some special circumstances outside of the tendency of the act, for which no generalized explanation exists. I think that such a view is wrong, but it is familiar, and I dare say generally is accepted in England.

Everywhere the basis of principle is tradition, to such an extent that we even are in danger of making the rôle of history more important than it is. The other day Professor Ames wrote a learned article to show, among other things, that the common law did not recognize the defense of fraud in actions upon specialties, and the moral might seem to be that the personal character of that defense is due to its equitable origin. But if, as I have said, all contracts are formal, the difference is not merely historical, but theoretic, between defects of form which prevent a contract from being made, and mistaken motives which manifestly could not be considered in any system that we should call ra-

---

* An example of the law's refusing to protect the plaintiff is when he is interrupted by a stranger in the use of a valuable way, which he has traveled adversely for a week less than the period of prescription. A week later he will have gained a right, but now he is only a trespasser. Example of privilege I have given already. One of the best is competition in business.

tional except against one who was privy to those motives. It is not confined to specialties, but is of universal application. I ought to add that I do not suppose that Mr. Ames would disagree with what I suggest.

However, if we consider the law of contract, we find it full of history. The distinctions between debt, covenant, and assumpsit are merely historical. The classification of certain obligations to pay money, imposed by the law irrespective of any bargain as quasi contracts, is merely historical. The doctrine of consideration is merely historical. The effect given to a seal is to be explained by history alone. Consideration is a mere form. Is it a useful form? If so, why should it not be required in all contracts? A seal is a mere form, and is vanishing in the scroll and in enactments that a consideration must be given, seal or no seal. Why should any merely historical distinction be allowed to affect the rights and obligations of businessmen?

Since I wrote this discourse I have come on a very good example of the way in which tradition not only overrides rational policy, but overrides it after first having been misunderstood and having been given a new and broader scope than it had when it had a meaning. It is the settled law of England that a material alteration of a written contract by a party avoids it as against him. The doctrine is contrary to the general tendency of the law. We do not tell a jury that if a man ever has lied in one particular he is to be presumed to lie in all. Even if a man has tried to defraud, it seems no sufficient reason for preventing him from proving the truth. Objections of like nature in general go to the weight, not to the admissibility, of evidence. Moreover, this rule is irrespective of fraud, and is not confined to evidence. It is not merely that you cannot use the writing, but that the contract is at an end. What does this mean? The existence of a written contract depends on the fact that the offerer and offeree have interchanged their written expressions, not on the continued existence of those expressions. But in the case of a bond, the primitive notion was different. The contract was inseparable from the parchment. If a stranger destroyed it, or tore off the seal, or altered it, the obligee could not recover, however free from fault, because the defendant's contract, that is, the actual tangible bond which he had sealed, could not be produced in the form in which it bound him. About a hundred years ago Lord Kenyon undertook to use his reason on this tradition, as he sometimes did to the detriment of the law, and, not understanding it, said he could see no reason why what was true of a bond should not be true of other contracts. His decision happened to be right, as it concerned a promissory note, where again the common law regarded the contract as inseparable from the paper on which it was written, but the reasoning was general, and soon was extended to other written contracts, and various absurd and unreal grounds of policy were invented to account for the enlarged rule.

I trust that no one will understand me to be speaking with disrespect of the law, because I criticize it so freely. I venerate the law, and especially our system of law, as one of the vastest products of the human mind. No one knows better than I do the countless number of great intellects that have spent themselves in making some addition or improvement, the greatest of which is trifling when compared with the mighty whole. It has the final title to respect that it exists, that it is not a Hegelian dream, but a part of the lives of men. But one may criticize even what one reveres. Law is the business to which my life is devoted, and I should show less than devotion if I did not do what in me lies to improve it, and, when I perceive what seems to me the ideal of its future, if I hesitated to point it out and to press toward it with all my heart.

Perhaps I have said enough to show the part which the study of history necessarily plays in the intelligent study of the law as it is today. In the teaching of this school and at Cambridge it is in no danger of being undervalued. Mr. Bigelow here and Mr. Ames and Mr. Thayer there have made important contributions which will not be forgotten, and in England the recent history of early English law by Sir Frederick Pollock and Mr. Maitland has lent the subject an almost deceptive charm. We must beware of the pitfall of antiquarianism, and must remember that for our purposes our only interest in the past is for the light it throws upon the present. I look forward to a time when the part played by history in the explanation of dogma shall be very small, and instead of ingenious research we shall spend our energy on a study of the ends sought to be attained and the reasons for desiring them. As a step toward that ideal it seems to me that every lawyer ought to seek an understanding of economics. The present divorce between the schools of political economy and law seems to me an evidence of how much progress in philosophical study still remains to be made. In the present state of political economy, indeed, we come again upon history on a larger scale, but there we are called on to consider and weigh the ends of legislation, the means of attaining them, and the cost. We learn that for everything we have we give up something else, and we are taught to set the advantage we gain against the other advantage we lose, and to know what we are doing when we elect.

There is another study which sometimes is undervalued by the practical minded, for which I wish to say a good word, although I think a good deal of pretty poor stuff goes under that name. I mean the study of what is called jurisprudence. Jurisprudence, as I look at it, is simply law in its most generalized part. Every effort to reduce a case to a rule is an effort of jurisprudence, although the name as used in English is confined to the broadest rules and most fundamental conceptions. One mark of a great lawyer is that he sees the application of the broadest rules. There is a story of a Vermont justice of the peace before whom a suit was brought by one farmer against another for breaking a churn. The justice took time to consider, and then said that he had looked through the statutes and could find nothing about churns, and gave judgment for the defendant. The same state of mind is shown in all our common digests and textbooks. Applications of rudimentary rules of contract or tort are tucked away under the head of Railroads or Telegraphs or go to swell treatises on historical subdivisions such as Shipping or Equity, or are gathered under an arbitrary title which is thought likely to appeal to the practical mind, such as Mercantile Law. If a man goes into law it pays to be a master of it, and to be a master of it means to look straight through all the dramatic incidents and to discern the true basis for prophecy. Therefore it is well to have an accurate notion of what you mean by law, by a right, by a duty, by malice, intent, and negligence, by ownership, by possession, and so forth. I have in my mind cases in which the highest courts seem to me to have floundered because they had no clear ideas on some of these themes. I have illustrated their importance already. If a further illustration is wished, it may be found by reading the Appendix to Sir James Stephen's *Criminal Law* on the subject of possession, and then turning to Pollock and Wright's enlightened book. Sir James Stephen is not the only writer whose attempts to analyze legal ideas have been confused by striving for a useless quintessence of all systems, instead of an accurate anatomy of one. The trouble with Austin was that he did not know enough English law. But still it is a practical advantage to master Austin, and his predecessors, Hobbes and Bentham, and his worthy successors, Holland and Pollock. Sir Frederick Pollock's recent little book is touched with the felicity which marks all his works, and is wholly free from the perverting influence of Roman models.

The advice of the elders to young men is very apt to be as unreal as a list of the hundred best books. At least in my day I had my share of such counsels, and high among the unrealities I place the recommendation to study the Roman law. I assume that such advice means more than collecting a few Latin maxims with which to ornament the discourse—the purpose for which Lord Coke recommended Bracton. If that is all that is wanted, the title *De Regulis Juris Antiqui* can be read in an hour. I assume that, if it is well to study the Roman law, it is well to study it as a working system. That means mastering a set of technicalities more difficult and less understood than our own, and studying another course of history by which even more than our own the Roman law must be explained. If anyone doubts me, let him read Keller's *Der Römische Civil Process und die Actionen,* a treatise on the praetor's edict, Muirhead's most interesting *Historical Introduction to the Private Law of Rome,* and, to give him the best chance, Sohm's admirable *Institutes.* No. The way to gain a liberal view of your subject is not to read something else, but to get to the bottom of the subject itself. The means of doing that are, in the first place, to follow the existing body of dogma into its highest generalizations by the help of jurisprudence; next, to discover from history how it has come to be what it is; and, finally, so far as you can, to consider the ends which the several rules seek to accomplish, the reasons why those ends are desired, what is given up to gain them, and whether they are worth the price.

We have too little theory in the law rather than too much, especially on this final branch of study. When I was speaking of history, I mentioned larceny as an example to show how the law suffered from not having embodied in a clear form a rule which will accomplish its manifest purpose. In that case the trouble was due to the survival of forms coming from a time when a more limited purpose was entertained. Let me now give an example to show the practical importance, for the decision of actual cases, of understanding the reasons of the law, by taking an example from rules which, so far as I know, never have been explained or theorized about in any adequate way. I refer to statutes of limitation and the law of prescription. The end of such rules is obvious, but what is the justification for depriving a man of his rights, a pure evil as far as it goes, in consequence of the lapse of time? Sometimes the loss of evidence is referred to, but that is a secondary matter. Sometimes the desirability of peace, but why is peace more desirable after twenty years than before? It is increasingly likely to come without the aid of legislation. Sometimes it is said that, if a man neglects to enforce his rights, he cannot complain if, after a while, the law follows his example. Now if this is all that can be said about it, you probably will decide a case I am going to put, for the plaintiff; if you take the view which I shall suggest, you possibly will decide it for the defendant. A man is sued for trespass upon land, and justifies under a right of way. He proves that he has used the way openly and adversely for twenty years, but it turns out that the plaintiff had granted a license to a person whom he reasonably supposed to be the defendant's agent, although not so in fact, and therefore had assumed that the use of the way was permissive, in which case no right would be gained. Has the defendant gained a right or not? If his gaining it stands on the fault and neglect of the landowner in the ordinary sense, as seems commonly to be supposed, there has been no such neglect, and the right of way has not been acquired. But if I were the defendant's counsel, I should suggest that the foundation of the acquisition of rights by lapse of time is to be looked for in the position of the person who gains them, not in that of the loser. Sir Henry Maine has made it fashionable to connect the archaic notion of property with prescription. But the connection is further back than the first recorded history. It is in the nature of man's mind. A thing which you have enjoyed and used as your own for a long time, whether property or an opinion, takes root in your being and cannot be torn away without your resenting the act and trying to defend yourself, however you came by it. The law can ask no better justification than the deepest instincts of man. It is only by way of reply to the suggestion that you are disappointing the former owner, that you refer to his neglect having allowed the gradual dissociation between himself and what he claims, and the gradual association of it with another. If he knows that another is doing acts which on their face show that he is on the way toward establishing such an association, I should argue that in justice to that other he was bound at his peril to find out whether the other was acting under his permission, to see that he was warned, and if necessary, stopped.

I have been speaking about the study of the law, and I have said next to nothing of what commonly is talked about in that connection— textbooks and the case system, and all the machinery with which a student comes most immediately in contact. Nor shall I say anything about them. Theory is my subject, not practical details. The modes of teaching have been improved since my time, no doubt, but ability and industry will master the raw material with any mode. Theory is the most important part of the dogma of the law, as the architect is the most important man who takes part in the building of a house. The most important improvements of the last twenty-five years are improvements in theory. It is not to be feared as unpractical, for, to the competent, it simply means going to the bottom of the subject. For the incompetent, it sometimes is true, as has been said, that an interest in general ideas means an absence of particular knowledge. I remember in army days reading of a youth who, being examined for the lowest grade and being asked a question about squadron drill, answered that he never had considered the evolutions of less than ten thousand men. But the weak and foolish must be left to their folly. The danger is that the able and practical minded should look with indifference or distrust upon ideas the connection of which with their business is remote. I heard a story, the other day, of a man who had a valet to whom he paid high wages, subject to deduction for faults. One of his deductions was, "For lack of imagination, five dollars." The lack is not confined to valets. The object of ambition, power, generally presents itself nowadays in the form of money alone. Money is the most immediate form, and is a proper object of desire. "The fortune," said Rachel, "is the measure of the intelligence." That is a good text to waken people out of a fool's paradise. But as Hegel says,* "It is in the end not the appetite, but the opinion, which has to be satisfied." To an imagination of any scope the most far-reaching form of power is not money, it is the command of ideas. If you want great examples, read Mr. Leslie Stephen's *History of English Thought in the Eighteenth Century,* and see how a hundred years after his death the abstract speculations of Descartes had become a practical force controlling the conduct of men. Read the works of the great German jurists, and see how much more the world is governed today by Kant than by Bonaparte. We cannot all be Descartes or Kant, but we all want happiness. And happiness, I am sure from having known many successful men, cannot be won simply by being counsel for great corporations and having an income of fifty thousand dollars. An intellect great enough to win the prize needs other food besides success. The remoter and more general aspects of the law are those which give it universal interest. It is through them that you not only become a great master in your calling, but connect your subject with the universe and catch an echo of the infinite, a glimpse of its unfathomable process, a hint of the universal law.

* Phil. des Rechts, §190.

Lon L. Fuller

:

THE CASE OF THE SPELUNCEAN EXPLORERS

The defendants, having been indicted for the crime of murder, were convicted and sentenced to be hanged by the Court of General Instances of the County of Stowfield. They bring a petition of error before this court. The facts sufficiently appear in the opinion of the Chief Justice.

TRUEPENNY, C. J.: The four defendants are members of the Speluncean Society, an organization of amateurs interested in the exploration of caves. Early in May of 4299 they, in the company of Roger Whetmore, then also a member of the Society, penetrated into the interior of a limestone cavern of the type found in the Central Plateau of this Commonwealth. While they were in a position remote from the entrance to the cave, a landslide occurred. Heavy boulders fell in such a manner as to block completely the only known opening to the cave. When the men discovered their predicament they settled themselves near the obstructed entrance to wait until a rescue party should remove the detritus that prevented them from leaving their underground prison. On the failure of Whetmore and the defendants to return to their homes, the Secretary of the Society was notified by their families. It appears that the explorers had left indications at the headquarters of the Society concerning the location of the cave they proposed to visit. A rescue party was promptly dispatched to the spot.

The task of rescue proved one of overwhelming difficulty. It was necessary to supplement the forces of the original party by repeated increments of men and machines, which had to be conveyed at great expense to the remote and isolated region in which the cave was located. A huge temporary camp of workmen, engineers, geologists, and other experts was established. The work of removing the obstruction was several times frustrated by fresh landslides. In one of these, ten of the workmen engaged in clearing the entrance were killed. The treasury of the Speluncean Society was soon exhausted in the rescue effort, and the sum of eight hundred thousand frelars, raised partly by popular subscription and partly by legislative grant, was expended before the imprisoned men were rescued. Success was finally achieved on the thirty-second day after the men entered the cave.

Since it was known that the explorers had carried with them only scant provisions, and since it was also known that there was no animal or vegetable matter within the cave on which they might subsist, anxiety was early felt that they might meet death by starvation before access to them could be obtained. On the twentieth day of their imprisonment it was learned for the first time that they had taken with them into the cave a portable wireless machine capable of both sending and receiving messages. A similar machine was promptly installed in the rescue camp and oral communication established with the unfortunate men within the mountain. They asked to be informed how long a time would be required to release them. The engineers in charge of the project answered that at least ten days would be required even if no new landslides occurred. The explorers then asked if any physicians were present, and were placed in communication with a committee of medical experts. The imprisoned men described their condition and the rations they had taken with them, and asked for a medical opinion whether they would be likely to live without food for ten days longer. The chairman of the committee of physicians told them that there was little possibility of this. The wireless machine within the cave then remained silent for eight hours. When communication was re-established the men asked to speak again with the physicians. The chairman of the physicians' committee was placed before the apparatus, and Whetmore, speaking on behalf of himself and the defendants, asked whether they would be able to survive for ten days longer if they consumed the flesh of one of their number. The physicians' chairman reluctantly answered this question in the affirmative. Whetmore asked whether it would be advisable for them to cast lots to determine which of them should be eaten. None of the physicians present was willing to answer the question. Whetmore then asked if there were among the party a judge or other official of the government who would answer this question. None of those attached to the rescue camp was willing to assume the role of advisor in this matter. He then asked if any minister or priest would answer their question, and none was found who would do so. Thereafter no further messages were received from within the cave, and it was assumed (erroneously, it later appeared) that the electric batteries of the explorers' wireless machine had become exhausted. When the imprisoned men were finally released it was learned that on the twenty-third day after their entrance into the cave Whetmore had been killed and eaten by his companions.

From the testimony of the defendants, which was accepted by the jury, it appears that it was Whetmore who first proposed that they might find the nutriment without which survival was impossible in the flesh of one of their own number. It was also Whetmore who first proposed the use of some method of casting lots, calling the attention of the defendants to a pair of dice he happened to have with him. The defendants were at first reluctant to adopt so desperate a procedure, but after the conversations by wireless related above, they finally agreed on the plan proposed by Whetmore. After much discussion of the mathematical problems involved, agreement was finally reached on a method of determining the issue by the use of the dice.

Before the dice were cast, however, Whetmore declared that he withdrew from the arrangement, as he had decided on reflection to wait for another week before embracing an expedient so frightful and odious. The others charged him with a breach of faith and proceeded to cast the dice. When it came Whetmore's turn, the dice were cast for him by one of the defendants, and he was asked to declare any objections he might have to the fairness of the throw. He stated that he had no such objections. The throw went against him, and he was then put to death and eaten by his companions.

After the rescue of the defendants, and after they had completed a stay in a hospital where they underwent a course of treatment for malnutrition and shock, they were indicted for the murder of Roger Whetmore. At the trial, after the testimony had been concluded, the foreman of the jury (a lawyer by profession) inquired of the court whether the jury might not find a special verdict, leaving it to the court to say whether on the facts as found the defendants were guilty. After some discussion, both the Prosecutor and counsel for the defendants indicated their acceptance of this procedure, and it was adopted by the court. In a lengthy special verdict the jury found the facts as I have related them above, and found further that if on these facts the defendants were guilty of the crime charged against them, then they found the defendants guilty. On the basis of this verdict, the trial judge ruled that the defendants were guilty of murdering Roger Whetmore. The judge then sentenced them to be hanged, the law of our Commonwealth permitting him no discretion with respect to the penalty to be imposed. After the release of the jury, its members joined in a communication to the Chief Executive asking that the sentence be commuted to an imprisonment of six months. The trial judge addressed a similar communication to the Chief Executive. As yet no action with respect to these pleas has been taken, as the Chief Executive is apparently awaiting our disposition of this petition of error.

It seems to me that in dealing with this extraordinary case the jury and the trial judge followed a course that was not only fair and wise, but the only course that was open to them under the law. The language of our statute is well known: "Whoever shall willfully take the life of another shall be punished by death." N.C.S.A. (N.S.) §12-A. This statute permits of no exception applicable to this case, however our sympathies may incline us to make allowance for the tragic situation in which these men found themselves.

In a case like this the principle of executive clemency seems admirably suited to mitigate the rigors of the law, and I propose to my colleagues that we follow the example of the jury and the trial judge by joining in the communications they have addressed to the Chief Executive. There is every reason to believe that these requests for clemency will be heeded, coming as they do from those who have studied the case and had an opportunity to become thoroughly acquainted with all its circumstances. It is highly improbable that the Chief Executive would deny these requests unless he were himself to hold hearings at least as extensive as those involved in the trial below, which lasted for three months. The holding of such hearings (which would virtually amount to a retrial of the case) would scarcely be compatible with the function of the Executive as it is usually conceived. I think we may therefore assume that some form of clemency will be extended to these defendants. If this is done, then justice will be accomplished without impairing either the letter or spirit of our statutes and without offering any encouragement for the disregard of law.

FOSTER, J.: I am shocked that the Chief Justice, in an effort to escape the embarrassments of this tragic case, should have adopted, and should have proposed to his colleagues, an expedient at once so sordid and so obvious. I believe something more is on trial in this case than the fate of these unfortunate explorers; that is the law of our Commonwealth. If this court declares that under our law these men have committed a crime, then our law is itself convicted in the tribunal of common sense, no matter what happens to the individuals involved in this petition of error. For us to assert that the law we uphold and expound compels us to a conclusion we are ashamed of, and from which we can only escape by appealing to a dispensation resting within the personal whim of the Executive, seems to me to amount to an admission that the law of this Commonwealth no longer pretends to incorporate justice.

For myself, I do not believe that our law compels the monstrous conclusion that these men are murderers. I believe, on the contrary, that it declares them to be innocent of any crime. I rest this conclusion on two independent grounds, either of which is of itself sufficient to justify the acquittal of these defendants.

The first of these grounds rests on a premise that may arouse opposition until it has been examined candidly. I take the view that the enacted or positive law of this Commonwealth, including all of its statutes and precedents, is inapplicable to this case, and that the case is governed instead by what ancient writers in Europe and America called "the law of nature."

This conclusion rests on the proposition that our positive law is predicated on the possibility of men's coexistence in society. When a situation arises in which the coexistence of men becomes impossible, then a condition that underlies all of our precedents and statutes has ceased to exist. When that condition disappears, then it is my opinion that the force of our positive law disappears with it. We are not accustomed to applying the maxim *cessante ratione legis, cessat et ipsa lex* to the whole of our enacted law, but I believe that this is a case where the maxim should be so applied.

The proposition that all positive law is based on the possibility of men's coexistence has a strange sound, not because the truth it contains is strange, but simply because it is a truth so obvious and pervasive that we seldom have occasion to give words to it. Like the air we breathe, it so pervades our environment that we forget that it exists until we are suddenly deprived of it. Whatever particular objects may be sought by the various branches of our law, it is apparent on reflection that all of them are directed toward facilitating and improving men's coexistence and regulating with fairness and equity the relations of their life in common. When the assumption that men may live together loses its truth, as it obviously did in this extraordinary situation where life only became possible by the taking of life, then the basic premises underlying our whole legal order have lost their meaning and force.

Had the tragic events of this case taken place a mile beyond the territorial limits of our Commonwealth, no one would pretend that our law was applicable to them. We recognize that jurisdiction rests on a territorial basis. The grounds of this principle are by no means obvious and are seldom examined. I take it that this principle is supported by an assumption that it is feasible to impose a single legal order upon a group of men only if they live together within the confines of a given area of the earth's surface. The premise that men shall coexist in a group underlies, then, the territorial principle, as it does all of law. Now I contend that a case may be removed morally from the force of a legal order, as well as geographically. If we look to the purposes of law and government, and to the premises underlying our positive law, these men when they made their fateful decision were as remote from our legal order as if they had been a thousand miles beyond our boundaries. Even in a physical sense, their underground prison was separated from our courts and writ-servers by a solid curtain of rock that could be removed only after the most extraordinary expenditures of time and effort.

I conclude, therefore, that at the time Roger Whetmore's life was ended by these defendants, they were, to use the quaint language of nineteenth-century writers, not in a "state of civil society," but in a "state of nature." This has the consequence that the law applicable to them is not the enacted and established law of this Commonwealth, but the law derived from those principles that were appropriate to their condition. I have no hesitancy in saying that under those principles they were guiltless of any crime.

What these men did was done in pursuance of an agreement accepted by all of them and first proposed by Whetmore himself. Since it was apparent that their extraordinary predicament made inapplicable the usual principles that regulate men's relations with one another, it was necessary for them to draw, as it were, a new charter of government appropriate to the situation in which they found themselves.

It has from antiquity been recognized that the most basic principle of law or government is to be found in the notion of contract or agreement. Ancient thinkers, especially during the period from 1600 to 1900, used to base government itself on a supposed original social compact. Skeptics pointed out that this theory contradicted the known facts of history, and that there was no scientific evidence to support the notion that any government was ever founded in the manner supposed by the theory. Moralists replied that, if the compact was a fiction from a historical point of view, the notion of compact or agreement furnished the only ethical justification on which the powers of government, which include that of taking life, could be rested. The powers of government can only be justified morally on the ground that these are powers that reasonable men would agree upon and accept if they were faced with the necessity of constructing anew some order to make their life in common possible.

Fortunately, our Commonwealth is not bothered by the perplexities that beset the ancients. We know as a matter of historical truth that our government was founded upon a contract or free accord of men. The archeological proof is conclusive that in the first period following the Great Spiral the survivors of that holocaust voluntarily came together and drew up a charter of government. Sophistical writers have raised questions as to the power of those remote contractors to bind future generations, but the fact remains that our government traces itself back in an unbroken line to that original charter.

If, therefore, our hangmen have the power to end men's lives, if our sheriffs have the power to put delinquent tenants in the street, if our police have the power to incarcerate the inebriated reveler, these powers find their moral justification in that original compact of our forefathers. If we can find no higher source for our legal order, what higher source should we expect these starving unfortunates to find for the order they adopted for themselves?

I believe that the line of argument I have just expounded permits of no rational answer. I realize that it will probably be received with a certain discomfort by many who read this opinion, who will be inclined to suspect that some hidden sophistry must underlie a demonstration that leads to so many unfamiliar conclusions. The source of this discomfort is, however, easy to identify. The usual conditions of human existence incline us to think of human life as an absolute value, not to be sacrificed under any circumstances. There is much that is fictitious about this conception even when it is applied to the ordinary relations of society. We have an illustration of this truth in the very case before us. Ten workmen were killed in the process of removing the rocks from the opening to the cave. Did not the engineers and government officials who directed the rescue effort know that the operations they were undertaking were dangerous and involved a serious risk to the lives of the workmen executing them? If it was proper that these ten lives should be sacrificed to save the lives of five imprisoned explorers, why then are we told it was wrong for these explorers to carry out an arrangement which would save four lives at the cost of one?

Every highway, every tunnel, every building we project involves a risk to human life. Taking these projects in the aggregate, we can calculate with some precision how many deaths the construction of them will require; statisticians can tell you the average cost in human lives of a thousand miles of a four-lane concrete highway. Yet we deliberately and knowingly incur and pay this cost on the assumption that the values obtained for those who survive outweigh the loss. If these things can be said of a society functioning above ground in a normal and ordinary manner, what shall we say of the supposed absolute value of a human life in the desperate situation in which these defendants and their companion Whetmore found themselves?

This concludes the exposition of the first ground of my decision. My second ground proceeds by rejecting hypothetically all the premises on which I have so far proceeded. I concede for purposes of argument that I am wrong in saying that the situation of these men removed them from the effect of our positive law, and I assume that the Consolidated Statutes have the power to penetrate five hundred feet of rock and to impose themselves upon these starving men huddled in their underground prison.

Now it is, of course, perfectly clear that these men did an act that violates the literal wording of the statute which declares that he who "shall willfully take the life of another" is a murderer. But one of the most ancient bits of legal wisdom is the saying that a man may break the letter of the law without breaking the law itself. Every proposition of positive law, whether contained in a statute or a judicial precedent, is to be interpreted reasonably, in the light of its evident purpose. This is a truth so elementary that it is hardly necessary to expatiate on it. Illustrations of its application are numberless and are to be found in every branch of the law. In *Commonwealth v. Staymore* the defendant was convicted under a statute making it a crime to leave one's car parked in certain areas for a period longer than two hours. The defendant had attempted to remove his car, but was prevented from doing so because the streets were obstructed by a political demonstration in which he took no part and which he had no reason to anticipate. His conviction was set aside by this court, although his case fell squarely within the wording of the statute. Again, in *Fehler v. Neegas* there was before this court for construction a statute in which the word "not" had plainly been transposed from its intended position in the final and most crucial section of the act. This transposition was contained in all the successive drafts of the act, where it was apparently overlooked by the draftsmen and sponsors of the legislation. No one was able to prove how the error came about, yet it was apparent that, taking account of the contents of the statute as a whole, an error had been made, since a literal reading of the final clause rendered it inconsistent with everything that had gone before and with the object of the enactment as stated in its preamble. This court refused to accept a literal interpretation of the statute, and in effect rectified its language by reading the word "not" into the place where it was evidently intended to go.

The statute before us for interpretation has never been applied literally. Centuries ago it was established that a killing in self-defense is excused. There is nothing in the wording of the statute that suggests this exception. Various attempts have been made to reconcile the legal treatment of self-defense with the words of the statute, but in my opinion these are all merely ingenious sophistries. The truth is that the exception in favor of self-defense cannot be reconciled with the *words* of the statute, but only with its *purpose*.

The true reconciliation of the excuse of self-defense with the statute making it a crime to kill another is to be found in the following line of reasoning. One of the principal objects underlying any criminal legislation is that of deterring men from crime. Now it is apparent that if it were declared to be the law that a killing in self-defense is murder such a rule could not operate in a deterrent manner. A man whose life is threatened will repel his aggressor, whatever the law may say.

Looking therefore to the broad purposes of criminal legislation, we may safely declare that this statute was not intended to apply to cases of self-defense.

When the rationale of the excuse of self-defense is thus explained, it becomes apparent that precisely the same reasoning is applicable to the case at bar. If in the future any group of men ever find themselves in the tragic predicament of these defendants, we may be sure that their decision whether to live or die will not be controlled by the contents of our criminal code. Accordingly, if we read this statute intelligently it is apparent that it does not apply to this case. The withdrawal of this situation from the effect of the statute, is justified by precisely the same considerations that were applied by our predecessors in office centuries ago to the case of self-defense.

There are those who raise the cry of judicial usurpation whenever a court, after analyzing the purpose of a statute, gives to its words a meaning that is not at once apparent to the casual reader who has not studied the statute closely or examined the objectives it seeks to attain. Let me say emphatically that I accept without reservation the proposition that this court is bound by the statutes of our Commonwealth and that it exercises its powers in subservience to the duly expressed will of the Chamber of Representatives. The line of reasoning I have applied above raises no question of fidelity to enacted law, though it may possibly raise a question of the distinction between intelligent and unintelligent fidelity. No superior wants a servant who lacks the capacity to read between the lines. The stupidest housemaid knows that when she is told "to peel the soup and skim the potatoes" her mistress does not mean what she says. She also knows that when her master tells her to "drop everything and come running" he has overlooked the possibility that she is at the moment in the act of rescuing the baby from the rain barrel. Surely we have a right to expect the same modicum of intelligence from the judiciary. The correction of obvious legislative errors or oversights is not to supplant the legislative will, but to make that will effective.

I therefore conclude that on any aspect under which this case may be viewed these defendants are innocent of the crime of murdering Roger Whetmore, and that the conviction should be set aside.

TATTING, J.: In the discharge of my duties as a justice of this court, I am usually able to dissociate the emotional and intellectual sides of my reactions, and to decide the case before me entirely on the basis of the latter. In passing on this tragic case I find that my usual resources fail me. On the emotional side I find myself torn between sympathy for these men and a feeling of abhorrence and disgust at the monstrous act they committed. I had hoped that I would be able to put these contradictory emotions to one side as irrelevant, and to decide the case on the basis of a convincing and logical demonstration of the result demanded by our law. Unfortunately, this deliverance has not been vouchsafed me.

As I analyze the opinion just rendered by my brother Foster, I find that it is shot through with contradictions and fallacies. Let us begin with his first proposition: these men were not subject to our law because they were not in a "state of civil society" but in a "state of nature." I am not clear why this is so, whether it is because of the thickness of the rock that imprisoned them, or because they were hungry, or because they had set up a "new charter of government" by which the usual rules of law were to be supplanted by a throw of the dice. Other difficulties intrude themselves. If these men passed from the jurisdiction of our law to that of "the law of nature," at what moment did this occur? Was it when the entrance to the cave was blocked, or when the threat of starvation reached a certain undefined degree of intensity, or when the agreement for the throwing of the dice was made? These uncertainties in the doctrine proposed by my brother are capable of producing real difficulties. Suppose, for example, one of these men had had his twenty-first birthday while he was imprisoned within the mountain. On what date would we have to consider that he had attained his majority—when he reached the age of twenty-one, at which time he was, by hypothesis, removed from the effects of our law, or only when he was released from the cave and became again subject to what my brother calls our "positive law"? These difficulties may seem fanciful, yet they only serve to reveal the fanciful nature of the doctrine that is capable of giving rise to them.

But it is not necessary to explore these niceties further to demonstrate the absurdity of my brother's position. Mr. Justice Foster and I are the appointed judges of a court of the Commonwealth of Newgarth, sworn and empowered to administer the laws of that Commonwealth. By what authority do we resolve ourselves into a Court of Nature? If these men were indeed under the law of nature, whence comes our authority to expound and apply that law? Certainly *we* are not in a state of nature.

Let us look at the contents of this code of nature that my brother proposes we adopt as our own and apply to this case. What a topsy-turvy and odious code it is! It is a code in which the law of contracts is more fundamental than the law of murder. It is a code under which a man may make a valid agreement empowering his fellows to eat his own body. Under the provisions of this code, furthermore, such an agreement once made is irrevocable, and if one of the parties attempts to withdraw, the others may take the law into their own hands and enforce the contract by violence—for though my brother passes over in convenient silence the effect of Whetmore's withdrawal, this is the necessary implication of his argument.

The principles my brother expounds contain other implications that cannot be tolerated. He argues that when the defendants set upon Whetmore and killed him (we know not how, perhaps by pounding him with stones) they were only exercising the rights conferred upon them by their bargain. Suppose, however, that Whetmore had had concealed upon his person a revolver, and that when he saw the defendants about to slaughter him he had shot them to death in order to save his own life. My brother's reasoning applied to these facts would make Whetmore out to be a murderer, since the excuse of self-defense would have to be denied to him. If his assailants were acting rightfully in seeking to bring about his death, then of course he could no more plead the excuse that he was defending his own life than could a condemned prisoner who struck down the executioner lawfully attempting to place the noose about his neck.

All of these considerations make it impossible for me to accept the first part of my brother's argument. I can neither accept his notion that these men were under a code of nature which this court was bound to apply to them, nor can I accept the odious and perverted rules that he would read into that code. I come now to the second part of my brother's opinion, in which he seeks to show that the defendants did not violate the provisions of N.C.S.A. (N.S.) §12-A. Here the way, instead of being clear, becomes for me misty and ambiguous, though my brother seems unaware of the difficulties that inhere in his demonstrations.

The gist of my brother's argument may be stated in the following terms: No statute, whatever its language, should be applied in a way that contradicts its purpose. One of the purposes of any criminal statute is to deter. The application of the statute making it a crime to kill another to the peculiar facts of this case would contradict this purpose, for it is impossible to believe that the contents of the criminal code could operate in a deterrent manner on men faced with the alternative of life or death. The reasoning by which this exception is read into the statute is, my brother observes, the same as that which is applied in order to provide the excuse of self-defense.

On the face of things this demonstration seems very convincing indeed. My brother's interpretation of the rationale of the excuse of self-defense is in fact supported by a decision of this court, *Commonwealth v. Parry,* a precedent I happened to encounter in my research on this case. Though *Commonwealth v. Parry* seems generally to have been overlooked in the texts and subsequent decisions, it supports unambiguously the interpretation my brother has put upon the excuse of self-defense.

Now let me outline briefly, however, the perplexities that assail me when I examine my brother's demonstration more closely. It is true that a statute should be applied in the light of its purpose, and that *one* of the purposes of criminal legislation is recognized to be deterrence. The difficulty is that other purposes are also ascribed to the law of crimes. It has been said that one of its objects is to provide an orderly outlet for the instinctive human demand for retribution. *Commonwealth v. Scape.* It has also been said that its object is the rehabilitation of the wrongdoer. *Commonwealth v. Makeover.* Other theories have been propounded. Assuming that we must interpret a statute in the light of its purpose, what are we to do when it has many purposes or when its purposes are disputed?

A similar difficulty is presented by the fact that although there is authority for my brother's interpretation of the excuse of self-defense, there is other authority which assigns to that excuse a different rationale. Indeed, until I happened on *Commonwealth v. Parry* I had never heard of the explanation given by my brother. The taught doctrine of our law schools, memorized by generations of law students, runs in the following terms: The statute concerning murder requires a "willful" act. The man who acts to repel an aggressive threat to his own life does not act "willfully," but in response to an impulse deeply ingrained in human nature. I suspect that there is hardly a lawyer in this Commonwealth who is not familiar with this line of reasoning, especially since the point is a great favorite of the bar examiners.

Now the familiar explanation for the excuse of self-defense just expounded obviously cannot be applied by analogy to the facts of this case. These men acted not only "willfully" but with great deliberation and after hours of discussing what they should do. Again we encounter a forked path, with one line of reasoning leading us in one direction and another in a direction that is exactly the opposite. This perplexity is in this case compounded, as it were, for we have to set off one explanation incorporated in a virtually unknown precedent of this court, against another explanation, which forms a part of the taught legal tradition of our law schools, but which, so far as I know, has never been adopted in any judicial decision.

I recognize the relevance of the precedents cited by my brother concerning the displaced "not" and the defendant who parked overtime. But what are we to do with one of the landmarks of our jurisprudence, which again my brother passes over in silence? This is *Commonwealth v. Valjean*. Though the case is somewhat obscurely reported, it appears that the defendant was indicted for the larceny of a loaf of bread, and offered as a defense that he was in a condition approaching starvation. The court refused to accept this defense. If hunger cannot justify the theft of wholesome and natural food, how can it justify the killing and eating of a man? Again, if we look at the thing in terms of deterrence, is it likely that a man will starve to death to avoid a jail sentence for the theft of a loaf of bread? My brother's demonstrations would compel us to overrule *Commonwealth v. Valjean,* and many other precedents that have been built on that case.

Again, I have difficulty in saying that no deterrent effect whatever could be attributed to a decision that these men were guilty of murder. The stigma of the word "murderer" is such that it is quite likely, I believe, that if these men had known that their act was deemed by the law to be murder they would have waited for a few days at least before carrying out their plan. During that time some unexpected relief might have come. I realize that this observation only reduces the distinction to a matter of degree, and does not destroy it altogether. It is certainly true that the element of deterrence would be less in this case than is normally involved in the application of the criminal law.

There is still a further difficulty in my brother Foster's proposal to read an exception into the statute to favor this case, though again a difficulty not even intimated in his opinion. What shall be the scope of this exception? Here the men cast lots and the victim was himself originally a party to the agreement. What would we have to decide if Whetmore had refused from the beginning to participate in the plan? Would a majority be permitted to overrule him? Or, suppose that no plan were adopted at all and the others simply conspired to bring about Whetmore's death, justifying their act by saying that he was in the weakest condition. Or again, that a plan of selection was followed but one based on a different justification than the one adopted here, as if the others were atheists and insisted that Whetmore should die because he was the only one who believed in an afterlife. These illustrations could be multiplied, but enough have been suggested to reveal what a quagmire of hidden difficulties my brother's reasoning contains.

Of course I realize on reflection that I may be concerning myself with a problem that will never arise, since it is unlikely that any group of men will ever again be brought to commit the dread act that was involved here. Yet, on still further reflection, even if we are certain that no similar case will arise again, do not the illustrations I have given show the lack of any coherent and rational principle in the rule my brother proposes? Should not the soundness of a principle be tested by the conclusions it entails, without reference to the accidents of later litigational history? Still, if this is so, why is it that we of this court so often discuss the question whether we are likely to have later occasion to apply a principle urged for the solution of the case before us? Is this a situation where a line of reasoning not originally proper has become sanctioned by precedent, so that we are permitted to apply it and may even be under an obligation to do so?

The more I examine this case and think about it, the more deeply I become involved. My mind becomes entangled in the meshes of the very nets I throw out for my own rescue. I find that almost every consideration that bears on the decision of the case is counterbalanced by an opposing consideration leading in the opposite direction. My brother Foster has not furnished to me, nor can I discover for myself, any formula capable of resolving the equivocations that beset me on all sides.

I have given this case the best thought of which I am capable. I have scarcely slept since it was argued before us. When I feel myself inclined to accept the view of my brother Foster, I am repelled by a feeling that his arguments are intellectually unsound and approach mere rationalization. On the other hand, when I incline toward upholding the conviction, I am struck by the absurdity of directing that these men be put to death when their lives have been saved at the cost of the lives of ten heroic workmen. It is to me a matter of regret that the Prosecutor saw fit to ask for an indictment for murder. If we had a provision in our statutes making it a crime to eat human flesh, that would have been a more appropriate charge. If no other charge suited to the facts of this case could be brought against the defendants, it would have been wiser, I think, not to have indicted them at all. Unfortunately, however, the men have been indicted and tried, and we have therefore been drawn into this unfortunate affair.

Since I have been wholly unable to resolve the doubts that beset me about the law of this case, I am with regret announcing a step that is, I believe, unprecedented in the history of this tribunal. I declare my withdrawal from the decision of this case.

KEEN, J.: I should like to begin by setting to one side two questions which are not before this court.

The first of these is whether executive clemency should be extended to these defendants if the conviction is affirmed. Under our system of government, that is a question for the Chief Executive, not for us. I therefore disapprove of that passage in the opinion of the Chief Justice in which he in effect gives instructions to the Chief Executive as to what he should do in this case and suggests that some impropriety will attach if these instructions are not heeded. This is a confusion of governmental functions—a confusion of which the judiciary should be the last to be guilty. I wish to state that if I were the Chief Executive I would go farther in the direction of clemency than the pleas addressed to him propose. I would pardon these men altogether, since I believe that they have already suffered enough to pay for any offense they may have committed. I want it to be understood that this remark is made in my capacity as a private citizen who by the accident of his office happens to have acquired an intimate acquaintance with the facts of this case. In the discharge of my duties as judge, it is neither my function to address directions to the Chief Executive, nor to take into account what he may or may not do, in reaching my own decision, which must be controlled entirely by the law of this Commonwealth.

The second question that I wish to put to one side is that of deciding whether what these men did was "right" or "wrong," "wicked" or "good." That is also a question that is irrelevant to the discharge of my office as a judge sworn to apply, not my conceptions of morality, but the law of the land. In putting this question to one side I think I can also safely dismiss without comment the first and more poetic portion of my brother Foster's opinion. The element of fantasy contained in the arguments developed there has been sufficiently revealed in my brother Tatting's somewhat solemn attempt to take those arguments seriously.

The sole question before us for decision is whether these defendants did, within the meaning of N.C.S.A. (N.S.) §12-A, willfully take the life of Roger Whetmore. The exact language of the statute is as follows: "Whoever shall willfully take the life of another shall be punished by death." Now I should suppose that any candid observer, content to extract from these words their natural meaning, would concede at once that these defendants did "willfully take the life" of Roger Whetmore.

Whence arise all the difficulties of the case, then, and the necessity for so many pages of discussion about what ought to be so obvious? The difficulties, in whatever tortured form they may present themselves, all trace back to a single source, and that is a failure to distinguish the legal from the moral aspects of this case. To put it bluntly, my brothers do not like the fact that the written law requires the conviction of these defendants. Neither do I, but unlike my brothers I respect the obligations of an office that requires me to put my personal predilections out of my mind when I come to interpret and apply the law of this Commonwealth.

Now, of course, my brother Foster does not admit that he is actuated by a personal dislike of the written law. Instead he develops a familiar line of argument according to which the court may disregard the express language of a statute when something not contained in the statute itself, called its "purpose," can be employed to justify the result the court considers proper. Because this is an old issue between myself and my colleague, I should like, before discussing his particular application of the argument to the facts of this case, to say something about the historical background of this issue and its implications for law and government generally.

There was a time in this Commonwealth when judges did in fact legislate very freely, and all of us know that during that period some or our statutes were rather thoroughly made over by the judiciary. That was a time when the accepted principles of political science did not designate with any certainty the rank and function of the various arms of the state. We all know the tragic issue of that uncertainty in the brief civil war that arose out of the conflict between the judiciary, on the one hand, and the executive and the legislature, on the other.

There is no need to recount here the factors that contributed to that unseemly struggle for power, though they included the unrepresentative character of the Chamber, resulting from a division of the country into election districts that no longer accorded with the actual distribution of the population, and the forceful personality and wide popular following of the then Chief Justice. It is enough to observe that those days are behind us, and that in place of the uncertainty that then reigned we now have a clear-cut principle, which is the supremacy of the legislative branch of our government. From that principle flows the obligation of the judiciary to enforce faithfully the written law, and to interpret that law in accordance with its plain meaning without reference to our personal desires or our individual conceptions of justice. I am not concerned with the question whether the principle that forbids the judicial revision of statutes is right or wrong, desirable or undesirable; I observe merely that this principle has become a tacit premise underlying the whole of the legal and governmental order I am sworn to administer.

Yet though the principle of the supremacy of the legislature has been accepted in theory for centuries, such is the tenacity of professional tradition and the force of fixed habits of thought that many of the judiciary have still not accommodated themselves to the restricted role which the new order imposes on them. My brother Foster is one of that group; his way of dealing with statutes is exactly that of a judge living in the 3900's.

We are all familiar with the process by which the judicial reform of disfavored legislative enactments is accomplished. Anyone who has followed the written opinions of Mr. Justice Foster will have had an opportunity to see it at work in every branch of the law. I am personally so familiar with the process that in the event of my brother's incapacity I am sure I could write a satisfactory opinion for him without any prompting whatever, beyond being informed whether he liked the effect of the terms of the statute as applied to the case before him.

The process of judicial reform requires three steps. The first of these is to divine some single "purpose" which the statute serves. This is done although not one statute in a hundred has any such single purpose, and although the objectives of nearly every statute are differently interpreted by the different classes of its sponsors. The second step is to discover that a mythical being called "the legislator," in the pursuit of this imagined "purpose," overlooked something or left some gap or imperfection in his work. Then comes the final and most refreshing part of the task, which is, of course, to fill in the blank thus created. *Quod erat faciendum.*

My brother Foster's penchant for finding holes in statutes reminds one of the story told by an ancient author about the man who ate a pair of shoes. Asked how he liked them, he replied that the part he liked best was the holes. That is the way my brother feels about statutes; the more holes they have in them the better he likes them. In short, he doesn't like statutes.

One could not wish for a better case to illustrate the specious nature of this gap-filling process than the one before us. My brother thinks he knows exactly what was sought when men made murder a crime, and that was something he calls "deterrence." My brother Tatting has already shown how much is passed over in that interpretation. But I think the trouble goes deeper. I doubt very much whether our statute making murder a crime really has a "purpose" in any ordinary sense of the term. Primarily, such a statute reflects a deeply felt human conviction that murder is wrong and that something should be done to the man who commits it. If we were forced to be more articulate about the matter, we would probably take refuge in the more sophisticated theories of the criminologists, which, of course, were certainly not in the minds of those who drafted our statute. We might also observe that men will do their own work more effectively and live happier lives if they are protected against the threat of violent assault. Bearing in mind that the victims of murders are often unpleasant people, we might add some suggestion that the matter of disposing of undesirables is not a function suited to private enterprise, but should be a state monopoly. All of which reminds me of the attorney who once argued before us that a statute licensing physicians was a good thing because it would lead to lower life insurance rates by lifting the level of general health. There is such a thing as overexplaining the obvious.

If we do not know the purpose of § 12-A, how can we possibly say there is a "gap" in it? How can we know what its draftsmen thought about the question of killing men in order to eat them? My brother Tatting has revealed an understandable, though perhaps slightly exaggerated revulsion to cannibalism. How do we know that his remote ancestors did not feel the same revulsion to an even higher degree? Anthropologists say that the dread felt for a forbidden act may be increased by the fact that the conditions of a tribe's life create special temptations toward it, as incest is most severely condemned among those

whose village relations make it most likely to occur. Certainly the period following the Great Spiral was one that had implicit in it temptations to anthropophagy. Perhaps it was for that very reason that our
ancestors expressed their prohibition in so broad and unqualified a
form. All of this is conjecture, of course, but it remains abundantly
clear that neither I nor my brother Foster knows what the "purpose"
of § 12-A is.

Considerations similar to those I have just outlined are also applicable to the exception in favor of self-defense, which plays so large a
role in the reasoning of my brothers Foster and Tatting. It is of course
true that in *Commonwealth v. Parry* an obiter dictum justified this exception on the assumption that the purpose of criminal legislation is to
deter. It may well also be true that generations of law students have
been taught that the true explanation of the exception lies in the fact
that a man who acts in self-defense does not act "willfully," and that
the same students have passed their bar examinations by repeating
what their professors told them. These last observations I could dismiss,
of course, as irrelevant for the simple reason that professors and bar
examiners have not as yet any commission to make our laws for us.
But again the real trouble lies deeper. As in dealing with the statute, so
in dealing with the exception, the question is not the conjectural *purpose* of the rule, but its *scope*. Now the scope of the exception in favor
of self-defense as it has been applied by this court is plain: it applies
to cases of resisting an aggressive threat to the party's own life. It is
therefore too clear for argument that this case does not fall within the
scope of the exception, since it is plain that Whetmore made no threat
against the lives of these defendants.

The essential shabbiness of my brother Foster's attempt to cloak his
remaking of the written law with an air of legitimacy comes tragically
to the surface in my brother Tatting's opinion. In that opinion Justice
Tatting struggles manfully to combine his colleague's loose moralisms
with his own sense of fidelity to the written law. The issue of this struggle could only be that which occurred, a complete default in the discharge of the judicial function. You simply cannot apply a statute as it
is written and remake it to meet your own wishes at the same time.

Now I know that the line of reasoning I have developed in this opinion will not be acceptable to those who look only at the immediate
effects of a decision and ignore the long-run implications of an assumption by the judiciary of a power of dispensation. A hard decision is

never a popular decision. Judges have been celebrated in literature for their sly prowess in devising some quibble by which a litigant could be deprived of his rights where the public thought it was wrong for him to assert those rights. But I believe that judicial dispensation does more harm in the long run than hard decisions. Hard cases may even have a certain moral value by bringing home to the people their own responsibilities toward the law that is ultimately their creation, and by reminding them that there is no principle of personal grace that can relieve the mistakes of their representatives.

Indeed, I will go farther and say that not only are the principles I have been expounding those which are soundest for our present conditions, but that we would have inherited a better legal system from our forefathers if those principles had been observed from the beginning. For example, with respect to the excuse of self-defense, if our courts had stood steadfast on the language of the statute, the result would undoubtedly have been a legislative revision of it. Such a revision would have drawn on the assistance of natural philosophers and psychologists, and the resulting regulation of the matter would have had an understandable and rational basis, instead of the hodgepodge of verbalisms and metaphysical distinctions that have emerged from the judicial and professorial treatment.

These concluding remarks are, of course, beyond any duties that I have to discharge with relation to this case, but I include them here because I feel deeply that my colleagues are insufficiently aware of the dangers implicit in the conceptions of the judicial office advocated by my brother Foster.

I conclude that the conviction should be affirmed.

HANDY, J.: I have listened with amazement to the tortured ratiocinations to which this simple case has given rise. I never cease to wonder at my colleagues' ability to throw an obscuring curtain of legalisms about every issue presented to them for decision. We have heard this afternoon learned disquisitions on the distinction between positive law and the law of nature, the language of the statute and the purpose of the statute, judicial functions and executive functions, judicial legislation and legislative legislation. My only disappointment was that someone did not raise the question of the legal nature of the bargain struck in the cave—whether it was unilateral or bilateral, and whether Whetmore could not be considered as having revoked an offer prior to action taken thereunder.

What have all these things to do with the case? The problem before us is what we, as officers of the government, ought to do with these defendants. That is a question of practical wisdom, to be exercised in a context, not of abstract theory, but of human realities. When the case is approached in this light, it becomes, I think, one of the easiest to decide that has ever been argued before this court.

Before stating my own conclusions about the merits of the case, I should like to discuss briefly some of the more fundamental issues involved—issues on which my colleagues and I have been divided ever since I have been on the bench.

I have never been able to make my brothers see that government is a human affair, and that men are ruled, not by words on paper or by abstract theories, but by other men. They are ruled well when their rulers understand the feelings and conceptions of the masses. They are ruled badly when that understanding is lacking.

Of all branches of the government, the judiciary is the most likely to lose its contact with the common man. The reasons for this are, of course, fairly obvious. Where the masses react to a situation in terms of a few salient features, we pick into little pieces every situation presented to us. Lawyers are hired by both sides to analyze and dissect. Judges and attorneys vie with one another to see who can discover the greatest number of difficulties and distinctions in a single set of facts. Each side tries to find cases, real or imagined, that will embarrass the demonstrations of the other side. To escape this embarrassment, still further distinctions are invented and imported into the situation. When a set of facts has been subjected to this kind of treatment for a sufficient time, all the life and juice have gone out of it and we have left a handful of dust.

Now I realize that wherever you have rules and abstract principles lawyers are going to be able to make distinctions. To some extent the sort of thing I have been describing is a necessary evil attaching to any formal regulation of human affairs. But I think that the area which really stands in need of such regulation is greatly overestimated. There are, of course, a few fundamental rules of the game that must be accepted if the game is to go on at all. I would include among these the rules relating to the conduct of elections, the appointment of public officials, and the term during which an office is held. Here some restraint on discretion and dispensation, some adherence to form, some scruple for what does and what does not fall within the rule, is, I concede, essential. Perhaps the area of basic principle should be expanded to include certain other rules, such as those designed to preserve the free civilmoign system.

But outside of these fields I believe that all government officials, including judges, will do their jobs best if they treat forms and abstract concepts as instruments. We should take as our model, I think, the good administrator, who accommodates procedures and principles to the case at hand, selecting from among the available forms those most suited to reach the proper result.

The most obvious advantage of this method of government is that it permits us to go about our daily tasks with efficiency and common sense. My adherence to this philosophy has, however, deeper roots. I believe that it is only with the insight this philosophy gives that we can preserve the flexibility essential if we are to keep our actions in reasonable accord with the sentiments of those subject to our rule. More governments have been wrecked, and more human misery caused, by the lack of this accord between ruler and ruled than by any other factor that can be discerned in history. Once drive a sufficient wedge between the mass of people and those who direct their legal, political, and economic life, and our society is ruined. Then neither Foster's law of nature nor Keen's fidelity to written law will avail us anything.

Now when these conceptions are applied to the case before us, its decision becomes, as I have said, perfectly easy. In order to demonstrate this I shall have to introduce certain realities that my brothers in their coy decorum have seen fit to pass over in silence, although they are just as acutely aware of them as I am.

The first of these is that this case has aroused an enormous public interest, both here and abroad. Almost every newspaper and magazine has carried articles about it; columnists have shared with their readers confidential information as to the next governmental move; hundreds of letters-to-the-editor have been printed. One of the great newspaper chains made a poll of public opinion on the question, "What do you think the Supreme Court should do with the Speluncean explorers?" About ninety per cent expressed a belief that the defendants should be pardoned or let off with a kind of token punishment. It is perfectly clear, then, how the public feels about the case. We could have known this without the poll, of course, on the basis of common sense, or even by observing that on this court there are apparently four-and-a-half men, or ninety per cent, who share the common opinion.

This makes it obvious, not only what we should do, but what we must do if we are to preserve between ourselves and public opinion a reasonable and decent accord. Declaring these men innocent need not involve us in any undignified quibble or trick. No principle of statutory construction is required that is not consistent with the past practices of this court. Certainly no layman would think that in letting these men off we had stretched the statute any more than our ancestors did when they created the excuse of self-defense. If a more detailed demonstration of the method of reconciling our decision with the statute is required, I should be content to rest on the arguments developed in the second and less visionary part of my brother Foster's opinion.

Now I know that my brothers will be horrified by my suggestion that this court should take account of public opinion. They will tell you that public opinion is emotional and capricious, that it is based on half-truths and listens to witnesses who are not subject to cross-examination. They will tell you that the law surrounds the trial of a case like this with elaborate safeguards, designed to insure that the truth will be known and that every rational consideration bearing on the issues of the case has been taken into account. They will warn you that all of these safeguards go for naught if a mass opinion formed outside this framework is allowed to have any influence on our decision.

But let us look candidly at some of the realities of the administration of our criminal law. When a man is accused of crime, there are, speaking generally, four ways in which he may escape punishment. One of these is a determination by a judge that under the applicable law he has committed no crime. This is, of course, a determination that takes place in a rather formal and abstract atmosphere. But look at the other three ways in which he may escape punishment. These are: (1) a decision by the Prosecutor not to ask for an indictment; (2) an acquittal by the jury; (3) a pardon or commutation of sentence by the Executive. Can anyone pretend that these decisions are held within a rigid and formal framework of rules that prevents factual error, excludes emotional and personal factors, and guarantees that all the forms of the law will be observed?

In the case of the jury we do, to be sure, attempt to cabin their deliberations within the area of the legally relevant, but there is no need to deceive ourselves into believing that this attempt is really successful. In the normal course of events the case now before us would have gone on all of its issues directly to the jury. Had this occurred we can be confident that there would have been an acquittal or at least a division that would have prevented a conviction. If the jury had been instructed that the men's hunger and their agreement were no defense to the charge of murder, their verdict would in all likelihood have ignored this instruction and would have involved a good deal more twisting of the letter of the law than any that is likely to tempt us. Of course the only reason that didn't occur in this case was the fortuitous circumstance that the foreman of the jury happened to be a lawyer. His learning enabled him to devise a form of words that would allow the jury to dodge its usual responsibilities.

My brother Tatting expresses annoyance that the Prosecutor did not, in effect, decide the case for him by not asking for an indictment. Strict as he is himself in complying with the demands of legal theory, he is quite content to have the fate of these men decided out of court by the Prosecutor on the basis of common sense. The Chief Justice, on the other hand, wants the application of common sense postponed to the very end, though like Tatting, he wants no personal part in it.

This brings me to the concluding portion of my remarks, which has to do with executive clemency. Before discussing that topic directly, I want to make a related observation about the poll of public opinion. As I have said, ninety per cent of the people wanted the Supreme Court to let the men off entirely or with a more or less nominal punishment. The ten per cent constituted a very oddly assorted group, with the most curious and divergent opinions. One of our university experts has made a study of this group and has found that its members fall into certain patterns. A substantial portion of them are subscribers to "crank" newspapers of limited circulation that gave their readers a distorted version of the facts of the case. Some thought that "Speluncean" means "cannibal" and that anthropophagy is a tenet of the Society. But the point I want to make, however, is this: although almost every conceivable variety and shade of opinion was represented in this group, there was, so far as I know, not one of them, nor a single member of the majority of ninety per cent, who said, "I think it would be a fine thing to have the courts sentence these men to be hanged, and then to have another branch of the government come along and pardon them." Yet this is a solution that has more or less dominated our discussions and which our Chief Justice proposes as a way by which we can avoid doing an injustice and at the same time preserve respect for law. He can be assured that if he is preserving anybody's morale, it is his own, and not the public's, which knows nothing of his distinctions. I mention this matter because I wish to emphasize once more the danger that we may get lost in the patterns of our own thought and forget that these patterns often cast not the slightest shadow on the outside world.

I come now to the most crucial fact in this case, a fact known to all of us on this court, though one that my brothers have seen fit to keep under the cover of their judicial robes. This is the frightening likelihood that if the issue is left to him, the Chief Executive will refuse to pardon these men or commute their sentence. As we all know, our Chief Executive is a man now well advanced in years, of very stiff notions. Public clamor usually operates on him with the reverse of the effect intended. As I have told my brothers, it happens that my wife's niece is an intimate friend of his secretary. I have learned in this indirect, but I think, wholly reliable way, that he is firmly determined not to commute the sentence if these men are found to have violated the law.

No one regrets more than I the necessity for relying in so important a matter on information that could be characterized as gossip. If I had my way this would not happen, for I would adopt the sensible course of sitting down with the Executive, going over the case with him, finding out what his views are, and perhaps working out with him a common program for handling the situation. But of course my brothers would never hear of such a thing.

Their scruple about acquiring accurate information directly does not prevent them from being very perturbed about what they have learned indirectly. Their acquaintance with the facts I have just related explains why the Chief Justice, ordinarily a model of decorum, saw fit in his opinion to flap his judicial robes in the face of the Executive and threaten him with excommunication if he failed to commute the sentence. It explains, I suspect, my brother Foster's feat of levitation by which a whole library of lawbooks was lifted from the shoulders of these defendants. It explains also why even my legalistic brother Keen emulated Pooh-Bah in the ancient comedy by stepping to the other side of the stage to address a few remarks to the Executive "in my capacity as a private citizen." (I may remark, incidentally, that the advice of Private Citizen Keen will appear in the reports of this court printed at taxpayers' expense.)

I must confess that as I grow older I become more and more perplexed at men's refusal to apply their common sense to problems of law and government, and this truly tragic case has deepened my sense of discouragement and dismay. I only wish that I could convince my brothers of the wisdom of the principles I have applied to the judicial office since I first assumed it. As a matter of fact, by a kind of sad rounding of the circle, I encountered issues like those involved here in the very first case I tried as Judge of the Court of General Instances in Fanleigh County.

A religious sect had unfrocked a minister who, they said, had gone over to the views and practices of a rival sect. The minister circulated a handbill making charges against the authorities who had expelled him. Certain lay members of the church announced a public meeting at which they proposed to explain the position of the church. The minister attended this meeting. Some said he slipped in unobserved in a disguise; his own testimony was that he had walked in openly as a member of the public. At any rate, when the speeches began he interrupted with certain questions about the affairs of the church and made some statements in defense of his own views. He was set upon by members of the audience and given a pretty thorough pommeling, receiving among other injuries a broken jaw. He brought a suit for damages against the association that sponsored the meeting and against ten named individuals who he alleged were his assailants.

When we came to the trial, the case at first seemed very complicated to me. The attorneys raised a host of legal issues. There were nice questions on the admissibility of evidence, and, in connection with the suit against the association, some difficult problems turning on the question whether the minister was a trespasser or a licensee. As a novice on the bench I was eager to apply my law school learning and I began studying these questions closely, reading all the authorities and preparing well-documented rulings. As I studied the case I became more and more involved in its legal intricacies and I began to get into a state approaching that of my brother Tatting in this case. Suddenly, however, it dawned on me that all these perplexing issues really had nothing to do with the case, and I began examining it in the light of common sense. The case at once gained a new perspective, and I saw that the only thing for me to do was direct a verdict for the defendants for lack of evidence.

I was led to this conclusion by the following considerations. The melee in which the plaintiff was injured had been a very confused affair, with some people trying to get to the center of the disturbance, while others were trying to get away from it; some striking at the plaintiff, while others were apparently trying to protect him. It would have taken weeks to find out the truth of the matter. I decided that nobody's broken jaw was worth that much to the Commonwealth. (The minister's injuries, incidentally, had meanwhile healed without disfigurement and without any impairment of normal faculties.) Furthermore, I felt very strongly that the plaintiff had to a large extent brought the thing on himself. He knew how inflamed passions were about the affair, and could easily have found another forum for the expression of his views. My decision was widely approved by the press and public opinion, neither of which could tolerate the views and practices that the expelled minister was attempting to defend.

Now, thirty years later, thanks to an ambitious Prosecutor and a legalistic jury foreman, I am faced with a case that raises issues which are at bottom much like those involved in that case. The world does not seem to change much, except that this time it is not a question of a judgment for five or six hundred frelars, but of the life or death of four men who have already suffered more torment and humiliation than most of us would endure in a thousand years. I conclude that the defendants are innocent of the crime charged, and that the conviction and sentence should be set aside.

TATTING, J.: I have been asked by the Chief Justice whether, after listening to the two opinions just rendered, I desire to re-examine the position previously taken by me. I wish to state that after hearing these opinions I am greatly strengthened in my conviction that I ought not to participate in the decision of this case.

The Supreme Court being evenly divided, the conviction and sentence of the Court of General Instances is *affirmed*. It is ordered that the execution of the sentence shall occur at 6 A.M., Friday, April 2, 4300, at which time the Public Executioner is directed to proceed with all convenient dispatch to hang each of the defendants by the neck until he is dead.

POSTSCRIPT

Now that the court has spoken its judgment, the reader puzzled by the choice of date may wish to be reminded that the centuries which separate us from the year 4300 are roughly equal to those that have passed since the Age of Pericles. There is probably no need to observe that the *Speluncean Case* itself is intended neither as a work of satire nor as a prediction in any ordinary sense of the term. As for the judges who make up Chief Justice Truepenny's court, they are, of course, as mythical as the facts and precedents with which they deal. The reader who refuses to accept this view, and who seeks to trace out contemporary resemblances where none is intended or contemplated, should be warned that he is engaged in a frolic of his own, which may possibly lead him to miss whatever modest truths are contained in the opinions delivered by the Supreme Court of Newgarth. The case was constructed for the sole purpose of bringing into a common focus certain divergent philosophies of law and government. These philosophies presented men with live questions of choice in the days of Plato and Aristotle. Perhaps they will continue to do so when our era has had its say about them. If there is any element of prediction in the case, it does not go beyond a suggestion that the questions involved are among the permanent problems of the human race.

Jonathan Swift

:

ON ·THE SCIENCE OF THE LAW

from *Gulliver's Travels*

There was another Point which a little perplexed him at present. I had said, that some of our Crew left their Country on Account of being ruined by *Law:* That I had already explained the Meaning of the Word; but he was at a Loss how it should come to pass, that the *Law* which was intended for *every* Man's Preservation, should be any Man's Ruin. Therefore he desired to be farther satisfied what I meant by *Law,* and the Dispensers thereof, according to the present Practice in my own Country: Because he thought, Nature and Reason were sufficient Guides for a reasonable Animal, as we pretended to be in shewing us what we ought to do, and what to avoid.

I ASSURED his Honour, that *Law* was a Science wherein I had not much conversed, further than by employing Advocates, in vain, upon some Injustices that had been done me. However, I would give him all the Satisfaction I was able.

I SAID there was a Society of Men among us, bred up from their Youth in the Art of proving by Words multiplied for the Purpose, that *White* is *Black,* and *Black* is *White,* according as they are paid. To this Society all the rest of the People are Slaves.

For example. If my Neighbour hath a mind to my *Cow,* he hires a Lawyer to prove that he ought to have my *Cow* from me. I must then hire another to defend my Right; it being against all Rules of *Law* that any Man should be allowed to speak for himself. Now in this Case, I who am the true Owner lie under two great Disadvantages.

First, my Lawyer being practised almost from his Cradle in defending Falsehood; is quite out of his Element when he would be an Advocate for Justice, which as an Office unnatural, he always attempts with great Awkwardness, if not with Ill-will. The second Disadvantage is that my Lawyer must proceed with great Caution: Or else he will be reprimanded by the Judges, and abhorred by his Brethren, as one who would lessen the Practice of the Law. And therefore I have but two Methods to preserve my *Cow.* The first is to gain over my Adversary's Lawyer with a double Fee; who will then betray his Client, by insinuating that he hath Justice on his Side. The second Way is for my Lawyer to make my Cause appear as unjust as he can; by allowing the *Cow* to belong to my Adversary; and this, if it be skilfully done, will certainly bespeak the Favour of the Bench.

Now, your Honour is to know, that these Judges are Persons appointed to decide all Controversies of Property, as well as for Tryal of Criminals; and picked out from the most dextrous Lawyers who are grown old or lazy: And having been byassed all their Lives against Truth and Equity, lie under such a fatal Necessity of favouring Fraud, Perjury and Oppression; that I have known some of them to have refused a large Bribe from the Side where Justice lay, rather than injure the *Faculty,* by doing any thing unbecoming their Nature or their Office.

It is a Maxim among these Lawyers, that whatever hath been done before, may legally be done again: And therefore they take special Care to record all the Decisions formerly made against common Justice and the general Reason of Mankind. These, under the Name of *Precedents,* they produce as Authorities to justify the most iniquitous Opinions; and the Judges never fail of directing accordingly.

In pleading, they studiously avoid entering into the *Merits* of the Cause; but are loud, violent and tedious in dwelling upon all *Circumstances* which are not to the Purpose. For Instance, in the Case already mentioned: They never desire to know what Claim or Title my Adversary hath to my *Cow;* but whether the said *Cow* were Red or Black; her Horns long or short; whether the Field I graze her in be round or square; whether she were milked at home or abroad; what Diseases she is subject to, and the like. After which they consult *Precedents,* adjourn the Cause, from Time to Time, and in Ten, Twenty, or Thirty Years come to an Issue.

It is likewise to be observed, that this Society hath a peculiar Cant and Jargon of their own, that no other Mortal can understand, and wherein all their Laws are written, which they take special Care to multiply; whereby they have wholly confounded the very Essence of Truth and Falsehood, of Right and Wrong; so that it will take Thirty Years to decide whether the Field, left me by my Ancestors for six Generations, belongs to me, or to a Stranger three Hundred Miles off.

IN the Tryal of Persons accused for Crimes against the State, the Method is much more short and commendable: The Judge first sends to sound the Disposition of those in Power; after which he can easily hang or save the Criminal, strictly preserving all the Forms of Law.

HERE my Master interposing, said it was a Pity, that Creatures endowed with such prodigious Abilities of Mind as these Lawyers, by the Description I gave of them must certainly be, were not rather encouraged to be Instructors of others in Wisdom and Knowledge. In Answer to which, I assured his Honour, that in all Points out of their own Trade, they were usually the most ignorant and stupid Generation among us, the most despicable in common Conversation, avowed Enemies to all Knowledge and Learning; and equally disposed to pervert the general Reason of Mankind, in every other Subject of Discourse, as in that of their own Profession.

Justice Benjamin Cardozo

:

THE NATURE OF THE JUDICIAL PROCESS, PART I

I. INTRODUCTION

The Method of Philosophy

The work of deciding cases goes on every day in hundreds of courts throughout the land. Any judge, one might suppose, would find it easy to describe the process which he had followed a thousand times and more. Nothing could be farther from the truth. Let some intelligent layman ask him to explain: he will not go very far before taking refuge in the excuse that the language of craftsmen is unintelligible to those untutored in the craft. Such an excuse may cover with a semblance of respectability an otherwise ignominious retreat. It will hardly serve to still the pricks of curiosity and conscience. In moments of introspection, when there is no longer a necessity of putting off with a show of wisdom the uninitiated interlocutor, the troublesome problem will recur, and press for a solution. What is it that I do when I decide a case? To what sources of information do I appeal for guidance? In what proportions do I permit them to contribute to the result? In what proportions ought they to contribute? If a precedent is applicable, when do I refuse to follow it? If no precedent is applicable how do I reach the rule that will make a precedent for the future? If I am seeking logical consistency, the symmetry of the legal structure, how far shall I seek it? At what point shall the quest be halted by some discrepant custom, by some consideration of the social welfare, by my own or the common standards of justice and morals? Into that strange compound which is brewed daily in the caldron of the courts, all these ingredients enter in varying proportions. I am not concerned to inquire whether judges ought to be allowed to brew such a compound at all. I take judge-made law as one of the existing realities of life. There before us, is the brew. Not a judge on the bench but has had a hand in the making. The elements have not come together by chance. *Some* principle, how-ever unavowed and inarticulate and subconscious, has regulated the in-fusion. It may not have been the same principle for all judges at any time, nor the same principle for any judge at all times. But a choice there has been, not a submission to the decree of Fate; and the con-siderations and motives determining the choice, even if often obscure, do not utterly resist analysis. In such attempt at analysis as I shall make, there will be need to distinguish between the conscious and the subconscious. I do not mean that even those considerations and motives which I shall class under the first head are always in consciousness distinctly, so that they will be recognized and named at sight. Not in-frequently they hover near the surface. They may, however, with comparative readiness be isolated and tagged, and when thus labeled, are quickly acknowledged as guiding principles of conduct. More subtle are the forces so far beneath the surface that they cannot reasonably be classified as other than subconscious. It is often through these subcon-scious forces that judges are kept consistent with themselves, and in-consistent with one another. We are reminded by William James in a telling page of his lectures on Pragmatism that every one of us has in truth an underlying philosophy of life, even those of us to whom the names and the notions of philosophy are unknown or anathema. There is in each of us a stream of tendency, whether you choose to call it philosophy or not, which gives coherence and direction to thought and action. Judges cannot escape that current any more than other mortals. All their lives, forces which they do not recognize and cannot name, have been tugging at them—inherited instincts, traditional be-liefs, acquired convictions; and the resultant is an outlook on life, a conception of social needs, a sense in James's phrase of "the total push and pressure of the cosmos," which, when reasons are nicely balanced, must determine where choice shall fall. In this mental background ev-ery problem finds its setting. We may try to see things as objectively as we please. None the less, we can never see them with any eyes except our own. To that test they are all brought—a form of pleading or an act of parliament, the wrongs of paupers or the rights of princes, a village ordinance or a nation's charter.

I have little hope that I shall be able to state the formula which will rationalize this process for myself, much less for others. We must apply to the study of judge-made law that method of quantitative analysis. A richer scholarship than mine is requisite to do the work aright. But until that scholarship is found and enlists itself in the task, there may be a passing interest in an attempt to uncover the nature of the process by one who is himself an active agent day by day, in keeping the process alive. That must be my apology for these introspective searchings of the spirit.

Before we can determine the proportions of a blend, we must know the ingredients to be blended. Our first inquiry should therefore be: Where does the judge find the law which he embodies in this judgment? There are times when the source is obvious. The rule that fits the case may be supplied by the Constitution or by statute. If that is so, the judge looks no farther. The correspondence ascertained, his duty is to obey. The Constitution overrides a statute, but a statute, if consistent with the Constitution, overrides the law of judges. In this sense, judge-made law is secondary and subordinate to the law that is made by legislators. It is true that codes and statutes do not render the judge superfluous, nor his work perfunctory and mechanical. There are gaps to be filled. There are doubts and ambiguities to be cleared. There are hardships and wrongs to be mitigated if not avoided. Interpretation is often spoken of as if it were nothing but the search and the discovery of a meaning which, however obscure and latent, had none the less a real and ascertainable pre-existence in the legislator's mind. The process is, indeed, that at times, but it is often something more. The ascertainment of intention may be the least of a judge's troubles in ascribing meaning to a statute. "The fact is," says Gray in his lectures on the "Nature and Sources of the Law," "that the difficulties of so-called interpretation arise when the legislature has had no meaning at all; when the question which is raised on the statute never occurred to it; when what the judges have to do is, not to determine what the legislature did mean on a point which was present to its mind, but to guess what it would have intended on a point not present to its mind, if the point had been present." So Brütt: "One weighty task of the system of the application of law consists then in this, to make more profound the discovery of the latent meaning of positive law. Much more important however, is the second task which the system serves, namely the filling of the gaps which are found in every positive law in greater or less measure." You may call this process legislation, if you will. In any event, no system of *jus scriptum* has been able to escape the need of it. Today a great school of continental jurists is pleading for a still wider freedom of adaptation and construction. The statute, they say, is often fragmentary and ill-considered and unjust. The judge as the interpreter for the community of its sense of law and order must supply omissions, correct uncertainties and harmonize results with justice through a method of free decision—*"libre recherche scientifique."* That is the view of Gény and Ehrlich and Gmelin and others. Courts are to "search for light among the social elements of every kind that are the living force behind the facts they deal with." The power thus put in their hands is great and subject, like all power, to abuse; but we are not to flinch from granting it. In the long run "there is no guaranty of justice," says Ehrlich, "except the personality of the judge." The same problems of method, the same contrasts between the letter and the spirit, are living problems in our own land and law. Above all in the field of constitutional law, the method of free decision has become, I think, the dominant one today. The great generalities of the Constitution have a content and a significance that vary from age to age. The method of free decision sees through the transitory particulars and reaches what is permanent behind them. Interpretation, thus enlarged, becomes more than the ascertainment of the meaning and intent of lawmakers whose collective will has been declared. It supplements the declaration, and fills the vacant spaces, by the same processes and methods that have built up the customary law. Codes and other statutes may threaten the judicial function with repression and disuse and atrophy. The function flourishes and persists by virtue of the human need to which it steadfastly responds. Justinian's prohibition of any commentary on the product of his codifiers is remembered only for its futility.

I will dwell no further for the moment upon the significance of Constitution and statute as sources of the law. The work of a judge in interpreting and developing them has indeed its problems and its difficulties, but they are problems and difficulties not different in kind or measure from those besetting him in other fields. I think they can be better studied when those fields have been explored. Sometimes the rule of Constitution or of statute is clear, and then the difficulties vanish. Even when they are present, they lack at times some of that element of mystery which accompanies creative energy. We reach the land of mystery when Constitution and statute are silent, and the judge must look to the common law for the rule that fits the case. He is the "living oracle of the law" in Blackstone's vivid phrase. Looking at Sir Oracle in action, viewing his work in the dry light of realism, how does he set about his task?

The first thing he does is to compare the case before him with the precedents, whether stored in his mind or hidden in the books. I do not mean that precedents are ultimate sources of the law, supplying the sole equipment that is needed for the legal armory, the sole tools, to borrow Maitland's phrase, "in the legal smithy." Back of precedents are the basic juridical conceptions which are the postulates of judicial reasoning, and farther back are the habits of life, the institutions of society, in which those conceptions had their origin, and which, by a process of interaction, they have modified in turn. None the less, in a system so highly developed as our own, precedents have so covered the ground that they fix the point of departure from which the labor of the judge begins. Almost invariably, his first step is to examine and compare them. If they are plain and to the point, there may be need of nothing more. *Stare decisis* is at least the everyday working rule of our law. I shall have something to say later about the propriety of relaxing the rule in exceptional conditions. But unless those conditions are present, the work of deciding cases in accordance with precedents that plainly fit them is a process similar in its nature to that of deciding cases in accordance with a statute. It is a process of search, comparison, and little more. Some judges seldom get beyond that process in any case. Their notion of their duty is to match the colors of the case at hand against the colors of many sample cases spread out upon their desk. The sample nearest in shade supplies the applicable rule. But, of course, no system of living law can be evolved by such a process, and no judge of a high court, worthy of his office, views the function of his place so narrowly. If that were all there was to our calling, there would be little of intellectual interest about it. The man who had the best card index of the cases would also be the wisest judge. It is when the colors do not match, when the references in the index fail, when there is no decisive precedent, that the serious business of the judge begins. He must then fashion law for the litigants before him. In fashioning it for them, he will be fashioning it for others. The classic statement is Bacon's: "For many times, the things deduced to judgment may be meum and tuum, when the reason and consequence thereof may trench to point of estate." The sentence of today will make the right and wrong of tomorrow. If the judge is to pronounce it wisely, some principles of selection there must be to guide him among all the potential judgments that compete for recognition.

In the life of the mind as in life elsewhere, there is a tendency toward the reproduction of kind. Every judgment has a generative power. It begets in its own image. Every precedent, in the words of Redlich, has a "directive force for future cases of the same or similar nature." Until the sentence was pronounced, it was as yet in equilibrium. Its form and content were uncertain. Any one of many principles might lay hold of it and shape it. Once declared, it is a new stock of descent. It is charged with vital power. It is the source from which new principles or norms may spring to shape sentences thereafter. If we seek the psychological basis of this tendency, we shall find it, I suppose, in habit. Whatever its psychological basis it is one of the living forces of our law. Not all the progeny of principles begotten of a judgment survive, however, to maturity. Those that cannot prove their worth and strength by the test of experience, are sacrificed mercilessly and thrown into the void. The common law does not work from pre-established truths of universal and inflexible validity to conclusions derived from them deductively. Its method is inductive, and it draws its generalizations from particulars. The process has been admirably stated by Munroe Smith: "In their effort to give to the social sense of justice articulate expression in rules and in principles, the method of the lawfinding experts has always been experimental. The rules and principles of case law have never been treated as final truths, but as working hypotheses, continually retested in those great laboratories of the law, the courts of justice. Every new case is an experiment; and if the accepted rule which seems applicable yields a result which is felt to be unjust, the rule is reconsidered. It may not be modified at once, for the attempt to do absolute justice in every single case would make the development and maintenance of general rules impossible; but if a rule continues to work injustice, it will eventually be reformulated. The principles themselves are continually retested; for if the rules derived from a principle do not work well, the principle itself must ultimately be re-examined."

The way in which this process of retesting and reformulating works, may be followed in an example. Fifty years ago, I think it would have been stated as a general principle that A may conduct his business as he pleases, even though the purpose is to cause loss to B, unless the act involves the creation of a nuisance. Spite fences were the stock illustration, and the exemption from liability in such circumstances was supposed to illustrate not the exception, but the rule. Such a rule may have been an adequate working principle to regulate the relations between individuals or classes in a simple or homogeneous community. With the growing complexity of social relations, its inadequacy was revealed. As particular controversies multiplied and the attempt was made to test them by the old principle, it was found that there was something wrong in the results, and this led to a reformulation of the principle itself. Today, most judges are inclined to say that what was once thought to be the exception is the rule, and what was the rule is the exception. A may never do anything in his business for the purpose of injuring another without reasonable and just excuse. There has been a new generalization which, applied to new particulars, yields results more in harmony with past particulars, and, what is still more important, more consistent with the social welfare. This work of modification is gradual. It goes on inch by inch. Its effects must be measured by decades and even centuries. Thus measured, they are seen to have behind them the power and the pressure of the moving glacier.

We are not likely to underrate the force that has been exerted if we look back upon its work. "There is not a creed which is not shaken, not an accredited dogma which is not shown to be questionable, not a received tradition which does not threaten to dissolve." Those are the words of a critic of life and letters writing forty years ago, and watching the growing skepticism of his day. I am tempted to apply his words to the history of the law. Hardly a rule of today but may be matched by its opposite of yesterday. Absolute liability for one's acts is today the exception; there must commonly be some tinge of fault, whether willful or negligent. Time was, however, when absolute liability was the rule. Occasional reversions to the earlier type may be found in recent legislation. Mutual promises give rise to an obligation, and their breach to a right of action for damages. Time was when the obligation and the remedy were unknown unless the promise was under seal. Rights of action may be assigned, and the buyer prosecute them to judgment though he bought for purposes of suit. Time was when the assignment was impossible, and the maintenance of the suit a crime. It is no basis today for an action of deceit to show, without more, that there has been the breach of an executory promise; yet the breach of an executory promise came to have a remedy in our law because it was held to be a deceit. These changes or most of them have been wrought by judges. The men who wrought them used the same tools as the judges of today. The changes, as they were made in this case or that, may not have seemed momentous in the making. The result, however, when the process was prolonged throughout the years, has been not merely to supplement, or modify; it has been to revolutionize and transform. For every tendency, one seems to see a counter-tendency; for every rule its antinomy. Nothing is stable. Nothing absolute. All is fluid and changeable. There is an endless "becoming." We are back with Heraclitus. That, I mean, is the average or aggregate impression which the picture leaves upon the mind. Doubtless in the last three centuries some lines, once wavering, have become rigid. We leave more to legislatures today, and less perhaps to judges. Yet even now there is change from decade to decade. The glacier still moves.

In this perpetual flux, the problem which confronts the judge is in reality a twofold one: he must first extract from the precedents the underlying principle, the *ratio decidendi;* he must then determine the path or direction along which the principle is to move and develop, if it is not to wither and die.

The first branch of the problem is the one to which we are accustomed to address ourselves more consciously than to the other. Cases do not unfold their principles for the asking. They yield up their kernel slowly and painfully. The instance cannot lead to a generalization till we know it as it is. That in itself is no easy task. For the thing adjudged comes to us oftentimes swathed in obscuring dicta, which must be stripped off and cast aside. Judges differ greatly in their reverence for the illustrations and comments and side-remarks of their predecessors, to make no mention of their own. All agree that there may be dissent when the opinion is filed. Some would seem to hold that there must be none a moment thereafter. Plenary inspiration has then descended upon the work of the majority. No one, of course, avows such a belief, and yet sometimes there is an approach to it in conduct. I own that it is a good deal of a mystery to me how judges, of all persons in the world, should put their faith in dicta. A brief experience on the bench was enough to reveal to me all sorts of cracks and crevices and loopholes in my own opinions when picked up a few months after delivery, and reread with due contrition. The persuasion that one's own infallibility is a myth leads by easy stages and with somewhat greater satisfaction to a refusal to ascribe infallibility to others. But dicta are not always ticketed as such, and one does not recognize them always at a glance. There is the constant need, as every law student knows, to separate the accidental and the non-essential from the essential and inherent. Let us assume, however, that this task has been achieved, and that the precedent is known as it really is. Let us assume too that the principle, latent within it, has been skillfully extracted and accurately stated. Only half or less than half of the work has yet been done. The problem remains to fix the bounds and the tendencies of development and growth, to set the directive force in motion along the right path at the parting of the ways.

The directive force of a principle may be exerted along the line of logical progression; this I will call the rule of analogy or the method of philosophy; along the line of historical development; this I will call the method of evolution; along the line of the customs of the community; this I will call the method of tradition; along the lines of justice, morals and social welfare, the *mores* of the day; and this I will call the method of sociology.

I have put first among the principles of selection to guide our choice of paths, the rule of analogy or the method of philosophy. In putting it first, I do not mean to rate it as most important. On the contrary, it is often sacrificed to others. I have put it first because it has, I think, a certain presumption in its favor. Given a mass of particulars, a congeries of judgments on related topics, the principle that unifies and rationalizes them has a tendency, and a legitimate one, to project and extend itself to new cases within the limits of its capacity to unify and rationalize. It has the primacy that comes from natural and orderly and logical succession. Homage is due to it over every competing principle that is unable by appeal to history or tradition or policy or justice to make out a better right. All sorts of deflecting forces may appear to contest its sway and absorb its power. At least, it is the heir presumptive. A pretender to the title will have to fight his way.

Great judges have sometimes spoken as if the principle of philosophy *i.e.,* of logical development, meant little or nothing in our law. Probably none of them in conduct was ever true to such a faith. Lord Halsbury said in Quinn v. Leathem: "A case is only an authority for what it actually decides. I entirely deny that it can be quoted for a proposition that may seem to follow logically from it. Such a mode of reasoning assumes that the law is necessarily a logical code, whereas every lawyer must acknowledge that the law is not always logical at all." All this may be true but we must not press the truth too far. Logical consistency does not cease to be a good because it is not the supreme good. Holmes has told us in a sentence which is now classic that "the life of the law has not been logic; it has been experience." But Holmes did not tell us that logic is to be ignored when experience is silent. I am not to mar the symmetry of the legal structure by the introduction of inconsistencies and irrelevancies and artificial exceptions unless for some sufficient reason, which will commonly be some consideration of history or custom or policy or justice. Lacking such a reason, I must be logical, just as I must be impartial, and upon like grounds. It will not do to decide the same question one way between one set of litigants and the opposite way between another. "If a group of cases involves the same point, the parties expect the same decision. It would be a gross injustice to decide alternate cases on opposite principles. If a case was decided against me yesterday when I was defendant, I shall look for the same judgment today if I am plaintiff. To decide differently would raise a feeling of resentment and wrong in my breast; it would be an infringement, material and moral, of my rights." * Everyone feels the force of this sentiment when two cases are the same. Adherence to precedent must then be the rule rather than the exception if litigants are to have faith in the even-handed administration of justice in the courts. A sentiment like in kind, though different in degree, is at the root of the tendency of precedent to extend itself along the lines of logical development. No doubt the sentiment is powerfully reinforced by what is often nothing but an intellectual passion for *elegantia juris,* for symmetry of form and substance. That is an ideal which can never fail to exert some measure of attraction upon the professional experts who make up the lawyer class. To the Roman lawyers, it meant much, more than it has meant to English lawyers or to ours, certainly more than it has meant to clients. "The client," says Miller in his "Data of Jurisprudence," "cares little for a 'beautiful' case! He wishes it settled somehow on the most favorable terms he can obtain." Even that is not always true. But as a system of case law develops, the sordid controversies of litigants are the stuff out of which great and shining truths will ultimately be shaped. The accidental and the transitory will yield the essential and the permanent. The judge who molds the law by the method of philosophy may be satisfying an intellectual craving for symmetry of

* W. G. Miller.

form and substance. But he is doing something more. He is keeping the law true in its response to a deep-seated and imperious sentiment. Only experts perhaps may be able to gauge the quality of his work and appraise its significance. But their judgment, the judgment of the lawyer class, will spread to others, and tinge the common consciousness and the common faith. In default of other tests, the method of philosophy must remain the organon of the courts if chance and favor are to be excluded, and the affairs of men are to be governed with the serene and impartial uniformity which is of the essence of the idea of law.

You will say that there is an intolerable vagueness in all this. If the method of philosophy is to be employed in the absence of a better one, some test of comparative fitness should be furnished. I hope, before I have ended, to sketch, though only in the broadest outline, the fundamental considerations by which the choice of methods should be governed. In the nature of things they can never be catalogued with precision. Much must be left to that deftness in the use of tools which the practice of an art develops. A few hints, a few suggestions, the rest must be trusted to the feeling of the artist. But for the moment, I am satisfied to establish the method of philosophy as one organon among several, leaving the choice of one or the other to be talked of later.

Example, if not better than precept, may at least prove to be easier. We may get some sense of the class of questions to which a method is adapted when we have studied the class of questions to which it has been applied. Let me give some haphazard illustrations of conclusions adopted by our law through the development of legal conceptions to logical conclusions. A agrees to sell a chattel to B. Before title passes, the chattel is destroyed. The loss falls on the seller who has sued at law for the price. A agrees to sell a house and lot. Before title passes, the house is destroyed. The seller sues in equity for specific performance. The loss falls upon the buyer. That is probably the prevailing view, though its wisdom has been sharply criticized. These variant conclusions are not dictated by variant considerations of policy or justice. They are projections of a principle to its logical outcome, or the outcome supposed to be logical. Equity treats that as done which ought to be done. Contracts for the sale of land, unlike most contracts for the sale of chattels, are within the jurisdiction of equity. The vendee is in equity the owner from the beginning. Therefore, the burdens as well as the benefits of ownership shall be his. Let me take as another illustration of my meaning the cases which define the rights of assignees of choses in action. In the discussion of these cases, you will find much conflict of opinion about fundamental conceptions. Some tell us that the assignee has a legal ownership. Others say that his right is purely equitable. Given, however, the fundamental conception, all agree in deducing its consequences by methods in which the preponderating element is the method of philosophy. We may find kindred illustrations in the law of trusts and contracts and in many other fields. It would be wearisome to accumulate them.

The directive force of logic does not always exert itself, however, along a single and unobstructed path. One principle or precedent, pushed to the limit of its logic, may point to one conclusion; another principle or precedent, followed with like logic, may point with equal certainty to another. In this conflict, we must choose between the two paths, selecting one or other, or perhaps striking out upon a third, which will be the resultant of the two forces in combination, or will represent the mean between extremes. Let me take as an illustration of such conflict the famous case of Riggs v. Palmer. That case decided that a legatee who had murdered his testator would not be permitted by a court of equity to enjoy the benefits of the will. Conflicting principles were there in competition for the mastery. One of them prevailed and vanquished all the others. There was the principle of the binding force of a will disposing of the estate of a testator in conformity with law. That principle, pushed to the limit of its logic, seemed to uphold the title of the murderer. There was the principle that civil courts may not add to the pains and penalties of crimes. That, pushed to the limit of its logic, seemed again to uphold his title. But over against these was another principle, of greater generality, its roots deeply fastened in universal sentiments of justice, the principle that no man should profit from his own inequity or take advantage of his own wrong. The logic of this principle prevailed over the logic of the others. I say its logic prevailed. The thing which really interests us, however, is why and how the choice was made between one logic and another. In this instance, the reason is not obscure. One path was followed, another closed, because of the conviction in the judicial mind that the one selected led to justice. Analogies and precedents and the principles behind them were brought together as rivals for precedence; in the end, the principle that was thought to be most fundamental, to represent the larger and deeper social interests, put its competitors to flight. I am not greatly concerned about the particular formula through which justice was attained. Consistency was preserved, logic received its tribute, by holding that the legal title passed, but that it was subjected to a constructive trust. A constructive trust is nothing but "the formula through which the conscience of equity finds expression." Property is acquired in such circumstances that the holder of the legal title may not in good conscience retain the beneficial interest. Equity, to express its disapproval of his conduct, converts him into a trustee. Such formulas are merely the remedial devices by which a result conceived of as right and just is made to square with principle and with the symmetry of the legal system. What concerns me now is not the remedial device, but rather the underlying motive, the indwelling, creative energy, which brings such devices into play. The murderer lost the legacy for which the murder was committed because the social interest served by refusing to permit the criminal to profit by his crime is greater than that served by the preservation and enforcement of legal rights of ownership. My illustration, indeed, has brought me ahead of my story. The judicial process is there in microcosm. We go forward with our logic, with our analogies, with our philosophies, till we reach a certain point. At first, we have no trouble with the paths; they follow the same lines. Then they begin to diverge, and we must make a choice between them. History or custom or social utility or some compelling sentiment of justice or sometimes perhaps a semi-intuitive apprehension of the pervading spirit of our law, must come to the rescue of the anxious judge, and tell him where to go.

It is easy to accumulate examples of the process—of the constant checking and testing of philosophy by justice, and of justice by philosophy. Take the rule which permits recovery with compensation for defects in cases of substantial, though incomplete performance. We have often applied it for the protection of builders who in trifling details and without evil purpose have departed from their contracts. The courts had some trouble for a time, when they were deciding such cases, to square their justice with their logic. Even now, an uneasy feeling betrays itself in treatise and decision that the two fabrics do not fit. As I had occasion to say in a recent case: "Those who think more of symmetry and logic in the development of legal rules than of practical adaptation to the attainment of a just result" remain "troubled by a classification where the lines of division are so wavering and blurred." I have no doubt that the inspiration of the rule is a mere sentiment of justice. That sentiment asserting itself, we have proceeded to surround it with the halo of conformity to precedent. Some judges saw the unifying principle in the law of quasi-contracts. Others saw it in the distinction between dependent and independent promises, or between promises and conditions. All found, however, in the end that there *was* a principle in the legal armory which, when taken down from the wall where it was rusting, was capable of furnishing a weapon for the fight and of hewing a path to justice. Justice reacted upon logic, sentiment upon reason, by guiding the choice to be made between one logic and another. Reason in its turn reacted upon sentiment by purging it of what is arbitrary, by checking it when it might otherwise have been extravagant, by relating it to method and order and coherence and tradition.

In this conception of the method of logic or philosophy as one organon among several, I find nothing hostile to the teachings of continental jurists who would dethrone it from its place and power in systems of jurisprudence other than our own. They have combated an evil which has touched the common law only here and there, and lightly. I do not mean that there are not fields where we have stood in need of the same lesson. In some part, however, we have been saved by the inductive process through which our case law has developed from evils and dangers inseparable from the development of law, upon the basis of the *jus scriptum,* by a process of deduction. Yet even continental jurists who emphasize the need of other methods, do not ask us to abstract from legal principles all their fructifying power. The misuse of logic or philosophy begins when its method and its ends are treated as supreme and final. They can never be banished altogether. "Assuredly," says François Gény, "there should be no question of banishing ratiocination and logical methods from the science of positive law." Even general principles may sometimes be followed rigorously in the deduction of their consequences. "The abuse," he says, "consists, if I do not mistake, in envisaging ideal conceptions, provisional and purely subjective in their nature, as endowed with a permanent objective reality. And this false point of view, which, to my thinking, is a vestige of the absolute realism of the middle ages, ends in confining the entire system of positive law, *a priori,* within a limited number of logical categories, which are predetermined in essence, immovable in basis, governed by inflexible dogmas, and thus incapable of adapting themselves to the ever varied and changing exigencies of life."

In law, as in every other branch of knowledge, the truths given by induction tend to form the premises for new deductions. The lawyers and the judges of successive generations do not repeat for themselves the process of verification, any more than most of us repeat the demonstrations of the truths of astronomy or physics. A stock of juridical conceptions and formulas is developed, and we take them, so to speak, ready-made. Such fundamental conceptions as contract and possession and ownership and testament and many others, are there, ready for use. How they came to be there, I do not need to inquire. I am writing, not a history of the evolution of law, but a sketch of the judicial process applied to law full grown. These fundamental conceptions once attained form the starting point from which are derived new consequences, which at first tentative and groping, gain by reiteration a new permanence and certainty. In the end, they become accepted themselves as fundamental and axiomatic. So it is with the growth from precedent to precedent. The implications of a decision may in the beginning be equivocal. New cases by commentary and exposition extract the essence. At last there emerges a rule or principle which becomes a datum, a point of departure, from which new lines will be run, from which new courses will be measured. Sometimes the rule or principle is found to have been formulated too narrowly or too broadly, and has to be reframed. Sometimes it is accepted as a postulate of later reasoning, its origins are forgotten, it becomes a new stock of descent, its issue unite with other strains, and persisting permeate the law. You may call the process one of analogy or of logic or of philosophy as you please. Its essence in any event is the derivation of a consequence from a rule or a principle or a precedent which, accepted as a datum, contains implicitly within itself the germ of the conclusion. In all this, I do not use the word philosophy in any strict or formal sense. The method tapers down from the syllogism at one end to mere analogy at the other. Sometimes the extension of a precedent goes to the limit of its logic. Sometimes it does not go so far. Sometimes by a process of analogy it is carried even farther. That is a tool which no system of jurisprudence has been able to discard. A rule which has worked well in one field, or which, in any event, is there whether its workings have been revealed or not, is carried over into another. Instances of such a process I group under the same heading as those where the nexus of logic is closer and more binding. At bottom and in their underlying motives, they are phases of the same method. They are inspired by the same yearning for consistency, for certainty, for uniformity of plan and structure. They have their roots in the constant striving of the mind for a larger and more inclusive unity, in which differences will be reconciled, and abnormalities will vanish.

Piero Calamandrei

.

THE CRISIS IN THE REASONED OPINION

from *Procedure and Democracy*

The most important and most typical indication of the rationality of the judicial function is the reasoned opinion.

In all modern codes of procedure, whether civil or criminal, a reasoned opinion is prescribed as one of the requisites of the decision. The person who is interested only in the logical aspect of the decision finds the statement of the premises of the syllogism in the reasoned opinion and the conclusion of the syllogism in the judgment. The requirement that there be a reasoned opinion is considered so important in Italy that it has been placed in the Constitution, where it is stated that "all judicial acts must be reasoned" (Art. 111).

The major function of the reasoned opinion is an explanatory or, one might say, a pedagogical one. No longer content merely to command, to proclaim a *sic volo, sic iubeo* from his high bench, the judge descends to the level of the parties, and although still commanding, seeks to impress them with the reasonableness of the command. The reasoned opinion is above all the justification of the decision and as such it attempts to be as persuasive as it can. Ever since justice descended from heaven to earth and the idea gained ground that the judge is a human being and not a supernatural and infallible oracle to be adored, whose authority is beyond question, man has felt the need of a rational explanation to give validity to the word of the judge. And the reasoned opinion is precisely that part of the decision that serves to demonstrate the justice of the decision, and to persuade the losing party that the

683

judgment against him was the inevitable conclusion of a logical process and not the result of oppressive and arbitrary improvisations. Even counsel for the losing party may find in the reasoned opinion the arguments that had previously escaped his attention and that convince him of the error of the position he had sustained. In this way losing a case after coming to the conclusion that it was justly lost is almost as satisfying as winning a case when we are convinced that the right is on our side.

But besides this psychological function of justification and persuasion the reasoned opinion has a more strictly juridical use, that of enabling the parties to determine whether or not there may lie within the reasoning on which the judge bases his decision any of those defects that make the decision susceptible to revision on appeal.

In the majority of cases the various appeals that the losing party may bring, before either the same or a higher court, are based on some error or omission constituting a departure from the logical *iter* followed by the judge, leading him astray and causing him to reach a mistaken conclusion in the judgment, that is, a conclusion other than the just one. Now the reasoned opinion, which is the written account of the issues of fact and of law that have led the judge to his conclusion (one might almost call it the log of his logical journey), is indispensable as a means of introducing the reader into the thought processes of the judge, of enabling him to ascertain whether or not at some point in his chain of syllogisms there is an error or a missing link. The reasoned opinion might be called a mirror that reveals the errors of the judge. When a lawyer studies a decision in search of grounds for appeal, he pays particular attention to the reasoning, dissecting its every paragraph, sentence by sentence, word by word, because there he may find hidden in a single word or grammatical construction a minute break in the logical continuity into which can be inserted the blade of appeal that may bring down the whole edifice. The importance of the reasoning as grounds for appeal is shown by the fact that in Italian law, as well as in that of other countries, any omission, insufficiency, or contradiction in the opinion concerning a point at issue may be sufficient grounds for quashing the judgment, whether the objection is raised in appellant's brief or is adduced by the reviewing court (Code of Civil Procedure, Art. 360, No. 5).

Reasoned opinions and appellate review are in a certain sense parallel institutions in the laws of procedure. As a general rule, where a reasoned opinion is not required, no appellate review is provided; for an appeal presupposes a criticism and a censure of the act appealed against, and this is hardly possible when the reasons and the justification for the act are not stated.

For this reason the decisions of the Courts of Assizes were final as long as the jury system was in effect in Italy. Since the verdict of the jury was not reasoned it could not be criticized, and therefore the decision based on such verdict was not appealable. The jurors replied yes or no to the questions put to them by the presiding judge, and the reasoning behind their answers was never made public. Unlike the judge, they were not required to seek to encase in cold syllogisms the impulses of sentiment, which, rather than reason, are often the basis of the decision. The unreasoned verdict of the jury, however, determined only questions of fact and their criminal classification. It was the task of the judge to assign the proper punishment for the facts ascertained and classified by the jury, in this way integrating the decision by supplying the essential elements not found in the verdict, and he was required to give the reasoning for his findings. Thus the reasoning was necessarily limited to the question of the punishment to be applied, and only within this narrow field was the decision susceptible to appeal.

The jury system was abolished in Italy by the Fascist regime, primarily for political reasons, because it appeared to be one of those institutions inspired by the nineteenth-century doctrine of popular sovereignty, anathema to the Fascist dictatorship; and in place of the jury system, in which the decision is formulated in two chronologically distinct steps, through the joint efforts of two different bodies operating independently, a single body with mixed membership was formed, composed of regular judges and so-called assessors, whose decisions were required to be reasoned on questions of fact and of law, according to the regular rules.

The jury system was not re-established after the fall of Fascism. Although the political factors that led to its abolition were no longer valid, there remained technical reasons that counseled against its reintroduction. The present Constitution has re-established the principle of the "direct participation of the people in the administration of justice" (Art. 102); but since according to Article 111 of the same Constitution all judicial decisions without exception must include a reasoned opinion, it has been held that this unqualified constitutional provision prevents the reintroduction of the unreasoned jury verdict. Thus the decisions of the Courts of Assizes must be fully reasoned today in fact and in law, and appeal is granted against any part of them. Perhaps this was a wise move, since the traditional jury system, in which the jurors were called on to judge without giving the reasons for their verdict, seems to have been fashioned—as experience has borne out—for the very purpose of encouraging the jurors to judge unreasonably; and so, rather than the faithful expression of the social conscience, their verdict often appeared to be the triumph of pure irrationality, an irrationality that was all the more dangerous in that it was not susceptible to appeal.

The reasoned opinion seems to offer proof *per tabulas* of the essentially logical nature of the decision. One might say that even before it appeared in legal theory, the judicial syllogism was found in judicial reality, since the law requires that every decision be accompanied by a kind of logical X-ray that discloses its rational framework. One might almost say that in requiring the judgment to be preceded by the reasoning in the final form of the decision, it was the intention of the law to make evident the syllogistic structure of the decision and to persuade the parties in judgment that there was no room for arbitrary action in the inflexible concatenation of logical vertebrae.

Nevertheless some doubt arises when we consider the fact that according to the same laws of procedure, instead of being a *posterius* of the reasoning, the judgment is normally a *prius*. As an act of will the decision is already born before the judge has clearly expressed the logical process that has led him to decide as he did; the conclusion of the syllogism is thus irrevocably determined before its premises are formulated.

According to Article 274 of the Code of Civil Procedure, which regulates the discussion of the decision in the judges' chambers, "When the voting is finished, the presiding judge writes and signs the judgment. The opinion is then prepared by the *relatore.*" Only after the opinion has been prepared can the decision be published (Code of Civil Procedure, Art. 133). And this may not occur until many days, sometimes many months, have passed after the decision has been reached. An even better example can be taken from criminal procedure, where the decision is announced at the close of the trial by the public reading of the judgment (Code of Criminal Procedure, Art. 472); while the complete opinion, including the reasoning that justifies it, is filed with the court clerk within a fortnight (Code of Criminal Procedure, Art. 151).

These laws leave us perplexed. Is the reasoned opinion really the logical premise from which the judgment is deduced as a necessary and inevitable consequence, or is it rather a kind of obligatory apology, by means of which the judge prepares ostensibly rational arguments in order to justify his decision in public, while his real motives are destined to remain hidden within his conscience?

The provisions of the laws of procedure mentioned above might lead us to suppose that the reasoned opinion is nothing other than a hypocritical expedient serving only, as it were, to give a logical disguise to an act impelled by quite different motives, perhaps even by arbitrariness and injustice.

These provisions are actually a candid recognition of the fact that the judge reaches his decision before he prepares the reasoned opinion; they are the clearest demonstration of the insufficiency and superficiality of those theories that reduce the decision to the form of a syllogism. In this instance the law itself is in contradiction to this theory. The accountant who attempted to determine the total before knowing the figures to be added would be ill advised; but, as I have already said, a judicial decision is no arithmetic operation. It is a far more complicated and mysterious act, rooted in moral consciousness and irreducible to numerical abstractions.

Rather than a preliminary study made by the judge to enable him to decide justly, the opinion is generally the expression of a soul-searching reappraisal made by the judge to convince himself that he has decided justly. Its purpose is to establish by logic the validity of a decision actually based on sentiment; it is the rationalization of the sense of justice, the demonstration of the *ratio scripta* that the judge prepares for his own peace of mind as much as for the parties, corroborating a discovery born of his intuition.

Even under the rule of law, when a judge decides a case he goes through basically much the same procedure as the lawyers do in pleading it. First comes intuition—one might almost say creative imagination—which suggests the thesis to sustain. Then comes the intellectual task of seeking legal grounds to support the thesis.

Those who have had experience in the legal profession know how the advice to give a client wishing to start a suit generally takes shape in the lawyer's mind (I am speaking of the honest lawyer, who realizes that he is his client's first judge): In first presenting his case to the lawyer the client lays before him an accumulation of disordered facts, from among which it is difficult to isolate the juridically relevant material. The lawyer sets himself patiently at the task of choosing, examining, and combining the separate pieces and of creating order out of the confusion. And finally there comes to him a flash of inspiration; that formless mass takes shape and acquires a significance, and in it there suddenly appears the outline of a familiar conformation, which gives juridical relevance to the case, much as Leonardo discerned human forms on walls cracked and discolored by dampness and age. Only after this relevance has been discovered, more through intuition than through reason, accompanied by an almost instinctive feeling of sympathy or repugnance, does the research work of consulting the law and the commentaries begin.

This "feeling" for the law is slowly acquired over years of practical experience at the bar. In its final stages it becomes a kind of clairvoyance. One of the happy moments in the life of a lawyer occurs when, thumbing through treatises and law reports, he finds the reasoned and rational confirmation of the correctness of the answer he reached intuitively through his "feeling" for the law. In this way he demonstrates that, rather than being a variable subjective illusion, the sense of justice, through a discipline of the spirit, is sharpened and perfected by experience so that the just solution, fully confirmed by the written commentaries, can be reached directly through intuition.

The uninitiated often believe that lawyers are omniscient beings who have memorized all the laws. How deserving of our pity lawyers would be were they expected to commit to memory the thousands of continually changing laws. But the lawyer is no legal handbook. He is the man who knows how to go about studying a case, who can discover what is juridically relevant in human problems, but above all he is the man who has a "feeling" for the just solution of a case. Often when one of my young assistants comes to ask my advice on a case he is preparing, I say to him, "I haven't studied the case and I don't know the pertinent law, but I *feel* that there *must be* a law setting forth this principle, or if there is no such law, there *must be* some legal precedent in this sense. . . ." I don't know the law and I haven't consulted the precedents; but when, after looking up the law on the points I suggested, my assistant comes to tell me that the provision I had imagined is actually to be found hidden in the labyrinth of special laws, or that in an old case book he has uncovered the very decision that confirms my diagnosis, mine is the same joy that the research worker in the laboratory experiences when his microscope gives him the empirical confirmation of the hypothesis suggested to him by his intuition.

Judges experience the same thing. For them the really decisive and culminating moment of their work is that of deciding the case; then if their legal sense is well developed the reasoning comes without effort. I have often heard judges who were called upon to decide a particularly complex and difficult case make the remark: "It is not hard to decide this case, but it is hard to give the reasoning." This explains the practice of the American courts, which not only permits dissenting opinions but allows the judges who concur in the judgment but not in the reasoning of the majority to write separate concurring opinions, basing the same conclusion on different grounds. This practice shows that a given judgment is not necessarily derived from a given reasoning; even among the footpaths of logic it may be that more than one road leads to Rome.

Naturally, if in the actual process of judging, the reasoning follows the decision and is an explanation of it rather than a preparation for it, the reasoning may become a screen to hide the real factors on which the judgment is based, covering with plausible reasoning the true motives for the decision, which cannot be admitted. Once a German jurist made a painstaking analysis of many decisions to show that the reasons alleged in the opinion were not the real motives that had actually led to the decision. This was a subtle study of psychology and of judicial logic, the purpose of which was to reveal the true motives beneath the apparent ones. The legal scholar with little experience in the courtroom reading the intricate reasoning of a decision as reported in a law review may often suspect, from the dialectical contortions and subtleties that the judge uses to justify his decision, that not even he was fully convinced by what he was writing, and that those arguments, couched in legal language, serve merely as a façade to hide from view the intrigue or partiality that was the true motivating factor of the decision.

In order to obtain the desirable fusion between the intuition that suggests the decision and the reasoning that verifies it (and consequently to make certain that the reasoned opinion be a true explanation and not a fallacious travesty of the decision), it is necessary that the judge's "feeling" and reasoning faculties be "in unison"; or rather that the same sentiment of social solidarity that inspired the legislators to enact the laws be alive in the mind of the judge to suggest to him the decision that his reason will later confirm. This is what is meant by such expressions as *ratio legis,* "the spirit of the law," "the intention of the legislator." In democratic regimes the law is a product of the social conscience. The legislator in a democratic state is not free to enact laws arbitrarily, disregarding the needs of society (although a tyrant or a dictator is free to do so for a certain period of time through the use of force); he must seek inspiration (and this is the purpose of the parliamentary system) from the collective conscience of the society that he represents. The judge is also part of the society in which he lives, and when he interprets the law in applying it to a specific case, he must draw inspiration from the same sentiment of social utility on which the law is based; to determine "the intention of the legislator" one must understand fully the significance and force of the law; this can be done only by turning for inspiration to the same social or political sources that inspired the legislator.

When it is said (and even I have been guilty of this) that under a government of laws the law is a wall separating the judge from politics, only a half-truth is expressed, since a judge may be able to understand a law, interpret it faithfully, and feel in tune with it only by studying the political and social forces that created it. If a law is the result of a revolutionary change in government, the judge who applies it cannot be guided by counterrevolutionary and reactionary sentiments. Under a government of laws the judge's sentiments must serve as a stimulus for integrating the law, not as an excuse for evading it, abusing it, or defeating its purpose.

At this point, if space permitted me to make more than a passing reference to this question, it would be fitting to evaluate the accuracy of those Marxist criticisms that made "bourgeois" justice the butt of their attack, understanding by this, justice as it is organized in the states of western Europe, administered by corps of legally trained judges appointed for life, claiming to be independent of any other power, whose sole function is faithfully to apply the laws that parliament enacts. It is not necessary to seek these criticisms in an orthodox Soviet source such as Vyshinski; it is sufficient to read the writings of Harold Laski, an Englishman converted to Marxism, to find a demonstration that "bourgeois" justice is a "class" justice, in which the judge, like all other jurists, interprets laws enacted in the interest of wealth and privilege, and unconsciously becomes an instrument of this very tyranny, called on to justify by his subtle sophistry the selfish interests of the rich. In the struggle between the weak and the powerful that is at the core of Manzoni's immortal novel, *I promessi sposi,* the lawyer, Dr. Azzeccagarbugli, chose without hesitation the side of the powerful.

There is undoubtedly some truth in this criticism, not only because professionally trained jurists, who must have a university education that the sons of the poor are unable to afford, come from the so-called "bourgeois" class, but also because, if the law is an expression of the interests of the ruling class, it is inevitable that the judge, if he wishes to be a faithful interpreter of this law, becomes an instrument of the same interests and thus, unconsciously, an instrument for maintaining that class in power. Since it is through the judge that the oppressed classes feel the oppression that is only abstract and potential in the law, they may be led to concentrate their animosity on the judge rather than on the distant legislator, for it is the judge who affects them directly, taking the threats that in the law appear remote and innocuous and transforming them into personal suffering. Public opinion often condemns the judge for the sin of the legislator; he is called a class judge, because he interprets class laws; in the allegorical paintings with which Orozco has adorned the Supreme Court building in Mexico City, one can clearly see what the enchained people thought of the judges serving an oppressive regime.

This accusation loses much of its value, however, when applied to the judicial organization of democratic parliamentary states; where, even though the judges are appointed for life and generally come from the middle class, the constitutional mechanism so operates as to permit a continual change in the ruling class and therefore of the interests that it protects by legislation. In this way the gradual adaptation to the new social requirements that occurs in legislation is inevitably reflected (and sometimes foreseen) in the decisions of the judges, where one can follow more clearly than in the laws the slow, laborious but uninterrupted progress of social justice.

It might also be observed that when Marxists accuse "bourgeois" justice of being an instrument of political struggle which the ruling class uses to maintain its favorable position, they make an accusation that, even in part valid, can all the better be turned against them; because in the dictatorship of the proletariat justice is openly vaunted as a political weapon for the defense of socialism. The only difference is that although in the western system of a government of laws political pressure can affect the judge, before it reaches him it has been purified in passing through the filter of the law.

During periods of tranquillity and social stability, where a continuous peaceful social revolution obviates the necessity for abrupt changes, when the laws in effect are accepted by the majority as expressions of popular will, and the judge in applying them feels spiritually at one with the legislative voice of his people, the normal function of the reasoned opinion, which is to furnish a rational basis for the socially inspired feeling of justice that first prompted the judgment, is performed effectively and efficiently, in what might be called a physiological manner.

But the poignant potentialities of the reasoned opinion become apparent when the judge's sense of justice is not in harmony with that of the legislator; when as a result of abrupt political changes and a break in juridical continuity, the judge is called on to apply a law that he believes unjust. It is very well to say that under the rule of law the principle *dura lex sed lex* applies and that consequently the judge must take the law as he finds it, without judging it. But the judge is a human being, and as such he automatically judges the law before applying it; even if he is willing to obey it, he cannot avoid making a moral and political evaluation according to the dictates of his conscience. And even if he stifles the voice of his conscience, when he is obliged to apply a law in which he does not believe, it is only natural that he will apply it mechanically, as an official duty, with a cold bureaucratic pedantry; he cannot be expected to vivify or to re-create a law that is extraneous or actually hostile to his philosophy. When under these conditions the law is applied by a judge who does not approve of it and who is not in sympathy with the forces that gave it birth, it is reduced to a dry formula, to be applied literally.

It is on these occasions that those pathological conditions of conflict and disharmony occur between the judge and the law that cause the reasoned opinion to lose its physiological function and to become either a screen of studied hypocrisy designed to hide the true motives of the decision or a form of disguised protest, through which the judge, in the very act of formally deciding a case in accordance with the law, sees to it that by reading between the lines of the opinion that pretends to show the justice of the decision one can discover why the judge believes it unjust.

Then the crisis of legality, the cause of which is always a more or less acute incompatibility between the laws in effect and the needs of the society, takes the form of that singular phenomenon in judicial pathology that might be called "the crisis in the reasoned opinion."

Recently the causes of this crisis have been so numerous and have arisen from such varying sources that scholars have been able to distinguish and classify certain prevalent types much as if they were working in an experimental laboratory. In Italy, as elsewhere, this crisis has made itself felt repeatedly.

First of all, during the Fascist dictatorship and the German invasion there was the difficult moral decision to be made by the judges who were obliged by the foreign and domestic tyrants to apply cruel and senseless laws that were repugnant to their consciences (e.g., the so-called race laws persecuting the Jews). Even greater was the inner torment of the judges who in their official capacity were required to impose sentence for the violation of laws that as citizens they themselves were violating every day. I can never forget the pathetic case of a judge whose duty it was to sentence persons accused of buying food on the black market in violation of the rationing laws during the war, who every morning before coming to the court went the rounds of the city in frantic search of black market meat for his own sick child.

There has recently appeared in America a highly original study by Professor Cahn entitled *The Sense of Injustice,* which, in order to demonstrate pragmatically how the sense of justice arises and operates in society and in the realm of law, focuses on its negative aspect, on that natural rebellion that is awakened in the human conscience in the face of injustice. Like the illness that makes us appreciate the health we had previously taken for granted, or like the air for which we feel a need only when we are deprived of it, so the sense of injustice reveals to us the value of justice at the moment we are in danger of losing it. In reaction to inhuman laws like those of "racial" persecution there welled up an irrepressible sense of injustice, stronger than reason, leading the judges to seek ingenious pretexts for not applying those abominable laws. The opinion was often the cleverly camouflaged screen behind which this noble treason was accomplished. A study of great political and social interest could be made in attempting to show by an analysis of their opinions the great efforts the judges made to limit the application of those odious laws, against which their consciences rebelled. Such a study would show the moral level of the judges in that period.

But in the countries where the war brought about the fall of the dictatorships and the return of liberty the crisis of the reasoned opinion has now reappeared in another and quite different form.

The fall of the Fascist regime did not lead to a radical change of personnel in the judiciary, nor to major changes in legislation. Even after the promulgation of the republican constitution most of the old laws remained in force, and the same judges applied them who for twenty years had been accustomed to interpret them with a conformist spirit. In the long run habit becomes a form of sclerosis, for judges as well as for others. So long as the laws remain the same, even though the regime has fallen and the constitutional premises have been drastically changed, how can a judge who has grown old through twenty years of dictatorship be expected to interpret in a new democratic spirit the very laws that for twenty years he considered the expression of an authoritarian philosophy?

A judge who has not become irrevocably attached to the spirit of the old laws may have recourse to an evolutionary interpretation; in the elastic provisions of the laws that have remained apparently unchanged, a new spirit can enter through reference to the general principles of the new order. If only he is willing to take the trouble to raise his eyes from the Code before him and look for a moment out of the window at what is happening in the street, the interpreter can easily see that the significance of certain articles whose wording has not been changed is the exact opposite today of what it was under Fascism. For example, the crime of "subversive propaganda" (Art. 272 of the Criminal Code) actually means today quite the opposite of what it meant twenty years ago.

But not all judges are able to make this slight effort. Particularly those who have grown old in the service are likely to remain attached to the old fetishes. It is difficult, after having interpreted laws for twenty years according to one philosophy, to retain the mental agility necessary to break away from the old prejudices and adjust to the new philosophy. In the periods following an abrupt change, a strange assortment of illogical reasoning and of ill-assorted and incompatible conclusions may appear in the opinions of the judges: republican laws interpreted in a monarchist spirit, democratic laws interpreted in the Fascist spirit, laws designed to bring about innovations interpreted in a spirit of conservatism. In such cases the opinion is often at odds with the judgment and may even attempt to discredit it.

Theorists have long been aware of the so-called suicidal decisions, in which the judge is careful to let it be known by his opinion that although he has resigned himself to deciding the case in a certain way in deference to the spirit of conformism, he is nevertheless fully convinced in his own mind that this decision is unjust. In this way in order to save his soul he exhorts his readers not to take his decision seriously and to try to have it reversed on appeal.

In the last ten years all countries whose legal systems have undergone basic changes have experienced other misuses of the reasoned opinion, such as in the polemic decisions where the opinion has been used by certain nostalgic judges not to state the legal reasoning on which the decision is based, but as a pamphlet suitable for a political rally, serving only as an outlet for partisan feeling.

And there are other still less savory subterfuges, like that of a judgment absolving the accused and that he therefore has no interest in appealing, which is followed by an opinion of an almost libelous nature, made public only after the time limit for an appeal has elapsed.

But these, fortunately, are exceptional cases, isolated symptoms of that *malaise* occurring during the period of readjustment after rapid social changes and inevitably affecting the judiciary. Then gradually the old incorrigible judges retire, the younger judges who grew up in the new political atmosphere take their places, and there is established in the judiciary a harmonious relationship with the spirit of the new laws that had previously been lacking, and thus the "crisis in the reasoned opinion" is overcome.

We should not be discouraged. Merely because in periods of general social unrest judges also function less efficiently, we should not cease to have faith in justice.

A few years ago a French jurist, Georges Ripert, of the Law School of the University of Paris, wrote a book worthy of study, entitled *Le déclin du droit,* which sounded like a tocsin warning of the crisis in law from which Europe is suffering. Ripert makes an acute and careful analysis of this crisis: The law of the strongest, the degeneration of private law into public law, the spirit of disobedience, the discontinuity of the law, the uncertainty of the law, the weakening of individual liberty. The conclusion of the eminent jurist is rather pessimistic: The law is declining. But, with all due respect for this learned scholar's understandable and touching concern, his conclusion calls to mind an epigram that I learned as a child in an elementary school book.

> Sedeva in pianti e lai
> la signorina al mar;
> la commoveva assai
> del sole il tramontar.

> —Si calmi, signorina;
> l'affare così va:

il sol di qua declina,
e torna su di là.—*

The law is like the sun; after its decline it will rise again. And if we want to fulfill our social duties we jurists must not lament the twilight of the old justice. It is much more to the point to see to it that, rather than being an instrument for conservation, the law becomes an instrument for peaceful social evolution, capable of forestalling new catastrophes and guiding the world toward the dawn of a new justice.

* A little lady sat
  lamenting by the shore,
  deeply grievèd that
  she saw the sun no more.

"My lady, ease thy mind
and conquer thy despair;
the sun that here declined
will soon rise over there."

Judge Learned Hand

A N D

Judge Jerome Frank

:

OPINION AND DISSENTING OPINION IN
REPOUILLE v. UNITED STATES

JUDGE LEARNED HAND:

The District Attorney, on behalf of the Immigration and Naturalization Service, has appealed from an order, naturalizing the appellee, Repouille. The ground of the objection in the district court and here is that he did not show himself to have been a person of "good moral character" for the five years which preceded the filing of his petition. The facts were as follows. The petition was filed on September 22, 1944, and on October 12, 1939, he had deliberately put to death his son, a boy of thirteen, by means of chloroform. His reason for this tragic deed was that the child had "suffered from birth from a brain injury which destined him to be an idiot and a physical monstrosity malformed in all four limbs. The child was blind, mute, and deformed. He had to be fed; the movements of his bladder and bowels were involuntary, and his entire life was spent in a small crib." Repouille had four other children at the time towards whom he has always been a dutiful and responsible parent; it may be assumed that his act was to help him in their nurture, which was being compromised by the burden imposed upon him in the care of the fifth. The family was altogether dependent upon his industry for its support. He was indicted for manslaughter in the first degree; but the jury brought in a verdict of manslaughter in the second degree with a recommendation of the "utmost clemency"; and the judge sentenced him to not less than five years nor more than ten, execution to be stayed, and the defendant to be placed on probation, from which he was dis-

charged in December, 1945. Concededly, except for this act he conducted himself as a person of "good moral character" during the five
years before he filed his petition. Indeed, if he had waited before filing
his petition from September 22, to October 14, 1944, he would have
had a clear record for the necessary period, and would have been admitted without question.

Very recently we had to pass upon the phrase "good moral character"
in the Nationality Act; and we said that it set as a test, not those standards which we might ourselves approve, but whether "the moral feelings,
now prevalent generally in this country" would "be outraged" by the
conduct in question: that is, whether it conformed to "the generally
accepted moral conventions current at the time." In the absence of some
national inquisition, like a Gallup poll, that is indeed a difficult test to
apply; often questions will arise to which the answer is not ascertainable,
and where the petitioner must fail only because he has the affirmative.
Indeed, in the case at bar itself the answer is not wholly certain; for we
all know that there are great numbers of people of the most unimpeachable virtue, who think it morally justifiable to put an end to a life so
inexorably destined to be a burden to others, and—so far as any possible
interest of its own is concerned—condemned to a brutish existence,
lower indeed than all but the lowest forms of sentient life. Nor is it
inevitably an answer to say that it must be immoral to do this, until the
law provides security against the abuses which would inevitably follow,
unless the practice were regulated.

Many people—probably most people—do not make it a final ethical
test of conduct that it shall not violate law; few of us exact of ourselves
or of others the unflinching obedience of a Socrates. There being no
lawful means of accomplishing an end, which they believe to be righteous
in itself, there have always been conscientious persons who feel no scruple
in acting in defiance of a law which is repugnant to their personal convictions, and who even regard as martyrs those who suffer by doing so.
In our own history it is only necessary to recall the Abolitionists. It is
reasonably clear that the jury which tried Repouille did not feel any
moral repulsion at his crime. Although it was inescapable murder in the
first degree, not only did they bring in a verdict that was flatly in the face
of the facts and utterly absurd—for manslaughter in the second degree
presupposes that the killing has not been deliberate—but they coupled
even that with a recommendation which showed that in substance they
wished to exculpate the offender. Moreover, it is also plain, from the

sentence which he imposed, that the judge could not have seriously disagreed with their recommendation.

One might be tempted to seize upon all this as a reliable measure of current morals; and no doubt it should have its place in the scale; but we should hesitate to accept it as decisive, when, for example, we compare it with the fate of a similar offender in Massachusetts, who, although he was not executed, was imprisoned for life. Left at large as we are, without means of verifying our conclusion, and without authority to substitute our individual beliefs, the outcome must needs be tentative; and not much is gained by discussion. We can say no more than that, quite independently of what may be the current moral feeling as to legally administered euthanasia, we feel reasonably secure in holding that only a minority of virtuous persons would deem the practice morally justifiable, while it remains in private hands, even when the provocation is as overwhelming as it was in this instance.

However, we wish to make it plain that a new petition would not be open to this objection; and that the pitiable event, now long passed, will not prevent Repouille from taking his place among us as a citizen. The assertion in his brief that he did not "intend" the petition to be filed until 1945, unhappily is irrelevant; the statute makes crucial the actual date of filing.

Order reversed; petition dismissed without prejudice to the filing of a second petition.

JUDGE JEROME FRANK (dissenting):
This decision may be of small practical import to this petitioner for citizenship, since perhaps, on filing a new petition, he will promptly become a citizen. But the method used by my colleagues in disposing of this case may, as a precedent, have a very serious significance for many another future petitioner whose "good moral character" may be questioned (for any one of a variety of reasons which may be unrelated to a "mercy killing") in circumstances where the necessity of filing a new petition may cause a long and injurious delay.* Accordingly, I think it desirable to dissent.

The district judge found that Repouille was a person of "good moral character." Presumably, in so finding, the judge attempted to employ

* Consider, e.g., the case of a professional man, unable during a long delay, incident to his becoming a citizen, to practice his profession in certain states of this country.

that statutory standard in accordance with our decisions, i.e., as measured by conduct in conformity with "the generally accepted moral conventions at the time." My colleagues, although their sources of information concerning the pertinent mores are not shown to be superior to those of the district judge, reject his finding. And they do so, too, while conceding that their own conclusion is uncertain, and (as they put it) "tentative." I incline to think that the correct statutory test (the test Congress intended) is the attitude of our ethical leaders. That attitude would not be too difficult to learn; indeed, my colleagues indicate that they think such leaders would agree with the district judge. But the precedents in this circuit constrain us to be guided by contemporary public opinion about which, cloistered as judges are, we have but vague notions. (One recalls Gibbon's remark that usually a person who talks of "the opinion of the world at large" is really referring to "the few people with whom I happened to converse.")

Seeking to apply a standard of this type, courts usually do not rely on evidence but utilize what is often called the doctrine of "judicial notice," which, in matters of this sort, properly permits informal inquiries by the judges.* However, for such a purpose (as in the discharge of many other judicial duties), the courts are inadequately staffed, so that sometimes "judicial notice" actually means judicial ignorance.

But the courts are not utterly helpless; such judicial impotence has its limits. Especially when an issue importantly affecting a man's life is involved, it seems to me that we need not, and ought not, resort to our mere unchecked surmises, remaining wholly (to quote my colleagues' words) "without means of verifying our conclusions." Because court judgments are the most solemn kind of governmental acts—backed up as they are, if necessary, by the armed force of the government—they should, I think, have a more solid foundation. I see no good reason why a man's rights should be jeopardized by judges' needless lack of knowledge.

I think, therefore, that, in any case such as this, where we lack the means of determining present-day public reactions, we should remand to the district judge with these directions: The judge should give the petitioner and the government the opportunity to bring to the judge's attention reliable information on the subject, which he may supplement in any appropriate way. All the data so obtained should be put on

---

* In this very case, my colleagues have relied on informally procured information with reference to "the fate of a similar offender in Massachusetts."

record. On the basis thereof, the judge should reconsider his decision and arrive at a conclusion. Then, if there is another appeal, we can avoid sheer guessing, which alone is now available to us, and can reach something like an informed judgment.*

* Of course, we cannot thus expect to attain certainty, for certainty on such a subject as public opinion is unattainable.

Judge Learned Hand

:

OPINION ON SCHMIDT v. UNITED STATES

The petitioner has appealed from an order denying his petition for naturalization on the ground that he had failed to establish that he was a person of "good moral character" for the five years preceding the filing of the petition on July 5, 1944. He was a native of Germany, at that time thirty-nine years old, who had been admitted to the United States for permanent residence on January 17, 1939. He was a teacher of French and German in the College of the City of New York and was in every way qualified as a citizen, except that, in a moment of what may have been unnecessary frankness, he verified an affidavit before the examiner, which contained the following passage. "Now and then I engaged in an act in sexual intercourse with women. These women have been single and unmarried women. As to the frequency of these acts I can only state that they occurred now and then. My last such act took place about half a year ago with an unmarried woman." The only question in the case is whether by this admission the alien showed that he was not a person of "good moral character."

In United States ex rel. Iorio v. Day, a deportation case where the Commisioner of Immigration had held that a violation of the Prohibition Law was "a crime involving moral turpitude," we said that it was "impossible to decide at all without some estimate, necessarily based on conjecture, as to what people generally feel." The phrase, "good moral character," in the Naturalization Law, is of the same kind, and makes the same demand. It is true that in Estrin v. United States we held that a

702

single act of adultery, unexplained and unpalliated, was alone enough to prevent the alien's naturalization; but we refused to say whether under the "common standards of morality" there might not be "extenuating circumstances" for such a single lapse. In Petitions of Rudder et al. the question arose as to what those circumstances might be. Each of several aliens had been living for years with a single woman in an adulterous union, which apparently had not been concupiscent. Either the alien or the woman had been unable, for one reason or another, to get a divorce. We admitted them all because we did not "believe that the present sentiment of the community views as morally reprehensible such faithful and long continued relationships under the circumstances here disclosed." In United States v. Rubia the alien was admitted upon substantially the same facts, save that he had had a good war record. In United States v. Francioso we admitted an alien who had married, and was living with his niece under circumstances where we thought that "the moral feelings, now prevalent generally in this country" would not "be outraged because Francioso continued to live" with his wife and with four children whom he had had by her. The last case in which we passed on the clause was Repouille v. United States where the alien, in order to relieve his family of crushing expense, had killed his child who was a hopeless bedridden idiot. We thought that such conduct did not conform to "the generally accepted moral conventions current at the time"; but we added: "Left at large as we are, without means of verifying our conclusion, and without authority to substitute our individual beliefs, the outcome must needs be tentative; and not much is gained by discussion." In two very recent cases the Third Circuit by an equally divided court of all six judges, affirmed orders admitting two aliens in the following circumstances. In the first case, an unmarried man admitted that he had had occasional meretricious relations with a single woman for pay; in the second case, the facts were the same, except that the alien had a wife and children in Italy, from whom he had apparently not been legally separated.

The foregoing are the only cases that we have discovered in Courts of Appeal which touch nearly enough upon the case at bar to be important; and it must be owned that the law upon the subject is not free from doubt. We do not see how we can get any help from outside. It would not be practicable—even if the parties had asked for it, which they did not—to conduct an inquiry as to what is the common conscience on the point. Even though we could take a poll, it would not be enough merely to count heads, without any appraisal of the voters. A majority of the votes of those in prisons and brothels, for instance, ought scarcely to outweigh the votes of accredited churchgoers. Nor can we see any reason to suppose that the opinion of clergymen would be a more reliable estimate than our own. The situation is one in which to proceed by any available method would not be more likely to satisfy the impalpable standard, deliberately chosen, than that we adopted in the foregoing cases: that is, to resort to our own conjecture, fallible as we recognize it to be. It is true that recent investigations have attempted to throw light upon the actual habits of men in the petitioner's position, and they have disclosed—what few people would have doubted in any event—that his practice is far from uncommon; but it does not follow that on this point common practice may not have diverged as much from precept as it often does. We have answered in the negative the question whether an unmarried man must live completely celibate, or forfeit his claim to a "good moral character"; but, as we have said, those were cases of continuous, though adulterous, union. We have now to say whether it makes a critical difference that the alien's lapses are casual, concupiscent and promiscuous, but not adulterous. We do not believe that discussion will make our conclusion more persuasive; but, so far as we can divine anything so tenebrous and impalpable as the common conscience, these added features do not make a critical difference.

Order reversed; petition granted.

Justice William O. Douglas

A N D

Justice Robert H. Jackson

:

OPINION AND DISSENTING OPINION IN
TERMINIELLO v. CHICAGO

JUSTICE WILLIAM O. DOUGLAS:

Petitioner after jury trial was found guilty of disorderly conduct in violation of a city ordinance of Chicago and fined. The case grew out of an address he delivered in an auditorium in Chicago under the auspices of the Christian Veterans of America. The meeting commanded considerable public attention. The auditorium was filled to capacity with over eight hundred persons present. Others were turned away. Outside of the auditorium a crowd of about one thousand persons gathered to protest against the meeting. A cordon of policemen was assigned to the meeting to maintain order; but they were not able to prevent several disturbances. The crowd outside was angry and turbulent.

Petitioner in his speech condemned the conduct of the crowd outside and vigorously, if not viciously, criticized various political and racial groups whose activities he denounced as inimical to the nation's welfare.

The trial court charged that "breach of the peace" consists of any "misbehavior which violates the public peace and decorum"; and that the "misbehavior may constitute a breach of the peace if it stirs the public to anger, invites dispute, brings about a condition of unrest, or creates a disturbance, or if it molests the inhabitants in the enjoyment of peace and quiet by arousing alarm." Petitioner did not take exception to that instruction. But he maintained at all times that the ordinance as applied to his conduct violated his right of free speech under the Federal Constitution. The judgment of conviction was affirmed by the Illinois Appellate Court and by the Illinois Supreme Court. The case is here on a petition for certiorari which we granted because of the importance of the question presented.

The argument here has been focused on the issue of whether the content of petitioner's speech was composed of derisive, fighting words, which carried it outside the scope of the constitutional guarantees. We do not reach that question, for there is a preliminary question that is dispositive of the case.

As we have noted, the statutory words "breach of the peace" were defined in instructions to the jury to include speech which "stirs the public to anger, invites dispute, brings about a condition of unrest, or creates a disturbance. . . ."

That construction of the ordinance is a ruling on a question of state law that is as binding on us as though the precise words had been written into the ordinance.

The vitality of civil and political institutions in our society depends on free discussion. As Chief Justice Hughes wrote in De Jonge v. Oregon, it is only through free debate and free exchange of ideas that government remains responsive to the will of the people and peaceful change is effected. The right to speak freely and to promote diversity of ideas and programs is therefore one of the chief distinctions that sets us apart from totalitarian regimes.

Accordingly a function of free speech under our system of government is to invite dispute. It may indeed best serve its high purpose when it induces a condition of unrest, creates dissatisfaction with conditions as they are, or even stirs people to anger. Speech is often provocative and challenging. It may strike at prejudices and preconceptions and have profound unsettling effects as it presses for acceptance of an idea. That is why freedom of speech, though not absolute, is nevertheless protected against censorship or punishment, unless shown likely to produce a clear and present danger of a serious substantive evil that rises far above public inconvenience, annoyance, or unrest. There is no room under our Constitution for a more restrictive view. For the alternative would lead to standardization of ideas either by legislatures, courts, or dominant political or community groups.

The ordinance as construed by the trial court seriously invaded this province. It permitted conviction of petitioner if his speech stirred people to anger, invited public dispute, or brought about a condition of unrest. A conviction resting on any of those grounds may not stand.

The fact that petitioner took no exception to the instruction is immaterial. No exception to the instructions was taken in Stromberg v. California. But a judgment of conviction based on a general verdict under a state statute was set aside in that case, because one part of the statute was unconstitutional. The statute had been challenged as unconstitutional and the instruction was framed in its language. The Court held that the attack on the statute as a whole was equally an attack on each of its individual parts. Since the verdict was a general one and did not specify the ground upon which it rested, it could not be sustained. For one part of the statute was unconstitutional and it could not be determined that the defendant was not convicted under that part.

The principle of that case controls this one. As we have said, the gloss which Illinois placed on the ordinance gives it a meaning and application which are conclusive on us. We need not consider whether as construed it is defective in its entirety. As construed and applied it at least contains parts that are unconstitutional. The verdict was a general one; and we do not know on this record but what it may rest on the invalid clauses.

The statute as construed in the charge to the jury was passed on by the Illinois courts and sustained by them over the objection that as so read it violated the Fourteenth Amendment. The fact that the parties did not dispute its construction makes the adjudication no less ripe for our review, as the Stromberg decision indicates. We can only take the statute as the state courts read it. From our point of view it is immaterial whether the state law question as to its meaning was controverted or accepted. The pinch of the statute is in its application. It is that question which the petitioner has brought here. To say therefore that the question on this phase of the case is whether the trial judge gave a wrong charge is wholly to misconceive the issue.

But it is said that throughout the appellate proceedings the Illinois courts assumed that the only conduct punishable and punished under the ordinance was conduct constituting "fighting words." That emphasizes, however, the importance of the rule of the Stromberg Case. Petitioner was not convicted under a statute so narrowly construed. For all anyone knows he was convicted under the parts of the ordinance (as construed) which, for example, make it an offense merely to invite dispute or to bring about a condition of unrest. We cannot avoid that issue by saying that all Illinois did was to measure petitioner's conduct, not the ordinance, against the Constitution. Petitioner raised both points—that his speech was protected by the Constitution; that the inclusion of his speech within the ordinance was a violation of the Constitution. We would, therefore, strain at technicalities to conclude that the constitutionality of the ordinance as construed and applied to petitioner was not before the Illinois courts. The record makes clear that petitioner at all times challenged the constitutionality of the ordinance as construed and applied to him.

Reversed.

JUSTICE ROBERT H. JACKSON (dissenting):

The Court reverses this conviction by reiterating generalized approbations of freedom of speech with which, in the abstract, no one will disagree. Doubts as to their applicability are lulled by avoidance of more than passing reference to the circumstances of Terminiello's speech and judging it as if he had spoken to persons as dispassionate as empty benches, or like a modern Demosthenes practicing his Philippics on a lonely seashore.

But the local court that tried Terminiello was not indulging in theory. It was dealing with a riot and with a speech that provoked a hostile mob and incited a friendly one, and threatened violence between the two. When the trial judge instructed the jury that it might find Terminiello guilty of inducing a breach of the peace if his behavior stirred the public to anger, invited dispute, brought about unrest, created a disturbance or molested peace and quiet by arousing alarm, he was not speaking of these as harmless or abstract conditions. He was addressing his words to the concrete behavior and specific consequences disclosed by the evidence. He was saying to the jury, in effect, that if this particular speech added fuel to the situation already so inflamed as to threaten to get beyond police control, it could be punished as inducing a breach of peace. When the light of the evidence not recited by the Court is thrown upon the Court's opinion, it discloses that underneath a little issue of Terminiello and his hundred-dollar fine lurk some of the most far-reaching constitutional questions that can confront a people who value both liberty and order. This Court seems to regard these as enemies of each other and to be of the view that we must forego order to achieve liberty. So it fixes its eyes on a conception of freedom of speech so rigid as to tolerate no concession to society's need for public order.

An old proverb warns us to take heed lest we "walk into a well from looking at the stars." To show why I think the Court is in some danger of doing just that, I must bring these deliberations down to earth by a long recital of facts.

Terminiello, advertised as a Catholic Priest, but revealed at the trial to be under suspension by his Bishop, was brought to Chicago from Birmingham, Alabama, to address a gathering that assembled in response to a call signed by Gerald L. K. Smith, which, among other things, said:

". . . The same people who hate Father Coughlin hate Father Terminiello. They have persecuted him, hounded him, threatened him, but
he has remained unaffected by their anti-Christian campaign against him.
You will hear all sorts of reports concerning Father Terminiello. But
remember that he is a Priest in good standing and a fearless lover of
Christ and America."

The jury may have considered that this call attempted to capitalize the
hatreds this man had stirred and foreshadowed, if it did not intend to
invite, the kind of demonstration that followed.

Terminiello's own testimony shows the conditions under which he
spoke. So far as material it follows:

". . . We got there [the meeting place] approximately fifteen or
twenty minutes past eight. The car stopped at the front entrance. There
was a crowd of three or four hundred congregated there shouting and
cursing and picketing. . . .

"When we got there the pickets were not marching; they were body to
body and covered the sidewalk completely, some on the steps so that we
had to form a flying wedge to get through. Police escorted us to the
building, and I noticed four or five others there.

"They called us 'God damned Fascists, Nazis, ought to hang the so
and sos.' When I entered the building I heard the howls of the people
outside. . . . There were four or five plain-clothes officers standing at
the entrance to the stage and three or four at the entrance to the back
door.

"The officers threatened that if they broke the door again they would
arrest them and every time they opened the door a little to look out something was thrown at the officers, including ice-picks and rocks.

"A number of times the door was broken, was partly broken through.
There were doors open this way and they partly opened and the officers
looked out two or three times and each time ice-picks, stones and bottles
were thrown at the police at the door. I took my place on the stage,
before this I was about ten or fifteen minutes in the body of the hall.

"I saw a number of windows broken by stones or missiles. I saw the
back door being forced open, pushed open.

"The front door was broken partly open after the doors were closed.
There were about seven people seated on the stage. Smith opened the
meeting with prayer, the Pledge of Allegiance to the Flag and singing of
America. There were other speakers who spoke before me and before
I spoke I heard things happening in the hall and coming from the outside.

"I saw rocks being thrown through windows and that continued throughout at least the first half of the meeting, probably longer, and again attempts were made to force the front door, rather the front door was forced partly. The howling continued on the outside, cursing could be heard audibly in the hall at times. Police were rushing in and out of the front door protecting the front door, and there was a general commotion, all kinds of noises and violence—all from the outside.

"Between the time the first speaker spoke and I spoke, stones and bricks were thrown in all the time. I started to speak about 35 or 40 minutes after the meeting started, a little later than nine o'clock. . . ."

The court below, in addition to this recital, heard other evidence, that the crowd reached an estimated number of 1,500. Picket lines obstructed and interfered with access to the building. The crowd constituted "a surging, howling mob hurling epithets at those who would enter and tried to tear their clothes off." One young woman's coat was torn off and she had to be assisted into the meeting by policemen. Those inside the hall could hear the loud noises and hear those on the outside yell, "Fascists, Hitlers!" and curse words like "damn Fascists." Bricks were thrown through the windowpanes before and during the speaking. About 28 windows were broken. The street was black with people on both sides for at least a block either way; bottles, stink bombs and brickbats were thrown. Police were unable to control the mob, which kept breaking the windows at the meeting hall, drowning out the speaker's voice at times and breaking in through the back door of the auditorium. About 17 of the group outside were arrested by the police.

Knowing of this environment, Terminiello made a long speech, from the stenographic record of which I omit relatively innocuous passages and add emphasis to what seems especially provocative:

"Father Terminiello: Now, I am going to whisper my greetings to you, Fellow Christians. I will interpret it. I said, 'Fellow *Christians,*' and I suppose there are *some of the scum got in by mistake,* so I want to tell a story about *the scum:*

". . . And nothing I could say tonight could begin to express the contempt I have for the *slimy scum* that got in by mistake.

". . . The subject I want to talk to you tonight about is the attempt *that is going on right outside this hall tonight,* the attempt that is going on to *destroy America by revolution.* . . .

"My friends, it is no longer true that it can't happen here. It is happening here, and it only depends upon you, good people, who are here tonight, depends upon all of us together, as Mr. Smith said. The tide is changing, and if you and I turn and run from that tide, we will all be drowned in this tidal wave of communism which is going over the world.

". . . I am not going to talk to you about the menace of communism, which is already accomplished, in Russia, where from eight to fifteen million people were murdered in cold blood by their own countryman, and millions more through Eastern Europe at the close of the war are being murdered by these murderous Russians, hurt, being raped and sent into slavery. *That is what they want for you, that howling mob outside.*

"I know I was told one time that my winter quarters were ready for me in Siberia. I was told that. Now, I am talking about the fifty-seven varieties that we have in America, and we have fifty-seven varieties of pinks and reds and pastel shades in this country; and all of it can be traced back to the twelve years we spent under the New Deal, because that was the build-up for what is going on in the world today.

"Now, Russia promised us we would *ga* [sic] back to the official newspaper of Russia. Primarily it was back about 1929. They quoted the words of George E. Dimitroff, who at that time was the Executive Secretary of the Communist International. I only quote you this one passage. I could quote thousands of paragraphs for you. Let me quote you: 'The worldwide nature of our program is not mere talk, but an all embracing *blood-soaked reality.*' *That is what they want for us, a blood-soaked reality but it was promised to us by the crystal gazers in Washington;* and you know what I mean by the 'crystal gazers,' I presume.

"First of all, we had Queen Eleanor. Mr. Smith said, 'Queen Eleanor is now one of the world's Communists.' She is one who said this—imagine, coming from the spouse of the former President of the United States for twelve long years—this is what she said: 'The war is but a step in the revolution. The war is but one step in the revolution, and we know who started the war.'

"Then we have Henry Adolph Wallace, the sixty million job magician. You know we only need fifty-four million jobs in America and everybody would be working. He wants sixty million jobs, because some of the bureaucrats want two jobs apiece. Here he is, what he says about revolution: 'We are in for a profound revolution. Those of us who realize the inevitableness of the revolution, and are anxious that it be *gradual and bloodless* instead of *somewhat bloody. Of course, if necessary, we will have it more bloody.*'

"And then Chief Justice Stone had this to say: 'A way has been found for the effective suppression of speeches and press and religion despite constitutional guarantee,'—from the Chief Justice, from the Chief Justice of the United States.

"Now, my friends, they are planning another ruse; and if it ever happens to this cou-try [sic], God help America. They are going to try to put into Mr. Edgar Hoover's position a man by the name of *George Swarzwald.* I think even those who were uneducated on so-called sedition charges, that the majority of the individuals in this department, that Christ-like men and women who realize today what is going on in this country, men who are in this audience today, who want *to know the names of those people, before they are outside, they want to know the names if any. Did you hear any tonight that you recognized? Most of them probably are imported. They are imported from Russia, certainly. If you know the names, please send them to me immediately.* . . .

". . . Didn't you ever read the Morgenthau plan for the starvation of little babies and pregnant women in Germany? Whatever could a child that is born have to do with Hitler or anyone else at the beginning of the war? Why should every child in Germany today not live to be more than two or three months of age? Because Morgenthau wants it that way, and so did F.D.R. . . . *You will know who is behind it when I tell you the story* of a doctor in Akron, Ohio. He boasted to a friend of mine within the last few days, while he was in the service of this country as a doctor, he and others of his kind made it a practice—now, this was not only one man—made it a practice to amputate the limbs of every German they came in contact with whenever they could get away with it; so, that they could never carry a gun. Imagine men of that caliber, sworn to serve this beautiful country of ours, *why should we tolerate them?*

"My friends, this moment someone reminded me of the plan to sterilize them. The nurses, they tell me are going to inject diseases in them, syphilis and other diseases in *every one that came there all of one race, all non-Christians.*

"Now, we are going to get the threats of the people of Argentine, the people of Spain. We have now declared, according to our officials, to have declared Franco to have taken the place of Hitler. *Franco was the savior of what was left of Europe.*

"Now, let me say, I am going to talk about—I almost said, about the Jews. Of course, I would not want to say that. However, I am going to talk about some Jews. I hope that—I am a Christian minister. We must take a Christian attitude. I don't want you to go from this hall with hatred in your heart for any person, for no person. . . .

"Now, this danger which we face—let us call them Zionist Jews if you will, let's call them atheistic, communistic Jewish or Zionist Jews, then let us not fear to condemn them. You remember the Apostles when they went into the upper room after the death of the Master, they went in there, after locking the doors; they closed the windows. (At this time there was a very loud noise as if something was being thrown into the building.)

"Don't be disturbed. That happened by the way, while Mr. Gerald Smith was saying 'Our Father who art in heaven'; (just then a rock went through the window.) *Do you wonder they were persecuted in other countries in the world?*

"You know I have always made a study of the psychology, sociology of mob reaction. It is exemplified out there. Remember there has to be a leader of that mob. He is not out there. He is probably across the street, looking out the window. There must be certain things, money, other things, in order to have successful mob action; there must be rhythm. There must be some to beat a cadence. Those mobs are chanting; that is the caveman's chant. They were trained to do it. They were trained this afternoon. They are being led; *there will be violence.*

"That is why I say to you, men, don't you do it. Walk out of here dignified. The police will protect you. Put the women on the inside, where there will be no hurt to them. Just walk; don't stop and argue. . . . They want to picket our meetings. They don't want us to picket their meetings. It is the same kind of tolerance, if we said there was a bedbug in bed, 'We don't care for you,' or if we looked under the bed and found a snake and said, 'I am going to be tolerant and leave the snake there.' We will not be tolerant of that mob out there. We are not going to be tolerant any longer.

"We are strong enough. We are not going to be tolerant of their smears any longer. We are going to *stand up and dare them to smear us.*

"So, my friends, since we spent much time tonight trying to quiet the howling mob, I am going to bring my thoughts to a conclusion, and the conclusion is this. We must all be like the Apostles before the coming of the Holy Ghost. We must not lock ourselves in an upper room for fear of the Jews. I speak of the communistic Zionistic Jew, and those are not American Jews. We don't want them here; we want them to go back where they came from.

"Mr. Smith: I would like to ask that Miss Purcell would please go back to the front of the building and contact the police officer in charge of the detail. We are going to adjourn this meeting if and when Miss Purcell comes back and reports to me that the one in charge of the detail believes it is safe for us to go out on the street. I am sure it is. Sit still. We are not going to have anybody move. If there are any chiselers that want to go, we are going to take up an offering for Father Terminiello.

"(There was further discussion to stimulate this offering which was not reported.)"

Such was the speech. Evidence showed that it stirred the audience not only to cheer and applaud but to expressions of immediate anger, unrest and alarm. One called the speaker a "God damned liar" and was taken out by the police. Another said that "Jews, niggers and Catholics would have to be gotten rid of." One response was, "Yes, the Jews are all killers, murderers. If we don't kill them first, they will kill us." The anti-Jewish stories elicited exclamations of "Oh!" and "Isn't that terrible!" and shouts of "Yes, send the Jews back to Russia," "Kill the Jews," "Dirty kikes," and much more of ugly tenor. This is the specific and concrete kind of anger, unrest and alarm, coupled with that of the mob outside, that the trial court charged the jury might find to be a breach of peace induced by Terminiello. It is difficult to believe that this Court is speaking of the same occasion, but it is the only one involved in this litigation.

Terminiello, of course, disclaims being a Fascist. Doubtless many of the indoor audience were not consciously such. His speech, however, followed, with fidelity that is more than coincidental, the pattern of European Fascist leaders.

The street mob, on the other hand, included some who deny being Communists, but Terminiello testified and offered to prove that the demonstration was Communist-organized and Communist-led. He offered literature of left-wing organizations calling members to meet and "mobilize" for instruction as pickets and exhorting followers: "All out to fight Fascist Smith."

As this case declares a nationwide rule that disables local and state authorities from punishing conduct which produces conflicts of this kind, it is unrealistic not to take account of the nature, methods and objectives of the forces involved. This was not an isolated, spontaneous and unintended collision of political, racial or ideological adversaries. It was a local manifestation of a world-wide and standing conflict between two organized groups of revolutionary fanatics, each of which has imported to this country the strong-arm technique developed in the struggle by which their kind has devastated Europe. Increasingly, American cities have to cope with it. One faction organizes a mass meeting, the other organizes pickets to harass it; each organizes squads to counteract the other's pickets; parade is met with counterparade. Each of these mass demonstrations has the potentiality, and more than a few the purpose, of disorder and violence. This technique appeals not to reason but to fears and mob spirit; each is a show of force designed to bully adversaries and to overawe the indifferent. We need not resort to speculation as to the purposes for which these tactics are calculated nor as to their consequences. Recent European history demonstrates both.

Hitler summed up the strategy of the mass demonstration as used by both fascism and communism: "We should not work in secret conventicles but in mighty mass demonstrations, and it is not by dagger and poison or pistol that the road can be cleared for the movement but *by the conquest of the streets.* We must teach the Marxists that the future *master of the streets* is National Socialism, just as it will some day be the master of the state." [Emphasis supplied.] 1 Nazi Conspiracy & Aggression (GPO, 1946) 204, 2 id. 140, Docs 2760-PS, 404-PS, from "Mein Kampf." First laughed at as an extravagant figure of speech, the battle for the streets became a tragic reality when an organized *Sturmabterlung* began to give practical effect to its slogan that "possession of the streets is the key to power in the state." Ibid, also Doc 2168-PS.

The present obstacle to mastery of the streets by either radical or reactionary mob movements is not the opposing minority. It is the authority of local governments which represent the free choice of democratic and law-abiding elements of all shades of opinion, but who, whatever their differences, submit them to free elections which register the results of their free discussion. The Fascist and Communists groups, on the contrary, resort to these terror tactics to confuse, bully and discredit those freely chosen governments. Violent and noisy shows of strength discourage participation of moderates in discussions so fraught with violence, and real discussion dries up and disappears. And people lose faith in the democratic process when they see public authority flouted and impotent and begin to think the time has come when they must choose sides in a false and terrible dilemma such as was posed as being at hand by the call for the Terminiello meeting: "Christian Nationalism or World Communism—Which?"

This drive by totalitarian groups to undermine the prestige and effectiveness of local democratic governments is advanced whenever either of them can win from this Court a ruling which paralyzes the power of these officials. This is such a case. The group of which Terminiello is a part claims that his behavior, because it involved a speech, is above the reach of local authorities. If the mild action those authorities have taken is forbidden, it is plain that hereafter there is nothing effective left that they can do. If they can do nothing as to him, they are equally powerless as to rival totalitarian groups. Terminiello's victory today certainly fulfills the most extravagant hopes of both right and left totalitarian groups, who want nothing so much as to paralyze and discredit the only democratic authority that can curb them in their battle for the streets.

I am unable to see that the local authorities have transgressed the Federal Constitution. Illinois imposed no prior censorship or suppression upon Terminiello. On the contrary, its sufferance and protection was all that enabled him to speak. It does not appear that the motive in punishing him is to silence the ideology he expressed as offensive to the State's policy or as untrue, or has any purpose of controlling his thought or its peaceful communication to others. There is no claim that the proceedings against Terminiello are designed to discriminate against him or the faction he represents or the ideas that he bespeaks. There is no indication that the charge against him is a mere pretext to give the semblance of legality to a covert effort to silence him or to prevent his followers or the public from hearing any truth that is in him.

A trial court and jury has found only that in the context of violence and disorder in which it was made, this speech was a provocation to immediate breach of the peace and therefore cannot claim constitutional immunity from punishment. Under the Constitution as it has been understood and applied, at least until most recently, the State was within its powers in taking this action.

Rioting is a substantive evil, which I take it no one will deny that the State and the City have the right and the duty to prevent and punish. Where an offense is induced by speech, the Court has laid down and often reiterated a test of the power of the authorities to deal with the speaking as also an offense. "The question in every case is whether the words *used are used in such circumstances* and are of *such a nature* as to create a *clear and present danger* that they will bring about the substantive evils that Congress [or the State or City] has a right to prevent." Mr. Justice Holmes in Schenck v. United States. No one ventures to contend that the State on the basis of this test, for whatever it may be worth, was not justified in punishing Terminiello. In this case the evidence proves beyond dispute that danger of rioting and violence in response to the speech was clear, present and immediate. If this Court has not silently abandoned this long standing test and substituted for the purposes of this case an unexpressed but more stringent test, the action of the State would have to be sustained.

Only recently this Court held that a state could punish as a breach of the peace use of epithets such as "damned racketeer" and "damned Fascists," addressed to only one person, an official, because likely to provoke the average person to retaliation. But these are mild in comparison to the epithets "slimy scum," "snakes," "bedbugs," and the like, which Terminiello hurled at an already inflamed mob of his adversaries. Mr. Justice Murphy, writing for a unanimous Court in Chaplinsky v. New Hampshire, said:

"There are certain well-defined and narrowly limited classes of speech, the prevention and punishment of which have never been thought to raise any Constitutional problem. These include the lewd and obscene, the profane, the libelous, and the insulting or 'fighting' words—those which by their very utterance inflict injury or tend to incite an immediate breach of the peace. It has been well observed that such utterances are no essential part of any exposition of ideas, and are of such slight social value as a step to truth that any benefit that may be derived from them is clearly outweighed by the social interest in order and morality. 'Resort to epithets or personal abuse is not in any proper sense communication of information or opinion safeguarded by the Constitution, and its punishment as a criminal act would raise no question under that instrument.' Cantwell v. Connecticut.

In the latter case Mr. Justice Roberts for a unanimous Court said:

"The offense known as breach of the peace embraces a great variety of conduct destroying or menacing public order and tranquility. It includes not only violent acts but acts and words likely to produce violence in others. No one would have the hardihood to suggest that the principle of freedom of speech sanctions incitement to riot or that religious liberty connotes the privilege to exhort others to physical attack upon those belonging to another sect. When clear and present danger of riot, disorder, interference with traffic upon the public streets, or other immediate threat to public safety, peace, or order, appears, the power of the State to prevent or punish is obvious."

How this present decision, denying state power to punish civilly one who precipitated a public riot involving hundreds of fanatic fighters in a most violent melee, can be squared with those unanimous statements of law, is incomprehensible to me. And the Court recently cited these two statements as indicating that "The essential rights of the First Amendment in some instances are subject to the elemental need for order without which the guarantees of civil rights to others would be a mockery."

However, these wholesome principles are abandoned today and in their place is substituted a dogma of absolute freedom for irresponsible and provocative utterance which almost completely sterilizes the power of local authorities to keep the peace as against this kind of tactics.

Before giving the First and Fourteenth Amendments to the Constitution this effect, we should recall that our application of the First Amendment to Illinois rests entirely on authority which this Court has voted to itself. The relevant parts of the First Amendment, with emphasis supplied, reads: "*Congress* shall make *no* law . . . abridging the freedom of speech." This restrains no authority except Congress. Read as literally as some would do, it restrains Congress in terms so absolute that no legislation would be valid if it touched free speech, no matter how obscene, treasonable, defamatory, inciting or provoking. If it seems strange that no express qualifications were inserted in the Amendment, the answer may be that limitations were thought to be implicit in the definition of "freedom of speech" as then understood. Or it may have been thought unnecessary to delegate to *Congress* any power over abuses of free speech. The Federal Government was then a new and experimental authority, remote from the people, and it was supposed to deal with a limited class of national problems. Inasmuch as any breaches of peace from abuse of free speech traditionally were punishable by state governments, it was needless to reserve that power in a provision drafted to exclude only Congress from such a field of law-making.

The Fourteenth Amendment forbade states to deny the citizen "due process of law." But its terms gave no notice to the people that its adoption would strip their local governments of power to deal with such problems of local peace and order as we have here. Nor was it hinted by this Court for over half a century that the Amendment might have any such effect. In 1922, with concurrence of the most liberty-alert Justices of all times—Holmes and Brandeis—this Court declared flatly that the Constitution does not limit the power of the state over free speech. Prudential Ins. Co. v. Cheek. In later years the Court shifted its dogma and decreed that the Constitution does this very thing and that state power is bound by the same limitation as Congress. Gitlow v. New York. I have no quarrel with this history. I recite the method by which the right to limit the state has been derived only from this Court's own assumption of the power, with never a submission of legislation or amendment into which the people could write any qualification to prevent abuse of this liberty, as bearing upon the restraint I consider as becoming in exercise of self-given and unappealable power.

It is significant that provisions adopted by the people with awareness that they applied to their own states have universally contained qualifying terms. The Constitution of Illinois is representative of the provisions put in nearly all state constitutions and reads (Art. 2, § 4): "Every person may freely speak, write and publish on all subjects, *being responsible for the abuse of that liberty.*" [Emphasis added.] That is what I think is meant by the cryptic phrase "freedom of speech," as used in the Federal Compact, and that is the rule I think we should apply to the states.

This absence from the Constitution of any expressed power to deal with abuse of freedom of speech has enabled the Court to soar aloof from any consideration of the abuses which create problems for the states and to indulge in denials of local authority, some of which seem to me improvident in the light of functions which local governments must be relied on to perform for our free society. Quite apart from any other merits or defects, recent decisions have almost completely immunized this battle for the streets from any form of control.

Streets and parks maintained by the public cannot legally be denied to groups "for communication of ideas." Hague v. Congress for Industrial Organization. Cities may not protect their streets from activities which the law has always regarded subject to control, as nuisances. Cities may not protect the streets or even homes of their inhabitants from the aggressions of organized bands operating in large numbers. Douglas v. Jeannette. As in this case, the facts are set forth fully only in the dissent. Neither a private party nor a public authority can invoke otherwise valid state laws against trespass to exclude from their property groups bent on disseminating propaganda. Picketing is largely immunized from control on the ground that it is free speech, and police may not regulate sound trucks and loud-speakers, though the Court finds them an evil that may be prohibited altogether. And one-third of the Court has gone further and declared that a position "that the state may prevent any conduct which induces people to violate the law, or any advocacy of unlawful activity, cannot be squared with the First Amendment. . . ." And it is only we who can decide when the limit is passed. Whatever the merits of any one of these decisions in isolation, and there were sound reasons for some of them, it cannot be denied that their cumulative effect has been a sharp handicap on municipal control of the streets and a dramatic encouragement of those who would use them in a battle of ideologies.

I do not think we should carry this handicap further, as we do today, but should adhere to the principles heretofore announced to safeguard our liberties against abuse as well as against invasion. It should not be necessary to recall these elementary principles, but it has been a long time since some of them were even mentioned in this Court's writing on the subject and results indicate they may have been overlooked.

I begin with the oft-forgotten principle which this case demonstrates, that freedom of speech exists only under law and not independently of it. What would Terminiello's theoretical freedom of speech have amounted to had he not been given active aid by the officers of the law? He could reach the hall only with their help, could talk only because they restrained the mob, and could make his getaway only under their protection. We would do well to recall the words of Chief Justice Hughes in Cox v. New Hampshire, "Civil liberties, as guaranteed by the Constitution, imply the existence of an organized society maintaining public order without which liberty itself would be lost in the excesses of unrestrained abuses. . . ."

This case demonstrates also that this Court's service to free speech is essentially negative and can consist only of reviewing actions by local magistrates. But if free speech is to be a practical reality, affirmative and immediate protection is required; and it can come only from nonjudicial sources. It depends on local police, maintained by law-abiding taxpayers, and who, regardless of their own feelings, risk themselves to maintain supremacy of law. Terminiello's theoretical right to speak free from interference would have no reality if Chicago should withdraw its officers to some other section of the city, or if the men assigned to the task should look the other way when the crowd threatens Terminiello. Can society be expected to keep these men at Terminiello's service if it has nothing to say of his behavior which may force them into dangerous action?

No one will disagree that the fundamental, permanent and overriding policy of police and courts should be to permit and encourage utmost freedom of utterance. It is the legal right of any American citizen to advocate peaceful adoption of fascism or communism, socialism or capitalism. He may go far in expressing sentiments whether pro-Semitic or anti-Semitic, pro-Negro or anti-Negro, pro-Catholic or anti-Catholic. He is legally free to argue for some anti-American system of government to supersede by constitutional methods the one we have. It is our philosophy that the course of government should be controlled by a consensus of the governed. This process of reaching intelligent popular decisions requires free discussion. Hence we should tolerate no law or custom of censorship or suppression.

But we must bear in mind also that no serious outbreak of mob violence, race rioting, lynching or public disorder is likely to get going without help of some speech-making to some mass of people. A street may be filled with men and women and the crowd still not be a mob. Unity of purpose, passion and hatred, which merges the many minds of a crowd into the mindlessness of a mob, almost invariably is supplied by speeches. It is naïve, or worse, to teach that oratory with this object or effect is a service to liberty. No mob has ever protected any liberty, even its own, but if not put down it always winds up in an orgy of lawlessness which respects no liberties.

In considering abuse of freedom by provocative utterances it is necessary to observe that the law is more tolerant of discussion than are most individuals or communities. Law is so indifferent to subjects of talk that I think of none that it should close to discussion. Religious, social and political topics that in other times or countries have not been open to lawful debate may be freely discussed here.

Because a subject is legally arguable, however, does not mean that public sentiment will be patient of its advocacy at all times and in all manners. So it happens that, while peaceful advocacy of communism or fascism is tolerated by the law, both of these doctrines arouse passionate reactions. A great number of people do not agree that introduction to America of communism or fascism is even debatable. Hence many speeches, such as that of Terminiello, may be legally permissible but may nevertheless in some surroundings, be a menace to peace and order. When conditions show the speaker that this is the case, as it did here, there certainly comes a point beyond which he cannot indulge in provocations to violence without being answerable to society.

Determination of such an issue involves a heavy responsibility. Courts must beware lest they become mere organs of popular intolerance. Not every show of opposition can justify treating a speech as a breach of peace. Neither speakers nor courts are obliged always and in all circumstances to yield to prevailing opinion and feeling. As a people grow in capacity for civilization and liberty their tolerance will grow, and they will endure, if not welcome, discussion even on topics as to which they are committed. They regard convictions as tentative and know that time and events will make their own terms with theories, by whomever and by whatever majorities they are held, and many will be proved wrong. But on our way to this idealistic state of tolerance the police have to deal with men as they are. The crowd mind is never tolerant of any idea which does not conform to its herd opinion. It does not want a tolerant effort at meeting of minds. It does not know the futility of trying to mob an idea. Released from the sense of personal responsibility that would restrain even the worst individuals in it if alone and brave with the courage of numbers, both radical and reactionary mobs endanger liberty as well as order. The authorities must control them and they are entitled to place some checks upon those whose behavior or speech calls such mobs into being. When the right of society to freedom from probable violence should prevail over the right of an individual to defy opposing opinion, presents a problem that always tests wisdom and often calls for immediate and vigorous action to preserve public order and safety.

I do not think that the Constitution of the United States denies to the states and the municipalities power to solve that problem in the light of local conditions, at least so long as danger to public order is not invoked in bad faith, as a cover for censorship or suppression. The preamble declares domestic tranquility as well as liberty to be an object in founding a Federal Government and I do not think the Forefathers were naïve in believing both can be fostered by the law.

Certain practical reasons reinforce the legal view that cities and states should be sustained in the power to keep their streets from becoming the battleground for these hostile ideologies to the destruction and detriment of public order. There is no other power that can do it. Theirs are the only police that are on the spot. The Federal Government has no police force. The Federal Bureau of Investigation is, and should remain, not a police but an investigative service. To date the only federal agency for preserving and restoring order when local authority fails has been the Army. And when the military steps in, the court takes a less liberal view of the rights of the individual and sustains most arbitrary exercises of military power. Every failure of local authority to deal with riot problems results in a demand for the establishment of a federal police or intervention by federal authority. In my opinion, locally established and controlled police can never develop into the menace to general civil liberties that is inherent in a federal police.

The ways in which mob violence may be worked up are subtle and various. Rarely will a speaker directly urge a crowd to lay hands on a victim or class of victims. An effective and safer way is to incite mob action while pretending to deplore it, after the classic example of Antony, and this was not lost on Terminiello. And whether one may be the cause of mob violence by his own personification or advocacy of ideas which a crowd already fears and hates, is not solved merely by going through a transcript of the speech to pick out "fighting words." The most insulting words can be neutralized if the speaker will smile when he says them, but a belligerent personality and an aggressive manner may kindle a fight without use of words that in cold type shock us. True judgment will be aided by observation of the individual defendant, as was possible for this jury and trial court but impossible for us.

There are many appeals these days to liberty, often by those who are working for an opportunity to taunt democracy with its stupidity in furnishing them the weapons to destroy it as did Goebbels when he said: "When democracy granted democratic methods for us in times of opposition, this [Nazi seizure of power] was bound to happen in a democratic system. However, we National Socialists never asserted that we represented a democratic point of view, but we have declared openly that we used democratic methods only in order to gain the power and that, after assuming the power, we would deny to our adversaries without any consideration the means which were granted to us in times of [our] opposition." 1 Nazi Conspiracy & Aggression (GPO 1926) 202, Docs 2500-PS, 2412-PS.

Invocation of constitutional liberties as part of the strategy for overthrowing them presents a dilemma to a free people which may not be soluble by constitutional logic alone.

But I would not be understood as suggesting that the United States can or should meet this dilemma by suppression of free, open and public speaking on the part of any group or ideology. Suppression has never been a successful permanent policy; any surface serenity that it creates is a false security, while conspiratorial forces go underground. My confidence in American institutions and in the sound sense of the American people is such that if with a stroke of the pen I could silence every Fascist and Communist speaker, I would not do it. For I agree with Woodrow Wilson, who said:

"I have always been among those who believed that the greatest freedom of speech was the greatest safety, because if a man is a fool, the best thing to do is to encourage him to advertise the fact by speaking. It cannot be so easily discovered if you allow him to remain silent and look wise, but if you let him speak, the secret is out and the world knows that he is a fool. So it is by the exposure of folly that it is defeated; not by the seclusion of folly, and in this free air of free speech men get into that sort of communication with one another which constitutes the basis of all common achievement." Address at the Institute of France, Paris, May 10, 1919. 2 Selected Literary and Political Papers and Addresses of Woodrow Wilson (1926) 333.

But if we maintain a general policy of free speaking, we must recognize that its inevitable consequence will be sporadic local outbreaks of violence, for it is the nature of men to be intolerant of attacks upon institutions, personalities and ideas for which they really care. In the long run, maintenance of free speech will be more endangered if the population can have no protection from the abuses which lead to violence. No liberty is made more secure by holding that its abuses are inseparable from its enjoyment. We must not forget that it is the free democratic communities that ask us to trust them to maintain peace with liberty and that the factions engaged in this battle are not interested permanently in either. What would it matter to Terminiello if the police batter up some Communists or, on the other hand, if the Communists batter up some policemen? Either result makes grist for his mill; either would help promote hysteria and the demand for strong-arm methods in dealing with his adversaries. And what, on the other hand, have the Communist agitators to lose from a battle with the police?

This Court has gone far toward accepting the doctrine that civil liberty means the removal of all restraints from these crowds and that all local attempts to maintain order are impairments of the liberty of the the citizen. The choice is not between order and liberty. It is between liberty with order and anarchy without either. There is danger that, if the Court does not temper its doctrinaire logic with a little practical wisdom, it will convert the constitutional Bill of Rights into a suicide pact.

I would affirm the conviction.

Felix Frankfurter

:

ADVICE TO A YOUNG MAN INTERESTED IN GOING INTO LAW

In May 1954 a twelve-year-old boy living in Alexandria, Virginia, sent a letter to Mr. Justice Frankfurter in which he wrote that he was "interested in going into law as a career" and requested advice as to "some ways to start preparing myself while still in junior high school." He received this reply.

My dear Paul:

No one can be a truly competent lawyer unless he is a cultivated man. If I were you, I would forget all about any technical preparation for the law. The best way to prepare for the law is to come to the study of the law as a well-read person. Thus alone can one acquire the capacity to use the English language on paper and in speech and with the habits of clear thinking which only a truly liberal education can give. No less important for a lawyer is the cultivation of the imaginative faculties by reading poetry, seeing great paintings, in the original or in easily available reproductions, and listening to great music. Stock your mind with the deposit of much good reading, and widen and deepen your feelings by experiencing vicariously as much as possible the wonderful mysteries of the universe, and forget all about your future career.

With good wishes,

Sincerely yours,

[*Signed*] Felix Frankfurter

Master M. Paul Claussen, Jr.

Justice Oliver Wendell Holmes, Jr.

·

LETTER TO HAROLD LASKI

Washington, D. C., May 27, 1921

Dear Laski: Your letter of 12 V. 21 (I can copy if I cannot emulate) came this P.M. too late for me to catch the boat that I still imagine to sail every Saturday. Your tale of negotiations was most interesting but I fear from what little I have heard or seen later that it did not succeed. With us the main event has been the death of the Chief Justice.* Poor man, he suffered long and bore up against it heroically—but life could not have been satisfactory longer, even if his pain had ceased. He had, beside the trouble of which he died, cataracts on both eyes and had grown very deaf. I cannot judge whether his delaying any operation was due to determination not to give the appointment to Wilson or to love of the office or to mistaken sense of duty—possibly all combined. For I think he loved the office as an end in itself. There is a queer difference in people about that. The only thing that gives me appreciable pleasure is when people—the rare ones that I care about and whose judgment I respect—tell me that I have hit the *ut de poitrine* in my work. Then for half an hour I feel that the long struggle has been rewarded—and then comes again the doubt—will the next one do the trick. As I may have written, the last year or two has brought more of the feeling of reward than ever before—and I fully appreciate the part that you have played in bringing that about. Now people speculate as to who will take White's

---

* Mr. Chief Justice White had died on May 19. The vacancy was filled at the end of June by the appointment of William Howard Taft.

place—Taft is much mentioned. I would rather have Hughes but I think he doesn't want it. Hughes is very hard working. Taft is said to be indolent. He has been out of judicial place for 20 years or so—and though he did well as a Circuit Judge I never saw anything that struck me as more than first rate second rate. I have heard it said and denied that he is hard to get along with if you don't agree with him. I assume that the President will be impressed by political experience (which of course is valuable) and popular prominence. You may wonder if I am thinking of it. Not in any sense except that all possibilities occur to one and that no doubt a few here and there have named me. They would not appoint so old a man—and although I think I know my place with regard to the higher aspects of the law, I should not expect it of the appointing power. That is not the kind of thing that excites me much. I take it for granted that Brandeis's chance died with Wilson's departure. I wonder how many men are pulling wires now. I give you my word of honor that I am not. I don't even know what, if any, wires I could pull —I haven't lifted a finger. When White was appointed I told McKenna that I believed that he and I were the only justices who hadn't got a little boom of greater or less magnitude. *Quam parva sapientia regitur mundus.* The funeral was preceded and followed by garden parties at the White House. I went yesterday from a sense of duty and found it both pleasant and beautiful. I hoped I might meet the Princess Bibesco (Mrs. Asquith's daughter) whom I have not yet seen—but I didn't. The colors of some dresses and many ladies' faces were bright and it is always agreeable to see some one brighten up with a friendly look. I had a short talk with Cabot Lodge whom I hadn't seen for a long time. He looked tired. There are not many now with whom one has had a lifelong familiarity and he is ten years younger than I. Mrs. Gray* is here and the other day I took her out to my private show—Fort Stevens where I saw Lincoln when the big guns were firing and our skirmishers going up the opposite slope and the enemy got their nearest to Washington. It is a hidden spot that few know and I was posing as the last survivor in the little cemetery nearby when we met 3 80-year olders two at least of whom I believe were there—and we held a little reunion that pleased Mrs. Gray and them. My work is pretty nearly done. We expect to go to Beverly Farms or Boston rather June 15, and oh, how I shall miss you there.

Compliments to the missus.   *Affectionately yours, O. W. Holmes*

* Mrs. John Chipman Gray, an intimate friend of Holmes's.

Justice Oliver Wendell Holmes, Jr.

:

OPINION IN BUCK v. BELL

This is a writ of error to review a judgment of the supreme court of appeals of the state of Virginia, affirming a judgment of the circuit court of Amherst county, by which the defendant in error, the superintendent of the State Colony for Epileptics and Feeble Minded, was ordered to perform the operation of salpingectomy upon Carrie Buck, the plaintiff in error, for the purpose of making her sterile. The case comes here upon the contention that the statute authorizing the judgment is void under the 14th Amendment as denying to the plaintiff in error due process of law and the equal protection of the laws.

Carrie Buck is a feeble minded white woman who was committed to the State Colony above mentioned in due form. She is the daughter of a feeble minded mother in the same institution, and the mother of an illegitimate feeble minded child. She was eighteen years old at the time of the trial of her case in the circuit court, in the latter part of 1924. An Act of Virginia approved March 20, 1924, recites that the health of the patient and the welfare of society may be promoted in certain cases by the sterilization of mental defectives, under careful safeguard, etc.; that the sterilization may be effected in males by vasectomy and in females by salpingectomy, without serious pain or substantial danger to life; that the Commonwealth is supporting in various institutions many defective persons who if now discharged would become a menace but if incapable of procreating might be discharged with safety and become self-supporting with benefit to themselves and to society; and that experience has

728

shown that heredity plays an important part in the transmission of insanity, imbecility, etc. The statute then enacts that whenever the superintendent of certain institutions including the above named State Colony shall be of opinion that it is for the best interests of the patients and of society that an inmate under his care should be sexually sterilized, he may have the operation performed upon any patient afflicted with hereditary forms of insanity, imbecility, etc., on complying with the very careful provisions by which the act protects the patients from possible abuse.

The superintendent first presents a petition to the special board of directors of his hospital or colony, stating the facts and the grounds for his opinion, verified by affidavit. Notice of the petition and of the time and place of the hearing in the institution is to be served upon the inmate, and also upon his guardian, and if there is no guardian the superintendent is to apply to the circuit court of the county to appoint one. If the inmate is a minor, notice also is to be given to his parents if any with a copy of the petition. The board is to see to it that the inmate may attend the hearings if desired by him or his guardian. The evidence is all to be reduced to writing, and after the board has made its order for or against the operation, the superintendent, or the inmate, or his guardian, may appeal to the circuit court of the county. The circuit court may consider the record of the board and the evidence before it and such other admissible evidence as may be offered, and may affirm, revise, or reverse the order of the board and enter such order as it deems just. Finally any party may apply to the supreme court of appeals, which, if it grants the appeal, is to hear the case upon the record of the trial in the circuit court and may enter such order as it thinks the circuit court should have entered. There can be no doubt that so far as procedure is concerned the rights of the patient are most carefully considered, and as every step in this case was taken in scrupulous compliance with the statute and after months of observation, there is no doubt that in that respect the plaintiff in error has had due process of law.

The attack is not upon the procedure but upon the substantive law. It seems to be contended that in no circumstances could such an order be justified. It certainly is contended that the order cannot be justified upon the existing grounds. The judgment finds the facts that have been recited and that Carrie Buck "is the probable potential parent of socially inadequate offspring, likewise afflicted, that she may be sexually sterilized without detriment to her general health and that her welfare and that of society will be promoted by her sterilization," and thereupon makes the order. In view of the general declarations of the legislature and the specific findings of the court obviously we cannot say as matter of law that the grounds do not exist, and if they exist they justify the result. We have seen more than once that the public welfare may call upon the best citizens for their lives. It would be strange if it could not call upon those who already sap the strength of the state for these lesser sacrifices, often not felt to be such by those concerned, in order to prevent our being swamped with incompetence. It is better for all the world, if instead of waiting to execute degenerate offspring for crime, or to let them starve for their imbecility, society can prevent those who are manifestly unfit from continuing their kind. The principle that sustains compulsory vaccination is broad enough to cover cutting the Fallopian tubes. Three generations of imbeciles are enough.

But, it is said, however it might be if this reasoning were applied generally, it fails when it is confined to the small number who are in the institutions named and is not applied to the multitudes outside. It is the usual last resort of constitutional arguments to point out shortcomings of this sort. But the answer is that the law does all that is needed when it does all that it can, indicates a policy, applies it to all within the lines, and seeks to bring within the lines all similarly situated so far and so fast as its means allow. Of course so far as the operations enable those who otherwise must be kept confined to be returned to the world, and thus open the asylum to others, the equality aimed at will be more nearly reached.

Judgment affirmed.

Jerome Frank

.

ON LAWSUITS AS INQUIRIES
INTO THE TRUTH

from *Courts on Trial*

When we say that present-day trial methods are "rational," presumably we mean this: The men who compose our trial courts, judges and juries, in each lawsuit conduct an intelligent inquiry into all the practically available evidence, in order to ascertain, as near as may be, the truth about the facts of that suit. That might be called the "investigatory" or "truth" method of trying cases. Such a method can yield no more than a guess, nevertheless an educated guess.

The success of such a method is conditioned by at least these two factors: (1) The judicial inquirers, trial judges or juries, may not obtain all the important evidence. (2) The judicial inquirers may not be competent to conduct such an inquiry. Let us, for the time being, assume that the second condition is met—i.e., that we have competent inquirers—and ask whether we so conduct trials as to satisfy the first condition, i.e., the procuring of all the practically available important evidence.

The answer to that question casts doubt on whether our trial courts do use the "investigatory" or "truth" method. One mode of trials is commonly known as "contentious" or "adversary." It is based on what I would call the "fight" theory, a theory which derives from the origin of trials as substitutes for private out-of-court brawls.

Many lawyers maintain that the "fight" theory and the "truth" theory coincide. They think that the best way for a court to discover the facts in a suit is to have each side strive as hard as it can, in a keenly partisan spirit, to bring to the court's attention the evidence favorable to that side. Macaulay said that we obtain the fairest decision "when two men argue, as unfairly as possible, on opposite sides," for then "it is certain that no important consideration will altogether escape notice."

Unquestionably that view contains a core of good sense. The zealously partisan lawyers sometimes do bring into court evidence which, in a dispassionate inquiry, might be overlooked. Apart from the fact element of the case, the opposed lawyers also illuminate for the court niceties of the legal rules which the judge might otherwise not perceive. The "fight" theory, therefore, has invaluable qualities with which we cannot afford to dispense.

But frequently the partisanship of the opposing lawyers blocks the uncovering of vital evidence or leads to a presentation of vital testimony in a way that distorts it. I shall attempt to show you that we have allowed the fighting spirit to become dangerously excessive.

This is perhaps most obvious in the handling of witnesses. Suppose a trial were fundamentally a truth-inquiry. Then, recognizing the inherent fallibilities of witnesses, we would do all we could to remove the causes of their errors when testifying. Recognizing also the importance of witnesses' demeanor as clues to their reliability, we would do our best to make sure that they testify in circumstances most conducive to a revealing observation of that demeanor by the trial judge or jury. In our contentious trial practice, we do almost the exact opposite.

No businessman, before deciding to build a new plant, no general before launching an attack, would think of obtaining information on which to base his judgment by putting his informants through the bewildering experience of witnesses at a trial. "The novelty of the situation," wrote a judge, "the agitation and hurry which accompanies it, the cajolery or intimidation to which the witness may be subjected, the want of questions calculated to excite those recollections which might clear up every difficulty, and the confusion of cross-examination . . . may give rise to important errors and omissions." "In the court they stand as strangers," wrote another judge of witnesses, "surrounded with unfamiliar circumstances giving rise to an embarrassment known only to themselves."

In a book by Henry Taft (brother of Chief Justice Taft, and himself a distinguished lawyer) we are told: "Counsel and court find it necessary through examination and instruction to induce a witness to abandon for an hour or two his habitual method of thought and expression, and conform to the rigid ceremonialism of court procedure. It is not strange that frequently truthful witnesses are . . . misunderstood, that they nervously react in such a way as to create the impression that they are either evading or intentionally falsifying. It is interesting to account for some of the things that witnesses do under such circumstances. An honest witness testifies on direct examination. He answers questions promptly and candidly and makes a good impression. On cross-examination, his attitude changes. He suspects that traps are being laid for him. He hesitates; he ponders the answer to a simple question; he seems to 'spar' for time by asking that questions be repeated; perhaps he protests that counsel is not fair; he may even appeal to the court for protection. Altogether the contrast with his attitude on direct examination is obvious; and he creates the impression that he is evading or withholding." Yet on testimony thus elicited courts every day reach decisions affecting the lives and fortunes of citizens.

What is the role of the lawyers in bringing the evidence before the trial court? As you may learn by reading any one of a dozen or more handbooks on how to try a lawsuit, an experienced lawyer uses all sorts of stratagems to minimize the effect on the judge or jury of testimony disadvantageous to his client, even when the lawyer has no doubt of the accuracy and honesty of that testimony. The lawyer considers it his duty to create a false impression, if he can, of any witness who gives such testimony. If such a witness happens to be timid, frightened by the unfamiliarity of courtroom ways, the lawyer, in his cross-examination, plays on that weakness, in order to confuse the witness and make it appear that he is concealing significant facts. Longenecker, in his book *Hints On The Trial of a Law Suit* (a book endorsed by the great Wigmore), in writing of the "truthful, honest, over-cautious" witness, tells how "a skilful advocate by a rapid cross-examination may ruin the testimony of such a witness." The author does not even hint any disapproval of that accomplishment. Longenecker's and other similar books recommend that a lawyer try to prod an irritable but honest "adverse" witness into displaying his undesirable characteristics in their most unpleasant form, in order to discredit him with the judge or jury. "You may," writes Harris, "sometimes destroy the effect of an adverse witness by making him appear more hostile than he really is. You may make him exaggerate or unsay something and say it again." Taft says that a clever cross-examiner, dealing with an honest but egotistic witness, will "deftly tempt the witness to indulge in his propensity for exaggeration, so as to make him 'hang himself.' And thus," adds Taft, "it may happen that not only is the value of his testimony lost, but the side which produces him suffers for seeking aid from such a source"—although, I would add, that may be the only source of evidence of a fact on which the decision will turn.

"An intimidating manner in putting questions," writes Wigmore, "may so coerce or disconcert the witness that his answers do not represent his actual knowledge on the subject. So also, questions which in form or subject cause embarrassment, shame or anger in the witness may unfairly lead him to such demeanor or utterances that the impression produced by his statements does not do justice to its real testimonial value." Anthony Trollope, in one of his novels, indignantly reacted to these methods. "One would naturally imagine," he said, "that an undisturbed thread of clear evidence would be best obtained from a man whose position was made easy and whose mind was not harassed; but this is not the fact; to turn a witness to good account, he must be badgered this way and that till he is nearly mad; he must be made a laughing-stock for the court; his very truths must be turned into falsehoods, so that he may be falsely shamed; he must be accused of all manner of villainy, threatened with all manner of punishment; he must be made to feel that he has no friend near him, that the world is all against him; he must be confounded till he forget his right hand from his left, till his mind be turned into chaos, and his heart into water; and then let him give his evidence. What will fall from his lips when in this wretched collapse must be of special value, for the best talents of practiced forensic heroes are daily used to bring it about; and no member of the Humane Society interferes to protect the wretch. Some sorts of torture are as it were tacitly allowed even among humane people. Eels are skinned alive, and witnesses are sacrificed, and no one's blood curdles at the sight, no soft heart is sickened at the cruelty." This may be a somewhat overdrawn picture. Yet, referring to this manner of handling witnesses, Sir Frederic Eggleston recently said that it prevents lawyers from inducing persons who know important facts from disclosing them to lawyers for litigants. He notes, too, that "the terrors of cross-examination are such that a party can often force a settlement by letting it be known that a certain . . . counsel has been retained."

The lawyer not only seeks to discredit adverse witnesses but also to hide the defects of witnesses who testify favorably to his client. If, when interviewing such a witness before trial, the lawyer notes that the witness has mannerisms, demeanor-traits, which might discredit him, the lawyer teaches him how to cover up those traits when testifying. He educates the irritable witness to conceal his irritability, the cocksure witness to subdue his cocksureness. In that way, the trial court is denied the benefit of observing the witness's actual normal demeanor, and thus prevented from sizing up the witness accurately.

Lawyers freely boast of their success with these tactics. They boast also of such devices as these: If an "adverse," honest witness, on cross-examination, makes seemingly inconsistent statements, the cross-examiner tries to keep the witness from explaining away the apparent inconsistencies. "When," writes Tracy, counseling trial lawyers, in a much-praised book, "by your cross-examination, you have caught the witness in an inconsistency, the next question that will immediately come to your lips is, 'Now, let's hear you explain.' Don't ask it, for he may explain and, if he does, your point will have been lost. If you have conducted your cross-examination properly (which includes interestingly), the jury will have seen the inconsistency and it will have made the proper impression on their minds. If, on re-direct examination the witness does explain, the explanation will have come later in the case and at the request of the counsel who originally called the witness and the jury will be much more likely to look askance at the explanation than if it were made during your cross-examination." Tracy adds, "Be careful in your questions on cross-examination not to open a door that you have every reason to wish kept closed." That is, don't let in any reliable evidence, hurtful to your side, which would help the trial court to arrive at the truth.

"In cross-examination," writes Eggleston, "the main preoccupation of counsel is to avoid introducing evidence, or giving an opening to it, which will harm his case. The most painful thing for an experienced practitioner . . . is to hear a junior counsel laboriously bring out in cross-examination of a witness all the truth which the counsel who called him could not" bring out "and which it was the junior's duty as an advocate to conceal." A lawyer, if possible, will not ask a witness to testify who, on cross-examination, might testify to true facts helpful to his opponent.

Nor, usually, will a lawyer concede the existence of any facts if they are inimical to his client and he thinks they cannot be proved by his adversary. If, to the lawyer's knowledge, a witness has testified inaccurately but favorably to the lawyer's client, the lawyer will attempt to hinder cross-examination that would expose the inaccuracy. He puts in testimony which surprises his adversary who, caught unawares, has not time to seek out, interview, and summon witnesses who would rebut the surprise testimony. "Of course," said a trial lawyer in a bar association lecture in 1946, "surprise elements should be hoarded. Your opponent should not be educated as to matters concerning which you believe he is still in the dark. Obviously, the traps should not be uncovered. Indeed, you may cast a few more leaves over them so that your adversary will step more boldly on the low ground believing it is solid."

These, and other like techniques, you will find unashamedly described in the many manuals on trial tactics written by and for eminently reputable trial lawyers. The purpose of these tactics—often effective—is to prevent the trial judge or jury from correctly evaluating the trustworthiness of witnesses and to shut out evidence the trial court ought to receive in order to approximate the truth.

In short, the lawyer aims at victory, at winning in the fight, not at aiding the court to discover the facts. He does not want the trial court to reach a sound educated guess, if it is likely to be contrary to his client's interests. Our present trial method is thus the equivalent of throwing pepper in the eyes of a surgeon when he is performing an operation.

However unpleasant all this may appear, do not blame trial lawyers for using the techniques I have described. If there is to be criticism, it should be directed at the system that virtually compels their use, a system which treats a lawsuit as a battle of wits and wiles. As a distinguished lawyer has said, these stratagems are "part of the maneuvering . . . to which [lawyers] are obliged to resort to win their cases. Some of them may appear to be tricky; they may seem to be taking undue advantage; but under the present system it is part of a lawyer's duty to employ them because his opponent is doing the same thing, and if he refrains from doing so, he is violating his duty to his client and giving his opponent an unquestionable advantage. . . ." These tricks of the trade are today the legitimate and accepted corollary of our fight theory.

However, some tactics, unfortunately too often used, are regarded as improper by decent members of the legal profession. We know, alas, that an immense amount of testimony is deliberately and knowingly false. Experienced lawyers say that, in large cities, scarcely a trial occurs, in which some witness does not lie. Perjured testimony often goes undetected by trial courts and therefore often wins cases. Judge Dawson of the Kansas Supreme Court found one of the "real and crying hindrances to a correct and efficient administration of justice . . . the widespread prevalence of perjury practiced with impunity by litigants and witnesses. . . ." A wag has it that courts decide cases according to the "preponderance of the perjury." Some—not all—of that lying testimony results from coaching of witnesses by dishonest lawyers.

But much inaccurate testimony, not to be classified as perjurious, results from a practice that is not dishonest: Every sensible lawyer, before a trial, interviews most of the witnesses. No matter how scrupulous the lawyer, a witness, when thus interviewed, often detects what the lawyer hopes to prove at the trial. If the witness desires to have the lawyer's client win the case, he will often, unconsciously, mold his story accordingly. Telling and re-telling it to the lawyer, he will honestly believe that his story, as he narrates it in court, is true, although it importantly deviates from what he originally believed. So we have inadvertent but innocent witness-coaching. The line, however, between intentional and inadvertent grooming of witnesses cannot easily be drawn. Now, according to many lawyers of wide experience, the contentious method of trying cases augments the tendency of witnesses to mold their memories to assist one of the litigants, because the partisan nature of trials tends to make partisans of the witnesses. They come to regard themselves, not as aids in an investigation bent on discovering the truth, not as aids to the court, but as the "plaintiff's witnesses" or the "defendant's witnesses." They become soldiers in a war, cease to be neutrals.

"I do not think I am exaggerating," wrote Eggleston in 1947, after a résumé of the ways of trial lawyers and trial courts, "when I say that the evidence contains only kaleidoscopic fragments of the facts. It is as if a checker of light and dark patches were held over reality. All that gets down in the record is that seen through the light patches. It is quite clear," he continues, "that reality does not survive in the process of analysis to which" the contending lawyers "submit it from opposite poles. Cases are won by the exercise of the last degree of ingenuity, and this marginal utility makes the contest highly artificial."

In 1906, the French lawyer, De la Grasserie, said that, in a modern (civil) trial, "deceit" has "succeeded to . . . force, bringing with it al-

most the same disasters. It is . . . a conflict . . . which has been substituted for the primitive conflict of force. . . . Its wounds are often
as deep, its risks as serious. . . . The battle of craft is enacted by the
parties under the eyes of the judge. . . . Each [party] strives to conceal what is contrary to his interests and to take advantage of everything that helps his cause. . . . No doubt craft is preferable to violence from the point of view of the social order, but the risk that judgment is wrong is at times as great." An English lawyer, at about the
same time, said that, in litigation, "one party or the other is always
supremely interested in misrepresenting, exaggerating, or suppressing
the truth"; and he spoke "of the characteristic dangers of deception
. . . to which judicial tribunals are exposed . . ." As applied to all
contemporary American trials, these statements are excessive, misde-
scriptive. Yet one who visits many of our trial courts, or who reads the
books and articles on practical trial techniques to which I have referred,
will perhaps incline to believe that, in many cases, matters are not altogether different in this country today. The views of so competent a
student of trials as Judge Learned Hand (whom I shall quote in a moment) tend to support such a depressing belief.

The effects of the contemporary American fighting or adversary
method must sorely puzzle many a litigating citizen. The parties to a
suit, remarks Eggleston, "know exactly what they are fighting about
when the writ is issued, but find themselves fighting a very different case
when the trial is actually launched. It is a wise litigant who knows his
own quarrel when he sees it in court." "If," said Judge Learned Hand
to the lawyer, "you lead your client into the courtroom with you . . .
you will, if you have the nerve to watch him, see in his face a baffled
sense that there is going on some kind of game which, while its outcome
may be tragic to him in its development, is incomprehensible." The
legal profession should not take much pride in a system which evokes
from Judge Hand the remark, "About trials hang a suspicion of trickery
and a sense of result depending upon cajolery or worse." To Judge
Hand's comments I would add that, were it impossible to contrive a
better system, we lawyers could legitimately defend ourselves, saying,
"We do the best we can." But I think such a defense not legitimate because I think we do not do the best we can, since an improved system
can be contrived.

Mr. Justice Frankfurter recently observed that a criminal statute is not unconstitutional merely because in one trial under that statute a man goes scot-free while in another trial under the same statute another man is sent to jail for "similar conduct." Such "diversity in result . . . in different trials," said the Justice, is "unavoidable," because, in each trial, the ascertainment of the facts must be left to "fallible judges and juries." He concluded that "so long as the diversities are not designed consequences, they do not deprive persons of due process of law." This statement by Justice Frankfurter—which I think correctly states the judicial attitude towards trials—has such significance that I want the reader thoroughly to understand it. When, in that context, the Justice spoke of "due process of law," he meant a "fair trial," that is, one which meets the minimum test of fairness required by the Constitution. The Supreme Court holds that a trial is constitutionally "fair," if only it does not depart from the methods usually employed in our trial courts. I am not criticizing the Supreme Court when I suggest that one imbued with a lively sense of justice will not be satisfied with that minimal constitutional test. A particular trial may be thus minimally "fair" when measured by the standard of our present usual trial practices. But the question remains whether those usual practices can be regarded as actually fair when, due to practically *avoidable* human errors, they deprive men of life or liberty in criminal proceedings, or of property or money in civil suits. I would answer, No. Our mode of trials is often most unfair. It will, I think, continue to be, until everything feasible has been done to prevent avoidable mistakes. Only avoidless mistakes should we accept among life's necessary dangers.

After careful scrutiny of the record of the famous Sacco-Vanzetti case, lawyers of experience have concluded that those men received an egregiously unfair trial, because obviously the trial judge was poisonously biased against the accused, and the prosecutors hit below the belt, resorting to measures which violated the Marquis of Queensberry rules governing courtroom bouts. However, in the case of Campbell, and many others like it, innocent men have been convicted after trials from which such glaring defects were absent. Were those trials fair? Yes, in a constitutional sense. They would be pronounced technically fair by the lawyers who criticize the Sacco-Vanzetti decision. But forget the lawyer's perspective. In terms of common sense, how can we say that those trials were fair since, almost surely, in their course, the government lawyers utilized some of the legitimized lawyer-tactics which were likely to mislead the trial courts? Intelligent laymen should insist that it is not enough that a trial seem fair to many lawyers, who, indurated to the techniques of their trade, have become so calloused that they acquiesce in needless judicial injustices.

Take, for instance, a speech made last year, before a bar association, by a highly respected judge. He began by saying, "We start with the fundamental conception that a trial, under our procedure, is not a game or battle of wits but a painstaking, orderly inquiry for the discovery of the truth." Now that judge, I have no doubt, believed that statement—or, rather, believed that he believed it. Yet a few minutes later in his speech, he cautioned the lawyer never on cross-examination "thoughtlessly [to] ask the one question which will supply an omission in your opponent's case." He quoted, with approval, the remark of an expert cross-examiner that, if you put such a question, "you may find the witness has had time to think, and you will get an answer" that hurts your client. So here you have a judge who, after seriously depicting a trial as "an inquiry for the discovery of truth," goes on to encourage lawyers to avoid bringing out the truth. That bewildered judge—and alas there are too many like him—will make no serious effort to change a system which permits a lawyer to act as did Mr. Chaffanbrass in another of Trollope's novels: "Nothing would flurry this [witness he was cross-examining], force her to utter a word of which she herself did not know the meaning. The more he might persevere in such an attempt, the more dogged and steady she would become. He therefore soon gave that up . . . and resolved that, as he could not shake her, he would shake the confidence the jury might place in her. He could not make a fool of her, and therefore he would make her out a rogue. . . . As for himself, he knew well enough that she had spoken nothing but the truth. But he . . . so managed that the truth might be made to look like falsehood—or at any rate to have a doubtful air."

I repeat that we ought not to blame the trial lawyers for employing such tactics. Yet the legal profession is somewhat responsible for the fact that non-lawyers do sometimes assess such blame. For lawyers and judges declare solemnly that every lawyer is an "officer of the court." So to designate the lawyer, said one court, "is by no means a figure of speech," since "it is his duty to help save the court from error and imposition, and to aid the court to a proper determination of the law and the facts. Theoretically, at least, it is counsel's first duty to see that the issue is justly decided, however his client is affected." His "office" is "indispensable to the administration of justice. . . ." But these words mean only that a lawyer must not affirmatively mislead a court, must not introduce in evidence, at a trial, documents which he knows to be false, testimony which he knows to be perjured. Most courts do not effectively disapprove of the lawyers' wiles I have described. Little wonder, then, if laymen sometimes smile cynically when they hear lawyers called court "officers," think it a strange sort of judicial officer who is authorized ingeniously to obscure the facts from trial judges and juries.

The layman's bafflement at the workings of the judicial system has been remarkably described by Kafka, in his book, *The Trial*. There, too, he gives a layman's attitude towards the apathy of many lawyers concerning reforms of the system. Although "the pettiest Advocate," he writes, "might be to some extent capable of analyzing the state of things in the Court, it never occurred to the Advocates that they should suggest or insist on any improvements in the system, while—and this was very characteristic—almost every accused man, even quite ordinary people among them, discovered from the earliest stages a passion for suggesting reforms which often wasted time and energy that [the Advocate's thought] could have been better employed in other directions. The only sensible thing [for an Advocate] was to adapt oneself to existing conditions. . . . One must lie low, no matter how much it went against the grain. Must try to understand that this great organization remained, so to speak, in a state of delicate balance, and that if someone took it upon himself to alter the disposition of things around him . . . the organization would simply right itself by some compensating reaction in another part of its machinery—since everything interlocked—and remain unchanged, unless, indeed, which was very probable, it became still more rigid, more vigilant, more severe, and more ruthless."

Kafka's reaction is one of mild bitterness. Jonathan Swift was more vitriolic. He referred to lawyers as "a society of men . . . bred up from their youth in the art of proving by words, multiplied for the purpose"—and in "a jargon of their own that no other mortal can understand"—that "white is black, and black is white, according as they are paid." Kipling talks of "the tribe who describe with a jibe the perversions of justice"; and Soddy calls lawyers "charlatans" who aim to "mystify the public." Those strictures are altogether too severe; their analyses of lawyers' motivations are inaccurate. And such writers, being uninformed laymen, cannot be constructively critical. What we need today is the kind of vigorous, patient, reformist zeal of a knowing critic like Jeremy Bentham, whose untiring attacks (in the late 18th and early 19th centuries) on lawyers' complacency in the face of judicial injustice, led to the elimination of some of the worst features of judicial procedure.

Our contentious trial method, I have said, has its roots in the origin of court trials as substitutes for private brawls. But that does not altogether explain its survival. Wigmore (following up a suggestion made by Bentham) suggested that "the common law, originating in a community of sports and games, was permeated by the instinct of sportsmanship" which led to a "sporting theory of justice," a theory of "legalized gambling." This theory, although it had some desirable effects, "has contributed," said Wigmore, "to lower the system of administering justice and in particular of ascertaining truth in litigation, to the level of a mere game of skill or chance . . ." in which lawyers use evidence "as one plays a trump card, or draws to three aces, or holds back a good horse till the home-stretch. . . ."

Damon Runyon had much the same idea. "A big murder trial," he wrote, "possesses some of the elements of a sporting event. I find the same popular interest in a murder trial that I find . . . on the eve of a big football game, or a pugilistic encounter, or a baseball series. There is the same conversational speculation on the probable result, only more of it. . . . The trial is a sort of game, the players on the one side the attorneys for the defense, and on the other side the attorneys for the State. The defendent figures in it merely as the prize. . . . And the players must be men well-schooled in their play. They must be crafty men. . . . The game of murder trial is played according to very strict rules, with stern umpires, called judges, to prevent any deviations from these rules. . . ." The players "are supposed to be engaged in a sort of common cause, which is to determine the guilt or innocence of the defendant. . . . A player . . . for the State represents the people. His function, as I understand it," Runyon continued, "is to endeavor to convict any person who has transgressed the law. . . . It is inconceivable that he would wish to convict an innocent person. But it has been my observation that the player or attorney for the State is quick to take any advantage of the rules . . . that puts his side in front, and equally quick to forestall any moves by the other side."

This Wigmore-Runyon explanation may be partially sound, but it seems to me to over-emphasize sportsmanship. I suggest, as an additional partial explanation of the perpetuation of the excessive fighting method of trials, both civil and criminal, the belief in uncontrolled competition, of unbridled individualism. I suggest that the fighting theory of justice is not unrelated to, and not uninfluenced by, extreme laissez-faire in the economic field.

"Classical" laissez-faire economic theory assumed that, when each individual, as an "economic man," strives rationally, in the competitive economic struggle or "fight," to promote his own self-interest, we attain public welfare through the wisest use of resources and the most socially desirable distribution of economic goods. The "fight" theory of justice is a sort of legal laissez-faire. It assumes a "litigious man." It assumes that, in a lawsuit, each litigious man, in the courtroom competitive strife, will, through his lawyer, intelligently and energetically try to use the evidential resources to bring out the evidence favorable to him and unfavorable to his courtroom competitor; that thereby the trial court will obtain all the available relevant evidence; and that thus, in a socially beneficial way, the court will apply the social policies embodied in the legal rules to the actual facts, avoiding the application of those rules to a mistaken version of the facts. Legal laissez-faire theory therefore assumes that the government can safely rely on the "individual enterprise" of individual litigants to ensure that court orders will be grounded on all the practically attainable relevant facts.

Most of us have come to distrust, in the economic field, ultra let-alone-ism, the ultra laissez-faire theory with its anti-social concept of an "economic man." For observation of social realities has shown that the basic postulates of that theory, although in part correct, are inadequate as exclusive postulates. I think that, in like fashion, observation of courtroom realities shows that the postulates of legal laissez-faire are insufficient as exclusive postulates. We should retain what there is of value in the fighting theory of justice, eliminating what is socially harmful. We should retain, I repeat, so much of "individual initiative" in the trial of cases as serves to bring out evidence that might be overlooked and the niceties of legal rules a court might otherwise ignore. But the fight should not so dominate a lawsuit that it leads to the non-discovery of important evidence and the distortion of testimony.

*

The fighting theory has, in part, broken down. Time was when a litigant could refuse to disclose evidence in his possession to the adversary party before trial. But so-called "discovery" procedure has been developed which requires such disclosure in non-criminal cases. The federal courts are particularly energetic in compelling such "discovery." Thus far, at least, have we advanced towards effectuating the "truth" theory.

There have been other advances, such as increased insistence on the power and right of the trial judge to take a hand in examining witnesses, and even to summon witnesses of whom he is aware and whom neither litigant has called. I must add, however, that regrettably (as I see it) few judges avail themselves of that power. Judge Shientag, a learned and respected judge, recently said that "a litigant has the right to expect . . . that the judge will not interfere in the examination of witnesses, even though he believes he can do a better job than counsel, except to correct patent errors, misconceptions or misrepresentations. . . ." Some bolder trial judges disagree.

But even if the judge does "interfere," and even if "discovery" procedure is open, the trial court may fail to learn of crucial evidence. Partly this may be due to the incompetence of the lawyer for one side. For lack of means to retain an able lawyer, the impecunious litigant may here be singularly disadvantaged. To some extent we are overcoming that handicap, through Legal Aid Services, although much remains to be done before the legal procession catches up with the medical profession in assisting the indigent and the "white-collar" men.

Apart from failure to bring out the evidence, the mistakes of a man's lawyer may cause him to lose his case—a proper result under strict legal laissez-faire theory. But is it fair that a litigant should be punished because he retained an incompetent lawyer? When an error of a trial court, resulting from a lawyer's blunder, is egregious, the upper courts sometimes relieve the litigant. But there persists a reluctance to grant such relief. Maybe that reluctance is justified. I am not sure.

There is one most serious handicap in litigation that has received little attention: With the ablest lawyer in the world, a man may lose a suit he ought to win, if he has not the funds to pay for an investigation, before trial, of evidence necessary to sustain his case. I refer to evidence not in the files of the other party and therefore not obtainable by "discovery" procedure. What I mean is this: In order to prove his claim, or to defend against one, a man may need to hire detectives to scour the country—even sometimes foreign countries—in order to locate witnesses who alone may know of events that occurred years ago, or to unearth letters or other papers which may be in distant places. Or, again, he may need the services of an engineer, or a chemist, or an expert accountant, to make an extensive—and therefore expensive— investigation. Without the evidence which such an investigation would reveal, a man is often bound to be defeated. His winning or losing may therefore depend on his pocketbook. He is out of luck if his pocketbook is not well lined with money. For neither his lawyer nor any legal-aid institution will supply the needed sums. For want of money, expendable for such purposes, many a suit has been lost, many a meritorious claim or defense has never even been asserted.

Let me illustrate. Fisher, in his recent excellent book, *The Art of Investigation,* writes: "The percentage of witnesses who cannot be found if enough effort is exerted is infinitesimal. A famous investigator once said that the man who could not be found is the man at the bottom of the sea, and even then he must be at the bottom at its points of greatest depth. Anyone alive can be found if enough effort is put forth." That statement may be exaggerated. But you get the point: Suppose there is one man, John Brown, who alone could testify to a crucial event—such as that Sam Jones was in New York City on June 12, 1948. Brown is missing. He may be in China, India or Peru. If he can be found, and if he testifies, the plaintiff will win his suit; otherwise he will lose it. If the plaintiff can afford to pay enough to investigators to scour the world for the missing witness, he may be located. If the plaintiff is a man of means, he will hire such investigators. But if he has little money, he can't do so—and will lose his case which may involve all his worldly goods.

That is not true justice, democratic justice. This defect in our judicial system makes a mockery of "equality before the law," which should be one of the first principles of a democracy. That equality, in such instances, depends on a person's financial condition. The tragedy of such a situation is etched in irony when a man's impoverished condition has resulted from a wrong done him by another whom he cannot successfully sue to redress the wrong. Many of our state constitutions contain a provision that "every person ought to obtain justice freely and without being obliged to purchase it." But, as things stand, this is too often a provision in words only. For the advantage in litigation is necessarily on the side of the party that can "purchase justice" by hiring private assistance in obtaining evidence when his adversary cannot. Unless we contrive some method to solve the problem I have posed, we must acknowledge that, in a very real sense, frequently we are "selling justice," denying it to many under-incomed persons. It should shock us that judicial justice is thus often an upper-bracket privilege. Here we have legal laissez-faire at its worst.

That brings me to a point which the fighting theory obscures. A court's decision is not a mere private affair. It culminates in a court order which is one of the most solemn of governmental acts. Not only is a court an agency of government, but remember that its order, if not voluntarily obeyed, will bring into action the police, the sheriff, even the army. What a court orders, then, is no light matter. The court represents the government, organized society, in action.

Such an order a court is not supposed to make unless there exist some facts which bring into operation a legal rule. Now any government officer, other than a judge, if authorized to do an act for the government only if certain facts exist, will be considered irresponsible if he so acts without a governmental investigation. For instance, if an official is empowered to pay money to a veteran suffering from some specified ailment, the official, if he does his duty, will not rely solely on the applicant's statement that he has such an ailment. The government officer insists on a governmental check-up of the evidence. Do courts so conduct themselves?

In criminal cases they seem to, after a fashion. In such cases, there is some recognition that so important a governmental act as a court decision against a defendant should not occur without someone, on behalf of the government itself, seeing to it that the decision is justified by the actual facts so far as they can be discovered with reasonable diligence. For, in theory at least, usually before a criminal action is begun, an official investigation has been conducted which reveals data sufficient to warrant bringing the defendant to trial. In some jurisdictions, indigent defendants charged with crime are represented by a publicly paid official, a Public Defender—a highly important reform which should everywhere be adopted. And the responsibility of government for mistakes of fact in criminal cases, resulting in erroneous court judgments, is recognized in those jurisdictions in which the government compensates an innocent convicted person if it is subsequently shown that he was convicted through such a mistake.

In civil cases (non-criminal cases), on the whole a strikingly different attitude prevails. Although, no less than in a criminal suit, a court's order is a grave governmental act, yet, in civil cases, the government usually accepts no similar responsibilities, even in theory. Such a suit is still in the ancient tradition of "self help." The court usually relies almost entirely on such evidence as one or the other of the private parties to the suit is (a) able to, and (b) chooses to, offer. Lack of skill or diligence of the lawyer for one of those parties, or that party's want of enough funds to finance a pre-trial investigation necessary to obtain evidence, may have the result, as I explained, that crucial available evidence is not offered in court. No government official has the duty to discover, and bring to court, evidence, no matter how important, not offered by the parties.

In short, the theory is that, in most civil suits, the government, through its courts, should make orders which the government will enforce, although those court orders may not be justified by the actual facts, and although, by reasonable diligence, the government, had it investigated, might have discovered evidence—at variance with the evidence presented—coming closer to the actual facts.

Yet the consequence of a court decision in a civil suit, based upon the court's mistaken view of the actual facts, may be as grave as a criminal judgment which convicts an innocent person. If, because of such an erroneous decision, a man loses his job or his savings and becomes utterly impoverished, he may be in almost as serious a plight as if he had been jailed. His poverty may make him a public charge. It may lead to the delinquency of his children, who may thus become criminals and go to jail. Yet in no jurisdiction is a man compensated by the government for serious injury to him caused by a judgment against him in a non-criminal case, even if later it is shown that the judgment was founded upon perjured or mistaken testimony.

I suggest that there is something fundamentally wrong in our legal system in this respect. If a man's pocket is picked, the government brings a criminal suit, and accepts responsibility for its prosecution. If a man loses his life's savings through a breach of a contract, the government accepts no such responsibility. Shouldn't the government perhaps assume some of the burden of enforcing what we call "private rights"?

Some few moves have been made in the right direction. In an English divorce court, an official, the King's Proctor, brings forward evidence, bearing on possible collusion, not offered by either contestant; some American states provide that the public prosecutor shall do likewise in divorce actions. In our own Domestic Relations Courts, government officers procure and present most of the evidence. Lawyers for any of the parties may cross-examine any witness, may offer additional evidence, and may argue about the applicable legal rules. The advantages of the adversary method are fully preserved, but the fighting spirit is much diminished. Under the Chandler Act, enacted in 1938, in certain types of cases relating to corporate reorganization, the SEC, at large public expense, uses its expert staff to obtain and present to the court evidence which usually no private party could afford to procure; the judge and the private parties may treat this evidence like any other evidence, and the parties may introduce further supplementary or conflicting evidence.

Many of our administrative agencies have large and efficient staffs to conduct investigations in order to ferret out evidence put before those agencies in their own administrative proceedings. I know, from personal experience, that not much evidence escapes an agency like the SEC. Mr. Justice Jackson has said: "Such a tribunal is not as dependent as the ordinary court upon the arguments of skilled counsel to get at the truth. Skilled advocacy is neither so necessary to keep such a body informed nor is stupid or clever advocacy so apt to blur the merits of a controversy."

I do not suggest that courts, like such administrative bodies, conduct their own investigations through their own employees. I do suggest that we should consider whether it is not feasible to provide impartial government officials—who are not court employees, and who act on their own initiative—to dig up, and present to the courts, significant evidence which one or the other of the parties may overlook or be unable to procure. No court would be bound to accept that evidence as true. Nor would any of the parties be precluded from trying to show the unreliability of such evidence (by cross-examination or otherwise) or from introducing additional evidence. Trials would still remain adversary. As I concede that to use that device in all civil cases would lead to many complications, I do not urge that it be at once generally adopted. But I think experiments along those lines should now be made.

This proposal resembles somewhat the procedures long used in criminal cases on the European continent. Critics may oppose it on that ground, saying that we should not take over ideas from countries which have been less democratic than ours. To any such argument, Woodrow Wilson gave the answer: "But why should we not use such parts of foreign contrivances as we want if they may be in any way serviceable? We are in no danger of using them in a foreign way. We borrowed rice, but we do not eat it with chopsticks."

It will also be said that any such proposal is absurdly radical. Yet something of the sort was endorsed by President Taft, by no means a radical. More than thirty years ago he said: "Of all the questions . . . before the American people I regard no one as more important than this, the improvement of the administration of justice. We must make it so that the poor man will have as nearly as possible an opportunity in litigating as the rich man, and under present conditions, ashamed as we may be of it, this is not the fact." Moreover, we now have public-utility commissions which, on behalf of private persons, bring rate-suits against utility companies. With that in mind, Willoughby wrote a book, published in 1927 by the conservative Brookings Institution, in which he proposed the appointment of a "public prosecutor of civil actions." If a complaint were made to the prosecutor, he would first try to settle the matter or to have the parties agree to submit the dispute to arbitration. Only if these efforts failed would he bring that suit. No one would be obliged to retain that prosecutor; his employment would be optional; and, if an action were brought on a person's behalf by the prosecutor, that person would be at liberty to retain a private lawyer to assist in the preparation for, and conduct of, the trial. That idea, I think, merits public discussion and consideration. Were it adopted, it should perhaps be supplemented to include a practice now adopted, in some states, by the Public Defender in criminal actions: That official is authorized to expend public funds to seek out and procure what he regards as essential evidence.

Statutes in some jurisdictions authorize the trial judge to call as a witness an expert selected by the judge. Judges might sometimes avail themselves of that power to help indigent or under-incomed litigants. But I believe that none of those statutes, as they now read, provides for payment by the government to judge-called experts in non-criminal suits. Moreover, those statutes will not meet the difficulties of a prospective litigant when making up his mind whether to bring or defend a suit. Nor do they permit expenditures for detectives and other investigators not regarded as "experts." Nevertheless, this expedient might be expanded so as partially to solve the problem I have presented.

None of these proposals, if adopted, would usher in the millenium. Official evidence gatherers, or public prosecutors of civil actions, will make mistakes, or become excessively partisan. The trial process is, and always will be, human, therefore fallible. It can never be a completely scientific investigation for the discovery of the true facts.

I said that, in theory, in criminal suits the government seems to take greater responsibility than in civil suits, that theoretically, in each criminal trial, the public prosecutor has made a pre-trial investigation and that he brings out, at the trial, the evidence he has uncovered. Actually, many prosecutors, infected badly by the fighting spirit, in partisan manner produce only the evidence they think will cause convictions. In most jurisdictions, "discovery" in criminal cases is denied; even where permitted it is narrowly limited. We should, I think, follow the practice now well settled in England where, before trial, the prosecutor must disclose to the accused all evidence the prosecutor intends to offer.

The "third degree" is widely employed by our police, too often with the tacit approval of prosecutors, to extort confessions which, obtained by physical or mental torture, are not infrequently untrue. To our shame be it said that the English, who do not tolerate the "third degree," call it the "American method." Competent American police— such as the FBI force—do not resort to that outrageous device. To rid ourselves of it, we must have a public demand for properly trained police forces. And to rid ourselves of unfair prosecutors, we should not permit any man to hold that office who has not been specially educated for that job and passed stiff written and oral examinations demonstrating his moral and intellectual fitness.

It has been suggested that trained psychologists, called by trial judges as the court's experts, be permitted to testify as "testimonial experts" concerning the witnesses. Such an expert, it is proposed, having interviewed and examined the witness out of court, would testify at the trial about the witness's capacity for hearing, seeing, touching, tasting, his capacity for attention and memory, and any "abnormal" tendencies (such as "pathological lying," for instance).* The expert would be subjected to cross-examination, and his testimony about a witness would not be binding on the trial judge or jury.

Applied to every witness at every trial, this proposal (of which Wigmore approves) is open to the objection that it would make trials endless. Yet I think we ought to experiment with the idea. Aware that judges and juries lack competence in medicine, physics, chemistry, and a host of other subjects, we now use expert witnesses to guide our trial courts. Sizing up a witness from his statements and demeanor when on the witness-stand is a difficult task at best, and one at which juries and most judges are amateurs. Expert aid in the discharge of that task might do much to minimize mistakes in fact-finding.

Suppose that, in a crude "primitive" society, A claims that B took A's pig. If that is true, B violated a well-settled tribal rule. But B denies that he took the pig. A attacks B and kills him. Does A's killing of B prove that B was wrong about the facts? Does that killing constitute the enforcement of the tribal rule? Now suppose somewhat the same sort of dispute in the U.S.A. A sues B, claiming that, by fraud and deceit, B got A's pig. A legal rule says that if B did those acts, then A has a legal right to get back the pig or its money value. If A wins that suit, does the decision in his favor constitute the enforcement of that legal rule, even if A won through perjured testimony or because the trial court erroneously believed an honest but mistaken witness?

A lawyer friend of mine, to whom I put this question, replied, "Yes, in theory. In theory, the facts as found must be assumed to be true." His answer does not satisfy me. That we must accept the facts found by a trial court does not mean that a rule against fraud is really enforced when a court holds a man liable for a fraud he did not commit. My friend is saying, in effect, that, even were it true that the courts misfound the facts in 90% of all cases, still the courts would be enforcing the rules.

That conclusion does not bother the hardened cynic. "In the long run," one may imagine him saying, "what is the difference whether courts make many mistakes in fact-finding, and, as a result, render er-

---

* In some cities, applicants for drivers' licenses are examined by experts to determine whether they are neurotic or psychotic, for such persons will be menaces if they drive cars. Yet we now allow men's lives and fortunes to be menaced by witnesses of that sort whose defects are undisclosed.

roneous decisions—as long as the public generally doesn't learn of these mistakes? Take, for instance, all this to-do about 'convicting the innocent.' One of the important purposes of punishing a man for a crime is to deter others from becoming criminals. Conviction and punishment of the innocent serve just as effectively as if they were guilty to deter others from crime—provided only the errors are not, too frequently, later discovered and publicized. It's tough on the innocent; but we can afford to sacrifice them for the public good. In the same way, if a non-criminal legal rule is of a desirable kind—for instance, a rule concerning the duty of a trustee to the beneficiaries of a trust— why bother whether, in particular lawsuits, the courts, through failure to discover the actual facts, apply it to persons who haven't violated it? Public respect for that rule, and its infiltration into community habits, will come just as well from its misapplications as from its correct applications—if only the public doesn't learn of its misapplications. If you call it injustice to punish the innocent or mistakenly to enter money judgments against men who have done no legal wrongs, then I answer that effectively concealed instances of injustice are not only harmless but socially beneficial. They serve as useful examples. Don't get squeamish about such mistakes." I doubt whether any reader will agree with the cynic.

No one can doubt that the invention of courts, which preserve the peace by settling disputes, marked a great step forward in human progress. But are we to be so satisfied with this forward step that we will rest content with it? Should not a modern civilized society ask more of its courts than that they stop peace-disrupting brawls? The basic aim of the courts in our society should, I think, be the just settlement of particular disputes, the just decision of specific lawsuits.

The just settlement of disputes demands a legal system in which the courts can and do strive tirelessly to get as close as is humanly possible to the actual facts of specific courtroom controversies. Courthouse justice is, I repeat, done at retail, not at wholesale. The trial court's job of fact-finding in each particular case therefore looms up as one of the most important jobs in modern courthouse government. With no lack of deep admiration and respect for our many able trial judges, I must say that that job is not as well done as it could and should be. No wonder it is not, when a leading law-teacher, Professor Morgan of Harvard, a close student of trials, can write that a lawsuit, as most lawsuits are now required to be conducted, is not "a proceeding for the discovery of truth," but "a game in which the contestants are not the litigants but the lawyers." Reviewing a book on trial techniques by an experienced trial lawyer, which revealed in detail the tactics of courtroom fighting—tactics considered entirely legitimate, but which patently impede the discovery of the true facts, so far as they are practically discoverable—Morgan commented sadly, "If only a reviewer could assert that this book is a guide not to the palaces of justice but to the red-light districts of the law. But a decent respect for the truth compels the admission that [the author] has told his story truly."

A distinguished legal historian, Vinagradoff, has said that an "ancient trial" was little more than a "formally regulated struggle between the parties in which the judge acted more as an umpire or warden of order and fair play than as an investigator of truth." To continue that ancient tradition, unmodified, to treat a lawsuit as, above all, a fight, surely cannot be the best way to discover the facts. Improvement in factfinding will necessitate some considerable diminution of the martial spirit in litigation.

Montaigne

:

There is no desire more natural than the desire for knowledge. We try all the ways that can lead us to it. When reason fails us, we use experience—

> Experience, by example led,
> By varied trials art has bred
>
> MANILIUS

—which is a weaker and less dignified means. But truth is so great a thing that we must not disdain any medium that will lead us to it. Reason has so many shapes that we know not which to lay hold of; experience has no fewer. The inference that we try to draw from the resemblance of events is uncertain, because they are always dissimilar: there is no quality so universal in this aspect of things as diversity and variety.

Both the Greeks and the Latins, and we ourselves, use eggs for the most express example of similarity. However, there have been men, and notably one at Delphi, who recognized marks of difference between eggs, so that he never took one for another; and although there were many hens, he could tell which one the egg came from.

Dissimilarity necessarily intrudes into our works; no art can attain similarity. Neither Perrozet nor any other can smooth and whiten the backs of his cards so carefully that some gamesters will not distinguish them simply by seeing them slip through another man's hands. Resemblance does not make things so much alike as difference makes them

754

unlike. Nature has committed herself to make nothing separate that was not different.

Therefore I do not much like the opinion of the man who thought by a multiplicity of laws to bridle the authority of judges, cutting up their meat for them. He did not realize that there is as much freedom and latitude in the interpretation of laws as in their creation. And those people must be jesting who think they can diminish and stop our disputes by recalling us to the express words of the Bible. For our mind finds the field no less spacious in registering the meaning of others than in presenting its own. As if there were less animosity and bitterness in commenting than in inventing!

We see how mistaken he was. For we have in France more laws than all the rest of the world together, and more than would be needed to rule all the worlds of Epicurus: *As formerly we suffered from crimes, so now we suffer from laws* [Tacitus]. And yet we have left so much room for opinion and decision to our judges, that there never was such a powerful and licentious freedom. What have our legislators gained by selecting a hundred thousand particular cases and actions, and applying a hundred thousand laws to them? This number bears no proportion to the infinite diversity of human actions. Multiplication of our imaginary cases will never equal the variety of the real examples. Add to them a hundred times as many more: and still no future event will be found to correspond so exactly to any one of all the many, many thousands of selected and recorded events that there will not remain some circumstance, some difference, that will require separate consideration in forming a judgment. There is little relation between our actions, which are in perpetual mutation, and fixed and immutable laws. The most desirable laws are those that are rarest, simplest, and most general; and I even think that it would be better to have none at all than to have them in such numbers as we have.

Nature always gives us happier laws than those we give ourselves. Witness the picture of the Golden Age of the poets, and the state in which we see nations live which have no other laws. Here are some who employ, as the only judge in their quarrels, the first traveler passing through their mountains. And these others on market day elect one of themselves who decides all their suits on the spot. What would be the danger in having our wisest men settle ours in this way, according to the circumstances and at sight, without being bound to precedents, past or future? For every foot its own shoe. King Ferdinand, when he sent colonists to the Indies, wisely provided that no students of jurisprudence should accompany them, for fear that lawsuits might breed in this new world, this being by nature a science generating altercation and division; judging, with Plato, that lawyers and doctors are a bad provision for a country.

Why is it that our common language, so easy for any other use, becomes obscure and unintelligible in contracts and wills, and that a man who expresses himself so clearly, whatever he says or writes, finds in this field no way of speaking his mind that does not fall into doubt and contradiction? Unless it is that the princes of this art, applying themselves with particular attention to picking out solemn words and contriving artificial phrases, have so weighed every syllable, so minutely examined every sort of combination, that here they are at last entangled and embroiled in the endless number of figures and in such minute partitions that they can no longer fall under any rule or prescription or any certain interpretation. *What is broken up into dust becomes confused* [Seneca].

Who has seen children trying to divide a mass of quicksilver into a certain number of parts? The more they press it and knead it and try to constrain it to their will, the more they provoke the independence of this spirited metal; it escapes their skill and keeps dividing and scattering in little particles beyond all reckoning. This is the same; for by subdividing these subtleties they teach men to increase their doubts; they start us extending and diversifying the difficulties, they lengthen them, they scatter them. By sowing questions and cutting them up, they make the world fructify and teem with uncertainty and quarrels, as the earth is made more fertile the more it is crumbled and deeply plowed. *Learning makes difficulties* [Quintilian].

We were perplexed over Ulpian, we are still perplexed over Bartolus and Baldus. We should have wiped out the traces of this innumerable diversity of opinions, instead of wearing them as decoration and cramming the heads of posterity with them.

I do not know what to say about it, but it is evident from experience that so many interpretations disperse the truth and shatter it. Aristotle wrote to be understood; if he did not succeed, still less will another man, less able, and not treating his own ideas. By diluting the substance we allow it to escape and spill it all over the place; of one subject we make a thousand, and, multiplying and subdividing, fall back into Epicurus' infinity of atoms. Never did two men judge alike about the same thing, and it is impossible to find two opinions exactly alike, not only in different men, but in the same man at different times. Ordinarily I find subject for doubt in what the commentary has not deigned to touch on. I am more apt to trip on flat ground, like certain horses I know which stumble more often on a smooth road.

Who would not say that glosses increase doubts and ignorance, since there is no book to be found, whether human or divine, with which the world busies itself, whose difficulties are cleared up by interpretation? The hundredth commentator hands it on to his successor thornier and rougher than the first one had found it. When do we agree and say, "There has been enough about this book; henceforth there is nothing more to say about it"?

This is best seen in law practice. We give legal authority to numberless doctrines, numberless decisions, and as many interpretations. Do we therefore find any end to the need of interpreting? Do we see any progress and advance toward tranquillity? Do we need fewer lawyers and judges than when this mass of law was still in its infancy? On the contrary, we obscure and bury the meaning; we no longer find it except hidden by so many enclosures and barriers.

Men do not know the natural infirmity of their mind: it does nothing but ferret and quest, and keeps incessantly whirling around, building up and becoming entangled in its own work, like our silkworms, and is suffocated in it. *A mouse in a pitch barrel* [Erasmus]. It thinks it notices from a distance some sort of glimmer of imaginary light and truth; but while running toward it, it is crossed by so many difficulties and obstacles, and diverted by so many new quests, that it strays from the road, bewildered. Not very different from what happened to Aesop's dogs, who, discovering something that looked like a dead body floating in the sea, and being unable to approach it, attempted to drink up the water and dry up the passage, and choked in the attempt. To which may be joined what a certain Crates said of the writings of Heraclitus, that they needed a good swimmer for a reader, so that the depth and weight of Heraclitus' learning should not sink him and drown him.

It is only personal weakness that makes us content with what others or we ourselves have found out in this hunt for knowledge. An abler man will not rest content with it. There is always room for a successor, yes, and for ourselves, and a road in another direction. There is no end to our researches; our end is in the other world. It is a sign of contraction of the mind when it is content, or of weariness. A spirited mind never stops within itself; it is always aspiring and going beyond its strength; it has impulses beyond its powers of achievement. If it does not advance and press forward and stand at bay and clash, it is only half alive. Its pursuits are boundless and without form; its food is wonder, the chase, ambiguity. Apollo revealed this clearly enough, always speaking to us equivocally, obscurely, and obliquely, not satisfying us, but keeping our minds interested and busy. It is an irregular, perpetual motion, without model and without aim. Its inventions excite, pursue, and produce one another.

> So in a running stream one wave we see
> After another roll incessantly,
> And line by line, each does eternally
> Pursue the other, each the other flee.
> By this one, that one ever on is sped,
> And this one by the other ever led;
> The water still does into water go,
> Still the same brook, but different waters flow.
>
> LA BOÉTIE

It is more of a job to interpret the interpretations than to interpret the things, and there are more books about books than about any other subject: we do nothing but write glosses about each other. The world is swarming with commentaries; of authors there is a great scarcity.

Is it not the chief and most reputed learning of our times to learn to understand the learned? Is that not the common and ultimate end of all studies?

Our opinions are grafted upon one another. The first serves as a stock for the second, the second for the third. Thus we scale the ladder, step by step. And thence it happens that he who has mounted highest has often more honor than merit; for he has only mounted one speck higher on the shoulders of the next last.

How often and perhaps how stupidly have I extended my book to make it speak of itself! Stupidly, if only for this reason, that I should have remembered what I say of others who do the same: that these frequent sheep's eyes at their own work testify that their heart thrills with love for it, and that even the rough, disdainful blows with which they beat it are only the love taps and affectations of maternal fondness; in keeping with Aristotle, to whom self-appreciation and self-depreciation often spring from the same sort of arrogance. For as for my excuse, that I ought to have more liberty in this than others, precisely because I write of myself and my writings as of my other actions, because my theme turns in upon itself—I do not know whether everyone will accept it.

I have observed in Germany that Luther has left as many divisions and altercations over the uncertainty of his opinions, and more, as he raised about the Holy Scriptures.

Our disputes are purely verbal. I ask what is "nature," "pleasure," "circle," "substitution." The question is one of words, and is answered in the same way. "A stone is a body." But if you pressed on: "And what is a body?"—"Substance."—"And what is substance?" and so on, you would finally drive the respondent to the end of his lexicon. We exchange one word for another word, often more unknown. I know better what is man than I know what is animal, or mortal, or rational. To satisfy one doubt, they give me three; it is the Hydra's head.

Socrates asked Meno what virtue was. "There is," said Meno, "the virtue of a man and of a woman, of a magistrate and of a private individual, of a child and of an old man." "That's fine," exclaimed Socrates; "we were in search of one virtue, and here is a whole swarm of them."

We put one question, they give us back a hive of them. As no event and no shape is entirely like another, so none is entirely different from another. An ingenious mixture on the part of nature. If our faces were not similar, we could not distinguish man from beast; if they were not dissimilar, we could not distinguish man from man. All things hold together by some similarity; every example is lame, and the comparison that is drawn from experience is always faulty and imperfect; however, we fasten together our comparisons by some corner. Thus the laws serve, and thus adapt themselves to each of our affairs, by some roundabout, forced, and biased interpretation.

Since the ethical laws, which concern the individual duty of each man in himself, are so hard to frame, as we see they are, it is no wonder if those that govern so many individuals are more so. Consider the form of this justice that governs us: it is a true testimony of human imbecility, so full it is of contradiction and error. What we find to be leniency and severity in justice—and we find so much of them that I do not know whether the mean between them is met with as often—are sickly parts and unjust members of the very body and essence of justice.

Some peasants have just informed me hastily that a moment ago they left in a wood that belongs to me a man stabbed in a hundred places, who is still breathing, and who begged them for pity's sake to bring him some water and help him to get up. They say that they did not dare go near him, and ran away, for fear that the officers of the law would catch them there and hold them accountable for the accident—as is done with those who are found near a murdered man—to their total ruin, since they had neither ability nor money to defend their innocence. What could I say to them? It is certain that this act of humanity would have got them into trouble.

How many innocent people we have found to have been punished— I mean by no fault of their judges—and how many there have been that we have not found out about! Here is something that happened in my time. Certain men are condemned to death for a murder, the sentence being, if not pronounced, at least decided and determined. At this point the judges are informed by the officers of an inferior court nearby that they have some prisoners who confess outright to this murder and throw a decisive light on the whole business. They deliberate whether because of this they should interrupt and defer the execution of the sentence passed upon the first accused. They consider the novelty of the case and the precedent it would set in suspending the execution of sentences; that the sentence has been passed according to law, and that the judges have no right to change their minds. In short, these poor devils are sacrificed to the forms of justice.

Philip, or some other, took care of a similar problem in this manner. He had sentenced a man, by a definitive judgment, to pay a heavy fine to another. The truth came to light some time after, and it turned out that he had decided unfairly. On one side were the rights of the case, on the other side the rights of judicial forms. He gave some satisfaction to both, letting the sentence stand and compensating the loss of the convicted man out of his own purse. But he was dealing with a reparable accident; my men were irreparably hanged. How many condemnations I have seen more criminal than the crime!

All this reminds me of these ancient notions: that a man is forced to do wrong in detail if he wants to do right in gross, and injustice in little things if he wants to achieve justice in great ones; that human justice is formed on the model of medicine, according to which all that is useful is also just and honest; and what the Stoics hold, that Nature herself goes against justice in most of her works; and what the Cyrenaics hold, that there is nothing just in itself, that customs and laws shape justice; and the Theodorians, who consider theft, sacrilege, and every sort of lechery just for a wise man, if he knows that it is profitable for him.

There is no remedy. My position, like that of Alcibiades, is this: I shall never turn myself over, if I can help it, to a man who can dispose of my head, where my honor and my life depend on the skill and diligence of my attorney more than on my innocence. I would risk a kind of justice that would take into account my good deeds as well as my bad, from which I would have as much to hope as to fear. Lack of punishment is not sufficient pay for a man who does better than not doing wrong. Our justice offers us only one of her hands, and the left at that. Whoever he is, he comes out of it with a loss.

In China—a kingdom whose government and arts, without dealings with and knowledge of ours, surpass our examples in many branches of excellence, and whose history teaches me how much ampler and more varied the world is than either the ancients or we ourselves understand— the officers deputed by the prince to inspect the state of his provinces, even as they punish those who are corrupt in their office, also reward, from pure liberality, those who have conducted themselves better than the average and better than the requirements of their duty. People come before them not merely to defend themselves, but to gain by it, and not simply to be paid, but also to receive presents.

No judge has yet, thank God, spoken to me as a judge in any cause whatever, my own or another man's, criminal or civil. No prison has received me, not even for a visit. Imagination makes the sight of one, even from the outside, unpleasant to me. I am so sick for freedom, that if anyone should forbid me access to some corner of the Indies, I should live distinctly less comfortably. And as long as I find earth or air open elsewhere, I shall not lurk in any place where I have to hide. Lord, how ill could I endure the condition in which I see so many people, nailed down to one section of this kingdom, deprived of the right to enter the principal towns and the courts and to use the public roads, for having quarreled with our laws! If those that I serve threatened even the tip of my finger, I should instantly go and find others, wherever it might be. All my little prudence in these civil wars in which we are now involved is employed to keep them from interrupting my freedom of coming and going.

Now laws remain in credit not because they are just, but because they are laws. That is the mystic foundation of their authority; they have no other. And that is a good thing for them. They are often made by fools, more often by people who, in their hatred of equality, are wanting in equity; but always by men, vain and irresolute authors.

There is nothing so grossly and widely and ordinarily faulty as the laws. Whoever obeys them because they are just, does not obey them for just the reason he should. Our French laws, by their irregularity and lack of form, rather lend a hand to the disorder and corruption that is seen in their administration and execution. Their commands are so confused and inconsistent that they are some excuse for both disobedience and faulty interpretation, administration, and observance.

Then whatever may be the fruit we can reap from experience, what we derive from foreign examples will hardly be much use for our education, if we make such little profit from the experience we have of ourselves, which is more familiar to us, and certainly sufficient to inform us of what we need.

James Boswell

:

FROM THE *LIFE OF JOHNSON*

I asked him whether, as a moralist, he did not think that the practice
of the law, in some degree, hurt the nice feeling of honesty. JOHNSON.
"Why no, Sir, if you act properly. You are not to deceive your clients
with false representations of your opinion: you are not to tell lies to a
Judge." BOSWELL. "But what do you think of supporting a cause which
you know to be bad?" JOHNSON. "Sir, you do not know it to be good or
bad till the Judge determines it. I have said that you are to state facts
fairly; so that your thinking, or what you call knowing, a cause to be
bad, must be from reasoning, must be from your supposing your arguments to be weak and inconclusive. But, Sir, that is not enough. An argument which does not convince yourself, may convince the Judge to whom
you urge it: and if it does convince him, why, then, Sir, you are wrong,
and he is right. It is his business to judge; and you are not to be confident
in your own opinion that a cause is bad, but to say all you can for your
client, and then hear the Judge's opinion." BOSWELL. "But, Sir, does not
affecting a warmth when you have no warmth, and appearing to be
clearly of one opinion when you are in reality of another opinion, does
not such dissimulation impair one's honesty? Is there not some danger
that a lawyer may put on the same mask in common life, in the intercourse with his friends?" JOHNSON. "Why no, Sir. Everybody knows you
are paid for affecting warmth for your client; and it is, therefore, properly
no dissimulation: the moment you come from the bar you resume your
usual behavior. Sir, a man will no more carry the artifice of the bar into

the common intercourse of society, than a man who is paid for tumbling upon his hands will continue to tumble upon his hands when he should walk on his feet."

.   .   .   .

SIR A. "I think, Sir, almost all great lawyers, such at least as have written upon law, have known only law, and nothing else." JOHNSON. "Why no, Sir; Judge Hale was a great lawyer, and wrote upon law; and yet he knew a great many other things, and has written upon other things. Selden too." SIR A. "Very true, Sir; and Lord Bacon. But was not Lord Coke a mere lawyer?" JOHNSON. "Why, I am afraid he was; but he would have taken it very ill if you had told him so. He would have prosecuted you for scandal." BOSWELL. "Lord Mansfield is not a mere lawyer." JOHNSON. "No, Sir. I never was in Lord Mansfield's company; but Lord Mansfield was distinguished at the University. Lord Mansfield, when he first came to town, 'drank champagne with the wits,' as Prior says. He was the friend of Pope." SIR A. "Barristers, I believe, are not so abusive now as they were formerly. I fancy they had less law long ago, and so were obliged to take to abuse, to fill up the time. Now they have such a number of precedents, they have no occasion for abuse." JOHNSON. "Nay, Sir, they had more law long ago than they have now. As to precedents, to be sure they will increase in course of time; but the more precedents there are, the less occasion is there for law; that is to say, the less occasion is there for investigating principles."

.   .   .   .

Before leaving London this year, I consulted him [Johnson] upon a question purely of Scotch law. It was held of old, and continued for a long period, to be an established principle in that law, that whoever intermeddled with the effects of a person deceased, without the interposition of legal authority to guard against embezzlement, should be subjected to pay all the debts of the deceased, as having been guilty of what was technically called *vicious intromission*. The Court of Session had gradually relaxed the strictness of this principle, where the interference proved had been inconsiderable. In a case* which came before that Court the preceding winter, I had labored to persuade the Judges to return to the ancient law. It was my own sincere opinion, that they ought to adhere to it; but I had exhausted all my powers of reasoning in vain. Johnson thought as I did; and in order to assist me in my application to the Court for a

* Wilson against Smith and Armour.

revision and alteration of the judgment, he dictated to me the following argument:

"This, we are told, is a law which has its force only from the long practice of the Court: and may, therefore, be suspended or modified as the Court shall think proper.

"Concerning the power of the Court to make or to suspend a law, we have no intention to inquire. It is sufficient for our purpose that every just law is dictated by reason; and that the practice of every legal Court is regulated by equity. It is the quality of reason to be invariable and constant; and of equity, to give to one man what, in the same case, is given to another. The advantage which humanity derives from law is this: that the law gives every man a rule of action, and prescribes a mode of conduct which shall entitle him to the support and protection of society. That the law may be a rule of action, it is necessary that it be known; it is necessary that it be permanent and stable. The law is the measure of civil right; but if the measure be changeable, the extent of the thing measured never can be settled.

"To permit a law to be modified at discretion, is to leave the community without law. It is to withdraw the direction of that public wisdom, by which the deficiencies of private understanding are to be supplied. It is to suffer the rash and ignorant to act at discretion, and then to depend for the legality of that action on the sentence of the Judge. He that is thus governed, lives not by law, but by opinion: not by a certain rule to which he can apply his intention before he acts, but by an uncertain and variable opinion, which he can never know but after he has committed the act on which that opinion shall be passed. He lives by a law (if a law it be), which he can never know before he has offended it. To this case may be justly applied that important principle, *misera est servitus ubi jus est aut incognitum aut vagum.* If Intromission be not criminal till it exceeds a certain point, and that point be unsettled, and consequently different in different minds, the right of Intromission, and the right of the Creditor arising from it, are all *jura vaga,* and, by consequence, are *jura incognita;* and the result can be no other than a *misera servitus,* an uncertainty concerning the event of action, a servile dependence on private opinion.

"It may be urged, and with great plausibility, that there may be Intromission without fraud; which, however true, will by no means justify an occasional and arbitrary relaxation of the law. The end of law is protection as well as vengeance. Indeed, vengeance is never used but to strengthen protection. That society only is well governed, where life is freed from danger and from suspicion; where possession is so sheltered by salutory prohibitions, that violation is prevented more frequently than punished. Such a prohibition was this, while it operated with its original force. The creditor of the deceased was not only without loss but without fear. He was not to seek a remedy for an injury suffered; for injury was warded off.

"As the law has been sometimes administered, it lays us open to wounds, because it is imagined to have the power of healing. To punish fraud when it is detected, is the proper act of vindictive justice; but to prevent frauds, and make punishment unnecessary, is the great employment of legislative wisdom. To permit Intromission, and to punish fraud, is to make law no better than a pitfall. To tread upon the brink is safe; but to come a step further is destruction. But, surely, it is better to enclose the gulf, and hinder all access, than by encouraging us to advance a little, to entice us afterwards a little further, and let us perceive our folly only by our destruction.

"As law supplies the weak with adventitious strength, it likewise enlightens the ignorant with extrinsic understanding. Law teaches us to know when we commit injury, and when we suffer it. It fixes certain marks upon actions, by which we are admonished to do or to forbear them. *Qui sibi bene temperat in licitis,* says one of the fathers, *nunquam cadet in illicita.* He who never intromits at all, will never intromit with fraudulent intentions.

"The relaxation of the law against vicious intromission has been very favorably represented by a great master of jurisprudence,* whose words have been exhibited with unnecessary pomp, and seem to be considered as irresistibly decisive. The great moment of his authority makes it necessary to examine his position. 'Some ages ago,' (says he) 'before the ferocity of the inhabitants of this part of the island was subdued, the utmost severity of the civil law was necessary, to restrain individuals from plundering each other. Thus, the man who intermeddled irregularly with the moveables of a person deceased, was subjected to all the debts of the deceased without limitation. This makes a branch of the law of Scotland, known by the name of *vicious intromission;* and so rigidly was this regulation applied in our Courts of Law, that the most trifling moveable abstracted *malâfide,* subjected the intermeddler to the fore-

---

* Lord Kames, in his *Historical Law Tracts.*

going consequences, which proved in many instances a most rigorous punishment. But this severity was necessary, in order to subdue the undisciplined nature of our people. It is extremely remarkable, that in proportion to our improvement in manners, this regulation has been gradually softened, and applied by our sovereign Court with a sparing hand.'

"I find myself under a necessity of observing, that this learned and judicious writer has not accurately distinguished the deficiencies and demands of the different conditions of human life, which, from a degree of savageness and independence, in which all laws are vain, passes or may pass, by innumerable gradations, to a state of reciprocal benignity, in which laws shall be no longer necessary. Men are first wild and unsocial, living each man to himself, taking from the weak, and losing to the strong. In their first coalitions of society, much of this original savageness is retained. Of general happiness, the product of general confidence, there is yet no thought. Men continue to prosecute their own advantages by the nearest way; and the utmost severity of the civil law is necessary to restrain individuals from plundering each other. The restraints then necessary, are restraints from plunder, from acts of public violence, and undisguised oppression. The ferocity of our ancestors, as of all other nations, produced not fraud, but rapine. They had not yet learned to cheat, and attempted only to rob. As manners grew more polished, with the knowledge of good, men attain likewise dexterity in evil. Open rapine becomes less frequent, and violence gives way to cunning. Those who before invaded pastures and stormed houses, now begin to enrich themselves by unequal contracts and fraudulent intromissions. It is not against the violence of ferocity, but the circumventions of deceit, that this law was framed; and I am afraid the increase of commerce, and the incessant struggle for riches which commerce excites, give us no prospects of an end speedily to be expected of artifice and fraud. It therefore seems to be no very conclusive reasoning, which connects those two propositions—'the nation is become less ferocious, and therefore the laws against fraud and *covin* shall be relaxed.'

"Whatever reason may have influenced the Judges to a relaxation of the law, it was not that the nation was grown less fierce; and, I am afraid, it cannot be affirmed, that it is grown less fraudulent.

"Since this law has been represented as rigorously and unreasonably penal, it seems not improper to consider what are the conditions and qualities that make the justice or propriety of a penal law.

"To make a penal law reasonable and just, two conditions are neces-

sary, and two proper. It is necessary that the law should be adequate
to its end; that, if it be observed, it shall prevent the evil against which
it is directed. It is, secondly, necessary that the end of the law be of such
importance, as to deserve the security of a penal sanction. The other
conditions of a penal law, which though not absolutely necessary, are to
a very high degree fit, are, that to the moral violation of the law there
are many temptations, and that of the physical observance there is great
facility.

"All these conditions apparently concur to justify the law which we
are now considering. Its end is the security of property; and property
very often of great value. The method by which it effects the security
is efficacious, because it admits, in its original rigor, no gradations of
injury; but keeps guilt and innocence apart, by a distinct and definite
limitation. He that intromits, is criminal; he that intromits not, is innocent. Of the two secondary considerations it cannot be denied that both
are in our favor. The temptation to intromit is frequent and strong; so
strong and so frequent, as to require the utmost activity of justice, and
vigilance of caution, to withstand its prevalence; and the method by
which a man may entitle himself to legal intromission, is so open and
so facile, that to neglect it is a proof of fraudulent intention: for why
should a man omit to do (but for reasons which he will not confess)
that which he can do so easily, and that which he knows to be required
by the law? If temptation were rare, a penal law might be deemed unnecessary. If the duty enjoined by the law were of difficult performance,
omission, though it could not be justified, might be pitied. But in the
present case, neither equity nor compassion operate against it. A useful,
a necessary law is broken, not only without a reasonable motive, but
with all the inducements to obedience that can be derived from safety
and facility.

"I therefore return to my original position, that a law, to have its
effect, must be permanent and stable. It may be said, in the language of
the schools, *Lex non recipit majus et minus*—we may have a law, or
we may have no law, but we cannot have half a law. We must either have
a rule of action, or be permitted to act by discretion and by chance.
Deviations from the law must be uniformly punished, or no man can be
certain when he shall be safe.

"That from the rigor of the original institution this Court has sometimes departed, cannot be denied. But, as it is evident that such deviations, as they make law uncertain, make life unsafe, I hope, that of de-

parting from it there will now be an end; that the wisdom of our ancestors will be treated with due reverence; and that consistent and steady decisions will furnish the people with a rule of action, and leave fraud and fraudulent intromission no future hope of impunity or escape."

With such comprehension of mind, and such clearness of penetration, did he thus treat a subject altogether new to him, without any other preparation than my having stated to him the arguments which had been used on each side of the question. His intellectual powers appeared with peculiar luster, when tried against those of a writer of so much fame as Lord Kames, and that too in his Lordship's own department.

This masterly argument, after being prefaced and concluded with some sentences of my own, and garnished with the usual formularies, was actually printed and laid before the Lords of Session, but without success. My respected friend Lord Hailes, however, one of that honorable body, had critical sagacity enough to discover a more than ordinary hand in the *Petition*. I told him Dr. Johnson had favored me with his pen. His Lordship, with wonderful *acumen,* pointed out exactly where his composition began, and where it ended. But that I may do impartial justice, and conform to the great rule of the Courts, *suum cuique tribuito,* I must add, that their Lordships in general, though they were pleased to call this "a well-drawn paper," preferred the former very inferior petition which I had written; thus confirming the truth of an observation made to me by one of their number, in a merry mood: "My dear Sir, give yourself no trouble in the composition of the papers you present to us; for, indeed, it is casting pearls before swine."

.   .   .   .

SIR JOSHUA REYNOLDS. "I do not perceive why the profession of a player should be despised; for the great and ultimate end of all the employments of mankind is to produce amusement. Garrick produces more amusement than anybody." BOSWELL. "You say, Dr. Johnson, that Garrick exhibits himself for a shilling. In this respect he is only on a footing with a lawyer who exhibits himself for his fee, and even will maintain any nonsense or absurdity, if the case requires it. Garrick refuses a play or a part which he does not like; a lawyer never refuses." JOHNSON. "Why, Sir, what does this prove? Only that a lawyer is worse. Boswell is now like Jack in *The Tale of a Tub,* who, when he is puzzled by an argument, hangs himself. He thinks I shall cut him down, but I'll let him hang." (laughing vociferously.) SIR JOSHUA REYNOLDS. "Mr. Boswell thinks that the profession of a lawyer being unquestionably honorable, if he can show the profession of a player to be more honorable, he proves his argument."

. . . .

I introduced the subject of toleration. JOHNSON. "Every society has a right to preserve public peace and order, and therefore has a good right to prohibit the propagation of opinions which have a dangerous tendency. To say the *magistrate* has this right, is using an inadequate word: it is the *society* for which the magistrate is agent. He may be morally or theologically wrong in restraining the propagation of opinions which he thinks dangerous, but he is politically right." MAYO. "I am of opinion, Sir, that every man is entitled to liberty of conscience in religion; and that the magistrate cannot restrain that right." JOHNSON. "Sir, I agree with you. Every man has a right to liberty of conscience, and with that the magistrate cannot interfere. People confound liberty of thinking with liberty of talking; nay, with liberty of preaching. Every man has a physical right to think as he pleases; for it cannot be discovered how he thinks. He has not a moral right, for he ought to inform himself, and think justly. But, Sir, no member of a society has a right to *teach* any doctrine contrary to what the society holds to be true. The magistrate, I say, may be wrong in what he thinks: but while he thinks himself right, he may and ought to enforce what he thinks." MAYO. "Then, Sir, we are to remain always in error, and truth never can prevail; and the magistrate was right in persecuting the first Christians." JOHNSON. "Sir, the only method by which religious truth can be established is by martyrdom. The magistrate has a right to enforce what he thinks; and he who is conscious of the truth has a right to suffer. I am afraid there is no other way of ascertaining the truth, but by persecution on the one hand and enduring it on the other." GOLDSMITH. "But how is a man to act, Sir? Though firmly convinced of the truth of his doctrine, may he not think it wrong to expose himself to persecution? Has he a right to do so? Is it not, as it were, committing voluntary suicide?" JOHNSON. "Sir, as to voluntary suicide, as you call it, there are twenty thousand men in an army who will go without scruple to be shot at, and mount a breach for five-pence a day." GOLDSMITH. "But have they a moral right to do this?" JOHNSON. "Nay, Sir, if you will not take the universal opinion of mankind, I have nothing to say. If mankind cannot defend their own way of thinking, I cannot defend it. Sir, if a man is in doubt whether it would be better for him to expose himself to martyrdom or not, he should not do it. He must be convinced that he has a delegation from heaven." GOLDSMITH. "I would consider whether there is the greater chance of good or evil upon the whole. If I see a man who had fallen into a well, I would wish to help him out; but if there is a greater probability that he shall pull me in, than that I shall pull him out, I would not attempt it. So were I to go to Turkey, I might wish to convert the Grand Signor to the Christian faith; but when I considered that I should probably be put to death without effectuating my purpose in any degree, I should keep myself quiet." JOHNSON. "Sir, you must consider that we have perfect and imperfect obligations. Perfect obligations, which are generally not to do something, are clear and positive; as, 'thou shalt not kill.' But charity, for instance, is not definable by limits. It is a duty to give to the poor; but no man can say how much another should give to the poor, or when a man has given too little to save his soul. In the same manner it is a duty to instruct the ignorant, and of consequence to convert infidels to Christianity; but no man in the common course of things is obliged to carry this to such a degree as to incur the danger of martyrdom, as no man is obliged to strip himself to the shirt in order to give charity. I have said, that a man must be persuaded that he has a particular delegation from heaven." GOLDSMITH. "How is this to be known? Our first reformers, who were burnt for not believing bread and wine to be CHRIST"—JOHNSON (interrupting him). "Sir, they were not burnt for not believing bread and wine to be CHRIST, but for insulting those who did believe it. And, Sir, when the first reformers began, they did not intend to be martyred: as many of them ran away as could." BOSWELL. "But, Sir, there was your countryman, Elwal, who you told me challenged King George with his black-guards, and his red-guards." JOHNSON. "My countryman, Elwal, Sir, should have been put in the stocks; a proper pulpit for him; and he'd have had a numerous audience. A man who preaches in the stocks will always have hearers enough." BOSWELL. "But Elwal thought himself in the right." JOHNSON. "We are not providing for mad people; there are places for them in the neighborhood" (meaning Moorfields). MAYO. "But, Sir, is it not very hard that I should not be allowed to teach my children what I really believe to be the truth?" JOHNSON. "Why, Sir, you might contrive to teach your children *extrà scandalum;* but, Sir, the magistrate, if he knows it, has a right to restrain you. Suppose you teach your children to be thieves?" MAYO. "This is making a joke of the subject." JOHNSON. "Nay, Sir, take it thus: —that you teach them the community of goods; for which there are as many plausible arguments as for most erroneous doctrines. You teach them that all things at first were in common, and that no man had a right to any thing but as he laid his hands upon it; and that this still is, or ought to be, the rule amongst mankind. Here, Sir, you sap a great principle in society—property. And don't you think the magistrate would have a right to prevent you? Or, suppose you should teach your children the notion of the Adamites, and they should run naked into the streets, would not the magistrate have a right to flog 'em into their doublets?" MAYO. "I think the magistrate has no right to interfere till there is some overt act." BOSWELL. "So, Sir, though he sees an enemy to the state charging a blunderbuss, he is not to interfere till it is fired off?" MAYO. "He must be sure of its direction against the state." JOHNSON. "The magistrate is to judge of that.—He has no right to restrain your thinking, because the evil centers in yourself. If a man were sitting at this table, and chopping off his fingers, the magistrate, as guardian of the community, has no authority to restrain him, however he might do it from kindness as a parent. Though, indeed, upon more consideration, I think he may; as it is probable, that he who is chopping off his own fingers, may soon proceed to chop off those of other people. If I think it right to steal Mr. Dilly's plate, I am a bad man; but he can say nothing to me. If I make an open declaration that I think so, he will keep me out of his house. If I put forth my hand, I shall be sent to Newgate. This is the gradation of thinking, preaching, and acting: if a man thinks erroneously, he may keep his thoughts to himself, and nobody will trouble him; if he preaches erroneous doctrine, society may expel him; if he acts in consequence of it, the law takes place, and he is hanged." MAYO. "But, Sir, ought not Christians to have liberty of conscience?" JOHNSON. "I have already told you so, Sir. You are coming back to where you were." BOSWELL. "Dr. Mayo is always taking a return post-chaise, and going the stage over again. He has it at half price." JOHNSON. "Dr. Mayo, like other champions for unlimited toleration, has got a set of words. Sir, it is no matter, politically, whether the magistrate be right or wrong. Suppose a club were to be formed, to drink confusion to King George the Third, and a happy restoration to Charles the Third, this would be very bad with respect to the State; but every member of that club must either conform to its rules, or be turned out of it. Old Baxter, I remember, maintains, that the magistrate should 'tolerate all things that are tolerable.' This is no good definition of toleration upon any principle; but it shows that he thought some things were not tolerable." TOPLADY. "Sir, you have untwisted this difficult subject with great dexterity."

.   .   .   .

We got into an argument whether the Judges who went to India might with propriety engage in trade. Johnson warmly maintained that they might. "For why," (he urged) "should not Judges get riches, as well as those who deserve them less?" I said, they should have sufficient salaries, and have nothing to take off their attention from the affairs of the public. JOHNSON. "No Judge, Sir, can give his whole attention to his office; and it is very proper that he should employ what time he has to himself, to his own advantage, in the most profitable manner." "Then, Sir," (said Davies, who enlivened the dispute by making it somewhat dramatic) "he may become an insurer; and when he is going to the bench, he may be stopped—'Your Lordship cannot go yet: here is a bunch of invoices: several ships are about to sail.' " JOHNSON. "Sir, you may as well say a Judge should not have a house; for they may come and tell him, 'Your Lordship's house is on fire'; and so, instead of minding the business of his Court, he is to be occupied in getting the engine with the greatest speed. There is no end of this. Every Judge who has land, trades to a certain extent in corn or in cattle; and in the land itself, undoubtedly. His steward acts for him, and so do clerks for a great merchant. A Judge may be a farmer; but he is not to geld his own pigs. A Judge may play a little at cards for his amusement; but he is not to play at marbles, or at chuck-farthing in the Piazza. No, Sir; there is no profession to which a man gives a very great proportion of his time. It is wonderful when a calculation is made, how little the mind is actually employed in the discharge of any profession. No man would be a Judge, upon the condition of being totally a Judge. The best employed lawyer has his mind at work but for a small proportion of his time: a great deal of his occupation is merely mechanical. I once wrote for a magazine: I made a calculation, that if I should write but a page a day, at the same rate, I should, in ten years, write nine volumes in folio, of an ordinary size and print." BOSWELL. "Such as Carte's *History?*" JOHNSON. "Yes, Sir. When a man writes from his own mind, he writes very rapidly.* The greatest part of a writer's time is spent in reading, in order to write: a man will turn over half a library to make one book."

I argued warmly against the Judges trading, and mentioned Hale as an instance of a perfect Judge, who devoted himself entirely to his office. JOHNSON. "Hale, Sir, attended to other things besides law: he left a great

* Johnson certainly did, who had a mind stored with knowledge, and teeming with imagery: but the observation is not applicable to writers in general.

estate." BOSWELL. "That was, because what he got, accumulated without any exertion and anxiety on his part."

While the dispute went on, Moody once tried to say something upon our side. Tom Davies clapped him on the back, to encourage him. Beauclerk, to whom I mentioned this circumstance, said, that "he could not conceive a more humiliating situation than to be clapped on the back by Tom Davies."

. . . .

After supper I accompanied him to his apartment, and at my request he dictated to me an argument in favor of the Negro who was then claiming his liberty, in an action in the Court of Session in Scotland. He had always been zealous against slavery in every form, in which I, with all deference, thought that he discovered "a zeal without knowledge." Upon one occasion, when in company with some very grave men at Oxford, his toast was, "Here's to the next insurrection of the Negroes in the West Indies." His violent prejudice against our West Indian and American settlers appeared whenever there was an opportunity. Towards the conclusion of his *Taxation no Tyranny,* he says, "How is it that we hear the loudest *yelps* for liberty among the drivers of Negroes?" and in his conversation with Mr. Wilkes, he asked, "Where did Beckford and Trecothick learn English?" That Trecothick could both speak and write good English is well known. I myself was favored with his correspondence concerning the brave Corsicans. And that Beckford could speak it with a spirit of honest resolution even to his Majesty, as his "faithful Lord-Mayor of London," is commemorated by the noble monument erected to him in Guildhall.

The argument dictated by Dr. Johnson was as follows:—

"It must be agreed that in most ages many countries have had part of their inhabitants in a state of slavery; yet it may be doubted whether slavery can ever be supposed the natural condition of man. It is impossible not to conceive that men in the original state were equal; and very difficult to imagine how one would be subjected to another but by violent compulsion. An individual may, indeed, forfeit his liberty by a crime; but he cannot by that crime forfeit the liberty of his children. What is true of a criminal seems true likewise of a captive. A man may accept life from a conquering enemy on condition of perpetual servitude; but it is very doubtful whether he can entail that servitude on his descendants; for no man can stipulate without commission for another. The condition which he himself accepts, his son or grandson perhaps would have rejected. If we should admit, what perhaps may with more reason be denied, that there are certain relations between man and man which may make slavery necessary and just, yet it can never be proved that he who is now suing for his freedom ever stood in any of those relations. He is certainly subject by no law, but that of violence, to his present master; who pretends no claim to his obedience, but that he bought him from a merchant of slaves, whose right to sell him never was examined. It is said that, according to the constitutions of Jamaica, he was legally enslaved; these constitutions are merely positive; and apparently injurious to the rights of mankind, because whoever is exposed to sale is condemned to slavery without appeal; by whatever fraud or violence he might have been originally brought into the merchant's power. In our own time Princes have been sold, by wretches to whose care they were entrusted, that they might have an European education; but when once they were brought to a market in the plantations, little would avail either their dignity or their wrongs. The laws of Jamaica afford a Negro no redress. His color is considered as a sufficient testimony against him. It is to be lamented that moral right should ever give way to political convenience. But if temptations of interest are sometimes too strong for human virtue, let us at least retain a virtue where there is no temptation to quit it. In the present case there is apparent right on one side, and no convenience on the other. Inhabitants of this island can neither gain riches nor power by taking away the liberty of any part of the human species. The sum of the argument is this:—No man is by nature the property of another: The defendant is, therefore, by nature free: The rights of nature must be some way forfeited before they can be justly taken away: That the defendant has by any act forfeited the rights of nature we require to be proved; and if no proof of such forfeiture can be given, we doubt not but the justice of the court will declare him free."

I record Dr. Johnson's argument fairly upon this particular case; where, perhaps, he was in the right. But I beg leave to enter my most solemn protest against his general doctrine with respect to the *Slave Trade*. For I will resolutely say—that his unfavorable notion of it was owing to prejudice, and imperfect or false information. The wild and dangerous attempt which has for some time been persisted in to obtain an act of our Legislature, to abolish so very important and necessary a branch of commercial interest, must have been crushed at once, had not the insignificance of the zealots who vainly took the lead in it, made the vast body of Planters, Merchants, and others, whose immense properties are involved in that trade, reasonably enough suppose that there could be no danger. The encouragement which the attempt has received excites my wonder and indignation: and though some men of superior abilities have supported it; whether from a love of temporary popularity, when prosperous; or a love of general mischief, when desperate, my opinion is unshaken. To abolish a *status,* which in all ages GOD has sanctioned, and man has continued, would not only be *robbery* to an innumerable class of our fellow-subjects; but it would be extreme cruelty to the African Savages, a portion of whom it saves from massacre, or intolerable bondage in their own country, and introduces into a much happier state of life; especially now when their passage to the West-Indies and their treatment there is humanely regulated. To abolish that trade would be to

—*shut the gates of mercy on mankind.*

Whatever may have passed elsewhere concerning it, The HOUSE OF LORDS is wise and independent:

Intaminatis fulget honoribus;
Nec sumit aut ponit secures
Arbitrio popularis auræ.

I have read, conversed, and thought much upon the subject, and would recommend to all who are capable of conviction, an excellent Tract by my learned and ingenious friend John Ranby, Esq., entitled *Doubts on the Abolition of the Slave Trade.* To Mr. Ranby's *Doubts* I will apply Lord Chancellor Hardwicke's expression in praise of a Scotch Law Book, called *Dirleton's Doubts;* his *Doubts* (said his Lordship), are better than most people's *Certainties.*

When I said now to Johnson, that I was afraid I kept him too late up. "No, Sir," (said he) "I don't care though I sit all night with you." This was an animated speech from a man in his sixty-ninth year.

Had I been as attentive not to displease him as I ought to have been, I know not but this vigil might have been fulfilled; but I unluckily entered upon the controversy concerning the right of Great Britain to tax America, and attempted to argue in favor of our fellow-subjects on the other side of the Atlantic. I insisted that America might be very well governed, and made to yield sufficient revenue by the means of *influence,* as exemplified in Ireland, while the people might be pleased with the imagination of their participating of the British constitution, by having a body of representatives, without whose consent money could not be exacted from them. Johnson could not bear my thus opposing his avowed opinion, which he had exerted himself with an extreme degree of heat to enforce; and the violent agitation into which he was thrown, while answering, or rather reprimanding me, alarmed me so, that I heartily repented of my having unthinkingly introduced the subject. I myself, however, grew warm, and the change was great, from the calm state of philosophical discussion in which he had a little before been pleasingly employed.

W. H. Auden

:

LAW LIKE LOVE

Law, say the gardeners, is the sun,
Law is the one
All gardeners obey
Tomorrow, yesterday, today.

Law is the wisdom of the old
The impotent grandfathers shrilly scold;
The grandchildren put out a treble tongue,
Law is the senses of the young.

Law, says the priest with a priestly look,
Expounding to an unpriestly people,
Law is the words in my priestly book,
Law is my pulpit and my steeple.

Law, says the judge as he looks down his nose,
Speaking clearly and most severely,
Law is as I've told you before,
Law is as you know I suppose,
Law is but let me explain it once more,
Law is The Law.

Yet law-abiding scholars write;
Law is neither wrong nor right,

Law is only crimes
Punished by places and by times,
Law is the clothes men wear
Anytime, anywhere,
Law is Good-morning and Good-night.

Others say, Law is our Fate;
Others say, Law is our State;
Others say, others say
Law is no more
Law has gone away.

And always the loud angry crowd
Very angry and very loud
Law is We,
And always the soft idiot softly Me.

If we, dear, know we know no more
Than they about the law,
If I no more than you
Know what we should and should not do
Except that all agree
Gladly or miserably
That the law is
And that all know this,
If therefore thinking it absurd
To identify Law with some other word,
Unlike so many men
I cannot say Law is again,
No more than they can we suppress
The universal wish to guess
Or slip out of our own position
Into an unconcerned condition.
Although I can at least confine
Your vanity and mine
To stating timidly
A timid similarity,
We shall boast anyway:
Like love I say.

Like love we don't know where or why
Like love we can't compel or fly
Like love we often weep
Like love we seldom keep.